WITHDRAWN
Wilmette Public Library

Dictionary of Literary Biography

1 *The American Renaissance in New England,* edited by Joel Myerson (1978)

2 *American Novelists Since World War II,* edited by Jeffrey Helterman and Richard Layman (1978)

3 *Antebellum Writers in New York and the South,* edited by Joel Myerson (1979)

4 *American Writers in Paris, 1920-1939,* edited by Karen Lane Rood (1980)

5 *American Poets Since World War II,* 2 parts, edited by Donald J. Greiner (1980)

6 *American Novelists Since World War II, Second Series,* edited by James E. Kibler Jr. (1980)

7 *Twentieth-Century American Dramatists,* 2 parts, edited by John MacNicholas (1981)

8 *Twentieth-Century American Science-Fiction Writers,* 2 parts, edited by David Cowart and Thomas L. Wymer (1981)

9 *American Novelists, 1910-1945,* 3 parts, edited by James J. Martine (1981)

10 *Modern British Dramatists, 1900-1945,* 2 parts, edited by Stanley Weintraub (1982)

11 *American Humorists, 1800-1950,* 2 parts, edited by Stanley Trachtenberg (1982)

12 *American Realists and Naturalists,* edited by Donald Pizer and Earl N. Harbert (1982)

13 *British Dramatists Since World War II,* 2 parts, edited by Stanley Weintraub (1982)

14 *British Novelists Since 1960,* 2 parts, edited by Jay L. Halio (1983)

15 *British Novelists, 1930-1959,* 2 parts, edited by Bernard Oldsey (1983)

16 *The Beats: Literary Bohemians in Postwar America,* 2 parts, edited by Ann Charters (1983)

17 *Twentieth-Century American Historians,* edited by Clyde N. Wilson (1983)

18 *Victorian Novelists After 1885,* edited by Ira B. Nadel and William E. Fredeman (1983)

19 *British Poets, 1880-1914,* edited by Donald E. Stanford (1983)

20 *British Poets, 1914-1945,* edited by Donald E. Stanford (1983)

21 *Victorian Novelists Before 1885,* edited by Ira B. Nadel and William E. Fredeman (1983)

22 *American Writers for Children, 1900-1960,* edited by John Cech (1983)

23 *American Newspaper Journalists, 1873-1900,* edited by Perry J. Ashley (1983)

24 *American Colonial Writers, 1606-1734,* edited by Emory Elliott (1984)

25 *American Newspaper Journalists, 1901-1925,* edited by Perry J. Ashley (1984)

26 *American Screenwriters,* edited by Robert E. Morsberger, Stephen O. Lesser, and Randall Clark (1984)

27 *Poets of Great Britain and Ireland, 1945-1960,* edited by Vincent B. Sherry Jr. (1984)

28 *Twentieth-Century American-Jewish Fiction Writers,* edited by Daniel Walden (1984)

29 *American Newspaper Journalists, 1926-1950,* edited by Perry J. Ashley (1984)

30 *American Historians, 1607-1865,* edited by Clyde N. Wilson (1984)

31 *American Colonial Writers, 1735-1781,* edited by Emory Elliott (1984)

32 *Victorian Poets Before 1850,* edited by William E. Fredeman and Ira B. Nadel (1984)

33 *Afro-American Fiction Writers After 1955,* edited by Thadious M. Davis and Trudier Harris (1984)

34 *British Novelists, 1890-1929: Traditionalists,* edited by Thomas F. Staley (1985)

35 *Victorian Poets After 1850,* edited by William E. Fredeman and Ira B. Nadel (1985)

36 *British Novelists, 1890-1929: Modernists,* edited by Thomas F. Staley (1985)

37 *American Writers of the Early Republic,* edited by Emory Elliott (1985)

38 *Afro-American Writers After 1955: Dramatists and Prose Writers,* edited by Thadious M. Davis and Trudier Harris (1985)

39 *British Novelists, 1660-1800,* 2 parts, edited by Martin C. Battestin (1985)

40 *Poets of Great Britain and Ireland Since 1960,* 2 parts, edited by Vincent B. Sherry Jr. (1985)

41 *Afro-American Poets Since 1955,* edited by Trudier Harris and Thadious M. Davis (1985)

42 *American Writers for Children Before 1900,* edited by Glenn E. Estes (1985)

43 *American Newspaper Journalists, 1690-1872,* edited by Perry J. Ashley (1986)

44 *American Screenwriters, Second Series,* edited by Randall Clark, Robert E. Morsberger, and Stephen O. Lesser (1986)

45 *American Poets, 1880-1945, First Series,* edited by Peter Quartermain (1986)

46 *American Literary Publishing Houses, 1900-1980: Trade and Paperback,* edited by Peter Dzwonkoski (1986)

47 *American Historians, 1866-1912,* edited by Clyde N. Wilson (1986)

48 *American Poets, 1880-1945, Second Series,* edited by Peter Quartermain (1986)

49 *American Literary Publishing Houses, 1638-1899,* 2 parts, edited by Peter Dzwonkoski (1986)

50 *Afro-American Writers Before the Harlem Renaissance,* edited by Trudier Harris (1986)

51 *Afro-American Writers from the Harlem Renaissance to 1940,* edited by Trudier Harris (1987)

52 *American Writers for Children Since 1960: Fiction,* edited by Glenn E. Estes (1986)

53 *Canadian Writers Since 1960, First Series,* edited by W. H. New (1986)

54 *American Poets, 1880-1945, Third Series,* 2 parts, edited by Peter Quartermain (1987)

55 *Victorian Prose Writers Before 1867,* edited by William B. Thesing (1987)

56 *German Fiction Writers, 1914-1945,* edited by James Hardin (1987)

57 *Victorian Prose Writers After 1867,* edited by William B. Thesing (1987)

58 *Jacobean and Caroline Dramatists,* edited by Fredson Bowers (1987)

59 *American Literary Critics and Scholars, 1800-1850,* edited by John W. Rathbun and Monica M. Grecu (1987)

60 *Canadian Writers Since 1960, Second Series,* edited by W. H. New (1987)

61 *American Writers for Children Since 1960: Poets, Illustrators, and Nonfiction Authors,* edited by Glenn E. Estes (1987)

62 *Elizabethan Dramatists,* edited by Fredson Bowers (1987)

63 *Modern American Critics, 1920-1955,* edited by Gregory S. Jay (1988)

64 *American Literary Critics and Scholars, 1850-1880,* edited by John W. Rathbun and Monica M. Grecu (1988)

65 *French Novelists, 1900-1930,* edited by Catharine Savage Brosman (1988)

66 *German Fiction Writers, 1885-1913,* 2 parts, edited by James Hardin (1988)

67 *Modern American Critics Since 1955,* edited by Gregory S. Jay (1988)

68 *Canadian Writers, 1920-1959, First Series,* edited by W. H. New (1988)

69 *Contemporary German Fiction Writers, First Series,* edited by Wolfgang D. Elfe and James Hardin (1988)

70 *British Mystery Writers, 1860-1919,* edited by Bernard Benstock and Thomas F. Staley (1988)

71 *American Literary Critics and Scholars, 1880-1900,* edited by John W. Rathbun and Monica M. Grecu (1988)

72 *French Novelists, 1930-1960,* edited by Catharine Savage Brosman (1988)

73 *American Magazine Journalists, 1741-1850,* edited by Sam G. Riley (1988)

74 *American Short-Story Writers Before 1880,* edited by Bobby Ellen Kimbel, with the assistance of William E. Grant (1988)

75 *Contemporary German Fiction Writers, Second Series,* edited by Wolfgang D. Elfe and James Hardin (1988)

76 *Afro-American Writers, 1940-1955,* edited by Trudier Harris (1988)

77 *British Mystery Writers, 1920-1939,* edited by Bernard Benstock and Thomas F. Staley (1988)

78 *American Short-Story Writers, 1880-1910,* edited by Bobby Ellen Kimbel, with the assistance of William E. Grant (1988)

79 *American Magazine Journalists, 1850-1900,* edited by Sam G. Riley (1988)

80 *Restoration and Eighteenth-Century Dramatists, First Series,* edited by Paula R. Backscheider (1989)

81 *Austrian Fiction Writers, 1875-1913,* edited by James Hardin and Donald G. Daviau (1989)

82 *Chicano Writers, First Series,* edited by Francisco A. Lomelí and Carl R. Shirley (1989)

83 *French Novelists Since 1960,* edited by Catharine Savage Brosman (1989)

84 *Restoration and Eighteenth-Century Dramatists, Second Series,* edited by Paula R. Backscheider (1989)

85 *Austrian Fiction Writers After 1914,* edited by James Hardin and Donald G. Daviau (1989)

86 *American Short-Story Writers, 1910-1945, First Series,* edited by Bobby Ellen Kimbel (1989)

87 *British Mystery and Thriller Writers Since 1940, First Series,* edited by Bernard Benstock and Thomas F. Staley (1989)

88 *Canadian Writers, 1920-1959, Second Series,* edited by W. H. New (1989)

89 *Restoration and Eighteenth-Century Dramatists, Third Series,* edited by Paula R. Backscheider (1989)

90 *German Writers in the Age of Goethe, 1789-1832,* edited by James Hardin and Christoph E. Schweitzer (1989)

91 *American Magazine Journalists, 1900-1960, First Series,* edited by Sam G. Riley (1990)

92 *Canadian Writers, 1890-1920,* edited by W. H. New (1990)

93 *British Romantic Poets, 1789-1832, First Series,* edited by John R. Greenfield (1990)

94 *German Writers in the Age of Goethe: Sturm und Drang to Classicism,* edited by James Hardin and Christoph E. Schweitzer (1990)

95 *Eighteenth-Century British Poets, First Series,* edited by John Sitter (1990)

96 *British Romantic Poets, 1789-1832, Second Series,* edited by John R. Greenfield (1990)

97 *German Writers from the Enlightenment to Sturm und Drang, 1720-1764,* edited by James Hardin and Christoph E. Schweitzer (1990)

98 *Modern British Essayists, First Series,* edited by Robert Beum (1990)

99 *Canadian Writers Before 1890,* edited by W. H. New (1990)

100 *Modern British Essayists, Second Series,* edited by Robert Beum (1990)

101 *British Prose Writers, 1660-1800, First Series,* edited by Donald T. Siebert (1991)

102 *American Short-Story Writers, 1910-1945, Second Series,* edited by Bobby Ellen Kimbel (1991)

103 *American Literary Biographers, First Series,* edited by Steven Serafin (1991)

104 *British Prose Writers, 1660-1800, Second Series,* edited by Donald T. Siebert (1991)

105 *American Poets Since World War II, Second Series,* edited by R. S. Gwynn (1991)

106 *British Literary Publishing Houses, 1820-1880,* edited by Patricia J. Anderson and Jonathan Rose (1991)

107 *British Romantic Prose Writers, 1789-1832, First Series,* edited by John R. Greenfield (1991)

108 *Twentieth-Century Spanish Poets, First Series,* edited by Michael L. Perna (1991)

109 *Eighteenth-Century British Poets, Second Series,* edited by John Sitter (1991)

110 *British Romantic Prose Writers, 1789-1832, Second Series,* edited by John R. Greenfield (1991)

111 *American Literary Biographers, Second Series,* edited by Steven Serafin (1991)

112 *British Literary Publishing Houses, 1881-1965,* edited by Jonathan Rose and Patricia J. Anderson (1991)

113 *Modern Latin-American Fiction Writers, First Series,* edited by William Luis (1992)

114 *Twentieth-Century Italian Poets, First Series,* edited by Giovanna Wedel De Stasio, Glauco Cambon, and Antonio Illiano (1992)

115 *Medieval Philosophers,* edited by Jeremiah Hackett (1992)

116 *British Romantic Novelists, 1789-1832,* edited by Bradford K. Mudge (1992)

117 *Twentieth-Century Caribbean and Black African Writers, First Series,* edited by Bernth Lindfors and Reinhard Sander (1992)

118 *Twentieth-Century German Dramatists, 1889-1918,* edited by Wolfgang D. Elfe and James Hardin (1992)

119 *Nineteenth-Century French Fiction Writers: Romanticism and Realism, 1800-1860,* edited by Catharine Savage Brosman (1992)

120 *American Poets Since World War II, Third Series,* edited by R. S. Gwynn (1992)

121 *Seventeenth-Century British Nondramatic Poets, First Series,* edited by M. Thomas Hester (1992)

122 *Chicano Writers, Second Series,* edited by Francisco A. Lomelí and Carl R. Shirley (1992)

123 *Nineteenth-Century French Fiction Writers: Naturalism and Beyond, 1860-1900,* edited by Catharine Savage Brosman (1992)

124 *Twentieth-Century German Dramatists, 1919-1992,* edited by Wolfgang D. Elfe and James Hardin (1992)

125 *Twentieth-Century Caribbean and Black African Writers, Second Series,* edited by Bernth Lindfors and Reinhard Sander (1993)

126 *Seventeenth-Century British Nondramatic Poets, Second Series,* edited by M. Thomas Hester (1993)

127 *American Newspaper Publishers, 1950-1990,* edited by Perry J. Ashley (1993)

128 *Twentieth-Century Italian Poets, Second Series,* edited by Giovanna Wedel De Stasio, Glauco Cambon, and Antonio Illiano (1993)

129 *Nineteenth-Century German Writers, 1841-1900,* edited by James Hardin and Siegfried Mews (1993)

130 *American Short-Story Writers Since World War II,* edited by Patrick Meanor (1993)

131 *Seventeenth-Century British Nondramatic Poets, Third Series,* edited by M. Thomas Hester (1993)

132 *Sixteenth-Century British Nondramatic Writers, First Series,* edited by David A. Richardson (1993)

133 *Nineteenth-Century German Writers to 1840,* edited by James Hardin and Siegfried Mews (1993)

134 *Twentieth-Century Spanish Poets, Second Series,* edited by Jerry Phillips Winfield (1994)

135 *British Short-Fiction Writers, 1880-1914: The Realist Tradition,* edited by William B. Thesing (1994)

136 *Sixteenth-Century British Nondramatic Writers, Second Series,* edited by David A. Richardson (1994)

137 *American Magazine Journalists, 1900-1960, Second Series,* edited by Sam G. Riley (1994)

138 *German Writers and Works of the High Middle Ages: 1170-1280,* edited by James Hardin and Will Hasty (1994)

139 *British Short-Fiction Writers, 1945-1980,* edited by Dean Baldwin (1994)

140 *American Book-Collectors and Bibliographers, First Series,* edited by Joseph Rosenblum (1994)

141 *British Children's Writers, 1880-1914,* edited by Laura M. Zaidman (1994)

142 *Eighteenth-Century British Literary Biographers,* edited by Steven Serafin (1994)

143 *American Novelists Since World War II, Third Series,* edited by James R. Giles and Wanda H. Giles (1994)

144 *Nineteenth-Century British Literary Biographers,* edited by Steven Serafin (1994)

145 *Modern Latin-American Fiction Writers, Second Series,* edited by William Luis and Ann González (1994)

146 *Old and Middle English Literature,* edited by Jeffrey Helterman and Jerome Mitchell (1994)

147 *South Slavic Writers Before World War II,* edited by Vasa D. Mihailovich (1994)

148 *German Writers and Works of the Early Middle Ages: 800-1170,* edited by Will Hasty and James Hardin (1994)

149 *Late Nineteenth- and Early Twentieth-Century British Literary Biographers,* edited by Steven Serafin (1995)

150 *Early Modern Russian Writers, Late Seventeenth and Eighteenth Centuries,* edited by Marcus C. Levitt (1995)

151 *British Prose Writers of the Early Seventeenth Century,* edited by Clayton D. Lein (1995)

152 *American Novelists Since World War II, Fourth Series,* edited by James and Wanda Giles (1995)

153 *Late-Victorian and Edwardian British Novelists, First Series,* edited by George M. Johnson (1995)

154 *The British Literary Book Trade, 1700-1820,* edited by James K. Bracken and Joel Silver (1995)

155 *Twentieth-Century British Literary Biographers,* edited by Steven Serafin (1995)

156 *British Short-Fiction Writers, 1880-1914: The Romantic Tradition,* edited by William F. Naufftus (1995)

157 *Twentieth-Century Caribbean and Black African Writers, Third Series,* edited by Bernth Lindfors and Reinhard Sander (1995)

158 *British Reform Writers, 1789-1832,* edited by Gary Kelly and Edd Applegate (1995)

159 *British Short-Fiction Writers, 1800-1880,* edited by John R. Greenfield (1996)

160 *British Children's Writers, 1914-1960,* edited by Donald R. Hettinga and Gary D. Schmidt (1996)

161 *British Children's Writers Since 1960, First Series,* edited by Caroline Hunt (1996)

162 *British Short-Fiction Writers, 1915-1945,* edited by John H. Rogers (1996)

163 *British Children's Writers, 1800-1880,* edited by Meena Khorana (1996)

164 *German Baroque Writers, 1580-1660,* edited by James Hardin (1996)

165 *American Poets Since World War II, Fourth Series,* edited by Joseph Conte (1996)

166 *British Travel Writers, 1837-1875,* edited by Barbara Brothers and Julia Gergits (1996)

167 *Sixteenth-Century British Nondramatic Writers, Third Series,* edited by David A. Richardson (1996)

168 *German Baroque Writers, 1661-1730,* edited by James Hardin (1996)

169 *American Poets Since World War II, Fifth Series,* edited by Joseph Conte (1996)

170 *The British Literary Book Trade, 1475-1700,* edited by James K. Bracken and Joel Silver (1996)

171 *Twentieth-Century American Sportswriters,* edited by Richard Orodenker (1996)

172 *Sixteenth-Century British Nondramatic Writers, Fourth Series,* edited by David A. Richardson (1996)

173 *American Novelists Since World War II, Fifth Series,* edited by James R. Giles and Wanda H. Giles (1996)

174 *British Travel Writers, 1876-1909,* edited by Barbara Brothers and Julia Gergits (1997)

175 *Native American Writers of the United States,* edited by Kenneth M. Roemer (1997)

176 *Ancient Greek Authors,* edited by Ward W. Briggs (1997)

177 *Italian Novelists Since World War II, 1945-1965,* edited by Augustus Pallotta (1997)

178 *British Fantasy and Science-Fiction Writers Before World War I,* edited by Darren Harris-Fain (1997)

179 *German Writers of the Renaissance and Reformation, 1280-1580,* edited by James Hardin and Max Reinhart (1997)

180 *Japanese Fiction Writers, 1868-1945,* edited by Van C. Gessel (1997)

181 *South Slavic Writers Since World War II,* edited by Vasa D. Mihailovich (1997)

182 *Japanese Fiction Writers Since World War II,* edited by Van C. Gessel (1997)

183 *American Travel Writers, 1776-1864,* edited by James J. Schramer and Donald Ross (1997)

184 *Nineteenth-Century British Book-Collectors and Bibliographers,* edited by William Baker and Kenneth Womack (1997)

185 *American Literary Journalists, 1945-1995, First Series,* edited by Arthur J. Kaul (1998)

186 *Nineteenth-Century American Western Writers,* edited by Robert L. Gale (1998)

187 *American Book Collectors and Bibliographers, Second Series,* edited by Joseph Rosenblum (1998)

188 *American Book and Magazine Illustrators to 1920,* edited by Steven E. Smith, Catherine A. Hastedt, and Donald H. Dyal (1998)

189 *American Travel Writers, 1850-1915,* edited by Donald Ross and James J. Schramer (1998)

190 *British Reform Writers, 1832-1914,* edited by Gary Kelly and Edd Applegate (1998)

191 *British Novelists Between the Wars,* edited by George M. Johnson (1998)

192 *French Dramatists, 1789-1914,* edited by Barbara T. Cooper (1998)

193 *American Poets Since World War II, Sixth Series,* edited by Joseph Conte (1998)

194 *British Novelists Since 1960, Second Series,* edited by Merritt Moseley (1998)

195 *British Travel Writers, 1910-1939,* edited by Barbara Brothers and Julia Gergits (1998)

196 *Italian Novelists Since World War II, 1965-1995,* edited by Augustus Pallotta (1999)

197 *Late Victorian and Edwardian British Novelists, Second Series,* edited by George M. Johnson (1999)

198 *Russian Literature in the Age of Pushkin and Gogol: Prose,* edited by Christine A. Rydel (1999)

199 *Victorian Women Poets,* edited by William B. Thesing (1999)

200 *American Women Prose Writers to 1820,* edited by Carla J. Mulford, with Angela Vietto and Amy E. Winans (1999)

201 *Twentieth-Century British Book Collectors and Bibliographers,* edited by William Baker and Kenneth Womack (1999)

202 *Nineteenth-Century American Fiction Writers,* edited by Kent P. Ljungquist (1999)

203 *Medieval Japanese Writers,* edited by Steven D. Carter (1999)

204 *British Travel Writers, 1940–1997,* edited by Barbara Brothers and Julia M. Gergits (1999)

Documentary Series

1 *Sherwood Anderson, Willa Cather, John Dos Passos, Theodore Dreiser, F. Scott Fitzgerald, Ernest Hemingway, Sinclair Lewis,* edited by Margaret A. Van Antwerp (1982)

2 *James Gould Cozzens, James T. Farrell, William Faulkner, John O'Hara, John Steinbeck, Thomas Wolfe, Richard Wright,* edited by Margaret A. Van Antwerp (1982)

3 *Saul Bellow, Jack Kerouac, Norman Mailer, Vladimir Nabokov, John Updike, Kurt Vonnegut,* edited by Mary Bruccoli (1983)

4 *Tennessee Williams,* edited by Margaret A. Van Antwerp and Sally Johns (1984)

5 *American Transcendentalists,* edited by Joel Myerson (1988)

6 *Hardboiled Mystery Writers: Raymond Chandler, Dashiell Hammett, Ross Macdonald,* edited by Matthew J. Bruccoli and Richard Layman (1989)

7 *Modern American Poets: James Dickey, Robert Frost, Marianne Moore,* edited by Karen L. Rood (1989)

8 *The Black Aesthetic Movement,* edited by Jeffrey Louis Decker (1991)

9 *American Writers of the Vietnam War: W. D. Ehrhart, Larry Heinemann, Tim O'Brien, Walter McDonald, John M. Del Vecchio,* edited by Ronald Baughman (1991)

10 *The Bloomsbury Group,* edited by Edward L. Bishop (1992)

11 *American Proletarian Culture: The Twenties and The Thirties,* edited by Jon Christian Suggs (1993)

12 *Southern Women Writers: Flannery O'Connor, Katherine Anne Porter, Eudora Welty,* edited by Mary Ann Wimsatt and Karen L. Rood (1994)

13 *The House of Scribner, 1846-1904,* edited by John Delaney (1996)

14 *Four Women Writers for Children, 1868-1918,* edited by Caroline C. Hunt (1996)

15 *American Expatriate Writers: Paris in the Twenties,* edited by Matthew J. Bruccoli and Robert W. Trogdon (1997)

16 *The House of Scribner, 1905-1930,* edited by John Delaney (1997)

17 *The House of Scribner, 1931-1984,* edited by John Delaney (1998)

18 *British Poets of The Great War: Sassoon, Graves, Owen,* edited by Patrick Quinn (1999)

19 *James Dickey,* edited by Judith S. Baughman (1999)

Yearbooks

1980 edited by Karen L. Rood, Jean W. Ross, and Richard Ziegfeld (1981)

1981 edited by Karen L. Rood, Jean W. Ross, and Richard Ziegfeld (1982)

1982 edited by Richard Ziegfeld; associate editors: Jean W. Ross and Lynne C. Zeigler (1983)

1983 edited by Mary Bruccoli and Jean W. Ross; associate editor: Richard Ziegfeld (1984)

1985 edited by Jean W. Ross (1986)

1986 edited by J. M. Brook (1987)

1987 edited by J. M. Brook (1988)

1988 edited by J. M. Brook (1989)

1989 edited by J. M. Brook (1990)

1990 edited by James W. Hipp (1991)

1991 edited by James W. Hipp (1992)

1992 edited by James W. Hipp (1993)

1993 edited by James W. Hipp, contributing editor George Garrett (1994)

1994 edited by James W. Hipp, contributing editor George Garrett (1995)

1995 edited by James W. Hipp, contributing editor George Garrett (1996)

1996 edited by Samuel W. Bruce and L. Kay Webster, contributing editor George Garrett (1997)

1997 edited by Matthew J. Bruccoli and George Garrett, with the assistance of L. Kay Webster (1998)

Concise Series

Concise Dictionary of American Literary Biography, 6 volumes (1988-1989): *The New Consciousness, 1941-1968; Colonization to the American Renaissance, 1640-1865; Realism, Naturalism, and Local Color, 1865-1917; The Twenties, 1917-1929; The Age of Maturity, 1929-1941; Broadening Views, 1968-1988.*

Concise Dictionary of British Literary Biography, 8 volumes (1991-1992): *Writers of the Middle Ages and Renaissance Before 1660; Writers of the Restoration and Eighteenth Century, 1660-1789; Writers of the Romantic Period, 1789-1832; Victorian Writers, 1832-1890; Late-Victorian and Edwardian Writers, 1890-1914; Modern Writers, 1914-1945; Writers After World War II, 1945-1960; Contemporary Writers, 1960 to Present.*

Dictionary of Literary Biography® • Volume Two Hundred Four

British Travel Writers, 1940–1997

Dictionary of Literary Biography® • Volume Two Hundred Four

British Travel Writers, 1940–1997

Edited by
Barbara Brothers
and
Julia M. Gergits
Youngstown State University

A Bruccoli Clark Layman Book
The Gale Group
Detroit, Washington, D.C., London

WILMETTE PUBLIC LIBRARY

Advisory Board for
DICTIONARY OF LITERARY BIOGRAPHY

John Baker
William Cagle
Patrick O'Connor
George Garrett
Trudier Harris

Matthew J. Bruccoli and Richard Layman, Editorial Directors
C. E. Frazer Clark Jr., Managing Editor
Karen Rood, Senior Editor

Printed in the United States of America

The paper used in this publication meets the minimum requirements of American National Standard for Information Sciences–Permanence Paper for Printed Library Materials, ANSI Z39.48-1984. ∞™

This publication is a creative work fully protected by all applicable copyright laws, as well as by misappropriation, trade secret, unfair competition, and other applicable laws. The authors and editors of this work have added value to the underlying factual material herein through one or more of the following: unique and original selection, coordination, expression, arrangement, and classification of the information.

All rights to this publication will be vigorously defended.

Copyright © 1999 by The Gale Group
27500 Drake Road
Farmington Hills, MI 48331

All rights reserved including the right of reproduction in whole or in part in any form.

Library of Congress Cataloging-in-Publication Data

British travel writers, 1940–1997 / edited by Barbara Brothers and Julia M. Gergits.
p. cm.–(Dictionary of literary biography; v. 204)
"A Bruccoli Clark Layman book."
Includes bibliographical references and index.
ISBN 0-7876-3098-5 (alk. paper)
1.Travelers' writings, English–Bio-bibliography–Dictionaries. 2. British–Travel–Foreign countries–History–20th century–Dictionaries. 3. English prose literature–20th century–Bio-bibliography–Dictionaries. 4. Authors, English–20th century–Biography–Dictionaries. 5. Travelers–Great Britain–Biography–Dictionaries. 6. Travel writing–Bio-bibliography–Dictionaries. I. Brothers, Barbara, 1937– . II. Gergits, Julia Marie. III. Series.
PR788.T72B745 1999
820.9'355
[B]–DC21 98-51321
CIP

10 9 8 7 6 5 4 3 2 1

R
920
DI
444 4003

To Past Travelers—
William Price (1912–1996) and Mary Ella Bingham Hoover (1915–)
Leo John (1923–1979) and Mary Jane Hansen Gergits (1930–)

Gale Group 03/18/99 cont.

Contents

Plan of the Series

... Almost the most prodigious asset of a country, and perhaps its most precious possession, is its native literary product—when that product is fine and noble and enduring.

Mark Twain*

The advisory board, the editors, and the publisher of the *Dictionary of Literary Biography* are joined in endorsing Mark Twain's declaration. The literature of a nation provides an inexhaustible resource of permanent worth. We intend to make literature and its creators better understood and more accessible to students and the reading public, while satisfying the standards of teachers and scholars.

To meet these requirements, *literary biography* has been construed in terms of the author's achievement. The most important thing about a writer is his writing. Accordingly, the entries in *DLB* are career biographies, tracing the development of the author's canon and the evolution of his reputation.

The purpose of *DLB* is not only to provide reliable information in a convenient format but also to place the figures in the larger perspective of literary history and to offer appraisals of their accomplishments by qualified scholars.

The publication plan for *DLB* resulted from two years of preparation. The project was proposed to Bruccoli Clark by Frederick C. Ruffner, president of the Gale Research Company, in November 1975. After specimen entries were prepared and typeset, an advisory board was formed to refine the entry format and develop the series rationale. In meetings held during 1976, the publisher, series editors, and advisory board approved the scheme for a comprehensive biographical dictionary of persons who contributed to North American literature. Editorial work on the first volume began in January 1977, and it was published in 1978. In order to make *DLB* more than a reference tool and to compile volumes that individually have claim to status as literary history, it was decided to organize volumes by topic, period, or genre. Each of these freestanding volumes provides a biographical-bibliographical guide and overview for a particular area of literature. We are convinced that this organization—as opposed to a single alphabet method—constitutes a valuable innovation in the presentation of reference material. The volume plan necessarily requires many decisions for the placement and treatment of authors who might properly be included in two or three volumes. In some instances a major figure will be included in separate volumes, but with different entries emphasizing the aspect of his career appropriate to each volume. Ernest Hemingway, for example, is represented in *American Writers in Paris, 1920–1939* by an entry focusing on his expatriate apprenticeship; he is also in *American Novelists, 1910–1945* with an entry surveying his entire career, as well as in *American Short-Story Writers, 1910–1945, Second Series* with an entry concentrating on his short stories. Each volume includes a cumulative index of the subject authors and articles. Comprehensive indexes to the entire series are planned.

Since 1981 the series has been further augmented by the *DLB Yearbooks,* which update published entries and add new entries to keep the *DLB* current with contemporary activity. There have also been *DLB Documentary Series* volumes which provide biographical and critical source materials for figures whose work is judged to have particular interest for students. One of these companion volumes is entirely devoted to Tennessee Williams.

We define literature as the *intellectual commerce of a nation:* not merely as belles lettres but as that ample and complex process by which ideas are generated, shaped, and transmitted. *DLB* entries are not limited to "creative writers" but extend to other figures who in their time and in their way influenced the mind of a people. Thus the series encompasses historians, journalists, publishers, book collectors, and screenwriters. By this means readers of *DLB* may be aided to perceive literature not as cult scripture in the keeping of intellectual high priests but firmly positioned at the center of a nation's life.

DLB includes the major writers appropriate to each volume and those standing in the ranks behind

**From an unpublished section of Mark Twain's autobiography, copyright by the Mark Twain Company*

them. Scholarly and critical counsel has been sought in deciding which minor figures to include and how full their entries should be. Wherever possible, useful references are made to figures who do not warrant separate entries.

Each *DLB* volume has an expert volume editor responsible for planning the volume, selecting the figures for inclusion, and assigning the entries. Volume editors are also responsible for preparing, where appropriate, appendices surveying the major periodicals and literary and intellectual movements for their volumes, as well as lists of further readings. Work on the series as a whole is coordinated at the Bruccoli Clark Layman editorial center in Columbia, South Carolina, where the editorial staff is responsible for accuracy and utility of the published volumes.

One feature that distinguishes *DLB* is the illustration policy–its concern with the iconography of literature. Just as an author is influenced by his surroundings, so is the reader's understanding of the author enhanced by a knowledge of his environment. Therefore *DLB* volumes include not only drawings, paintings, and photographs of authors, often depicting them at various stages in their careers, but also illustrations of their families and places where they lived. Title pages are regularly reproduced in facsimile along with dust jackets for modern authors. The dust jackets are a special feature of *DLB* because they often document better than anything else the way in which an author's work was perceived in its own time. Specimens of the writers' manuscripts and letters are included when feasible.

Samuel Johnson rightly decreed that "The chief glory of every people arises from its authors." The purpose of the *Dictionary of Literary Biography* is to compile literary history in the surest way available to us–by accurate and comprehensive treatment of the lives and work of those who contributed to it.

The *DLB* Advisory Board

Introduction

The publication of W. H. Auden and Christopher Isherwood's appropriately titled *Journey to a War* on 16 March 1939 marked the end of an era in travel writing. An account of Auden and Isherwood's 1938 visit to China during the Second Sino-Japanese War, the book appeared six months before the outbreak of World War II. No country, even the so-called neutral ones, escaped the effects of this global conflict. War correspondents, military troops, support personnel, and refugees were the travelers of the years 1939 to 1945. The few travel essays and books that were published during this period were mostly reports from those who journeyed to the war. World War II and the events it set in motion shaped the destinations of British travel writers during the second half of the twentieth century as powerfully as the concerns of empire had shaped those of the nineteenth-century traveler.

When World War II ended in 1945, the world began to divide into opposing camps. As the United States and the Soviet Union vied to extend their spheres of influence, Communists and Nationalists began fighting in northern China; Yugoslavia was formed as a Communist country; and the Arab League was founded to oppose the creation of a Jewish state in Palestine. On 5 March 1946, at Westminster College in Fulton, Missouri, Winston Churchill gave the famous speech in which he proclaimed, "From Stettin in the Baltic to Trieste in the Adriatic, an iron curtain has descended," dividing the Communist states of the East and the free nations of the West. The Cold War had begun. In July 1947 Parliament passed the India Independence Act, beginning the gradual dissolution of the British Empire. In 1950 Chinese forces occupied Tibet, replacing religious restrictions on travel within her borders with equally stringent political limitations. In Africa battles for independence from colonial powers were followed by equally violent disputes over control of newly formed nations. Localized revolutions also occurred in South America during this period.

After World War II political and social changes and the proliferation of communications media had more influence over who traveled and where they went than did advances in the technology of travel. In 1936 BBC London inaugurated television broadcasting, and color television was introduced in 1951 in the United States. Later in the century home video and the Worldwide Web joined television, motion pictures, and the print media in bringing people pictures from around the world, whetting their desire to read about distant places and to experience them firsthand.

Stimulated by visual images and affordable prices for transportation and lodging, people in greater and greater numbers visited Italy, Egypt, Indonesia, Patagonia, Zimbabwe, and other countries that nineteenth- and early-twentieth-century travelers had traversed only with difficulty. By 1990 travel had become the second-largest American industry. According to the United States Travel Data Center, Americans made 44 million trips abroad for business and pleasure in 1993. Mark Cocker opens *Loneliness and Time* (1992), his study of twentieth-century British travel writing, with similarly impressive statistics on travel to and from Great Britain. For much of the world, travel has become part of everyday existence. In 1998 a journey around the world on the Concorde, as advertised in *The New Yorker,* took only twenty-four days and cost $56,000. Some commentators, such as Paul Fussell in *Abroad* (1980), continue the nineteenth-century tradition of distinguishing between the tourist and the traveler, decrying as mere tourists those whose mode of travel seems too easy or whose knowledge of the place visited is deemed too superficial. Cocker summarizes this distinction by saying that "tourists seek . . . an environment in which the characteristics that render a country distinct and even alien, are carefully controlled or totally eliminated." In contrast, travelers "generally insist that their activity depends upon the absence of the familiar"; they value "the very otherness of the visited country." Yet, Cocker argues, in the late twentieth century touring and traveling "now merge imperceptibly."

British travel and travel writing were also affected by changes in the social-class system. In 1944 the Butler Education Act inaugurated a system of universal secondary education, and in the 1960s seven new universities were established in Great Britain to answer the growing demand for postsecondary education. The extension of education to members of all classes contributed to an increase in the numbers and a greater diversity in the social status of British travelers. Broadening educational opportunities changed the market for travel books, as well as for those who wrote these books.

While it entertained and educated increasing numbers of readers following the war, travel writing received little critical attention. Modernism dominated the academy. Academics sought to distinguish what they studied and wrote from books produced for the masses, focusing their attention on fiction, poetry, and drama. The neglect of these travel writers in academe reveals much about the lingering denigration of travel writing as a lower art form than so-called imaginative literature. Travel writers who do achieve renown do so most often for other accomplishments. Lawrence Durrell, who won the Duff Cooper Prize in 1957 for his travel book *Bitter Lemons,* achieved a literary reputation on the basis of his novels. The same is true of V. S. Naipaul. Leigh Fermor, who received the Duff Cooper Prize for *Mani* in 1959, achieved fame as a war hero and has received little attention in literary studies. Newby is another example of a popular and distinguished travel writer who is not listed in most companions and guides to English writers in the twentieth century. Moorehead received the Duff Cooper Prize for *Gallipoli* (1956) and has been elected to the Royal Society for Literature; Mayle won a British Book Award for *A Year in Provence;* but, like Newby, they are not recognized as literary figures by literary historians. Geoffrey Moorhouse is a fellow of the Royal Society of Literature and the Royal Geographic Society. Though he has also written fiction, he is known primarily for his nonfiction prose and is thus generally ignored by literary scholars.

In the last quarter of the twentieth century, however, scholars who see literature as a part of and a reflection of the culture by and in which it is produced have broadened the definition of literature to include nonfiction prose works, including travel books. Distinguishing these works from guidebooks, Fussell has explained: "Travel books are a sub-species of memoir in which the autobiographical narrative arises from the speaker's encounter with distant or unfamiliar data. . . ." This definition often applies when a travel writer examines the seemingly familiar from an unfamiliar perspective, as when Jonathan Raban explores the land of his birth, Great Britain, from the sea in *Coasting* (1986). In this sort of travel writing the author enables readers to see places in new ways, to notice what they have not observed before.

Travel literature has also grown in popularity with the general public. In fact, Evelyn Waugh's prediction in 1946 that he did "not expect to see many travel books in the near future" has been proven wrong many times over. Guidebooks, the poor stepsisters of travel literature, account for significant shelf space in contemporary bookstores, testifying to the increasing number of tourists, if not travelers. According to *Travel Books Worldwide* (1991), of the more than two thousand travel books available each year in the United States, approximately 80 percent are guidebooks. (There are even guides to the guidebooks, including *The Guide to Travel Guides, The Traveler's Reading Guide,* and *Good Books for the Curious Traveler,* and the remainder are books that describe living in various places, such as Peter Mayle's *A Year in Provence* [1990] or Frances Mayes's *Under the Tuscan Sun* [1996]. Another 10 percent are travelogues. There are also magazines and newsletters devoted to travel.

The popularity of travel writing in Great Britain is evident from the works appearing on the best-seller lists. For example, on 7 December 1997 the list of best-selling hardbacks in the London *Sunday Times* included two travel books: Michael Palin's *Full Circle,* a description of a journey around the Pacific, and Bill Bryson's *A Walk in the Woods,* about his hiking the Appalachian Trail. These works beat out books about such pop-culture heroes and heroines as a famous cricketer and Princess Diana. During the same week a travel book held second place on the *Sunday Times* paperback list: Bryson's *Notes from a Small Island* (1995), about his walking tour of Great Britain.

Readers are drawn not only to new travel books but also to the works of earlier travelers. New books about earlier journeys–such as Peter Raby's *Bright Paradise* (1996), which describes the travels of Victorian scientists Charles Darwin, Henry Walter Bates, Alfred Russel Wallace, and Richard Spruce–demonstrate strong interest in travelers and their stories.

Another indicator of the widespread interest in travel writing was the establishment of the Thomas Cook Award, specifically for travel writing, in 1980. The first award went to Robyn Davidson for *Tracks,* her description of her trek across the Australian desert.[1] Some British newspapers, including *The Sunday Times* and *The Independent,* also have travel-writing competitions and awards. During the years since World War II travel books have won general literary awards, including the Hawthornden Prize, the Duff Cooper Memorial Prize, and the Somerset Maugham Award.

New media have broadened the audience for travel accounts. For example, there is a CD-ROM version of Davidson's *Tracks,* narrated by Davidson; and during Timothy Severin's 1996 journey, which he wrote about in *The Spice Islands Voyage: In Search of Wallace* (1997), he posted regular reports on the Worldwide Web and exchanged e-mail messages with schoolchildren around the world. Videos, audio books, television specials, and a cable network dedicated exclusively to travel also supplement traditional forms of travel reporting, such as the anthologies *Travelers' Tales,* specialized travel magazines such as *National Geographic* and *Condé Nast Traveler,* issues of *Granta* devoted to travel writing, and columns or articles in magazines such as *Gourmet* and *Bon Appétit.*

While the media through which travel writers can describe their journeys became more varied during the final decades of the twentieth century, writers' motives for traveling throughout the years since the end of World War II have remained much the same as their predecessors'. Intellectual curiosity, the desire for adventure, and even pure escapism remain high on the list of reasons for travel, even for professional travel writers.

A short stint at writing for a newspaper may launch a career as a travel-book writer, as in the case of William Dalrymple. Others combine work as newspaper travel correspondents with writing travel books. Alexander Frater of *The Observer* (London) produced five travel books between 1983 and 1993. Earlier Eric Newby worked as travel editor for *The Observer* (1964–1973) while continuing to write successful travel books.

Another professional travel writer, Stephen Brook, has worked as an editor and restaurant critic. In addition to producing some twenty books over a period of twenty-four years, he has written articles for magazines such as *Chef, Vogue,* and *Decanter,* as well as for British newspapers, including *The Times, The Independent,* and *The Sunday Express.*

Bruce Chatwin began his career as a professional travel writer in 1966, after he left Sotheby's, where at age twenty-six he had become the youngest director in the history of that auction house. Chatwin is known as a stylist whose works are full of literary references to writers and travelers. Like V. S. Naipaul, whose fiction and travel books are explorations of the postcolonial world, Chatwin challenges the boundaries between fact and fiction.

In addition to works by men and women who earn a living by traveling for its own sake, travel books are also written by people who go abroad for other professional reasons: for example, anthropologists, archaeologists, business executives, engineers, geologists, and journalists.

What might be best labeled as political travel has been popular throughout the twentieth century. Before World War II many British writers and intellectuals traveled to the Soviet Union to see the Communist political system in action. In *Political Pilgrims: Travels of Western Intellectuals to the Soviet Union, China, and Cuba 1928–1978* (1981) Paul Hollander discusses leftist sympathizers who, he believes, were so intent on defending the socialist experiment that they saw little that did not support their preconceptions. Yet, most of the books he examines are social or political histories. Both before and after the war most travel writers, even those who were favorably disposed to the Soviet system, did not necessarily describe it as the new heaven on earth. In fact, travel writers of the Cold War era, including those discussed in this volume, found much to fear in the Soviet Union, China, Cuba, and other Communist countries, and they were quick to describe the physical and emotional discomforts they experienced there.

In his *Among the Russians* (1983) Colin Thubron describes his travels by automobile in the Soviet Union toward the end of the Cold War as a journey undertaken in dread. Eric Newby's *The Big Red Train Ride* (1978), describing his journey across the Soviet Union from west to east on the Trans-Siberian Railway, is less overtly political than Thubron's book but is critical of Soviet attempts at censorship and limiting the traveler's movements. Florence Farmborough's *Nurse at the Russian Front: A Diary, 1914–18* (1974) and *Russian Album 1914–1918* (1975), accounts of her experiences as a nurse on the Russian Front during World War I, are also in keeping with the political mood of the Cold War era. In *The Best of Granta Travel* (1991), for which editors of *Granta* magazine selected twenty-one travel articles from their first thirty-five issues, more than a third of the essays are best described as political travel writing–from Martha Gelhorn's "Cuba Revisited" to Graham Swift's "Looking for Jiri Wolf," a description of a 1988 visit to Czechoslovakia.

The challenges facing the traveler-adventurer in the post-1950s world have less to do with the sort of physical unknowns faced by the explorers of earlier times than with political uncertainties. The hazards Patrick Marnham confronted in Uganda in 1973 were posed by government immigration and police squads, officials of dictator Idi Amin. A fellow of the Royal Society of Literature, Marnham is a journalist turned "swashbuckling" travel writer.

Even when travel writers least expect them, political adventures may await. In 1978, on his way to the airport in Dahomey, Bruce Chatwin found himself in the center of a coup and was imprisoned on suspicion of being a mercenary. In Iran during the late 1980s Christina Dodwell was arrested three times in less than a month by Revolutionary Guards who suspected her motives for traveling in their country.

Some political travel literature is by foreign correspondents for major newspapers. Gavin Young covered at least fifteen wars and revolutions in his thirty years as foreign correspondent for *The Observer* and wrote books about his travels in the Middle and Far East before turning his attention to the United States. Other travel writers who have worked as foreign correspondents include Jan Morris, Alan Moorehead, and Laurens van der Post.

Scientists and social scientists also write travel books. Nigel Barley went to Africa for anthropological fieldwork and began a parallel career as a travel writer. *A Plague of Caterpillars: A Return to the African Bush* (1986), his second book on Cameroon, is a wonderful example of travel humor. Redmond O'Hanlon, a reviewer of natural-history books, traveled to uncomfortable and unsafe places, such as Borneo, and treated his difficulties with humor in *In Trouble Again* (1988). Elspeth Huxley's studies in agricultural science inform her travel writings on Africa and Australia. Gavin Maxwell fits in the nineteenth-century tradition of nature and travel writer. Sheila Paine also fits the mold of amateur scientist. While she writes about social and political issues in her travel writings, her area of expertise is peasant embroidery. Her research trips to study it around the world inspired her to branch out into travel writing. Her travel essays won third prize in *The Sunday Times* Travel Writing Competition in 1989 and first prize in *The Independent* competition in 1991. In *The Afghan Amulet: Travels from the Hindu Kush to Razgrad* (1994) Paine describes the social and political life of people in remote regions of politically volatile nations such as Pakistan, Afghanistan, Iran, and Iraq.

Because it remains cut off from the rest of the world, Tibet is still a popular destination for travel writers. In fact, according to Cocker, only Tibet comes close to Greece in the twentieth century "in terms of the sheer volume of travel books" written about it. *Seven Years in Tibet* (1953), German traveler Heinrich Harrer's account of life in Tibet during the years immediately preceding the Chinese invasion of 1950, continues to attract readers, in part because of the 1997 movie version. Western fascination with Tibet owes much to its long history as a forbidden territory. Among the British travelers who have written about Tibet since 1950 are G. Stuart and Roma Gelder, who wrote *The Timely Rain* (1964) and *Memories for a Chinese Grand-daughter* (1967); Vikram Seth, whose *From Heaven Lake* (1983) won a Thomas Cook Award; and Vanya Kewley, whose *Tibet: Behind the Ice Curtain* (1990) is an account of her visit to a land that remains off limits to the casual tourist.

Travel is still not easy in some parts of Africa, contributing to reader interest in books about that continent. For Laurens van der Post, born in South Africa, and Elspeth Huxley, who spent much of her childhood in Kenya, travel to Africa is returning home. In his books about Africa, van der Post searches for his roots while attempting to understand the now-defunct South African policy of apartheid, which he deplored. In her memoirs and travel writing about Africa, Huxley domesticized the Africa of the male explorers. Beryl Markham's *West with the Night* (1942) is another memoir of growing up in a primitive, but nevertheless domestic, East Africa.

The continuing isolation of some parts of Africa is apparent in two recent books about the continent. Daisy Waugh, who traveled to Africa alone at age twenty-three, taught school in Isiolo, a remote Kenyan village, and wrote about her adventures in *A Small Town in Africa* (1994). In *Our Grandmothers' Drums* (1989), which won Somerset Maugham and Thomas Cook awards, Mark Hudson describes going to Gambia to research women's circumcision rites and spending a year in Dulaba, a village in which there was "nothing between one and the rough, dry surfaces of the people's lives."

Much travel writing since World War II has been marked by a search for the primitive, for places that have survived largely untouched by modern conveniences. Born in present-day Ethiopia, explorer Wilfred Thesiger made Arabia his spiritual home. Though he began his explorations during the 1930s, his first book, *Arabian Sands,* was not published until 1959. Since the 1960s much of Thesiger's time has been spent in Kenya, which in 1980 he decided to make his home. Patrick Leigh Fermor explored remote regions of the eastern Mediterranean before settling on the geographically isolated Greek peninsula of Mani. Cocker says that Thesiger, Leigh Fermor, and van der Post "found societies against which they could measure deficiencies in the home country[;] these places and their peoples were alien utopias." As Thesiger, citing Claude Lévi-Strauss's *Tristes Tropiques* (1955), has said of several writers on Arabia, they have created "the illusion of something that no longer exists but should exist."

Leigh Fermor was one of many British travel writers who wrote about the Mediterranean region after World War II. Rather than Italy, the destination of the eighteenth-century gentleman on the Grand Tour, or the French Riviera, favored by Edwardian and post–World War I socialites, these postwar travelers preferred the secluded spots of Greece or southeastern France. While Spain and Italy represented the fuller life to writers before World War II–such as Gamel Woolsey, Gerald Brenan, D. H. Lawrence, and Norman Douglas–the wartime allegiances of Spain and Italy made them unappealing, at least temporarily, to Lawrence Durrell and many other postwar writers.

Some critics consider Norman Lewis the best travel writer of the twentieth century, not because of his stylistic contributions to the genre but because of his skillful evocation of people and places–the attribute that many critics and writers consider the essential of good travel writing. Lewis had established himself as a travel writer before serving with the British Army in North Africa and Naples, which he described years later in *Naples '44* (1979). The Spain about which he had written in his first book, *Spanish Adventure* (1935), was essentially destroyed by the Spanish Civil War (1936–1939). The old Spain was his version of a place whose roots were in an ancient civilization and whose ways were little affected by the contemporary world. After World War II Lewis roamed further afield in his travels.

According to Cocker, enthusiasm for Greek travel books "reached its peak in a twenty-year period after the Second World War." (The travel writer who is credited with turning the attention of the British to Greece was Robert Byron, who published his books between 1929 and 1937 and was killed during World War II.) Several of these writers–including Leigh Fermor, Eric Newby, Alan Moorehead, and Norman Lewis–discovered the region during the war.

Leigh Fermor, whom Cocker identifies as one of the four most prominent writers on Greece (the others are Byron, Durrell, and the American Henry Miller), was a war hero. He fought in Crete and became famous for capturing a German general. His memoirs and travel books have been compared with writings of T. E. Lawrence (Lawrence of Arabia) for their scholarship and attention to detail. Leigh Fermor's books are eyewitness accounts of cultures that have in many cases changed dramatically or disappeared since he visited them.

Eric Newby escaped from an Italian prisoner-of-war camp and was given refuge by a farmer in the mountains of northern Italy until he was recaptured and sent to Germany. After the war he married a woman he had met while in hiding, and years later they began spending part of each year in a Tuscany farmhouse. He has written about the Mediterranean region in his war memoir, *Love and War in the Apennines* (1971), and in the travel book *On the Shores of the Mediterranean* (1984). Newby has ranged widely in his travels, and he is well known for his descriptions, not only of Italy but also of India, the Hindu Kush, and the Soviet Union.

Alan Moorehead covered the war as a correspondent for *The Daily Express* (London) and wrote books about it: *Mediterranean Front* (1941), *A Year of Battle* (1942), *The End of Africa* (1943), and *Eclipse* (1945). As David Callahan, who wrote the Moorehead entry in this volume, states, Moorehead's travel books are not conventional, but they "involve ceaseless travel" and "the fascination of being placed within an alien environment." As in many travel narratives, experience rather than history is the basis for Moorehead's war books. Moorehead returned to the Mediterranean after the war but to revisit battle sites and places he had seen in wartime.

For travel writers of the World War II generation and for those of later generations the isolated villages in the Mediterranean region have answered the desire to escape from the frenetic pace of modern life. While these writers were not the first to engage in a nostalgic search for a precontemporary world, this quest intensified after World War II. Peter Mayle, born during the war, left a job as an advertising copywriter to live in a two-hundred-year-old house in Provence. The popularity of his *A Year in Provence* (1989) and *Toujours Provence* (1991) is evidence of the enduring desire to get away from it all. For the most part, however, the Mediterranean has become the destination of the tourist who has bought a package tour. Those who want to escape from modernity in the late twentieth century have had to seek out more-remote places.

In twentieth-century travel writing, the means of travel has increasingly become the motivation for travel as well as the subject of travel writing. Timothy Severin, an historian of travel and exploration, has traced the steps of Marco Polo and re-created ancient shipboard journeys to test the veracity of legends about the travels of Brendan, Sinbad, Jason, and Ulysses. Building the ships and studying winds and tides to reconstruct hypothetically the courses he follows, Severin has introduced a new kind of travel into the genre of travel narratives.

The fascination of the first half of the twentieth century with the new motorcar and the fast, luxurious trains that crisscrossed Europe has been replaced in the second half of the century by a nostalgia for older means of travel. Alexander Frater's *Stopping-Train Britain: A Railway Odyssey* (1983) and *Beyond the Blue Horizon: On the Track of Imperial Airways* (1986) are travel books and histories of travel. Dervla Murphy traveled by bicycle, as did Eric Newby.

In other books, including Newby's *Slowly Down the Ganges* (1966), Naomi James's *At One with the Sea* (1979), and Gavin Young's *Slow Boats to China* (1981), boat travel gives authors a way to get to interior space and to re-examine the past. Beryl Bainbridge has described Jonathan Raban's *Coasting* (1986) as part travel book, part autobiography, and part novel.

During the second half of the twentieth century more and more women travel writers have undertaken dangerous journeys. Women such as Robyn Davidson, who was twenty when she began her expedition across the Aboriginal desert interior of Australia on camelback, and Sheila Paine, who was sixty when she went behind the Islamic curtain, have become known for travels in which they deliberately put themselves at risk, particularly because of their gender.

Sarah Hobson, a producer of documentary films as well as a writer of travel narratives, has disguised herself as a man to visit the Iranian shrine of Qum, which females are forbidden to enter. She has also traveled to Peru, India, Gambia, and Senegal and made documentaries on such dangerous subjects as the Cocaine War in South America. Christina Dodwell traveled by Land Rover, horse, bicycle, dugout, and airplane during her first, three-year "extraordinary odyssey" in Africa, which she described in *Travels with Fortune* (1979). Newspaper accounts published in French Equatorial Africa labeled her an "intrepid explorer." She lived up to that label by setting out next for Papua New Guinea, and she has since written about journeys to China, Turkey, Iran, Siberia, and Madagascar–as well as a second trip to West Africa, which she re-explored from a Pegasus XL Microlight airplane.

Naomi James tested herself by sailing around the world solo in 1977, becoming the first woman to do so, and wrote about her adventures in two books: *Woman Alone* (1978) and *At One with the Sea* (1979). Another woman sailor-writer is Rosie Swale, who wrote about her voyages in the catamaran *Anneliese* in *Children of Cape Horn* (1974) and *Back to Cape Horn* (1986).

Another solo traveler is Barbara Toy, whose journeys have been on land. Toy, who says her "one and only love" is the desert, received the Rover Award from the Long-Distance Land-Rover Association for making a journey "of outstanding initiative and enterprise" from the Niger River northeast to the Mediterranean. She wrote about it in *The Way of the Chariots* (1964). Like those earlier travelers whose writings she admires–Wilfred Thesiger, Freya Stark, and Charles Doughty–Toy is a lover of adventure.

Several women have become known for their travels by bicycle. Josie Dew describes bicycling through India in *The Wind in My Wheels* (1992) and through the United States in *Travels in a Strange State* (1994). Bettina Selby has also traveled alone and by bicycle, touring places as diverse as the British Isles, India, Africa, and the Middle East. Another frequent bicyclist is Dervla Murphy, an intrepid traveler who has used the means by which she travels to demonstrate her independence. Traveling in India, Tibet, Nepal, Pakistan, Africa, and the Andes, she makes light of the dangers she has encountered. Cocker identifies her as one of those travel writers for whom the "quest for knowledge can be a physically satisfying, all-absorbing lifelong adventure."

Not all women travel writers of the second half of the twentieth century have been adventurous. Grace Dibble, who taught at teacher's colleges in Canada, India, and Nigeria, most often traveled with tour groups. She began traveling in 1935 and eventually visited some sixty countries. After she retired in 1965, she began writing about her travels, publishing her first book three years later. Her books have been favorites among armchair travelers.

As Dennis Porter has observed in *Haunted Journeys* (1991), travel writers from James Boswell to V. S. Naipaul have submitted themselves to the challenge of travel, "if not always to make themselves over" or escape, "then at least to know themselves differently." In many ways Naipaul stands as the quintessential late-twentieth-century traveler and writer. Not only is it difficult to separate fact from fiction in his works and in those of many of his contemporaries among travel writers, but it is also more and more difficult to place such peripatetic individuals, born in one place and living in another, always seemingly engaged in the search for self and for home. The grandson of Indian Hindus, Naipaul was born in Trinidad, lives in England, and journeys to India on a quest for the home he knows only as a traveler.

In the late twentieth century academics have finally begun to treat travel writing as a genre worthy of examination from the viewpoint of literary history and critical theory. The few histories of travel writing focus on writers of a particular time, on women writers, or on writers about a particular place. Susan Morgan observes in *Place Matters* (1996) that "European travel literature on Borneo alone would require at least a book-length study." The twenty-first century should see many book-length studies of various aspects of travel literature.

–Barbara Brothers and Julia M. Gergits

1. The winners of Thomas Cook Awards for 1980 to 1997 are:

1980	Robyn Davidson, *Tracks*
1981	Jonathan Raban, *Old Glory*
1982	Tim Severin, *The Sindbad Voyage*
1983	Vikram Seth, *From Heaven Lake*
1984	Geoffrey Moorhouse, *To the Frontier*
1985	Patrick Marnham, *So Far From God*
1986–1987	Patrick Leigh Fermor, *Between the Woods and the Water*
1988	Colin Thubron, *Behind the Wall*
1989	Paul Theroux, *Riding the Iron Rooster*
1990	Mark Hudson, *Our Grandmothers' Drums*
1991	Jonathan Raban, *Hunting Mister Heartbreak*
1992	Norman Lewis, *A Goddess in the Stones*
	Gavin Young, *In Search of Conrad*
1993	Nik Cohn, *The Heart of the World*
1994	William Dalrymple, *City of Djins*
1995	Gavin Bell, In *Search of Tusitala*
1996	Stanley Stewart, *Frontiers of Heaven*
1997	Nicholas Crane, *Clear Waters Rising*

From 1980 to 1994 there were also Thomas Cook Awards for guidebooks, and from 1988 to 1992 there were separate awards for illustrated guides.

Acknowledgments

This book was produced by Bruccoli Clark Layman, Inc. Karen L. Rood, senior editor for the Dictionary of Literary Biography series, was the in-house editor.

Administrative support was provided by Ann M. Cheschi and Tenesha S. Lee.

Accountant is Neil Senol; assistant accountant is Angi Pleasant.

Copyediting supervisor is Phyllis A. Avant. The copyediting staff includes Brenda Carol Blanton, Thom Harman, Melissa D. Hinton, Beth Peters, Raegan E. Quinn, and Audra Rouse. Freelance copyeditors are Brenda Cabra, Rebecca Mayo, Nicole M. Nichols, and Jennie Williamson.

Editorial associate is Jeff Miller.

Layout and graphics staff includes Janet E. Hill and Mark J. McEwan.

Office manager is Kathy Lawler Merlette.

Photography editors are Margo Dowling, Charles Mims, Alison Smith, and Paul Talbot. Digital photographic copy work was performed by Joseph M. Bruccoli.

SGML supervisor is Cory McNair. The SGML staff includes Linda Drake, Frank Graham, Jennifer Harwell, and Alex Snead.

Systems manager is Marie L. Parker.

Database manager is Javed Nurani. Kimberly Kelly performed data entry.

Typesetting supervisor is Kathleen M. Flanagan. The typesetting staff includes Karla Corley Brown, Pamela D. Norton, and Patricia Flanagan Salisbury. Freelance typesetters include Deidre Murphy and Delores Plastow.

Walter W. Ross and Steven Gross did library research. They were assisted by the following librarians at the Thomas Cooper Library of the University of South Carolina: Linda Holderfield and the interlibrary-loan staff; reference-department head Virginia Weathers; reference librarians Marilee Birchfield, Stefanie Buck, Stefanie DuBose, Rebecca Feind, Karen Joseph, Donna Lehman, Charlene Loope, Anthony McKissick, Jean Rhyne, and Kwamine Simpson; circulation-department head Caroline Taylor; and acquisitions-searching supervisor David Haggard.

Dictionary of Literary Biography® • Volume Two Hundred Four

British Travel Writers, 1940–1997

Dictionary of Literary Biography

Stephen Brook

(20 June 1947–)

Brian D. Reed
Case Western Reserve University

BOOKS: *The Fine Art of Printing* (New York: Privately printed, 1974);

A Bibliography of the Gehenna Press: 1942–1975 (Northampton, Mass.: J. P. Dwyer, 1976);

New York Days, New York Nights (London: Hamilton, 1984; New York: Atheneum, 1985);

Honkytonk Gelato: Travels Through Texas (New York: Atheneum, 1985; London: Hamilton, 1985);

The Dordogne (London: George Philip, 1986; Topsfield, Mass.: Salem House, 1987);

Liquid Gold: Dessert Wines of the World (London: Constable, 1987; New York: Beech Tree Books, 1987);

Maple Leaf Rag: Travels Across Canada (London: Hamilton, 1987; New York: Vintage, 1988);

The Double Eagle: Vienna, Budapest and Prague (London: Hamilton, 1988); republished as *Vanished Empire: Vienna, Budapest, and Prague: Three Capital Cites of the Hapsburg Empire as Seen Today* (New York: Morrow, 1988);

The Club: The Jews of Modern Britain (London: Constable, 1989);

Winner Takes All: A Season in Israel (London: Hamilton, 1990; New York: Hamilton, 1991);

The Veneto: Venice to the Dolomites (London: George Philip, 1991);

L.A. Lore (London: Sinclair-Stevenson, 1992); republished as *L.A. Days, L.A. Nights* (New York: St. Martin's Press, 1993);

Prague: Architecture, History, Art (London: George Philip, 1992);

Claws of the Crab: Georgia and Armenia in Crisis (London: Sinclair-Stevenson, 1992);

Savignon Blanc and Semillon (London & New York: Viking, 1992);

Stephen Brook (photograph © Nicholas Cook)

Vienna (London & New York: Dorling Kindersley, 1994);

Sauternes and Other Sweet Wines of Bordeaux (London & Boston: Faber & Faber, 1995);

Class: Knowing Your Place in Modern Britain (London: Gollancz, 1997);

South of France: Southern Rhône, Provence, Languedoz-Roussillon Guide (London: De Agostini, 1997; New York: De Agostini, 1997);

God's Army: The Story of the Salvation Army (London: Macmillan, 1988);

Panillac: The Wines and Estates of a Renowned Bordeaux Commune (London: Mitchell Beazley, 1998).

OTHER: *The Oxford Book of Dreams,* edited by Brook (Oxford & New York: Oxford University Press, 1983; New York: Oxford University Press, 1983);

George Marciano, *The Panhandle,* introduction by Brook (Los Angeles: Guess?, 1988);

The Penguin Book of Infidelities, edited by Brook (London & New York: Penguin, 1994);

Opera: A Penguin Anthology, edited by Brook (London: Viking, 1995).

A meticulous observer with an acerbic wit, Stephen Brook is well known as a wine enthusiast, a restaurant critic, an editor, and a travel writer. Writing in an entertaining yet informative style, he synthesizes his own identity with the landscape and architecture around him, sampling and critiquing food and culture. Brook writes with humor and compassion while keeping a trenchant lookout for the sublime.

Stephen Brook was born on 20 June 1947 to Jewish parents in London. He "developed a taste for travel" as a child, when his parents took him on annual holidays through France, Switzerland, Germany, and Italy. Attending Trinity College, Cambridge, where he studied literature and philosophy, Brook graduated in the spring of 1969 and began a career in publishing. After a short stint as an editor with Cassell in London, he moved to Boston, Massachusetts, in December 1969 to join his American girlfriend. They were married a few months later. Brook prefers to keep his family life confidential, stating that "writers should be known for their writings more than the vagaries of their private lives."

Brook's time in the United States was well spent. He made important contacts with publishers in Boston and New York, and he became intrigued with the American psyche and lifestyle. While he was happy in his American setting, he also longed for familiar and comfortable British surroundings. In *Maple Leaf Rag* (1987) he explains that "I would occasionally drive up through Maine to Quebec City for a long weekend. Boston was a congenial city but an American one, and I missed Europe. I missed the texture of old stone and the scrawled plat du jour on a menu." Working as a staff editor for Little, Brown and *The Atlantic Monthly* in Boston from 1971 to 1973, Brook was also able to hone his writing skills while learning about the complex world of publishing. In 1973 he became editorial director at David R. Godine, where he remained through 1975. In that year Brook was divorced from his wife, and in 1976 he returned to London, taking up a position as editor with the academic publishing house Routledge & Kegan Paul, where he remained until 1980. He married Maria Lonstrup in 1987.

Brook began working as a freelance writer in 1982. While editing *The Oxford Book of Dreams* (1983) for Oxford University Press, he was also working on his first travel book, the critically acclaimed *New York Days, New York Nights* (1984). Relying on contacts he had made while living in America, Brook set out notebook in hand to write an honest assessment of a city he feels to be "pure magic."

Booked at the roach-infested Chelsea Hotel, made famous by earlier guests such as Andy Warhol, Bob Dylan, and Sid Vicious, Brook begins an amusing critique of his surroundings. At his best when he lets his sarcastic wit control his narrative, Brook enters the hotel lobby and comments on the "especially dull" paintings that adorned the "cheap" foyer. He continues this snobbish banter, claiming the receptionist "combined charm and ineptitude to a remarkable degree" when he informs Brook that his room key has been "mislaid." This news is not welcome to Brook (considering his concerns about the neighborhood), but he pushes onward. He is led down a "long corridor that has all the charm of a Victorian reformatory: the walls were coated with a rough beige plaster and the doors were painted a brown as pretty as creosote." He accepts a room that "had been untouched since the 1950's, that decade of exquisite taste." Even after an inspection of the refrigerator, which exposes a "cockroach convention," Brook seems to relish the experience as part of the New York culture, a necessary part of his quest to write a truthful account of one of the world's greatest cities.

The oddities of New York are an important part of its appeal for Brook. With his eye for uncommon detail, he describes an encounter in a coffee shop with a prostitute who "laid a hand on his thigh and slowly slid it in the direction of the organ in question" as he gulped down his milk before making a quick escape. He was also amused by Washington Square dope dealers, who openly hawk their wares "with considerable invention," using lines such as: "I've got the herb that's superb, the smoke that's no joke! Don't pass till you've tried my grass!" Seeking the unusual, Brook visited the "Erotic Bakery on Christopher Street" and recorded intriguing shop signs, including one in Greenwich Village that proclaims "EAR PIERCING. YOUR CHOICE: WITH OR WITHOUT PAIN." Perceiving the "style" of the panhandlers on chic Sixth Avenue, Brook reports an encounter with one who asked, "'I know that you

Austin to Dallas 1

Thex flight to Austin, they announced, would be delayed. Two colour television sets lurching off wall brackets kept a passive bunch of weary passengers quiet, if not happy, as we waited in the departure lounge at Houston for news. Businessmen sat bucketed in plastic, their briefcases and raincoats sloped over adjacent seats while they flicked the pages of <u>Texas Business</u>, <u>Fortune</u>, and <u>Money</u>. Heavily chinned women, bursting out of their blue jeans, had their noses into books with titles such as <u>Deafness</u> and <u>Shortness of Breath</u>. The men were making money; the women were reading about the health they so evidently neglected. And I was turning the pages of an especially minor Trollope nove, a small badge of Englishness I was carrying as a cultural St Christopher's medal on entering Texas.

Announcements from Southwest Airline officials kept us informed. Our plane ~~to Austin~~ was arriving via Dallas, but a norther had just struck that city. Northers are cold fronts that whoosh south across the great plains and hit the usually warm Texas air. The temperature can topple forty degrees in an hour or two, and if the cold norther hits a spongy xhumid tangle of warm Gulf air, all kinds of meteorol-ogical turbulence can result, and it was just such a change in the weather that had grounded our plane in Dallas.

Two pretty flight attnedants did their best to keep us cheerful. Eventually there was good news: "Just thought you folks'd like to know, the weather in Austin is just <u>beau</u>tiful." ~~Languid murmurings. "It's about eighty degrees this evening.~~ "And here's some more good news. We've been notified that the plane has just taken off from Dallas and is now airborne - somewhere or other." Cheers.

Half an hour later. "Ladies and gentleman, this is a final update. We expect to start boarding at 8.55. To pass the time until then we're offering a free ticket on this flight to the first person who correctly guesses our combined ages." We leapt from our seats and rushed to the counter, flinging numbers into thexx air.

"52!" I yelled.

Page from the typescript for Honkytonk Gelato *(Collection of Stephen Brook)*

have heard it a hundred times before, but have you a dime that you can spare?' I smiled and he promptly capitalized on his success: 'Or any multiple thereof?'" Brook inspected the workings of the "nerve-fraying" New York subway system, which, he decided, must be "sponsored by the city's cab drivers." Yet Brook does not necessarily dislike "the dirty, noisy, shabby, confusing" subways. Like many visitors to the city, he is excited by the "unsettling" experience of stepping "through psychedelically painted doors into an interior that itself resembles a hallucination." Writing that "everything about the trains is metallic and raucous. They're embellished, smeared, daubed with graffiti in a ferocious beauty of violent swirling color," he used the subway every day to better connect with this aspect of New York society.

As a food and wine critic, Brook wrote about more than twenty major dining establishments, including Bondini's, Sardi's, Elaine's, and the Four Seasons. His review of American fast food is the most telling:

> I . . . went in search of coffee, which, of course, is no problem in New York at 4:30 a.m. I found a Burger King, or one of its clones, and ordered a Breakfast Special that consisted of drinkable coffee, and a gelatination of egg, molten cheese and a whisper of ham, flattened between the halves of what Americans fondly think of as a bun, although scientific analysis suggests it is in fact a papier-mâché construct.

Continuing his travels in America, Brook's next book, *Honkytonk Gelato: Travels Through Texas* (1985), was successful with the critics if not with the public. In this witty narrative Brook looks beyond Texas folklore to discover the true essence of this complex state. The real Texas emerges in Brook's vivid descriptions and impressions of a culture that is modern and dynamic while still remaining true to its frontier roots. The consummate Englishman, Brook is delighted with cowboy culture and Southern hospitality, and his chatty style meshes well with his informative purpose.

While sitting in the Texas Lone Star Saloon in London with his friend Christopher Middleton, an expatriate English poet, Brook hatched the idea of writing a travel book on the "real" Texas. Middleton offered his house in Austin and promised "all night parties" and "women as beautiful as the climate."

Honkytonk Gelato presents a panorama of Texas from the large cities of Houston and Dallas to the small towns of Cross Plains and Marfa, from the sacredness of a Baptist revival meeting to the profaneness of cowboy speech, and from the wildness of the World Championship Chili Cookoff to the gentility of the Tyler Rose Festival. "The puzzle of Texas is that it is simultaneously diverse and unified," Brook claims:

> Texans' sense of themselves, their cultural identity, whether formed by a shared passion for football or Willie Nelson or frosted Margaritas, links the rancher from San Angelo with the timber merchant from Nacogdoches like mountaineers at different heights yet on the same rope.

Brook found Austin to be like any other university town in America, with its "bookshops, small cafes, boutiques, [and] street stalls." He decided not to spend much time there, for fear he would feel compelled to just "sip chilled wine on the patios of small restaurants" and would not find out much about the "real" Texas. So gathering supplies, "wine and fruit, a sleeping bag and tape recorder . . . maps and brochures," Brook set out in a rented car across the limestone hills toward Dallas and Houston.

Finding the larger cities of Texas not quite as enjoyable as New York, claiming that the Dallas Expressway was "suicidal" and its downtown laden with "architectural confusion" and slums like any "shantytowns of other Southern cities" and thinking Houston was full of "Whorehouse motels" where he was robbed of just about everything he had while he left to get a bite to eat, Brook spent most of his travels exploring the more remote areas. At the Texas Prison Rodeo in Huntsville, Brook became engrossed in the performances of the "Convict Cowboys," who rode Brahman bulls "like animated stick candy in their black and white stripes." Brook gleefully describes the action:

> "Would you believe it?" began the MC. "We have a thief in this prison. Yes we do, and they've stole our milk pails. So instead our Redshirts are gonna have to milk these cows into a Coke bottle. And to make it jest a bit harder, we've provided the meanest mama cows you ever seen."

Brook's eye for obscure but telling detail is apparent in his reporting on Texas bumper stickers. Claiming "bumper stickers invariably reflect the local culture," Brook quotes a Rockdale bumper sticker that said "HAPPINESS IS A WARM GUN," a sticker on a pickup truck in Hearne that stated "CRIME DOESN'T PAY . . . NEITHER DOES FARMING," one on a car in an Austin parking lot that proclaimed "EAT AMERICAN BEEF NOT FOREIGN BULL," another on a Dallas van stating "KEEP TEXAS BEAUTIFUL. PUT A YANKEE ON A BUS," and a sticker on a battered Chevy outside Laredo that called for the government to "DEREGULATE EVERYTHING." Such pieces of pop culture give the reader a better feel for the state than piles of scholarly publications.

Dust jacket for Brook's 1985 book, in which he concludes that "Texas has a vibrant character of its own, and a determined optimism that makes most Europeans look world-weary and effete"

Brook again took time to sample the local cuisine. In Texas the portions are large, hot, and beefy, and the restaurants are comfortable and hospitable. In Lubbock, Brook got some "serious" ribs at the "legendary" Stubb's, and in Coldwater he sampled "the purest beef jerky you can get." Neither dish is usual fare for Brook's refined tastes, but he seemed to enjoy the "hot intense spicy flavors." Not quite ready to embrace all Southern cooking, Brook also tried chicken-fried steak at a "hole in the wall," and he proclaims: "I'd think twice about serving the stuff to a dog."

Brook ended his stay in Texas by attending Willie Nelson's New Year's Eve concert in Houston. Claiming "the themes of the songs are both particularized and matched to the probable experiences of the audience," Brook sang along to songs about "love, loyalty . . . betrayal, drinking." With little else to listen to on the radio, he seems to have become "addicted" to country-western music during his stay in Texas.

"If Texas isn't a real place," muses Brook, "it is nevertheless a bag into which all its mythologies have been chucked over the years." Even if he does not agree with all Texas attitudes, biases, and ideas, he was won over by its warm hospitality and strong sense of place. Caught up in the "sentimentality," Brook ends his book by quoting from the lyrics of Waylon Jennings: "Ain't no easy way of saying goodbye, So be sure and tell them all down in Texas I Said Hi."

Brook's next publication, *The Dordogne* (1986), was the first book he wrote for George Philip's travel guide series, which also includes Brook's *The Veneto: Venice to the Dolomites* (1991) and *Prague: Architecture, History, Art* (1992). Filled with colorful photography, these books consist mostly of Brook's eyewitness accounts of his driving and walking tours. Sampling the local wine and cuisine, commenting on representative architecture, and rating the hospitality and cleanliness of hotels, Brook is quite comfortable in his role as critic. Peppering his guides with local history, Brook emphasizes following the unbeaten path. In *The Dordogne,* a title that refers to a section of southwest France, Brook makes recommendations with relish:

> From Bridaire there is a direct road to Eymet, but you may prefer a detour past the villages of Sadillac and Saint-Capraise-d'-Eymet. The church at Sadillac has been crudely stuccoed but it is a fine domed building that contains carved capitals of high quality.

Brook solidified his reputation as a wine critic in 1985, when he became the wine columnist for *The New*

Statesman. At this time he began work on *Liquid Gold: Dessert Wines of the World* (1987), a carefully researched and detailed guide that received acclaim from the established wine community.

Brook returned to North America for his next book, *Maple Leaf Rag: Travels Across Canada* (1987). He warns the reader:

> before I made these journeys across Canada, I subscribed to every prejudice going. . . . Canada in my mind was perceived as dull, decent, excessively forrested, culturally barren, politically timid, utterly overshadowed by its neighbor to the south. . . . On the rare occasions when I was required to think about Canada at all, it was impossible to do so without smugness.

Brook's honesty at the outset and his concern for the overwhelming size of the country (he says that getting "from A to B [is] always twice as far as you think") gives one the feeling that he was not as excited about this project as he was about his earlier travel books. He did not range far from the main roads of Canada; yet he took a side trip to Manhattan "to open up some space between Montreal and Toronto" and to regain "a sense of excitement" that he finds "wonderfully stimulating" in cultural centers such as London and New York City. Far from taking away from the book, these biases and Brook's curmudgeonly demeanor give spice and weight to his comments on long-debated and controversial Canadian issues.

Traveling through Ontario, Brook sums up the free-trade argument by saying "it certainly seems absurd that there should be trade barriers between two large countries with an extended common border and so many common interests." Discussing his feelings with an economics professor at the University of Toronto, Brook gets into the deeper concerns about free trade, including Canadian political and cultural independence from the United States. Because "the American domination of Canadian life [is] close to total," Brook believes, Canadian access to such a large market could only be beneficial. Brook also tackles the ethnocentric language laws of Quebec, describing how in many cases the "French only" law is "taken to extremes." Pointing out the absurdities of a law that "required companies with over fifty employees to conduct all their internal communications in French, even when all fifty were Anglophone," Brook is not afraid to address the important issues that have divided Canadian politics for decades. He also takes on the plight of the Native Canadian population, expressing his concerns about how the Canadian tribes "dwell wretchedly on remote northern reserves that lack proper roads and sewage systems."

Brook also scrutinizes the varied Canadian landscape. He is repulsed by the "tacky paraphernalia" that surrounds the Canadian side of Niagara Falls. He marvels at the vulgarity of the West Edmonton Mall, and he finds cities such as Toronto boring because "the unexpected doesn't happen." He even pokes fun at Canada's proud reputation for cleanliness. Claiming "the place just revels in . . . blandness," Brook contends that "if someone finds a gum wrapper on the subway platform, they phone their alderman to complain."

Even with these criticisms, Brook seems taken with the natural areas of Canada. He admires the awesome northern Canadian landscape, "with its formidable undergrowth and lofty trees." He also admits a fondness for the "European neatness" of rural Canadian villages "with the houses gathered tightly around the church, like piglets at teat," and he is exhilarated by the wide-open sky of the prairie. These views from a "confirmed urbanite" are surprising at first, but Brook seems to have been genuinely moved at times by the majesty of the great outdoors and "Canadian good-heartedness."

Leaving North America, Brook decided to journey next to "the uncertain center of Europe." His reasons for going there were twofold. He had a personal interest in the region because his father's family had lived in Prague during the 1930s, and his grandmother had been deported to a death camp in 1942. If it had not been for quick thinking in 1938, when Brook's father, mother, and grandmother escaped through Czechoslovakia and Austria toward safety in England, Brook may have never had the comfortable life that he was enjoying. Brook was also interested in examining the distinctive architecture, wine, and cultural life of the three great cities of the region: Vienna, Budapest, and Prague. Therefore, in 1986 Brook set out for the land of his parents to write a travel book about the rapidly changing countries of Austria, Hungary, and Czechoslovakia and to "flesh out the stories" he had heard about his ancestors. *The Double Eagle: Vienna, Budapest and Prague* (1988) is a personal exploration and a narrative whose title alludes to the shared Hapsburg traditions of the region.

Brook feels that the dissolution of the Hapsburg Empire after World War I, the upheavals of World War II, and the tensions of the Cold War in central Europe have "diminished" the three cities. Feeling that "Prague and Budapest are no longer the glittering cultural centres they once were" and that Vienna, "despite the return to prosperity," was "physically diminished" by its dwindling population and lack of prewar grandeur, Brook had some reservations about what he would find on his journey. Yet he discovered Vienna was "beautiful" and "as rich and sustaining as its pastries and cui-

Dust jacket for Brook's 1990 book, in which he expresses the fear that the "great dream" of a Zionist state "seems to be turning into a nightmare"

sine"; Budapest was "more unbuttoned" and "imaginative" than he had thought, and Prague was mysterious and "courageous" in its quest for freedom.

As always, Brook comments on the regional architecture, admiring the ceiling at the famous Winter Riding School in Vienna and the "elaborately turned and curved" ironwork that covers the windows of Budapest with a "gracefulness that masks their defensive function," and he is delighted by the "budding magnolias and squadrons of scarlet tulips" that cover the peacock-filled gardens of the palaces of Prague.

Relishing the local cuisine, Brook sampled gigantic dumplings, thick gravy, fresh pâté, stuffed pork, and rich pastries and washed it all down with local beer or wine. On a particularly memorable evening of "unrestrained gluttony" in Vienna, Brook followed the recommendations of the locals and visited Haller's restaurant to enjoy dining, good music, and dancing. The restaurant's owner, fifty-year-old "determinedly pudgy" Frau Haller, was much more entertaining than the menu:

> Her eyes gleamed, and her mouth was half-open with a permanent merriment whenever she flounced through the room with another tray heaped with plates from which schnitzels poked over the sides just as beer bellies loom over belts. She swung her hips provocatively, and there was plenty of hip to swing.

His equally lovable landlady in Prague was just as detrimental to his waistline. As if the only way to eat in the region was to excess, she offered Brook a daily breakfast of "a tub of yogurt, a ham omelette, two rolls, and two or sometimes three slices of cheese or nut cake, usually all but invisible beneath an avalanche of whipped cream."

The final chapter, "Coda: The Dead," describes Brook's visit to the graves of his ancestors near Vienna and in Prague. In Vienna he had to scale a wall of the locked and unused cemetery to visit the unkempt grave of his mother's little sister. In Prague, Brook found the grave of his grandfather, and in Terezin he found the deserted crematorium where his great-grandmother was "reduced to ashes" in 1942. Later, visiting the Central Cemetery in Vienna, Brook walked through the large Jewish section, where graves were untended, knocked over, and littered with debris. When asked about the conditions of the cemetery, the municipal authorities claimed the upkeep of the graves is the responsibility of the descendants. About two hundred thousand Jews lived in Vienna before the war. In the late 1980s there were about seven thousand.

Brook next wrote *The Club: The Jews of Modern Britain* (1989), a widely reviewed and controversial look at English Jewry. Reviewing the book for *New Statesman Society* (21 April 1989), Bernard Kops, while otherwise impressed with Brook's scholarship, was concerned "the title will set the tone and help to compound the stereotype image that the Jews are . . . aloof." In a scathing review for *The Spectator* (13 May 1989), Anthony Blond fumed, "whoever at Constables . . . decided to call this account of a tiny number of British citizens . . . *The Club,* should have his nose tweaked." Brook has remained interested in understanding his identity as an Anglo Jew. Soon after finishing *The Club,* Brook traveled to Israel to wrestle with his complex feelings about a nation he found fascinatingly heterogeneous but unusually neurotic. Brook had no "Zionist yearnings" to travel to Israel and had always felt "it was too far" to travel there. Also, because his "appetites and instincts were European rather than Levantine," he never saw any need to subject himself to the catastrophes of a troubled nation. Claiming he was uncomfortable with the whole idea of a Jewish state, Brook deduced, "it was only a matter of time before my canny editor sensed a Project in this deep reluctance of mine," so he was shipped off to better "understand Israel."

In the middle of all his careful research on past and present Jewish history, Brook continued writing about wine. In 1988 he became the wine critic for *Vogue* magazine.

In the midst of these changes Brook's focus remained on his heritage. *Winner Takes All: A Season in Israel* (1990) is an unsentimental travelogue full of rational, sensible discussions of the Israeli-Palestinian problem, but it offers few analytical or political observations that point toward any solution. Not until the final chapter, which in many ways seems out of place, does the book seem to have any polemical agenda. The bulk of his narrative is light and humorous, concerned with portraying the positive social aspects of a fascinatingly diverse people.

Brook's narrative begins by sifting through the cultures of the old city of Jerusalem. He is amazed that Jews, Greek Orthodox, Armenians, and Muslims can coexist at all when they must share sacred landmarks, but he is still disappointed in the way they handle themselves:

> Religious Jews are forbidden to approach the holy Moslem places on the Temple Mount lest they inadvertently encroach on the Holy of Holies. Moslems are hypersensitive to any archaeological explorations that come too close to their holy sites. And the numerous Christian denominations that guard the church of the Holy Sepulchre are forever squabbling.

In fact, "one gets used to seeing grown men and women standing on the street screaming at each other." Brook seems to have been overwhelmed by these troublesome problems, which may explain why he described what he saw rather than commenting on it and why he chose an amusing and upbeat approach to highlight the positive aspects of this complex country.

Brook mixes his light approach with serious discussions, however. He includes the conversations of disgruntled Arabs in the occupied territories and a chapter on Ultra-Orthodox Jews. Explaining that "there is nothing little about Bethlehem" and "Manger Square is a car park," he nonetheless speaks with poignancy about the pilgrims who journey there. With each chapter Brook's picture of Israel becomes more complex, until Brook finally concludes, "The problems seem too great, the will to solve them too feeble, and my own prescriptions altogether inadequate. . . . I came away from Israel with relief."

Brook had made his first visit to Los Angeles as a student in the 1960s, when he and three British companions lived with a film producer in a posh Beverly Hills mansion and attended pool parties at Zsa Zsa Gabor's house complete with "snacks, an impromptu basement disco, and motoring services." During this time he "reveled in the explosion of unforeseen luxury." Twenty-five years later, Brook returned to Los Angeles to search for more "preposterous yet satisfying excess," to reexamine the familiar landmarks, and to deal with the mystique as he had previously tackled that of New York. While gathering information for *L.A. Lore* (1992), Brook had many contacts and renewed friendships. At a famous Los Angeles restaurant he and his friends discussed the local culture, street crime, Rodney King, and the food and wine. The book is structured as a series of adventures interrupted by gastronomic interludes. During trekking and dining Brook tried to understand his irrational fondness for a great American city.

Before he began writing the book, Brook lived in Los Angeles for three months, renting a car and spending much time driving great distances. Despite getting lost and panicking in traffic, Brook embraced this "culture of the freeway" and drove everywhere, even when it was a longer walk to the car than to the place he was driving. Calling Los Angeles "a horizontal city, an urban omelette, an epic concrete smear," he felt he must move all over the city to best discover its significance. He visited a Korean massage spa, Disneyland, the Crystal Cathedral, the South Central neighborhood, the

Nixon Library, Mount Wilson, Knott's Berry Farm, and all the major film studios. Humorously and reverently, he critiques the art and architecture, the restaurants and nightclubs, the paranoia and arrogance, and the absurdity of living in a city that seems like a Hollywood movie set.

Brook's narrative takes a Los Angeles tone from the outset. He parodies Hollywood producers and memoirists when he provides "really sincere winsome Hollywood-style acknowledgments," including one "to my cat Phylloxera, and the ghost of my previous cat Lola, for showing respect." Later in the book he reports in television talkshow style: "Hi. . . . It's coming up to the top of the hour and Janey [a fictional cohost] and I are getting ready to bring you the first lines of this new chapter. We'll be updating you on all the latest plot developments, and we have a few real twists and turns up ahead."

Serious sections on race relations, politics, and unemployment give readers a balanced look at the "City of Dreams." Possibly the finest chapter is "Rodney King Drives Too Fast," which deals with the issues surrounding the police beating of an African American stopped for speeding. "For years there have been allegations of police brutality on this scale," Brook states, "but they were often dismissed as the whinings of wrongdoers who, if they hadn't been up to no good, would never have attracted the overenthusiastic attention of the forces of law and order." He brings out the fact that "in 1990 alone the Los Angeles Police Department (LAPD) paid out $11.3 million in damages to settle law suits brought by victims of police brutality" and suggests that these cases must be "merely the tip of the iceberg." After attending a demonstration against Chief Daryl Gates in front of police headquarters, Brook noticed a billboard for the Steven Seagal movie *Out for Justice* (1991), which read: "He's a cop. It's a dirty job . . . but somebody's got to take out the garbage." Brook suggests, "If police brutality is endemic to Los Angeles, then it is not the LAPD alone that bears the responsibility."

Brook planned a trip to Armenia and Georgia in the autumn of 1991 just after both republics declared their independence from the Soviet Union. Despite the political upheaval and the outbreak of civil war, his trek was "intended as a jaunt that would include visits to the dazzling High Caucasus, leisurely inspections of early medieval churches, a thorough sampling of the celebrated local gastronomy, and a study of the problems inevitably encountered by two small nations seeking independence." In the book that resulted from this unusual excursion, *Claws of the Crab: Georgia and Armenia in Crisis* (1992), Brook begins his narrative by maintaining that the two republics "became the prisoners of their histories and cultures" as they asserted their independence.

One of the major problems for the breakaway republics was the lack of food. Shortages of good quality meats and other staples made it difficult for Brook to sample the national cuisine in which he was so interested. The women in the fish shops sat "behind the counters reading the newspapers, as there was no fish to sell." Most restaurants were uncertain if they "would open at all." The renown regional wine shops "were locked and the shelves empty." Often he ignored the violence, and once he even wondered if nearby gunfire "was fighting or an accident or a domestic squabble . . . or a party." Despite all obstacles he sipped wine on a country estate in Tsinindali, where he "lied about its excellence" to appease his host, and he found a cellar in Kakheti, where he sampled wine that was "rich" and "full-bodied." In fact, much of his travels in the region are geared toward finding available wineries, and much of his text describes the bouquet, color, and taste of local vintages. He also enjoyed the local architecture despite the problems of coming under siege. He toured Armenian cathedrals with particular enjoyment and rated their carvings and windows in careful detail. While many critics panned *Claws of the Crab* because of Brook's uneasy response to the historical events that were unfolding around him, his insistence on maintaining his original plans provides the quirky charm of the narrative. By critiquing the Georgian hotels, the rude drivers, the gastronomic availabilities, and the cultural offerings, Brook creates an interesting perspective.

In 1991 Brook turned his attention again to publishing wine books. His critically acclaimed *Savignon Blanc and Semillon* (1992), his award-winning *Sauternes and Other Sweet Wines of Bordeaux* (1995), his *South of France* (1997), and his comprehensive study of the celebrated wines in *Panillac* (1998) further cemented his reputation as a wine critic. He also edited two important anthologies, *The Penguin Book of Infidelities* (1994) and *Opera: A Penguin Anthology* (1995), and in 1997 he published a scholarly study of the social-class system in Great Britain. Brook continues to write about travel and wine while also producing book reviews and gastronomy columns for *Chef, Cigar Aficionado, Vogue, Condé Nast Traveller,* and *Decanter* magazines and London newspapers, including *The Times, The Independent,* and *Sunday Express.* He lives in London with his second wife and his stepdaughter.

Brook's keen eye for telling detail, his good ear for local dialect, and his insatiable appetite for excellence in wine and food, make his books entertaining and valuable. Certainly, he is one of the most knowledgeable British travel writers.

Bruce Chatwin

(13 May 1940 – 18 January 1989)

James J. Schramer
Youngstown State University

See also the Chatwin entry in *DLB 194: British Novelists Since 1960, Second Series.*

BOOKS: *Animal Style Art from East to West,* by Chatwin, Emma C. Bunker, and Ann R. Farkas (New York: Asia Society, 1970);

In Patagonia (London: Cape, 1977; New York: Summit, 1979);

The Viceroy of Ouidah (London: Cape, 1980; New York: Summit, 1981);

On the Black Hill (London: Cape, 1982; New York: Viking, 1983);

Patagonia Revisited, by Chatwin and Paul Theroux, illustrated by Kyffin Williams (Salisbury: Michael Russell, 1985; Boston: Houghton Mifflin, 1986); republished as *Nowhere Is a Place: Travels in Patagonia,* with a new foreword and photographs by Jeff Gnass (San Francisco: Sierra Club, 1992);

The Songlines (London: Cape, 1987; New York: Viking, 1987);

Utz (London: Cape, 1988; New York: Viking, 1989);

What Am I Doing Here (London: Cape, 1989; New York: Viking, 1989);

Bruce Chatwin: Photographs and Notebooks, edited by David King and Francis Wyndham (London: Cape, 1993); republished as *Far Journeys: Photographs and Notebooks* (New York: Viking, 1993);

Anatomy of Restlessness: Selected Writings, 1969–1989, edited by Jan Borm and Matthew Graves (London: Cape, 1996; New York: Viking, 1996).

OTHER: Osip Mandelstam, *Journey to Armenia,* translated by Clarence Brown, introduction by Chatwin (London: Next Editions, 1980);

Robert Byron, *The Road to Oxiana,* introduction by Chatwin (London: Picador, 1981);

"An Eye and Some Body," introduction to *Lady: Lisa Lyon,* by Robert Mapplethorpe (New York: Viking, 1983; London: Blond & Briggs, 1983);

Sybille Bedford, *A Visit to Don Otavio,* introduction by Chatwin (London: Folio Society, 1990).

Bruce Chatwin in the Hindu Kush in 1964 (photograph by David Nash)

SELECTED PERIODICAL PUBLICATIONS–UNCOLLECTED: "Postscript to a Thousand Pictures," *Sunday Times Magazine,* 26 August 1973, pp. 48–51;

"The Albatross" and "Chiloe," *Granta,* 24 (Summer 1988): 11–13, 166–170.

Despite the critical acclaim for his travel sketches and books, Bruce Chatwin disliked being labeled a travel writer. He conceded, however, that travel was central to his writing and that he could not write unless he traveled. Asked by interviewer Michael Ignatieff what travel meant to him, Chatwin replied: "The word travel is the same as the French *travail.* It means hard work, penance, and finally a journey." The result of that travail is a body of work that resists classification. Nicholas Murray argues that Chatwin's "books straddle the genres of novel and travel-writing and blur the distinction between fact and fiction." Peripatetic by nature, Chatwin ignored both the boundaries imposed by geography and those imposed by genre.

Charles Bruce Chatwin was born in Sheffield, England, on 13 May 1940 to Charles Chatwin, a lawyer, and Margharita Turnell Chatwin. He began his nomadic way of life early; in *The Songlines* (1987) he writes about "the fantastic homelessness" of his early childhood: "My father was in the Navy, at sea. My mother and I would shuttle back and forth, on the railroads of wartime England, on visits to family and friends." He told Ignatieff that during the war, "while my father was away in the Navy, I lived in NAAFI [Navy, Army and Air Force Institutes] canteens and was passed around like a tea urn." What stability there was during the wartime years came during visits to his paternal maiden grandaunts, Janie and Gracie, who lived together in Stratford-upon-Avon (in *The Songlines* he changes their names to Katie and Ruth, respectively). Aunt Janie had served as a nurse in World War I and had traveled to Paris and Capri as a painter. According to Murray, it was from Aunt Janie, "a tireless reader of modern fiction," that Chatwin "first heard the name of Ernest Hemingway, his acknowledged mentor in prose style" and learned that "Americans wrote better, cleaner English than the English themselves." On the other hand, Aunt Ruth, Chatwin says in *The Songlines,* "had traveled only once in her life, to Flanders, to lay a wreath on a loved one's grave." From his aunts he learned about the men in his father's family who "were either solid and sedentary citizens–lawyers, architects, antiquaries–or horizon-struck wanderers who had scattered their bones in every corner of the earth." When his aunts talked about the "blighted destinies" of these wanderers, Gracie would hold him tight to protect him from the curse of wanderlust; but "from the way she lingered over words such as 'Xanadu' or 'Samarkand,'" he knew that she "also felt the trouble of the wanderer in her soul." She told him that the name Chatwin came from "Chettewynde, which meant the winding path in Anglo-Saxon."

In addition to Hemingway, Chatwin revered the writers Osip Mandelstam and Robert Byron. In his introduction to Clarence Brown's translation of Mandelstam's 1933 book of essays, *Journey to Armenia* (1980), Chatwin calls Mandelstam "the shaman and seer of his time." Exiled to Siberia because his poetry had offended Joseph Stalin, Mandelstam died in a transit camp near Vladivostock in 1938 and became, according to Chatwin, "our century's literary martyr. Another age would have made him a saint." In his introduction to the 1981 edition of Byron's *The Road to Oxiana* Chatwin says of that book, originally published in 1937: "Long ago, I raised it to the status of 'sacred text,' and thus beyond criticism. My own copy–now spineless and floodstained after four journeys to Central Asia–has been with me since the age of fifteen."

After preparatory school and Marlborough College–where, Murray quotes him as saying, he was thought of as "a dimwit and dreamer"–Chatwin decided against further university training; he told his university-bound friends that they were "boring." His family talked him out of a stage career, and he, in turn, rejected their suggestion that he become an architect. In 1958 he started at Sotheby and Company in London as a porter in the ceramics department at £6 a week. His superiors soon saw that Chatwin had what the fine-arts world referred to as "the eye," and by the time he was twenty-five he was the head of the Impressionist department and was on his way to becoming the youngest director in the history of the firm. In August 1965 he married Elizabeth Chanler, an American who had been educated at Radcliffe College and was the personal secretary of the chairman of Sotheby's.

Chatwin left Sotheby's in 1966. He spent the next several years studying archaeology at Edinburgh University; during this time he traveled to the Soviet Union, Czechoslovakia, the Ukraine, Afghanistan, Mauritania, and Dahomey. In 1970 he helped organize an exhibition of "Animal Style" art of nomadic peoples under the sponsorship of the New York-based Asia Society. Chatwin's contributions to the exhibition catalogue were the notes to the sections on Iron Age Europe and the Ipiutak people and an essay, "The Nomadic Alternative." In the introduction to the catalogue the director of Asia House Gallery, Gordon Bailey Washburn, notes: "Mr. Chatwin, an anthropologist at heart, is inclined to find shamanism the most likely explanation for the Animal Style . . . seeing in it the natural explanation for the style's apparent encirclement of the globe."

In "The Nomadic Alternative" Chatwin argues that the word *civilization* is encrusted with "moral and ethical overtones, the accumulated inheritance of our self-esteem." Although it is contrasted with "barbarism, savagery, and even bestiality," *civilization* "means nothing more than 'living in cities.'" Chatwin sees the nomad not as an invader but as a "stigmatized outsider" dwelling on lands that proved unsuitable to urban civili-

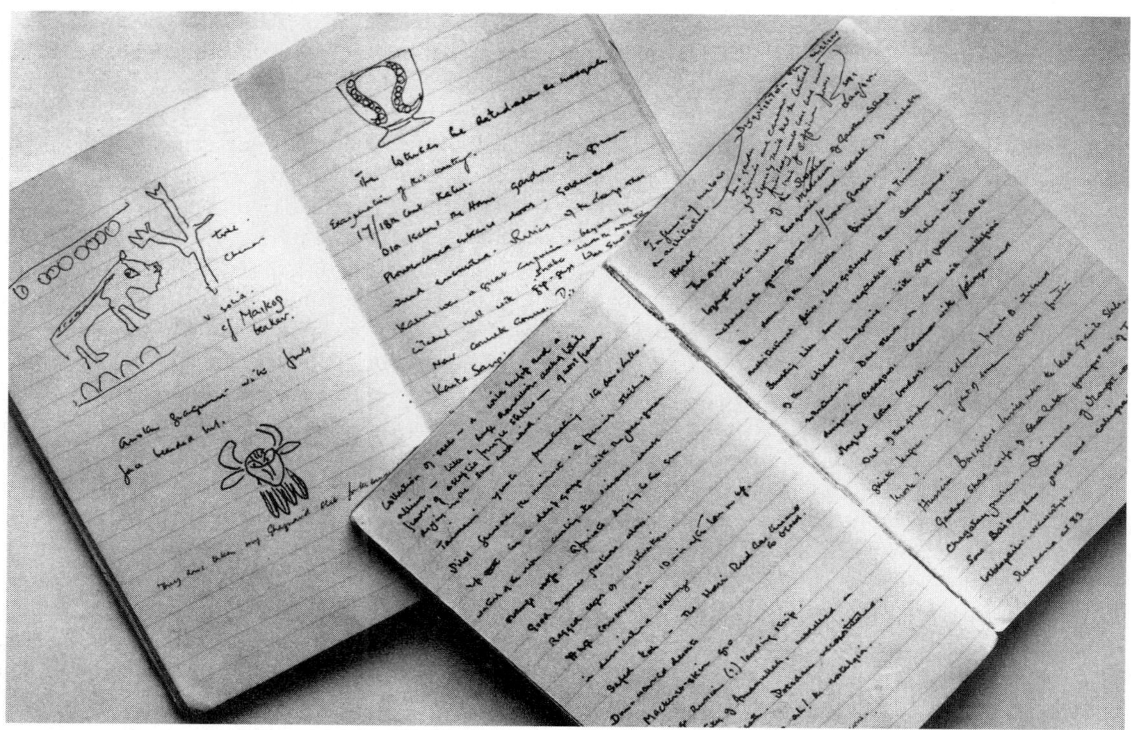

Two of the fifty notebooks in which Chatwin jotted down his impressions during his travels (Estate of Bruce Chatwin)

zation. Pointing out that *nomad* comes from Latin and Greek words meaning "to pasture," Chatwin observes that there is little that is random about the movements of nomadic peoples. "Pastoral tribes follow the most conservative patterns of migration, changing them only in times of drought or disaster."

A self-described "total failure at the age of 33," Chatwin was nearly out of money when Francis Wyndham, assistant editor of *The Sunday Times Magazine,* secured for him a position as an adviser on art and architecture. He soon became a free-roving journalist, interviewing such figures as André Malraux and Indira Gandhi; the interviews are collected in his *What Am I Doing Here* (1989). At the end of the interview with Malraux, Chatwin asks what the French writer thinks about the "prospects for an adventurer today." Malraux replies that there is "a faint possibility" for adventure in Central Asia but adds that "there are blocks of flats in Samarkand." They end their talk exchanging images of Afghanistan, "where eagles wheel over deodar forests and tribesmen carry copper battle-axes and wreathe vine leaves round their heads as they did in the time of Alexander." Gandhi is, at least initially, a less sympathetic character than Malraux. Observing her meeting with the widows of five workers gunned down by police, Chatwin reports: "She gave them no consolation. Instead she offered her jagged three-quarter profile to them and the photographers." Beneath that "jagged profile," however, Chatwin detects a more fragile Gandhi. "Notwithstanding the imperial nose and the great brooding eyes, she seemed small, frail and nervous. . . . My immediate impulse was to protect her." For Chatwin, the key to Gandhi's character is her fascination with the story of Joan of Arc, "the girl who gave up her life for her country." In a postscript in *What Am I Doing Here* to his piece on Gandhi, Chatwin recalls watching the television broadcast of her funeral after her assassination in 1984: "I felt immeasurably sad. . . . Yes. Indira had found her martyrdom. Politically, she was a catastrophe: yet she was still the little girl who wanted to be Joan of Arc."

In his essay "I Always Wanted to Go to Patagonia: The Making of a Writer," included in *Anatomy of Restlessness: Selected Writings, 1969–1989* (1996), Chatwin says that the idea of a trip to Patagonia resulted from his interview in late 1975 with the ninety-three-year-old architect and designer Eileen Grey. On the wall of her Paris salon hung a map of Patagonia she had painted in gouache. Chatwin told Grey that he "always wanted to go there"; Grey replied, "So have I. . . . Go there for me." After this meeting, Chatwin claims, he sent a one-sentence telegram from Paris to his bosses at *The Sunday Times Magazine:* "Gone to Patagonia for six months." It is doubtful, however, that Chatwin acted so precipitously. Wyndham, who would have been the recipient of the message, told Murray: "It must be a fiction." Hunter Davies, the editor, told Murray that Harold Evans, the general editor, had ordered him to cull writers, such as Chatwin, whose writing did not fit the magazine's new format, which emphasized shorter pieces with a domestic focus. Davies added, "I did not care for his purple prose, which I thought . . . self indulgent." Whatever the truth about Chatwin's departure from *The Sunday Times Magazine,* the book that resulted from his trip, *In Patagonia* (1977), marked his emergence as a rising star on the British literary scene.

For his travel reading on his Patagonia trip Chatwin took Mandelstam's *Journey to Armenia* and Hemingway's *In Our Time* (1925). If Mandelstam, who was exiled to Siberia for his anti-Stalinist poetry, was one of Chatwin's literary saints, Stalin was one of his personal devils. In the opening pages of *In Patagonia* Chatwin relates how the shadowy presence of the "Cannibal of the Kremlim" prompted him to develop an early interest in Patagonia as a refuge: growing up during the Cold War with the ever present fear that Stalin would set off a nuclear conflict, he had decided that Patagonia was "the safest place on earth." Even after Stalin's death, he "continued to hold Patagonia in reserve."

Journey to Armenia and *In Our Time* greatly influenced Chatwin's work. Both books are written in a terse, impressionistic style and are organized into short chapters, features that characterize the published version of *In Patagonia.* Chatwin's style may, however, have been as much the result of careful editing as of his emulating Mandelstam's or Hemingway's prose. In his 18 July 1996 review of the posthumously published *Anatomy of Restlessness* in *The Times* (London), John Ryle recalled that the manuscript for *In Patagonia* "was famously vast and unwieldy." The published version was "cut down to 97 laconic numbered sections, some only a paragraph long" by Chatwin and his editor at Jonathan Cape, Susannah Clapp.

The "laconic numbered sections" of *In Patagonia* are reminiscent of the interchapters of Hemingway's *In Our Time.* Chatwin weaves into the narrative of his travels through Argentina and Patagonia the story of the Western outlaws Butch Cassidy and the Sundance Kid (aliases of Robert Leroy Parker and Harry Longabaugh, respectively), who disappeared in South America in the early 1900s.

The structure of *In Patagonia* is not the only feature that can be traced to Hemingway's influence. The style of Chatwin's description of the books owned by Bill Philips, an English sheep rancher–"I looked at his shelf and saw all the best books. He had been reading Turgenev's *Sportsman's Sketches* and we talked about Turgenev"–is pure Hemingway, and so is its content: Ivan Turgenev was one of Hemingway's favorite authors. Chatwin's description of a young man in a tavern in Bahia Blanco seems to come right out of Hemingway's *The Sun Also Rises* (1926): "A country boy stood at the bar. He was shaky on his feet but kept his head up like a gaucho. He was a nice-looking boy with curly black hair and he really was very drunk." In this passage and elsewhere in the work Chatwin's interest in the male form is clear. Even a lunch in Buenos Aires becomes an occasion for a reflection on Latin machismo:

> At a lunch we sat under a painting of one of General Rosa's gauchos by Raymond Monvoisin, a follower of Delacroix. He lay swathed in a blood-red poncho, a male odalisque, cat-like and passively erotic.
>
> "Trust a Frenchman," I thought, "to see through all the cant about gauchos."

In this anecdote Chatwin turns the gaze of homoerotic desire on a figure–the gaucho–long associated with heterosexual virility. His "trust a Frenchman" remark is also a classic deflection in that it assigns to the more worldly–and, therefore, more carnal–French a knowledge of forbidden sexuality to which most English people would not admit.

Chatwin has an eye for distinctive details and an ability to detect a "story" in the most mundane facts. He is even able to uncover a tale in a telephone book: "The history of Buenos Aires is written in its telephone directory. Pompey Romanov, Emilio Rommel, Crispina D. Z. de Rose, Ladislao Radzwil, and Elizabeth Marta Callman de Rothschild–five names taken at random from the R's–told a story of exile, disillusion and anxiety behind lace curtains." He compares Buenos Aires with Russia, "Tsarist rather than Soviet Russia. . . . The Russia of greedy kulaks, corrupt officials, imported groceries and landowners asquint to Europe." A highly visual literary artist, Chatwin heightens some details and subdues others to help the story emerge from the canvas of daily life.

Perhaps because his style is so consciously visual, Chatwin seems to focus on the eyes of the people about whom he writes. When he meets an affluent young Persian who has come to Patagonia to recruit converts for the Baha'i faith, Chatwin concentrates on the man's "enormous syrupy eyes." He describes the "evil blue eyes" of the Sundance Kid. When he stays at a small hotel in Rio Pico, Argentina, run by a woman who is mourning the death of her firstborn son, her eyes catch his notice: "The owner was a brave and sorrowful woman in black, with heavy-lidded eyes, mourning with a Jewish mother's passion." Her remaining son is "an olive-skinned boy with the flickering eyes of the Semite." On a visit to Casimir Slapelič, a Lithuanian expatriate who discovered dinosaur bones in Patagonia,

Photograph taken by Chatwin during his 1971 visit to Abomey in Dahomey (Estate of Bruce Chatwin)

Chatwin feels himself being devoured by the "mica-shining eyes" of a young Indian woman Slapelič had adopted.

Chatwin's description of the Sundance Kid as a "Pennsylvania German with evil blue eyes" and his references to the "flickering eyes of the Semite" and the "mica-shining eyes" of the Indian woman suggest he was not above using ethnic or racial stereotypes to achieve his effects. Many people in Patagonia generously helped him, but Chatwin often repays their kindness by caricaturing them rather than capturing them as fully realized subjects. He writes that the hotel in Rio Pico was "run by a Jewish family who lacked even the most elementary notions of profit." When he cuts his hand in a fall from a horse, Chatwin is treated by a doctor who moves "with the slow fluidity that saves Russian women of bulk from ungainliness." Other people exist only as background. The reader learns about the Indian woman's eyes but nothing about her life. Chatwin is not without empathy for the poor, but he often glamorizes their poverty. Of spending a cold night in the peons' quarters on a ranch, he observes: "Apart from [their] ponchos, their maté equipment and their knives, the peons were free of possessions."

In fairness to Chatwin, he did not write *In Patagonia* as an ethnographic or sociological study. It is a book about the dreamers, eccentrics, and exiles who came to Patagonia to escape their pasts and work out their futures. Among the exiles who most appeal to Chatwin are the Welsh families who came to the Chubut Valley in 1865: "They were poor people in search of a New Wales, refugees from cramped coal-mining valleys, from a failed independence movement, and from Parliament's ban on Welsh in schools. Their leaders had combed the earth for a stretch of land uncontaminated by Englishmen." As often happens with immigrants determined to set themselves apart, the Welsh were only partially successful in maintaining their heritage. In the village of Gaimán, "the centre of Welsh Patagonia," Chatwin observes a society struggling to remain distinctive. He notes that Mrs. Jones's grandson, who helps run her tea shop, "called his grandmother 'Granny' but otherwise he did not speak English or Welsh." He spent the night at the Draigoch Guest House, "owned by Italians who played Neapolitan songs on the juke box late into the night." Not even converts to Welsh culture such as Mrs. Ivor Davies, whose parents were Genoese, can stop the cultural erosion: "She spoke Welsh and sang in Welsh. But, as an Italian, she couldn't make the boys Welsh. They were bored with the community and wanted to go to the States." A woman named Gwynneth Morgan tells him, "When Welshmen marry foreigners, they lose the tradition." She wants the valley to remain Welsh but believes that "it's all going to pieces."

Chatwin observes similar cases of ethnic isolation elsewhere in Patagonia. At Estancia Lochinver, an isolated sheep station, he meets a Scotsman who has lived in Patagonia for forty years but still dreams of Scotland. Inside the house are pictures of Scotland and photographs of the British royal family. Outside on the packed dirt that passes for a lawn is a wire-net cage. When Chatwin asks what was kept in the cage, the Scotsman grumbles, "Aagh, the bugger died on me." Chatwin looks closer and sees "Curled in the bottom of the cage . . . the dried-up skeleton of a thistle." Spending the night with a road construction gang, Chatwin meets another Scot, Robbie Ross, "with ginger hair and the physique of a caber thrower." The other workers, who are "Latins or Indian half-breeds," refer to Ross as an "Englishman." When Chatwin tells them that Ross is a Scotsman, Ross, who does not speak English, confirms: "Si, soy Escocés [Yes, I am Scotch]. . . . Mi Patria es la Inglaterra [My native country is England]." Ross does not distinguish between the two countries: "For him Scotland and England were an invisible blur."

One of Chatwin's reasons for going to Patagonia, he says, was to find the remains of a prehistoric animal. When he was a boy, his grandmother had kept a small piece of hide with reddish hair in a curio cabinet in her dining room. When he asked his mother what it was, she said that it was "a piece of brontosaurus." His grandmother's cousin, Charley Milward, had sent her the fascinating artifact. Milward, the captain of a merchant ship that had sunk in the Strait of Magellan, had settled near Punta Arenas, Chile. In the late 1890s he had helped an archaeological team explore a cave near Puerto Consuelo, and there he found his "brontosaurus"–which actually proved to be a "mylodon or Giant Sloth." Near the end of his travels in Patagonia, Chatwin enters the cave where his grandmother's cousin found the mylodon remains; there, amid the rubble, he spots "some strands of the coarse reddish hair" he remembers from his childhood.

The mylodon, Chatwin notes, disappeared from Patagonia ten thousand years ago, long before Europeans "discovered" South America. The ancestors of the Patagonian Indian tribes arrived shortly after the mylodon became extinct, but few of the Indians survived their confrontations with Europeans. In 1520 Ferdinand Magellan and his men made landfall at San Julián, where they "saw a giant dancing naked on the shore." When the man, a Tehuelche Indian, was brought before him, Magellan is said to have exclaimed, "'Ha! Patagon!' meaning 'Big-Foot' for the size of his moccasins." This phrase is widely believed to be the origin of the word *Patagonia,* but Chatwin disputes the theory. He admits that *pata* means "foot" in Spanish but argues that "the suffix *gon* is meaningless." He finds a more likely source in a chivalric romance, *Primaleon of Greece,* published in Castile in 1512. The knight-errant Primaleon lands on a faraway island inhabited by a savage people who fear a dog-headed monster, the Grand Patagon, that resides in the island's interior. Primaleon fights and wounds the monster and ships it "home to Polonia to add to the royal collection of curiosities." Chatwin argues that the dog-headed monster in *Primaleon of Greece* was the source not only for Magellan's "Patagon" but also for William Shakespeare's "puppy-headed monster," Caliban, in *The Tempest,* first staged in 1611.

Magellan, Chatwin points out, was also responsible for naming the island at the tip of South America. On 21 October 1521, as his ships navigated the dangerous waters of what would become known as the Strait of Magellan, the crews saw smoke from the campfires of Indians along the island's northern shore. They named the area Tierra del Fuego, the Land of Fire. Today the island is cold and forlorn: "The Fuegians are dead and all the fires snuffed out. Only the flares of oil rigs cast a pall over the night sky." A wealthy landowner in Punta Arenas tells Chatwin that it is ridiculous to make a fuss over the extermination of the Indians: "'All this business of Indian killing is being a bit overstretched. You see, these Indians were a pretty low sort of Indian. I mean they weren't like the Aztecs or the Incas. No civilization or anything. On the whole they were a pretty poor lot.'" Among those who would have agreed with this assessment of the Fuegians, Chatwin notes, was Charles Darwin, who described them as "the most abject and miserable creatures" he had ever seen. Chatwin writes that Darwin "lapsed into that common failing of naturalists: to marvel at the intricate perfection of other creatures and recoil from the squalor of man." Darwin even dismissed the Fuegians' language, which, he said, "scarcely deserves to be called articulate." That the Fuegians had a rich metaphoric vocabulary mattered little to Darwin. An obvious admirer of the richness of Fuegian metaphors, Chatwin asks: "What shall we think of a people who defined 'monotony' as 'an absence of male friends'? Or, for 'depression,' used the word that described the vulnerable phase in a crab's seasonal cycle, when it has sloughed off its old shell and waits for another to grow?"

Chatwin had visited Dahomey in 1971; he traveled there again in 1978 to do research for his next book, *The Viceroy of Ouidah* (1980), an historical novel about the slave trade. Chatwin describes the first visit in an essay, collected in *What Am I Doing Here,* on the German director Werner Herzog, whose movie *Cobra Verde* (1988) was based on the novel. In Ouidah, a decaying former slave port, he found two intriguing sites: "the Python Temple and Sigbomey, the Brazilian *case grande* built by the slaver millionaire Dom Francisco Felix de Souza." De Souza arrived on the Slave Coast in the early 1800s as a lieutenant assigned to the Portuguese fort. Masterminding a coup, he deposed the king of Dahomey and brought a new king, Ghezo, to the

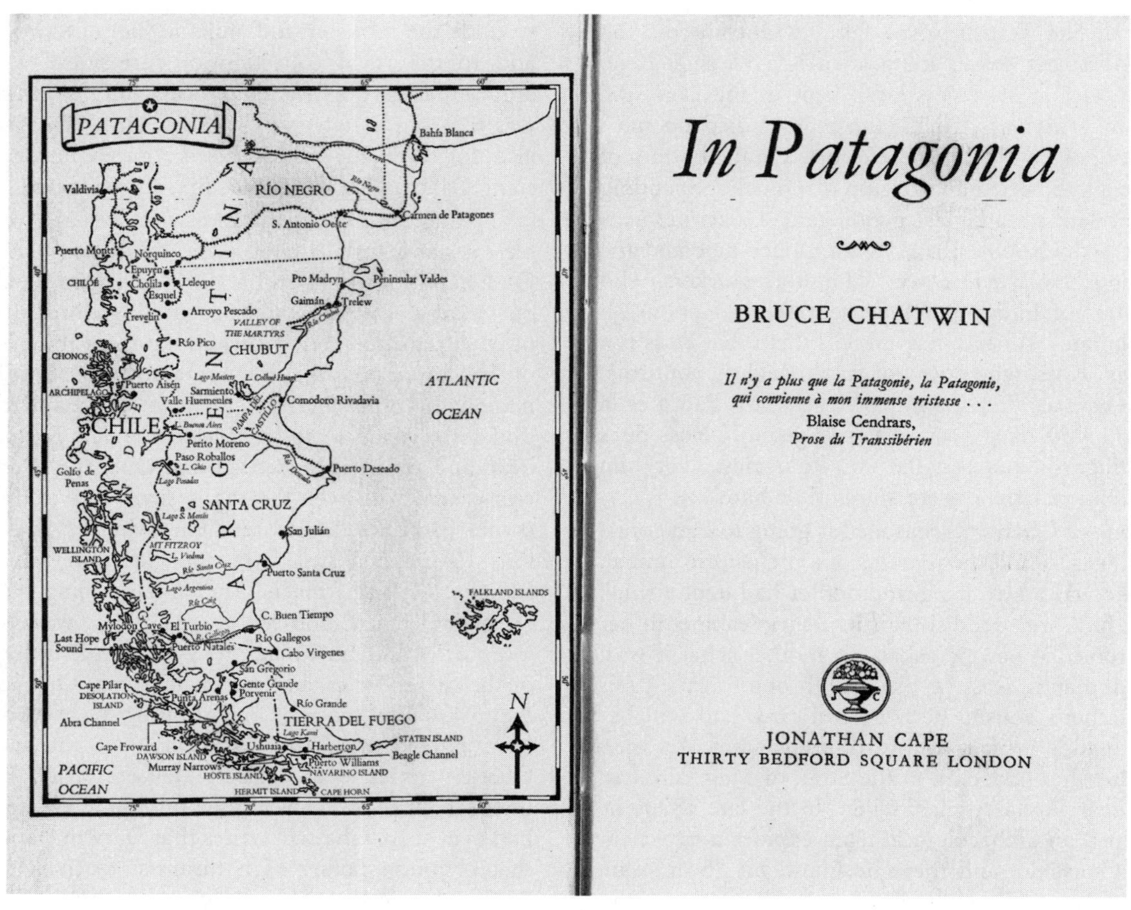

Frontispiece and title page for the book that established Chatwin as a rising star on the British literary scene

throne. De Souza then turned the Dahomean army, "with its core of Amazon warriors," into "the most efficient military machine in Africa." Ghezo rewarded De Souza with the "title of *chaca,* or viceroy, of Ouidah, and a monopoly over the sale of slaves." De Souza became fabulously wealthy from slave trading, but after his Brazilian partners cheated him and he had a falling out with Ghezo, he died an impoverished madman. "On Ghezo's orders" he "was buried in a barrel of rum, together with a beheaded boy and girl, under his Goanese four-poster bed."

When Chatwin returned to Dahomey in 1978, it had become the People's Republic of Benin, a Marxist state. He wrote about his experiences in Benin in "The Coup," which was published in *Granta* magazine in 1984 and reprinted in *What Am I Doing Here.* Chatwin's description of what it is like to be caught in a military takeover shows his style at its brittle best. As if to underscore how common coups have become in postcolonial Africa, Chatwin begins in an understated, matter-of-fact tone: "The coup began at seven on Sunday morning." Jailed as a suspected mercenary, Chatwin finds himself in a barracks guardroom with Jacques, a French water engineer who had made the mistake of dressing in camouflage hunting clothes when he went out to shoot game birds that morning. Jacques is an old Africa hand who has seen many coups. He assures Chatwin that the guards are "playing games" and will probably not shoot them–"That is, if they don't get drunk." Later, standing outside in his underwear against a mud-plaster wall with his arms above his head, Chatwin regrets having come to this part of Africa:

> This was not my Africa. Not this rainy, rotten-fruit Africa. Not this Africa of blood and laughter. The Africa I loved was the long undulating savannah country to the north, the "leopard-spotted land," where flat-topped acacias stretched as far as the eye could see.

Eventually Chatwin passes out from the heat and is carried back to the guardroom by Jacques and the corporal who had been guarding them. The French vice consul stops by; but when Chatwin asks the official to wire his name and passport number to the British embassy in Lagos, Nigeria, the vice consul refuses to "be mixed up in this affair." "Charming," Chatwin grumbles to Jacques, who replies: "Remember Waterloo. And besides, you may be a mercenary."

Jacques and the other French prisoners are released after the vice consul's visit; Chatwin is finally freed through the intervention of the German counselor. On his last morning in the country he goes to a bistro that had previously been run by a Corsican; the latter, however, "had gone back to Corsica while the going was good." There he encounters Jacques, who insists on buying him a farewell champagne. As they drink, Jacques tells Chatwin that the shooting he heard that morning was a settling of old scores. "This is Africa," Jacques says. "I know," replies Chatwin, "and I'm leaving."

In *The Viceroy of Ouidah* Chatwin changes de Souza's name to Dom Francisco Manoel da Silva and frames the story with events that occur in the twentieth century. In 1974 Dom Francisco's descendants gather at Ouidah to attend a requiem mass on the 117th anniversary of his death and to lay a wreath at the Portuguese fort. "It was the usual suffocating afternoon in March. . . . Turkey buzzards drifted in a milky sky. . . . Banana leafs hung in limp ribbons. There was no wind." At the end of the ceremony the da Silvas stand looking "at the grey lagoon, at the mangroves and the line of the surf beyond. . . . Soft lights were seen moving along the track to the beach, up which Dom Francisco had come, down which the word 'Voodoo' made its way to the Americas."

With the publication of *In Patagonia* and *The Viceroy of Ouidah* Chatwin found himself a celebrity, in demand for television appearances and as a writer of introductions to travel-writing classics. Among his first efforts as a writer of introductions is the sensitive essay that appears in the Picador edition of Byron's *The Road to Oxiana.* His worshipful attitude toward Byron's book suggests that Chatwin "read" central Asia as much through Byron's eyes as through his own observations. Romanticizing what he had seen in his travels in Afghanistan, Chatwin contrasts the country with Iran: to "cross the Afghan frontier, after the lowering fanaticism of Meshed, was like coming up for air." He agrees with Byron that "Here at last . . . is Asia without an inferiority complex." At the time Chatwin wrote the introduction Muslim fighters were battling the troops of the Soviet Union and the Soviet-backed Afghan army. The price of Afghanistan's emergence on the world stage was the loss of the world that writers such as Byron described:

> We shall not sleep in the nomad tents, or scale the Minaret of Jam. And we shall lose the tastes–the hot, coarse, bitter bread; the green tea flavoured with cardamoms; the grapes we cooled in the snow-melt; and the nuts and mulberries we munched for altitude sickness. Nor shall we get back the smell of the beanfields; the sweet, resinous smell of deodar wood burning, or the whiff of the snow leopard at 14,000 feet. Never. Never. Never.

Chatwin's next book was another novel, *On the Black Hill* (1982), set in the Welsh border country; the main characters are the twin brothers Lewis and Benjamin Jones, who "for forty-two years . . . slept side by side in their parents' bed, at their farm which was known as 'The Vision.'" In the interview with Ignatieff, Chatwin explained: "It always irritated me to be called a travel writer. So I decided to write something about people who never went out." Chatwin knew the border country well; he had first visited Wales with his father and later made frequent trips there. Murray cites an interview with Melvyn Bragg on London Weekend Television's *South Bank Show* in which Chatwin referred to the border country as a "home base, a metaphorical home base if you like and it's the place I love."

Although Chatwin claimed that he wrote *On the Black Hill* to distance himself from travel writing, the novel includes many references to travel. The story opens in the present, then shifts to the last year of the nineteenth century to describe the meeting of Lewis and Benjamin's parents, Amos Jones and Mary Latimer. When Amos comes to court Mary, she is wearing a "Kashmiri shawl." Her father, an "Old Testament scholar . . . had retired from mission work in India." Mary's memories of India include a first love: "He was a Eurasian–a streak of a man with syrupy eyes and a mouth full of apologies." Lewis inherits his mother's passion for the world outside the Wye valley: "He would pester visitors for their opinions on 'them savages in Africky'; for news of Siberia, Salonika or Sri Lanka." His conception of the world is derived from a "Bartholomew's atlas of 1925 when the two great colonial empires were coloured pink and mauve, and the Soviet Union was a dull sage green; . . . it offended his sense of order to find that the planet was now full of bickering little countries with unpronounceable names." Other than a brief seaside holiday in 1910, Lewis and Benjamin never travel farther than Hereford; but Lewis dreams of a nomadic existence.

Chatwin's next book, *Patagonia Revisited* (1985), consists of alternating passages by Chatwin and his co-author, the travel writer Paul Theroux. In his first passage Chatwin says:

Remnant of a building in Patagonia; photograph by Chatwin (Estate of Bruce Chatwin)

> Paul and I went to Patagonia for very different reasons. But if we are travellers at all, we are literary travellers. A literary reference or connection is likely to excite us as much as a rare animal or plant; and so we touch on some of the instances in which Patagonia has affected the literary imagination.

Among the literary references to Patagonia that Chatwin and Theroux uncover are Jonathan Swift's *Gulliver's Travels* (1726), in which Swift's Brobdingnagians may have been inspired by tales of the Tehuelche Indians as a race of giants; Samuel Taylor Coleridge's *The Rime of the Ancient Mariner* (1798)–Chatwin cites Capt. George Shelvocke's account in his *A Voyage round the World* (1726) of one of his officers shooting an albatross; Edgar Allan Poe's *The Narrative of Arthur Gordon Pym* (1838); Darwin's *Journal of Researches into the Natural History and Geology of the Countries Visited during the Voyage round the World of H.M.S. Beagle* (1839); Lady Florence Douglas Dixie's *Across Patagonia* (1880); and W. H. Hudson's *Idle Days in Patagonia* (1893). Ever since Magellan's time, Chatwin points out, Patagonia has fascinated writers. It has come to represent a land of wonders: "the word 'Patagonia,' like Mandalay or Timbuctoo, lodged itself in the Western imagination as a metaphor for The Ultimate, the point beyond which one could not go." It was, he notes, "the attending marvels of a thousand Patagonian sights and sounds" that induced Ishmael to sign on for his fateful voyage in Herman Melville's *Moby-Dick* (1851).

Chatwin's obsession with nomadism led to his next book, *The Songlines*. In 1984 Chatwin had traveled to Australia to attend the Adelaide Literary Festival and to research aboriginal nomadism. In Adelaide he met Salman Rushdie, and after the festival ended, the two authors flew to Alice Springs and then traveled around the Outback in a pickup truck. In his *Imaginary Homelands: Essays and Criticism, 1981–1991* (1991) Rushdie, who is supposed to have been the model for Arkady Volchok in *The Songlines,* recalls: "I am a fairly garrulous person myself, but in Bruce's company I don't manage more than a few interruptions." Rushdie describes Chatwin as an immensely appealing person, a brilliant conversationalist, and a mesmerizing storyteller:

> He was a magnificent raconteur of Scheherazadean inexhaustibility, a gilt-edged name dropper, a voracious reader of esoteric texts, a scholar gypsy, a mimic–his Mrs. Gandhi was perfect–and a giggler of international class. He was as talkative as he was curious, and he was curious about everything.

On the concept behind *The Songlines,* Rushdie says: "The idea of the 'dreaming tracks' or 'songlines' captivates me as much as it does Bruce. How could writers fail to love a world which has been mapped by stories?"

Rushdie speculates that Chatwin's book on nomadism was "the burden he's been carrying all his writing life."

The Songlines was written while Chatwin was ill with what he said was a rare bone-marrow fungus that he had contracted in China. Murray detects a "terminal urgency" in the book, a "desire to get some of this material down before it is too late." Despite his illness, Chatwin continued to travel as he wrote. He took the unwieldy manuscript to India in 1985 and worked on it at the home of the travel writer Patrick Leigh Fermor in Greece. In the end he produced a restless, agitated book about the restlessness that he believed to be at the core of human experience.

The Songlines is a hybrid work that defies classification. The first half is mostly fiction with autobiographical interludes; the second half is a series of excerpts from Chatwin's notebooks. The two main characters are Arkady Volchok, an Australian of Cossack descent, and a "Pom"–Australian slang for Britisher–named Bruce, who is both the real Chatwin and an authorial persona. A footloose philosopher, Arkady studies what the Aborigines call the "Footprints of the Ancestors" or the "Way of the Law"; Europeans call them the "Dreaming-tracks" or "songlines." These are songs, thought to have been created by ancient totemic beings, the singing of which allows nomads to find their way across the continent. Under the Land Rights Act the Australian government had given "the Aboriginal 'owners' the title to their country, providing it lay untenanted." Because he knows about the songlines, Arkady has invented a job for himself: translating tribal law into Crown law. His latest assignment is to survey the route of a proposed rail line between Alice Springs and Darwin to ensure that it does not destroy any sacred sites. He tells Bruce that the project is "a bit rash" because to the Aborigines "the whole of bloody Australia is a sacred site."

In the first autobiographical interlude Bruce recalls that as a child "I never heard the word 'Australia' without calling to mind the eucalyptus inhaler and an incessant red country populated by sheep." His grandaunt Ruth (Gracie) had a picture book about Australia at which he used to "gaze in wonder." His favorite picture (which adorns the cover of the Viking paperback edition of *The Songlines*) was of "an Aboriginal family on the move." He connects the "fantastic homelessness" of his early years with this image of restlessness. The chapter ends with Bruce imagining a group of Aborigines working at a cattle station who suddenly decide to go "Walkabout," stepping out of their work clothes and walking off into the horizon. He imagines the station foreman, "a Scot perhaps . . . with blotchy skin and a mouthful of obscenities," shouting for his "boys." The only signs he finds of them are "their shirts and hats and boots sticking up through their trousers."

In the next two chapters Arkady and Bruce carry on a dialogue on the meaning of the songlines and the necessity of nomadism. Arkady explains that the songlines are like the musical tracks of totemic ancestors: "A song," he says, is "both map and direction-finder. Providing you knew the song, you could always follow your way across country. . . . In theory, at least, the whole of Australia could be read as musical score. There was hardly a rock or creek in the country that could not or had not been sung." The Aborigines not only sing about the land; they also sing it into existence. Once, when Arkady asks one of them what he is singing, the man replies, "Singing up the country, boss. Makes the country come up quicker." "Singing up the country" gives a purpose to the seemingly random walkabouts.

The Australian Outback is a dry and harsh place; those qualities are part of its attraction for Bruce. He tells Arkady that when he was an art appraiser, a doctor suggested that the eye problems of which he complained were caused by looking at pictures too closely; the doctor's prescription was for him to look at some "long horizons." Bruce's search for "long horizons" took him to the western Sahara, where he "slept in black tents, blue tents, skin tents, yurts of felt, and windbreaks of thorns" and one night, in a sandstorm, experienced the truth of "Muhammed's dictum" that "A journey is a fragment of hell."

A journey into the desert can also be a re-creative act. On the shore of the Timor Sea, Bruce talks with Father Terence, a hermit, about the early desert anchorites: "For seven years, the Desert Fathers had been his spiritual guides: to be lost in the desert was to find one's way to God." Bruce tells Father Terence that he believes "something similar about the desert. . . . Man was born in the desert, in Africa. By returning to the desert he rediscovers himself." Later, Bruce reflects on his travels and restlessness:

> I had a presentiment that the "travelling" phase of my life might be passing. I felt, before the malaise of settlement crept over me, that I should reopen [my] notebooks. I should set down a résumé of the ideas, quotations and encounters which had amused and obsessed me; and which I hoped would shed some light on what is, for me, the question of questions: the nature of human restlessness.

He recalls that among the seventeenth-century mathematician and philosopher Blaise Pascal's "gloomier *pensées*" was "why . . . must a man with sufficient to live on feel drawn to divert himself on long sea voyages? To dwell in another town? To go off in search of a peppercorn?" Bruce wonders if "our need for distraction, our mania for the new, was, in essence, an instinctive migratory urge akin to the birds in autumn." If humankind–"from the structure of our brain-cells to the structure of our big toe"–was designed to journey "*on foot,*" and if its true home was the desert, "then it is easier to understand why greener pastures pall on us; why possessions exhaust us, and why Pascal's imaginary man found his comfortable lodgings a prison."

In the "notebooks" section of *The Songlines* Chatwin records comments on human restlessness from various authors. From Pascal: "OUR NATURE LIES in movement; complete calm is death." According to Baudelaire, the "Great Malady" is "horror of home." Chatwin recalls reading lines from John Donne while riding a night express train from Moscow to Kiev: "To live in one land, is captivitie, / To runne all countries, a wild roguery." From Robert Burton's *The Anatomy of Melancholy* (1621): "There is nothing better than a change of air in this malady [melancholia], than to wander up and down, as those Tartari Zalmohenses that live in hordes, and take the opportunity of times, places, seasons." On the stasis of civilization, he cites Melville's *Journal Up the Straits, October 11, 1856–May 5, 1857* (1935): "Masonry, and is it man's? . . . I shudder at the thought of the ancient Egyptian's." Finally, there is Arthur Rimbaud, who writes in *Une Saison en enfer* (A Season in Hell, 1873): "I was forced to travel to ward off the apparitions assembled in my brain" and who wrote from Ethiopia, "What am I doing here?"

Chatwin's next work, *Utz* (1988), is a novel about a man who collects Meissen porcelains amid the Nazi madness of World War II and the bleak Stalinism of postwar Czechoslovakia. Kaspar Utz lives among his miniatures in a two-room flat in Prague, "a city of giants: giants in stone, in stucco or marble; naked giants; blackamoor giants; giants dressed as for a hurricane, not one of them in repose." During the Cold War, Utz makes a yearly "pilgrimage" to Vichy, France. Each time he leaves Prague he vows never to return, yet before each trip he books his return passage: "The collection held him prisoner." In 1967 the narrator, a writer for a London magazine, has his first meeting with Utz at a Prague restaurant. The diners are given menus in English in which *carp* has been consistently misspelled: among the offerings are "Crap soup with paprika," "Stuffed crap," "Crap cooked in beer," "Fried crap," "Crap balls," and "Crap à la juive." Toward the end of the book the narrator goes to visit Utz's widow, Marta, who is living in a village near the Austrian border. Here the reader gets a glimpse through Chatwin's traveler's eye of what he found exotic about Eastern Europe of the Cold War period:

Dust jacket for Chatwin's 1985 collaboration with an American travel writer

> The wheat fields have been invaded by biblical "tares": but the cornflowers, the poppies, knapweed, scabious, and larkspur make one rejoice in the beauty of a European countryside as yet unpoisoned by selective weed-killers. On the edge of the village there are water meadows and, beyond, there is a lake where carp are raised, half-encircled with a stand of pines.

In *Imaginary Homelands* Rushdie detects in *Utz,* which was published the year before Chatwin's death, the beginnings of a new phase in Chatwin's writing life: "*Utz* is all we have of what had become possible for him once his Australian odyssey helped him express the ideas which he'd carried about for so many years."

Shortly before his death on 18 January 1989 in Nice, France, apparently of AIDS, Chatwin collected many of his previously published shorter pieces into a volume he titled, with a nod to Rimbaud, *What Am I Doing Here*. In his introduction Chatwin notes that the word *story* in the titles of some of the pieces should alert the reader to "the fact that, however closely the narrative may fit the facts, the fictional process has been at work." When Ignatieff asked Chatwin if there was a "division between fiction and non-fiction" in his work, Chatwin replied:

> I don't think there is one. There definitely should be, but I don't know where it is. I've always written very close to the line. I've tried applying fiction techniques to actual bits of travel. I once made the experiment of counting up the lies in the book I wrote about Patagonia. It wasn't, in fact, too bad: there weren't too many.

Murray calls Chatwin "an accomplished escapologist–from a certain kind of Englishness." Ignatieff observed that Chatwin seemed to be on the run from himself: "The shooting jumpers, corduroys and walking shoes mark him down as English country middle class, an identity he has spent a lifetime escaping." Chatwin confessed to Ignatieff that he traveled to avoid being typecast as a middle-class Englishman: "Being an Englishman makes me uneasy. I find I can be English and behave like an Englishman only if I'm not here." He also said, "Travel was an immense relief–it got rid of the pressure from above and below."

In 1993 Wyndham and David King co-edited *Bruce Chatwin: Photographs and Notebooks,* a collection of color and black-and-white photographs taken by Chatwin on his travels complemented by excerpts from his travel notebooks. In his introduction Wyndham explains that Chatwin "left behind some fifty pocket-sized notebooks, most of them bound in the shiny imitation leather known in France as *moleskinne*." They are a writer's notebooks; they are not diaries, "although, sometimes, when travelling, he prefixed an entry with a date." Few of the notebook entries are directly linked to the photographs in the collection, but Wyndham believes that Chatwin's notes "contain the general nature of his visual appetite, the *kind* of colours, forms, and images which arrested the attention of his ever-curious gaze."

The notes from Chatwin's 1970 trip to Mauritania illustrate the highly visual quality of his written observations. Visiting Nouakchott, Chatwin describes the stalls in the local market: "The afternoon I spent examining the market–a close emplacement of shacks, wood and corrugated iron, often made with a deliberate collage of many coloured plates. Rauschenberg could do no better." It is when he is in open country that Chatwin feels most alive: "The happiness to be found sleeping under tents is unbelievable. One night in tents is worth three in town." Chatwin's notes reveal his love for the desert and his dislike of sub-Saharan Africa. In Bamako, Mali, he writes: "A nothing place–I hate the tropical vegetation, sweat and sickly fruit." He prefers "lands that are sucked dry. They suit me. We complement each other." On the road to Chinguetti, Mauritania, near the western edge of the Sahara, he describes "Occasional screes, rectangular blocks where the linear fortifications of the mountains have fallen away. Canyons the black of oxidised silver. Sands are golden with purplish stones giving the landscape the appearance of a tiger."

The publication of a substantial portion of Chatwin's previously uncollected magazine pieces in *Anatomy of Restlessness* was the occasion for considerable critical debate over the merit of his work. In his review of the book in *The Times* Ryle called Chatwin "an erratic stylist, whose writing did not so much evolve as mutate." He concluded that Chatwin's "books did not get better: in some respects they got worse, the modernist style battling against an archaic sensibility, with preciosity the constant danger." In a review for *The Sunday Times* (21 July 1966), on the other hand, William Dalrymple wrote that "in the hands of a wonder-writer such as Chatwin, even a tawdry collection of odds and ends from out-of-date glossies becomes strangely irresistible." Dalrymple found "something very unEnglish . . . something refreshingly cosmopolitan in Chatwin's brazen lack of embarrassment at being so openly intellectual, so ostentatiously showy in his learning." In the same issue of *The Sunday Times* Harvey Porlock describes Nigel Spivey's glowing account of reading *Anatomy of Restlessness* at one of Chatwin's favorite places (Mount Athos in Greece) as a "Chatwinesque swoon." Porlock also, however, quotes David Sexton's remark in *The Spectator* that "for all the recondite good taste of his prize items, there was a side to Chatwin that was pure Liberace."

Part Liberace, part Hemingway, part Rimbaud, Chatwin was an accomplished mimic and a gifted storyteller who helped revive twentieth-century travel writing. As Rushdie says, "What a voice we lost when his fell silent. How much he still had to say."

Interviews:

Mary Blume, "Bruce Chatwin: From Patagonia to the Slave Trade," *International Herald Tribune,* 1980, p. 7;

Maureen Cleave, "In Search of the Giant Sloth and Other Stories," *Observer* (London), 31 October 1982, pp. 32–33;

Michael Ignatieff, "An Interview with Bruce Chatwin," *Granta,* 21 (Spring 1987): 23–37;

Michael Davie, "Heard between the Songlines," *Observer* (London), 21 June 1987, p. 18;

Lucy Hughes-Hallett, "Songs of the Earth," *Evening Standard* (London), 24 June 1987, p. 33;

Colin Thubron, "Born under a Wandering Star," *Daily Telegraph* (London), Weekend Section, 27 June 1987, p. 1;

Michele Field, "Bruce Chatwin," *Publishers Weekly,* 231 (7 August 1987): 430–431.

Biographies:

Nicholas Murray, *Bruce Chatwin* (Mid Glamorgan, Wales: Seren, 1993);

Susannah Clapp, *With Chatwin: Portrait of a Writer* (London: Cape, 1997).

References:

David Birch, "Strategy and Contingency," in *Twentieth-Century Fiction: From Text to Context,* edited by Peter Verdonk and Jean Jacques Weber (London: Routledge, 1995), pp. 220–234;

Evan Eisenberg, "The Voyage Out: Bruce Chatwin's Long and Winding Road," *Village Voice Literary Supplement,* 72 (March 1989): 25–27;

David C. Estes, "Bruce Chatwin's *In Patagonia:* Traveling in Textualized Terrain," *New Orleans Review,* 18, no. 2 (1990): 67–77;

Graham Huggan, "Maps, Dreams, and the Presentation of Ethnographic Narrative: Hugh Brody's *Maps and Dreams* and Bruce Chatwin's *The Songlines,*" *Ariel: A Review of International English Literature,* 22 (January 1991): 57–69;

Patrick Meanor, *Bruce Chatwin,* Twayne English Authors Series, no. 542 (New York: Twayne, 1997);

Salman Rushdie, *Imaginary Homelands: Essays and Criticism, 1981–1991* (London: Granta, 1991; New York: Viking, 1991), pp. 226–231, 232–236, 237–240;

Paul Theroux, "Chatwin Revisited," *Granta,* 44 (1993): 211–221;

Mario Vargas Llosa, "Gentleman of the Road," *Island,* 59 (Winter 1994): 28-30;

Hart L. Wegner, "The Travel Writer as Missionary in Reverse: Bruce Chatwin's *Songlines,*" *West Virginia University Philological Papers,* 40 (1994): 77–81.

Papers:

Bruce Chatwin's papers are in the Bodleian Library, Oxford; his will stipulates that they are not to be made available until twenty years after his death (2009).

Robyn Davidson

(6 September 1950 –)

David Callahan
University of Aveiro, Portugal

BOOKS: *Tracks* (London: Cape, 1980; New York: Pantheon, 1980); excerpted in *From Alice to Ocean: Alone across the Outback,* photographs by Rick Smolan (Reading, Mass.: Addison-Wesley, 1992);

Australia: Beyond the Dreamtime, by Davidson, Thomas Keneally, and Patsy Adams-Smith (London: BBC Books, 1987; New York: Facts on File, 1987);

Ancestors (London: Cape, 1989; New York: Simon & Schuster, 1989);

Alice Springs (Sydney: Collins, 1989);

Travelling Light (Sydney: Collins, 1989; revised edition, Pymble, Australia: Angus & Robertson / London: HarperCollins, 1993);

Desert Places (London: Viking, 1996; New York: Viking, 1996).

OTHER: *From Alice to Ocean* [CD-ROM], narrated by Davidson (Sausalito: Against All Odds Productions, 1992);

Maybeth Bond, ed., *Travelers' Tales: A Woman's World,* introduction by Davidson (San Francisco: Travelers' Tales, 1995).

Robyn Davidson (photograph by Rick Smolan)

Robyn Davidson won immediate acclaim for her first book, *Tracks* (1980), which, like the best travel books, deals not only with the place its author visited but also with the difficulties she experienced while attempting to understand what she was doing and why. *Tracks* is as much about what it is to be a woman in Australia during the 1960s and 1970s as it is about the practical details of traveling by camel through central and western Australia. In fact, these two aspects of the book interact: as Davidson self-consciously questions her "unwomanly" activity, it becomes apparent that travel is experienced in terms of how one sees oneself as a man or woman.

Robyn Davidson was born on 6 September 1950 to Australian parents, Antil Guilford Davidson (known as Mark) and Margaret Harris Davidson, in the small town of Miles, two hundred miles west of Brisbane in the state of Queensland. The family homestead was near the even smaller locality of Guluguba, twenty-five miles north of Miles. Although the Davidsons left Guluguba when Robyn was four years old, she remembers it with nostalgia, writing of her life there in *Australia: Beyond the Dreamtime* (1987) as an experience that confirms her identity as Australian. Davidson's nostalgia, however, is ambiguous. Her sense of the significance of this period of her childhood is accompanied by memories of isolation and loneliness and by subsequent guilt about the treatment of the Aborigines in Australia, including a massacre that took place near the family's property some fifty years before her birth.

Davidson's parents seem to have contributed to her lifelong restlessness. Her father had spent years traveling around Africa looking for mines, on safari, and generally in the pursuits of the colonial man abroad. Davidson's mother, who was attracted to her husband by his unconventionality and independence, became unhappy living so far from the city and pined to be elsewhere. Davidson admired her mother's adaptability and fortitude, so often characteristic of Australian bush wives, as well as her father's dreamy whimsicality. Her father's qualities, however, were not those required to make a fortune or even a living in the difficult Australian interior. From Stanley Park cattle property, Davidson's family moved to the country town of Mooloolah, nearer the coast, on the railway line north and not far from the main north-south highway. Although her father's business choices rarely brought much success, Davidson's family was not poor.

Davidson's memories of this period include becoming aware of the increasingly varied cultural mix of Australia and sensing the loss and displacement that many immigrants felt. Davidson experienced something of this displacement when her family moved from Mooloolah to Redcliffe, the outer suburb of Brisbane, in 1959. The drabness of life there, her parents' restrictive attitudes toward whatever distractions were available, and the rebelliousness that Australian young people demonstrated in the 1960s helped to move Davidson toward a radical break with her background. Like many thoughtful young people of her generation, Robyn Davidson gravitated toward values distant from those of her parents, largely rejecting their political and social viewpoints.

After studying biology at the University of Queensland during 1967–1969, Davidson moved to Sydney, where she studied piano for a time at the Sydney Conservatorium of Music and became involved with the fringes of what is known as the "Sydney Push," which she described in *Beyond the Dreamtime* as "a loose confederation of intellectuals, artists, renegades, radicals, eccentrics, ex-cons, Commies, misfits and bon vivants of all types, ages and backgrounds." In *Beyond the Dreamtime,* Davidson describes this counterculture as not simply a shared experience with Western countries: "eastern mysticism continued to do very well in Australia long after it became passé in other western countries," as did other aspects of the 1960s and 1970s counterculture. The proximity of Asia, the ease with which "getting back to the land" can be achieved by Australians, and the confluence between certain hippie ideals and Australian pioneering myths have contributed to the continuing presence of these values, as have more mundane factors such as the Australian welfare society and the general prosperity of the country.

In 1972, after three years of immersion in Sydney counterculture, Davidson returned home and then went into the Queensland interior with her father, looking for opals and finding continuity with the past in spite of the sense of rupture that the age encouraged. This journey appears to be the prelude to Davidson's decision to explore the Australian desert at greater length. The landscape felt like "home," she says in *Beyond the Dreamtime;* the mineral and animal wonders were breathtaking, and solitude allowed a deeply meditative solidarity.

Even though she was attracted to the Queensland interior, her decision in 1974 to leave Brisbane and go to Alice Springs in the dry center of the country surprised everyone, even herself. Once in Alice Springs, Davidson was caught up in its intensity, from the beautiful land and its flora and fauna to the blatant racism of its white inhabitants. What Vijay Mishra and Bob Hodge have called "the dark side of the dream" in their 1991 book of that title, the cruel treatment of the Aborigines by white Australians was soon apparent to Davidson in a way she had not previously experienced.

The major themes of *Tracks* were ready to be assembled: the searching for an experience that would connect Davidson with herself and her country; the conflict between Davidson's independent feminism and the raw machismo of the interior; Davidson's encounter with the mythical desert landscape; and Davidson's meeting with and coming to a deeply felt relationship with Aborigines, Aboriginal ways of thinking, and the responsibility of white Australians toward this oppressed, yet sentimentalized, people. Of thematic importance as well is her embattled relationship with the camels she acquired, trained, and took from Alice Springs to the Indian Ocean.

Tracks at first seems unusual among travel books in that the actual movement across the desert with the camels occupies only half the book. The preparation for the journey, which is described in the first half, is not simply a long prelude. Her experiences in Alice Springs are intrinsic to the central idea that even within her own country she was "traveling." Even though Davidson did not leave Australia, by going to Alice Springs she placed herself in an alien situation similar to that of a travel writer who has journeyed to another land. In such a situation the writer must define herself or himself in the face of difference. *Tracks* is a book in which a particularly stubborn, brave, and honest member of the Australian disaffected counterculture faces the extreme conservatism she opposes, outflanking it while at the same time discovering forms of commonality. With a hard-nosed lack of self-delusion, the narrative chronicles the history of one person's beliefs and the limits of

Davidson and her father watching Sallay Mahomet make a pack saddle for a camel, a few days before she left on her journey by camelback from Alice Springs across the desert of Western Australia to the Indian Ocean, April 1977 (photograph by Rick Smolan)

her physical endurance. Her life had scarcely prepared her for the circumstances she faced. As she wrote in *Tracks:*

> if you are fragmented and uncertain it is terrifying to find the boundaries of yourself melt. Survival in a desert, then, requires that you lose this fragmentation, and fast. It is not a mystical experience, or rather, it is dangerous to attach these sorts of words to it.

The sensitive combination of inner and outer voyaging in *Tracks* made it popular with a wide audience. The book was reviewed in places where travel books are not usually reviewed and was immediately noticed outside Australia. Most reviewers were agreeably surprised. For example, Nancy Evans, who reviewed it for the American magazine *Glamour* (March 1981), an unlikely place to find a review of an Australian travel book, summed up what many people felt about *Tracks:* "Read it as an adventure story, as a search for self, as a travelogue, but above all, read *Tracks,* the woman's *Zen and the Art of Motorcycle Maintenance.*" Though Evans rightly calls *Tracks* a "woman's" book, it may also be read more generally as the investigation of being an outsider, an urban interloper in an environment where the liberal values of the city have been rejected. Riding camels across the desert is not a common experience for Australian men or women, nor is having to shoot enraged and charging bull camels or one's faithful canine companion because it has been poisoned. Survival in such circumstances strips away some of the societal distinctions between men and women. *Tracks* won the first Thomas Cook Travel and Guide Book Award in 1980. To date it is still the only book by a woman to have won the award. *From Alice to Ocean: Alone Across the Outback* (1992) is a collection of excerpts from *Tracks* with photographs by Rick Smolan, the photographer assigned by *National Geographic* to cover Davidson's trek. The excerpts were selected by Smolan, but Davidson narrates the widely distributed CD-ROM version, which Jennifer Reese has called "the first disk to show that CD-ROM technology could in fact enhance storytelling" (*Fortune,* 10 July 1995). Smolan was instrumental in publicizing *Tracks,* in which Davidson honestly reports her attraction to and irritation with Smolan, whose photographing of secret Aborigine ceremonies partially undermined her credibility with them.

Davidson's next book, *Ancestors* (1989), is a novel that examines family histories and their power. Although not a travel book and not set in the desert,

Davidson arriving at the Indian Ocean after six months in the Australian desert (photograph by Rick Smolan)

Ancestors is clearly related to *Tracks.* The journeys in the novel are principally journeys in time, attempts to connect events that have shaped the histories of the various family members, especially the life of the woman narrator. In a way the factual journey through space in *Tracks* and the fictional journey through time in *Ancestors* form a diptych through which Davidson examines a series of ruptures and continuities between her generation and those that preceded it.

At the same time as Davidson was working on *Ancestors,* she was writing occasional travel and cultural journalism for the *Sydney Morning Herald,* the *Age* (Melbourne), *Women's Day,* the *Sunday Times* (London), and the Australian *National Times.* Some of these articles were collected in *Travelling Light* (1989). In these essays Davidson reexamined outsiders' perceptions of the interior of Australia and Aborigines, a subject she had first explored in *Tracks.* One of the principal enlightenments Davidson experienced in her original journey was how she could or should relate to the original inhabitants of Australia and, by extension, what part they have in contemporary Australia. Davidson is obviously moved and impressed by Aboriginal people. She found that Eddie, a Pitjantjara elder, really does embody the close relationship between Aborigines and the landscape, and she observed, "I don't think I have ever felt so good in my entire life," because through Eddie's influence she "noticed things I had not noticed before–noises, tracks." Eddie even helped her to see "how it all fitted together." For her the land became "not wild but tame, bountiful, benign, giving, as long as you knew how to see it, how to be part of it." In this perception, which Davidson realizes is common to people who work with Aborigines, she is participating in a reassessment of their country that Australians in general made throughout the 1970s. The debunking of the myth of the intractable desert, indeed, has been dealt with at length in many places, including a popular television show of the early 1970s in which naturalist Harry Butler introduced city dwellers to the bounty and wonder of a land they barely knew. Few white Australians, however, had bothered to put this reassessment to the test in person.

Apart from writing about traveling in her native Australia, as well as in Great Britain and the United States, Davidson has also shown increasing interest in India. In *Travelling Light* (1989) there is a section titled "Rajasthan," in which Davidson admits that "unlike most other Australians of my generation and class, [India] held no fatal attractions for me." When she was given an assignment in Rajasthan because of her experience with camels, Davidson began "a long love affair" with the region. She became fascinated with the people she met and described most of them with a sympathetic largeness of heart.

These experiences led to Davidson's second major travel book, *Desert Places* (1996), in which Davidson recounted her efforts to locate and then travel for a year with a group of Rabari nomads in Rajasthan and Gujarat. As a record of Davidson's unsentimentally recalled intellectual and emotional struggles to derive meaning from her difficulties, *Desert Places* possesses all the strengths of *Tracks*. The "desert places" are both topographical and mental–the minutely described tribulations of sharing the Rabari's discomforts and the cultural and personal baggage that mocks her pretensions to any sharing with a people with whom she can scarcely communicate and whom she can leave for a hot shower whenever she weakens.

From the beginning of her travels in India, Davidson was faced with a profound cultural alienation as she attempted to locate a group of Rabari who still carried out the traditional nomadic patterns and were willing to allow her presence. Facing the multiple layers of social hierarchies in India, she found herself totally dependent on a series of mediations and assistants that diluted her dreams of a direct encounter with the Rabari. Moreover, when she found a group that would accept her, she discovered that she was caught between the sense of solitude caused by not knowing their language and the maddening impossibility of ever being really alone. The book is a record of the fragility of her acceptance of difference and the toughness of her determination to succeed. Out of the crucible of her experiences came a constantly intelligent chronicle about how levels of discomfort and alienation to which few people would willingly subject themselves became lessons in self-knowledge and cultural limitation. With a mixture of rage and humility, Davidson traversed internal and external desert places, finding that in both cases they never seem to end. Sitting with the Rabari at the end of the day, she observed, "in the light of the fire similarity shifted to difference and back again. Which was paramount: our similarities or our differences?" This eternal question of travel writers will never be answered, but Davidson's version of the quest is a wonderful attempt nonetheless.

Davidson's principal strengths as a travel writer lie in the connections she makes with people and the knowledge she brings to writing about people who are extremely different from her or with whom she does not get along. Rather than landscapes or customs, individuals–with their distinctive ways of life, of looking at the world, and of relating to others–fascinate her and provide the central paradox of her work: an activity that began as the discovery of self ended up as the discovery of other people. As in most countercultures, difference was little tolerated in the "Sydney Push" of Davidson's Australia. Indeed, the group existed to affirm its own difference in the face of a society that it regarded as mindless, materialistic, and hypocritical. One of the triumphs of *Tracks* and *Desert Places* is Davidson's ability to strip away some of the sentimental clichés of that counterculture, as well as her own defenses.

The reintegration of self, the basic material of which Davidson constructed *Tracks,* made it a raw and honest book, both a progression in space as well as into herself. Repeating such success might have presented a problem for future work. One cannot repeatedly reintegrate one's disintegrated self without compromising the supposed wisdom of the first occasion. The authority of *Tracks* lies partly in its questioning of authority. In the articles collected in *Travelling Light,* however, Davidson wrote with the more conventional authority of the exterior observer, one who was impassioned and intelligent, but an exterior observer nonetheless. With *Desert Places* she moved back to the uncertainties of the inner self to show how the authority of the speaking voice breaks down under the experience of extreme difference. The thought that anyone can travel light becomes highly ironic, and her ability to inspire empathy in her readers suggests that she will always have an honored place in the travel-writing genre.

Davidson lives in London and India and continues to travel frequently. Her other projects include a documentary film on Clara Schumann and a theater piece based on Italo Calvino's *Invisible Cities* (1972). Robyn Davidson is a travel writer whose work remains among the most thoughtful contemporary examinations of the inner experience of traveling.

L. Grace Dibble

(3 October 1902 – 3 September 1998)

Suzanne Ferriss
Nova Southeastern University

BOOKS: *Return Tickets,* 2 volumes (Ilfracombe, U.K.: Stockwell, 1968);

More Return Tickets (Ilfracombe, U.K.: Stockwell, 1979);

Return Tickets to Southern Europe (Ilfracombe, U.K.: Stockwell, 1980);

Return Tickets to Scandinavia (Ilfracombe, U.K.: Stockwell, 1982);

Return Tickets to Yugoslavia (Ilfracombe, U.K.: Stockwell, 1984);

Return Tickets Here and There (Ilfracombe, U.K.: Stockwell, 1988);

No Return Tickets! (Ilfracombe, U.K.: Stockwell, 1989);

Return Tickets to Africa (Ilfracombe, U.K.: Stockwell, 1992);

Return Tickets to Asia (Ilfracombe, U.K.: Stockwell, 1993);

Return Tickets in Pictures for Armchair Globetrotters (Ilfracombe, U.K.: Stockwell, 1993);

Return Tickets in Pictures for Globetrotting Naturalists (Ilfracombe, U.K.: Stockwell, 1994);

Return Tickets to Sacred Places (Ilfracombe, U.K.: Stockwell, 1996);

Return Tickets Worldwide (Ilfracombe, U.K.: Stockwell, 1998).

A self-described "lone wanderer," L. Grace Dibble spent her life traveling and working abroad. Trained as a geographer, she had posts at schools in Canada, India, and Nigeria. An early and dedicated traveler, she purchased her first round-trip (or return) ticket in the early 1930s. In thirteen books, written in diary form and illustrated with her own photographs, Dibble recounted her excursions to more than sixty countries in simple, straightforward prose that aptly captures the persevering spirit that made her a traveler well into her eighties and a published author into her nineties.

L. Grace Dibble at eighty-five

Born in Basingstoke, Sussex, on 3 October 1902, Lucy Grace Dibble moved as a child to Friningham farm, on the North Downs in Kent, and later to a nearby village, Bearsted. Finally, the family settled into Mount Pleasant, formerly the home of cricketer Alfred Mynn, in the village of Thurnham. Her father, George Dibble, a farmer, played cricket and worked for the local Conservative Party. To him Dibble owed her lifelong interest in natural history. On their weekend walks with the family dog, her father taught her to identify birds and animals. Until she was nine she was taught at home by her mother. In 1911 her mother joined the staff of Bearsted school, where Dibble and her sister,

Doris, were expected to serve as models to the other students. Her first travels were annual trips to her mother's home in Gloucestershire.

In 1914, at age twelve, Dibble was sent on scholarship to the Maidstone Girls' Grammar School, where she studied music, art, literature, French, geography, Latin, and chemistry, developing an early ambition to teach in India. Dibble served as a student teacher at Union Street Infants and Junior School before attending Homerton Training College, Cambridge, from 1922 to 1925. She was one of only five women studying for the Cambridge Diploma in geography at the School of Geography. Her early attempts to teach abroad were unsuccessful. She was turned down twice by the Universities Mission to Central Africa in London, first because she needed to obtain a degree and a second time for medical reasons. In 1929 she obtained an honors degree in geography, with a minor in medieval European history. In 1934 Dibble applied for an exchange teacher's post to New Zealand or Vancouver; instead she was offered a one-year post at the General Wolfe Junior High School in Winnipeg. In 1938 she realized her original ambition to teach in India, accepting an appointment to teach advanced English and geography at St. Mary's Training College in Poona, where she remained for eight years, having been delayed in returning to England by World War II. She next accepted a geography post at the United Missionary College, a training college in Ibadan, Nigeria, where she remained for the next fourteen years as teacher and principal. In the early 1960s she returned to England, teaching for several years before retiring in 1965 to Broadstairs in Kent where she lived and wrote until her death in 1998.

Dibble's experiences in India and Africa, as well as her excursions to other places, are recounted in the *Return Tickets* series, begun after her retirement, when she had the leisure to publish memoirs of her working life and her travel diaries. In the introduction to the first, published in 1968, Dibble termed her work the "jottings of a wanderer" written in response to "constant urgings by friends to record my wanderings in the different continents, so that they and others could enjoy them in the comfort of their armchairs, without the discomfort of tropic heat or ravages of insects." Infused by a Christian commitment to service, she also hoped to inspire young readers to "fulfil their ambitions by service abroad." As their titles suggest, the books are focused on Dibble's extensive travels. While the early volumes include narratives of her childhood, education, and working life, later volumes make only cursory references, if any, to her personal life or current affairs. Directed at an audience of armchair travelers, the books describe, often in voluminous detail, the particulars of travel, including the minutia of departures and arrivals. At their best they offer comprehensive portraits of major sites, supported by information about historical background and contemporary social, industrial, and agricultural practices. One would be hard-pressed to call Dibble an adventurer, despite the exotic nature and the extensiveness of her journeys. She stuck to the beaten path, choosing organized tours rather than striking out on her own. Still, she was always indefatigable, driven by a compelling urge to learn and to teach about the world.

Dibble's first work, *Return Tickets,* published in two volumes on 21 July 1968, takes the reader from her early childhood to 1968. The first volume briefly recounts her childhood and education, with diary accounts of her first travels. In the early 1930s she traveled to Europe–to Oberammergau, Germany, for the Passion Play and with the Co-operative Holidays Association to Italy, France, and Corsica. On 1 August 1932 she set sail for Norway, a voyage highlighted by trips across Loen Lake, visits to the glaciers, and the sight of a Lapp family in their tent.

The next year she traveled to Egypt, calling herself "La Petite Anglais Vagabonde" (the little English vagabond). Her naiveté is apparent in her remarks about bartering as an "unpleasant way of shopping" and her observation that "before entering the mosques, we had to put on slippers, primarily because they are places of worship, and also to keep the beautiful carpets clean, for when the Moslems pray they touch the ground several times with their forehead." She rode a camel from the pyramids to the Sphinx, in the first of her many encounters with exotic animals. Her account of an early visit to Israel reveals her Christian upbringing and faith, as she traces the religious history of the country before continuing on to Lebanon and Turkey. In Greece she visited the Acropolis, the Parthenon, and other significant literary sites, and her journal entries reveal her knowledge of Greek and British poetry.

Offered a position at the General Wolfe Junior High School in Winnipeg, in 1934 Dibble set sail for Canada, traveling down the St. Lawrence River with stops in Quebec City and Montreal before continuing by rail from Ottawa to Toronto and then to Winnipeg. Her first experience working abroad taught her that "the only way to know the people of a country is to work alongside them." "Letters from Canada, 1934–35" describe her delight in discovering hot dogs and snowshoeing. Leaving Winnipeg, she headed west, stopping at Banff, Calgary, and Vancouver, before purchasing a ticket to return to Britain by sea. Dibble spent eight weeks visiting the Hawaiian Islands, Japan, and China. The modernity of Tokyo left her "feeling that Japan, after all, was very much like America."

Dibble riding an elephant in Ceylon, 1968

During 1935 and 1936 Dibble took winter trips to Switzerland. In Arosa the athletic Dibble (a devotee of field hockey and other sports) learned to ski and to ice skate for the first time. On a summer-vacation course to Hungary and Yugoslavia in 1936 she traveled up the Danube from Austria to Budapest and then into the countryside. She also visited Venice for the first time before embarking on a one-week cruise down the Adriatic coast to Split and Dubrovnik.

Arriving in Nürnberg in 1936, Dibble was distressed to find hotel rooms all booked for the National Socialist Congress. After a passing reference to Adolf Hitler, she announced, "Never before have I seen a city so gaily decorated. Everywhere were the soldiers, airmen, Storm Troopers, and Hitler Youths, wearing the red Nazi armlet." Not until experiencing disruption of life in India during World War II did she reflect on Hitler's fascism.

At St. Mary's Training College in Poona, where Dibble received a four-year teaching appointment in 1938, she delighted in her students' thirst for knowledge and in the exotic plants and animals of India, making frequent excursions to Bombay, Delhi, and other sites. While she learned Hindustani, she clearly lived the life of an expatriate, joining fellow Britishers for tennis and tea and talking of "the disquieting news from Europe" over drinks. The war led to censorship of letters, disruption of mails, shortages (including paper), and the sinking of the *Yorkshire,* with tennis partners on board. Part of the school was turned into an emergency hospital, and Dibble became a member of the St. John's ambulance brigade.

This time was also one of personal difficulty. Dibble contracted jaundice over Christmas in 1940, and later she suffered from malaria. An earthquake marked her fortieth birthday in 1942. Following the war, which had delayed her return home by four years, Dibble was offered passage to England working as a nanny:

> That last night in India, I again thought what I should miss–the scent of garlands of frangipani and jasmine; the smoke from manure fires in the early evening; the soft padding of flat, bare feet; the whiteness of buffalo milk; the sweetness of jellabies and halva; the delicious dal and chupatties; the vocabulary which included the mali, the dhobi, the peon, the ayah and the cha, dhudh and pani of everyday life; rain, thunder, lightning would all seem tame; the friendly lizards skittering on the walls and the cheerful myna; the exquisite colour of sunbirds and the melodious song of the bulbuls; the friendliness of the Indian and Anglo-Indian peoples. All these would recreate India for me.

In 1946, after a summer of teaching geography, English, religious education, and gardening at her alma mater, the Maidstone Girls' Grammar School, Dibble set off for a geography post at the United Missionary College in Ibadan, Nigeria. She struggled to learn about the region and to master the "difficult, tonal Yoruba language." Largely responsible not only for teaching but for stocking the school with supplies, Dibble made frequent excursions, returning with books, clothes, and equipment (including a stove). She continued to devote herself to natural history, collecting specimens for class. As a missionary college, the school often hosted visitors, including the wife of Marcus Garvey, the leader of the "Back to Africa" movement in the United States. During trips through northern Nigeria, she learned Hausa and saw her first game of polo. As in India, life abroad brought hardship: she again contracted malaria and soon thereafter learned of her mother's sudden death.

During summers Dibble returned to Europe. In 1948 she toured Switzerland, stopping in Montreux, Chillon, Geneva, and farms in Gruyère, Basle, Lucerne, Weggis, and Brunnen before returning to Ibadan. During her second year in Nigeria, Dibble oversaw the building of a tennis court, organized motion-picture series for the students, and taught the "labourers" how to plant to prevent erosion. She continued to explore the country (Benin, Enuga, Calabar, and Mount Cameroon) and to learn about its people (meeting eminent Nigerians such as artist Ben Enwonwu).

In 1950 Dibble crossed the Sahara Desert by bus. Frequent breakdowns forced the small group of passengers to rough it, camping out in the desert. Along the way Dibble collected rock specimens for her classes. Her third tour in Nigeria was interrupted by news that her father was ill. She returned home to nurse him, but he died a scant two weeks later.

In 1952 Dibble was offered the position of acting principal at the new Women's Teacher Training College in Ilesha, Nigeria. This school was part of an effort to ensure equal education for Nigerian girls, who had only recently won the right to the same primary education as boys. As in Ibadan, Dibble was responsible for stocking the school, buying books, china, other furnishing and supplies, and a car. Conditions at the new school were significantly less modern than in Ibadan: there was no electricity, for instance. Still, she managed to teach geography, nature study, and physical education and appears to have been well-liked by students. One wrote of "our devoted Mother, Miss Dibble": "She is always directed by God. She is always occupied in the office throughout the school hours yet she will kick her car and came to the class at 5 o'clock to train us."

In the summer of 1954 Dibble traveled by railroad coach through the Normandy plain, Loire valley, and south of France into Spain, where she journeyed from San Sebastian through Basque country to Burgos, Castile, Madrid, and Valencia. She noted, "Barcelona would be much more attractive if the noisy trams could be replaced." In a rare political observation, she pointed out "posters and paintings . . . praising Franco, and also calling attention to British occupation of Gibraltar."

In 1955 Dibble left the Women's Teacher Training College in Ilesha to take a post at a new regional teacher-training college in Ibadan. Initially she was transferred to Queen's School, in Ede, to replace an English teacher. Her "temporary" assignment lasted until 1959.

A three-month journey in that year took Dibble through ten African countries. She voyaged up the Congo to Stanleyville, then by plane to Bukavu (a health resort for Belgians living in Leopoldville); by boat to Goma; and by car to Kisenyi and Kampala, rather than being forced to "thumb a lift" on a truck, something she had never done. She then embarked on a "thrilling voyage" up Murchison River, spotting elephants, hippopotamuses, buffalo, and baboons and eventually crossing Lake Victoria by steamer to Kisumu. In Nairobi she finally fulfilled her dream of seeing lions.

Another "cherished wish" was "to see the Matopos at the World View, with the grave of Cecil Rhodes." There she was struck by the forbidding mountains, "mostly bare rocks, with no sign of humanity." Another dream was realized when she visited Victoria Falls, which Africans call "the smoke that thunders." In South Africa she was taken aback by apartheid and modernization: "With trolley buses and escalators in the bank, and segregation of whites and 'nie blankes' in the buses and post office, I felt very far away from Nigeria."

In the second volume of *Return Tickets* Dibble recounts her life and travels from 1959 to 1968. The book opens with her recollections of fulfilling a "life-long wish to visit New Zealand," where she was captivated by the dramatic contrasts in scenery, from volcanoes and geysers to glaciers. Traveling with her sister, she sailed to Durban, South Africa, where she became a "real geographer, making two studies" of soap and sugar factories. On this trip she also made her first visit to a game reserve, which she later lauded as the best way to view wild animals in their natural habitat.

In 1961, during her last days in Nigeria after fourteen years of teaching, she was bitten by "a beautiful fly, which was later identified as simulium damnosum–a suitable name for a cause of 'River Blindness.'" She later discovered that she had contracted this disease.

Once back in England, Dibble kept her memories of Nigeria alive by giving talks, illustrated by slides, to friends and schools. Applying for positions in British schools, she was dismissed as too old: "One manager commented that as I had worked for twenty-two years

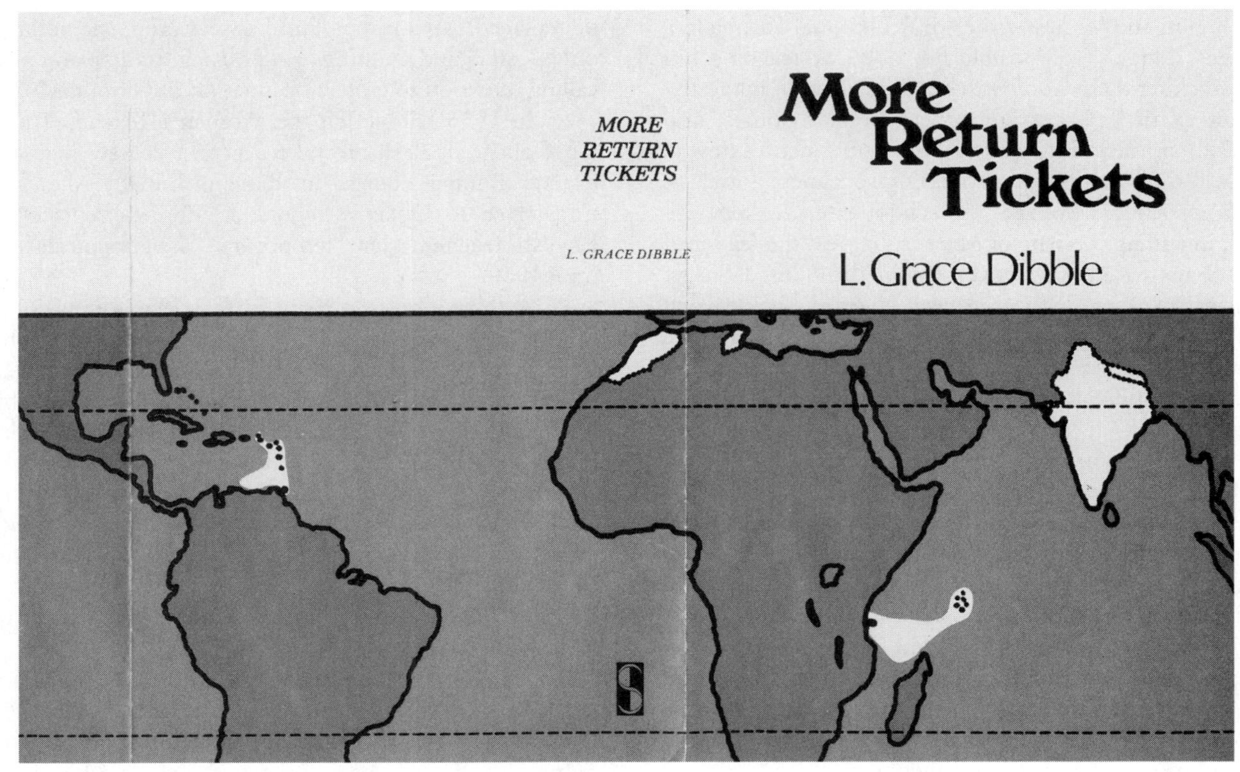

Dust jacket for Dibble's 1979 book about her 1969–1977 travels in South Asia and North Africa

in the Tropics, I could not be very healthy. I replied that it just went to prove how tough I was!" She finally found a job at Dane Court School for Girls in Broadstairs. Teaching British girls required some adjustment: "At once I was conscious that there was not the all-absorbing urge to learn, as I had known in Nigeria." At fifty-nine, she also belatedly began taking driving lessons, even though she had driven extensively in Nigeria, where a license was not required. She finally passed the driving test after she had turned sixty.

Still possessed of an irrepressible urge to travel, Dibble took the "Journey of a Life Time," returning to Israel on a pilgrimage in 1962. In *Return Tickets* she wrote movingly about modern Israel:

> I felt that it must be hard to be a Christian there, as that religion emphasises the faith of the individual, and in Israel there is a strong feeling of a collective mentality, coupled with an intense nationalistic spirit. There is little bridging of the wide gulfs between the three monotheistic faiths and the modern materialism. We were constantly switching mentally from the past to the present, and always there seemed to be an atmosphere of political, religious and cultural conflicts.

The next year, Dibble traveled to Turkey, following in the "footsteps of St. Paul." By bus she traced Paul's route, tying her own journey to the biblical past. In her account of the trip Dibble assumes her reader is possessed of the same knowledge and faith, devoting little space to reflect on biblical traditions or explain them for the benefit of nonbelievers.

In 1964 Dibble was hospitalized for twenty-one days with onchocerciasis, or "River Blindness," and she was then forced to make monthly visits to West Kent Hospital for treatment by intravenous injections to save her sight. This ordeal may have contributed to her decision to retire a year later.

Her illness did not, however, dampen her desire to travel and study. In the summer preceding her final year of teaching, she was "plunged into preparations for the Field Study Course in North America, organised by the Isle of Thanet Geographical Association." The trip took her back to Canada for the first time since her initial posting to Winnipeg more than thirty years before. The group traveled through Newfoundland and New Brunswick to Montreal, then on to Ottawa, Trenton, Toronto, and McMaster University in Hamilton. Crossing the border into New York State, Dibble encountered some of the tensions of the civil-rights era. Arriving late in Rochester, she wrote,

> At once we hurried out to get food and went into the first cafeteria in which there were folk who might have triggered off trouble at any moment, though we knew

> that the recent Race riots had been officially quelled. One man, who was wandering up and down and visiting the tables, was not drunk, as we had thought at first, but was "feeble minded" and really a harmless fellow. A Negro, very politely, asked to borrow the salt from our table.

Continuing to New York for a day at the World's Fair, the tour then paused for lessons in U.S. history in Washington, D.C., before passing through the Appalachian Mountains to Shenandoah National Park in Virginia.

Dibble's retirement to Broadstairs in 1965 brought the pleasures of leisure. Dibble devoted herself to gardening and discovered the lure of the cinema. She continued her language studies, adding Spanish to a list that already included German, French, Yoruba, and Hindi. Retirement also provided Dibble with the time for writing her *Return Tickets* series. Travel remained a preoccupation, though from this point forward her voyages were to warmer climes, often in the company of the members of the Isle of Thanet Geographical Association or the local United Nations Association. A Caribbean cruise in 1965 took her to Nassau, Miami, Jamaica (Kingston, Ochos Rios), Panama (Colon, Panama City), Venezuela, Trinidad, Barbados, Martinique, St. Thomas, and Madeira. In *Return Tickets* she writes that the Caribbean reminded her of "life in the West Coast of Africa–the happy friendly people, the tropical vegetation, and the hot sunny days."

In 1965 Dibble flew with the Geographical Association to Malta. The next year a military coup caused her to cancel a return visit to Nigeria, so she took another cruise instead. Her tour of the Mediterranean included stops in Pompeii, Athens, Alexandria, Cairo, Haifa, Jerusalem, Mount Zion, Nazareth, Sicily, Messina, Taormina, Tangier, and Lisbon. Later trips were the result of her rediscovered passion for gardening. Dibble visited Holland in the spring of 1966 before attending "summer school" in Puerto Rico later that year.

Dibble made her third visit to Nairobi in February 1967 for a week's safari. She photographed zebras, rhinoceroses, elephants, lions, and water buffalo, before fulfilling another dream, to visit the island of Mauritius. By summer she was in Switzerland for the United Nations Association summer school. There she walked in the mountains wearing her "boy's boots, now about fifty years old, having been preserved with Neat's foot oil!"

In 1968, after thirty-four years, Dibble returned to Ceylon (now Sri Lanka), "the pearl of the east," visiting places sacred to the Buddha, such as monasteries, temples, and ruins.

In the final sections of the book Dibble describes how she was possessed of a compelling urge to write, and her references to the act of writing become more frequent: "The 'spirit' drove me to writing my journal all the evening." The habit of reflection brought on by writing also yielded greater insights: "In my Paradise, there will be a sea–and a tropical one at that. I cannot share the feelings of the writer of 'Revelations,' 'there shall be no more sea.'" An account of a "sentimental safari" closes the second volume. In 1968 she returned to Nairobi to study the natural environment, suddenly deciding to return to Murchison Falls National Park in Uganda.

More Return Tickets (1979), like Dibble's previous work, combines diary entries for each voyage with brief narratives of Dibble's life. The reader learns that in 1968 she was busy attending "stimulating lectures in Canterbury Cathedral and also at the meetings of the Isle of Thanet Geographical Association; and the Archaeological, the Horticultural and the Natural History societies." She also served "on the Board of Managers of the local Church School." As she aged and devoted more of her time to writing, her journal entries became more detailed, including domestic trivia, such as what food she was served on the airplane and trips to hairdressers (dust being an enemy to a coiffure). Mentions of current affairs also increase, though typically these are cursory lists recapping major events. As in her previous books, Dibble's focus is emphatically on her travels.

As *More Return Tickets* recounts, in 1969 Dibble brushed up on her Hindi in preparation for a return trip to India. During her travels she contracted ptomaine poisoning and "thought that my ashes might be cast on the Jumana!" Quickly recovered, however, she embarked on an ambitious tour of temples, caves, and other sites along the Ganges. She found India changed: "it was most distressing to see so much poverty, so many hovels, so many apathetic and hungry people, alongside the obviously wealthy families. . . . I hated to see the women still engaged on road work and building sites–such hard and dirty jobs." Crossing into Nepal, she was again struck by the contrast between rich and poor.

No child of the 1960s, Dibble dismissed those engaged in transcendental meditation in Kathmandu and elsewhere in the Himalayas. Instead, she wrote contemptuously in her journals of the hippies she encountered, preferring the comfort of her faith and lauding the National Christian Council of India for its literacy campaign.

In the 1970s Dibble made several voyages to southern Europe (Greece, Italy, and Spain). They

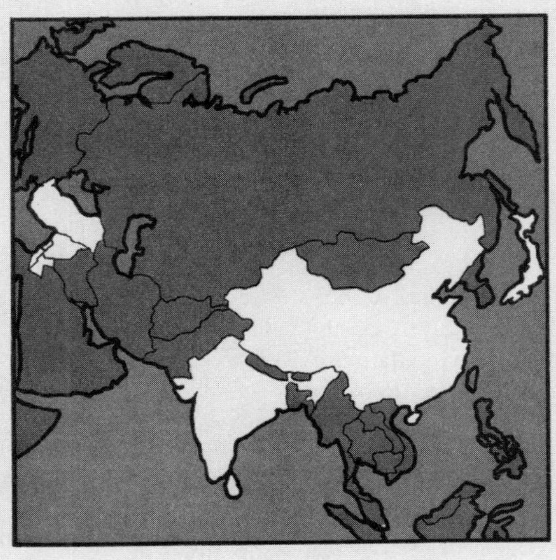

Front cover for Dibble's 1993 book, a collection of previously published travel writings

receive only passing reference in *More Return Tickets,* awaiting fuller discussion in a later volume of the series.

Traveling to Tunisia in 1975, Dibble visited markets, mosques, and museums, lingering over mosaics, which had become of special interest to her. Here she was asked for the first of many times why she was traveling alone, without her husband. In response to the question, "When are you going to marry?" she replied "Too old." In each book, her traveling companions, if any, remain shadowy figures identified only by their first names, if at all. Instead, Dibble stresses the advantage of traveling alone, explaining that it is easier to meet other people.

Her 1977 trip to Morocco completed her "visits to African countries bordering the Mediterranean Sea." During her account of the voyage, the reader learns of the "heart trouble" that increasingly interfered with her life and travels in later years.

Return Tickets to Southern Europe (1980) marks a bit of a departure for Dibble. For the first time she limited a book to a specific region, rather than covering her travels in chronological order. The book describes her journeys to northern Italy (1971), Greece (1972), Sicily (1973), southern Sardinia (1974), and southern Spain (1977). Again presented in diary form, the accounts track her tours of ruins, gardens, and churches, emphasizing her "special interest in mosaics." Typically, she wore her traveling uniform: cotton dress (often African), Italian rope-soled shoes, Indian Shan-style bag, and Nigerian hat. Her accounts in this volume are often more than recitations of fact, offering evidence of greater reflection and analysis.

Dibble's account of her trip to Rome, for instance, includes moving passages on artworks and literary history. Greatly affected by Michelangelo's *Pietà* in St. Peter's, she wrote,

> Mary is portrayed as a young, beautiful and sensitive woman–not as a mother in her fifties. She appears alone in the world, as she gazes downwards, with the weight of the head covering helping to bend her head. She is the embodiment of serene composure, with a

> grandeur of spirit. She is intensely alive and natural: the great artist did not need haloes and angels in this composition.

Her descriptions of visits to the Forum, the Colosseum, and other ruins are informed by references to writers who have preceded her, including Charles Dickens; George Gordon, Lord Byron; John Keats; and Percy Bysshe Shelley.

References to her advancing age also become more frequent. In Assisi, on 3 October 1971, she wrote, "My birthday! and alone!" The next year she wondered "if this would be my last chance to experience all the wonders and charm of Athens." Nonetheless, she still had her charms. In Greece she was approached by an amorous and insistent middle-aged man, who proposed marriage and entreated her to get off at his bus stop. Recalling the event, she puffed, "Such an experience even at 70 years!"

Such self-deprecating comments occasionally include elements of humor, as when she described a donkey ride on Crete: "As I approached the animals, I was suddenly picked up bodily and thrown across the padded back of a small mule, which immediately took off at a smart pace. . . . After what seemed an interminable climb, I reached the top and was unceremoniously hoisted off the poor beast!"

In 1982 Dibble again chose to limit her narrative to a particular region. *Return Tickets to Scandinavia* is the first of her books to include material previously published in the original *Return Tickets,* which was no longer in print. Accounts of her early voyages to Scandinavia are juxtaposed with new sections based on more recent travels. The diary of her 1932 trip to Norway is reprinted in its entirety, followed by "Norway Revisited," a narrative of a return trip taken in June 1978. Forty-six years later, Dibble was not quite as spry. She noted that her heart was "playing up" at one point, but later described a "taxing" two and one-half-hour climb to see the Brixdal glacier. Largely pleased with what she encountered in modern Norway, she emphasized that the people were still friendly, the scenery wonderful, and the city clean. Following a section about her 1976 visit to Denmark on the Garden News and Dobies' Seeds Garden Tour, Dibble included the section from *Return Tickets* about her 1937 trip to Sweden and then added "Sweden Revisited–1982," highlighted by her reacquaintance with a school friend.

Return Tickets to Yugoslavia (1984) collects daily chronicles of several trips to Yugoslavia between 1976 and 1983. Again returning to locales she had visited in the 1930s, Dibble devoted particular attention to the religious past and history of conflict in the region. Contemporary readers will envy her easy passage among Croatia, Herzegovina, Serbia, and Montenegro. A tour of the southeastern region in 1981 was the first in which she discovered evidence of the growing tensions. On hearing that the group would be unable to travel through Kosmet Province "owing to political disturbances," Dibble was distressed that "we would not see the famous monuments to the Serbs and the Turks, after the former had been conquered in 1389; nor could we visit the marvelous buildings in Peć, Priština and Gračinica. This had been my principal objective in joining this tour of South Yugoslavia!" At times the stress of walking caused her to ask, "Why do I do it at my age?" Still, in response to a seventy-six-year-old Canadian tourist who longed to return to her hotel, Dibble snapped, "This 79 year old still thrives on visiting such fabulous places as Venice."

In the 1980s Dibble remained a dedicated traveler, but she voyaged to less far-flung places and increasingly devoted her attentions to life in Broadstairs, winning an award for her service efforts in 1981. *Return Tickets Here and There* (1988), dedicated to the Isle of Thanet Geographical Association, recounts the last of her return tickets. In May 1980 she finally returned to Vienna, reminding readers that in 1936 she had been unable to disembark there because her currency had been confiscated at the Hungarian border.

As always, Dibble's motivation for traveling was study, with the United Nations Association to Vienna and elsewhere with other organizations to pursue her deepening interest in plants and animals. In 1984 and 1986 she attended garden festivals in Liverpool and Stoke-on-Trent. Trips to Jersey and Guernsey in 1985 with the Isle of Thanet Geographical Association also focused on the natural world: parks, gardens, butterfly farms, and nurseries. In 1984 Dibble fulfilled another wish in Tenerife: "I had long wished to visit this island, because we used to see the snow-capped peak of the volcano Teide, when sailing to and from Lagos in Nigeria." In her account of this trip she affirmed, "I am always happiest near the sea, where one can gaze at the ever-changing face of the ocean every day. This had been the fiftieth island which I have visited and the thirteenth on which I have stayed to explore."

Two tours of the Italian lakes in 1986 took Dibble to more islands: Baveno, Isola Bella, Isola Pescatori, and Isola Madre, with its famous botanical gardens. In 1987 she spent six days in the Coronary Unit in Margate Hospital. Continuing trouble with her heart appears to have diminished opportunities for travel beyond her eighty-fifth year.

Fittingly, *No Return Tickets!* was published in 1989. As its title suggests, this volume marks a significant departure. The centenary of the Maidstone Grammar School for Girls (to whom the book is dedicated) led

Dibble to reminisce about her pretravel days, 1902 to 1925. Returning to material originally published in the first volume of *Return Tickets,* Dibble here recounts her early childhood experiences.

Her next five books also cover well-worn territory. *Return Tickets to Africa* (1992) and *Return Tickets to Asia* (1993) gather previously published accounts of her travels to each region. *Return Tickets in Pictures for Armchair Globetrotters* (1993) and *Return Tickets in Pictures for Globetrotting Naturalists* (1994) present photographs from her various travels, introduced by brief essays in which Dibble reflects on the sights she was privileged to experience in seventy years of travel.

Failing eyesight meant that *Return Tickets to Sacred Places* (1996), like the previous volumes of the 1990s, republishes earlier accounts of journeys. By focusing in this book on holy sites in the Middle East and Asia, Dibble ended her publishing career by emphasizing her faith and dedication to God. (The book is dedicated to Holy Trinity Church, Broadstairs.) The first volumes of *Return Tickets* end with an epilogue that she also included in subsequent volumes: "I often recall the words of Bishop Kenneth E. Kirk: 'It remains in some mysterious way that the more we understand God's universe, the nearer we come to an understanding of God Himself.'"

Possessed of a "compelling urge to write," Dibble produced thirteen books that are a testament to her stamina and her "inexhaustible thirst for fresh geographical and natural history knowledge; . . . the attraction of islands; the love of new adventures; the love of the heat and colour of the tropics; the fun of meeting people of other races and nationalities; and the fresh scope for photography." A reviewer for *The Lady* (2 April 1981) noted that "the author is by no means a master of prose, but she is competent and industrious." In *Wayward Women* (1990) Jane Robinson calls Dibble "a traveller of the old traditional school: the cheerful maiden lady whose inveterate world-wending habits are harnessed to a clear sense of Christian duty, and whose prodigious books both edify and entertain." Undoubtedly Dibble will be remembered for the variety and scope of her travels, especially her journeys to destinations seldom chosen by single women of a certain age. Her manuscripts, to be housed in the Hypatia Trust at the University of Exeter, will remain as a testament to her unflagging desire to learn and teach about the world.

Reference:

Jane Robinson, *Wayward Women: A Guide to Women Travellers* (New York: Oxford University Press, 1990).

Christina Dodwell

(1 February 1951 –)

Syrine C. Hout
American University of Beirut

BOOKS: *Travels with Fortune: An African Adventure* (London: W. H. Allen, 1979);

In Papua New Guinea (Sparkford, Yeovil, U.K.: Oxford Illustrated Press, 1983);

An Explorer's Handbook: Travel, Survival and Bush Cookery (London: Hodder & Stoughton, 1984); republished as *An Explorer's Handbook: An Unconventional Guide for Travelers to Remote Regions* (New York: Facts on File, 1986);

A Traveller in China (London: Hodder & Stoughton, 1985; New York: Beaufort Books, 1985);

A Traveller on Horseback in Eastern Turkey and Iran (London: Hodder & Stoughton, 1987; New York: Walker, 1989);

Travels with Pegasus: A Microlight Journey across West Africa (London: Hodder & Stoughton, 1989; New York: Walker, 1990);

Beyond Siberia (London: Hodder & Stoughton, 1993);

Madagascar Travels (London: Hodder & Stoughton, 1995).

Three factors account for Christina Dodwell's renown as a traveler and writer: her parents' moral support, "a little cash and a powerful wanderlust." Because she is a member of a family of veteran voyagers, it seemed natural for her to revisit places where her family had lived (China and Nigeria) and to explore new territories.

Dodwell's maternal grandparents went to China in 1919. After a few years they settled briefly in Hankou (now part of Wuhan) and then moved to Beijing, where they stayed for seven years before they finally moved to Tianjin in 1932. Her grandfather, Lesley Beddow, was captured by Japanese invasion forces in 1941 and sent to an underground prison for seven months. Her grandmother, Doris Beddow, was a special correspondent for the *News Chronicle* and the *Daily News*. Beddow's articles on the besieged city of Hankou, warlord Chang Tso-lin, and the Kuomintang leader Sun Yat-sen's last days in 1925 have remained valuable to historians. Dodwell's mother was born in Hankou in 1924 and raised in Beijing.

Christina Dodwell, 1992 (courtesy of Christina Dodwell)

The daughter of Christopher and Evelyn Dodwell, Christina Dodwell was born on 1 February 1951 and brought up "deep in the bush" of Nigeria. When she was six, as the African nation loosened its ties to the British Empire, her family relocated to England for seven years. Her parents went back to Nigeria when Dodwell was thirteen years old, after her father had accepted a post offered by his company, but she stayed behind in England to continue her education and joined them only on holidays. During the Biafran War between the Ibo and Hausa tribes in Nigeria (1967–1970), Dodwell witnessed two military coups in Lagos. After the Africanization of industry, her family returned to England for good.

At the age of twenty-four Dodwell decided to give her life a new direction. In *Travels with Fortune* (1979) she wrote that by that time she had "held an assortment of jobs from secretary of a society column in a fashion magazine [*Queen*], advertising manager of an engineering firm, interior designer, to manager of the Mayfair branch of a car-hire company." Leaving behind her "home-loving, materialistic, possessive, insecure, and very afraid of the dark" nature, she decided to travel. A few years later, she wrote in her second book, *In Papua New Guinea* (1983), that "travelling round meant that home was simply a state of mind, and it often came in unexpected places."

Dodwell's books are a rich source of information about her actions, attitudes, and writing habits. In each of her travel books she refers repeatedly and specifically to the places and times where and when she carried out her writing.

The opening line of *Travels with Fortune: An African Adventure* states that Dodwell "left England on 11 March 1975 intending to spend a year as an overlander through Africa." She had three companions: "two boys," whom she contacted "through an advertisement in a travel magazine," and a twenty-eight-year-old New Zealand nurse, Lesley Jamieson, who had previously been to South America. In a late-model Land Rover they drove across Europe, through Spain, and ended up in Morocco. At a feast celebrating the birth of the Prophet Muhammad, to which they were invited by a Tuareg boy called Moktar, Dodwell learned to ululate, as local women typically do to express joy. Heading across Algeria and Niger to Nigeria, they crossed the Sahara Desert, "the land of thirst and mirages which is called Emptiness."

After they reached Kano, Nigeria, on 10 April, the future of the carefully planned expedition was suddenly thrown into uncertainty. After some searching, Dodwell and Jamieson found that "the boys" had sold the Land Rover for a ridiculously low price and that their capital, previously equivalent to £3,000, had dropped to £400. To make up for the lost money, they bartered some of their Western personal belongings, including a watch. Disregarding her parents' advice to fly to Nairobi and an Englishman's well-meaning but somewhat disingenuous suggestion to behave as civilized and prudent white ladies by keeping their distance from the Africans, Dodwell and Jamieson started hitchhiking "to see how things were, by looking at the difference in our cultures, not in terms of good and bad, superior or inferior, but as totally separate worlds."

"Our destination seemed irrelevant," Dodwell wrote, "it was the journey now which was an experience in itself." One such experience was learning about juju (West African medicine and magic) and the African mentality. Hitchhiking came to an end when gasoline became extremely scarce in Nigeria, so Dodwell and Jamieson started riding horses–Cara Mia and Diablo–that they were given by some Italian men. After learning a few words of Fulani, they entered Cameroon and sold their horses for £20. On 16 June they arrived in Bamenda, a town "with electricity, and many white faces." Dodwell "already felt a good deal older than the kid who had left England three months before."

In Ngaoundéré they borrowed bicycles to explore the town, and in Victoria, on 5 July, they read in the newspaper that London was in the throes of an IRA bombing campaign. Choosing at random which country to visit next by marking a set of matches with different names, they resolved to travel to Gabon and set out in a dugout that they located and purchased with the help of a group of Americans. On 4 August they left Bangui in the Central African Republic and began a difficult one-thousand-mile river journey, covering thirty-six miles a day at about four-and-a-half miles per hour. During a stop in the forest they met the president of the Republic of Congo. Jamieson contracted malaria but quickly recovered, after which she and Dodwell spent a pleasant time in Brazzaville, where they were interviewed on Congolese television and did a radio broadcast. The newspapers in French Equatorial Africa heralded the two women as "intrepid explorers" on an "extraordinary odyssey."

After selling the dugout for £2, Dodwell and Jamieson spent the next three months roaming through the jungles of Congo and Gabon. They then started hitchhiking rides on airplanes. Spinning a knife, they decided to go to Pointe-Noire on the Congo coast. At the end of October, they crossed the border into Gabon and arrived in Moanda, where a French pilot offered to fly them to Libreville, Gabon. There a postcard from a friend informed them that he had read about their river journey in the *South China Morning Post,* and Dodwell ran into her brother-in-law, who had come from Lagos to assure the family of their well-being. Another Frenchman helped arrange Dodwell and Jamieson's passage on a ship that was leaving on Christmas Day for Capetown, South Africa. On board *L'Augure* on New Year's Eve, Dodwell was sexually harassed and imprisoned by the captain. "The preservation of my virtue was not the thing that mattered–I was fighting for a principle that no one had the right to bully me," she later wrote. The horror came to an end after the ship turned back to

Dodwell setting up camp near the Pegasus XL Microlight airplane in which she and David Young flew around West Africa for four months in 1988–1989 (photograph by Young)

Libreville, and the two young women managed to get to an airport, flying from there to Johannesburg in South Africa.

Randomly again, they set out for Salisbury, Rhodesia (now Zimbabwe), where Dodwell celebrated her twenty-fifth birthday and said good-bye to Jamieson, who by that time was engaged to be married. After three months Dodwell left Hunter's Moon, a dog kennel in which she had been working for a while, for the eastern highland regions of Rhodesia, where Cecil Rhodes was buried. In mid December she traveled on horseback across the Zululand region of South Africa to reach the Transkei region. She spent her twenty-sixth birthday in Lesotho: "The future was wide open, every alternative route would in some way have different effects, every decision and change would alter my life."

From Capetown, Dodwell traveled through Namibia, Botswana, Zambia, Malawi, and Tanzania, and into Kenya, where she spent two months, leaving at the end of September 1977. An American primatologist named Toni agreed to accompany her on her journey north. Dodwell spent a third birthday in Africa while they were looking for horses. A bite from a poisonous spider debilitated her for a few days in early March 1978. Finally, on 27 April 1978, after "a three-year marathon," Dodwell flew back to England.

One year later *Travels with Fortune: An African Adventure* was published. Like all Dodwell's subsequent works, her first book is a delicate blend of anecdotal, autobiographical, and scientific information, allowing the reader to learn from her experiences and observations and to do so with genuine enjoyment. The twenty-seven chapters in *Travels with Fortune* are supplemented by three maps and thirteen photographs, some featuring Dodwell engaged in various activities.

To finance her next major trip, Dodwell worked with BBC radio, which produced four series of travel features for broadcasting and published articles in the *New Scientist.* Feeling restless in London before setting out in December 1979 on a two-year journey to Papua New Guinea–"the Last Unknown"–she toured France and Greece and then went by way of England to the United States and Mexico. Dodwell has not yet written about her travels in Europe and North America.

To reach Papua New Guinea, Dodwell flew to Thailand and spent her twenty-ninth birthday, which coincided with Thaipusam–a major Hindu festival dedicated to Siva, god of destruction–in Malaysia. After the celebration of the Chinese New Year, she left Malacca, went by bus to Singapore, and later by boat to Java in Indonesia, with its 13,500 islands peopled by more than 350 ethnic groups. Once in Papua New Guinea, a former Dutch colony, she picked up a few words of the local pidgin to help her get along. Choosing arbitrarily, as always, she flew to the highlands in the least-explored part of the country and was struck by the variety of reptiles and birds, whose presence she attributed to the sunken land bridge that once linked Australia to Asia.

While traveling on horseback, she remembered the child's rhyme that "Thursday's child has far to go," and since she had been born on a Thursday, she "never doubted that it referred to me." After a one-thousand-mile horseback journey and a four-month adventure in a canoe down the Sepik River and a raft down the white-water river Wahgi, she was known by the natives as the Horse Lady and "Sepik Woman." In 1983 BBC television filmed her descent of the Wahgi as *The Wahgi Eater of Men,* part of their award-winning *River Journeys* series, which had its premiere at the Royal Geographical Society. A picture of her at a rodeo appeared on the front page of a national newspaper and transformed her into something of a national celebrity. In an interview with *Geographical Magazine* she commented on her success: "I give a lot of respect to the people I travel among and demand a lot in return." In 1983 she published *In Papua New Guinea,* an account of her journey, which also includes a glossary, two maps, and twenty-six photographs. A second edition appeared in 1985.

Relying on her travel experiences, Dodwell sought to help fellow travelers by publishing *An Explorer's Handbook: Travel, Survival and Bush Cookery* (1984), filled with information about a wide range of topics–including how to look after traveling animals, how to cook meat, and to how to avoid being arrested as a foreign spy–occasionally illustrated by drawings and sketches. Two years later it was republished with a different subtitle in New York, where it won an Academy of Sciences award.

Next came Dodwell's trip to China. Supported financially by Dodwell International (a firm apparently unrelated to the Dodwell family) and equipped with the rudiments of Mandarin and an alien's travel card valid for four months, she flew in May 1984 to Urumqi, the capital of the Xinjiang Uygur region. There she embarked on a four-day bus journey to Kashgar (Kashi) on the Silk Road that Marco Polo had traveled in 1273. On the way, to break the "conversational ice," she employed a tactic that had previously been successful in bringing her closer to the natives of Africa and Papua New Guinea: she shared photographs of her family and postcards of England with the other passengers. As she wrote in *A Traveller in China* (1985), "Suddenly you are no longer just a foreign devil, you are also a person with a mother and father, like anyone else." Until seven years before her journey, China had kept out all Western influences. One thing that irritated her, until she realized it was culturally acceptable, was that people constantly stared at her.

More than once in *A Traveller in China,* Dodwell quotes Marco Polo. Dodwell demonstrates much book-bred knowledge of the many countries she visits, but her comments on any aspect of a culture, such as the sociopolitical situation in China, are primarily derived from conversations with people, both natives and Westerners, whom she has met along the way. On Lake Karakol she followed "in the wake of Sven Hedin," a Swedish geographer who surveyed the area in 1894, and Chris Bonington, the renowned climber of Mount Kongur in 1980. There she basked in solitude, which "gives time for thought," a luxury rarely enjoyed in a country of one billion people.

By asking natives direct questions about their religious beliefs, Dodwell found out how mixed their feelings were about the Communist Party and its efforts at modernization. While being driven around on a bicycle by a Chinese schoolteacher called Chen, who had been a victim of the Cultural Revolution of 1966–1976, she learned much about the educational system and the curriculum, which emphasized social conformity and submission to party ideology. In response to Chen's invitation, she spent an evening lecturing on history and geography to some fifty students. As these events attest, Dodwell's travel ethos is based on verbal and behavioral interaction, the giving and taking of information, and the exchange of ideas.

In Beijing, Dodwell followed in the footsteps of two pioneers: Marco Polo and her grandmother. Canoeing on the Yellow River (Huang), she discovered a hitherto unknown portion of the Great Wall. In Beijing she was entertained by Mr. Liu, the local manager of Dodwell International, who promised to help her locate her grandparents' house (which was locked when she arrived at it). Later, in a Tibetan nomad tent, she participated in the ornamentation ritual of a ladies' hairdressing session. From Beijing, Dodwell went to Canton (now Guangzhou), where she boarded a ship and "said goodbye to China." For her, "it had been many things but above all an overwhelming emotional experience." *A Traveller in China,* which includes thirty-one photographs, was published in London and New York in 1985.

After Africa and the Far East, Dodwell decided to explore the Middle East, and she wrote about it in *A Traveller on Horseback in Eastern Turkey and Iran* (1987). She began her journey to those parts in May 1986 by witnessing the Orthodox Church Easter celebrations in Athens. She also wanted to research her "great-many-times-great-uncle Edward Dodwell's journey by mule across Greece in the early nineteenth century. He had

A pygmy teaching Dodwell how to make turtle stew in Cameron, during her 1988-1989 travels in West Africa (photograph by David Young)

been travelling to find and record ruins of historical and religious interest." As a prisoner on parole, having been captured in France during the Napoleonic Wars and denied re-entry to England, he had found travel liberating. With some knowledge of Turkish but none of Farsi, Edward's descendant embarked on her journey to two major Muslim countries. In one the population was primarily Sunni (Turkey), and in the other the people were mainly Shiite (Iran).

From Greece, Dodwell crossed the Aegean Sea and landed in the Turkish port of Kusadasi, where she took a bus halfway across the country to Nevsehir. There she caught a *dolmus,* "the useful Turkish cross between a taxi and a minibus," to Ürgüp, a village in the middle of the region of Cappadocia, a former Roman province. On the first day of Ramadan, the holiest month in the Islamic calendar, she set out on a pony called Beyaz (white) to explore nearby villages. Wearing a cloth cap to protect herself from the sun, she was assumed by villagers to be a man, for a woman on horseback was an unusual sight. When asked where she was going, she replied "Gesiorum," which means to wander serendipitously. After visiting Erzurum and obtaining a visa for Iran, she crossed the border to spend a month exploring that country, then in the seventh year of its war with neighboring Iraq.

In the border village of Maku, Dodwell bought a bus ticket to Tehran. She admired the nomadic women in "gaudy full-skirted dresses, headbands and glittery gold scarves, making a contrast to all the other black hooded crows." Despite this initial description of women who wear the chador, she ended up appreciating it as a multipurpose garment. She was willing to shed preconceptions of the veil as a negative sign in favor of a more positive and contextualized understanding of this culture-specific item of feminine clothing. In Tehran she caught a bus and traveled along the Caspian shore to Gonbad-e-Kavus, the site of the Tomb of Kavus, which had been described by travel writer Robert Byron as one of the four most beautiful structures in all of Iran.

At one point Dodwell was arrested by Revolutionary Guards, who confiscated her passport and Farsi dictionary and threw her into a solitary cubicle because they suspected she had been in trouble with the police. After her release she went to visit an American woman who had married an Iranian and lived there since 1957. This woman had also recently suffered, like Dodwell, at the hands of the guards. To adapt to village life in Iran, Dodwell paid homage to the natives' belief in jinni (spirits of good and evil). She also showed deep appreciation for Persian carpets. Her passion for the truth led her to seek to resolve the controversial dispute between archaeologists and Turkomans about how far inland Alexander's Wall extended. She followed the wall beyond the point where it was said to have ended, but did not reach the point at which it stopped.

Talking to Iranians, she discovered how ambiguous their feelings were toward their past leader, the Westernized Shah Mohammad Reza Pahlavi, and their present leader, the Islamic fundamentalist Ayatollah Khomeini. Like some female Western travelers before her, she realized how prejudiced many modern feminists and orientalists had been in viewing the chador as a means of female oppression in male-oriented Muslim societies: "Actually I don't think the women mind as much as their liberated sisters would want them to. They quite enjoy wearing one as a means of flirtation, sometimes wearing little underneath, and it gives the plain girl the same start as the beauty." This comment is based on interviews: "Being female meant I could associate freely with Iranian women, and over the full course of my journey I talked with an enormous number, whose background varied from local bus passengers to the wealthy upper class." Nevertheless, Dodwell is well aware of the dangers women face should they openly protest: "Iranian women who resisted covering up risked having acid sprayed in their faces." Dodwell also praises Iranian music and dance, which have been prohibited by the Revolutionary Guards, commenting that it "seemed a shame that to display such grace was now a crime."

From Kerman she went by bus to Zahedan, near the Pakistani border, and then went on to Karachi, where she hoped to renew her almost expired visa. After doing so, she lunched at the Sind Club, the oldest polo and country club in Central Asia. In the bazaar she befriended local merchants, who invited her to listen to BBC World Service News and drink tea with them. A Scottish woman, Sheila, and her Zoroastrian Parsi husband, Jahansoz, took Dodwell to an Afghan refugee camp near the Afghan border. Dodwell was angered by the lack of Pakistani expertise in operating medical units and called it "a waste of foreign aid."

At this point in her journey only six weeks had passed since Dodwell had left Greece, "but somehow the time seemed to contain worlds travelled." She had visited a great many places and had met many people, including Jennifer Qazi Musa, the Irish widow of Qazi Musa, an associate of Mohammed Ali Jinnah, the founding father of the nation of Pakistan. At the festival celebrating the major Islamic holiday of the Eid, she met Gen. Mohammad Musa, governor of Baluchistan, who made sure she was taken care of by the festival's organizer. After obtaining her renewed visa and doing her Christmas shopping, Dodwell took a bus westward back to Iran.

Driven by curiosity about why she had found no descriptions of Cyrus's tomb that explained its simplicity, she "did some research" to find out if it "wasn't originally set inside an ornate exterior," and she "discovered that pillar bases of a superstructure had been noted around the tomb's exterior." As always, Dodwell used her skills as an observer to question or add to documented information.

On horseback she rode to Persepolis (a former capital of ancient Persia), hiding her face at times with a head scarf to protect her privacy. At the Palace of Darius she spoke to a few Iranian families and took some photographs. In Shiraz her passport was confiscated by the Revolutionary Guards because of the incongruity of the dates stamped therein. It was eventually accepted that the discrepancy was because of the differences between the Christian and Islamic calendars and not any attempt at forgery on her part.

Wherever she went, Dodwell saw pictures of Khomeini and thousands of young martyrs, who were willing to die because they had been promised the spiritual key to heaven, which was symbolized by those hung around their necks. She wrote sarcastically that they were enrolled by the mullahs because they were seen as potential troublemakers.

Next Dodwell rode to the Valley of the Assassins in the Elburz Mountains to visit a couple she had met earlier and to follow in the footsteps of travel writer Freya Stark, whom she had previously met in England. Inspired by Stark's belief that "the great and almost only comfort about being a woman is that one can always pretend to be more stupid than one is and no one will be surprised," Dodwell admits that this technique has helped her in several predicaments from China to Africa, except in Iran, where, she opined, stupidity is the monopoly of the Revolutionary Guards. While in the war zone Dodwell provided succinct histories of several groups that have lived in the region, including the Assassins of the late eleventh century; the present-day Mujahedin, who were fighting against the Revolutionary Guards; and the twenty million Kurds who have been denied a sovereign state by Western and Eastern powers.

Near Mahabad, Dodwell was arrested for a third time and held for twenty-one hours by the Revolutionary Guards, who confiscated nearly all her personal possessions except her diary. After her release she bought a ticket in Tabriz for the Turkish border. She left Iran in early July, hoping to fulfill one of the original purposes of her journey: to ride on horseback through eastern Turkey.

Dodwell digging for mammoth bones during her 1992 visit to the Kamchatka Peninsula (courtesy of Christina Dodwell)

In Turkey she bought a horse called Keyif and started her wanderings. To show her gratitude to a hospitable group of villagers, she gave some lighters to the men and earrings to the women. Although she found such gift giving a bit "neo-colonial," Dodwell said it gives "immediate pleasure to the locals." She next set off for eastern Turkey, touted by the tourist office as a "land of adventure." Her first adventure was witnessing a circumcision rite and being given a scrub bath by local women. Nevertheless, when Dodwell was fully dressed in pants and a shirt, they could not help but feel her breasts to reassure themselves she was a woman because in her dauntless roaming she was behaving like a man.

From Van to Hakkari, Dodwell followed Stark's route. Instead of traveling on muleback like Stark, Dodwell got a lift in a truck and was shown around the region by a Kurdish guide named Salih. Later she met a fugitive who had defected from the Iranian army and gave him directions and advice. Next she was attacked by three young shepherds, but she managed to defend herself. She finally made it on horseback to Mount Ararat–regarded as holy by Jews, Christians, and Muslims alike–and spent some time searching for Noah's ark.

In Kars she was arrested for the fourth time since her arrival in the Middle East, when police held her on suspicion of espionage. Her letter from the Royal Geographical Society, which stated that she was nonpolitical and interested only in studying ethnic customs and rural life, was of little use. What finally helped her obtain release was the chance showing on Turkish television of *River Journeys,* a movie that she had done for the BBC in 1983. Though she thought she was cleared of suspicion, Dodwell was arrested once more, this time, she believed, to allay Soviet concerns. Later Dodwell celebrated the feast of Bayram in a village before she said good-bye to "one of the happiest episodes of my life." She wrote about these travels in *A Traveller on Horseback in Eastern Turkey and Iran* (1987), which includes forty illustrations and several maps.

After twelve years of traveling on horseback and in motor vehicles, canoes, trains, and buses in several parts of the world, Dodwell returned to West Africa, which she reexplored from the vantage point of a 1984 Pegasus XL Microlight airplane. The result was *Travels with Pegasus: A Microlight Journey across West Africa* (1989). On her four-month, seven-thousand-mile trip, she was accompanied by David Young, the pilot whose duties included keeping the Microlight airworthy and teaching her how to fly. Their departure was scheduled for mid November 1988, when Dodwell and Young took a flight aboard a conventional airliner from Gatwick Airport in London to Douala, Cameroon. From the start she explained to Young that microlighting for her was a means, not an end, for travel. In the coastal town of

Kribi she paddled in a canoe and met a tribe of Pygmies. The chief's deputy taught her how to use a spear.

To allay official suspicion, Dodwell and Young flew the Microlight in Douala for journalists and in Yaoundé for Cameroon national television. Although they were discouraged by an attaché, who claimed that "she doesn't stand a snowball's chance of making it across West Africa," Dodwell was determined to do so.

Dodwell and Young took off from Koutaba, a military base, where a large crowd had gathered for the occasion. Then she had her first training session. Flying smoothly at six thousand feet, Dodwell insisted on landing so she could visit the ancient city of Foumban, where she talked with a local woman about their manners and customs. As always, Dodwell took full advantage of the opportunity to learn firsthand about a new culture.

The next day the pair encountered considerable turbulence during their flight to Tibati, where they took refuge in a Catholic mission and prepared for the next leg to Ngaoundéré. Looking down while flying, Dodwell recognized the line of her 1975 journey on horseback. In the village of Rhumsiki, Dodwell asked the local sorcerer if she would complete her journey without a plane crash and broken bones. After an elaborate ritual, he reassured her that her journey was going to be successful, but she did not believe him.

Because Young suffered from stomach pains for a while, Dodwell took on a greater part of the flying duties than planned. On stepping onto Nigerian soil, she experienced a great disappointment: "There was none of the fanfare I'd imagined on returning to the country of my birth. Just the hot dusty street with black-market money-changers sitting in the shade." Things got worse when she found out that Young had been arrested. After a twenty-four-hour ordeal, they were allowed to fly anywhere in Nigeria, except near Lake Chad. To satisfy her longing to see the lake again, Dodwell picnicked there on her own.

Dodwell and Young spent Christmas Eve at an Anglican church in Kano. The next day they flew to Daura to refuel before crossing the border to Niger, where they were welcomed by the local commandant and offered "a lovely cottage with a shady verandah which served as a government rest-house."

From Zinder, the former capital of Niger, they flew into Tuareg country. Over a cup of tea in Agadez, a Tuareg man called Sulieman explained to Dodwell why men of his tribe wear a *shesh* to cover their faces in the company of unknown women, a custom that is the opposite of the practice of traditional Muslim societies. They also discussed the upcoming Paris-Dakar air rally, which was due to leave Paris on 1 January and to come through Agadez within one or two weeks. The next day, New Year's Eve, Dodwell and Young set out on camelback to explore the desert in the Aïr Mountains. Later, because of a navigational error, Dodwell and Young found themselves flying north toward Algeria. Running low on fuel, they landed and spent a "peaceful night under the stars." In moments such as these, Dodwell took out her diary to jot down her impressions, observations, and experiences, and this night was no exception: "Small dead twigs on the fire gave enough light to write by."

After an "evil flight" that made Dodwell "never want to fly again," they reached Ingal. While touring the area, Dodwell came across large dinosaur bones, which she covered before leaving in order to protect them from the sun and windblown sand, as well as from the hands of collectors. "Obviously, from the undisturbed state of the dry mud we were the first to discover these bones," she wrote, continuing that she "felt stunned with the thrill of it but also with fears for their survival should the site be discovered." Over supper with their local host, Sidibe, they discussed the possibility of inviting an international group from university paleontology departments to conduct a professional excavation of the site. In Niamey the president of Niger thanked Dodwell for reporting the discovery of the bones. Her contribution to scientific knowledge proved significant when experts later confirmed that the bones belonged to a camarasaur, the first one to be positively identified in Africa. In addition, two new species were discovered among the bone fragments: a prehistoric fish and a kind of small crocodile.

Not all of Dodwell's experiences are left to chance. She plans many as well. Most of the time, however, they are a combination of planning and arbitrariness. For example, she hoped to meet "Woodabe cattle herders, famed for their face-painting and tribal male beauty contests." Instead, she encountered Peul tribesmen. In Kao a Peul man named Sambo told her about their tribal history and mythology. In Niamey, Dodwell was given something she "had always wanted to possess–one of the legendary black stones of Central Africa."

In Mali, Dodwell visited monuments of the Songhai kingdom, dating back to the thirteenth century. In Douentza she was welcomed by an Englishwoman, Fiona Patrick, who was working on a Save the Children project in Mali and taught Dodwell about humanitarian missions in West Africa. When Chief Marouchett Agdbossa of Inhabou told her about the restrictions placed on Tuareg women in their social interactions with men, Dodwell produced pictures of Queen Elizabeth and informed him that Britain's greatest chief and its prime minister were both women. Despite his shock, they con-

Down inside Koni crater it's like the
rest of the world is left behind, you
wouldn't know the place existed if you
passed by its outside, sealed off by
the crater walls. It's a secluded refuge,
with a profusion of edible plants:
king bananas, rare giant oranges still
green on the trees, manioc, mangoes, mostly
all endangered species.
The crater belongs to the village & 30 people
are appointed to tend the land & gather the
fruits. They can harvest a specific amount
per week to add to their small salary as guardians
As community projects go, it's an impressive example
of man in harmony with nature.
53.

Page from the manuscript for Island Hopping in the Indian Ocean, *Dodwell's forthcoming book about her travels in 1998 (Collection of Christina Dodwell)*

tinued to converse about Tuareg customs regarding labor and marriage.

On their way to Timbouctou (Tombouctou), Mali, Dodwell and Young landed in a small village, where a marriage was being celebrated. With reference to the history of Tombouctou, Dodwell quotes Leo Africanus, the Spanish Moor who visited the city in 1494 and recorded his observations in his *History and Description of Africa* (1550). She also pays homage to two more recent European explorers: the Scotsman Gordon Laing–who arrived there in 1826 but "did not live to bring back traveller's tales of the fabled city, as he was murdered by his Arab escort"–and German geographer Heinrich Barth, who visited the city in the 1850s.

On 16 February 1989, exactly three months after they had arrived in Africa, Young and Dodwell flew south back to Douentza. In Bandiagara, Dodwell witnessed a celebration to mark the circumcision of small girls. Later, while flying over a desert of dunes, she remembered Amelia Earhart, who in the 1930s, when she was the age of Dodwell, had flown east three-quarters of the way around the world before she crashed and disappeared somewhere in the Pacific Ocean.

In Ayoun, Mauritania, Dodwell borrowed a motorbike to explore the "amazing sandstone landscape" and was surprised that her guidebook had said "there was nothing worth seeing." To her "nature's creations are more impressive than anything man can build," and those natural monuments were a joy to contemplate from the bird's-eye perspective of an airplane because they might be "invisible to those who travel by road."

Two weeks before the journey was scheduled to end, Dodwell tried her hand at solo flying. On 9 March they left Nouakchott, Mauritania, and flew down the beach. The next leg took them to St. Louis, the old colonial capital of Senegal, from which it was only a one-day flight to Dakar, the modern capital. On the way to St. Louis, they celebrated Young's one-thousandth hour of flight.

After dismantling *Pegasus,* which Dodwell described as a "helicopter with a parasol," they flew back to England. While sitting comfortably in a jet plane, Dodwell thought to herself that after flying seven thousand miles, she "had perhaps earned the title of pilot." *Travels with Pegasus* was favorably reviewed in *TLS: The Times Literary Supplement.*

Dodwell's next trip, described in *Beyond Siberia* (1993), was perhaps the most daring of all. Thanks to glasnost, foreign travelers were finally being permitted to visit Kamchatka, "the thumb-shaped peninsula beyond Siberia which stretches north-east toward the Bering Strait," a location that had been an important site for Soviet efforts in the nuclear-arms race. Supported by a Russian shipping and trading company, Dodwell set out in winter 1992 on a three-month journey to "discover how that traditional side of Kamchatka life fitted into today's world." With no contemporary English book about the region to guide her, she arrived in Palana, the capital of the Koryak territory on the West coast of the peninsula, ready to travel by dogsled or reindeer sled in temperatures of approximately -20° Celsius. An elderly couple, Makar and Hilin, housed Dodwell, teaching her how to fish through the ice and to enjoy blood soup for supper.

With a dozen local people–including a pilot, Yuri; a thirty-two-year-old interpreter, Nadya; and a dance troupe of eight male and female performers–she flew in a helicopter to Manile to attend a show featuring portrayals of real-life events and local myths. By talking to the performers, she found out how their training since the age of seven had been strictly Russian, bent on making them unlearn their native tongue and habits. Although the Communist regime had seen this training as a means of saving ethnic minorities from extinction, Dodwell rightfully calls it "cultural genocide." One cultural aspect that did fade away under Soviet rule was shamanism. With the advent of glasnost, however, the Koryak National Association was founded to protect the rights of the indigenous people. Yuri and Nadya told Dodwell that they were alternately taught to hate and pity Westerners. Despite the recent reforms, both admitted that they liked neither Mikhail Gorbachev nor Boris Yeltsin because of the false promises and higher taxes they attributed to the two leaders.

Dodwell's next stop was Ayanka, where she caused a stir: she was the first foreigner ever to have visited the place, and she felt like a giant in comparison to the average Koryak. She felt more at home, however, when she met a four-year-old toddler who was named Christina. By spending much time with the locals, she gathered valuable sociological information about their marriage ceremonies, methods of contraception, sexual habits, burial procedures, and conceptions of the afterlife. After much anticipation, Dodwell finally saw a reindeer, the "most versatile creature of the far north, the tundra's answer to the camel," and she managed to take a picture before her camera froze up.

Back in Palana, Dodwell stayed with Big Taya, "a delightful huge fat Russian woman," who took her to the *banyo* (steam bath) and gave her a facial. She also skied with Alexandra, an Olympic slalom champion for the Soviet Union in 1965, and brushed up on her Russian. In addition, she attended the twelve-hundred-mile Beringei dogsled race when it passed through Palana. Vladoya, whose company had invited Dodwell to Kamchatka, summed up the experience of living in that region by telling her: "Day follows day . . . and you begin to think you could disappear forever in this boundless space, forgotten in the universe. . . . You have to believe you will go on forever. Otherwise you will be overwhelmed."

Dodwell left Palana on a plane to the largest city of Kamchatka, Petropavlovsk, which Danish explorer Vitus Jonassen Bering named after his two ships, *St. Peter* and *St. Paul,* in 1779. There, while having lunch with Vladoya and an interpreter, she experienced an earthquake that registered as a three on the Richter scale. A second unexpected event occurred when a Russian mafioso broke into her car looking for her camera. In mid April she visited a volcanic region, where she was shown around by Boris, who worked for the Institute of Volcanology. Next she spent ten days in the Kronotsky Preserve in the company of the ranger Vitali, who introduced her to bears. Dodwell tested her discoveries against Stepan Petrovich Krasheninnikov's *Description of the Land of Kamchatka* (1755), wherein the natives spotted a misprint of the local term for *cuckoo.*

Dodwell explored the Mutnofski region with a geologist named Valentin and an interpreter named Luda, with whom she recalled the fates of several people who had been exiled to Siberia at various times, including Joseph Stalin and Vladimir Ilich Lenin. There Dodwell enjoyed the best skiing of her life and drove the *vezdehod* (a truck with caterpillar tracks). Around Easter she set off for the reindeer-breeding region of Achai Vayam, where she spent the next month with a geologist named Leonid. There she encountered the Chukchi and Eveni ethnic groups. On one of her expeditions with her companions, Dodwell uncovered mammoth bones that were up to a quarter of a million years old. Before departing in the spring, she was told that since her arrival three months previously, the prices of certain items had risen by more than one thousand percent.

After Kamchatka, Dodwell set her eyes on the island of Madagascar and wrote about her four-month stay there in *Madagascar Travels* (1995). Her trip began in February 1994 in the highlands, where she traveled by horse-drawn stagecoach and met a wide range of local people, including a healer, a village poet, and families that practiced the cults of their ancestors. While paddling her canoe on the southeast coastal rivers and interacting with kings and wood-carvers, Dodwell obtained valuable information about taboos, fetishes, and astrology.

Dodwell also ventured to the unexplored Tsingy de Bemaraha (Tsingin' I Bemaraha) Nature Reserve, an area of limestone pinnacles classified as World Heritage and usually closed to nonscientists. There she found previously untested avenues of passage by connecting tunnels, caves, canyons, and river passages that were filled with crocodiles feeding on blind white fish. Delving deep into the many natural phenomena and mysteries of Madagascar, she traveled by oxcart and on foot. Pioneers in the forests, studying new species of wildlife, informed her that in spite of a spiral of environmental catastrophes in Madagascar, there still existed significant genetic banks of original plants, but their survival hung in the balance.

In the capital city of Antananarivo, Dodwell socialized with family friends who introduced her to members of noble, diplomatic, and nongovernmental-organization (NGO) circles. She attended a celebration of "turning the ancestors' bones," an important ceremony in which the bones are taken out of their old parcels and wrapped, and she went on a hunt for dinosaur bones and discovered some two-hundred-million-year-old petrified trees.

At what seemed the end of her journey, a BBC crew offered her the opportunity to go anywhere on the island to film a documentary. In response she mounted an expedition to search for one of the largest forests of petrified trees in the world. A radio series based on this expedition aired in February 1995, and a BBC movie was released that August. In October *Madagascar Travels* was published.

Several interviews with Dodwell have been published in *The Times* (15 May 1993), *The Guardian* (26 June 1993), *The Daily Telegraph* (27 November 1993), and *The Independent* (25 May 1994). In November 1993 she founded a charity called The Dodwell Trust, with a mission to educate Third World women about child care and family planning. Her first task was to set up a four-year project in Madagascar. In 1991 she married Stephen, an Englishman. They have a home in West London and a farm in the Chiltern Hills, surrounded by horses, highland cattle, and other animals.

Dodwell asserts that "having spent twenty years making new-ground journeys, the next ten years will hold some returnings." Nevertheless, she admits that "travel is a wonderful emptiness just waiting to be filled," and she "loves not knowing what will happen next." When asked once about how she would like to be remembered, she humbly replied, "as a friend by remote village groups throughout the world."

References:

Mary Morris, ed., *Maiden Voyages: Writings of Women Travelers* (New York: Vintage, Departures, 1993), pp. 374–389;

Jane Robinson, *Wayward Women: A Guide to Women Travellers* (New York: Oxford University Press, 1990), pp. 89–90;

Robinson, ed., *Unsuitable for Ladies: An Anthology of Women Travellers* (Oxford & New York: Oxford University Press, 1994), pp. 14–15, 338–339.

Lawrence Durrell

(27 February 1912 – 7 November 1990)

Steven E. Alford
Nova Southeastern University

See also the Durrell entries in *DLB 15: British Novelists, 1930–1959, DLB 27: Poets of Great Britain and Ireland, 1945–1960,* and *DLB Yearbook: 1990.*

BOOKS: *Quaint Fragment: Poems Written between the Ages of Sixteen and Nineteen* (London: Cecil Press, 1931);

Ten Poems (London: Caduceus Press, 1932);

Bromo Bombastes, as Gaffer Peeslake (London: Caduceus Press, 1933);

Transition: Poems (London: Caduceus Press, 1934);

Pied Piper of Lovers (London: Cassell, 1935);

Panic Spring, as Charles Norden (London: Faber & Faber, 1937; New York: Covici Friede, 1937);

The Black Book: An Agon (Paris: Obelisk, 1938; New York: Dutton, 1960; London: Faber & Faber, 1973);

A Private Country (London: Faber & Faber, 1943);

Prospero's Cell: A Guide to the Landscape and Manners of the Island of Corcyra (London: Faber & Faber, 1945); republished with *Reflections on a Marine Venus* (New York: Dutton, 1960);

Cities, Plains and People: Poems (London: Faber & Faber, 1946);

Zero and Asylum in the Snow: Two Excursions into Reality (Rhodes: Privately printed, 1946); republished as *Two Excursions into Reality* (Berkeley, Cal.: Circle Editions, 1947);

Cefalû (London: Editions Poetry London, 1947); republished as *The Dark Labyrinth* (London: Ace, 1958; New York: Dutton, 1962);

On Seeming to Presume (London: Faber & Faber, 1948);

A Landmark Gone (Los Angeles: Reuben Pearson, 1949);

Deus Loci: A Poem (Ischia: Di Maio Vito, 1950);

Sappho: A Play in Verse (London: Faber & Faber, 1950; New York: Dutton, 1958);

Key to Modern British Poetry (London & New York: Nevill, 1952); republished as *A Key to Modern British Poetry* (Norman: University of Oklahoma Press, 1952);

Reflections on a Marine Venus: A Companion to the Landscape of Rhodes (London: Faber & Faber, 1953); republished with *Prospero's Cell* (New York: Dutton, 1960);

Lawrence Durrell (photograph © Jerry Bauer)

The Tree of Idleness, and Other Poems (London: Faber & Faber, 1955);

Private Drafts (Nicosia, Cyprus: Proodos Press, 1955);

Selected Poems (London: Faber & Faber, 1956; New York: Grove, 1956);

Justine (London: Faber & Faber, 1957; New York: Dutton, 1957);

White Eagles Over Serbia (London: Faber & Faber 1957; New York: Criterion, 1958);

Bitter Lemons (London: Faber & Faber, 1957; New York: Dutton, 1958);

Esprit de Corps: Sketches from Diplomatic Life (London: Faber & Faber, 1957; New York: Dutton, 1958);
Balthazar (London: Faber & Faber, 1958; New York: Dutton, 1958);
Mountolive (London: Faber & Faber, 1958; New York: Dutton, 1959);
Stiff Upper Lip: Life Among the Diplomats (London: Faber & Faber, 1958; New York: Dutton, 1959);
Clea (London: Faber & Faber, 1960; New York: Dutton, 1960);
Collected Poems (London: Faber & Faber, 1960; New York: Dutton, 1960);
Penguin Modern Poets 1, by Durrell, Elizabeth Jennings, and R. S. Thomas (Harmondsworth, U.K.: Penguin, 1962);
The Alexandria Quartet (London: Faber & Faber, 1962; New York: Dutton, 1962)–comprises *Justine, Balthazar, Mountolive,* and *Clea;*
An Irish Faustus: A Morality in Nine Scenes (London: Faber & Faber, 1963; New York: Dutton, 1964);
Selected Poems 1935–1963 (London: Faber & Faber, 1964);
Acte: A Play (London: Faber & Faber, 1965; New York: Dutton, 1965);
Sauve Qui Peut (London: Faber & Faber, 1966; New York: Dutton, 1967);
The Ikons and Other Poems (London: Faber & Faber, 1966; New York: Dutton, 1967);
Tunc: A Novel (London: Faber & Faber, 1968; New York: Dutton, 1968);
Collected Poems. New and Revised Edition (London: Faber & Faber, 1968; New York: Dutton, 1968);
Spirit of Place: Letters and Essays on Travel, edited by Alan G. Thomas (London: Faber & Faber, 1969; New York: Dutton, 1969);
Nunquam: A Novel (London: Faber & Faber, 1970; New York: Dutton, 1970);
The Red Limbo Lingo: A Poetry Notebook for 1968–1970 (London: Faber & Faber, 1971; New York: Dutton, 1971);
Le Grand Suppositoire: Entreiens avec Marc Alyn (Paris: Pierre Belfond, 1972); translated by Francine Barker as *The Big Supposer: A Dialogue with Marc Alyn* (London: Abelard-Shuman, 1973; New York: Grove, 1973);
Vega and Other Poems (London: Faber & Faber, 1973; Woodstock, N.Y.: Overlook Press, 1973);
The Revolt of Aphrodite (London: Faber & Faber, 1974)–comprises *Tunc* and *Nunquam;*
Monsieur, or The Prince of Darkness (London: Faber & Faber, 1974; New York: Viking, 1975);
The Best of Antrobus (London: Faber & Faber, 1974);
Blue Thirst (Santa Barbara, Cal.: Capra Press, 1975);
Sicilian Carousel (London: Faber & Faber, 1977; New York: Viking, 1977);
Selected Poems, edited by Alan Ross (London: Faber & Faber, 1977);
The Greek Islands (London: Faber & Faber, 1978; New York: Viking, 1978);
Livia, or Buried Alive (London: Faber & Faber, 1978; New York: Viking, 1979);
Collected Poems: 1931–1974, edited by James A. Brigham (London: Faber & Faber, 1980; New York: Viking, 1980);
A Smile in the Mind's Eye (London: Wildwood House, 1980; New York: Universe, 1980);
Constance, or, Solitary Practices (London: Faber & Faber, 1982; New York: Viking, 1982);
Sebastian, or, Ruling Passions: A Novel (London & Boston: Faber & Faber, 1983; New York: Viking, 1983);
Quinx, or, The Ripper's Tale: A Novel (London & Boston: Faber & Faber, 1985; New York: Viking Penguin, 1985);
Antrobus Complete (London & Boston: Faber & Faber, 1985);
Caesar's Vast Ghost: Aspects of Provence, text by Durrell and photographs by Henry Peccinotti (London: Faber & Faber, 1990; New York: Arcade, 1990); republished as *Provence* (New York: Arcade, 1994);
The Avignon Quintet (London: Faber & Faber, 1992)–comprises *Monsieur, Livia, Constance, Sebastian,* and *Quinx.*

TRANSLATION: Emmanouel Rhoïdes, *Pope Joan: A Romantic Biography,* translated by Durrell (London: Verschoyle, 1954; revised edition, London: Deutsch, 1960; New York: Dutton, 1961).

Until 1957 Lawrence Durrell was an ordinary disaffected Englishman with a passion for writing, seemingly destined to live his life in a series of remote Mediterranean isles in the shadow of his renowned brother Gerald. In that year, however, he achieved recognition of his own with the publication of four books: his novel *Justine,* his Cyprus narrative *Bitter Lemons,* his diplomatic satire *Esprit de Corps,* and his adolescent adventure story *White Eagles Over Serbia. Bitter Lemons* won the Duff Cooper Award that year, presented to him by the Queen Mother. It was *Justine,* however, and the three subsequent novels in *The Alexandria Quartet*–*Balthazar* (1958), *Mountolive* (1958), and *Clea* (1960)–that defined him forever in the mind of the reading public. This tetralogy established the unreliable narrator as a metaphysical, as well as literary, issue. It dramatized the question of point of view, situating Durrell in a tradition that stretches from Friedrich Nietzsche's perspectivism to the deconstructionist's *differance.* In his introduction

Durrell in Corfu, circa 1938 (Estate of Lawrence Durrell)

to *Critical Essays on Lawrence Durrell* (1987) Allan Warren Friedman has concluded that Durrell ranks "not with the truly great British novelists of the century–Conrad, Joyce, Lawrence, Woolf–but with those of the next order: Cary, Greene, Huxley, Waugh, writers of distinction and enduring interest and worth." Yet, the extensive discussion of Durrell the novelist has obscured his exceptional ability as a travel writer. From the mid 1930s to the late 1980s Durrell recorded the attraction of the Mediterranean basin with a vigor and affection matched by few writers of the twentieth century.

Lawrence George Durrell was born in Jullundur, India, on 27 February 1912, one of four children of Englishman Lawrence Samuel and his Irish wife, Louise Florence Dixie Durrell. His engineer father was responsible for several important building projects in India for the Tata Iron and Steel Works and the Darjeeling-Himalayan Railway. Durrell attended the Jesuit College at Darjeeling until age eleven, leaving India on 18 March 1923, when he was sent to England to continue his education. There he attended St. Olaf's and St. Saviour's Grammar School in Southwark (September 1925–June 1926) and St. Edmund's, Canterbury (September–December 1927). After he left St. Edmund's, he was sent to study with a tutor. Following the death of his father on 16 April 1928, Durrell received an annual income of £150, and by the beginning of 1930 he had abandoned his schooling–an activity he was to hate throughout his lifetime. He eventually ended up in London, where he spent much of his time in Bloomsbury, writing and playing jazz piano at nightclubs. By mid 1932 he had met Nancy Meyers.

After secretly marrying Nancy on 22 January 1935, Durrell took his new wife to live on Corfu, where they had been invited by expatriate friends. His mother and three siblings soon followed them to the island, but they did not share living quarters. His experiences there were the basis for Durrell's first travel book, *Prospero's Cell* (1945).

Durrell believed in environmental determinism–that place shapes character–and he convincingly demonstrated that travel writing and his kind of reportage are not necessarily the same thing. He made the distinction between the two in "Landscape and Character," an essay first published in *The New York Times Magazine* (12 June 1960) and later collected in *Spirit of Place* (1969):

> I have evolved a private notion about the importance of landscape, and I willingly admit to seeing "characters" almost as functions of a landscape. This has only come about in recent years after a good deal of travel–though here again I doubt if this is quite the word, for I am not really a "travel-writer" so much as a "residence-writer." My books are always about living in places, not just rushing through them. But as you get to know Europe slowly, tasting the wines, cheeses and characters of the different countries you begin to realize that the important determinant of any culture is after all–the spirit of place. Just as one particular vineyard will always give you a special wine with discernible characteristics so a Spain, an Italy, a Greece will always give you the same type of culture–will express itself through the human being just as it does through its wild flowers. We tend to see "culture" as a sort of historic pattern dictated by the human will, but for me this is no longer absolutely true.

This environmental determinism leads in some cases to what sounds like condescension toward those of other cultures, and indeed some of his portraits of foreign people emerge as caricatures. To understand his purpose one must consider his attitude toward travel writing in general. For Durrell travel writing is an eclectic genre capacious enough to include within the same work reportage, fiction (epistolary inventions and fictional characters), casual historical narration (for example, classical writers' reports go unchallenged; scholarly disputes are swept aside as hairsplitting), autobiography (one of Durrell's important evaluative criteria for the traveler seems to be how well one sleeps in a particular locale), philosophical speculation, the typologies of national and regional "characters," and the author's dreams and their function in evaluating the travel experience. The resulting hodgepodge is charming and, like his best fiction, evocative of the truth of a landscape and its people, while not necessarily toeing the factual line. What he says of Alexandria in *The Alexandria Quartet* could be true of all his travel books: only the city is real.

Durrell's first and last books are about Greece, which is only appropriate, as the whole of his work is infused with the sun-filled humor and Mediterranean resignation characteristic of that country. His first book, *Prospero's Cell,* takes the form of a series of journal entries dated from late 1937 to early 1941, followed by an epilogue and an "appendix for travellers." Like all his travel books, *Prospero's Cell* is neither guidebook nor history nor sociological tract, but the tale of a foreigner, armed with surprising (to the locals) linguistic competence, who affectionately sets about to do some living in the locale. He rents a house, buys a boat, has the locals work on his dwelling, gets drunk and philosophizes with everyone, reads books on the island while writing his own, swims naked and fishes for octopus, and uses the contrast of the Mediterranean's affirmative response to sex, food, and intoxication as a cheerful tongue waggle to what he sees as the dank and cheerless Britain he feels so lucky to have escaped.

This idyll of friendship and love of landscape is dedicated to four friends–characters developed from people he knew would be a more accurate description of them–Theodore Stephanides, Zarian, The Count D., and Max Nimiec. While they offer him the gift of camaraderie and conversation, Durrell isolates what is special about Greece: "Other countries may offer you discoveries in manners or lore or landscape; Greece offers you something harder–the discovery of yourself." In Greece, life is reduced to its essentials, which are enumerated by Father Nichols. "What more does a man want than an olive-tree, a native island, and woman from his own place?" Durrell had all these, and it remained for him, through exploring the island, to discover himself.

In writing about Corfu, however, Durrell found he could not simply write a history (although he did that), nor simply an autobiographical sketch of his experiences (although he did that as well). Instead, as he states in *Prospero's Cell,* "If I wrote a book about Corcyra [the Greek name for Corfu] it would not be a history but a poem."

This "poem" explores the characters on the island, its history, its festivals, its social practices, and Durrell's own experiences. He wrote, for example, that he had discovered "perhaps the loveliest beach in the world. Its name is Myrtiotissa." The thread linking his descriptions connects all Durrell's travel books, the quest to discover the spirit of the place and one's relation to it. In Corfu the spirit is linked to the olive tree: "Under Venice she prospered–at least in forests; for the Venetians gave ten gold pieces for every grove of a hundred olive-trees planted, until when they left, it is said, the islanders possessed nearly two million trees." Hence, for the islanders, the olive is the center of their culture. For Durrell, it is something more:

> The whole Mediterranean–the sculptures, the palms, the gold beads, the bearded heroes, the wine, the ideas, the ships, the moonlight, the winged gorgons, the bronze men, the philosophers–all of it seems to rise in the sour, pungent taste of these black olives between the teeth. A taste older than meat, older than wine. A taste as old as cold water.

Like all idylls, this one had to end, and it was ended, by war. Although autobiographically inexact–Durrell described himself as escaping Corfu for Crete–his paean to Corfu is one of powerful emotion recollected in tranquillity. Durrell thought of the island "with a regret so luxurious and so deep that it did not stir the emotions at all. Seen through the transforming lens of memory the past seemed so enchanted that even thought would be unworthy of it."

While living in Corfu, the Durrells made frequent visits to Paris, where Durrell met American novelist Henry Miller in 1937 and helped him to edit a short-lived avant-garde magazine. Following a move to Athens in September 1939 to work for the British Embassy Information Services and the British Council, Durrell taught in Kalamata, on the southern coast of the Peloponnese peninsula, until shortly before the Germans invaded Greece in April 1941. Fleeing with their infant daughter, Penelope (born 4 June 1940), the Durrells reached Crete and then Cairo, where Durrell again found work, first as a journalist, then as a foreign press officer for the British. In July 1942 Nancy and Penelope Durrell moved to Palestine owing to the Nazi threat to Egypt, and the marriage soon broke up. The following October, Durrell was transferred to Alexandria, where he remained until June 1945. There Durrell became romantically involved with Yvette (Eve) Cohen, daughter of a Jewish businessman in Tunisia. In June 1945 the two traveled to Rhodes, where Durrell worked as a public information officer. This position involved running three newspapers (in Greek, Italian, Turkish), and it permitted him to travel around the Dodecanese islands, gathering material for his second travel book, *Reflections on a Marine Venus: A Companion to the Landscape of Rhodes* (1953).

Some critics have regarded this book as inferior to *Prospero's Cell.* In his "Place and Durrell's Island Books" Friedman comments that *Reflections on a Marine Venus* is "not so much of Rhodes as simply about it," while "*Prospero's Cell* seems of the very essence of Corfu." *Reflections on a Marine Venus* is still an engaging work, however, with several extensive set pieces on the history of Rhodes. Primarily the book was another occasion for Durrell to develop further an idea he had originated in *Prospero's Cell,* "a rare but by no means unknown affliction of spirit": islomania. In Durrell's words, "There are people . . . who find islands somehow irresistible. The mere knowledge that they are on an island, a little world surrounded by the sea, fills them with an indescribable intoxication. These [are] born 'islomanes.'"

Islomania determines the narrative style. Durrell believed that "Only by a strict submission to the laws of inconsequence can one ever write about an island–as an islomane, that is." Hence, in *Marine Venus* the reader

Photograph in Durrell's album of the house on Corfu where he lived from October 1935 until April 1941 (Estate of Lawrence Durrell)

follows Durrell around Rhodes and other islands in the Dodecanese group, among them Symi (Sími), Kalymnos, Cos (Kos), Leros, and Patmos. On one of his trips among the islands as public information officer, Durrell learned of the large sales of his newspapers among the mostly illiterate islanders. Owing to a paper shortage, they found his newspapers useful for wrapping their fish. In his book Durrell wrote: "It is one of the anomalies of war that the daily newspaper which we issue at a penny is worth two pence as wrapping paper, and already in Rhodes our receipts for scrapped issues are greater than our receipts on current sales. It puts journalism in its right perspective somehow."

As in *Prospero's Cell,* Durrell introduces the reader to his friends: in this case Mills, a doctor; and two aspiring writers, Gideon and Hoyle. When they learn Durrell is writing a book about Rhodes, they have decided opinions as to its direction. Mills hopes the book will be neither "history or myth–but landscape and atmosphere somehow," one that would be "some sort of effective monument to all the charm and grace of our stay there in Rhodes."

Durrell found the symbolic center of the island, the Marine Venus, in the island museum. For him this statue embodied the spirit of Rhodes and evoked the possibility for self-knowledge implicit in all travel. The Marine Venus "sits up there alone in the museum, disregarded, sightless; yet somehow we have learned to share that timeless, exact musical contemplation–the secret of her self-sufficiency–which has helped her to outlive the savage noise of wars and change, to maintain unbroken the fine thread of her thoughts through the centuries past." This isolation and independence provides the visitor with a sense of continuity, "not only with the past–but also with the future–for surely history's evaluations are wrong in speaking of civilized and

Staff at the British Office of Information in Alexandria, circa 1942–1945: Miss Philpott, Durrell, Milto Axelos, and Miss Palli (courtesy of Faber & Faber)

barbaric ages succeeding or preceding one another, surely they have always co-existed–for one is the measure of the other?"

Alongside Durrell's narrative of his contemporary concerns–such as the newspapers, his friends, and the best places for swimming–he included some lengthy set pieces about the history of Rhodes. The most famous artwork associated with the island is, of course, the Colossus, and Durrell wrote a detailed description of the siege of the town by Demetrius Polyorcites, beginning in 305 B.C. The heroic defense of the city resulted in a treaty, the terms of which specified that the revenue from the sale of Demetrius's siege equipment should be used to erect a statue in memory of the battle. The result was the Colossus, which stood for fifty-six years. This tale, along with Durrell's investigation into the relationship of Rhodes and the medieval Knights of St. John, gives the sense that the book is more a "companion" to living in Rhodes than a travel book.

Durrell and Eve Cohen were married in February 1947 and left soon thereafter for England. They remained there until 28 October, when they left for Argentina, where Durrell spent time lecturing for the British Council at Cordoba and elsewhere. Deeply unhappy in Argentina, the Durrells returned to England a year later. In July 1949 they left for Yugoslavia, where he worked for three years as a press attaché. On 30 May 1951 Eve gave birth to Durrell's second child, Sappho Jane. In December 1952, just before the Durrells were to leave Yugoslavia for his next posting in Cyprus, Eve had a mental breakdown and was sent to a British Army hospital in Hanover and then for further treatment in England. She joined Durrell in Cyprus for a time in 1954 and 1955, before deciding to seek a divorce.

Arriving in Cyprus in late January 1953, Durrell completed a draft of *Justine,* and in late 1955 he met Claude-Marie Vincendon, an Alexandrian French woman who later became his third wife. In August 1956 they moved to England, where Durrell completed his account of his experiences in Cyprus, a work that most critics regard as his best travel book: *Bitter Lemons.*

This prize-winning work is also the saddest of Durrell's books, chronicling as it does the violence that attended the postwar waning of British power over the opposing populations of Turkish and Greek Cypriots. In his introduction to the 1996 edition of the book, Ian MacNiven points out that because the Queen Mother

Lawrence and Eve Durrell at the Parthenon, circa 1949 (courtesy of Faber & Faber)

presented the Duff Cooper Award to Durrell, "it carried a strong flavor of official approval" for *Bitter Lemons*. In addition he notes that *Bitter Lemons* was "equally well received in the United States" and that contemporary American reviewers considered the book "accurate, 'authentic,' moving, and politically fair." Such was not the case among Cypriot readers. MacNiven notes that many Cypriots and Greeks found *Bitter Lemons* "a devastatingly clever apologia for British policy," a book that did little to help create a national identity for the Cypriots, one that could withstand the pressures of political self-interest, not only from the Greeks and Turks but from the British as well.

Bitter Lemons continues Durrell's theme of travel as means of inner discovery, in which "journeys, like artists, are born and not made." For Durrell, travels "flower spontaneously out of the demands of our natures–and the best of them lead us not only outwards in space, but inwards as well." Durrell's initial occupation on Cyprus was that of an English teacher to the local Cypriots, beginning at seven each morning with girls' sixth form. During one lesson, Durrell recounted, while he was trying to help his students understand the difference between the English words *love, adore,* and *dote,* his student Chloe said of the king and queen of Greece that "when they married they were in a great dote. He was so excitement and she was so excitement. They were both excitement." *Bitter Lemons* also chronicles Durrell's efforts to buy a house in the village of Bellapaix, above Nicosia. Employing the Turkish character Sabri Tahir, Durrell leads the reader through the psychological and familial intricacies of the negotiations, a comedy with the happy ending of his purchase.

Here as elsewhere in Durrell's writings the sensitive reader may recoil from his caricatures of the locals, which seem to emerge from an imperialist's conde-

Greek poet and diplomat Giorgos Seferiades (George Seferis) and Durrell in Cyprus, 1953 (courtesy of Faber & Faber)

scending vision. Yet, in outlining the "blameless monotony" of the British colony, Durrell's perspective from his residence in a small village permitted him to argue that the "British saw a one-dimensional figure in the Cypriot." For him the locals were recognizable as "the very sort of characters who rejoice the English heart in a small country town–the rogue, the drunkard, the singer, the incorrigible." Any one of them derived his integrity from "belonging truly to his landscape." Here one can see that Durrell's view of the inhabitants of a foreign country is lodged not so much in the national disdain sometimes evident in British attitudes toward the people of its colonial possessions in Africa and India, but as a view of nations possessing eternal Theophrastian types, ones formed by the spirit of place.

The book turns somber when it begins to cover events after August 1954, when Durrell became director of public information for the British Embassy. His new job required him to move to Nicosia, and over time many of his Greek friends became alienated from him because he had become a representative of a foreign government that was no longer supported by the Cypriots. Visiting prisons, he encountered former students who had been caught in acts of terrorist violence. The heart-rending set piece that concludes the book dramatizes Durrell's final walk with his Cypriot friend Panos, a schoolteacher who was subsequently shot dead apparently for fraternizing with a representative of the Crown, Lawrence Durrell.

In February 1957 Durrell and Claude Vincendon went to live in Sommières, Provence, the setting for his fourth travel book, *Caesar's Vast Ghost: Aspects of Provence* (1990), and the place where Durrell lived for most of the remainder of his life. He and Claude were married on 27 March 1961 and remained together until her death from cancer on 1 January 1967. In November 1973 Durrell married Ghislaine de Boissons. They were divorced five years later.

From his base in Provence, Durrell produced the bulk of his literary output over the next three decades. He wrote the rest of the *Alexandria Quartet: Balthazar, Mountolive,* and *Clea,* as well as his less-celebrated linked novels, *The Revolt of Aphrodite: Tunc* (1968) and *Nunquam* (1970), and *The Avignon Quintet: Monsieur* (1974), *Livia* (1978), *Constance* (1982), *Sebastian* (1983), and *Quinx* (1985).

In 1969 Durrell's friend Alan G. Thomas, a London bookseller, edited *Spirit of Place,* a collection of Dur-

Gouache by Durrell of Kyrenia, Cyprus (Estate of Lawrence Durrell)

rell's letters and travel writings, along with excerpts from his early novels. The first section, "Letters by Lawrence Durrell," brings together a series of letters written to Thomas and others, with biographical observations by Thomas. The reader follows Durrell from his first breathlessly happy reports from Corfu, through his escape to Egypt and his foreign service in Rhodes, to Argentina (with a climate like "a piece of wet meat laid across the nervous system"), Yugoslavia and Cyprus, and finally France. The second section, "Essays, Travel Pieces, Selections from Early Novels," includes the important essay "Landscape and Character"; the amusing "Reflections on Travel" (first published in *The Sunday Times* [London], 27 December 1959); the memorable "Three Roses of Grenoble" (*Holiday,* January 1959), in which Durrell locates an apartment once occupied by Stendhal; and the diverting "The Gascon Touch" (*Holiday,* January 1963). In "The Gascon Touch" Durrell accompanies a "Knight of the Road," a traveling salesman who is peddling Savegoose (a medicine for overstuffed geese), through the restaurants and small hotels of Gascony.

In a 1949 letter written from Yugoslavia, the reader discovers Durrell's incipient conservatism. While they seldom manifested themselves in his writing, his political leanings may well be the source of the unease expressed by the Cypriot critics of *Bitter Lemons.* According to the letter, political events have made Durrell "firmly reactionary and Tory." Labour, in his view, has produced "this machine state, with its censored press, its long marching columns of political prisoners guarded by tommy guns," which results in nothing other than "Philistinism, puritanism and cruelty." For Durrell "the whole edifice has begun to crumble, and one has the pleasurable job of aiding and abetting this blockheaded people to demolish their own ideological Palace of Pleasures."

A 1957 letter reveals the development of the attitude toward the French that is expressed in the publication of *Caesar's Vast Ghost: Aspects of Provence.* Durrell found strange "the disparity between their character and the character of France itself." In France there was still "genuine unfeatherbedded peasantry" and "the values of ordinary life flow from them–in food and similar things."

In "Women of the Mediterranean" (*Réalités,* June 1961) he noted the seemingly unbridgeable cultural gap between the England he left behind and the Mediterranean region he embraced. As a teacher in the Mediterranean, he could never make his students understand fully "the literary notions which have grown up about two northern concepts: namely 'Spleen' and 'Ennui.' As for 'Angst' I did not even dare to try."

The concluding essay, "Reflections on Travel," proposes a series of books to be written and assembled by a group of travelers to a specific place, giving advice on details such as seasons and prices. Nostalgic for travel and critical of the tourist, he allows that the tourist should be "cushioned against misadventure" but that the genuine traveler "will not feel that he has had his money's worth unless he brings back a few scars like that hole in his trousers which comes from striking Italian matches towards instead of away from oneself." For Durrell, "the mishaps and disappointments only lend relief to the splendours of the voyage." *Spirit of Place* is a valuable compilation of stray pieces of Durrell's travel writing that would not have otherwise been preserved. It does not establish, however, any significant new directions in Durrell's attitudes toward travel.

Durrell's next travel book, *Sicilian Carousel* (1977), did not appear until twenty years after the publication of *Bitter Lemons.* With the exception of Paul Fussell, most critics consider *Sicilian Carousel* Durrell's weakest travel book. Unlike his previous books of "foreign residence," *Sicilian Carousel* follows Durrell through a planned, tourist's bus holiday among a motley, multinational group recognizable to anyone who has ever signed up for a "vacation package."

While waiting in Rome for passage to Catania, Durrell began to encounter some of his fellow travelers: "Immediately next to me was an aggrieved French couple with a small child who looked around with a rat-like malevolence. He had the same face as his father. They looked like very cheap microscopes." This family was only one set of colorful companions. Among others were "the Anglican Bishop who had developed

Doubts," "the French couple of a vaguely diplomatic persuasion," and his boon companion:

> Colonel Deeds, D.S.O., late Indian Army, later still, Desert Rat. Nowadays I suppose they have broken the mould of that most recognisable of species, the Eighth Army veteran. The clipped moustache, the short back and sides haircut.

There as the tour guide is the charming and educated Roberto, who develops a crush on the young female German passenger, a beauty who is romantically interested in another passenger, much to Roberto's pain and sorrow. Finally, what tour would be complete without someone like the officious and arrogant Beddoes, whose mean-spirited complaints and noisome pipe make the trip miserable for everyone?

Durrell contrasted lighthearted and invented stories about his fellow bus passengers with truths about their pasts and characters that emerged during the inconveniences and rigors of the tour. While critics justly chide such a distinguished intellect and writer for squandering his descriptive resources on writing about a package tour, readers less familiar with Durrell's other work may well find his tone and stories engaging.

The tour began in Catania, moving south through Syracuse, up into the broad back of mountains of the island, to Agrigento, over to Palermo, and concluding at Taormina. Durrell had been drawn to Sicily by the letters of "Martine," who once lived there. The text provides a counterpoint between her epistolary account of the island and Durrell's ongoing experience. For him the true lure of Sicily was its connection with Greece. Like the southern islands of Greece, "it was, like them, an island of the mid-channel–the front line of defence against the huge seas coming up from Africa." He recognized Sicily as a part of Magna Graecia.

Along the way Durrell indulged in speculation about two of his favorite topics. First, he examined islomania and his regrets at the outcome of his previous travel books. Unwittingly, in his search to isolate "the virus of islomania," he had discovered that "*Club Mediterranee* had even adopted the phrase as a *cri de guerre*–blessed by the French glossies. I had the impression that it had all but made the *Medical Encyclopedia.*" Second, he continued to explore his conviction that place–not nation, culture, or race–determines the character of a people. He noted that when thinking about the character of a group that "it was hard to shed the tough little carapace of the national ego and to begin to see them as the bare products of the soil, just like the wild flowers or the wines, just like the crops."

Durrell's next travel book was the profusely illustrated *The Greek Islands* (1978). This work has the look and feel of a coffee-table book; yet, the text is inimitably Durrellian. As Edward A. Hungerford has noted, the book covers fifty-six Greek islands with incidental references to "a few tiny rocks and atolls." With *The Greek Islands* Durrell moved far afield from the "poem" of *Prospero's Cell.* As he wrote,

Watercolor by Durrell of Sommières, France, where he settled in 1957 (Estate of Lawrence Durrell)

> The idea was not to compete [with tourist guidebooks], but simply to endeavour to answer two questions. What would you have been glad to know when you were on the spot? What would you feel sorry to have missed while you were there? A guide, yes, but a very personal one.

Indeed, *The Greek Islands* is a guidebook, but one oriented toward the personal preferences of the author, which incline toward parsimony and solitude. On the island of Ios one can find "the calm poetry of its quiet green glens and vineyards, its tiny spotless town, its safe and beautiful small harbour," a place where "one sleeps the full sleep of early childhood." Along with solitude, Durrell did not want the traveler to miss the local libations: "*Rezina* may well taste 'like pure turpentine which has been strained through the socks of a bishop,' as someone wrote to me; but it is to be recommended

Durrell and Henry Miller with a bust of Bigot de Préameneu, Sommière, 1967 (photograph by Baylis Glascock)

most warmly." In addition to the sights, sounds, and drinks, Durrell also reflected on what kind of mental attitude is appropriate to bring to a country so linked with the development of all Western civilization. For him

> A fondness for mythology and folklore is perhaps a handicap when one visits classical sites. It is unwise to spend too much time contrasting the present with the past, since it leads inevitably to dissatisfaction with the present for not being romantic enough.

While breaking little new ground–other than to reveal the author's predilections–*The Greek Islands* remains a valuable guidebook. It is a fitting summation of an islomane's forty years of experience of Greece.

Durrell's last companion in Sommières and environs was Françoise Kestsman, to whom he dedicated *Caesar's Vast Ghost: Aspects of Provence,* his final travel book, which reached bookstores just before his death in 1990. After his lengthy sojourn among the Greeks, Durrell had chosen to live in Provence because it reminded him of the Mediterranean basin, and it held him in its thrall for the final thirty years of his life. *Caesar's Vast Ghost: Aspects of Provence* neatly dovetails with Durrell's first travel book, *Prospero's Cell,* in establishing the writer's obligation toward the region as poetic instead of journalistic, through a "system of poetical collage." In writing of Provence, he sought to "capture the poetic quiddity of this extraordinary cradle of romantic dissent without sentimentalizing it."

In Provence, Durrell found a "brutality and extremism" at odds with the "luxuriance and efflorescence of Mediterranean culture." He also discovered that seeming oppositions of license and frugality "were sisters under the skin–like poetry and mathematics." Unlike Greece, however, whose language and soil provide the substance of the Greek people, Provence is more protean in its influences, not "a separated, self-realized soul as, say, Switzerland is."

Owing ultimately to Caesar's presence, Provence is "a beautiful metaphor born of Caesar's impatience with a geographical corridor stacked with the ruins of a hundred cultures, a hundred nations and tribes, a hundred armies." Caesar brought with him the roads that, "when they came did much to render the place coherent, and to clarify the prevailing doctrine and predisposition of the country's inner being, its true soul which could be summed up by the word dissent." Like other regions only nominally under the control of a nation-state, Provence draws its character not from national affiliation so much as from language and poetry. Durrell considered Provence a companion to Wales–neither is part of the geographical area in which it finds itself. Instead, "the demographic myth is a convenience accepted with a cheerful unwillingness: the post office decrees it!" Like the Welsh, the people of Provence have their own language and "a poet or two like Mistral to sanctify it."

As in his other travel books–particularly *Prospero's Cell* and *Bitter Lemons*–in *Caesar's Vast Ghost* the reader follows Durrell as he purchases a house, tries to fix it up, immerses himself in books and stories about the region, and makes new friends (whose peculiarities represent "types" exemplifying the Provençal Spirit of Place). The book includes some stories of the region that are bound to inspire wonder, such as a meeting between Buffalo Bill and the Provençal poet Mistral. Arcade Publishing republished the book in 1994 under the title *Provence,* probably an attempt to ally Durrell's work with Peter Mayle's enormously popular series of books on the region.

Lawrence Durrell died on 7 November 1990 at age seventy-eight. From the outset Durrell defined his life in terms of negation. A British subject not born in Britain, Durrell was the perpetual outsider who sought in his travel writing to establish how soil and language define a person–he who shared neither soil nor language with virtually any place he lived throughout his life. He rejected the popular literary values of his time to embrace a literary universe established by an American living in Paris, Henry Miller. He was a traveler who, when traveling, rejected the concept of his foreignness within the country and instead sought to disappear into the identity of his residence by living like the locals. Yet, while speaking Greek or French, he chose to write in English. Durrell seems to have found his identity wherever he was not, a psychological stance that allies him with many postmodern writers; yet, his writing remains firmly in the modern mold.

Harry R. Stoneback has argued that the "fundamental Durrellian stance, in much of the poetry and fiction, in all the island books and in the essays, is that of pilgrim, sailor, shepherd and finally, settler, who attends carefully to what the land is saying." Stoneback claims that Durrell's travel writing should be understood in terms of tension: "It is precisely here, in this tension between pastoral and tragedy, in the tension between the romantic mistranslation of the phrase–'I too have been in Arcadia'–and the older, darker, correct rendering–'Even in Arcadia, there am I' (that is, Death)–that I would locate the center of Durrell's vision." Edward A. Hungerford claims that "for his travel writing alone, Durrell belongs among the significant names of the last hundred years." Without question Durrell remains a significant travel writer. In his attempts to capture the spirit of Greece he stands with writers such as Robert Byron, Patrick Leigh Fermor, Robert Liddell, Henry Miller, and Colin Thubron. Durrell's strong insistence on environmental determinism and his idiosyncratic method of "residence writing" make his writing distinctive, yet problematic. The debate over whether his portrayal of foreign people is jingoistic or a proper understanding of the effects of the spirit of place will continue, but Durrell's travel writing will still inspire writers and travelers intoxicated by the siren song of the Mediterranean.

Letters:

Art and Outrage: A Correspondence about Henry Miller between Alfred Perles and Lawrence Durrell (London: Putnam, 1959; New York: Dutton, 1960);

Lawrence Durrell and Henry Miller. *The Durrell-Miller Letters, 1935–1980,* edited by Ian MacNiven (London: Faber & Faber, 1988; New York: New Directions, 1988).

Bibliographies:

Alan G. Thomas and James A. Brigham, *Lawrence Durrell: An Illustrated Checklist* (Carbondale & Edwardsville: Southern Illinois University Press, 1983);

Daniel Ray Todd, "An Annotated, Enumerative Bibliography of the Criticism of Lawrence Durrell's Alexandria Quartet and His Travel Works," dissertation, Tulane University, 1985.

Biographies:

Gordon Bowker, *Through the Dark Labyrinth: A Biography of Lawrence Durrell* (New York: St. Martin's Press, 1997);

Ian S. MacNiven, *Lawrence Durrell: A Biography* (London: Faber & Faber, 1998).

References:

Mark Cocker, *Loneliness and Time: British Travel Writing in the Twentieth Century* (London: Secker & Warburg, 1992);

Gregory Dickson, "Lawrence Durrell and the Tradition of Travel Literature" in *On Miracle Ground II: Second International Lawrence Durrell Conference Proceedings,* edited by Lawrence W. Markert and Carol Peirce, *Deus Loci: The Lawrence Durrell Quarterly Special Issue,* 7, no. 5 / University of Baltimore Monograph Series (1984): 43–50;

Gerald Durrell, "My Brother Larry," *Twentieth Century Literature: A Scholarly and Critical Journal,* 33 (Fall 1987): 262–265;

Durrell, *My Family and Other Animals* (Harmondsworth, U.K.: Penguin, 1959);

Patrick Leigh Fermor, "Observations on a Marine Vulcan," *Twentieth Century Literature: A Scholarly and Critical Journal,* 33 (Fall 1987): 305–307;

Alan Warren Friedman, "Place and Durrell's Island Books," in *Critical Essays on Lawrence Durrell,* edited by Friedman (Boston: G. K. Hall, 1987), pp. 59–70;

Paul Fussell, "Durrell Incognito," *Saturday Review,* 4 (September 1977): 24–26;

Edward A. Hungerford, "Durrell's Mediterranean Paradise," in *Studies in the Literary Imagination,* 24 (Spring 1991): 57–69;

Ian S. MacNiven, "Lawrence Durrell Discovers Greece," *Studies in the Literary Imagination,* 24 (Spring 1991): 83–99;

Peter T. Newby, "Literature and the Fashioning of Tourist Taste," in *Humanistic Geography and Literature: Essays on the Experience of Place,* edited by Douglas C. D. Pocock (Totowa, N.J.: Barnes & Noble, 1981), pp. 130–141;

Roger J. Porter, "Durrell and the Dilemmas of Travel Writing," *Deus Loci: The Lawrence Durrell Journal,* 3 (1994): 51–59;

Julius Rowan Raper, Melody L. Enscore, and Paige Matthey Bynum, eds., *Lawrence Durrell: Comprehending the Whole* (Columbia: University of Missouri Press, 1995);

Harry R. Stoneback, "*Et in Alexandria Ego:* Lawrence Durrell and the Spirit of Place," *Mid-Hudson Language Studies,* 5 (1982): 115–128;

John A. Weigel, *Lawrence Durrell,* revised edition (Boston: Twayne, 1989).

Papers:

There are collections of Lawrence Durrell's papers at the University of California, Los Angeles; the University of Illinois, Urbana; and the Harry Ransom Humanities Research Center, University of Texas, Austin.

Florence Farmborough

(15 April 1887 – 18 August 1978)

Cecile M. Jagodzinski
Illinois State University

BOOKS: *Life and People in National Spain* (London: Sheed & Ward, 1938);

Nurse at the Russian Front: A Diary, 1914–18 (London: Constable, 1974); republished as *With the Armies of the Tsar: A Nurse at the Russian Front, 1914–18* (New York: Stein & Day, 1975); abridged as *Russian Album 1908–1918,* edited by John Jolliffe (Salisbury: Michael Russell, 1979).

SELECTED PERIODICAL PUBLICATIONS–UNCOLLECTED: "Moscow As It Is. Picture of Soviet Misrule. An Englishwoman's Experience," anonymous, *Times* (London), 13 July 1918, p. 5;

"Through Siberia. An Englishwoman's Adventures. Bolshevist Ways," anonymous, *Times* (London), 29 July 1918, p. 5;

"Three Weeks in a Coal-Siding. The Last of Russia," anonymous, *Times* (London), 11 September 1918, p. 7.

As the discipline of history has turned from the study of great men to the examination of the everyday lives of ordinary people, the writings of such authors as Florence Farmborough have taken on increasing importance. In general, travelers' accounts convey two kinds of information: what the individuals saw and how they reacted to their experiences. Travelers enhance their credibility not only by being informed about what they view but also by thoughtfully comparing foreign cultures to their own. When these criteria are met, the traveler's account transcends the genre of travelogue to become a unique primary resource. Farmborough's *Nurse at the Russian Front: A Diary, 1914–18* (1974) is just such a resource. Her memoirs, based on a diary kept while she served as a nurse with the Russian army during World War I, report on war from the viewpoint of an idealistic, sometimes naive, and politically conservative young Englishwoman of the first decades of the twentieth century. Unlike the published narratives of generals and common soldiers, which typically deal with military tactics, the horrors of war, and the camaraderie of men at arms, Farmborough's report of her three-and-a-half-year experience focuses not on the war, but upon the Russian soldiers and civilians whose lives are disrupted by war.

Florence Farmborough in her Red Cross nurse's uniform at the Russian Front during World War I

Farmborough was born 15 April 1887 in Steeple Claydon, Buckinghamshire, and her parents, in a bit of prescience, named her after Florence Nightingale. At the age of twenty-one, Farmborough went to Kiev to teach English, fulfilling what was apparently a lifelong desire to travel, as she writes in the preface to *Nurse at the Russian Front*:

> I always knew that I should have to travel. The longing was strong within me from my earliest years. As the fourth of a family of six children, there were few obstacles in my way when, still in my teens, I expressed the wish to go abroad. My feet were restless with the urge to wander and my eyes strained after the veiled ways ahead, eager to behold all that the wide, wonderful world held in store for me . . .

After two years in Kiev, she went to Moscow where she served as companion and teacher to the two daughters of a Russian heart specialist, Pavel Sergeyevich Usov. When World War I broke out in August 1914, Farmborough and her two students, imbued with a youthful enthusiasm to do good, volunteered to become hospital aides.

Following six months of training, Farmborough was accepted into the Red Cross as a qualified surgical nurse. Traveling with the Tenth Field Surgical *Otryad* [Unit], this young woman (who until then had never seen a sick adult in bed) was at first full of confidence. The neophyte nurse's description in *Nurse at the Russian Front* of their temporary hospital illuminates her state of mind in April 1915:

> We have already chosen our hospital; it is a well built house, with several nice, airy rooms. Everything is being scrubbed, painted and white-washed; the operating room will be a splendid sight when finished; our *apteka* [pharmacy] is already full of medicinal and surgical material and there are rows of labelled bottles on the shelves.

Her pride in this small hospital space is mirrored by the natural spaces about her; the Carpathian Mountains in the background underscore the writer's serenity and confidence that she and her comrades will help, but Farmborough quickly realizes that goodwill and primitive battlefield medical care are insufficient to save hundreds of wounded. Not ten days after settling into their new hospital, Farmborough is shaken into reality by the army's retreat as the medical staff is forced to abandon not only their hospital and equipment but even the wounded:

> They shouted to us when they saw us leaving; called out to us in piteous language to stop–to take them with us; not to forsake them, for the love of God; not to leave them–our brothers–to the enemy. Those who could walk, got up and followed us; running, hopping, limping, by our sides. The badly crippled crawled after us; all begging, beseeching us not to abandon them in their need. And, on the road, there were others, many others; some of them lying down in the dust, exhausted. They too called after us. They held on to us; praying us to stop with them. We had to wrench our skirts from their clinging hands. Then their prayers were intermingled with curses; and, far behind them, we could hear the curses repeated by those of our brothers whom we had left to their fate.

Such experiences comprise much of Farmborough's journey through Russia. Retreat, poor planning by the military, and medical triage (which meant treating only those who had a chance of survival) became facts of life in wartime; and the voices of the wounded, cursing those from whom they had expected care and relief, ring through Farmborough's memories.

The diary, written in lined notebooks and on scraps of paper–sometimes jottings of only a word or two–reflects upon both the large and small events of war. Like the photographs that she took and developed, the diary is filled with both panoramic views of masses of soldiers and peasants, and intimate portraits of the soldiers and common people with whom Farmborough came into contact.

Nurse at the Russian Front is the story of battle and of people in what seems a distant past. It is also a revelation of Farmborough's views on religion, culture, and politics. Without a great deal of anxious self-examination or self-pity (save under the most extreme circumstances), Farmborough lays bare her soul and character. Religion is a key barometer of change throughout the narrative, both for the Russians and for Farmborough. Despite her Englishness, she is highly sympathetic to the Orthodox faith. Farmborough's promotion to nurse is accompanied by an Orthodox religious ceremony; on the departure of the Red Cross Unit for the Galician front, there is an elaborate send-off accompanied by priests, icons, benediction, and the kissing of crucifixes. Her descriptions of these religious ceremonies evoke memories of a holier, more orderly past; this spiritual conservatism re-emerges in political form in her writings on the Spanish Civil War during the 1930s when she decries the disastrous effects of the 1917 revolution.

Even when Farmborough participates in Orthodox religious ceremonies in deference to her Russian friends, her sentiments are inextricably linked to her consciousness of her English heritage. Her Russian experiences and her native culture may happily coincide, as they do, for instance, when she creates her own name day. Unable to locate a Russian "Saint Florence" in the Russian calendar, she chooses 24 May, her mother's and Queen Victoria's birthday, and not coincidentally, Empire Day. But a clash of cultures is inevitable, and for Farmborough it occurs within the space of her mind and conscience. In 1917, after nearly three years at the front, a bout with typhoid, the death of her father, and continuing Russian losses, Farmborough's "English" self-control slips:

> Some of our Sisters and Brothers were not noted for their self-control and when they began to throw nasty, biting words at each other, I would tell myself: "It is lack of education," or "It is the Russian temperament." And now, I am doing the same thing! And I am English! We English have a reputation here for having our feelings well under control. I really am ashamed of myself and must take myself in hand.

Such displays of chauvinism are uncharacteristic of Farmborough, though she is certainly a political and social conservative. Before she goes off to the front, she mentions an incident where an old man, attempting to present a petition to the czar, is whisked away by police agents. Without comment, she also records the story of a general who strikes a wounded soldier whose only fault is not having been issued new (and scarce) boots. The soldiers serving in the Imperial Army are "heroic," while the same men serving under the Bolsheviks are undisciplined radicals.

Farmborough is impressed by the socialist Alexander Kerensky's talk of freedom when she hears him at the front but regards the more left-wing followers of the Bolsheviks Vladimir Lenin and Leon Trotsky as "mutinous sailors and soldiers." After a Russian victory she is saddened by, and fails to comprehend, the fact that drunkenness could provide release from the war to the Russian troops: "It was not the best way to celebrate victory, but perhaps those poor, illiterate recruits knew no better." This moral and political conservatism is balanced, however, by a real concern and empathy for the individuals she deals with as a nurse. She strives to understand the psychological conditions of the many soldiers who come into their makeshift hospitals with self-inflicted wounds, and she recognizes that a young prostitute whom the medical staff treats is as much a victim of war as is any soldier.

A wartime awareness of "the enemy" and the clinical medical standards of the day often presented Farmborough with ethical dilemmas that she could not satisfactorily resolve. Human emotion and her role as nurse conflicted with her duty to obey her superiors. In one incident, she is told not to offer comfort to a wounded Austrian soldier by speaking to him in German. At another time, she is severely reprimanded by the head doctor, who reminds her of their duty to preserve life; she had suggested that the routine injection of camphor or caffeine (to restore the heartbeat) be dispensed with because it only revived the patient to experience more pain. After Farmborough gives a cup of forbidden water to a dying man and he dies more quickly as a result, she is accused of murder by the head pharmacist. The psychological and spiritual struggles are as wearying as are the ethical ones. She is nearly overcome by the sight of amputated limbs piled up in a storage shed awaiting burial; she reflects that without religious faith all the frightful sights of death and dying "would work havoc with one's brain; and one's heart would faint with the depth of its despair."

Farmborough in the pharmacy of her Red Cross unit on the Russian Front

By December 1917, Farmborough's medical unit had been disbanded, and the unstable conditions of the new Russia compelled her to return to England. She describes her seven-day train ride from Romania to Moscow, complete with the dangers from spies in the new regime, the ubiquity of the military police, the confiscation of private property, and the mutual distrust between bourgeois Russians and former peasants. Farmborough's trip across Russia and through Siberia to the port of Vladivostok, marks both the end of her diary and her parting from a Russia that is gradually disappearing. The twenty-seven-day journey by rail closing the book is a physical, historical, and psychological passage. As she views the frozen tundra, she finds in the landscape a cure for her soul:

> As we gradually make our way across this mighty land of Siberia so, gradually, do my overwrought feelings find solace. The unusual train, the proximity of compatriots, the familiar mother tongue, the discomforts we are sharing; all these help. And strange though it may sound–Siberia is for me the greatest tonic of all. I begin to love this immense spacious land, with its wealth of weird and rare lineaments. I know that its very name conjures up torment for thousands of Russians, but, I tell myself, that misery comes from the harassed people, not from the land; these wide, changeless spaces can bring only comfort and peace.

Farmborough closes the book mourning the "surpassingly beautiful land which had been laid waste, for

Farmborough photographing Russian soldiers in the snow

a mighty Empire which had been brought low–by its own sons." This unhesitating condemnation of the new Bolshevik government was even more pronounced in a series of articles published, without byline, in *The Times* (London) shortly after Farmborough returned to England.

Farmborough did not prepare her diary for publication until the 1970s. An exhibition of her Russian photographs and memorabilia in April 1971 at Heswall, Cheshire, was the impetus for the publication of her diary; a second exhibit in August 1974 coincided with the publication of her book on 26 August of that year. Farmborough recalled in a 1974 interview:

> I had a little exhibition of Russian souvenirs and photographs. Constable, my publishers, asked if they might send someone from London to take down my memoirs on tape. They didn't know about the diaries. I said I would like to write the book myself, and I did. It took me thirteen months working everyday from morning till night.

Much of the actual writing of the book was thus done nearly sixty years after the events it covers, and in the editing process nearly half of the four hundred thousand words Farmborough wrote were deleted. Nevertheless, the power of Farmborough's words remains in this seamless blending of memoir and daily journal.

Nurse at the Russian Front was well received by reviewers. The reviewer for *TLS: The Times Literary Supplement* (4 October 1975) called it "compelling reading" and "a most enthralling, moving, and valuable piece of historical testimony." *The Times,* on 1 December 1974, went so far as to name it one of the outstanding books of 1974.

After her return to England from Russia, Farmborough became a fellow of the Royal Geographical Society. She moved to Spain, probably in the early 1930s, where she taught English for nine years at the University of Luis Vives in Valencia. During the Spanish Civil War, Farmborough supported the Nationalist cause, seeing it as a defense of religion and order against bolshevism, and became the English language newsreader in Salamanca for broadcasts on the progress of the war, making the official English language announcement that the war had ended on 1 April 1939. She revised some of her broadcasts into a book, *Life and People in National Spain* (1938).

In the dedication to *Life and People in National Spain,* Farmborough praises the Nationalist leader, Generalissimo Franco, as a "great Spanish soldier and patriot, whose faith, nobility and courage have made him and his brave armies invincible in the Crusade against the Common Foe of Civilisation." The introduction to the book makes clear that her position derives from her memories of the Russian Revolution and from contemporary accounts of the godlessness of communism. More interestingly, however, Farmborough opens her book with a declaration of her identity:

> I am an Englishwoman. I introduce myself to you in this way so that you will readily understand that a person born and bred in the quietness and beauty of the English countryside, and whose father and forefathers have been true to their country and county's soil for many centuries, must remain, despite much travel and despite life's vicissitudes, wholly English.
>
> Therefore it is not a foreigner writing, although I write from a foreign land; it is an Englishwoman who, knowing her country well, is devoted to it and has its welfare ever at heart.

This traveler must convince her English readers that travel had not erased her English character, that the understanding and tolerance produced by contact with foreign peoples and lands had not changed her essential nature or made her incapable of discriminating between civilization and barbarism.

The propagandistic intent of the book is apparent; it is a series of attacks on the tactics of the Left and emotional and overblown praise for the leaders on the Right. Farmborough, for example, recounts the romaticized account of the death of a Nationalist leader's son at the siege of Alcázar–a story largely concocted by Nationalist propagandists–and repeatedly castigates the British press for its attacks on Franco and the British people for their materialist capitalism.

Farmborough returned to England after the outbreak of World War II, working first for the Women's Voluntary Service in London and then for the postal service as a linguist in Jamaica, censoring foreign correspondence to South America. (She was fluent in Russian and German, and knew smatterings of Italian, Polish, and Latin.) Farmborough continued her travels even into old age, visiting the Soviet Union in 1962 and Israel in 1966. After the success of *Nurse at the Russian Front,* a selection of photographs from the book was published in 1979 as *Russian Album 1908–1918.* The album, with its enlarged photos and sharply abridged text, serves as a fine visual counterpart to the complete text.

Florence Farmborough died in Heswall on 18 August 1974 at the age of ninety-one. In a 1974 interview the author spoke of her 1966 visit to the Holy Land and the role travel had played in her own life, saying, "I went in humble thanksgiving for travelling for 60 years and meeting wonderful people and seeing wonderful things. I still think that travelling is one of the greatest joys and means of education that life can offer."

The self-effacing nature of Farmborough's comment is contradicted by the insights of her diary, for *Nurse at the Russian Front* does more than treat the reader to "wonderful people" and "wonderful things." More effectively than do news accounts or official histories, Florence Farmborough's writings demonstrate how wars and revolutions affect the personal histories of individuals and how the great events of history can transform or destroy the lives of ordinary people.

Interview:

Shona Crawford Poole, "Florence Farmborough: Diary of a Woman at War," *Times* (London), 19 August 1974, p. 6.

References:

Christopher Walker, "A Remarkable View of Front-line Service in Imperial Russia: First Exhibition of Souvenirs and Photographs Collected by Nurse," *Times* (London), 15 April 1971, p. 4;

Stanley Weintraub, *The Last Great Cause: The Intellectuals and the Spanish Civil War* (New York: Weybright & Talley, 1968), pp. 170–171.

Patrick Leigh Fermor

(11 February 1915 –)

Anita G. Gorman
Slippery Rock University of Pennsylvania

and

Hariclea Zengos
American College of Greece

BOOKS: *The Traveller's Tree: A Journey Through the Caribbean Islands* (London: Murray, 1950; New York: Harper, 1950);

A Time to Keep Silence (London: Queen Anne Press, 1953);

The Violins of Saint-Jacques: A Tale of the Antilles (London: Murray, 1953; New York: Harper, 1954);

Mani: Travels in the Southern Peloponnese (London: Murray, 1958; New York: Harper, 1958);

Roumeli: Travels in Northern Greece (London: Murray, 1966; New York: Harper & Row, 1966);

A Time of Gifts: On Foot to Constantinople from the Hook of Holland to the Middle Danube (London: Murray, 1977; New York: Harper & Row, 1977);

Between the Woods and the Water: On Foot to Constantinople from the Hook of Holland: The Middle Danube to the Iron Gates (London: Murray, 1986; New York: Viking, 1986);

Three Letters from the Andes (London: Murray, 1991).

OTHER: Konstantinos P. Rhodokanakes, *No Innocent Abroad: A Novel,* translated by Leigh Fermor (London & Toronto: Heinemann, 1937); republished as *Forever Ulysses* (New York: Viking, 1938);

Colette, *Julie de Carneilhan* [and] *Chance Acquaintances,* translated by Leigh Fermor (London: Secker & Warburg, 1952);

George Psychoundakis, *The Cretan Runner: His Story of the German Occupation,* translated, with an introduction, by Leigh Fermor, annotated by Leigh Fermor and Xan Fielding (London: Niko Murray, 1955);

Niko Ghika (Nikolaos Chatzekyriakos-Ghikas), *India,* translated by Leigh Fermor (Athens: Icaros, 1959);

Patrick Leigh Fermor

Matila Ghyka, *The World Mine Oyster: Memoirs,* introduction by Leigh Fermor (London: Heinemann, 1961);

"Gluttony," in *The Seven Deadly Sins* (London: Sunday Times Publications, 1962; New York: Morrow, 1962);

Ghika, *Ghika: Paintings, Drawings, Sculpture,* texts by Leigh Fermor and Stephen Spender (London: Lund Humphries, 1964; Boston: Boston Book & Art Shop, 1965);

Miles Reid, *Into Colditz,* introduction by Leigh Fermor (Salisbury, U.K.: Michael Russell, 1983);

David Smiley, *Albanian Assignment,* foreword by Leigh Fermor (London: Chatto & Windus, 1984);

Roger Hinks, *The Gymnasium of the Mind: The Journals of Roger Hinks 1933–1963,* edited by John Goldsmith, with a memoir by Leigh Fermor (Salisbury, U.K.: Michael Russell, 1984);

"Greece," in *The Englishman's Room,* edited by Alvilde Lees-Milne (Topsfield, Mass.: Salem House, 1986), pp. 91–95; republished as "Sash Windows on the Sea: Patrick Leigh Fermor at Home in Greece," *Architectural Digest,* 43 (November 1986): 178–181, 226, 228;

Freya Stark, *Over the Rim of the World: Selected Letters,* edited by Caroline Moorehead, foreword by Leigh Fermor (London: Murray in association with Michael Russell, 1988);

Sacheverell Sitwell, *Roumanian Journey,* introduction by Leigh Fermor (Oxford: Oxford University Press, 1992);

Nicolas Bouvier, *The Way of the World,* translated by Robyn Marsack, introduction by Leigh Fermor (Edinburgh: Polygon, 1992; Marlboro, Vt.: Marlboro Press, 1992);

Xan Fielding, *A Hideous Disguise,* foreword by Leigh Fermor (Francestown, N.H.: Typographeum, 1994);

Marianna Koromela, *In the Trail of Odysseus,* introduction by Leigh Fermor (Norwich, U.K.: Michael Russell, 1994).

SELECTED PERIODICAL PUBLICATIONS–UNCOLLECTED: "Entrance to Hades," *Cornhill,* 169 (Spring 1957): 166–177;

"The Black Departers: An Adventure in Greece," *Cornhill,* 173 (Autumn 1963): 295–327;

"On Prospero's Island: Balancing Splendor and Rusticity in a Corfu Villa," *Architectural Digest,* 43 (June 1986): 152–157, 212;

"Observations on a Marine Vulcan," *Twentieth Century Literature,* 33 (Fall 1987): 305–307;

"A Clean Sheet for Paeonia; Patrick Leigh Fermor Defends Greece Against Accusations of Bullying Macedonia," *Spectator,* 269 (12 September 1992): 24–26;

"Some Architectural Notes," *Spectator,* 273 (24 September 1994): 46.

Patrick Leigh Fermor's life and travel books have earned him comparison with T. E. Lawrence (Lawrence of Arabia) and a reputation as one of the foremost travel writers of the twentieth century. Writing in *The New York Times* (5 December 1986), John Gross called Leigh Fermor "the preeminent English travel writer of his generation." Leigh Fermor's writing often focuses on areas not particularly well known to American and western European readers, including the Balkans, prewar Slovakia and Hungary, the southern Peloponnese, and the Andes. Leigh Fermor's meticulousness, attention to detail, scholarship, and wide-ranging interests make his books valuable eyewitness accounts of cultures that have changed dramatically or even disappeared since his visits to them.

In *Abroad: British Literary Traveling Between the Wars* (1980) Paul Fussell defines travel books (as opposed to guidebooks) as "a sub-species of memoir in which the autobiographical narrative arises from the speaker's encounter with distant or unfamiliar data, and in which the narrative–unlike that in a novel or romance–claims literal validity by constant reference to actuality." Fussell's definition not only explains how travel writing conjoins the personal and the literal but also suggests how travel writing reveals as much, if not more, about the traveler than the travels. Such is the case with Leigh Fermor. While his books describe his journeys to far-flung areas of the world, they do more than catalogue places seen and people met. Leigh Fermor's works constitute a portrait of himself as a scholar, artist, traveler, and man. As a scholar, he possesses a vivid imagination that is preoccupied with capturing the people and events of the past. As an artist and writer, Leigh Fermor is lyrical, reveling in the love of words for their own sake. Using sensory details, he vividly re-creates moods, impressions, and experiences for his readers. As a traveler, Leigh Fermor undertakes a journey not with the end in view but in search of strange happenings along remote and unfamiliar paths. As a man, Leigh Fermor emerges from his works as an engaging personality: intellectually curious, sensitive, and confident, with a passion for scholarship, languages, literature, art, architecture, and geography and–most important for a traveler–a love of adventure and the unknown.

Patrick Michael Leigh Fermor was born in London on 11 February 1915 to Muriel Eileen Taaffe Ambler Fermor and Sir Lewis Leigh Fermor, Order of the British Empire and fellow of the Royal Society. Shortly after her son's birth, Muriel Leigh Fermor sailed to India to be reunited with her husband, who at the time was heading the Geological Survey of India. Because of the dangers of travel during World War I, Leigh Fermor's parents, like other colonials at the time, thought it best to leave their young son in England. His mother intended to return for him at the end of the war, not knowing that it would last for nearly four more years.

In "Introductory Letter to Xan Fielding," which prefaces *A Time of Gifts* (1977), Leigh Fermor described himself during his formative years as "a small farmer's

Leigh Fermor in 1936 (photograph by Valasa Cantacuzene)

child run wild." He spent a blissful early childhood with permissive foster parents on a Northamptonshire farm, where "I was allowed to do as I chose in everything." These "marvellously lawless years," he wrote, made him unfit for the constraints of any school, save for the rather unorthodox Salsham Hall, near Bury St. Edmunds, a coeducational school for "difficult children" aged four to twenty, where Leigh Fermor was sent at age ten. Its unorthodox educational methods included students and teachers country dancing in the nude. When Salsham closed, Leigh Fermor was sent to a more conventional preparatory school. After the freedom of Salsham, he found this school unbearable, and so he left. Passing his common entrance exams, he gained entrance to King's School, Canterbury, where he again proved unable to live by constraints. (One of Leigh Fermor's friends there was Alan Watts, later well known for his writings on Zen Buddhism.) Leigh Fermor wrote later that his housemaster saw him as "a dangerous mixture of sophistication and recklessness." After a series of misdeeds, Leigh Fermor was dismissed.

At seventeen Leigh Fermor found himself in London and spent the next two years studying for the London Certificate, which he hoped would eventually clear the way for entry to Sandhurst and a military career. The bohemian world of London, however, seduced him away from his plans to join the army. The publication of a poem fired him with the idea of becoming a writer. In the summer of 1933, after passing the London Certificate exam, Leigh Fermor attempted to live the London writer's life, renting a room in a Shepherd Market boardinghouse, but he spent his time socializing with his friends more than writing. By the winter of the same year, Leigh Fermor decided to "abandon London and England and to set out like a tramp–or, . . . like a pilgrim or a palmer, an errant scholar" to cross Europe by foot and reach Constantinople (renamed Istanbul in 1930). On 8 December 1933 Leigh Fermor set out on this great adventure. Far from giving up his dream of becoming an author, he saw his travels as a way of realizing it. His journeys would give him something to write about and give him the needed solitude, time for reflection, freedom, and inspiration to create. In fact, throughout his sojourn, Leigh Fermor recorded his experiences in notebooks from which he later reconstructed part of his journey in *A Time of Gifts* and *Between the Woods and the Water* (1986).

During the years before the outbreak of World War II in September 1939, Leigh Fermor found time to translate Konstantinos Rhodokanakes's novel *No Innocent Abroad* (1937) from the original Greek. In 1939, after extensive travel in Central Europe, the Balkans, and Greece, Leigh Fermor enlisted in the Irish Guards. His military career during World War II was distinguished. He served as a lieutenant in the British Military Mission in Greece and Crete and as a liaison officer to the Greek headquarters in Albania. He fought in the campaigns of Greece and Crete. After the fall of Crete to the Germans, he organized the resistance movement there and, disguised as a shepherd, oversaw guerrilla operations on the island from 1942 to 1944. Leigh Fermor's friend and fellow soldier Xan Fielding has written an account of the Cretan resistance, *Hide and Seek: The Story of a War-time Agent* (1954).

In 1944 Leigh Fermor led a successful expedition to seize Maj. Gen. Heinrich Kreipe, commander of the twenty-two thousand German troops on Crete. The operation is recounted in several books, including *Ill Met By Moonlight* (1950) by Maj. W. Stanley Moss. (The 1957 movie version starred Dirk Bogarde as Leigh Fermor.) In Moss's book Leigh Fermor is referred to as Paddy and described as a dashing, adventurous, and charming friend who looked "Teutonic" in his disguise

W. Stanley Moss and Leigh Fermor disguised as German soldiers during their 1944 expedition to kidnap Maj. Gen. Heinrich Kreipe, commander of the German troops on Crete (from Moss's Ill Met by Moonlight, *1950)*

as a German soldier. He was also an inspiration to his cohorts: "The morale of our own little band continues to be as high as ever, but Paddy is forever having to give pep-talks to the outsiders, telling them not to give up hope and that the end of the world is not yet upon us." Another account of the expedition is found in George Psychoundakis's *The Cretan Runner* (1955), a book translated, with an introduction, by Leigh Fermor. Psychoundakis functioned as a guide and runner for the British officers hiding on the island. In Psychoundakis's narrative, Leigh Fermor is called Mr. Michali by the Cretans and described as "a tall man, full of life, with a beautiful moustache and curly brown hair. He wore Cretan breeches and boots, a black shirt and a fringed turban, and he had dyed his whiskers and hair in such a way that he seemed the image of a true Cretan."

Leigh Fermor, Moss, and their British and Cretan associates captured General Kreipe and escaped through the Nazi-occupied capital city of Iráklion, passing through German roadblocks with Leigh Fermor posing as the general. Then with the aid of Cretan runners they contacted radio operators who could transmit messages to Cairo and facilitate their escape from the island. David Smiley's *Albanian Assignment* (1984) reports that when Leigh Fermor and Moss had spoken to their friends in Cairo about their intended capture of the general, their military associates had registered alarm, but their "social contacts" had laughed at what they considered a joke.

At the end of the war Leigh Fermor was in North Germany as the team commander of the Special Allied Airborne Reconnaissance Force. He was discharged from military service in 1945. For his service to the

Map from Leigh Fermor's 1958 book, Mani: Travels in the Southern Peleponnese

Crown he was awarded the Order of the British Empire in 1943 and the Distinguished Service Order in 1944. The people of Crete showed their thanks for his contribution to the resistance effort by making Leigh Fermor an honorary citizen of Iráklion in 1947.

By 1947 Leigh Fermor had met the Honorable Mrs. Joan Rayner, born Joan Elizabeth Eyres Monsell, daughter of Henry Bolton Graham Eyres Monsell, first Viscount Monsell; she became Leigh Fermor's wife in 1968. A 19 June 1947 letter from Freya Stark to Sir Sydney Cockerell reported that "a young buccaneering Irishman called Leigh Fermor is coming to lunch with Joan Rayner, who was Osbert Lancaster's secretary in Athens." Stark's letters during the postwar period show Leigh Fermor to have been a friend as well as an intriguing figure to her. On 27 August 1950, she wrote to her husband, Stewart Perowne, "Yesterday we had a cheerful party down here with Patrick Leigh Fermor and Joan and two young Pallisers–Paddy looking in this wine dark sea *so* like a Hellenistic lesser sea-god of a rather low period, and I do like him; he is the genuine buccaneer."

In 1947–1948 Leigh Fermor spent a year as deputy director of the British Institute in Athens, Greece, and then resumed his travels. During the late 1940s he and two companions, one of whom was Joan Rayner, journeyed to the Caribbean and the West Indies, island travels that he recorded in detail in his first book, *The Traveller's Tree* (1950). They also inspired his first and only novel, *The Violins of Saint-Jacques* (1953).

The Traveller's Tree takes its title from a plant commonly known as the traveler's tree. Like the people who inhabit the Antilles, it was originally a stranger to that region. As the preface explains, the book concerns life on the islands "as it impinges on an interested stranger, their buildings and food and religions, their history and the perceptible texture of their existence." *The Traveller's Tree* received immediate critical acclaim, earning Leigh Fermor the Heinemann Foundation Prize for Literature in 1950 and the Kemsley Prize in 1951.

Leigh Fermor wrote in his introduction that he felt no compunction to treat political problems, but he could not avoid offering passing opinions on racial conflict. For example, in Martinique he met a civil engineer, formerly from Lyons, who "embarked upon a hymn of hate against the Negroes." Leigh Fermor concluded that the Frenchman was a "little madman." In Barbados Leigh Fermor encountered a more subtle form of discrimination, discovering that the places of entertainment for "whites only" are called clubs. "Thanks to the clarity of our complexions," Leigh Fermor wrote, "we were automatically members." A white Barbadian friend later described this unspoken system of discrimination to Leigh Fermor as one of the advantages of the island, and when Leigh Fermor asked where a white and a black Barbadian could meet for dinner, his friend made it clear that whites and blacks did not meet. Leigh Fermor called this system "disgustingly hypocritical" and more despicable and loathsome than the laws of segregation then in effect in the United States.

The Traveller's Tree is a penetrating account of travel in the Caribbean, probing the mixed heritage and varied history of each island and offering readers an unforgettable picture of the islands before they were transformed largely into resorts and spas for tourists. The book includes vivid descriptions of Guadeloupe, Martinique, Dominica, Barbados, Trinidad, Grenada, St. Lucia, Antigua, St. Kitts, St. Eustatius, Saba, St. Martin, St. Thomas, Haiti, and Jamaica. Leigh Fermor was interested in the landscape and architecture of each island, but above all he focused on the unusual groups of people that populate this region. In Dominica, for example, he encountered Caribs, members of a nearly extinct group of Native Americans. *The Traveller's Tree* details the history of these warrior peoples and describes with particular relish their cannibalistic habits of yore. Though they were initially difficult to subdue, by the eighteenth century the Caribs were nearly eliminated by white colonists. By the late 1950s there were only five hundred Caribs left, and of these, Leigh Fermor noted, only one hundred were of pure blood. Leigh Fermor felt privileged to have met these members of a nearly extinct people. In Jamaica he encountered the Kingston Pocomaniacs, who–like Haitians who believe in voodoo and Christianity–practice a curious religion that mixes Christianity with surviving remnants of African religion. Leigh Fermor witnessed late-night rites of Haitians and Pocomaniacs, rituals that result in the participants experiencing ecstasy and possession by spirits. Not only are Leigh Fermor's accounts of voodoo highly detailed and extensive, but they also abound with interesting conclusions, including his assessment that it "was the unifying force of Voodoo, far more than the advent of New Ideas from Europe, that impelled the slaves at the time of the French Revolution to revolt."

Writing in *Library Journal* (15 December 1951), W. K. Harrison called *The Traveller's Tree* "one of the most rewarding travel books published in many years," and *The Sunday Times* said Leigh Fermor was a "born writer," the "ideal traveller, inquisitive, humorous, interested in everything." Reviewing the book for the *New Statesman and Nation* (13 January 1951), Dorothy Carrington termed Leigh Fermor's account of voodoo "the most intelligent I have read on the subject." The reviewer for *The Times Literary Supplement* (*TLS*) judged the chapter on voodoo one of the best in the book, citing as well Leigh Fermor's "keen eye for such vestiges of splendour and prosperity as have survived the depredations of tropical nature and the collapse of an economy based on slavery" (29 December 1950).

Leigh Fermor's translations of Colette's *Julie de Carneilhan* and *Chambre d'Hotel,* published in 1952, were followed by his novel, *The Violins of Saint-Jacques,* in 1953. The book was inspired by the volcanic destruction of St. Pierre, the capital of Martinique, in 1902. Leigh Fermor gave a realistic sense to a fantastic tale employing a frame narrator, an Englishman, who relates the early history of the island. Then the scene switches to the Greek Aegean island of Mitylene, where the English narrator meets Berthe de Rennes, a woman past seventy, who eventually tells him the story of her youth on the island of Saint-Jacques at the turn of the century and of the tragedy that befell her the last night of Mardi Gras. Antonia White in the *New Statesman and Nation* (5 December 1953) described the writing as "deliberate, sometimes overconscious artifice, scattered with French and native words and adorned with litanies of picturesque names." Yet, she complimented Leigh Fermor on his "fine visual imagination, shown to the full in the description of the fiery destruction of St. Jacques as seen from a small schooner." While White admired Leigh Fermor for his "erudition," "delight in exotic sights, sounds, faces and dresses," and the "skill

Leigh Fermor in Phlomochori, Greece, during the travels he described in Mani *(photograph by Joan Eyres Monsell)*

with which he builds up to his grand climax," the novel remained for her "little more than a splendid spectacle." *The Violins of Saint-Jacques* inspired a successful three-act opera, composed by Malcolm Williamson, with libretto by William Chappell. It had its premiere at Sadler's Wells Theatre in London, on 29 November 1966.

In *A Time to Keep Silence* (1953) Leigh Fermor described his extended sojourns in two French monasteries, the Abbey of St. Wandrille de Fontanelle and La Grande Trappe, and the abandoned rock monasteries of Cappadocia in Turkey. Not a believer, Leigh Fermor initially went to the monasteries because he was in search of a quiet, inexpensive place to stay while he wrote. As the title suggests, the main theme of the work is the effect of silence and solitude on the human consciousness and spirit. In 1952 Leigh Fermor, on a friend's recommendation, visited St. Wandrille de Fontanelle, one of the oldest Benedictine abbeys in France. At first, he wrote, the peaceful solitude and pervading silence of the abbey did not calm his spirit but made him melancholy, lonely, and unproductive: "So much silence and sobriety! The place assumed the character of an enormous tomb, a necropolis of which I was the only living inhabitant." His feelings about the abbey underwent a change, however, as he learned to turn inward and to be with and by himself.

While the transition from "urban excess to a life of rustic solitude" was painful and slow, Leigh Fermor came to see the monastery as a "silent university" at which he learned much about himself and his unsuspected capacity for silence, contemplation, and solitude. In his introduction to the 1957 edition of the book Leigh Fermor wrote that the seclusion, silence, and solitariness of the monastery eventually allowed him to reach "a state of peace that is unthought of in the ordinary world," a clarity of mind and spirit that made him feel as if he were "the beneficiary . . . of a supernatural windfall."

Leigh Fermor's next encounter with monasticism occurred at the Abbey of Solesmes in western France, where he remained for two weeks, "established in a warm cell, writing hard in front of a blazing log fire, enjoying the amenities of a library that must be one of the largest of any monastery." His visit to Solesmes was followed by a more extended stay at La Grande Trappe, where Leigh Fermor encountered the rigorous rule of the Cistercians, with its sacrifice, deprivation, penance, physical hardship, and "the unbroken cycle of contemplation, prayer and back-breaking toil." Although Leigh Fermor admired the difficulties of Trappist life, he also questioned them in his analysis of the paradoxes inherent in such an existence.

In the final section of *A Time to Keep Silence* Leigh Fermor recorded his visit to the rock monasteries of Cappadocia, no longer inhabited by monks but by doves. Arriving in the "derelict town" of Urgub (Urgüp), in which he saw "the last vestiges of humanity," Leigh Fermor and his companion descended into a "tormented ravine" of "wild strangeness." The landscape seemed to Leigh Fermor to be almost extraterrestrial, like "the surface of the Moon or Mars or Saturn: a dead, ashen world, lit with the blinding pallor of a waste of asbestos, filled, not with craters and shell-holes, but with cones and pyramids and monoliths." Within these geological formations tenth- and twelfth-century monks had constructed detailed replicas of Byzantine churches. Leigh Fermor describes the silence that pervades the rock monasteries of Cappadocia as of a different kind than that he had found at the monasteries in France. It is the silence of ruin, desertion, abandonment, and mystery. The "rock monasteries keep their secret almost as closely guarded as Stonehenge. . . ."

Leigh Fermor's next travel book, *Mani: Travels in the Southern Peloponnese* (1958), was well received by critics, inspiring reviewer John Raymond to write in the *New Statesman* (6 December 1958) that "Mr. Leigh Fermor is the best travel writer of his generation." Classical scholar Gilbert Highet praised the book in a blurb printed on the dust jacket: "It is a really beautiful book of travel in an almost wholly unknown part of Europe, among people who still belong largely to the tough simple Middle Ages; and it shows not only their charm and vigor, but the delights which still await the explorer of Greece." Part travelogue, part an inspired evocation of the past, *Mani,* which won the Duff Cooper Memorial Prize, is a fusion of scholarship, imagination, and history.

Desolate, rocky, and isolated, Mani is generally considered the southernmost extension of continental Europe in the Mediterranean–though Leigh Fermor noted in a later interview (*New York Review of Books,* 8 February 1987) that a village near Gibraltar "beats it by a sixth of a mile." In his account of his journeys about this rocky peninsula in the Peloponnese, Leigh Fermor captured the rugged beauty of this once remote and wild region of Greece and the toughness and endurance of its people, whose roots stretch back to Byzantium. The dominant theme of the book is the contrast between the Greek present and its mythic past. Leigh Fermor sought out this remote area of Greece to explore the relationship between contemporary Greeks and their history, believing that in still untouched areas this relationship would be undisturbed by "the butt of a Coca-cola bottle." Hanging over the narrative is a pervading sense of doom and impending loss. Much of the past remains alive in contemporary Greece, particularly in rural areas, in the form of traditions, customs, and rituals, but much has also been lost in the process of growth and Westernization and in the name of progress.

The book reveals the vibrant folk culture of Mani, the poetic dirges of the wailing women at funerals, the propensity of the citizenry to blood feuds, and their hospitality. In this book, as elsewhere in his writings, Leigh Fermor reveals his fascination with the mix of pagan and Christian elements in folk culture. "The clergy did what they could to reduce the pagan characteristics" of Greek culture, Leigh Fermor wrote, "but there was more truth in the gods' claims to immortality than is generally thought." Among the most valuable sections of *Mani* are Leigh Fermor's careful analyses of the persistence of pre-Christian beliefs in modern Greek society.

In 1964 Leigh Fermor and Rayner built a house in the town of Kardamyli in Mani, which he described in an essay collected in *The Englishman's Room* (1986). The essay, which was republished in *Architectural Digest* (November 1986) with photographs by Derry Moore, describes the appearance of the house as "like a monastery which had been crumbling for centuries."

On 27 September 1958, while in the middle of reading *Mani,* Freya Stark wrote to John Grey Murray that Leigh Fermor's book was "first rate." "I think he writes better than I do–more consciously and with a fine choice of words," she exclaimed, adding that he "gives wonderful descriptions of rock and sky and the gauntness and intensity of this land–I do hope it will be liked as it deserves."

In 1962 Leigh Fermor contributed an essay on "Gluttony" to a series on the seven deadly sins in *The Times* (London). Also boasting essays by Angus Wilson, Edith Sitwell, Cyril Connolly, Evelyn Waugh, Christopher Sykes, and W. H. Auden, the series was later published as a book. Leigh Fermor's humorous insights

Patrick and Joan Leigh Fermor in the library of their house in Kardamyli, Greece

into gluttony includes a cigar-smoking character named Mr. Vortigern, who blames pasta for the decline of Italian culture:

> The piazzas were a tragic squirming tangle of spaghetti and lasagne, the lagoon ran red with tomato sauce. Italy's genius was dead, laid low by her own gluttony . . . not only Italy's painting, but Italian thought and poetry and literature and rhetoric and even Italian architecture. Everything was turned into macaroni.

In 1966 Leigh Fermor published *Roumeli: Travels in Northern Greece,* an account of a journey "undertaken a few years ago," according to Leigh Fermor. Again his traveling companion was Joan Rayner, who as Joan Eyres Monsell had taken the photographs for *Mani* and did so again for *Roumeli.* The colloquial designation for a region of northern Greece, the name Roumeli is not found on present-day maps. Its boundaries have changed over the centuries, and it is now generally understood to be that region of northern Greece that lies south of the Agrapha Mountains. Leigh Fermor's introduction refers to Roumeli as a "contracting wilderness," expressing his displeasure that "progress" is stripping the region and its people of their connection to the past: "Monasteries and temples which, almost yesterday, were only to be reached by solitary and exacting climbs are now the brief staging points of highly organized and painless tourism in multitudes."

According to Fussell, tourists insist on visiting the known and the familiar, while travelers relish the unknown and the absence of the familiar. Leigh Fermor is the epitome of the traveler and a critic of the tourist. Tourism "destroys the object of its love," and it saddened Leigh Fermor to see that Greece had become the "most recent, most beautiful, and perhaps its most fragile victim." Tourism has turned "dignified islands and serene coasts into polluting hells." It has changed delightful, old Athenian taverns into "an alien nightmare of bastard folklore and bad wine." Some inns survive unpolluted, Leigh Fermor discovered, but soon, he predicted, guidebook writers would tell their readers where to find these last bastions of Greek culture. For Leigh Fermor, who believes that such guidebooks should be "publicly burnt," "Greece is suffering its most dangerous invasion since the time of Xerxes." Leigh Fermor's statements have proven prophetic.

Roumeli describes the wedding celebrations Leigh Fermor attended among the Sarakatsan nomads, his visit to the monastery of St. Barlaam in the Meteora, and his search for George Gordon, Lord Byron's shoes in Missolonghi. The dominant theme of the work is the decline or loss of traditional ways of life. For example, his narrative of his sojourn at the monastery of St. Barlaam focuses on the reasons for the decline and decay of Orthodox monasticism. In the eleventh century hermits and ascetics first began to occupy the pinnacles and crevices of the Meteora, and by the sixteenth century a powerful community of twenty-six monasteries was flourishing there. At the time of Leigh Fermor's visit only four were still active. Of the others only occasional ruins remained. Leigh Fermor attributed the decline to two causes: legislation that stripped the monasteries of much of their wealth and the impact of Western materialism.

Leigh Fermor's two books on Greece have contributed to the general reader's understanding and love of the country. Leigh Fermor traces the roots of his philhellenism to the years he spent in German-occupied Crete, which mark the beginning of his many years of study, experience, and observation of the Greek environment. Cocker argues that Leigh Fermor "is the most obvious heir to [Robert] Byron's pre-war mantle as leading philhellene amongst British writers." Certainly Leigh Fermor, along with Lawrence Durrell, writes in the tradition of the British travel writer Robert Byron.

Leigh Fermor also owes a debt to another philhellene, the poet Byron. In *Roumeli* Leigh Fermor wrote that "every English traveler, however humble or unimpressive, and whether he knows or deserves or wants it or not, is the beneficiary of some reflected fragment of his glory." Byron is revered even today as a national hero by the Greeks, and Leigh Fermor, too, has been honored by the Greeks for his service to their country. As if in tribute to Byron's memory, during a trip to Turkey in October 1986, Leigh Fermor at age sixty-nine repeated Byron's 1810 swim across the Hellespont.

Writing in *The New York Times* (28 August 1966), Stark praised Leigh Fermor's ability to present people "as they are" as well as his "brilliance, the felicitous profusion, the exuberance of learning and information, wayward as a gossamer, from what one soon comes to realize is a very solid store." In the *New Statesman* (13 May 1966) V. S. Pritchett expressed reservations about Leigh Fermor's "greed for detail" that at times overburdened his style but praised his ability to present fully realized human beings and their conversation, concluding that Leigh Fermor "probably knows Greece better than anybody." The *TLS* (7 July 1966) writer, in addition to praising Leigh Fermor, indulged in a more personal analysis of the author:

> Mr. Leigh Fermor has acquired an enormous fund of esoteric knowledge during his wanderings, and writes like a baroque angel; but when one closes his enchantingly digressive book it is not the objective or historical passages that stick in the mind so much as the oblique self-portrait he has built up, of a traveller as nomadic and untrammelled as the Saracatsani themselves, riding through Macedonia in his teens, an eyewitness of the 1935 Venizelos revolution, with Cretan comrades in the White Mountains during the German occupation, playing billiards with Lady Wentworth, hunting for Byron's shoes in Missolonghi, always a little elusive and tangential, writing a testament the centre of which is never, one feels, plumb in the middle.

Leigh Fermor's knowledge of Greece is amply demonstrated in the essay he wrote for *Ghika: Paintings, Drawings, Sculpture* (1964), a book of Niko Ghika's art work with text by Leigh Fermor and Stephen Spender. Leigh Fermor's essay, "The Background of Niko Ghika," notes that Greece is "wilder and harder, less vegetated and more precipitous" than Italy, that rich source of great painters. The light in Greece is also different, less diffuse and less soft than in Italy: "Low and bright, the large sun spins in a sky of pale and unfathomable blue drained of all but radiance." He was made an honorary citizen of Gytheion, Laconia, in 1966 and of Kardamyli in 1967.

Leigh Fermor's next book, *A Time of Gifts* (1977), won the W. H. Smith and Son Literary Award in 1978. This volume is the first in a projected trilogy about his travels in central Europe during the 1930s, part travelogue, part interpretative autobiography, and an important historical narrative that documents what the region was like before the storm of World War II. The title of *A Time of Gifts* comes from lines in Louis MacNeice's poem "Twelfth Night": "For now the time of gifts is one / O boys that grow, O snows that melt." The book chronicles the first leg of Leigh Fermor's trip across Europe to Istanbul, taking the reader from Rotterdam to the Hungarian border. Using diaries he kept on his journey and the resources of his memory, Leigh Fermor re-created his young self at eighteen, offering his readers his perspective on the past and an image of the young man he was.

As an author of fiction creates a character, so an autobiographer creates a persona, a version of himself or herself that may or may not coincide with life as it was lived but that captures meaning or significance. The young Leigh Fermor is a captivating figure. A lover of history, he is attracted by strange place names and haunts the libraries of his hosts in search of knowledge. Showing remarkable poise and self-confidence for his age, he is just as comfortable in the company of swineherds as he is in the company of nobility. With his

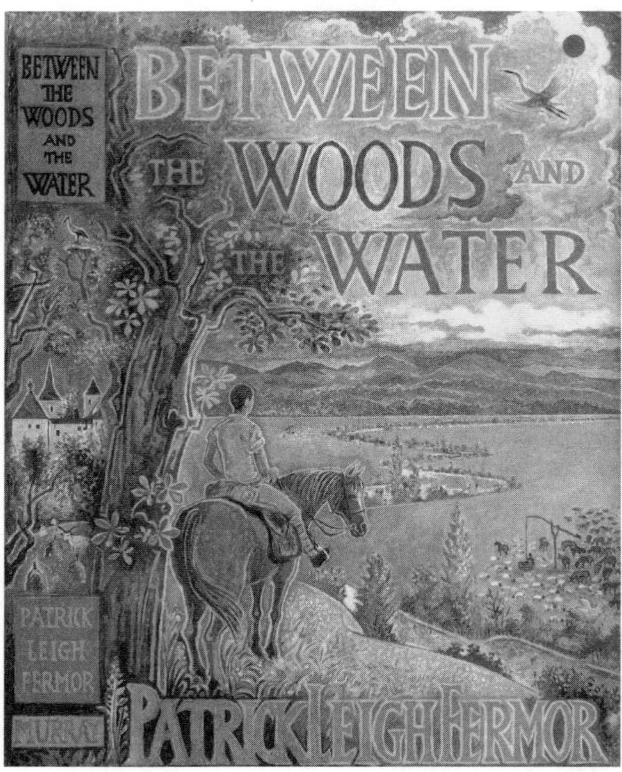

Dust jacket for Leigh Fermor's 1986 book, the second memoir in a projected trilogy about his travels across Europe to Istanbul during the 1930s

knowledge of languages he is able to break barriers between himself and his hosts, who find him so engaging that he becomes a lifelong friend. He is eager to experience the strange and exotic and curious enough to ask questions. He can be reserved at times and at others a reveler. Leigh Fermor does not look on this younger self with nostalgia or regret. He acknowledges that time is irredeemable, but because he still possesses youthful enthusiasm and avidity, he does not seem to be saddened by the passage of years.

To avoid giving his narrative a melancholic cast, Leigh Fermor tries not to compare the central Europe of the past with that of the present. Such comparisons would be "like having a skeleton at the feast," Leigh Fermor later told an interviewer (*New York Review of Books,* 8 February 1987). Instead the book is an enchanting portrait of a Europe that was destroyed by totalitarianism and world war. In much of Europe young Leigh Fermor discovers a tradition of hospitality and benevolence toward wandering young people. In Holland, for instance, he learns that humble travelers can find refuge for the night in police stations. A local constable lets him spend the night in a cell and gives him a bowl of coffee and some bread. In Germany–after having been robbed of the rucksack that contained his books, passport, money, and diary of his trip to that point Leigh Fermor is treated with kindness and generosity by Baron Rheinhard von Liphardt-Ratshoff, who re-equips him with a rucksack and clothes, presents him with a seventeenth-century, leather-bound copy of Horace's odes and epodes, and sends him off with letters of introduction to fellow members of the gentry.

Leigh Fermor sleeps at times in barns and at other times in fairy-tale castles and learns from a Burgermeister that as a student he is entitled to expect and even demand a free supper, a mug of beer, a bed for the night, and bread and a bowl of coffee for breakfast in every town or village in Germany. Nor is such hospitality unique to Germany. In Vienna he is befriended by Konrad, a Frisian who helps him find subjects to sketch in order to earn some much-needed pocket money. Leigh Fermor attributes his success in selling these sketches not to his talent but to "kind Viennese hearts."

A Time of Gifts lingers on what was golden about pre–World War II Europe: the landscapes, arts, architecture, history, literature, and, above all, the people. Still, neither the reader nor Leigh Fermor can ignore that Adolf Hitler has come to power in Germany and that signs of war are gathering. In Germany, Leigh Fermor sees framed photographs of Hitler in inns and store windows, swastika armbands and flags, Hitler Youth and Maidens, and he is aware of the persecution of the Jews, finding striking the ordinariness of individuals capable of such inhumanity. In one inn young Leigh Fermor sees a dozen SA men, who, after a few mugs of beer, begin to sing German folk songs. Leigh Fermor notes that "the charm" of their singing "made it impossible, at that moment, to connect the singers with organized bullying and the smashing of Jewish shop windows and nocturnal bonfires of books."

Leigh Fermor's digressions, which make each of his works seem spontaneous, immediate, and unstructured, take various forms–historical background and information, philosophical musings, postscripts and asides that create a sense of intimacy between Leigh Fermor and his audience, flashbacks, flash forwards, and flights of the imagination. Rather than being peripheral to the works, these digressions are the heart of each book. As Mark Cocker observes in *Loneliness and Time* (1994), "a single linear narrative is never quite adequate to contain the burning multiplicity of ideas exercising him at any one moment."

The master of digression, Leigh Fermor jokingly apologizes for interrupting his narrative with Proustian associations, making comments such as "We shall never get to Constantinople like this. I know I ought to be moving on. . . . But I can't–not for a page or two." In one moment of free association he flashes forward to the kidnapping of General Kreipe in the mountains of Crete during World War II, commenting that, though they were enemies, he and the general had felt a strange connection and mutual respect, perhaps because they shared a knowledge of Horace's odes. The reader is unlikely to want Leigh Fermor to move on during such digressions, for they are an integral part of the experience of traveling with him.

Writing in *The New York Times Book Review* (27 November 1977), Raymond Sokolov declared that Leigh Fermor had re-created "historically irreplaceable impressions of Central European Jews waking up to Hitler's menace, of the last days of the charming, Hapsburgian petty nobility and of the pre-Communist landscape of Hungary and Rumania." Yet he added some mild reservations about the "prose of preening but often magnificent richness" and Leigh Fermor's "(perhaps excessively) literate mind." Reviewing the book for *Library Journal* (1 September 1997), A. M. Robinson called the volume "pure gold, most highly recommended," while Jan Morris in *The Spectator* (24 September 1977) called the work "nothing short of a masterpiece."

Winner of the 1987 Thomas Cook Travel Book Award and the 1987 International Time-Life Silver Pen Award, *Between the Woods and the Water* (1986), the long-awaited second volume of Leigh Fermor's trilogy, picks up where *A Time of Gifts* leaves off. Leigh Fermor's journey now takes him down the Danube from Budapest, across the great Hungarian plain by horseback, and over the Romanian border into legendary and mysterious Transylvania, a wild and beautiful region of forests and mountains, which at that time was secluded from Western eyes. The woods of the title are in Transylvania, and the water is the Danube and its tributaries. The book ends with young Leigh Fermor at the Iron Gates, where the Balkans begin. As in *A Time of Gifts, Between the Woods and the Water* records a dual perspective, that of a young and enthusiastic eighteen-year-old and the older, septuagenarian Leigh Fermor. Reviewing the book for the *Los Angeles Times* (28 December 1986), Richard Eder described it as "as much an old man's encounter with his young self as it is an account of sights and people."

Leigh Fermor "meant to live like a tramp or a pilgrim or a wandering scholar, sleeping in ditches and ricks and only consorting with birds of the same feather," but while he found himself some nights with Romanian-speaking shepherds whom he fancied as lineal descendants of Vlachs and Dacians or with peasant farmers or even sleeping alone in the mountains, at other times he found himself "strolling from castle to castle, sipping Tokay out of cut-glass goblets and smoking pipes a yard long with archdukes instead of halving gaspers with tramps." His portrait of a rural Hungarian aristocracy captures a world that perished in the rubble of World War II.

Leigh Fermor describes a learned, elegant, and eccentric class of people whose homes were filled with antiques and large libraries. Leigh Fermor captures the appealing eccentricities of the Hungarian gentry without making them seem petty or frivolous. One host kept a shotgun by his piano while he played Bach fugues. Every few minutes he broke off, rushed to the window, and shot "a bird from the enormous rookery that overlooked the house." A Hungarian count, who collected moths, spoke English fluently, but–thanks to a Highland nanny–with a Scottish accent. ("I'll dree on own weird," he tells Leigh Fermor as he thinks over a difficult decision.) Leigh Fermor also had the unusual experience of playing bicycle polo with a count and his entourage.

Between the Woods and the Water also explores the power and art of memory. Leigh Fermor's diary entries were "backed up by a collection of clear visions." Leigh Fermor is quick to confess to lapses in memory, discovering that memory is often selective and untrustworthy, but he is also surprised by some of the moments that he does remember vividly. For example, in re-creating an evening at a Hungarian castle, Leigh Fermor recalls the members of the party and the piano music, but not what was discussed or what was played. In his mind's eye, however, is a clear vision of a bowl of "enormous white and red peonies" from which "a few petals have dropped on the polished floor." These retained concrete images or visions, which capture poetically and concisely the essence of the remembered experience, are akin to William Wordsworth's "spots of time" in which the imagination and memory transcend time.

For the eighteen-year-old Leigh Fermor life is akin to a golden age, but the septuagenarian Leigh Fermor writes with the knowledge of what the future held for his cast of characters and for their region. In the narrative there is a sense of impending catastrophe. The people young Leigh Fermor meets sense the threat of war. While they do not know when catastrophe will strike, they just know that it will. "Everything is going to vanish," an Austrian friend laments at the prospect of a power dam. Leigh Fermor, given the benefit of retrospection, knows that most of it did. At times, because of Leigh Fermor's knowledge of the future, a bit of melancholy seeps into the narrative. In fact, few of the friends Leigh Fermor mentions survived World War II. "Every part of Europe I had crossed so far was to be torn and shattered by war," he sadly explains to his readers, "and when war broke out, all these friends vanished into darkness."

As in his earlier works, Leigh Fermor mixes history with description and takes delight in details. He responds with equal sensitivity to the richness and variety of human life and the beauty of the landscape. For Phoebe-Lou Adams, whose review of the book appeared in *The Atlantic Monthly* (March 1987), *Between the Woods and the Water* "is just as charming as its predecessor, for young Mr. Fermor was observant, well informed, discreetly inquisitive, sympathetic, and ready for any action that came up, while the older Mr. Fermor adds to the tale worldly experience and a wryly humorous view of his juvenile self." There were still some reviewers, however, who felt his writing lacked restraint in the description and information it provided.

In 1987 Leigh Fermor wrote "Observations on a Marine Vulcan," a tribute to Lawrence Durrell, whom he first met during World War II in Cairo and later encountered in Rhodes. The following year Leigh Fermor received the Municipality of Athens Gold Medal of Honour.

Three Letters from the Andes was published in 1991, the same year Leigh Fermor received an honorary doctorate in literature from the University of Kent. The book describes a 1971 journey he took with five friends. As the group traveled from Lima into increasingly remote parts of Peru, Leigh Fermor chronicled his experiences in a series of letters to his wife in Greece. These letters, somewhat revised, are the basis for the book. The lively epistolary form creates a sense of intimacy. Lacking Leigh Fermor's characteristic digressions, asides, and footnotes, *Three Letters from the Andes* is perhaps the most linear of his narratives. It is a slim work, lacking the development and the attention to minute detail that a reader expects from him. While reviews for the book were generally favorable, Charles Solomon pointed out in the 11 July 1993 issue of the *Los Angeles Times* that the gear these upper-class British adventurers took with them included Charvet pajamas and fourteen bottles of airport whiskey. Solomon also criticized the "droll, impractical tone that suggests the Pickwickians at Machu Picchu."

While Leigh Fermor reveled in the beauties of the Andean landscape, the Inca ruins, and the Spanish baroque churches, for him the high point of the journey was crossing a glacier for the first time. Reaching a height of just over fifteen thousand feet, Leigh Fermor discovered "an undulating, brilliantly sparkling" stark white wilderness–empty, uninterrupted stretches of snow and ice that were strangely beautiful. A novice climber, Leigh Fermor described reaching the peak of the glacier as "a moment of great euphoria, and . . . near intoxication. . . ." He also recounted the joys and rigors of camp life. Although they had some creature comforts, such as whiskey, the expedition team washed in cold streams and huddled in tents against the cold, snow, hail, and wind. Leigh Fermor found himself "Lord of the Primus," tending to the lighting and cleaning of the stove and the brewing of the tea. After his adventures in the high Andes exploring some of the least known and remotest parts of the region, he was saddened to find himself "down to earth," enduring local hotels without hot water (and, at times, without running water) and badly boiled eggs for breakfast. This book includes fewer memorable encounters with people than do most of his previous works, and, except for occasional vivid evocations of nature, it does not quite reach the breadth and depth of Leigh Fermor's previous works.

In 1992 Leigh Fermor published "A Clean Sheet for Paeonia," an article in which he defended Greece against charges of "bullying" the former Yugoslav Republic of Macedonia. In the same year he received the Prix Jacques Audiberti, Ville d'Antibes, and he contributed a foreword to a new edition of Sacheverell Sitwell's *Roumanian Journey* (first published in 1938). In 1993 Leigh Fermor received an honorary doctorate from the American College of Greece.

A fellow of the Royal Geographical Society and of the Royal Society of Literature, Leigh Fermor is also a patron of the Friends of Mount Athos, a visiting member of the Athens Academy. He and his wife, Joan, still live in Mani.

Mainland Greece and its islands, Romania and other countries of central Europe, the islands of the Caribbean, and the Andes Mountains have all inspired Leigh Fermor's romantic imagination. His extraordinary contribution to twentieth-century travel literature can only be enhanced by the long-awaited publication of the final volume of his travels in the 1930s from Holland to Constantinople.

Interviews:

Nicholas Shakespeare, "Walking Back to Happiness," *Times* (London), 16 October 1986, p. 17;

R. W. Apple Jr., "Skeletons at the Feast," *New York Times Book Review,* 8 February 1987, p. 31.

References:

Maurice Cardiff, *Friends Abroad: Memories of Lawrence Durrell, Freya Stark, Patrick Leigh-Fermor, Peggy Guggenheim and Others* (New York: St. Martin's Press, 1997);

Mark Cocker, *Loneliness and Time: British Travel Writing in the Twentieth Century* (London: Secker & Warburg, 1994), pp. 195–202;

Xan Fielding, *Hide and Seek: The Story of a War-time Agent* (London: Secker & Warburg, 1954);

Greg Keeton, "They Kidnapped a General," *Reader's Digest,* 63 (September 1953): 121–125;

Verlyn Klinkenborg, "A Time of Gifts," *New Republic,* 196 (19 January 1987): 36–38;

W. Stanley Moss, *Ill Met by Moonlight* (London: Harrap, 1950);

David Smiley, *Albanian Assignment* (London: Chatto & Windus, 1984);

Alan Watts, *In My Own Way: An Autobiography 1915–1965* (New York: Random House, 1972);

Paul West, *The Modern Novel,* 2 volumes (London: Hutchinson University Library, 1963), I: 147;

Simon Winchester, Epilogue to *The Violins of Saint-Jacques* (Oxford: Oxford Univerity Press, 1985).

Graham Greene

(2 October 1904 – 3 April 1991)

John Boening
University of Toledo

See also the Greene entries in *DLB 13: British Dramatists Since World War II; DLB 15: British Novelists, 1930–1959; DLB 77: British Mystery Writers, 1920–1939; DLB 100: Modern British Essayists: Second Series; DLB 162: British Short-Fiction Writers, 1915–1945; DLB Yearbook: 1985; DLB Yearbook: 1991;* and *DLB 201: Twentieth-Century British Book Collectors and Bibliographers.*

BOOKS: *Babbling April* (Oxford: Blackwell, 1925);

The Man Within (London: Heinemann, 1929; Garden City, N.Y.: Doubleday, Doran, 1929);

The Name of Action (London: Heinemann, 1930; Garden City, N.Y.: Doubleday, Doran, 1931);

Rumour at Nightfall (London: Heinemann, 1931; Garden City, N.Y.: Doubleday, Doran, 1932);

Stamboul Train (London: Heinemann, 1932); republished as *Orient Express* (Garden City, N.Y.: Doubleday, Doran, 1933);

It's a Battlefield (London: Heinemann, 1934; Garden City, N.Y.: Doubleday, Doran, 1934; revised edition, London & Toronto: Heinemann, 1948);

England Made Me: A Novel (London & Toronto: Heinemann, 1935; Garden City, N.Y.: Doubleday, Doran, 1935); republished as *The Shipwrecked* (New York: Viking, 1953);

The Bear Fell Free (London: Grayson & Grayson, 1935);

The Basement Room, and Other Stories (London: Cresset, 1935);

Journey Without Maps (London & Toronto: Heinemann, 1936; Garden City, N.Y.: Doubleday, Doran, 1936);

A Gun for Sale: An Entertainment (London & Toronto: Heinemann, 1936); republished as *This Gun for Hire* (Garden City, N.Y.: Doubleday, Doran, 1936);

Brighton Rock: An Entertainment (New York: Viking, 1938); republished as *Brighton Rock: A Novel* (London & Toronto: Heinemann, 1938);

The Lawless Roads: A Mexican Journey (London, New York & Toronto: Longmans, Green, 1939); republished as *Another Mexico* (New York: Viking, 1939);

Graham Greene in 1934

The Confidential Agent: An Entertainment (London & Toronto: Heinemann, 1939; New York: Viking, 1939);

The Power and the Glory (London & Toronto: Heinemann, 1940); published simultaneously as *The Labyrinthine Ways* (New York: Viking, 1940); republished as *The Power and the Glory* (New York: Viking, 1946);

British Dramatists, The British People in Pictures series (London: Collins, 1942);

The Ministry of Fear: An Entertainment (London & Toronto: Heinemann, 1943; New York: Viking, 1943);

The Little Train, anonymous, with Dorothy Craigie (London: Eyre & Spottiswoode, 1946; as Greene, New York: Lothrop, Lee & Shepard, 1958);

Nineteen Stories (London & Toronto: Heinemann, 1947; New York: Viking, 1949); revised and enlarged as *Twenty-One Stories* (London, Melbourne & Toronto: Heinemann, 1954); republished as *21 Stories* (New York: Viking, 1962);

The Heart of the Matter (Melbourne, London & Toronto: Heinemann, 1948; New York: Viking, 1948);

Why Do I Write? An Exchange of Views between Elizabeth Bowen, Graham Greene, & V. S. Pritchett, by Greene, Elizabeth Bowen, and V. S. Pritchett (London: Marshall, 1948);

The Third Man and The Fallen Idol (Melbourne, London & Toronto: Heinemann, 1950); abridged as *The Third Man* (New York: Viking, 1950);

The Little Fire Engine, by Greene and Craigie (London: Parrish, 1950); republished as *The Little Red Fire Engine* (New York: Lothrop, Lee & Shepard, 1953);

The Lost Childhood, and Other Essays (London: Eyre & Spottiswoode, 1951; New York: Viking, 1952);

The End of the Affair (Melbourne, London & Toronto: Heinemann, 1951; New York: Viking, 1951);

The Little Horse Bus, by Greene and Craigie (Norwich, U.K.: Jarrold / London: Parrish, 1952; New York: Lothrop, Lee & Shepard, 1954);

The Living Room: A Play in Two Acts (Melbourne, London & Toronto: Heinemann, 1953; New York: Viking, 1954);

The Little Steamroller: A Story of Adventure, Mystery and Detection, by Greene and Craigie (London: Parrish, 1953; New York: Lothrop, Lee & Shepard, 1955);

Graham Greene: Essais Catholiques, translated into French by Marcelle Sibon (Paris: Editions du Seuil, 1953);

Loser Takes All (Melbourne, London & Toronto: Heinemann, 1955; New York: Viking, 1957);

The Quiet American (Melbourne, London & Toronto: Heinemann, 1955; New York: Viking, 1956);

The Potting Shed: A Play in Three Acts (New York: Viking, 1957; revised edition, London, Melbourne & Toronto: Heinemann, 1958);

Our Man in Havana: An Entertainment (London, Melbourne & Toronto: Heinemann, 1958; New York: Viking, 1958);

The Complaisant Lover: A Comedy (London, Melbourne & Toronto: Heinemann, 1959; New York: Viking, 1961);

A Visit to Morin (London, Melbourne & Toronto: Heinemann, 1960);

A Burnt-Out Case (London, Melbourne & Toronto: Heinemann, 1961; New York: Viking, 1961);

In Search of a Character: Two African Journals (London: Bodley Head, 1961; New York: Viking, 1962);

Introductions to Three Novels (Stockholm: Norstedt, 1962);

A Sense of Reality (London: Bodley Head, 1963; New York: Viking, 1963);

The Revenge: An Autobiographical Fragment (Barnet, U.K.: Privately printed, 1963);

Carving a Statue: A Play (London: Bodley Head, 1964);

The Comedians (London: Bodley Head, 1966; New York: Viking, 1966);

May We Borrow Your Husband? And Other Comedies of the Sexual Life (London, Sydney & Toronto: Bodley Head, 1967; New York: Viking, 1967);

The Third Man: A Film, by Greene and Carol Reed, Modern Film Scripts, no. 13 (London: Lorrimer, 1968; New York: Simon & Schuster, 1969);

Graham Greene: Collected Essays (London, Sydney & Toronto: Bodley Head, 1969; New York: Viking, 1969);

Travels With My Aunt: A Novel (London, Sydney & Toronto: Bodley Head, 1969; New York: Viking, 1970);

A Sort of Life (London, Sydney & Toronto: Bodley Head, 1971; New York: Simon & Schuster, 1971);

Graham Greene: Collected Stories (London: Bodley Head / Heinemann, 1972; New York: Viking, 1973);

The Pleasure-Dome: The Collected Film Criticism 1935–40, edited by John Russell Taylor (London: Secker & Warburg, 1972); republished as *Graham Greene on Film: Collected Film Criticism 1935–1940* (New York: Simon & Schuster, 1972);

The Virtue of Disloyalty (London: Bodley Head, 1972);

The Honorary Consul (London, Sydney & Toronto: Bodley Head, 1973; New York: Simon & Schuster, 1973);

Lord Rochester's Monkey: Being the Life of John Wilmot, Second Earl of Rochester (London, Sydney & Toronto: Bodley Head, 1974; New York: Viking, 1974);

The Return of A. J. Raffles: An Edwardian Comedy in Three Acts Based Somewhat Loosely on E. W. Hornung's Characters in "The Amateur Cracksman" (London, Sydney & Toronto: Bodley Head, 1975; New York: Simon & Schuster, 1976);

The Human Factor (London, Sydney & Toronto: Bodley Head, 1978; New York: Simon & Schuster, 1978);

Doctor Fischer of Geneva, or the Bomb Party (London: Bodley Head, 1980; New York: Simon & Schuster, 1980);

How Father Quixote Became a Monsignor (Los Angeles: Sylvester & Orphanos, 1980);

Ways of Escape (London: Bodley Head, 1980; New York: Simon & Schuster, 1981);

The Great Jowett (London: Bodley Head, 1981);

Monsignor Quixote (Toronto: Lester & Orpen Dennys, 1982; London: Bodley Head, 1982; New York: Simon & Schuster, 1982);

J' Accuse: The Dark Side of Nice (London: Bodley Head, 1982);

A Quick Look Behind: Footnotes to an Autobiography (Los Angeles: Sylvester & Orphanos, 1983);

Yes and No; and, For Whom the Bell Chimes (London: Bodley Head, 1983);

Getting to Know the General: The Story of an Involvement (London: Bodley Head, 1984; New York: Simon & Schuster, 1984);

The Monster of Capri (Helsinki: Eurographica, 1985);

The Tenth Man (London: Bodley Head/Anthony Blond, 1985; New York: Simon & Schuster, 1985);

The Captain and the Enemy (London: Reinhardt, 1988; New York: Viking, 1988);

Reflections on Travels with My Aunt (New York: Firsts & Company, 1989);

Why the Epigraph? (London: Nonesuch, 1989);

Yours, Etc.: Letters to the Press, 1945–1989, edited by Christopher Hawtree (London: Reinhardt, 1989; New York: Viking, 1989);

A Weed Among the Flowers, afterword by Stephen Spender (Los Angeles: Sylvester & Orphanos, 1990);

The Last Word and Other Stories (Toronto: Lester & Orpen Dennys, 1990; London: Reinhardt, 1990; New York: Viking, 1991);

Reflections, edited, with an introduction, by Judith Adamson (London: Reinhardt / New York: Viking, 1990);

A World of My Own: A Dream Diary, edited by Yvonne Cloetta (London: Reinhardt / New York: Viking, 1992).

Editions and Collections: Uniform Edition, 14 volumes (London: Heinemann, 1947–1960);

Three by Greene (New York: Viking, 1952)–comprises *This Gun for Hire; The Confidential Agent; The Ministry of Fear;*

Three Plays (London: Mercury, 1961)–comprises *The Living Room; The Potting Shed; The Complaisant Lover;*

The Travel Books (London: Heinemann, 1963)–comprises *Journey Without Maps; The Lawless Road;*

Graham Greene: The Collected Edition, 22 volumes, introductions by Greene (London: Heinemann/Bodley Head, 1970–1982);

Triple Pursuit: A Graham Greene Omnibus (New York: Viking, 1971)–comprises *This Gun For Hire; The Third Man; Our Man in Havana;*

The Portable Graham Greene, edited by Philip Stratford (New York: Viking, 1973; Harmondsworth, U.K.: Penguin, 1977; revised edition, New York & London: Penguin, 1994);

Shades of Greene: The Televised Stories of Graham Greene (London: Bodley Head/Heinemann, 1975; New York: Penguin, 1977);

Author's Choice: Four Novels by Graham Greene (Harmondsworth, U.K.: Penguin, 1985)–comprises *The Power and the Glory; The Quiet American; Travels with My Aunt; The Honorary Consul;*

The Collected Plays of Graham Greene (Harmondsworth, U.K.: Penguin, 1985)–comprises *The Living Room; The Potting Shed; The Complaisant Lover; Carving a Statue; The Return of A. J. Raffles; The Great Jowett; Yes and No; For Whom the Bell Chimes;*

Fragments of Autobiography (London: Penguin, 1991)–comprises *A Sort of Life* and *Ways of Escape;*

The Graham Greene Film Reader: Mornings in the Dark, edited by David Parkinson (Manchester, U.K.: Carcanet, 1993).

PLAY PRODUCTIONS: *The Living Room,* London, Wyndham's Theatre, 16 April 1953;

The Potting Shed, New York, Bijou Theatre, 29 January 1957; London, Globe Theatre, 5 February 1958;

The Complaisant Lover: A Comedy, London, Globe Theatre, 18 June 1959; New York, Ethel Barrymore Theatre, 1 November 1961;

Carving a Statue, London, Haymarket Theatre, 17 September 1964; New York, Gramercy Arts Theatre, 30 April 1968;

The Return of A. J. Raffles, London, Aldwych Theatre, 4 December 1975;

Yes and No and *For Whom the Bell Chimes,* Leicester, Haymarket Studio, 20 March 1980.

MOTION PICTURES: *Twenty-One Days,* screenplay adapted by Greene and Basil Dean from John Galsworthy's short story "The First and the Last," Denham, 1937; rereleased as *21 Days Together,* Columbia, 1940; rereleased as *The First and the Last,* 1940;

The Future's in the Air, commentary written by Greene, Strand Film Unit, 1937;

The Green Cockatoo, screenplay by Greene, Edward O. Berkman and Arthur Wimperis, New World, 1940;

The New Britain, commentary written by Greene, Strand Film Unit, 1940;

Brighton Rock, screenplay by Greene and Terence Rattigan, Associated British Pictures, 1946; rereleased as *Young Scarface,* Mayer-Kingsley, 1952;

The Fallen Idol, adaptation by Greene, from his "The Basement Room," London Films, 1948; rereleased as *The Lost Illusion,* Selznick International, 1949;

The Third Man, screenplay by Greene, London Films, 1949; rereleased, Selznick International, 1950;

The Stranger's Hand, produced by Greene, Peter Moore, and John Stafford, London Films, 1954; rereleased, Distributors Corporation of America, 1955;

Loser Takes All, screenplay by Greene, IFP, 1956; rereleased, Distributors Corporation of America, 1957;

Saint Joan, screenplay adapted by Greene from George Bernard Shaw's play, Wheel Productions, 1957;

Our Man in Havana, screenplay by Greene, Columbia, 1960;

The Comedians, screenplay by Greene, M-G-M, 1967.

OTHER: *The Old School: Essays by Divers Hands,* edited by Greene (London: Cape, 1934);

Henry James, *The Portrait of a Lady,* introduction by Greene, The World's Classics, no. 509 (Oxford: Oxford University Press, 1947);

Herbert Read, *The Green Child,* introduction by Greene, Century Library, no. 4 (London: Eyre & Spottiswoode, 1947);

H. H. Munro, *The Best of Saki,* introduction by Greene (London: John Lane, 1950; New York: Viking, 1961);

John Gerard, *John Gerard: The Autobiography of an Elizabethan,* introduction by Greene, translated from the Latin by Philip Caraman (London & New York: Longmans, Green, 1951);

R. K. Narayan, *The Financial Expert: A Novel,* introduction by Greene (London: Methuen, 1952);

The Spy's Bedside Book: An Anthology, edited by Greene and Hugh Greene (London: Hart-Davis, 1957; New York: Carrol & Graf, 1985);

Marjorie Bowen, *The Viper of Milan: A Romance of Lombardy,* introductory note by Greene (London: Bodley Head, 1960);

Frederick Franck, *African Sketchbook,* preface by Greene (New York: Holt, Rinehart & Winston, 1961; London: Peter Davies, 1962);

Ford Madox Ford, *The Bodley Head Ford Madox Ford,* volumes 1–4, edited by Greene, with introductions in volumes 1 and 3 by Greene (London: Bodley Head, 1962–1963);

Eric Osborne, ed., *Victorian Detective Fiction: A Catalogue of the Collection Made by Dorothy Glover & Graham Greene. Bibliographically Arranged by Eric Osborne and Introduced by John Carter with a Preface by Graham Greene,* preface by Greene (London: Sydney & Toronto: Bodley Head, 1966);

Kim Philby, *My Silent War,* introduction by Greene (London: MacGibbon & Kee, 1968);

Bernard Diederich and Al Burt, *Papa Doc: Haiti and Its Dictator,* foreword by Greene (London: Bodley Head, 1969);

David Low, *With All Faults,* introduction by Greene (Tehran: Amate Press, 1973);

Arthur Conan Doyle, *The Sign of Four,* introduction by Greene (London: Murray/Cape, 1974; Garden City, N.Y.: Doubleday, 1977);

An Impossible Woman: The Memories of Dottoressa Moor of Capri, edited, with an epilogue, by Greene (London, Sydney & Toronto: Bodley Head, 1975; New York: Viking, 1976);

Victorian Villainies, edited by Greene and Hugh Greene (Harmondsworth, U.K. & New York: Viking Penguin, 1984);

Paul Hogarth, *Graham Greene Country Visited by Paul Hogarth,* foreword and commentary by Greene (London: Pavilion, 1986);

John Medcalf, *Letters from Nicaragua,* foreword by Greene (London: CIIR, 1988);

Dermot Keogh, *Church and Politics in Latin America,* foreword by Greene (New York: St. Martin's Press, 1990).

Graham Greene's career spanned a global stage, with his works set in locales as disparate as Hanoi and Havana, Liberia and Lithuania, Mexico and Malaya. Greene also deliberately sought out hazardous and physically demanding journeys. In *Journey Without Maps* (1936), his first and arguably his finest travel book, Greene writes, "There are times . . . when one is willing to suffer some discomfort for the chance of finding–there are a thousand names for it, King Solomon's Mines, the 'heart of darkness' if one is romantically inclined, or more simply, as Herr [Kurt] Heuser puts it in his African novel, *The Inner Journey,* one's place in time. . . ." Paul Fussell, in *Abroad: English Literary Traveling Between the Wars* (1980), calls this "real" travel, as opposed to tourism, and connects it to its etymology of *travail:* "travel is work–the traveler is a student of what he sees." Greene's travel writings are usually thought of as consisting principally of *Journey Without Maps,* his account of a West African safari undertaken in the company of his cousin Barbara Greene in 1935, and *The Lawless Roads: A Mexican Journey* (or *Another Mexico,* its U.S. title, 1939), the story of his travels through postrevolutionary Mexico. The other Greene book commonly included among his travel writings is *In Search of a Character: Two African Journals* (1961), which makes available in published form two of Greene's notebooks, one kept on a convoy to Sierra Leone in 1941 during his wartime service, the second a record of his stay in the Congo in 1959. But any enumeration of Greene's travel writings should also include mention of the dozens of sketches and articles on foreign travels he contributed to various periodicals throughout his career, from his reports on visits to Ireland and the occupied Ruhr in the early 1920s to his sketch of a trip to China in the 1980s (*A Weed Among the Flowers,* 1990). It should

Greene and his cousin Barbara Greene in 1935, on board the David Livingstone *en route to Africa on the trip Greene described in* Journey Without Maps *(1936)*

also include *Getting to Know the General: The Story of an Involvement* (1984), Greene's account of a series of visits to Panama in the 1970s and 1980s at the invitation of Panamanian strongman Omar Torrijos. As Patrick Marnham pointed out in his review in *The Spectator* (29 September 1984), this book "is not simply about Panama, it is about Central America."

Henry Graham Greene was born 2 October 1904 at Berkhamstead, England, the son of Charles Henry Greene and Marion Raymond Greene. He came from a large and worldly family (Graham's great-grandfather Benjamin Greene owned a sugar plantation on St. Kitts). From 1915 to 1921 he attended Berkhamstead School, where his father was headmaster. His memory of his early school experience was to become, as it was for many of his generation, a powerful admixture of loathing and nostalgia. For Greene, because of his father's position, it was especially fraught with ambivalent feelings. Throughout Greene's life these feelings were never far below the surface, and they had a powerful effect on his writing, including his travel writing. It was at school that his awareness of borders, of frontiers, was sharpened. In the opening passages of *The Lawless Roads* Greene recalls his double life as the headmaster's son, symbolized by a green baize door in a hallway by his father's study. The door represented the frontier between one world, that of the family, in which his father was just his father, and another, that of school: "One was an inhabitant of both countries: on Saturday and Sunday afternoons of one side of the baize door, the rest of the week of the other. How can life on a border be other than restless? You are pulled by different ties of hate and love." For the rest of his life, as Philip Stratford writes in his introduction to *The Portable Graham Greene* (1973), where frontiers "didn't exist, he invented them; where they did, he sought out some of the least accessible of them; once across, he hearkened back to the place he left."

Greene continued his education at Oxford, where his contemporaries and friends included Louis MacNeice, Peter Quennell, W. H. Auden, C. Day Lewis, and Edmund Blunden, and where he received a B. A. from Balliol College, in 1925. His restlessness and sense of adventure, however, had already taken hold. While still a student, he made a long walking trip in Ireland. Judith Adamson, in her introduction to Greene's *Reflections* (1990), writes that then, as later, "he travelled light and apparently without fear, absorbing the myriad details from which he would re-create the essence of contemporary life. June 1923 was a precarious time for an Englishman to walk from Dublin to Waterford," an especially dangerous time, as Greene's biographer Norman Sherry notes, for "meddling Englishmen" to be questioning strangers about the strength of Republican feeling. He published an account of part of the trip, "Impressions of Dublin," in the *Weekly Westminster Gazette* (25 August 1923).

In 1924 Greene, together with his Oxford friend Claud Cockburn and his cousin "Tooter" Greene, traveled to the troubled Ruhr area of Germany, then under French occupation. Although Greene could not speak German, he persuaded Count von Bernstorff of the German Embassy that if the German secret service financed the trip, he would write articles that would counteract pro-French sentiment in Oxford. The trip did result in articles for the *Oxford Chronicle* ("In the Occupied Area," 9 May 1924) and *Oxford Outlook* ("The French Peace," June 1924), both of which were later collected, as was the article on Dublin, in Greene's *Reflections.* Greene also set his poorly received early novel, *The Name of Action* (1930), in the Ruhr. According to Adamson, "the seeds of Greene's double-life as a novelist-reporter are in these early journeys," and they set the tone for Greene's itinerant career.

At Oxford, Greene also met Vivien Dayrell-Browning, a Roman Catholic whom he married 15 October 1927 (after converting to Catholicism the year

Native bearers crossing a river in Liberia during Greene's trek into the interior of Africa, 1935

before). His Catholicism would become one of the dominant forces in his life and work. Graham and Vivien Greene had a daughter, Lucy Caroline, born 28 December 1933, and a son, Francis, born 13 September 1936. From 1926 to 1930 Greene worked as a journalist and editor at *The Times* (London). In 1929 he turned to writing fiction and in that year published the novel *The Man Within,* following it up in the 1930s with other novels: *Rumour at Nightfall* (1931); *Stamboul Train* (1932), published in the U.S. as *Orient Express* (1933); *It's a Battlefield* (1934); *England Made Me: A Novel* (1935); *A Gun for Sale: An Entertainment* (1936), published in the U.S. as *This Gun for Hire;* and *The Confidential Agent: An Entertainment* (1939), as well as several short stories.

The adventure from which Greene's first travel book, *Journey Without Maps,* was to emerge began 4 January 1935, when he left for Liberia with his twenty-three-year-old cousin Barbara Greene. He had a book in mind from the outset, and he chose his destination because Liberia remained one of the few unmapped places on the African continent, a part of the world to which his imagination had already been drawn. Greene had read a government Blue Book that described the primitive conditions to be found in that country, including scores of dread diseases and rampant political anarchy, especially in the interior, compared to which "the little injustices of Kenya became shoddy and suburban."

Significantly, Greene wrote in *Journey Without Maps* that "there seemed to be a seediness about the place you couldn't get to the same extent elsewhere, and seediness has a very deep appeal. . . . It seems to satisfy, temporarily, the sense of nostalgia for something lost; it seems to represent a stage further back." He rejected South Africa, Kenya, and Rhodesia as simply British colonial institutions in a new setting: for Greene, "a quality of darkness is needed," a look at "brutality," to see "from what we have come, to recall at which point we went astray." With such a program in mind, Greene and his cousin made landfall at Freetown, Sierra Leone, and set off into the interior, first on a short rail journey and then, having engaged bearers and guides, on foot, describing an eastward arc through part of French Guinea and the Liberian back country, emerging again at the coastal town of Grand Bassa. There they caught a ship for Monrovia, the Liberian capital, a few miles up the coast. The overland trek, as recounted in *Journey Without Maps,* took them through some of the

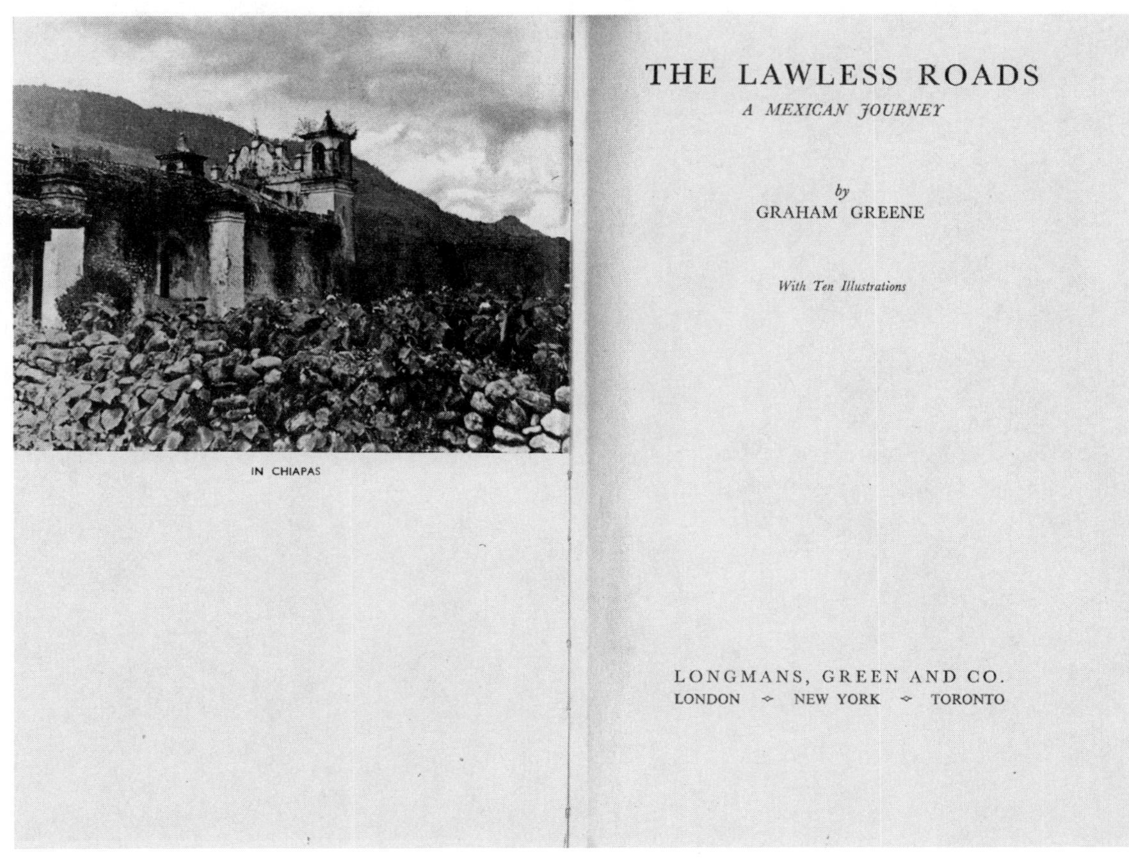

IN CHIAPAS

THE LAWLESS ROADS

A MEXICAN JOURNEY

by

GRAHAM GREENE

With Ten Illustrations

LONGMANS, GREEN AND CO.

LONDON ◇ NEW YORK ◇ TORONTO

Frontispiece photograph by Greene and title page for his book about his 1938 travels in Mexico

most desolate and mind-numbingly boring terrain on the African continent, relieved only by increasingly squalid mud villages and a constant battle with rats, dust, ants, and roaches. Graham had a particular curiosity about witchcraft and secret societies, and his account of the cult of the Bush Devil provides one of the few digressions from the seemingly endless trekking from one cluster of huts to the next. At the end of his inland journey, Greene finds Monrovian society a kind of parody of European civilization in which the corruption is merely more explicit, populated by a cast of characters which would be funny if it were not so sad. The city on the coast, however, is clearly not the Africa he wishes to emphasize. Greene made clear what he was looking for in the Liberian journey in an article, "Analysis of a Journey," published in *The Spectator* (27 September 1935) upon his return: "The choice of a journey often deserves a writer's attention quite as much as the journey itself. . . . When X chose West Africa, and in West Africa Liberia, for the object of his journey, it interested me to try to trace in his sub-conscious mind the reason of his choice." As was Joseph Conrad–whose novel *Heart of Darkness* (1902) is mentioned three times in the book–Greene is drawn to the continent's interior in the hope of discovering something about himself. As he puts it in the passage from which the book's title is taken, "in Africa one couldn't avoid the supernatural. The method of psychoanalysis is to bring the patient back to the idea which he is repressing: a long journey backwards without maps, catching a clue here and a clue there, as I caught the names of villages from this man and that, until one has to face the general idea, the pain or the memory."

Once back in England, Greene faced the formidable problem of producing a readable travel book–he had, after all, accepted a publisher's advance–about a country that, as Meyers puts it, "had perhaps the least interesting indigenous culture in West Africa." Many years later, in *Ways of Escape* (1980), the second installment of his memoirs, Greene compared the account he had written of the Liberian journey with that published by his cousin Barbara, who had–unknown to him–also been keeping a diary. Barbara Greene's account first appeared as *Land Benighted* in 1938 and was republished, with an introduction by Paul Theroux, as *Too Late to Turn Back: Barbara and Graham Greene in Liberia* (1981). In the course of this comparison, Greene writes:

> It had seemed simple, before I set out, to write a travel book, but when I returned and was faced with my material I had a moment of despair and wished to abandon the project. A diary written in pencil with increasing fatigue and running to less than eighty quarto pages of a loose-leaf notebook . . . and memories, memories chiefly of rats, of frustration, and of deeper boredom on the long forest trek than I had ever experienced before–how was I, out of all this, to make a book?

Whatever the book would be, Greene writes, it

> could not be written in the manner of a European tour: there was no architecture to describe, no famous statuary . . . if this was an adventure, it was only a subjective adventure, three months of virtual silence, of "being out of touch." This thought gave me a clue to the form I needed. The account of a journey–a slow, footsore journey into an interior literally unknown–was only of interest if it paralleled another journey. It would lose the triviality of a personal travel diary only if it became more completely personal. It is a disadvantage to have an "I" who is not a fictional figure, and the only way to deal with "I" was to make him an abstraction.

In this way, Greene justifies his erasure of his cousin, who is mentioned only three or four times in passing in *Journey Without Maps:* "To all intents I eliminated my companion of the journey and supported the uneventful record with memories, dreams, word associations: if the book in one sense became more personal, the journey become more general."

Although perhaps unjust to Barbara Greene (who did, after all, nurse Graham back to health when he fell seriously ill on the trek), Greene's transformation made *Journey Without Maps* one of the landmarks of British travel literature. According to Fussell, the book helped to define a kind of travel writing that came into its own in the twentieth century and that has, for all intents and purposes, disappeared with the advent of regular air routes and the rise of mass tourism. Samuel Hynes has written, in *The Auden Generation: Literature and Politics in England in the 1930's* (1976), that "the travel book, traditionally a mode of reportage that depends for its principal interest on the exotic nature of its literal content," was transformed in the 1930s, principally by Greene, W. H. Auden, Christopher Isherwood, and Louis MacNiece, into a record of "interior journeys and parables of their times, making landscape and incident–the factual materials of *reportage*–do the work of symbol and myth–the materials of *fable*." And since the journey, as Fussell notes, is "the most insistent of 'thirties metaphors, . . . one might say that the travel books simply act out, in the real world, the basic trope of the generation." Contemporary reviewers of *Journey Without Maps* were hardly oblivious to this: Guy Hunter wrote in the *London Mercury* (June 1936), "In the midst of the African forest we are made aware not of Sir James Frazier's study of comparative religion, but of those famous notes to *The Waste Land,* of 'the seediness of civilization.'"

If the book resulting from Greene's Liberian travels is often held up as one of the high points of "literary traveling," the results of his journey to Mexico in 1938 are nonetheless more famous: they include not only *The Lawless Roads* in 1939 but also, in March of the following year, *The Power and the Glory,* simultaneously published in New York as *The Labyrinthine Ways,* which critics have called Greene's finest novel. Unlike his trip to Liberia, which was a destination of his own choosing, Greene traveled to Mexico with a contract from his British publishers, Heinemann, to make notes for a book on the suppression of the Catholic Church by the Mexican government. The trip lasted six weeks, following an itinerary that began at Laredo on the U.S. border and took him south on what became a circular journey through Monterrey, San Luis Potosí, Mexico City, to the gulf coast at Vera Cruz, then by boat to landfall at Frontera and an arduous overland journey through the remote areas of Tabasco and Chiapas (in the far south, where Mexico borders Guatemala), then by air from Tuxtla to Oaxaca and back to Mexico City, visiting the tourist area of Puebla, Taxco, and Cuernevaca before boarding a German steamer at Vera Cruz for the return to Europe.

Although a handful of years–and the novel *Brighton Rock: An Entertainment* (1938)–had come between Greene's African and Mexican journeys, the latter seems in many ways to have picked up where the earlier itinerary had left off. Certainly many of the same motifs recur: scenes of squalor, disease, and poverty relieved occasionally by arresting scenery or pockets of human privilege, usually corrupt. In Mexico, as in Africa, Greene fights bouts of illness and exhaustion (depression, really), and, as in Africa, almost everything he sees and everyone he encounters recalls for him some element of his past, his childhood, or his own psyche. Even more than in Africa, though, Greene is here obsessed with the notion of the border and the frontier, which he explicitly connects to the memory of his father's study. And whereas Greene's preconceptions of Africa were met by what he found there (he made certain of that in his choice of landfall), the physical reality of Mexico presented him with a stark contrast to the European image of the country as a colorful, exotic, even romantic destination. Greene finds the cities and countryside nearly uniformly "dreary," "grim," or simply "ugly." The loathing for Mexico that Greene accumulates in the course of his travels–by the end of

Yajalon in Northern Chiapas; photograph by Greene for The Lawless Roads (1939)

The Lawless Roads he admits to an almost pathological hatred of the place–was not without precedent. Jeffrey Meyers, in his essay "Greene's Travel Books"(1990), has pointed out that *The Lawless Roads* and *The Power and the Glory* "belong to a distinguished but consistently negative tradition of English books on Mexico," ranging from D. H. Lawrence's *The Plumed Serpent* (1926) to Malcolm Lowry's *Under the Volcano* (1947). The epigraph of *The Lawless Roads,* however, suggests its real subject: Greene's obsession with the Fall and the fact of evil. Quoting Cardinal Newman, it reads, in part "either there is no Creator, or this living society of men is in a true sense discarded from his presence. . . . if there be a God, *since* there is a God, the human race is implicated in some terrible aboriginal calamity." To Greene, Mexico becomes the emblem of this abandonment.

Despite its merits as a travelogue, *The Lawless Roads* is seriously marred by Greene's heavy-handed and tiresome propagandizing. As Meyers notes, "Greene has the convert's zealous outrage. And his didactic–and curiously insular–book . . . reeks of propaganda and piety." Greene's claim that persecution under the Cárdenas government was extreme, Meyers says, is contradicted "by the fact that Greene traveled openly as a Catholic and as a foreigner investigating the 'war for the soul of the Indian.'" This view of *The Lawless Roads* is shared by Paul Fussell, who contrasts it to *Journey Without Maps:* "Just three years before, in West Africa, Greene had looked, accepted, and learned. Now he is angry and truculent. . . ." Fussell continues,

> His power of noticing nasty details is undiminished, but now it is enlisted in the service of a crude "point," and anomalies like the cock-fights and the "dead fleas dressed up as little people inside walnuts" as well as the constant "heat and flies, heat and flies," are deployed to dramatize the "useless cruelty" and pervasive anarchy [of Mexico].

Its flaws notwithstanding, *The Lawless Roads* laid the groundwork for *The Power and the Glory,* in which the Mexican setting becomes a substantive part of a powerful and nuanced story, though in a world now leavened with the possibility of redemption. Perhaps this transformation owes something to the fact that, as Gwen Boardman contends, by 1940 Greene had "gained the necessary artistic distance" between the Mexico he had painted so simplistically and its fictional re-emergence as the land of the hunted "whiskey priest." Though the lasting critical success of *The Power and the Glory* has assured that there will always be an interest in *The Lawless Roads,* it has also assured that the earlier book would suffer by unfair comparison.

The Lawless Roads was the last full-scale, book-length travel narrative Greene would write, but he continued throughout his life to publish dispatches from one part of the world or another, many of them later collected in *Reflections.* During World War II, Greene served as an intelligence officer in Sierra Leone in West Africa from 1941 to 1943. After the war he worked as an editor and director of the publishing house of Eyre and Spottiswoode (from 1944 to 1948) and The Bodley Head (from 1958 to 1968).

In the decades following World War II, Greene also became one of the world's most celebrated literary figures. The film *The Third Man,* for which Greene wrote the screenplay, was a triumphant success, winning the Grand Prix at Cannes in 1949. He and Vivien permanently separated in 1947 after she discovered he had a mistress, the American Catherine Walston. Greene was later involved with a Swedish actress, Anita Bjork, and from 1966 until his death, with a married Frenchwoman, Yvonne Cloetta, who lived near his villa in Antibes.

In 1961 Greene published a third "travel book," though not one with a sustained narrative: *In Search of a Character: Two African Journals.* This thin volume (ninety-seven pages, including the introduction) brings together two journals not originally intended for publication: one kept on a trip Greene took to the Belgian Congo in 1959 with the conscious purpose of collecting medical background for a novel already germinating; the other kept on a wartime convoy to West Africa in 1941, solely "for my own amusement at the period of the war when life and a future seemed uncertain for all of us." The former provided the raw material for the 1961 novel *A Burnt-Out Case,* set in a leprosarium in the Congo; the latter prefigures, though it was not the basis for, *The Heart of the Matter,* Greene's 1948 novel about a British colonial officer in Sierra Leone.

In his introduction to *In Search of a Character,* Greene writes that these journals "may have some interest as an indication of the kind of raw material a novelist accumulates." In fact, each of these journals is fascinating in its own right, and the coupling of the two in a single volume only multiplies the effect. The notes taken in the Congo cover a five-week period in early 1959 and take up three-quarters of the book. They comprise a true writer's notebook, interleaving sketches of conversations, characters, and medical lore with "brilliant descriptive writing" as Maurice Richardson noted in his review in *The New Statesman* (27 October 1961). The second journal takes up a little over twenty pages in printed form and covers the progress of a freighter convoy from Liverpool and Belfast, via the Azores, to West Africa and the Cape in December of 1941. In constant danger from German U-boats, the passengers on Greene's ship volunteer to stand submarine and machine-gun watches. In this journal, as in the sea-voyage passages of *Journey Without Maps* and *The Lawless Roads,* Greene has captured a sense of what shipboard life was then like, with its tedium, its little rituals, and its enforced camaraderie.

In the 1960s and 1970s Greene's popularity continued to grow with the success of such works of fiction as *The Comedians* (1966), *Travels With My Aunt: A Novel* (1969), and *The Honorary Consul* (1973). Although he also produced two volumes of memoirs, *A Sort of Life* in 1971 and *Ways of Escape* in 1980, Greene undertook no further travel narratives as such, but he did write one extended "biography-travel book escapist yarn memoir," as J. D. Reed, the reviewer for *Time* magazine (27 October 1984), jokingly called it. Published in 1984, *Getting to Know the General,* Greene's account of his friendship with Panamanian strongman Omar Torrijos, is in many ways of a piece with *Journey Without Maps* and *The Lawless Roads,* if only because it once again takes Greene back to the borderland between privilege and squalor, idealism and cynicism he had encountered in West Africa and Mexico.

The book stemmed from an unexpected invitation, which led eventually to five trips to Central America between 1976 and 1983. By this time in his life, Greene's leftist politics and anti-Americanism had turned into an almost unqualified enthusiasm for revolutionary causes, and he went to Central America, as he later told an interviewer, Marie-Françoise Allain, because he wanted "to be near the action." From his Panamanian base he immersed himself in the politics of the region–in Nicaragua, Cuba, El Salvador, and elsewhere–even becoming, at the invitation of Torrijos, a member of the Panamanian delegation to the signing of the Canal Treaty.

In explaining why he felt a need to keep a diary of his trip to Panama, Greene writes, "For the first time in many years, since I had been oversaturated by air travel to Africa, Malaya and Vietnam, I felt again a certain sense of adventure," doubtless at least partially because of childhood reading about the Spanish Main. He saw his visits to Panama as an opportunity to write a new novel, and became as fascinated by the local color as he was by the political situation: "the Republic was to me an unknown land, and my voyage there was a voyage of discovery," he writes. Greene abandoned the novel but took long drives around the countryside in the company of a guide and chauffeur known as Chuchu, a member of Torrijos's security detail, who was in reality the Marxist poet and professor José de Jesus Martinez and may have engineered Greene's invitation to Panama. Typical of their destinations, and particularly memorable to Greene, was a "haunted house" not far from the U. S. Canal Zone but "undeniably in Panama. Nothing could be less American than the bar next door, decorated with cabalistic signs and bearing a name in Spanish meaning The Bewitched." It is in descriptions of such places that the old Graham Greene,

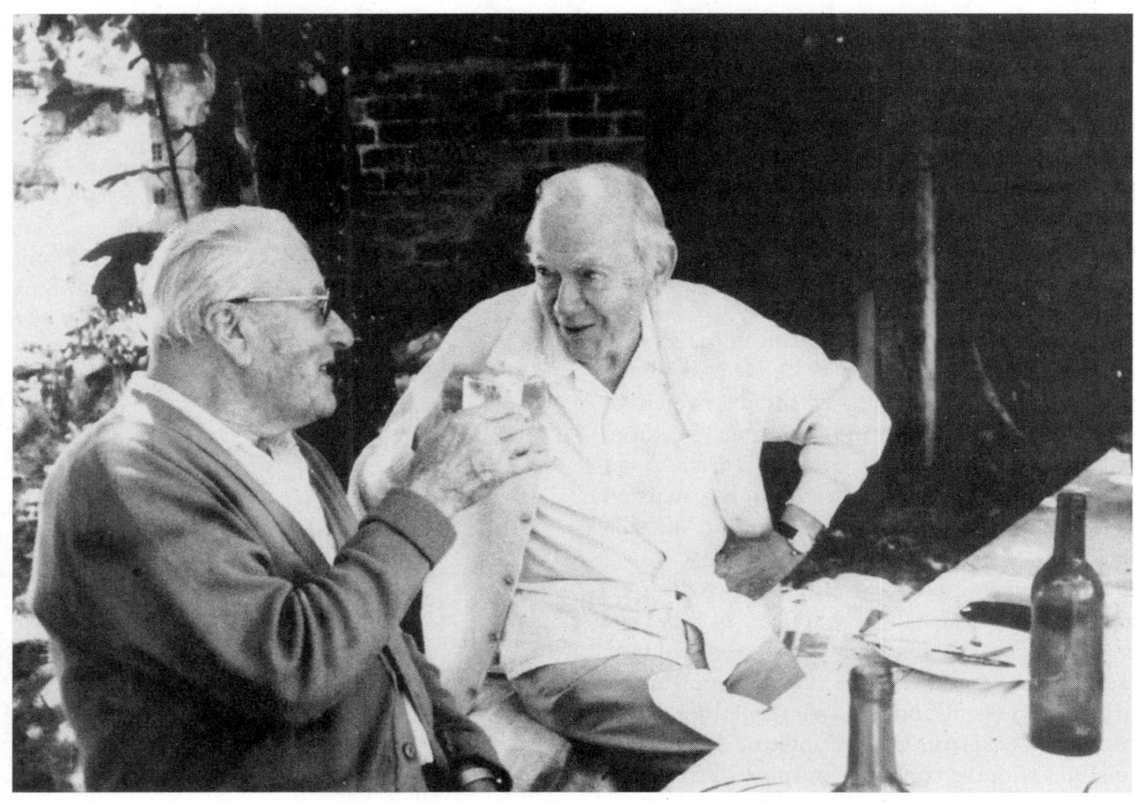

Greene and his friend Antonio Nogueiras, a wine grower in Las Regadas, Spain, 1985 (photograph by Leopoldo Duran)

with his sharp eye for local color and the picturesque, still emerges.

Reviewers were quick to point out that Greene's peregrinations, within Panama and into neighboring countries, seem disconnected and haphazard, but that is because they seem to have expected a political book rather than a travelogue. For Greene, however, the human situation in Central America was inextricable from the sense of place. Revealingly, Greene recounts how, on one of his side trips to a small jungle island off the Panamanian coast, while reflecting on his captivation by "the struggle with the United States, by the peasants barking like dogs, . . . by the drumbeats on the slums of El Chorillo," he is once again rereading Conrad's *Heart of Darkness.* In some ways *Getting to Know the General* seems an almost nostalgic attempt by Greene, in his old age, to relive and recapture some of the excitement and mystery of his earlier journeys, though he was still, as Reed commented, "a master of contradictions . . . the aging writer who still manages to offer a volume as odd, vigorous and entertaining as anything he has recently produced."

To the very end of his life, Greene remained a citizen of the world. By the time of his death in Vevey, Switzerland, on 3 April 1991, he had accumulated awards and honors from more than a dozen countries, cities, and universities, perhaps as often for his politics as for his art (one of the last of these was a doctorate, *honoris causa,* from Moscow State University). While Greene's reputation rests chiefly on his novels and stories, his travel writings are considered not only among the best, but perhaps among the last of their kind. Fussell contends that "literary traveling" flourished for a relatively short period, roughly the twenty years between the two world wars, and that even by the late 1930s British travel writing, including Greene's, had lost its subtlety and wit, becoming tendentious and even "preachy." At their strongest (as in *Journey Without Maps*), but even when they are flawed (as in *The Lawless Roads*), Greene's travel books, like his novels and stories, remind the reader of the interrelationship between persons and places, between the world within and the world outside. The settings of Greene's fiction, as a reviewer in *The Times Literary Supplement* (17 September 1971) once put it,

> have been so consistently vivid and actual that they have been given a collective name–"Greeneland"–and a descriptive adjective–"seedy." Greene objects to both the noun and the adjective, but he can scarcely deny that his world *is* consistently seedy, sordid, violent and cruel. These qualities are part of the legend; they describe not an actual environment, but an image of a spiritual condition–a world abandoned by God.

For Greene, however, this spiritual condition is always reflected in the specifics of place. As John Spurling notes, in his *Graham Greene* (1983), one of the qualities that makes Greene "more than a temporary phenomenon is, paradoxically, what is most contemporary about him: his settings and situations. In spite of its distortions, Greeneland is real. No European writer since Conrad has put the hot, poor and foully governed places of the earth on paper as vividly as Greene." Few European travel writers have lingered so intently, and so memorably (if not always so generously), on the borders between the European world and the "other" world abroad, two worlds once distant but now at each other's doorstep.

Interviews:

Robert Osterman, "Interview With Graham Greene," *Catholic World,* 170 (February 1950): 356–361;

Martin Shuttleworth and Simon Raven, "The Art of Fiction III: Graham Greene," *Paris Review,* 1 (1953): 24–41;

"New Honor and a New Novel: Interview," *Life,* 60 (4 February 1966): 43–44;

Christopher Birstall, "Graham Greene Takes the Orient Express," *Listener,* 80 (21 November 1968): 672–674, 676–677;

Gene D. Phillips, "Graham Greene: On the Screen," *Catholic World,* 209 (August 1969): 218–221;

Phillips, "Graham Greene Interview," *Twentieth Century,* 25 (Summer 1970): 111–117;

Michael Mewshaw, "Greene in Antibes," *London Magazine,* 17 (June–July 1977): 35–45;

Pierre Joannon, "Graham Greene's Other Island: An Interview," *Etudes Irlandaises,* 6 (December 1981): 157–169;

Marie-Françoise Allain, *The Other Man: Conversations with Graham Greene,* translated by Guido Waldman (London: Bodley Head, 1983; New York: Simon & Schuster, 1983);

Karel Kynel, "A Conversation with Graham Greene," *Index on Censorship,* 13 (June 1984): 2–6;

A. F. Cassis, *Graham Greene: Man of Paradox* (Chicago: Loyola University Press, 1994).

Bibliographies:

William Birmingham, "Graham Greene Criticism: A Bibliographical Study," *Thought,* 27 (Spring 1952): 72–100;

Francis Wyndham, *Graham Greene,* Bibliographical Series of Supplements to *British Book News* on Writers and Their Work, no. 67 (London: Longmans, 1955);

Maurice Beebe, "Criticism of Graham Greene: A Selected Checklist with an Index to Studies of Separate Works," *Modern Fiction Studies,* 3 (Autumn 1957): 281–288;

Phyllis Hargreaves, "Graham Greene: A Selected Bibliography," *Modern Fiction Studies,* 3 (Autumn 1957): 269–280;

Neil Brennan, "Bibliography," in *Graham Greene: Some Critical Considerations,* edited by R. O. Evans (Lexington: University of Kentucky Press, 1967);

Jerry Don Vann, *Graham Greene: A Checklist of Criticism* (Lexington: University of Kentucky Press, 1970);

Robert H. Miller, *Graham Greene: A Descriptive Catalog* (Lexington: University of Kentucky Press, 1979);

R. A. Wobbe, *Graham Greene: A Bibliography and Guide to Research* (New York & London: Garland, 1979);

A. F. Cassis, *Graham Greene: An Annotated Bibliography of Criticism* (Metuchen, N.J. & London: Scarecrow Press, 1981);

Richard Costa, "Graham Greene: A Checklist," *College Literature,* 12 (Winter 1985): 85–94;

Robert Murray Davis, "Greene Criticism in the Seventies: 'That's a Lot,'" in *Essays in Graham Greene: An Annual Review,* edited by Peter Wolfe, volume 1 (1987): 187–201;

Neil Brennan and Alan R. Radway, *A Bibliography of Graham Greene* (New York: Oxford University Press, 1990);

Alan W. Friedman, "The Status of Graham Greene Studies," *Library Chronicle of the University of Texas at Austin,* 20, no. 4 (1991): 36–67.

Biographies:

Norman Sherry, *The Life of Graham Greene. Volume I: 1904–1939; Volume II: 1939–1955* (New York: Viking, 1989, 1994);

Leopoldo Duran, *Graham Greene: Friend and Brother,* translated by Evan Cameron (London: HarperCollins, 1994); republished as *Graham Greene: An Intimate Portrait by His Closest Friend and Confidant,* (San Francisco: HarperSanFrancisco, 1994);

Anthony Mockler, *Graham Greene: Three Lives* (New York: Hunter Mackay, 1995);

Michael Shelden, *Graham Greene: The Enemy Within* (London: Heinemann / New York: Random House, 1995).

References:

Judith Adamson, *Graham Greene: The Dangerous Edge: Where Art and Politics Meet* (New York: St. Martin's Press, 1990);

Gwenn R. Boardman, *Graham Greene: The Aesthetics of Exploration* (Gainesville: University of Florida Press, 1971);

Lawrence Cunningham, "The Alter-Ego of Greene's 'Whiskey Priest'," *English Language Notes,* 8 (1970): 50–52;

Robert Murray Davis, "The Rhetoric of Mexican Travel: Greene and Waugh," *Renascence,* 38 (Spring 1986): 160–169;

André Dedet and Christian Petr, "Le voyageur en Afrique et son regard sur l'autre," *Journal of European Studies,* 22, no. 4 (1992): 323–336;

Philip Dodd, "The Views of Travellers: Travel Writing in the 1930s," *Prose Studies,* 5 (May 1982): 127–138;

R. O. Evans, *Graham Greene: Some Critical Considerations* (Lexington: University of Kentucky Press, 1963);

Paul Fussell, *Abroad: English Literary Traveling Between the Wars* (New York: Oxford University Press, 1980);

Barbara Greene, *Too Late to Turn Back: Barbara and Graham Greene in Liberia,* introduction by Paul Theroux (London: Settle Bendall, 1981);

Richard Hoggart, "The Force of Caricature: Aspects of the Art of Graham Greene, with Particular Reference to *The Power and the Glory,*" in his *Speaking to Each Other* (London: Oxford University Press/ Chatto & Windus, 1970), pp. 40–55;

Samuel Hynes, "1936," in his *The Auden Generation: Literature and Politics in England in the 1930s* (London: Bodley Head, 1976), pp. 193–241;

Thomas R. Knipp, "Gide and Greene: Africa and the Literary Imagination," *Serif* (Ohio), 6, no. 2 (1969): 3–14;

Francis L. Kunkel, *The Labyrinthine Ways of Graham Greene,* revised edition (Mamaroneck, N.Y.: Paul J. Appel, 1973);

Eric J. Leed, *The Mind of the Traveler: From Gilgamesh to Global Tourism* (New York: Basic Books, 1991);

R. W. B. Lewis, "The Trilogy," in *Graham Greene: A Collection of Critical Essays,* edited by Samuel Hynes (Englewood Cliffs, N. J.: Prentice-Hall, 1973), pp. 49–74;

M. M. Mahood, "The Possessed: Greene's *The Comedians,*" in her *The Colonial Encounter: A Reading of Six Novels* (London: Rex Collings, 1977), pp. 115–141;

Patrick Marnham, "Sergeant Chuchu's Guest," *Spectator,* 253 (29 September 1984): 25–26;

Patrick McCarthy, "Camus, Orwell and Greene: The Impossible Fascination of the Colonised," in *Camus' L'Etranger: Fifty Years On,* edited by Adele King (New York: St. Martin's Press, 1992), pp. 221–231;

Jeffrey Meyers, "Graham Greene: The Decline of the Colonial Novel," in his *Fiction and the Colonial Experience* (Totowa, N. J.: Rowman & Littlefield, 1973), pp. 97–115;

Meyers, "Greene's Travel Books," in his *Graham Greene: A Revaluation. New Essays* (New York: St. Martin's Press, 1990), pp. 47–67;

Jean-Yves Monnier, "Myth and Reality: Graham Greene's View of Africa in *Journey Without Maps,*" in *Commonwealth Essays and Studies* (Dijon), 11, no.1 (1988): 61–69;

Sheryl S. Pearson, "'Is There Anybody There'?: Graham Greene in Mexico," *Journal of Modern Literature,* 9 (May 1982): 277–290;

John Spurling, *Graham Greene* (London & New York: Methuen, 1983);

Spurling, "Panamania," *New Statesman,* 108 (14 October 1984): 31–32;

Douglas W. Veitch, *Lawrence, Greene and Lowry: The Fictional Landscape of Mexico* (Waterloo, Ontario: Wilfred Laurier University Press, 1978).

Papers:

The John J. Burns Library of Rare Books and Special Collections, Boston College, holds most of Graham Greene's personal library and many letters. The Catherine Walston/Graham Greene Papers, with some Greene manuscripts and letters, are in the Special Collections of the Lauinger Library, Georgetown University, Washington, D.C. The Harry Ransom Humanities Research Center, University of Texas at Austin, holds manuscripts and typescripts for most of Greene's books, working drafts and final manuscripts of various short stories and articles, and many letters. Greene collections are also held by the Library of Congress; the Lilly Library, Indiana University, Bloomington; the Rare Book Library of Pennsylvania State University; and the Special Collections of the University Libraries, University of Louisville, Kentucky. Important British collections are at the University of Bristol; the University of Reading; and the British Library, London.

Sarah Hobson

(17 April 1947 –)

Sherrie A. Inness
Miami University

BOOKS: *Through Persia in Disguise* (London: Murray, 1973); revised as *Masquerade, an Adventure in Iran* (Chicago: Academy Chicago, 1979); republished as *Through Iran in Disguise* (Chicago: Academy Chicago, 1982);

Belts for All Occasions (London: Mills & Boon, 1975);

Family Web: A Story of India (London: Murray, 1978; Chicago: Academy Chicago, 1982);

Two-Way Ticket (London: Macdonald, 1982).

TELEVISION: *The Crossroads of Civilisation,* researched and co-written by Hobson, David Paradine Productions, 1976–1978;

Two-Way Ticket, written and presented by Hobson, Yorkshire Television, 1981–1982;

The Lost Harvest, written and presented by Hobson, BBC Global Report, 1983;

The Tin Trap, written and presented by Hobson, BBC Global Report, 1983;

Behind the Cocaine War, produced by Hobson, Patricia Castano, and Adelaida Trujillo, Equal Media Ltd., 1990.

OTHER: *Where Did You Say?: A Report on Broadcasting in Britain–Its Coverage of Developing Countries and World Development Issues in 1978/79, Particularly in Programmes Used by Young People,* written and compiled by Hobson (London: Centre for World Development Education, 1980);

"The Mountain Child–Oscar of Peru," written and compiled by Hobson, UNICEF Development Education Kit, no. 14 (New York: The Centre, 1982);

"The Desert Child–Fatimettou of Mauritania," written and compiled by Hobson, UNICEF Development Education Kit, no. 15 (New York: The Centre, 1982);

"The Rainforest Child–Pauline of Malaysia," written and compiled by Hobson, UNICEF Development Education Kit, no. 16 (New York: The Centre, 1983);

Sarah Hobson (courtesy of Sarah Hobson)

"Hardships of Rural Living," with Sumi Krishna, in *India,* edited by Gillian Moore (Amsterdam: Time-Life Books, 1986), pp. 110–125;

"Child Abuse in Great Britain," in *Betrayal: A Report on Violence Toward Children in Today's World,* edited by Caroline Moorehead (New York: Doubleday, 1990), pp. 112–140;

Revelation and the Environment, AD 95–1995, edited by Hobson and Jane Lubchenco (Singapore & River Edge, N.J.: World Scientific, 1997);

Religion, Science and the Environment: The Black Sea in Crisis, edited by Hobson and Laurence Mee (London: World Scientific, 1998).

SELECTED PERIODICAL PUBLICATIONS–UNCOLLECTED: "Ruled by Land and Men," *New Internationalist,* 23 (January 1975): 19–21;

"Planning a Family of 26," *People* (London), 3, no. 4 (1976): 4–13;

"Life in Rural Iran," *New Society,* 46 (30 November 1978): 510–512;

"Iran: New Perceptions," *Blackwood's Magazine,* 326 (October 1979): 292–301;

"Becoming an Agent of Change," *Action for Development,* 103 (October 1982): 6–7;

"Bulldozed," *New Internationalist,* 131 (January 1984): 21–22;

"Bitter Rice?" *International Agricultural Development,* 4 (March–April 1984): 5–6;

"The Lost Harvest: A Case for Women's Land Rights in the Gambia," *Wiser Links,* 7 (November–December 1985): 16;

"Empowering the Village through Video," *Inquiry,* 3 (July 1986): 76–77;

"Into the Heart of Darkness," *New Statesman and Society,* 2 (17 March 1989): 28–31;

"U.S. Attacks Kuwait," *New Statesman and Society,* 2 (29 January 1993): 10;

"Communication Development," *Zebra News,* 1 (March 1994): 16–23;

"Confronting Famine in Africa," *IDS Policy Briefing,* 3 (April 1995).

Sarah Hobson, a travel writer and television producer, has long sought to explore different cultures as a participant, not merely as a viewer. Whether she is masquerading as a boy in Iran or living with a rural family in India, she submerges herself in the societies that she visits, hoping more accurately to describe their cultures. Although her home is in Northamptonshire, England, Hobson's work spans the globe from Iran to Peru.

Sarah Hobson was born on 17 April 1947 to John Gardner Sumner Hobson, a lawyer and member of parliament, and Beryl Marjorie Johnson, a winner of the junior doubles tennis tournament at Wimbledon and daughter of a successful factory owner. As a child, Hobson lived in Northamptonshire and vacationed with her family in Scotland. Hobson describes her education as "erratic in quality and quantity," with her parents sending her to six schools in twelve years. Her early mobility and education gave her the resilience and the adaptability she was later to need in her wide-ranging travels.

Equally important to her development as a traveler and writer were Hobson's teenage years, during which she rebelled against her comfortable background and her mother's hopes that her daughter would marry well. Resenting the expectations placed upon her as an upper-middle-class woman, Hobson sought personal freedom through travel and work abroad. By the age of seventeen she was working at a Russian Orthodox convent in Jordan. At nineteen she traveled through Africa, visiting Ethiopia, Kenya, Uganda, Tanzania, Malawi, and Rhodesia (now Zimbabwe), for eighteen months. These experiences developed her interests in travel and rural development. As she writes, "It was these early journeys which more than anything alerted me to the richness of different cultures and gave me a perspective on my own background and culture. . . . It was also the beginnings of my passionate quest to understand better why people in rural areas seem so rich in their lives yet are so poorly treated."

Hobson's first travel book is *Through Persia in Disguise* (1973). Seeking to learn more about Iranian culture and art, Hobson took a trip that refuted many of her preconceived Western notions of the Islamic world. In *Through Persia in Disguise* she tells of her adventures in Iran, which she explored at the age of twenty-three dressed as a boy, an experience that reveals her driving curiosity to see places from the standpoint of their local inhabitants. Her story starts in England, where she first decided to masquerade as a boy, when necessary, in order to travel more freely in Islamic countries. After hitchhiking to Istanbul, Hobson gradually becomes more adept at mimicking a boy's actions and behaviors, but she still is confronted with unexpected complications, as when a homosexual man, thinking her a young boy, propositions her.

Through Persia in Disguise is at its strongest when Hobson describes her arrival and stay in Iran. She creates a vivid, fascinating view of Islamic culture. Because she is considered a boy, she has a unique view of Iranian culture and gender roles. Her unusual position is clear when she ventures to Qum, a center for Muslim religious activity. She passes as a nineteen-year-old *Khajeh* (eunuch), demonstrating her ability to blend into the cultures that she studies. She constantly risks discovery, however, as when her host notices her pierced ears–which Hobson explains away by claiming that they are a Scottish custom. In Qum, she strives to achieve not only artistic but also spiritual understanding of Islam; in fact, the two elements seem intertwined for her. Masquerading as "John," Hobson is given an introduction to Islamic spirituality by her new friend

Hasan-'Ali, an experience that would have been denied to her if she had traveled as a woman.

Leaving Qum behind, Hobson journeys to Isfahan: "From Qum, the city of Isfahan seemed a natural progression, a transition from theory and reflection to practice and organic expression, where the effects of doctrines and disciplines are seen in building, in decoration, in craftsmanship." The author discovers the poetic beauty of Islam through the study of art, and one of the book's strengths is her frequent allusion to art and reflections on what makes Islamic art unique. Hobson later used the artistic inspiration she gained from her trip in her small belt-making business, as well as in *Belts for All Occasions* (1975), a crafts book she wrote about the history and design of belts.

Through Persia in Disguise is also about the construction of gender, and what it means for a woman to pass as a man. Hobson becomes more aware of the gender inequities in Iran when she dresses as a woman to discuss with craftsmen the shipping of their goods to England. She is treated with condescension and becomes angry because she believes she would have been treated with greater respect had she been a man. On another occasion she is sexually propositioned by a group of men who have discovered from her passport that she is a woman. She also relates an incident in which she overhears two men quarreling over the attributes of one of their sisters. One brother comments, "She's a good cook, and she can milk, and she can weave, *and* she's got big breasts. What else do you want in a woman?"

Hobson also describes positive aspects of the condition of women in Iran, showing her determination to reveal the multifaceted nature of Iranian culture. One of her Iranian friends from Qum informs her that women are given an equal place in Islam and that they can get divorces and help to decide the rules of the marital contract. Contrary to Western stereotypes about Islamic cultures, Hobson thinks that some Islamic women are actually better off and more independent than Western women.

Besides allowing her an opportunity to see how differently men and women are treated in Iran, Hobson's masquerade shapes her personality and character, as she reflects at one point: "I no longer felt concerned about my disguise; indeed I sometimes felt the disguise had taken over, that I really was a boy. . . . Quite unconsciously I would size up the shape of a woman's legs, or speculate, with the other boys, as to what important jobs we would soon secure as men." Hobson also thinks about how her clothing changed her when she visited the Turkmen, a tribal group: "And it was strange, I thought, how when I was a boy I could fall in with their callousness, but the moment I was a girl, I felt humiliated and powerless." For Hobson, male attire not only conceals one identity but also creates an entirely new one, which forces her to question exactly how men and women construct their different identities.

Turkmen tribesman in Iran; photograph by Hobson for Through Persia in Disguise *(1973)*

In *Through Persia in Disguise* Hobson's male disguise enables her to go on adventures. She buys a dilapidated old motorbike to reach the homes of tribal dwellers in Fars, a distant southern province. The bike also proves a convenient sign of her masculine identification. As she travels, she continues to discover the contradictions that make up Iranian society: sheep sharing the road with buses and cars, heavy machinery tearing up roads next to irreplaceable old mosques with delicate and intricate tile work. Increasingly, she discovers that the real Iran is nothing like the idealized, mythic version she had visualized from studying its artwork. Hobson shows what it means to experience the reality of a country and compare it to one's preconceptions.

Although traveling as a boy does have advantages, Hobson must always be on her guard from what she describes as the "natural inquisitiveness" of many Iranians, which often makes her journey hazardous as she has to dodge questions that might give her away. She has to decline an invitation to go swimming; deal with the come-ons of a prostitute; and devise plausible excuses when men suggest that she wrestle, weight lift, or go running with them. Sometimes her attire puts her in real danger, such as when an Iranian policeman accuses her of being a Russian spy because of her disguise.

The epilogue to *Masquerade, an Adventure in Iran,* the revised 1979 edition of the book, focuses on Hobson's return to Iran eight years after she traveled as a boy. Her return trip is just before the shah is deposed, and she sees the violence breaking out in the streets of Tehran; however, she discovers that Iranian life, despite political upheavals, still goes along the course it has followed for hundreds of years. Ultimately, Hobson argues that no amount of study or travel will help her to come entirely to terms with the meaning of Iran and its Islamic way of life. She reflects,

> My main feeling was one of confusion, so that I found it hard to draw conclusions, or even to draw together the multiple strands I had gathered. Besides, the country seemed composed of far more strands than I had seen, so that my thoughts on character only skimmed reality.

Iran eludes Hobson, but for her this very elusiveness helps to embody the character of the country. Unlike some people who refer to the "mysterious East," Hobson acknowledges her inability to understand fully Iranian culture, without the condescension expressed by such a cliché.

In 1974 Hobson married Tony Mayer; the couple divorced in 1988. From 1976 to 1978 Hobson was increasingly involved in writing for television. She was head of research and coscriptwriter for the eight-part television series *The Crossroads of Civilisation,* a groundbreaking study of 2,500 years of the history of Iran, demonstrating her continuing interest in cross-cultural interpretation.

Like Iran, India proved to have far too many threads to untangle, which Hobson recognized in her second travel book, *Family Web: A Story of India* (1978), a narrative about her experiences living for several months with a poor village family in southern India. What started off as a documentary film project by Hobson's husband, Tony, evolved to include Hobson's book, which provides an in-depth examination of the Gowda family and its day-to-day life. Again, one of Hobson's strengths in her travel writing is that she allows people to speak for themselves.

In *Family Web* she often finds Indian family life even more baffling than her experiences in Iran. She learns the difficulties of understanding a culture in which Western logic frequently does not apply. Even finding out factual details is difficult or impossible in a society where "facts," such as birth and death dates, are interpreted in numerous ways. Only with painstaking slowness does Hobson begin to learn how convoluted the Indian social system is, fragmented by culture, class, religion, caste, and language.

Family Web focuses on one extended family, exploring how the family both helps and hurts its members. On the positive side, the extended family gives its members a degree of financial security in the community. On the negative side, the family is a hotbed of intrigue, with different members doing whatever is necessary, no matter how manipulative, in order to get their individual needs met. Hobson tries to understand this complex family system by immersing herself in the family's life, even helping with the domestic chores, such as planting, cooking, and housecleaning.

Doing such duties brings her closer to the family's members, particularly the women with whom she frequently works, and she presents a sensitive, perceptive study of the difficulties facing these women. One woman, for instance, has a husband who beats her; she has borne three sons within three years, but they have all died within a day of birth. Another woman considers her husband her intellectual inferior and wants to leave the family, but there is little an uneducated village woman can do besides become a prostitute. Hobson's narrative illustrates the differences between the lives of village men and women, while depicting the relative lack of freedom that women have in a society that is based on male rule and authority.

Hobson's observation of the family's life is made more difficult when her husband's film crew arrives and she is torn between her allegiance to the Gowda family and her status as an unofficial member of the film crew. The documentary film crew's arrival, however, does allow her to show how disparate the views of members of two different cultures can be. Ironically, while the Gowda family thinks the crew wishes to produce a documentary about the family's successful life, the crew sees the family as living in dire poverty. In addition, the family is proud of its many members, while the film crew is puzzled as to why Indian villagers have large families despite the availability of contraceptives. Hobson's writing focuses on the meeting of different cultures, showing how each culture acts in ways that it perceives as "logical."

Ultimately, Hobson is left feeling that an understanding of Indian culture might be as elusive as an understanding of Iranian culture. Living with the family has taught her about the significance of family bonds, but at the same time she feels ambivalent about her stay: "It is hard to show . . . the obsession and repetition of the family's daily life, and the difficulties I felt in trying to become part of it." She has made close

One of the cousins started a fire to heat the water, snapping the twigs into kindling: smoke and flames began to rise. The old lady placed a small wooden board auspiciously painted with ~~white~~ rice paste near the feet of Susheelamma; then she seated herself at the grinding stone to urge on Lakshmi. The cattle moved restlessly, dropped their dung with a splatter, heaved themselves up and down, ~~fretting~~ against their ropes. The children continued to sleep in the bedroom. The fire burned strongly.

At 4.05, Susheelamma sat on the board, with her mother in front between her outstretched legs, and the midwife behind supporting her back. Together they groped through her sari, feeling their way to the head of the baby as it began to emerge; they told her to breathe, to push out with all her strength. They worked together, easing the baby out, first the head, then the torso, finally the legs. It gave a soft cry.

The old lady hurried over, peered forward, pushing the legs of the baby apart. A hint of disappointment skimmed her face: Susheelamma had delivered a daughter.

The midwife lay the child on a tossing basket, its grey cord trailing through blood to its mother who sat motionless, exhausted, her head bent onto her knees. The midwife cleaned the baby, wiping away the blood with a rag; she tied some cotton round the cord, pulled it tight, and cut through with a billhook. She burnt the end with a candle ad tied a rough knot.

Susheelamma sat silently slumped against a pillar disregarded by everyone. The smell of blood was almost stench and the cattle chafed wildly. The room shook with the shadows from the flames of the fire and the door was kept firmly closed against the intrusion of men.

Page from the typescript for "Birth" from Hobson's 1978 book, Family Web: A Story of India *(Collection of Sarah Hobson)*

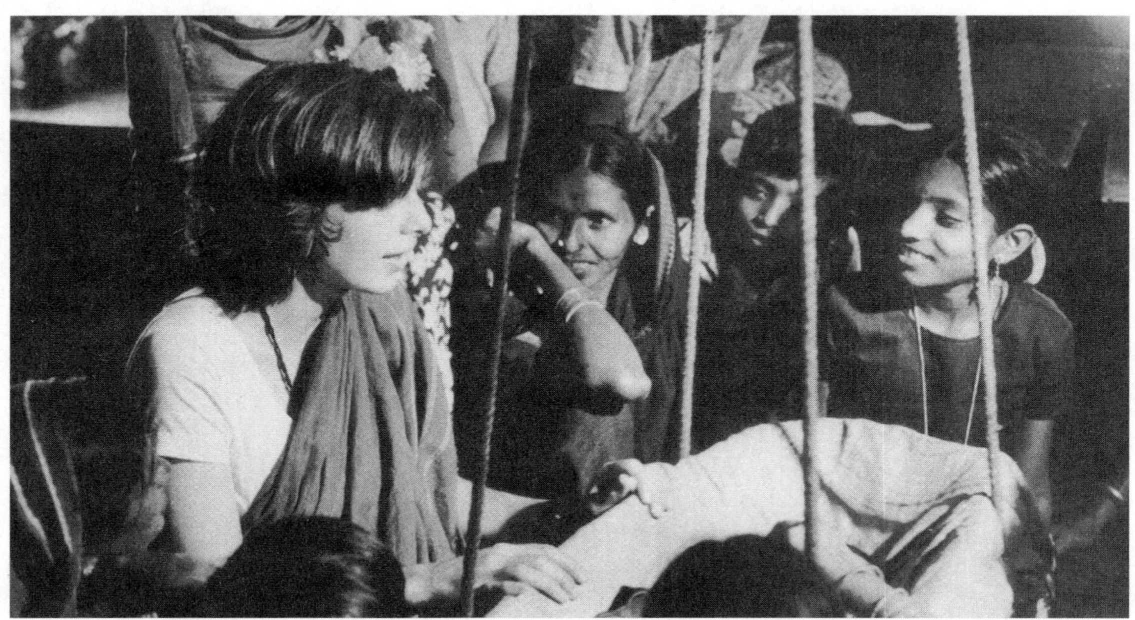

Hobson at a naming ceremony with members of the Indian family she lived with while researching Family Web

friends and considers the Indian family in many ways to be her family, yet she is annoyed and frustrated by the family's endless demands for more money and more goods from the film crew. Rather than being a flaw, Hobson's ambivalence is one of the strengths of her writing since it helps to point out the complexity of different cultures.

Hobson's interest in cultural exploration has continued. From 1981 to 1982 she wrote and presented a six-part series for Yorkshire Television. *Two-Way Ticket* allowed six young people from rural areas around the world to talk about their lives and their reactions to England where they visit. Hobson wrote a book, *Two-Way Ticket* (1982), based on this series and developed three education kits, published by UNICEF, on life in Mauritania, Peru, and Malaysia. One of the book's strengths is that Hobson allows children from different parts of the world to speak about their experiences themselves. As she puts it in her preface, "The book tries to look at our world not from the outside but from within." In 1982–1983 Hobson produced television programs for the BBC. In *The Lost Harvest* and *The Tin Trap* she again focused on Third World concerns, this time traveling to Gambia and Bolivia. In the late 1980s Hobson's interest in international issues, particularly as they relate to women, found expression in "Equal Media," a company that she started with another woman, producer Parminder Vir, to produce documentary television programs in partnership with Third World moviemakers.

Hobson has worked to understand the concerns of societies in a variety of locations around the world. Through her writing and her work with documentaries she has explored the contact zones between different cultures, in the process illuminating how essential it is for people to tell their own stories if others are to reach some understanding of their reality.

Reference:

Jane Robinson, *Wayward Women: A Guide to Women Travellers* (Oxford: Oxford University Press, 1990), p. 48.

Elspeth Huxley

(23 July 1907 – 10 January 1997)

Victoria Carchidi
Massey University

See also the Huxley entry in *DLB 77: British Mystery Writers, 1920–1939.*

BOOKS: *White Man's Country: Lord Delamere and the Making of Kenya,* 2 volumes (London: Macmillan, 1935; New York: Macmillan, 1935);

Murder at Government House (London: Methuen, 1937; New York & London: Harper, 1937);

Murder on Safari (London: Methuen, 1938; New York & London: Harper, 1938);

Red Strangers (London: Chatto & Windus, 1939; New York & London: Harper, 1939);

Death of an Aryan (London: Methuen, 1939); republished as *The African Poison Murders* (New York & London: Harper, 1940);

East Africa, The British Commonwealth in Pictures (London: Published for Penns in the Rock Press by William Collins, 1941);

The Story of Five English Farmers (London: Sheldon Press, 1941);

Atlantic Ordeal: The Story of Mary Cornish (London: Chatto & Windus, 1941; New York & London: Harper, 1942);

English Women (London: Sheldon Press, 1942);

Brave Deeds of the War (London: Sheldon Press, 1943);

Race and Politics in Kenya: A Correspondence between Elspeth Huxley and Margery Perham (London: Faber & Faber, 1944; Westport, Conn.: Greenwood Press, 1975);

Colonies: A Reader's Guide (London: Published for the National Book League by Cambridge University Press, 1947);

The Walled City (London: Chatto & Windus, 1948; Philadelphia & New York: Lippincott, 1949);

Settlers of Kenya (Nairobi: Highway Press / London, New York & Toronto: Longmans, Green, 1948; Westport, Conn.: Greenwood Press, 1975);

African Dilemmas (London, New York & Toronto: Longmans, Green, 1948);

The Sorcerer's Apprentice: A Journey through East Africa (London: Chatto & Windus, 1948; Westport, Conn.: Greenwood Press, 1975);

I Don't Mind If I Do (London: Chatto & Windus, 1950);

Four Guineas: A Journey through West Africa (London: Chatto & Windus, 1954; Westport, Conn.: Greenwood Press, 1974);

A Thing to Love (London: Chatto & Windus, 1954);

Kenya Today (London: Lutterworth Press, 1954);

What Are Trustee Nations? (London: Batchworth Press, 1955);

The Red Rock Wilderness (London: Chatto & Windus, 1957; New York: Morrow, 1957);

No Easy Way: A History of the Kenya Farmers' Association and Unga Limited (Nairobi: East African Standard, 1957);

The Flame Trees of Thika: Memories of an African Childhood (London: Chatto & Windus, 1959; New York: Morrow, 1959);

A New Earth: An Experiment in Colonialism (London: Chatto & Windus, 1960; New York: Morrow, 1960);

The Mottled Lizard (London: Chatto & Windus, 1962); republished as *On the Edge of the Rift: Memories of Kenya* (New York: Morrow, 1962);

The Merry Hippo (London: Chatto & Windus, 1963); republished as *The Incident at the Merry Hippo* (New York: Morrow, 1964);

Forks and Hope: An African Notebook (London: Chatto & Windus, 1964); republished as *With Forks and Hope* (New York: Morrow, 1964);

A Man from Nowhere (London: Chatto & Windus, 1964; New York: Morrow, 1965);

Suki: A Little Tiger, text by Huxley and photographs by Laelia Goehr (London: Chatto & Windus, 1964; New York: Morrow, 1964);

Back Street New Worlds: A Look at Immigrants in Britain (London: Chatto & Windus, 1964; New York: Morrow, 1965);

Brave New Victuals: An Inquiry into Modern Food Production (London: Chatto & Windus, 1965);

Their Shining Eldorado: A Journey through Australia (London: Chatto & Windus, 1967; New York: Morrow, 1967);

Love Among the Daughters (London: Chatto & Windus, 1968); republished as *Love Among the Daughters: Memories of the Twenties in England and America* (New York: Morrow, 1968);

The Challenge of Africa, Aldus Encyclopedia of Discovery and Exploration Series (London: Aldus, 1971);

Livingstone and His African Journeys, The Great Explorers (London: Weidenfeld & Nicolson, 1974; New York: Saturday Review Press, 1974);

Florence Nightingale (London: Weidenfeld & Nicolson, 1975; New York: Putnam, 1975);

Gallipot Eyes: A Wiltshire Diary (London: Weidenfeld & Nicolson, 1976);

Scott of the Antarctic (London: Weidenfeld & Nicolson, 1977; New York: Atheneum, 1978);

Whipsnade: Captive Breeding for Survival (London: Collins, 1981);

The Prince Buys the Manor: An Extravaganza (London: Chatto & Windus, 1982);

Last Days in Eden, text by Huxley and photographs by Hugo van Lawick (London: Harvill, 1984; New York: Amaryllis Press, 1984);

Out in the Midday Sun: My Kenya (London: Chatto & Windus, 1985; New York: Viking, 1987);

Peter Scott: Painter and Naturalist (London & Boston: Faber & Faber, 1993; Golden, Colo.: Fulcrum, 1995).

OTHER: *The Kingsleys: A Biographical Anthology,* edited, with a preface, by Huxley (London: Allen & Unwin, 1973);

Mary H. Kingsley, *Travels in West Africa,* edited, with an introduction, by Huxley (London: Folio Society, 1976);

Isak Dinesen (Karen Blixen), *Out of Africa,* introduction by Huxley (London: Folio Society, 1980);

Nellie Grant, *Nellie: Letters from Africa,* edited, with a memoir, by Huxley (London: Weidenfeld & Nicolson, 1980); republished as *Nellie's Story, With a Memoir by Her Daughter Elspeth Huxley* (New York: Morrow, 1981);

Pioneers' Scrapbook: Reminiscences of Kenya, 1890–1968, edited by Huxley and Arnold Curtis (London: Evans, 1980);

Nine Faces of Kenya, edited by Huxley (London: Collins Harvill, 1990; New York: Viking, 1991).

SELECTED PERIODICAL PUBLICATIONS–UNCOLLECTED: "The Nature of the Native," *Times* (London), 28 July 1936, pp. 15–16;

"Soil Erosion in America," *Times* (London), 11 September 1936, p. 10;

"'Making Deserts' 1. The Other Aspect of Agriculture," *Times* (London), 10 June 1937, pp. 17–18;

"'Making Deserts' 2. The Exhausted Pasture," *Times* (London), 11 June 1937, pp. 17–18;

"Agricultural wages," letter to the editor, *Times* (London), 23 July 1953, p. 9;

"Africa's wild life: need to preserve game sanctuary," *Times* (London), 19 August 1958, p. 9;

"Threat to game in Africa," *Times* (London), 24 October 1959, pp. 7, 14.

From her youth in Kenya through her adult life in Wiltshire, Elspeth Josceline Huxley faithfully recorded some of the most significant developments in Africa during the twentieth century. Noted for her forthright statements, her "sociological" sharpness of insight, and her intense involvement in environmental issues long before the ecological movement began, Huxley wrote about the personal impact of "the winds of change" that swept across the British Empire.

Huxley's travel writing includes not only her accounts of travel in Africa and Australia but also her other nonfiction works and her novels, all of which carry the reader imaginatively to a land far from Britain. Because Huxley's parents were settlers in Kenya, her travel writing has a less Eurocentric perspective than that of her contemporary male adventurer-explorers. Although her viewpoint is consistently British, Huxley had an affinity for Africa that stems from happy childhood memories. She also avoided the critical trap caused by expectations that travel literature should be "objectively true" despite the difficulties of translating a foreign land into one's vocabulary. As Sara Mills has noted, this trap ensnares female writers whose anecdotal, personal approach to describing their travels is more subjective than that of male traveler-adventurers. Huxley embraced the complexity of truth and fiction. Calling her autobiographies of her life in Kenya "half fiction," she offered subjective visions of foreign places, in a personal, accessible tone. By declaring her freedom from conventional definitions of travel literature, Huxley offered new views of Africa to the British public through genres not always considered travel writing.

Elspeth Josceline Grant was born on 23 July 1907 in London to Maj. Josceline (Jos) Grant and his wife, Eleanor (Nellie) Lillian Grosvenor Grant, a year after their marriage. Jos Grant, from eastern Scotland, had no property or profession. Although Nellie Grant was the daughter of Lord Richard de Aquila Grosvenor (later Baron Stalbridge), younger brother of Hugh Lupus Grosvenor, first Duke of Westminster, she was equally impoverished at the time of her marriage. She had been brought up in lavish surroundings, but her family had fallen on straitened circumstances. In 1912

Elspeth Huxley

Jos and Nellie Grant immigrated to East Africa, leaving behind their young daughter until they could build a suitable house on their land. Elspeth joined them the following year and spent her early childhood on Kitimuru, their coffee plantation at Thika, thirty-five miles outside Nairobi, Kenya. After World War I, which Elspeth and Nellie spent in England, the family was reunited in Thika in 1919. They moved in 1922 to a more fertile site in Njoro, where they established Gikammeh farm. Much of Huxley's early education was garnered from odd assortments of books. She attended a boarding school at Aldeburgh in Suffolk during the war and then studied at the Government European School in Nairobi. While there she began her writing career with articles on polo playing, many published under the pen name Bamboo, in the *Kenya Sunday Times & Sporting News,* the *East African Standard,* and the *East African Observer* newspapers. Huxley amusingly described some of the motives for those early efforts in *The Mottled Lizard* (1962): they included a need for pocket money and the pleasure of criticizing the playing of her family and their friends.

Huxley returned to England in 1925 to study agriculture at Reading University, earning a diploma in 1927. She then spent the 1927–1928 academic year at Cornell University in the United States, the period covered in her autobiographical volume *Love Among the Daughters* (1968). Back in England, Huxley found work as a press officer at the Empire Marketing Board, summarizing and popularizing scientific articles for newspapers, a position she held from 1929 until 1932. At the Empire Marketing Board she met Gervas Huxley, head of the publicity division and thirteen years her senior. They were married on 12 December 1931. Gervas Huxley was a grandson of Thomas Henry Huxley and a cousin to Aldous and Julian Huxley. In a 16 September 1968 interview published in *The Times* (London) Elspeth Huxley commented, "I'm a bogus Huxley. . . . When I married Gervas I found it very useful to climb on the Huxley bandwagon." After their marriage, Gervas Huxley joined the Ceylon Tea Propaganda Board, the purpose of which was to encourage tea consumption. In 1935 he became organizing director of the International Tea Market Expansion Board, a position he held until 1967.

By 1933 Elspeth Huxley had arranged to write the biography of Hugh Cholmondeley, Baron Delamere (1870–1931), Kenyan pioneer and politician. So that she could research the work, which became the two-volume *White Man's Country: Lord Delamere and the Making of Kenya* (1935), the Huxley's separated temporarily; he went to Ceylon (now Sri Lanka), while she went to Kenya to work in Nairobi. There, in what Huxley described as "a cheerful little town, at a half-way stage between pioneer squalor and the urban sophistication that was to transform it," she delved into Delamere's papers and government archives. Huxley also collected memories from Delamere's widow and those who remembered the early days of British settlement, thus establishing the pattern of reliance on the intimate and the anecdotal that is both the strength and weakness of all Huxley's writing. Though this method results in a firsthand account of events as described by the people who experienced them, it risks perpetuating the errors and exaggerations of the self-interested.

White Man's Country was praised for its range and readability. A review in the 13 June 1935 issue of *The Times Literary Supplement* (*TLS*) called the book "an accurate, discriminating and comprehensive contribution to the history of the Empire in Africa" and praised Huxley's decision to put the man in the context of the colony: Huxley "is right and successful in giving her biography the broad setting of the whole Colony's varied and struggling life." This work also established Huxley as "white Kenya's leading writer," a stature reaffirmed in a 1991 article by C. J. Duder: not "until the 1930s and Elspeth Huxley's biography of Lord Delamere" did the settler community of Kenya "gain an advocate as eloquent and as persuasive as any of the critics arrayed against them." Writing for the 3 August 1935 issue of *Nature,* W. Ormsby-Gore praised Huxley's work as "the most comprehensive account of the pioneer activities in farming and politics of European colonisation" in Kenya. Further, Ormsby-Gore called Huxley "young and intelligent" and said that the book is "cleverly and attractively written, and admirably produced"–praise, indeed, albeit not in the most intellectual vein. Mills has found that this focus on the person rather than the work is a marked feature of many reviews of female travel writers' accounts.

In a statement published in *Twentieth-Century Crime and Mystery Writers* (1985) Huxley explained the origin of her next books, a series of mystery novels: "my husband's job took us both on many journeys . . . and I took to writing crime stories to pass the time on shipboard." Earl F. Bargainnier has said that one reason Huxley deserves to "rank high" as a mystery writer is her "massive knowledge of Africa, which informs the novels without turning them into travel books." *Murder at Government House* (1937), *Murder on Safari* (1938), and *Death of an Aryan* (1939) are all set in the fictional African country of Chania. Their hero is a policeman, Superintendent Vachell, who has recently arrived from the United States and Canada and struggles to make sense of the strange country and its customs. Vachell is less successful at disentangling the larger mystery of Africa itself than he is at unraveling the European snarls of jealousy and bitterness characteristic of the "Happy Valley" sections of Kenya.

In these early works, especially in *Murder on Safari,* Huxley began to shape the lush descriptions of scenery that later characterize her travel writing. The nature of the mystery novel also encouraged a focus on the exotic, which also marks Huxley's later work. Local color includes the description of a young African girl killed for suspected witchcraft, a crime that is not investigated because the Europeans never learn about it, and an African "witch doctor" who utters recondite riddles that must be fathomed before they reveal clues to a mystery.

Many readers have found Huxley's mysteries an interesting window into the culture of white settlers. In an overview of the representation of Kenya in literature, Duder praises Huxley's accurate representation of settler society, noting that she "catches both the isolation of settler life and some of the strains" of that society. Duder points out that although Huxley's writings are far more sophisticated and polished than the typical "Kenya novel" of the time, the depiction in *Murder at Government House* of a secret African society with rituals modeled on government ceremonies furthered "the image of Africans trying to assimilate the trappings of European civilization while failing to grasp its essentials." Precisely because such literature was not written as deliberate propaganda but as entertainment, it spread such messages to an audience that was far wider than that reached by more sober government papers. Despite the aesthetic superiority of Huxley's writings, Duder finds that "even in Huxley's work, the world of the settlers is familiar and comprehensible, while that of the Africans is not."

A surprising element is the brutality toward animals in *Death of an Aryan.* The 28 October 1939 *TLS* review noted that some readers might find "the cruelty to animals too nauseating," a warning repeated in an 18 July 1986 *TLS* review of a new edition of the novel, which states "the assault on animals are rather hard to stomach." This mistreatment anticipates the Mau Mau brutality to animals in Huxley's novel *A Man from Nowhere* (1964) and in her nonfiction book *No Easy Way* (1957), but in *Death of an Aryan* the atrocities are placed at the feet of a European. In fact, readers can find in Huxley's murder mysteries some stereotypes that are common to travel literature, including the idea of the foreign land as a place of brutality and disorder; yet, strikingly, Huxley does not attribute these qualities to the Africans but to the Europeans abroad. Huxley's three African mysteries have remained popular. Between 1986 and 1988 Dent republished all three of the early mysteries in Great Britain, and Penguin followed suit in the United States between 1988 and 1990.

In her "documentary" novel *Red Strangers* (1939) Huxley worked hard to overcome the inevitably peripheral and superficial depictions of Africans in her mysteries. She researched *Red Strangers,* a fictional account of Kikuyu life and how it changed in reaction to European arrival, in 1937, when she and her mother, Nellie Grant, camped for several months in Kikuyuland, the highland region of south central Kenya, near Mount Kenya. After this trip Huxley enrolled in a course in anthropology taught by Bronislaw Malinowski at the London School of Economics. In *Nellie* (1980) she described her pleasure at finding another Kenyan in the class, with whom she had lunch several times: "this was none other than Johnstone Kenyatta, as he was then known." As Jomo Kenyatta, he was jailed in 1953 as the leader of the Mau Mau rebellion against British colonial rule in Kenya and later became prime minister (1963–1964) and president (1964–1978) of Kenya. When Huxley met Kenyatta, he was also working on a book about his tribe, the Kikuyu: *Facing Mount Kenya* (1938).

A reviewer for *The New York Times* (10 September 1939) praised *Red Strangers* for having "almost the value of an anthropological study," but a *TLS* reviewer (3 June 1939) wrote that the characters in the novel fail to come alive; instead, they "are subordinate to the incidents in which they take part . . . ritual observances, episodes illustrating custom, hunting scenes," circumcision, and battle raids. Huxley's efforts at "objectivity" in describing the incidents succeed less well than might a more honest portrayal. The treatment of animals offers the best example, particularly the ritual sacrifice of live goats. Huxley observed such rituals, and, as she recounted in *Out in the Midday Sun* (1985), they left a mark on her. In *The Flame Trees of Thika* (1959) the young narrator sees a similar scene and fears that a similar agony will befall her pet duiker (a small African antelope). Her reaction instantly develops a contrast between African and European attitudes toward animals and increases the interest of the book. In *Red Strangers* the scene is presented with no analysis or reaction. Rather than explaining the cultural practice in a

Nellie and Elspeth Grant in 1908 (Estate of Elspeth Huxley)

nuanced way, acknowledging both her difficulty with the practice and the illumination it casts on a different set of values, Huxley's attempt at objectivity silenced her own voice and distanced readers brought up in other cultures.

A reviewer in the 13 February 1954 issue of *The Times* assessed the novel highly: "When Mrs. Huxley wrote *Red Strangers* she produced what must rank with Alan Paton's *Cry the Beloved Country* [1948] as about the most sensitive and interpretative fictional account of race relations ever given by a European." In a later comparison of Huxley's novel and *The River Between* (1965) by Ngugi wa Thiong'o (James Ngugi), however, Reinhard Sander is not as complimentary, quoting Ezekiel Mphalele's observation that the major Kikuyu characters in the novel "display 'a moonstruck pursuit of things European.'" Certainly by the end of the novel, when a newborn child is named "Airplane," the symbolism of African customs merging with European values becomes so overt as to almost undercut the dominant theme. Sander finds Huxley's work full of superficial descriptions, such as "primitive savages," and self-serving vignettes. For example, the arguments put forward during a land dispute between two Kikuyu echo the European rationale for substituting a different piece of land for an area under claim: "Thus Mrs Huxley defends the British practice of establishing reserves for the various tribes in Kenya." Sander sees *Red Strangers* not as the record of a dying culture but as "a defense of British colonialism in East Africa" in which events incomprehensible to the Kikuyu are presented as serving "the interests of all people in Kenya, including the Kikuyu."

The accuracy of Sander's interpretation of Huxley's beliefs is borne out in *Race and Politics in Kenya* (1944), which warrants close attention from those interested in Huxley's philosophy on Kenya. Recording two views on Kenya, the book is based on letters exchanged between Huxley and Margery Perham in 1942 and 1943 and includes an introduction by Frederick John Dealtry, Baron Lugard (1858–1945), a British colonial administrator who had served as governor general of Nigeria (1912–1919). The first view of Kenya, with which Huxley sympathized, held that Kenya had been a land awaiting the arrival of British husbandry to develop it fully for the sake of European and African alike; the other held that European settlers were exploiting the country and its population. Perham, another frequent traveler to and writer about Africa, held that the British role in Kenya should be only to prepare its indigenous population for self-government. The terms of the debate have shifted dramatically in the last half century; yet, Huxley's beliefs were widely held at the time. A contemporary reviewer in *TLS* (17 June 1944) gave Perham "the better of the argument" but found Huxley's eloquence "extraordinarily attractive." Huxley continued the argument in *The Sorcerer's Apprentice* (1948).

In 1938 Elspeth and Gervas Huxley bought a seventeenth-century farmhouse in North Wiltshire, but during World War II they could spend only weekends there. During the war Elspeth Huxley worked for the British Broadcasting Corporation (BBC) as news talks assistant (1941–1943) and as a liaison officer between the BBC and the Colonial Office (1943–1944). After the birth of their only child, Charles Grant Huxley, in 1944, the Huxleys settled in Wiltshire, farming and writing. While working for the BBC, Huxley also published several books: *East Africa* (1941), *The Story of Five English Farmers* (1941), *Atlantic Ordeal: The Story of Mary Cornish* (1941), *English Women* (1942), and *Brave Deeds of the War* (1943). *East Africa* set the tone for Huxley's position as a guide to Kenya, Uganda, and Tanganyika (now part of Tanzania). In 1947 Huxley became a justice of the peace for Wiltshire, and she later became magistrate, serving until 1977. Huxley continued radio broadcasting and freelance journalism for *The Times* and other newspapers and magazines.

In 1945 Huxley helped to establish the foundations for what became in 1948 the East African Literature Bureau, founded to promote literacy in the region. The work required visiting Kenya, Uganda, and Tanganyika. Her mother's letters and other trips to Kenya, including a final visit to her father before his death on 7 April 1947, allowed Huxley to monitor changes taking place in Africa, leading to a report published in 1947. During the twelve years from 1948 to 1960 Huxley published thirteen books, including three travel books–*The Sorcerer's Apprentice* (1948), *Four Guineas* (1954), and *A New Earth* (1960). During this period Huxley also wrote the work for which she is best known: *The Flame Trees of Thika* (1959), her retrospective look at the Africa of her childhood.

The Sorcerer's Apprentice: A Journey through East Africa comprises six parts: Kenya, Tanganyika, Zanzibar, Tanganyika, Uganda, and Kenya again. This circular structure of opening and closing the book with Kenya reveals Huxley's unsurprising affinity for the land of her childhood, one that at times lends the book a slightly contemptuous tone toward the worries of Uganda and Tanganyika about federation with Kenya and its racial policies. The main theme, perhaps sparked by the creation of the sovereign state of India in 1947, is how "the sorcerer's apprentice"–that is, indigenous Africans–would be able to manage the fragile environment of Africa. Huxley's implication is that–like the sorcerer's apprentice whose failure to learn his master's wizardry leads to catastrophe–they cannot. Huxley reiterated time and again the danger of the population "pullulating" beyond all measure and thereby devastating even the rich, Eden-like regions of Africa.

A comparison of this book to Huxley's "Making Deserts," a two-part article published in *The Times* on 10–11 June 1937, reveals a hardening of Huxley's position. In the earlier piece Huxley identified the warning symptoms of land exhaustion coming out of the American dust bowl and saw a similar situation developing in Africa. She urged restraint on British policies such as the widespread dispersal of hoes, which allowed more soil to be exposed to erosion, and the introduction of European-style monocultural practices, which exhausted the soil more quickly than did the indigenous mixed-crop practice. A decade later, in *The Sorcerer's Apprentice,* Huxley blamed the land abuse not on foolhardy British intervention but on the Africans. In this book, more than in any of her other works, she presented Africans in stereotype: lazy, irresponsible, rapacious, and thoughtless. These views are at times tempered by an acknowledgment that all groups of human beings share these failings; yet, the work as a whole undercuts that simple truth. One must go back to Huxley's early articles or to her later works for a more complete and balanced picture of the forces contributing to the deleterious treatment of arable land in Africa.

The Sorcerer's Apprentice also presents Indians as duplicitous, hypocritical, pushy, and dangerous, stating that the "White Highlands" of Kenya are reserved for

Nellie, Josceline, and Elspeth Grant at Kitimuru Farm in Thika, 1922 (Estate of Elspeth Huxley)

Europeans mainly to keep them out of the grips of the Indians who are planning to make Kenya an Indian colony. Throughout the volume is a barely suppressed resentment of any criticism of white settlers or administrators in Kenya. Yet, Huxley acknowledged racial disparity in Kenya even as she criticized Tanganyika and Uganda for their uneasiness about Kenyan racial policies. She saw them as inevitable. For example, she justified paying Africans less than Europeans for the same work on the grounds that to do otherwise would cause unspeakable inflation.

The Sorcerer's Apprentice also attempts to answer the hypothetical question "who is being exploited?" Huxley responded:

> The British, shivering with meagre fuel . . . shorn by vicious taxes of what they should be putting by for a little comfort in their old age, and themselves grossly overcrowded . . . are paying for these Mombasa Africans to live almost rent free on their sun-warmed island . . . never cold and seldom hungry, a six-hour day the most that is ever asked of them. Fair enough, perhaps–restitution for past neglect, fulfillment of colonial responsibilities?–but it does seem hard that the British should be accused of exploiting Africans.

Huxley finds East Africa lacking in industry; yet, when she encountered native industries such as fishing and salt collecting, Huxley disparaged the work as unacceptably backward for a modern country:

> If Uganda is to be developed, the latent wealth of these waters must be exploited no less than the resources of the land. It is certain that this wealth cannot be fully exploited by those crude go-as-you-please native methods which served well enough before Africa was sucked into the stream of world economics and world history.

Huxley does acknowledge different standards, pointing out that salt collecting, like fishing, "is a real native industry: according to our standards, wasteful of labour, crude and inefficient, but exactly right according to theirs, yielding minimum needs for minimum effort–the servant, in fact, and not the master, of their lives." The emphasis on "crude and inefficient" lingers, despite an implied critique of European and American obsession with capital.

The attitudes Huxley expressed in this book are belied by her actions as a founder of the East African Literature Bureau and as a woman of letters. Although

African literacy might seem to lead to enlightenment, Huxley wrote in *The Sorcerer's Apprentice* that it really exposes more innocent souls to the poison distilled by "vernacular" newspapers.

An animosity toward educated Africans who question their "colonial masters" also appears in Huxley's novel *The Walled City* (1948). Benjamin Morris, an African, is rescued as a child from a ritual sacrifice, raised by a priest, and sent abroad to be educated. When he returns as a reporter, he foments a riot in which one of the heroes of the novel, a European, is killed. The novel was a Book Society choice.

In 1952 Huxley became a member of the general advisory council for the BBC, continuing to broadcast as part of "The Critics" program and on African matters. In 1953 she spent several months in Kenya, visiting her mother and gathering material for several articles, the novel *A Thing to Love* (1954)–set during the Mau Mau Emergency, which began in 1952–and her travel book *Four Guineas: A Journey through West Africa* (1954). To research *Four Guineas* Huxley traveled to the "Guinea Coast" of West Africa, where she visited Gambia, Sierra Leone, the Gold Coast (now Ghana), and Nigeria–all of which were then British protectorates. Huxley explained her title, which alludes to the British coins called guineas because the source of the gold from which they were minted was supposed to be West Africa: "Guinea Coast gold was considered so much purer than any other that a sovereign minted from it was worth an extra shilling." The four countries thus reflect the "little extra" Africans put into life.

Each of the four sections is prefaced by a brief summary of statistics relating to the country in question, identifying its capital, population, area, trade, history, and government. The histories begin with European discovery, usually around the fifteenth century, and the governmental synopses focus on the 1940s and 1950s. Only Nigeria is acknowledged to have had a civilization before European settlement. It is said to have had a "crude form of government" from the thirteenth century. The focus of the volume, as the reviewer for *The Times* (13 February 1954) described it, is on "the purely African democracies hastening towards self-government." (the Gold Coast achieved independence as Ghana in 1957, and Nigeria, Sierra Leone, and Gambia became independent nations in 1960, 1961, and 1963 respectively.) The reviewer also praised Huxley's "descriptive powers" but noted that "in West Africa an East African is just as much a stranger as someone fresh from Britain" and that Huxley had not quite acknowledged new developments in those countries.

Huxley focused less on hopes for the future than on describing her travels and what she saw. Gambian women supplement the landscape as they "look like flowers on the move"; a "Tough, stocky" Welshman, "intolerant of slovenly standards, a glutton for work . . . has galvanized the sleepy Gambia." In Sierra Leone Huxley commented that the typical male posture is reclining in a hammock and a photograph is included to illustrate the point. The reader is also told that after puberty African students become dull: the "usual explanation is that, onwards from fourteen, a busy sex life uses up" the students' energy. In one town Huxley found every female, whether a teenager or a granny, pregnant.

African dances, Huxley wrote, have "a rough, cruel humour. . . . they aim to threaten and to terrify." In Sierra Leone she reported that leopard killings of human beings were staged for cannibalistic and magical reasons. In Kumasi, just fifty years earlier, she noted, "the delight in cruelty, bloodshed and excess" led to human sacrifice on a vast scale–three thousand victims for one queen's funeral. The brutality of one form of execution is described as "not for the squeamish." The footnote that describes it takes up most of a page: "A favourite method" for executing slaves, "when they were not needed for funeral sacrifices, was to smear them with honey and peg them to an ant-heap." In 1950, she reported, a huge massacre was followed by an active meat trade. In consequence, local laws were passed "obliging butchers to sell meat with the hide still on, the better to identify its origin." Huxley commented that such activity "must have been a factor in keeping population numbers level, " and she added, such slaughter provided excitement in lives (presumably for those not slaughtered) that seemed "how monotonous, how anaemic, how inert!"

Huxley also devoted many pages to animal abuse. She noted, for example that the "progressive Ibo" beat to death, hanged, or otherwise tortured old, worn-out horses; "This is no relic of barbarism; it is a recognized social custom of the new middle class." In fact, wrote Huxley, "We have never faced the fact that a great many people, including a lot of Africans, enjoy inflicting cruelty and find bloodshed stimulating, not appalling."

The volume is framed by two passages that encapsulate the unfathomable qualities of Africa for Huxley. The book begins, "It has been said that Africa is the only continent without a history. Not because history has not been made here: because Africa devours its history as it goes along, eats up its monuments, destroys its artifacts and absorbs its invaders, like a boa constrictor that swallows a kid." The book ends with the observation that "from the days of ancient Egypt and Phoenicia until modern times," the waves of immigrants that have flowed across Africa have been

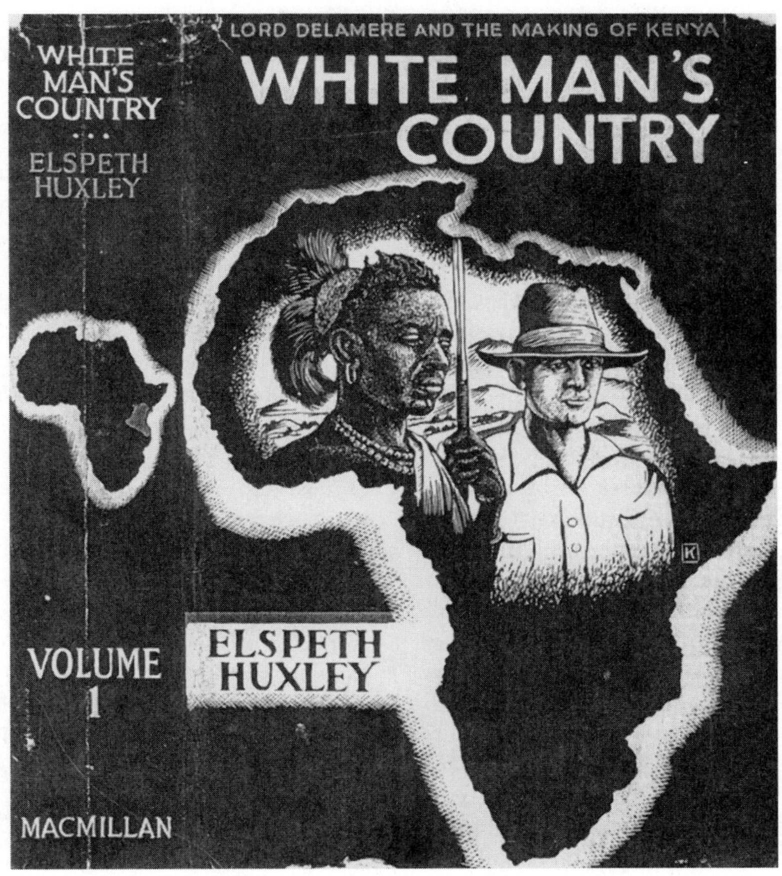

Dust jacket for Huxley's first book (1935), a biography that established her as an authority on Kenya

"absorbed into that great conglomeration of races labelled 'African.' From all these, the jackdaw continent has picked out the bits that caught her fancy and built them into a subtle, ruthless and ancient society. . . . The rest has disintegrated, leaving little trace." These beautifully written passages reflect common views of Africa among Huxley's contemporaries, visions of African society as cruel, primitive, and erecting nothing of lasting value, "a subtle and ruthless" society with few needs. Huxley acknowledged historical traces of a great era of African art, the source of the "distorted later art of West Africa," adding that this art is "so European, so classical in form, that all sorts of speculations were set loose as to forgotten civilizations and links with the antique world."

Huxley recognized that to read one culture in light of another does both a disservice, acknowledging, "Foreign parts seem often to provoke in English people the most inappropriate comparisons." Nonetheless, she said, Gambia "reminded me of East Anglia," and Efik society is divided into houses "like Montagues and Capulets." She also decided that Ashanti girls understood the ancient Greek drama *Antigone* better than English girls because of African family solidarity. This equation of the classical world with contemporary Africa suggests admiration, but elsewhere Huxley criticized the African focus on the family. For her, "So long as the African family system continues–and it is the core and soul of African life–so long will bribery and corruption . . . flourish."

Travel writing about Africa often asserts a sense of the organic nature of the people as well as the land. Huxley praised the spartan simplicity of African life and criticized the imperial monuments being erected to education. Teachers trained at colleges "for which the British taxpayer has found about a quarter of a million pounds" would be teaching in far less luxurious surroundings, she pointed out. "Is it, then, wise to break these shoots off the branch that bore them and for two years to pamper them in such artificial surroundings, and then to plant them out again in stony ground?" This metaphor relies less on botany than on the concept of the African as part of African flora and fauna.

Huxley's concern with African overpopulation, central to all her nonfiction writings about the continent, led to "unsentimental" ambiguous attitudes toward statistics such as the reduction of infant mortality in Gambia from 50 percent. The babies that survived, Huxley pointed out, needed to eat, and hypothetically they ate a vast amount over a period of twenty years. Then "the saved ones have in their turn started breeding, and soon the process gets out of hand, as threatening as a cancerous tumour." Famine, she warned, is the result: "Slavery, epidemic and famine" are "triple guardians of the balance" between land and population.

Not all reviewers were sympathetic to Huxley's point of view. Some of the sharpest criticism was leveled by the reviewer for *The Listener* (2 September 1954), who called the book "vivid and unfair." "Mrs. Huxley goes too far," the reviewer continued, and "has failed to bring out . . . the very real achievements, the substantial degree of mutual understanding and co-operation among Africans of many different cultures and still more between them and Europeans." In the 20 March 1954 issue of *The New Statesman,* Kingsley Martin commented that Huxley began from "all the prejudices that one might expect" and that "she everywhere emphasises the primitive nature of the cultures upon which Western ideas had been only recently imposed. But she has done her best to be fair."

Certainly Huxley could identify unfair practices and see their contribution to food shortages. *No Easy Way* (1957) documents blatantly discriminatory practices in the Kenya Farmers' Association and in soil conservation practices. Ian Spencer's later "Settler Dominance, Agricultural Production and the Second World War In Kenya," a detailed economic account in the *Journal of African History* (1980), describes racially discriminatory practices in Kenya from 1941 on, which led to a famine in 1943 and "the abandonment of all programmes of soil conservation." The conscription of labor and livestock led to a "movement from willing co-operation in the early years of the war to concerted resistance by the end." These tensions contributed to support for the Mau Mau rebellion. Huxley's response to the growing resistance to European measures follows a classic pattern: placing blame on Africans, not Europeans. Such thinking accounts for Huxley's celebration of the British in Kenya, a viewpoint that she moderated in her later writings.

Toward the end of one eulogy to British efforts in Kenya, Huxley described an encounter with a scientist who handed her a mud brick used to build African huts and explained, "That is impregnated with DDT. . . . It kills all mosquitoes within fifteen seconds of their contact with the walls. The incidence of malarial infection in the blood of children fell by half after one application." Since malaria was a major health problem, Huxley praised his efforts. Yet, with current knowledge of the deleterious effects of DDT on human health, this public-health effort demonstrates how Europeans' good intentions did not always succeed in Africa.

Huxley's point of view may be disturbing to many readers in the 1990s, but the contemporary audience for *No Easy Way* responded positively. The *TLS* review (5 February 1949) described the book as "most entertaining and full of exceptionally good pictures of life in East Africa. . . . The author writes objectively, accurately and amusingly with an impeccably liberal generosity and balance." The reviewer's only criticism was "Possibly the comic and farcical in the background of some of her stories will be lost on strangers to the Black Continent, and for them the humour of the scene might have been pointed more plainly on occasion. The black man's smile, the temper of a child that laughs almost too readily, win affection and long-enduring patience from Englishmen."

In *Four Guineas* Huxley began looking back on her experiences in Kenya, a description of the life of an American family suddenly blossoming into a comparison with Huxley's childhood. In 1959 she published a full-length memoir, *The Flame Trees of Thika,* the work most responsible for her enduring fame. Critics often refer to this book and its sequel, *The Mottled Lizard,* as her best-loved descriptions of Africa. A semifictional autobiography, *The Flame Trees of Thika* tells of Huxley's life until the advent of World War I, when she and her mother, called Tilly in this book, leave for England, while her father, here called Robin, goes off to fight in the war.

Flame Trees is marked by a child's innocence. Politics are absent. The child cares about the landscape and the wildlife, from tawny sunsets to chameleons changing color, from sleepy lions to shy but haughty gazelles. The Africans she meets are her parents' servants and their families. Rather than judging them by European standards, the little girl sees them as demonstrating interesting new ways of living. They remain figures of some mystery to her, even though the servants reveal things to her that they keep hidden from adult Europeans. The child finds Europeans slightly less intriguing than the Africans. Some of their doings and conversations are recorded as well, including those that reveal a love affair that some readers see as parallel to that between Denys Finch-Hatton and Karen Blixen. (Under her pen name Isak Dinesen, Blixen described the relationship in *Out of Africa* [1937]). *Flame Trees of Thika* creates what Dorothy Hammond and Alta Jablow call a vision of "the land in amber"–or, as Mary Louise Pratt calls it, the special or marginal space in which the romance of Africans as nurturing caretakers to Europeans can be enacted. Africa is an Eden before the fall. The first critic, Huxley's mother, who had disapproved of the project, wrote Huxley on 8 July 1958, "Have read two-thirds of the typescript and like it very much. I am *not* like Tilly."

In a 1990 essay that compares *The Flame Trees of Thika* to Dinesen's *Out of Africa* and Mary S. Lovell's *Straight on Till Morning: A Biography of Beryl Markham* (1987), Knipp observes that the three books share a sense of Africa as pristine but are "marked by adventure, freedom and power." The overall tone is "elegiac–a kind of collective cultural nostalgia, a longing that author and original audience share for a younger world that is not crowded, stuffy, and emotionally and experientially diminished." Admiring its humor and satire, Knipp considered Huxley's work the best of the three, but he criticized its tired ways of presenting the other: Africa is a utopian feudal society in which Africans are part of the natural fauna, not people in their own rights. Thus, he argued, Huxley's book reveals the "need in the Western world for justifying images and narrative formulations of white power and the consequent nostalgic persistence in the white imagination of a mythic Africa."

In January 1959 Huxley flew to Kenya to visit her seventy-five-year-old mother and to gather material for articles and another book about Africa, *A New Earth: An Experiment in Colonialism* (1960). By the end of 1959, Nellie Grant had sold most of her land at Njoro, keeping only enough to provide for herself and her servants. At home in Britain, Gervas Huxley had become a published author with the appearance of *Endymion Porter: The Life of a Courtier, 1587–1649* (1959).

A New Earth: An Experiment in Colonialism contrasts interestingly with *The Sorcerer's Apprentice,* Huxley's earlier overview of Kenya. The reader is taken on a "tour: not of the whole of Kenya, but of most of the African land units." The controlling image is the giant Progress, striding across the country, bringing change for good or ill, sometimes moving quickly and at other times slowly as it encounters impediments. The seventeen chapters move methodically from location to location, introducing the reader to "Better Farmers"–those who had adopted the government suggestions for land use–and their families and cattle. In areas where conservation programs are not accepted, the book repeats the theme of the selfless British colonial officer spurned by suspicious Africans. Writing of a scheme to terrace hillsides and settle landless Africans at a spot called Makueni, Huxley commented that after Kenyatta visited the district, "everyone boycotted Makueni. And the land went from bad to worse, if that was possible." Of the Luo the reader is told,

> Their obstinacy is legendary, they are inclined to be sullen and suspicious. . . . No spontaneous wish for any branch of Progress except the political seems to have gripped the collective Luo mind. Here, on these hot and apathetic lakeland flats, all the impetus has come from Europeans.

Huxley talking to Kikuyu women in Njoro, Kenya, circa 1936 (Estate of Elspeth Huxley)

A New Earth asks the question of whether government should push for change where it is not wanted: "It is an old story: should nanny sit by and watch Master Robert break up his toys–in this case, ruin the soil, create acute erosion, turn the whole of Nyanza province, which contains one-third of Kenya's population, into a great rural slum?" This grim possibility, Huxley warns, is already becoming a reality: "All the evils of land abuse were here displayed in concentrated form. . . . Famine was beginning to threaten these overcrowded areas–for the one thing the people continued to produce more and more of was their own kind." These statements sit oddly against Huxley's fair-minded acknowledgments of weakness among the colonizers, as when she comments that "nothing has been more characteristic of the half-century of European intervention in Africa than the slap-happy introduction of bright, well-meaning ideas by enthusiasts of all kinds, without any regard for their long-term consequences." Yet, one of the efforts she seems to criticize is improved public health: "To apply death control so drastically without restraining births, to fill the human reservoir while stopping its normal outlets, appears folly."

Huxley's views on literacy changed between 1948 and 1960. In *A New Earth* she praised the results of education, remarking that "how much the people seem able and willing to do for themselves" may be a result of their schooling. "The educational harvest is now starting to come in," she wrote, warning that the lack of places in schools for everyone created the danger of "turning loose" the uneducated or only slightly educated.

Huxley's attitude also changed toward efforts to eradicate the tsetse fly by the wholesale slaughtering of wildlife. She had written favorably and at length on these efforts in *The Sorcerer's Apprentice,* but in *A New Earth* she pointed out that since the tsetse fly is discriminating in its eating habits, "many of the species mowed down . . . need never have been shot at all"– unless researchers discovered that tsetse flies would switch their diet. "And tsetse flies are, in general, very conservative," she notes.

Throughout Huxley's work runs a moral imperative to use or lose the resources of the land. It is that land and its teeming life that draws Huxley's greatest interest, as shown in a passionate letter to *The Times* (24 October 1959) in which she deplored poaching in African national parks and begged the Western world to fund them. The letter ends with a prophecy: "For want of a nail, the kingdom of the beasts is in deadly peril. Nature does not recreate what man has destroyed."

The power of nature shimmers through Huxley's prose: "the sunset blazed across the water and lit the whole sky . . . everything burned with a wild, dramatic evening glow. . . . There was something about this excess of royal colour, the crimsons and purples and the gold, that disturbed the heart." Drama is wedded to scale: "To see a tropical sunset in a sky full of cumulus magnified by a lake the size of Ireland is almost too much for the human eye." This scale evokes grand, Romantic comparisons: "The saplings grow on a Gothic pinnacle high above a blue, speckled distance which stretches northwards apparently for ever; in that vast trough, enormous mountains lie like dice thrown by a god on the table of the universe."

As in Huxley's earlier works *A New Earth* presents Africans as one with their stark landscape. Commenting on a colonial administrator's speech, Huxley wrote: "A few of the seeds he planted in the minds of the Tugen lay dormant, like those of grass, for many years, to germinate when conditions were right." Huxley believed that Africans, like the barren land, had to be coaxed to grow:

> The Tugen are not impressive physically, being rather scrawny and with no distinctive cast of feature. The Masai pushed them into poorer regions because they lacked spirit and cunning to stand up to the aggressors, and they have not done much since.

Yet, the Tugen have embraced European values: "The bug has bitten, Progress has come, wants are poking forth like grass beneath the thorn: even among the Tugen, an unambitious tribe."

In *A New Earth* Huxley moved away from the defensive tone of *The Sorcerer's Apprentice,* a striking development given that the book was published in the same year as the convening of the Lancaster House Conference, signaling the arrival of African self-rule in Kenya more quickly than many, including Huxley, anticipated. (Kenya became an independent member of the British Commonwealth of Nations in 1963.) Huxley ended her book by reiterating that politics lie outside the scope of her investigation. Yet, as a reviewer wrote in the 15 July 1960 *TLS,* politics "are not absent from it." The sympathetic review went on to record three political threads running through *A New Earth:* if anything goes wrong with the crops or markets, the government will be blamed; African nationalists, called simply "politicians," oppose land reforms; and "if European influence is removed from the scene, as it might be when an African Government takes charge, then many schemes . . . may collapse." The review closes with praise for the brilliance of Huxley's "description of a largely undiscovered country."

In 1962 Huxley was named a Commander of the British Empire (CBE), and she published another autobiographical perspective on her "undiscovered country." *The Mottled Lizard,* a sequel to *The Flame Trees of Thika,* was published in the United States as *On the Edge of the Rift.* This volume covers Huxley's adolescent years at Thika and the move to Njoro. The tone is similar to *The Flame Trees of Thika,* equally lighthearted and engaging, with the same love of landscape and tamed animals permeating the pages. For example, Huxley wrote of Rupert, a pet cheetah:

> To begin with he rollicked with the dachshunds, but when he grew bigger and rolled them over roughly they wisely refused any further dealings, and would lie motionless gazing at him with a look of obstinate entreaty if he invited them to play. Should he refuse to take no for an answer, they would snarl and give a warning snap. This was always enough to quell Rupert. He was not an aggressive type, but rather humble.

Because the heroine is older than in *The Flame Trees of Thika,* there is a greater focus on people in this book, which includes an account of her first infatuation.

"Ex-slave making twine: African settlement, Gedi" and "Produce market, Zanzibar," photographs by Huxley for her 1948 book, The Sorcerer's Apprentice: A Journey through East Africa

A *TLS* reviewer (6 July 1962) called *The Mottled Lizard* "one of the few books that really smells of Africa. . . . it brings back the taste." Nonetheless, critics have argued about the characterization of white society in Kenya and about Huxley's decision to once again narrate her tale in novelistic form. Reviewing the book for *The New Statesman* (25 May 1962), Colin Haycroft noted the "endearing accounts" of raising pet animals and the "unflagging humour" of the settlers but commented that an "unsympathetic critic might well doubt that any group of people could have been so consistently goodhearted and courageous, or so amiable in their eccentricities, as those represented in these evocative pages." Certainly some of the same eccentrics have less benign avatars elsewhere in Huxley's writing; the unbearable governess Miss Cooper, who yammers on at Elspeth, first appears in *Death of an Aryan,* where her single state leads to obsession and mayhem. Huxley's hindsight perhaps lent the characters benignity. Thomas Hinde, writing for *The Spectator* (11 May 1962), praised the characterizations. For him the Kenyan settlers who "have come to symbolise reactionary colonial sentiment at its most stupid . . . become real and human; not all nice people" but sympathetic. Hinde also praised the natural descriptions, which he found vivid and compelling; yet, he criticized the repetitiveness of the book, "like Hebrew poetry." Hinde also questioned its veracity, particularly in Huxley's novelistic creation of long conversations that she could not have remembered verbatim from girlhood. Hinde called these passages "often stilted and artificial" and said that they create "a continuous sense of suspicion."

The role of Africans in the book is minor. While attesting to their centrality, the book leaves the farm workers offstage. For example, the narrator tells the reader, "Every day a cup of tea arrived before sunrise." The African servant who brewed and served that cup of tea is not described. Nonetheless, *The Mottled Lizard* has been widely admired for the world it creates. Writing in *The New York Times Book Review* (23 September 1962), South African novelist Nadine Gordimer praised it for recollecting "the look and smell and feel of the land itself, the physical Africa and the quality of the experience it gives."

This eloquent elegy to Huxley's youth was followed by *The Merry Hippo* (1963), a mystery that presents a different view of Africa. In 1959 and 1960 Huxley had served as a member of the Monckton Advisory Commission on Central Africa, visiting Northern Rhodesia (now Zambia) and Nyasaland (now Malawi) to try to reconcile those holding nationalist African views with those set on racial separation. *The Times* reported on 12 October 1960 that twenty-three of the twenty-five commission members signed the final report, but fifteen had "appended reservations on various sections." Huxley seems to have borrowed from her experiences on this commission when writing the satirical mystery *The Merry Hippo.*

This novel opens in London, where the Commission is assembled, and then moves to the imaginary African protectorate of Hapana, where murder and other mayhem unfold. *The Merry Hippo* expresses far greater cynicism than Huxley's previous nonfiction or her semifictional memoirs. In *The Merry Hippo* Africans are central characters. When they become suspects, it is not as a result of bigotry but of politics and personal characteristics. They are neither more nor less noble than any European character. The reviewer for *TLS* (5 April 1963) called the novel "a delight to read," and Orville Prescott, writing for *The New York Times* (12 January 1964), praised "its examples of African politics, African pride and African prejudice."

Huxley's next novel, *A Man From Nowhere* (1964), is a more serious look at African and British politics than *The Merry Hippo.* The hero of *A Man From Nowhere,* Dick Heron, travels from southern Africa to England to kill Peter Buckle, a British cabinet minister who has supported the African leader of a violent independence movement. Heron holds Buckle responsible for unleashing atrocities in his country–including the maiming of animals, the brutal murder of Heron's crippled brother, the loss of Heron's farm, and the resultant suicide of Heron's wife. Heron is particularly angry that the attackers were not punished but instead were politically rewarded. Some critics appreciated the "colonial" views of England expressed by Heron, as well as the emotional development in this work as Heron comes to terms with his complex motives for revenge. Others found its fictional presentation of issues raised by the Mau Mau uprising salutary. Most agreed, however–as Elizabeth Jennings put it in *The Listener* (18 June 1964)–that the book failed because Huxley "has been unable to weld together the horrific and the ordinary; her style and attitude are not really suited to the macabre."

In 1963 Huxley made another trip to East Africa, which resulted in the travel book *Forks and Hope: An African Notebook* (1964). The title comes from Lewis Carroll's "The Hunting of the Snark" (1867), in which the hunters seek the elusive Snark "with forks and hope." The allusion suggests that Africans are condemned to futility. The reviewer for *The Times* (6 February 1964) captured the main theme of the book in praising Huxley's description of "African settlers swarming on the farms from which the white man . . . is in retreat after having made the soil productive as it had never been before and may never be again." The book expresses Huxley's fear that the "land-hungry black flood" would swamp the "White Highlands" of Kenya

THE FLAME TREES OF THIKA
Memories of an African Childhood
Elspeth Huxley
1959
CHATTO & WINDUS
LONDON

Frontispiece and title page for Huxley's somewhat fictionalized account of her childhood in Kenya before World War I

and strip them bare. Yet, the tone is not strident, and her justification of the white settlers' actions–"they took over forest, bush and plain almost empty of humans, whatever African politicians May subsequently have claimed"–is briefer than in previous volumes.

In writing *Forks and Hope* Huxley drew on visits to parts of Tanganyika, Uganda, and of course Kenya, after the first two achieved independence in 1961 and 1962, respectively, and just months before Kenyan independence in 1963. Huxley's descriptions reveal her awareness of positive change. For example, two dormitories at the Royal College in Kenya, which had been segregated by race when they were built six years earlier, had been integrated: "No one can envisage anything else. So quickly has opinion changed." Huxley again enlivened her writing with exotic details. The reader learns of the lion-men, who are kidnapped and raised from childhood to believe they are lions and to kill on command.

The book also repeats Huxley's warning about the threat of overpopulation by indigenous groups. At one point she puzzles over Asians' desires for rhinoceros horn as an aphrodisiac, which leads to poaching of the animals in Africa:

> Not only is the superstition false, but how can there be a *need* to stimulate the sexual potency of Asian males? With a birth-rate like India's Pakistan, and south-east Asia's? Had the rhinos been slaughtered in the hope of damping down their ardour there might have been more excuse."

The reviewer for *The Times* called the book "completely without bias," but Huxley acknowledges its political stance, blaming liberals for the racial and nationalist tensions in Africa. Huxley argued that British liberals had stripped Africans of their readiness "to serve, to imitate and to follow the European," and, quoting Laurens van der Post, "to love and be loved." The "root of nationalist bitterness," she wrote, "is not that independence was once taken away, but that Europeans have insisted on abruptly restoring it."

Huxley's delight in the African wildlife provides a positive focus to counterbalance her political views. She visited the national parks in Uganda, writing yet again about Africa's age and mystery–embodied in the "*barkans:* the most peculiar sand-dunes I have ever seen" that creep along the plain, with no "rhyme or reason" for their formation or eventual disappearance. Huxley also visited naturalist Joy Adamson, who looked as leonine as her famous lion Elsa, and a game warden who lived with mongooses, zebra foals, and a baby rhinoceros named Rufus, who demanded peppermint drops. Her educated, Western eye captured scenes of great beauty: "A frieze of storks and cranes was outlined against the satin-smooth blue waters." Yet, the sight of flamingos in flocks up to a million "defies the pen." Not all wildlife seemed beautiful to Huxley, however: "a concentration of hippos" wallowing in Nile cabbage looked repulsive, "their backs glistening like aluminium blisters, or like silvery pustules on the flesh of some stricken mammoth–a revolting sight."

The sublime glory of the wildlife led Huxley to touch on the difficulty of maintaining beast and human in coexistence. Culling offers one answer, turning poachers into licensed executioners and ensuring that the animals are killed humanely and fully used, from the meat to the hooves and hides, rather than being caught in snares where they die painfully, by inches, until what is left is hardly fit for even a poacher. Huxley saw such a practice as the only way to encourage farmers with scant land to share it with animals other than cattle. Similarly, within the game parks, culling forestalls the protected animals from overgrazing and destroying their precious habitats in the same way that cattle overgrazing has resulted in land erosion outside the parks. Huxley discusses the Ngorongoro crater with admirable restraint; its excision from the national park for use as Masai grazing land had caused her to write an impassioned letter to *The Times* on 19 August 1958, pleading that it be preserved as a source of tourist income as well as for land and animal causes. *Forks and Hope* details the plight of animals directly and compassionately. Huxley even wrote of her regret at the advance of cultivation in Njoro, where she and her parents had lived after Thika, but her regret is tempered with a sense of inevitability. No matter how beautiful the trees or how hospitable the hyraxes, they had to give way to species that can be farmed productively. The book also includes some delightful accounts of Huxley's childhood, including some lively accounts of her tangles with a pet hyrax who wanted to sleep on her neck.

The men of power discussed in *Forks and Hope* are no longer chiefs under British government whose effectiveness can be judged in terms of British plans, but the leaders of new countries. President Julius Nyerere of Tanganyika and Jomo Kenyatta and Tom Mboya of Kenya may–as Huxley says in some bewilderment–imitate figures from fairy tales in their rises to power; but whatever Europeans thought of their plans for one-party states or affirmative action, Huxley presented them as making their own roads. Huxley explored some of the beginnings of what has come to be called "post-coloniality," looking briefly at the philosophy of negritude and discussing Octave Mannoni's theses about the psychological impact of colonialism in *Prospero and Caliban* (1956).

Huxley also asserted that Africans had pioneered civilization: "The great Egyptian monuments have always been there to prove it, and now we can add the achievements of Meroe and Kush, and the Nok cultures of the Niger and Benue valleys dating back beyond 2000 B.C." Huxley believed that these civilizations had little impact; yet, her acknowledgment of them does add to the "historical" summary given in *Four Guineas.*

Forks and Hope marks Huxley's acceptance of the independence of former British colonies, an acceptance that is all the more admirable when viewed in comparison to Huxley's earlier views. The reviewer for *TLS* (13 February 1964) remarked that *Forks and Hope* "may make some old Empire hands turn in their grave," but "truth shines through the whole of Mrs. Huxley's book."

In 1965 Nellie Grant acknowledged that new land-management practices boded ill for her old age. She sold her remaining land in Kenya to her servants and moved to Portugal. Huxley also turned her attention to other regions. Her next travel book, *Their Shining Eldorado: A Journey through Australia,* her only non-African work in the genre, was published on 11 May 1967, the same day that Gervas Huxley published *Victorian Duke,* a biography of Elspeth Huxley's maternal granduncle, the first Duke of Westminster.

Critics praised *Their Shining Eldorado.* J. Bernhard Burnham exclaimed in *National Review* (3 October 1967) that "among travel writers Elspeth Huxley knows no peer," and R. C. Scriven, writing in *Punch* (19 July 1967), praised Huxley's "brilliantly equipped mind [that] expresses her curiosity about the problems of the ancient, brand-new continent" compellingly.

Their Shining Eldorado focuses less on political issues than on what Burnham called "the constant struggle between man and his environment." Thus, although some chapters address Australian cities, more focus on regions. Others, such as "Kangaroos" and "The Golden Fleece," reveal Huxley's true love. Furthermore, the discussions of cities are often limited to information about their founding and typical architecture. In Sydney, Huxley "battles" her way out of an art show and goes to the zoo; in Canberra she courts lyre and bower birds; and in Melbourne she tells the reader, as Clive James put it in *The New Statesman* (7 July 1967),

Frontispiece and title page for Huxley's 1976 book, a record of one year of her life in rural England

"as much about the Mallee-Fowl as I will need." Writing in *The Times* (18 May 1967), Judy Egerton cited "nasty" and "impertinent" bits, but acknowledged, "No pommie book about Australia ever pleased all Australians." (*Pommie* is an Australian slang term for the English.) Egerton praised the "entrancing descriptions" of Australia's fauna. Indeed, the reviewer for *TLS* (25 May 1967) argued, "it might have been better if the Australian wild life, which already hogs the book, had been allowed to have the lot." Huxley probably agreed: the last chapter of the book is "Birds and Beasts."

The book also continued Huxley's campaign for proper land management. Just as in Africa, land clearance and overgrazing had led to desertification. Huxley quoted a botanist who told her, "Australia is creating the biggest desert in the world in the shortest space of time ever known." Yet the enormous scale of Australia filled Huxley with utopian visions of how the "millions of unused acres" could fulfill their potential. With enough determination, Australians could "flood the whole of central Australia, irrigating millions of square miles and feeding everyone who needs to be fed." Indeed, Huxley saw this move as inevitable: one day "the call of seabirds will again be heard, fish swim above the Simpson desert and trees be reflected in mighty reservoirs." Huxley also bemoaned the dwindling of the dry-land wildlife in the face of people who, according to one scientist, "look on reserves as potentially vacant land held in cold storage until some 'useful' purpose can be found for it." The purpose need not even be food, Huxley noted, but amusement centers or worse. Nostalgia contrasted uneasily with Huxley's demands for progress.

Clive James admired Huxley's thorough regard for Australian natural life–her ability to make "the wild life seem very attractive, warm, pouched, cuddly and somehow rather English"–but added: "The book's strength is all in the closeness to the soil. Its weakness is in the distance from human beings, which brings with it misunderstandings on the grand scale." He cited some minor errors but said the real fault in the book is a fundamental misunderstanding of the Australian social system. James found Huxley's views on Aborigines rather "sympathetic and on the whole wise, but she caps it by talking about the difficulties of educating them to their political responsibilities. About the political responsibilities of the white Australians, nothing is said."

James's critique echoed concerns raised in Huxley's African writings, and the parallel is not hard to find in the book itself. At times Huxley contrasts Australia to Africa. Picnicking by a river, Huxley comments, "In Africa you would expect crocodiles, but here is nothing dangerous or vicious, not even crabs." The similarities come through more strongly: "'The Government is going too fast.' How often have I heard the same complaint in Africa!"; the diary of a legendary robber is written "in the blood of kangaroos, full of fantasies of power and doom and strangely akin to the screeds 'posted' in trees by Mau Mau leaders in Africa." Even the indigenous people are compared: "the women have enormous buttocks where they store fat against lean times, as the Hottentots do"; each tribe of Aborigines "has its explanations of such phenomena as fire, death and the emergence of man"; their similarity "to those of many African tribes is remarkable." These passages show Huxley's continuing tendency to distance herself from the exotic other. The descriptions categorize indigenous creation tales as quaint, ignoring their parallels to the Western stories of Adam and Eve or Prometheus. This approach–coupled with statements such as her explanation that the "White Australia policy" has less to do with a belief in "coloured races" being inferior than with a fear that Chinese power would swamp British initiative–once again left Huxley open to the charge of being an apologist for British colonialism.

In *Love Among the Daughters* (1968) Huxley returned to autobiography. It is a travel book in reverse, recounting Huxley's journey to England from Kenya to study Agriculture at Reading University, her discoveries about the British class system between the wars, and her year at Cornell University in Ithaca, New York. Writing in *Book World* (3 November 1968), Peggy Shonbrun found the work charming and stated that with "her eye for the patterns of English country manners and morals" Huxley could be compared to Jane Austen.

In the same year Huxley's son, Charles, married. As a wedding gift Nellie Grant gave the couple most of her silver and her dead husband's gold watch, which, Huxley noted in *Nellie,* "had survived fifty-three years of hazard in Africa. So it was ironical" that the watch was stolen (along with the silver) just a few months later in London. The next decade held sorrow. Gervas Huxley's health was failing, and in 1970 the Huxleys sold their farmhouse, Woodfolds, and moved to a nearby cottage. In April 1971 Gervas Huxley died a few days before his seventy-seventh birthday. In August 1977 Huxley flew to Portugal to help her ninety-two-year-old mother pack up her belongings and move to England. When she arrived in Portugal, Huxley saw that her mother was more ill than she had reported, and, before they could return to England, Nellie Grant died in Lisbon on 21 August.

Huxley continued to write. In 1971 she published *The Challenge of Africa,* an illustrated overview of the history of Africa from the perspective of European exploration. The first chapter is titled "The Dark Continent"; the second is "First Reports." The book then chronicles the quests to find the sources of the Nile and Congo Rivers, introducing the reader to Sir Richard Francis Burton and John Hanning Speke, Henry Morton Stanley and David Livingstone. Huxley next turned to biographies of pioneering figures: *Livingstone and His African Journeys* (1974), *Florence Nightingale* (1975), and *Scott of the Antarctic* (1977). Published to warm acclaim, these books are notable for their readability and sympathetic but unsentimental portraits of their subjects. A review of *Livingstone and His African Journeys* in *TLS* (11 October 1974) reported: "Huxley tells Livingstone's extraordinary story without embellishments, and without concealing his weaknesses–his irresponsibility towards his family, for example. The result is a fascinating account of one of the world's most remarkable men." A few years later a reviewer for *The Economist* (12 November 1977) gave similarly glowing praise to *Scott of the Antarctic,* saying that the "book is one of the finest to be written about the Antarctic and it certainly towers above any other biography of Scott."

Huxley claimed that her hobbies were resting, gossiping, and gardening, but she continued to work at her writing in the 1980s and 1990s. She was quoted in a 16 September 1968 *Times* article as saying, "I don't think I shall write any more autobiography," because her later life was "more ordinary" than her early years; but in 1976 she produced *Gallipot Eyes,* a diary account of a year in Wiltshire, and in 1980 she edited and wrote a long memoir and her mother's letters from Africa, as *Nellie. Nellie* has received high praise for both Huxley and her mother. In the *Journal of African History* (1981) Anthony Clayton celebrated its "zest," describing it as a work that will make historians wiser as well as engaging them. Finally, *Out in the Midday Sun* (1985) completes the record of Huxley's experiences in Kenya. Robert Baldock wrote in *TLS* (31 January 1986) that "Kenya has been lucky in its interpreters. If Karen Blixen is its most elegant, Elspeth Huxley is its most humane." He describes *Out in the Midday Sun* as "a rambling and disorganized book, part collection of anecdotes, but warm, generous, humorous, wise and packed with life on every page." Perhaps in keeping with shifting perspectives, not all reviewers were as sympathetic. In *The New York Times Book Review* (22 March 1987) Louisa Dawkins asked, "Were Africans really as peripheral to Mrs. Huxley's Kenyan experience as one would conclude from this book?" and ended the review by stating "her Kenya emerges as very much a 'white man's country.'"

Nine Faces of Kenya (1990), an anthology of writing about that nation, suffers from the same limitation as *Out in the Midday Sun.* Perhaps Huxley's most ambitious

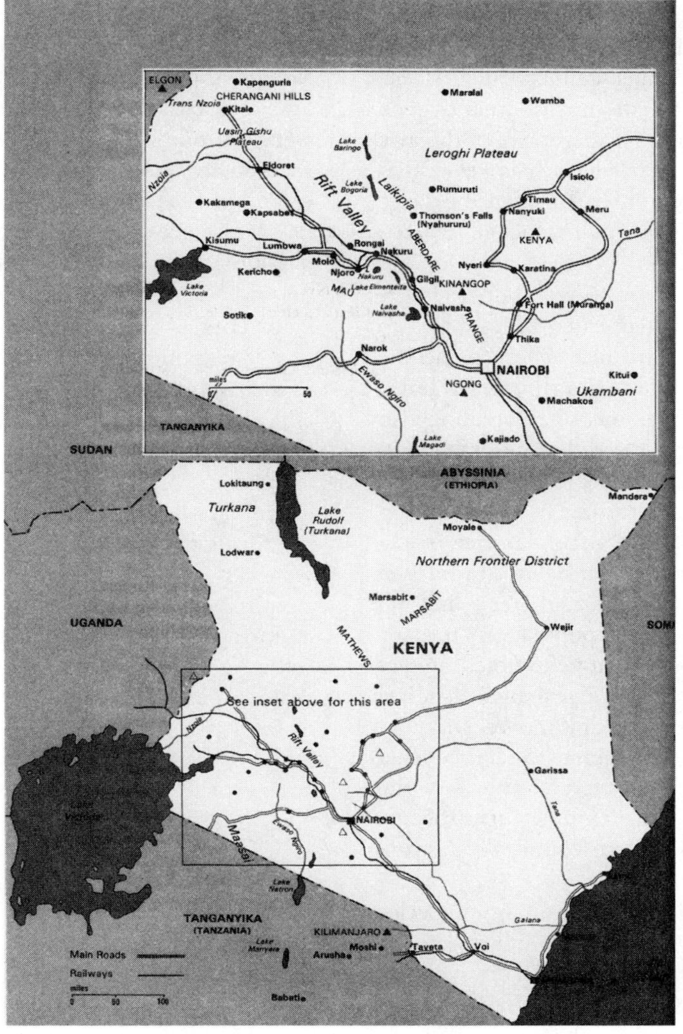

Map from Huxley's 1985 book, Out in the Midday Sun: My Kenya

attempt to present an overview of Kenya, the book is a collection of nine writers' views of historical aspects of the country: "Explorations," "Travel," "Settlers," "Wars," "Environment," "Wildlife," "Hunting," "Life-styles," and "Legend and Poetry." Yet, when one reads these sections, one may agree with Abdulrazak Gurnah (*TLS,* 12 October 1990), who wrote "that this anthology has been put together with affection, but it reveals only one face of Kenya." "Explorations," for example, focuses on Europeans' first sighting of landmarks such as Mount Kilimanjaro. The introduction says that Huxley intended the work for the "Young Kenyan with only a sketchy knowledge of his country's past, its peoples and its potentialities," but only the section on legends and poetry gives voice to the indigenous culture. Roughly the same length as the other sections, this chapter is too short to cover the range from creation myths to contemporary written poetry.

Huxley's Africa is gone. Some question if it ever existed. Her most poignant and effective writing acknowledges that loss. *Last Days in Eden* (1984), with text by Huxley and photographs by Hugo van Lawick, laments the passing of the days when Africa teemed with wildlife. At the same time it offers hope for the resurgence of some species through careful management, culling by license to create a sustainable economy and to maintain the animals' health. Like *Whipsnade, Last Days in Eden* attests to Huxley's reportorial strengths and her ability to present complicated situations without reducing them to false alternatives.

Huxley's ability to describe the beauty of the natural world without resorting to sentimentality has drawn praise throughout her career, and that skill comes to the fore in *Whipsnade: Captive Breeding for Survival* (1981), about the country branch of the London Zoo that carries out research and breeding programs.

The book allowed Huxley to engage her readers' attention in serious questions about captive breeding, and she contrasted the lives of some animals, such as elephants, kept in zoos–a form of imprisonment, even when benignly intended–with her memories of the awe they evoked in the wild. Huxley believed, however, that true freedom would never come again for the large mammals and for those whose environment has been taken for the human population.

Whipsnade echoes Huxley's travel books in its emphasis that people must be educated in how best to use their land, and again it warns that as long as people believe in the aphrodisiacal qualities of rhinoceros horn, the rhinoceros is in danger of extinction. The book also includes quick sketches of dedicated, hardworking British zookeepers and scientists whose studies and care have gone into the successful raising of animals in a country unlike their natural habitats. As in her works on Africa, Huxley noted that human habits are responsible for turning rainforest to desert, thereby limiting the possibility of returning captive populations to their natural environments. On a more hopeful note, Huxley acknowledged that human opinion can change, as it has from the game-hunting attitude of "if it moves, shoot it" to an aesthetic appreciation of animals and the belief that they must be guarded against exploitation–for the tangible human benefits of their previously unsuspected roles in the environment, as well as for morally responsible reasons.

Whipsnade raises an ethical question about species whose habitats are already irretrievably lost: ought these species be preserved for purely decorative purposes? Pointing out that wholly zoo-reared animals begin to evolve to suit the zoo, the book cautions against a Godlike approach to animal management. The volume ends with a clear acknowledgment that continuing such efforts and research is expensive. Yet, funding for such research can also further human goals, Huxley pointed out, as learning how best to manage land or investigating the possible use of formerly wild or "game" animals as farm stock can benefit agriculture. The book also asks why British zoos must charge admission to remain operational while art museums in Britain do not. The question pointedly illuminates the differing treatment of human and natural artifacts.

Huxley was at her best in her nature writing, and her last book, *Peter Scott: Painter and Naturalist* (1993); displays her strengths to the utmost. She continued her research for her biography of Robert Falcon Scott to tell the life of his son, a traveler, painter, and conservationist. The book captures the rugged landscape Scott encountered in his quests to find wildlife on its home ground. Iceland provided variety: "Strong winds stirred the lava-dust into gritty sand-storms. In the few hours of darkness a fierce cold gripped the members of the party in their tents, whereas in day-time, if it wasn't raining, they sunbathed and suffered from heat." Huxley's sense of the lively anecdote is put to good use as well. On one excursion, "Peter and Philippa procured two smelly sheepskins and, armed with cameras and disguised as sheep, stalked a flock of geese feeding in a field. The geese rumbled them." Sharing her subject's passion for the natural world, Huxley shone in this volume.

Huxley's place as a writer is secure. Her mystery novels remain popular, and her nostalgic look at Africa in the two early autobiographical works, *The Flame Trees of Thika* and *The Mottled Lizard,* has earned Huxley stature as more than a "popular" writer. Her nonfiction works on Africa offer insight into attitudes prevalent among Huxley's contemporaries in Europe and America during the 1950s and 1960s, when African countries were struggling to gain independence and the British Empire was beginning to crumble. Huxley's most enduring legacy, however, is her lyrical description of setting and wildlife, providing records of a landscape that was, even as Huxley described it, being altered by technology.

Interviews:

"Ahead For Africa: Dictators . . . Tribal Wars . . . Red Influence," *U.S. News & World Report,* 49 (12 September 1960): 82–87;

"An Authority on Africa Looks at the Road Ahead," *U.S. News & World Report,* 50 (6 March 1961): 53–55;

"Why Africa is in Chaos," *U.S. News & World Report,* 56 (17 February 1964): 46–49;

"What A Top Authority Says About Africa's Future," *U.S. News & World Report,* 60 (14 March 1966): 56–57;

Pamela Coleman, "Writing is a Huxley Habit," *Times* (London), 16 September 1968, p. 7.

Bibliographies:

P. A. Empson, *Papers of Elspeth Josceline Huxley, Mss. Afr. s 782 Kept in Rhodes House Library, Oxford,* University of Oxford Colonial Records Project (Oxford: Bodleian Library, 1966);

Robert S. Cross and Michael Perkin, *Elspeth Huxley: A Bibliography* (Winchester, U.K.: St Paul's Bibliographies, 1996).

References:

Earl F. Bargainnier, "The African Mysteries of Elspeth Huxley," *Clues: A Journal of Detection,* 5, no. 2 (1984): 35–47;

C. J. D. Duder, "Love and the Lions: The Image of White Settlement in Kenya in Popular Fiction, 1919–39," *African Affairs,* 90 (1991): 427–438;

Micere Githae-Mugo, *Visions of Africa: The Fiction of Chinua Achebe, Margaret Laurence, Elspeth Huxley and Ngugi wa Thiong'o* (Nairobi: Kenya Literature Bureau, 1978);

Ethel Waddell Githii, "Literary Imperialism in Kenya: Elements of Imperial Sensibility in the African Works of Isak Dinesen and Elspeth Huxley," dissertation, Tufts University, 1980;

Dorothy Hammond and Alta Jablow, *The Africa That Never Was: Four Centuries of British Writing about Africa* (New York: Twayne, 1970);

Thomas R. Knipp, "Kenya's Literary Ladies and the Mythologizing of the White Highlands," *South Atlantic Review,* 55 (1990): 1–16;

Sara Mills, *Discourses of Difference: An Analysis of Women's Travel Writing and Colonialism* (London & New York: Routledge, 1991);

Mary Louise Pratt, *Imperial Eyes: Travel Writing and Transculturation* (London & New York: Routledge, 1992);

Sharon A. Russell, "Elspeth Huxley's Africa: Mystery and Memory," in *Mysteries of Africa,* edited by Eugene Schleh (Bowling Green, Ohio: Bowling Green State University Popular Press, 1991), pp. 21–34;

Reinhard Sander, "Two Views of the Conflict of Cultures in Pre-Emergency Kenya: A Comparative Study of James Ngugi's *The River Between* and Elspeth Huxley's *Red Strangers,*" *Literary Half Yearly,* 19, no. 2 (1978): 27–48;

Marion Tinling, "Elspeth Josceline Huxley: Of Men and Animals in Africa," in her *Women into the Unknown: A Sourcebook on Women Explorers and Travelers* (New York: Greenwood Press, 1989), pp. 133–139;

Hariclea Zengos, "'A World without Walls': Race, Politics and Gender in the African Works of Elspeth Huxley, Isak Dinesen and Beryl Markham," dissertation, Tufts University, 1989.

Papers:

Elspeth Huxley's papers are in the Rhodes House Library at the University of Oxford.

Naomi James

(2 March 1949 –)

Marcia B. Dinneen
Bridgewater State College

BOOKS: *Woman Alone* (London: Daily Express, 1978);

At One with the Sea: Alone Around the World (London: Hutchinson, 1979; republished as *Alone Around the World* (New York: Coward, McCann & Geoghegan, 1979);

At Sea on Land (London: Hutchinson / Stanley Paul, 1981);

Courage at Sea: Tales of Heroic Voyages (London: Stanley Paul, 1987; Topsfield, Mass.: Salem House, 1988).

Naomi James (photograph by Alastair Black)

Naomi James was the first woman to sail around the globe single-handedly. In June 1978, on her fifty-three-foot sloop *Express Crusader,* she completed her voyage after 272 days at sea, shaving two days off the record Sir Francis Chichester set in the *Gypsy Moth IV* in 1967. Her only disappointment was that she could not complete her journey nonstop. In 1980 James broke the women's record for sailing single-handedly across the Atlantic, and in 1982 she and her husband, Rob James, won the Round Britain Race.

Born in Gisborne, New Zealand, on 2 March 1949, Naomi Christine Power is the daughter of Charles Robert Power and Joan Doherty Power. James spent her childhood with her parents, brother, and two sisters on a remote dairy farm in Hawkes Bay, New Zealand. They seldom saw people and visited the nearest town only once a year. James's early life gives no indication that she might someday accomplish major feats of seamanship, but it does reveal the development of the courage and self-reliance that made her journeys possible.

James, who has written about her childhood in *At One with the Sea* (1979), describes herself at that time as "a timid, shy little girl" who loved to daydream. She and her three siblings enjoyed farm life and exploring the countryside, although James notes that she frequently got lost. The children were "landlubbers," and their major sporting interest was riding horses. Money was tight, so they did not have the best horses or equipment, but "what we lacked in finery we make up in tenacity." Some neighbors described the Power children as "wild Indians." Reading was also a favorite pastime, and the children "lived" the books, acting out fictional or historical characters in their games. There was no television to dull their imaginations.

Between the ages of five and twelve James attended a tiny local school, devoting her time to play and daydreaming, not arithmetic and spelling. When she was twelve, the family moved to a larger farm in the Bay of Plenty district, and James was sent to the local intermediate school, where her lack of scholastic preparation was evident. In addition to not being much of a scholar, James was also a "loner," not getting along well with the other students.

When James was thirteen, she was given her first horse, a hand-me-down from her older sister Juliet. The horse was newly broken in and mean. Juliet had been thrown several times and had given up on the horse, but James persisted and discovered her obstinate streak. Soon, she and the horse established a working relationship.

James attended Rotorua Girls' High School but dropped out at age fifteen and worked as an apprentice to a local hairdresser during the years 1965–1971. The work suited her because she liked doing things with her hands, and it also cured her shyness. At age seventeen she returned to high school, taking night classes and passing her "O" level examinations in art and design.

Then she took up German, planning to travel to Austria. For the next three years, until she was twenty-one, James saved for the trip. Looking forward, she saw her life as a "blank," but she knew that she "wanted to choose, not accept."

James and her sister Juliet left New Zealand on New Year's Eve 1970. After ten months in England, where James worked as a hairdresser and a barmaid, she traveled to Vienna. There she also worked as a hairdresser and took classes at the university in German, painting, and clay modeling. By the beginning of summer 1973 James had given up her job, bought a motorized bicycle, and left Vienna. She traveled through Austria to Switzerland and Greece before returning to Vienna in September to teach at the Berlitz Language School.

In June 1975 James bicycled out of Vienna for the last time. After traveling through Austria, Switzerland, and France, she headed for St. Malo to take the ferry to England. There she met Robert Alan James.

It was a case of instant attraction. Rob James, a racing yachtsman, was skipper of the yacht *British Steel* and signed on James for his next charter as deckhand/cook. In *At One with the Sea,* James observes, "It was an ambitious title since I didn't know the front end of a boat from the back and, in addition, I couldn't cook." She was also "paralytically seasick," a problem she continued to have throughout her yachting career. Rob James allowed her on deck to ease the sickness and took over the cooking himself. He also taught her the ropes of sailing. They finished the summer charters in September, when Rob James had to start preparing for the Atlantic Triangle Race, which would last about six months. Unhappy at being separated from Rob, James returned to New Zealand to see her parents. She had been away for five years.

To earn money for her ticket back to England, James worked for her brother as a "fleeco" in his sheep-shearing gang, lugging pounds of fleece, sorting the wool, and sweeping. The work was physically demanding, but it gave her time to daydream about the future. At this time she first conceived the idea of sailing around the world alone. She had been reading about a young Frenchwoman who was planning to sail around the world solo, stopping at various ports and taking three years to make the circumnavigation. Fascinated with the concept, James read books by all the well-known single-handed sailors, including Sir Francis Chichester, Robin Knox-Johnson, and David Lewis. The more she read, the more the idea seemed feasible, even though she was frightened of falling overboard.

Although she wanted eventually to talk it over with Rob James, James kept the idea of sailing around the world to herself, knowing that once the subject was broached, she would feel committed to go through with the trip:

> What had begun in my childhood–little dares, like crossing a bridge from underneath by swinging along the supports, or riding a pony every day knowing she would throw me–had developed into a code of personal ethics which . . . I felt I had to follow, and failure to do so would make me lose faith in myself.

By the end of March 1976 James had returned to England. While staying with Rob's parents, she discovered how to modify a seat belt into a workable safety harness that would allow the mobility required for sailing. Her reservation about sailing alone, her fear of falling overboard, was removed, and she made up her mind to sail single-handedly around the world.

Naomi and Rob James were married on 29 May 1976, and during their honeymoon James mentioned her desire to sail around the world to her new husband. He was enthusiastic, and planning for her journey began in earnest.

Part of the problem was raising funds. At one point it appeared that the project would not get off the ground. Chay Blyth, who had previously sailed around the world solo, loaned her his sloop *Spirit of Cutty Sark.* The boat was refitted and renamed *Express Crusader* to acknowledge the financial support of the *Daily Express* (London), which stipulated that James take lots of pictures and write articles about her adventure. The articles became her first book, *Woman Alone* (1978), which

James's homecoming in Dartmouth, England, after her solo sailing voyage around the world, 8 June 1977 (courtesy of Naomi James)

includes excerpts from the journal she kept during her voyage. It is not intended as an in-depth account of the voyage, which James later detailed in *At One with the Sea* (1979).

Once she had sponsors, a boat, and insurance underwritten by Rob James's parents and other friends, James was ready to leave in less than five weeks. She was set to sail from Dartmouth on Wednesday, 7 September 1976, but before she was able to leave, the engine stopped, and a faulty fuel pump had to be replaced. On 9 September, as the Royal Dart Yacht Club fired a starting gun, James was on her way, with thirty thousand miles of ocean ahead "and no turning back. Not that I wanted to."

The *Express Crusader* had been modified for single-handed sailing with powerful self-tailing winches to handle the "rather large" sails. James is not a small woman at five feet, eight and one-half inches and weighing 140 pounds, but she did not have "the strength of Hercules." The winches were a necessity, as was the Sailomat self-steering gear.

Food, water, and clothing were also major concerns. James left Dartmouth with 200 gallons of fresh water and 1,008 bottles of fruit juices, in addition to tins of tea, chocolate, and coffee. Fresh food included 50 pounds each of potatoes, carrots, onions, apples, oranges, and grapefruit. Packaged foods included 200 pickled eggs, 48 pounds of sugar, 23 jars of jam, honey, and peanut butter, and an astonishing number of cans of meat, soup, and kippers. James also took some of her favorite foods, such as gherkins, beetroot, pickled onions, and piccalilli, as well as Christmas cake and Christmas pudding.

Clothing included a bikini, two "Polar wear" suits, two sets of oilskins with built-in safety harnesses, and twenty-eight pairs of socks. James also packed more than one hundred books. Another addition was Boris, a kitten that was supposed to serve as a "radar detector" to alert James when another boat was too close.

Only a few days out of Dartmouth, James had serious problems in the Bay of Biscay. Because of a heavy wind, the self-steering gear rudder broke free. Attempting to repair it, she pulled the rudder inboard and dropped a vital pin. As James noted, "one mistake invariably follows another," and the next "mistake" forced her to climb the mast to retrieve a loose halyard. Remembering Chay Blyth's advice, James cooked at least one hot meal a day, even if it were only a can of soup and another of peas: "Working on the foredeck and feeling weak from lack of food was inviting disaster," she wrote.

During quiet times James thought about the past and read: novels, autobiographies, and "a dozen or so about art and antiques." Yet "after nearly a month at sea and with the longest and worst part of the journey still ahead," the autobiographies interested her most, particularly those by adventurers. She was surprised to find that Chris Bonington's reasons for climbing Annapurna were "almost exactly the same as my motives for wishing to sail around the world: 'The satisfaction of exploring new ground . . . and perhaps even more important, of exploring one's own reactions to new, at times exacting, experience.'"

South of the Cape Verde Islands, the weather turned hot, and everything on board, including James, became covered with the "fine Sirocco dust that was blowing from the Spanish Sahara." Bothered by the heat, James found it hard to tend to her duties. The heat also affected Boris, although he always accompanied James when she was changing sails. The kitten became protective of his "territory," and when birds or flying fish landed on deck, "they would be speedily and noisily evicted." Also during this time James was visited by dolphins, "their noisy squeaking was unmistakable," and they would leap into the air together, all thirty or forty of them, and come down with a huge splash.

"Boris did not approve; his fur stood on end, and resembling a cactus he fled below."

James kept in touch with shore, specifically her father-in-law, by radio. She also had radio conversations with her husband, who was concurrently sailing around the world in the Whitbread Race. On 7 October, however, the radio went dead. She was unable to fix it, and her "link with the outside world" was severed. The broken radio, combined with the "feckless winds" and her "miserably slow progress," contributed to her depression: "I had read that people frequently suffered such moods in the Doldrums, and it was certainly affecting me." She was making careless mistakes, but forcing herself to eat properly. Yet, her mood lightened on the sixteenth, when she crossed the equator, "going like a rocket." Her sister Juliet had packed five "special" packages to be opened on specific days. Within the "Happy First Equator Crossing" parcel was a book of D. H. Lawrence short stories and a sticky lollipop, which James ate immediately. In honor of the occasion she also cooked herself a three-course dinner and drank a small bottle of French champagne, as "the gloom of the previous day disappeared."

On 30 October James's initial fear of going over the side became a reality, but it was Boris who fell into the sea. After searching for two and a half hours, James forced herself to continue. Now alone, she realized how much she had laughed with the kitten's antics and "after he'd gone I hardly spoke aloud."

James experienced her first real gale on 4 November and fearfully weathered the storm. Disaster struck on 18 November, when the bolt connecting the self-steering rudder to the gear box snapped. She had already used her only spare, and reasoning that "it would be unrealistic to attempt going on without self-steering with three-quarters of the way still ahead," she decided to make port. She had failed in one of her goals: to make the trip nonstop.

Because she had been having problems with navigation, she was also worried about making landfalls, writing, "I am either nowhere near South Africa or else I'm about to trip over it in the dark." Fortunately her navigation put her right at Cape Town, where she docked for repairs. A crowd met James on the dock. Her radio silence had caused concern, and she was greeted with relief as well as enthusiasm. Rob had spoken highly of the hospitality and helpfulness of the people of Cape Town, and James experienced it herself: "Everyone wanted to help." She especially appreciated a hot bath "smelling of all the beautiful things I'd forgotten over the last nine weeks." Yet, she continued to sleep aboard the *Express Crusader,* feeling that "it would be a mistake to upset the rapport I felt with the sea and the boat."

After sixty hours in port the repairs were completed, and with 8,000 miles already behind her, James was "more than ready to face the 7,000 miles to Australia." Leaving Cape Town, James entered the "Roaring Forties," on the lookout for icebergs: "I have never seen an iceberg and I didn't particularly want to." With the radio fixed, she was able to talk to Rob James again, and she kept her mind occupied by re-reading Chichester's and Knox-Johnson's books as well as enjoying the sea birds, particularly "one little grey thing" that kept trying to land on the mast. "Poor thing," she wrote, "the Southern Ocean is no place to be if you're likely to get tired!"

As the *Express Crusader* "cavorted, swayed and lurched her way towards Tasmania," James grew increasingly confident in the ability of the boat to survive "all situations." She also became proficient and innovative in repairs and jury rigging. Since it was impossible to be on the helm constantly during nine-to-twelve-hour-long gales, she devised a rig whereby the *Express Crusader* would steer herself, running "happily dead down wind without the self-steering gear."

With the weather continuing "cold, wet and nasty," James had to fashion yet another self-steering rudder from the broken ones. She wrote, "The effort of trying to do this and prevent myself from being hurled from one end of the boat to the other was exhausting." On 20 December, day 103 of her voyage, "the weather became worse." The *Express Crusader* suffered a major knockdown, lying over on her side. She did right herself, but water was everywhere, and the rudder had to be removed, yet again, for repairs.

On Christmas Eve day the weather was "fairly kind," and James climbed the mast to retrieve a lost halyard. "Three-quarters of the way up, I had to force myself to keep going." When she got to the top, she was seasick and exhausted. The trip took just over an hour. Covered with new blisters on her hands and bruises on her arms and legs, James felt a sense of "personal triumph" and was "amazed at myself for doing it." Then she began preparations for Christmas, which included cleaning up the boat and listening to Christmas cards from Radio Australia.

Yet, James's log records her continuing anxiety:

> I am reading Irving Stone's *Greek Treasurer,* and it's either that or the reminder of Christmas with all its family connections that has made me feel both emotional and morbid. No matter how much I try to think of the good things and what I shall do when I get home, these thoughts are overshadowed by the fear that I might find death instead.

She took small comfort in the fact that she was already one-third of the way around the world. After a good

James aboard Kriter Lady *(courtesy of Naomi James)*

sleep and with steady wind, however, James's spirit revived for Christmas Day, and the Southern Ocean provided her with the gift of good weather. She had packed special food for the holiday: chicken, mangoes, asparagus, and turtle soup. A bottle of wine was cooled in the ocean. Her midday call to her husband and his gift of a book on antiques contributed to her cheerfulness, as did the gift from her sister, a book and a lollipop that had "gone a bit sticky."

At a rendezvous in Tasmania, James picked up a new Sailomat rudder, which had been redesigned by the company and was much stronger. She hoped it would solve her problems with the self-steering gear. James chose to sail south of New Zealand, aware that Chichester had kept further north. She was racing against his time, and even though his boat was faster than the *Express Crusader,* he had stopped in Sydney for several weeks. James felt that she still had a chance to beat his record.

As she left Tasmania, the weather turned ugly yet again. She thought that before Tasmania "the weather was about as bad as it could get. I was wrong." Frightened, she was continually on the helm. When the storm jib disintegrated, she had to crawl up to the foredeck to pull it down. She was constantly apprehensive that the mast might come down. Although there was a period of respite, James encountered yet another gale, and the plate joining the wires to the mast sheared off. At this point the mast was held only at the top and bottom and "was bowing either side as we rolled." James climbed the mast and used "a couple of heavy ropes" as jury shrouds around the spreaders and down to the deck. With the mast straight once again she went to her bunk to think over the situation, which "could have been worse but not much; 2,800 miles from New Zealand and 2,200 from the Horn and probably not a ship within hundreds of miles." The barometer was also taking another drastic plunge.

As the barometer continued to drop, James prepared for the next storm as well as she could. She also made a list of her options. It seemed wisest to turn back to New Zealand for proper repairs and then continue the circumnavigation through the Panama Canal. The next morning, 27 February 1977, day 173, she capsized. Immediately she started pumping; then she went on deck to see if the mast was still standing. It was.

James wrote that the "next nine hours were the most hair-raising I'd ever experienced. Waves roared up astern and we were occasionally picked up bodily and hurtled forward." The feeling of being out of control affected her so profoundly that she "sat and had a good howl." Between cleaning up on deck and pumping below deck, James kept the *Express Crusader* afloat. Once the winds and waves subsided, she assessed the damage to the boat and herself and made a cup of tea. She decided, finally, to turn back and began to steer north.

It felt wrong, however, and once again she wrote down the reasons for continuing or going back. In her log she wrote: "I'm going on. I'm only frightened of the weather really which is illogical."

Her ability to survive the capsizing of her boat eliminated the fear that had been "dogging me for so long." The worst had happened. Although her mood continued to shift between elation and depression, she set her course for Cape Horn, which she rounded on 19 March. Known for its hazardous waters, it had been the "focal point of all my fears and apprehensions of the previous four months," and now it was behind her.

The next rendevous was at the Falkland Islands, three hundred miles away. En route, the "sea was alive not with expected dolphins but with leaping pilot whales, hundreds of them." James discovered that the islands were just as she had imagined them, "wind-swept, barren of trees, bleak"; in contrast, the people greeted her warmly. That evening she enjoyed a long hot bath and a roast lamb dinner. A sailor from HMS *Endurance* repaired the mast, and three days later James was on her way, filled with appreciation for the kindness of the Falkland Islanders.

On 1 April the weather was becoming warm enough to do without the oilskins on deck, and James reflected on whether "these past six months have really been well spent, or whether I would have been better off with Rob on *Great Britain II,* or at home?"

> But whatever else I have had six months doing what I like doing–with the exception perhaps of those three weeks when I was approaching the Horn. I've been at ease and happy with myself. . . .

With good winds James covered just under one thousand miles that week, gaining time on Chichester. Then the wind died. During this lull James cleaned the boat. Hanging by her toes, she hung over the side and scrubbed the thick green weed from the waterline. On 30 April, day 235, she "slipped back across the equator." The changeable winds required frequent sail changes, and James's log reads: "I feel that I have had just about all I can take. . . . At the moment I have had enough of sailing." She was also anxious to see Rob James, who was meeting her in the Azores with the newspaper and television crews.

Because of the rules of single-handed sailing, Rob James was not allowed to climb aboard the *Express Crusader,* but they talked to one another from the decks of their respective boats "till dawn broke." When it was light enough, the television filming was completed, and James began the last 1,200 miles of her journey. Allowing for changes in the weather, she expected to end it on 8 June, two days within Chichester's time. On 6 June she was met by the minesweeper HMS *Walkerton,* with Rob James aboard. With the sounds of "Land of Hope and Glory" coming from the loudspeakers and cheering and waving from the crew, James had a chance to talk again with her husband before continuing to Dartmouth. That night she anchored under the Devon hills, a few miles southwest of Dartmouth. At 9:15 A.M. on 8 June she crossed the finish line.

James's first book about her circumnavigation, *Woman Alone* was written hastily, and James has described it as a "picture and story book about the voyage." *At One with the Sea* was written more deliberately as James reflected on her journey. Both books are based on her log entries, but the second includes more of James's feelings and reflections during the voyage. *At One with the Sea* also provides autobiographical material about James's life before her voyage around the world and insight into why she felt able to undertake such a challenge.

At Sea on Land (1981) begins where *Woman Alone* and *At One with the Sea* left off, at the finishing gun. On land James faced a new challenge: fame. The commotion, the crowds, and the demands for speeches were a new series of obstacles, and in many ways they were more difficult for James to endure than the privations aboard the *Express Crusader.* For a truly private person, facing the media was frightening. James developed a roaring in her ears from the unaccustomed sounds: "At first this was the only obvious effect of plunging from deep solitude into the thick of society." Reality intruded, however; the trip had cost much more than what was budgeted for it, and bills had to be paid.

Her fame resulted in a variety of invitations. On 3 July 1977 she attended a tea party at 10 Downing Street and met Prime Minister James Callaghan, and the following day she was introduced to Katharine Worsley, Duchess of Kent. In August the Jameses left England to stay with her sister in Vienna, where Naomi concentrated on writing. James had already warned her editor that "Speling is my weekest point." He replied, "Yes, I'd noticed."

Between public appearances James worked on her first book. Once it was published, she was required to promote it with book signings and other activities. In addition to paying bills James hoped that the sales of the book might allow her to buy the *Express Crusader,* to which she was understandably attached.

James was also thinking about entering the *Observer* Single-Handed Trans-Atlantic Race and was looking for a sponsor. Kriter, a producer of French sparkling wines, provided the funds, stipulating that she sail two more races. James was able to purchase the *Express Crusader,* which she renamed *Kriter Lady.* "Although I had certain misgivings about furthering a

Naomi and Rob James, 1982 (courtesy of Naomi James)

career in the public eye, the fact that the boat would be mine and I would be doing two long trips well away from the hectic life ashore" was "reward enough."

Before she could begin sailing again, James had further commitments ashore, one of which was being made a Dame Commander of the Order of the British Empire (DBE) by Queen Elizabeth II. A worldwide trip to promote the book was the next endeavor. Before leaving on the trip, the Jameses vacationed in Ireland and found Curraghbinny. Enchanted with the place, they decided to make it their home base and eventually purchased a cottage there.

The book tour took her to New York City, cities in Canada, and back to New Zealand, where she was reunited with family and friends in Rotorua. At her old school she "experienced a strong urge" to reach out to the girls and "reassure them that all would be well, that even the most insignificant girl at the back could do whatever she wanted if she could just learn that she was capable of it."

On 7 June 1980 James left Dartmouth again on *Kriter Lady,* this time to race across the Atlantic in the OSTAR (*Observer* Single-Handed Trans-Atlantic Race). James's major concern now was not distance but speed. The boat had been refitted to help her cross the Atlantic at the best speed, but during the first major gale she encountered she elected to sail safe rather than push the boat hard. Another major concern was that Rob James was also sailing in the race, in a trimaran called *Boatfile,* "a frail little thing compared to *Kriter Lady.*"

During her first few days at sea James experienced a gale. After it gradually blew itself out on the ninth day, much of the fleet had been damaged, and on the eleventh day the wind was still heavy. James wrote in her log: "I spend almost all my time in the bunk, the only place I can relax the muscles tensed waiting for the next fall downwards." Days later, she was forced to climb the mast to fix a sail. On 22 June, off the Newfoundland Bank, the fog rolled in. Close to land, James had to "find my way around the Nantucket shoals to Newport and the finishing line."

Apprehensive of icebergs and uncertain of her navigation, James continued to have trouble with her sails and had to climb the mast yet again. At the same time high winds often confined her to her bunk, "chewing on cream crackers and drinking tea" in an effort to combat seasickness. When the fog closed in again, James almost ran into the Brenton Reef tower, "above me, silent as death." The tower marked the end of the finish line off Newport, Rhode Island.

James was the only woman to finish the race, and she broke the course record for women by more than three days, finishing in twenty-five days, nineteen hours, and twelve minutes. When asked if she would ever do it again, James answered no: "The North Atlantic to my mind is the most horrible, cold, evil place to hold a race."

James's *Courage at Sea: Tales of Heroic Voyages* (1987) includes a series of chapters on famous and not-so-famous seafaring travelers, ranging from Ferdinand Magellan and Sir Ernest Shackleton to her contemporaries. Some stories are of "immense heroism"; others are of "pain and failure and a sanity capsized." The last chapter describes James's final sailing journey: the 1982 Double-Handed Round Britain race with Rob James.

James anticipated the race with dread. Their boat was a trimaran, *Colt Cars,* "very light but very wide." Space was limited, and James saw the boat as "alien, unpredictable, and unruly." Her sea sickness was also a problem; nothing seemed to help this condition. On her own on a slower boat, she had had time to cope with it, but there would be no time to get over sickness on this race. Yet, she wrote, "As time went on, I stopped worrying about disaster." They won the race, sailing into Plymouth Harbor in the dark. When asked if she enjoyed the race, James answered "No. It was too hard, both physically and mentally," and announced her retirement from racing "while I'm ahead."

James's decision to retire was reconfirmed on 22 March 1983, when Rob James fell into the sea and drowned off the South Devon coast when the netting between the hull of the trimaran *Colt Cars* broke as he was trying to lower the mainsail. They had one child, a daughter. James lives in Curraghbinny, Ireland. She married Eric G. Haythorne in 1990. They were divorced in 1993.

As a travel writer, James focused on the accomplishments of the "traveler" rather than what she saw along the way. Scenery is only a backdrop for her journeys, and the stops she made were dictated by the need for repairs, not to explore uncharted territory or meet new people. Her books cover her moments of victory, but they also describe her fears and uncertainties, human reactions to such journeys. Her own words describe her travels best: "I didn't see myself as some kind of pioneer, going out to prove that women can do as well as men on the sea. I wasn't interested in proving anything to anyone except myself."

References:

Fred Hauptfuhrer, "Adventure," *People Weekly,* 12 (10 December 1979): 99, 102, 105;

Jane Robinson, *Wayward Women: A Guide to Women Travellers* (New York: Oxford University Press, 1990), p. 18.

Norman Lewis

(28 June 1908 –)

Dennis M. Read
Denison University

BOOKS: *Spanish Adventure* (London: Gollancz, 1935; New York: Holt, 1935);

Sand and Sea in Arabia (London: Routledge, 1938);

Samara (London: Cape, 1949);

Within the Labyrinth (London: Cape, 1950; New York: Carroll & Graf, 1986);

A Dragon Apparent: Travels in Indo-China (London: Cape, 1951; New York: Scribners, 1951);

Golden Earth: Travels in Burma (London: Cape, 1952; New York: Scribners, 1952);

A Single Pilgrim: A Novel (London: Cape, 1953; New York: Rinehart, 1954);

The Day of the Fox: A Novel (London: Cape, 1955; New York: Rinehart, 1955);

The Volcanoes above Us: A Novel (London: Cape, 1957; New York: Pantheon, 1957);

The Changing Sky: Travels of a Novelist (London: Cape, 1959; New York: Pantheon, 1959);

Darkness Visible: A Novel (London: Cape, 1960; New York: Pantheon, 1960);

The Tenth Year of the Ship: A Novel (London: Collins, 1962; New York: Harcourt, Brace & World, 1962);

The Honoured Society: The Mafia Conspiracy Observed (London: Collins, 1964); republished as *The Honored Society: A Searching Look at the Mafia* (New York: Putnam, 1964);

A Small War Made to Order: A Novel (London: Collins, 1966; New York: Harcourt, Brace & World, 1966);

Every Man's Brother: A Novel (London: Heinemann, 1967; New York: Morrow, 1968);

Flight from a Dark Equator: A Novel (London: Collins, 1972; New York: Putnam, 1972);

The Sicilian Specialist: A Novel (New York: Random House, 1974; London: Collins, 1975);

Naples '44 (London: Collins, 1978; New York: Pantheon, 1979);

The German Company: A Novel (London: Collins, 1979);

Cuban Passage: A Novel (London: Collins, 1982; New York: Pantheon, 1982);

Norman Lewis (photograph © Jerry Bauer)

A Suitable Case for Corruption: A Novel (London: Hamilton, 1984); republished as *The Man in the Middle* (New York: Pantheon, 1984);

Voices of the Old Sea (London: Hamilton, 1984; New York: Viking, 1985);

Jackdaw Cake: An Autobiography (London: Hamilton, 1985; New York & Harmondsworth: Penguin, 1987); enlarged as *I Came, I Saw: "An Autobiography"* (London: Picador, 1994);

A View of the World: Selected Journalism (London: Eland / New York: Hippocrene, 1986);

The March of the Long Shadows: A Novel (London: Secker & Warburg, 1987);

The Missionaries (London: Secker & Warburg, 1988; New York: McGraw-Hill, 1988);

To Run across the Sea (London: Cape, 1989);

A Goddess in the Stones: Travels in India (London: Cape, 1991; New York: Holt, 1992);

An Empire of the East: Travels in Indonesia (London: Cape, 1993; New York: Holt, 1994);

The World, the World (London: Cape, 1996; New York: Holt, 1997).

Collection: *Norman Lewis Omnibus* (London: Picador, 1995)–comprises *A Dragon Apparent, Golden Earth, A Goddess in the Stones.*

Norman Lewis has received high praise from many prominent literary figures. In *The Observer* (London) Anthony Burgess called him "the doyen of English travel writers." After reading *The Changing Sky: Travels of a Novelist* (1959) V. S. Pritchett proclaimed in *The New Statesman* (11 July 1959): "I have never travelled in my armchair so fast, variously and well." Reviewing *Golden Earth: Travels in Burma* (1952) in *The Sunday Times* (London) on 3 September 1952, Cyril Connolly exclaimed, "Mr. Lewis can make even a lorry interesting." Eric Newby, reviewing *The Honoured Society: The Mafia Conspiracy Observed* (1964) in *The Observer,* said that Lewis is "one of the great travel writers of our time"; Graham Greene, reviewing *The Missionaries* (1988) in *The Daily Telegraph* (London), called him "one of the best writers not of any particular decade, but of our century"; Auberon Waugh, topping them all in his review of *Golden Earth* in *Business Traveller,* wrote: "Norman Lewis is the best travel writer of our age, if not since Marco Polo."

Over the course of his long writing career, which now surpasses sixty years, Lewis has published some thirty books. A dozen of them are travel narratives of countries in Europe, the Near East, and Asia. Three–*The Changing Sky, A View of the World: Selected Journalism* (1986), and *To Run across the Sea* (1989)–are collections of essays on travel in these areas, as well as in Africa and South America, that were first published in magazines and newspapers. Four–*Naples '44* (1978), *Jackdaw Cake: An Autobiography* (1985), *The Missionaries,* and *The World, the World* (1996)–are autobiographical volumes. Finally, fifteen are novels, of which only one is set in his native Great Britain. Travel permeates all of his writings and, indeed, his life. As he explains in *Jackdaw Cake,* it has become "an almost indispensable stimulant" to him.

Several of Lewis's works have enjoyed great success. *A Dragon Apparent: Travels in Indo-China* (1951) and *Golden Earth* were best-sellers and are now widely regarded as classics of travel literature. His novel *The Volcanoes above Us* (1957), based on his experiences in revolutionary Guatemala, sold six million paperback copies in the Soviet Union. His report on the extermination of Indians in Brazil, "Genocide in Brazil," published in *The Sunday Times* in 1969, led to the establishment of Survival International, an organization working to protect and preserve indigenous populations that is currently active in sixty-seven countries. His *A Goddess in the Stones: Travels in India* (1991) won the 1991 Thomas Cook Travel Book Award.

With such an impressive output and such strong endorsements by august writers, one might wonder why Lewis is not as well known as his fellow travel writers Newby or Patrick Leigh Fermor. It may have to do with a lack of momentum in his writing career, with interruptions keeping his titles from accumulating steadily. It may also have to do with his aversion to self-promotion and his reticence regarding his personal life. Because his writings include little personal information or introspection, readers may find it difficult to feel close to him.

Norman Lewis was born on 28 June 1908 in Enfield, a suburb of London, to Richard and Louisa Lewis, née Evans. He was the last of four sons; the first two had died before his birth, and the third, Monty, died at seventeen in 1917, leaving Norman the only surviving offspring of the family.

William Zinsser quotes Lewis as describing his childhood as "outstandingly terrible." His father, a pharmacist, would often attempt to talk customers out of filling their prescriptions; failing that, he would sell them, Lewis says in *Jackdaw Cake,* his own concoction of "garlic flavoured water, and a touch of quinine to impart the bitterness people demanded of anything they imagined likely to do them any good." Remarkably, this potion became successful; the formula was purchased by a pharmaceutical company, and the proceeds kept the family solvent for many years.

Lewis writes in *Jackdaw Cake* that when he was nine his parents sent him to live with his paternal grandfather and three maiden aunts in Carmarthen, Wales; typically, he does not give a reason for the move. The grandfather, David Lewis, a stern, humorless tea merchant, had made a tidy sum many years earlier by purchasing the cargo of a wrecked merchantman from India and selling it in small packages–"at a profit," Lewis notes, "of several thousand percent." A widower for twenty-five years at the time Lewis went to live with him, he was attended by two of his daughters: Annie, who dressed in strange costumes, such as a wedding gown, and Li, who was given to continual weeping. The third daughter, Polly, suffered frequent epileptic seizures that sometimes caused her to fall into the hearth fire; her face was severely disfigured by burn scars. Each week the aunts would bake "a cake of exceptional richness" for the village jackdaws. "For some hours after this weekly event," Lewis recalls, "the atmosphere was one of calm and contentment, and then

A DRAGON
APPARENT

Travels in Indo-China

by

NORMAN LEWIS

JONATHAN CAPE
THIRTY BEDFORD SQUARE
LONDON

facing: LAOTIAN DANCERS

Frontispiece and title page for Lewis's 1951 narrative of his experiences in Southeast Asia from January to March 1950

the [hysterical] laughter and weeping would start again."

Lewis's residence with his grandfather and aunts was abruptly terminated about a year and a half after his arrival when Polly attempted suicide after she was accused of writing poison-pen letters and Li was forcibly institutionalized because she was suspected of having crushed the head of her father's prize king bird. Lewis returned to his parents' home to find them embarked on a career as spiritualist mediums. Although he did not believe in spiritualism, throughout his adolescence he assisted them in séances and healings. After graduating from Enfield Grammar School he became a wedding photographer, supplementing his income by buying items at auctions and selling them at a profit.

Lewis's first book, *Spanish Adventure* (1935), recounts his travels in September, October, and November 1934 through France, Spain, Portugal, and Morocco and is illustrated with twenty-five of his photographs. He was accompanied on the entire trip by Eugene Corvaja, whose sister, Ernestina, joined them midway. Lewis had met Ernestina on a blind date and had become friendly with the Corvaja family. Early in *Spanish Adventure* Lewis advises, "if you want to see the world, now is the time. There are omnipresent signs of a wrath to come, embracing the possibility, at least, of a return to the Dark Ages."

Lewis and Eugene Corvaja originally intended to canoe on French waterways and live off the land to hold down expenses; but drought and hunger scuttled their plans, and they abandoned their canoe to travel by bus and train to Spain. There they visited San Sebastián, Pamplona, and Zaragoza, where they were joined by Ernestina. Thus far their difficulties in Spain involved only terrible hotels and unpalatable food, but in Madrid they encountered gunfire and bombs as the civil war broke out. After short visits to Toledo and Salamanca they took a train to Portugal–which Lewis was disappointed to find English in look and feel–then traveled south to Cádiz, Spain. Sailing to Morocco, they saved a third on their lodgings in Casablanca by agreeing to put their rooms, in Lewis's delicately comic phrasing, "at the temporary disposition of certain ladies and gentlemen who might wish to drop in for a private chat." After exploring Marrakech and Tangier they returned to Spain and then to France.

Spanish Adventure, while lively and entertaining, bears the marks of a young writer attempting to sound older and more urbane. For instance, when Lewis and the Corvajas find themselves in a restaurant that turns out to be a tourist trap, he comments: "we resented having to pay a comparatively high sum in order to experience the accurately reproduced culinary hardships of a past age." The comment seems a pale imitation of a quip from Evelyn Waugh's *Labels: A Mediterranean Journal* (1930) or *Remote People* (1931). Reviews, however, were generally favorable. *The Times Literary Supplement* (*TLS*) for 26 September 1935 said that Lewis's style "is compounded of sharp observation, fine indignation and over-ponderous irony." In *The Spectator* (11 October 1935) John Marks said: "The fact that his book is snobbish and ingenious makes it all the more entertaining."

Lewis and Ernestina Corvaja were married soon after their return from Spain. Lewis describes their relationship in *The World, the World* as "not quite a love match but an arrangement we thought of as a partnership of similar minds."

In the early summer of 1936 the Lewises returned to Spain, where they stayed with friends of Ernestina's in Seville, but the civil war cut their visit short. The following spring Lewis embarked on a trip to North Yemen with Ladislas Farago and Rex Stevens. They sailed along the coasts of the Gulf of Aden and the Red Sea in a sambuk and a cargo steamer, stopping at many ports, but they were denied entry into North Yemen when the harbormaster realized that he was mistaken in his assumption that they were arms merchants. Lewis nevertheless recalls the trip fondly: "Never . . . was a journey richer in experience," he writes in *Jackdaw Cake,* "and the fact that the avowed object of the expedition remained unfulfilled was of little importance."

The journey resulted in two books: Lewis's *Sand and Sea in Arabia* (1938) and Farago's *The Riddle of Arabia* (1939). Lewis's book is a collection of his photographs, one on each of the 123 pages, accompanied by short explications. He describes the toilet on the sambuk as "a kind of boxed-in platform with a hole in its bottom, suspended precariously over the sea and known as the 'place of ease.' . . . In bad weather an enforced visit became an adventure." He graphically describes the Somali practice of female circumcision:

> During childhood the labiae are scraped and then sewn together until the bleeding surfaces are completely united. Marriage involves violent defibulation, and the birth of each child a further use of the knife, followed by partial re-infibulation. This perpetually recurring anguish in their relations with the other sex may have had a slightly dehumanizing effect on Somali women.

The journey included stops at Lahej, Sheikh Othman (or Shaykh Uthman), and Aden, South Yemen; Jiddah, Saudi Arabia; and Suakin, Sudan. Lewis provides extensive photographs of and commentaries on the people and customs of these places, as well as life aboard ship. Lewis now considers neither *Sand and Sea in Arabia* nor *Spanish Adventure* worth mentioning, and he usually omits them from lists of his works.

In 1938 Lewis and his wife undertook an ambitious trip through central Europe and the Balkans to the Black Sea, returning through Yugoslavia and Hungary, in what he describes in *Jackdaw Cakes* as "an elderly Ford V8 costing £31, bought expressly for the journey and thrown away at the end." No book came out of this experience.

During the 1930s Lewis bought a series of motorcycles and sports and racing cars. The first such automobile he bought was a Bugatti that had been idiosyncratically altered and adorned with small statues of Hindu gods by its previous owner, a wealthy Indian. In 1937, in Italy, he bought the Alfa Romeo that had won the twenty-four-hour Le Mans race and had it shipped back to England. When Lewis was driving it one afternoon, it attracted the attention of a rich young man from Singapore, Loke Wan Tho, who offered to swap his 1936 Mercedes Grand Tourer for it. Lewis declined–a decision he regretted when he read that another 1936 Grand Tourer, in decrepit condition, was sold at Christie's in the 1980s for £1,595,000. The incident did begin a friendship that endured until Loke's death in a plane crash in Taiwan in 1956. Early in 1939 Lewis raced a Bugatti Type 51 at Brooklands, but he did not finish the race and barely avoided serious injury. That experience ended his racing career but not his fast driving. On 23 December 1953 the humorist S. J. Perelman wrote to his wife that Lewis had driven him in Lewis's Porsche "at a nervewracking rate around London and I thought my hour had come the last night I was there when he picked me up at the theater and we drove to Soho for supper."

In July 1939 the Lewises sailed to New York City and then to Havana, Cuba, where they stayed with Spanish exiles named Castaña. When England declared war on Germany later that year, Lewis sensed, he writes in *Jackdaw Cake,* that if he remained in Cuba "great experiences might be missed." Accordingly, on 10 November he left Ernestina in Cuba, sailed to New York, and returned to England aboard the SS *President Harding,* arriving in Tilbury on 29 November.

Lewis had difficulty finding a way to contribute to the war effort. Finally, in January 1942 he was inducted into the army intelligence corps. Because he had acquired a rudimentary knowledge of Arabic at the School of Oriental Studies in London several years earlier, after basic training he was assigned to the Field Security Service and stationed in Algeria and Tunisia. Little of military consequence occurred at the places he was stationed, but he followed his wanderlust by visit-

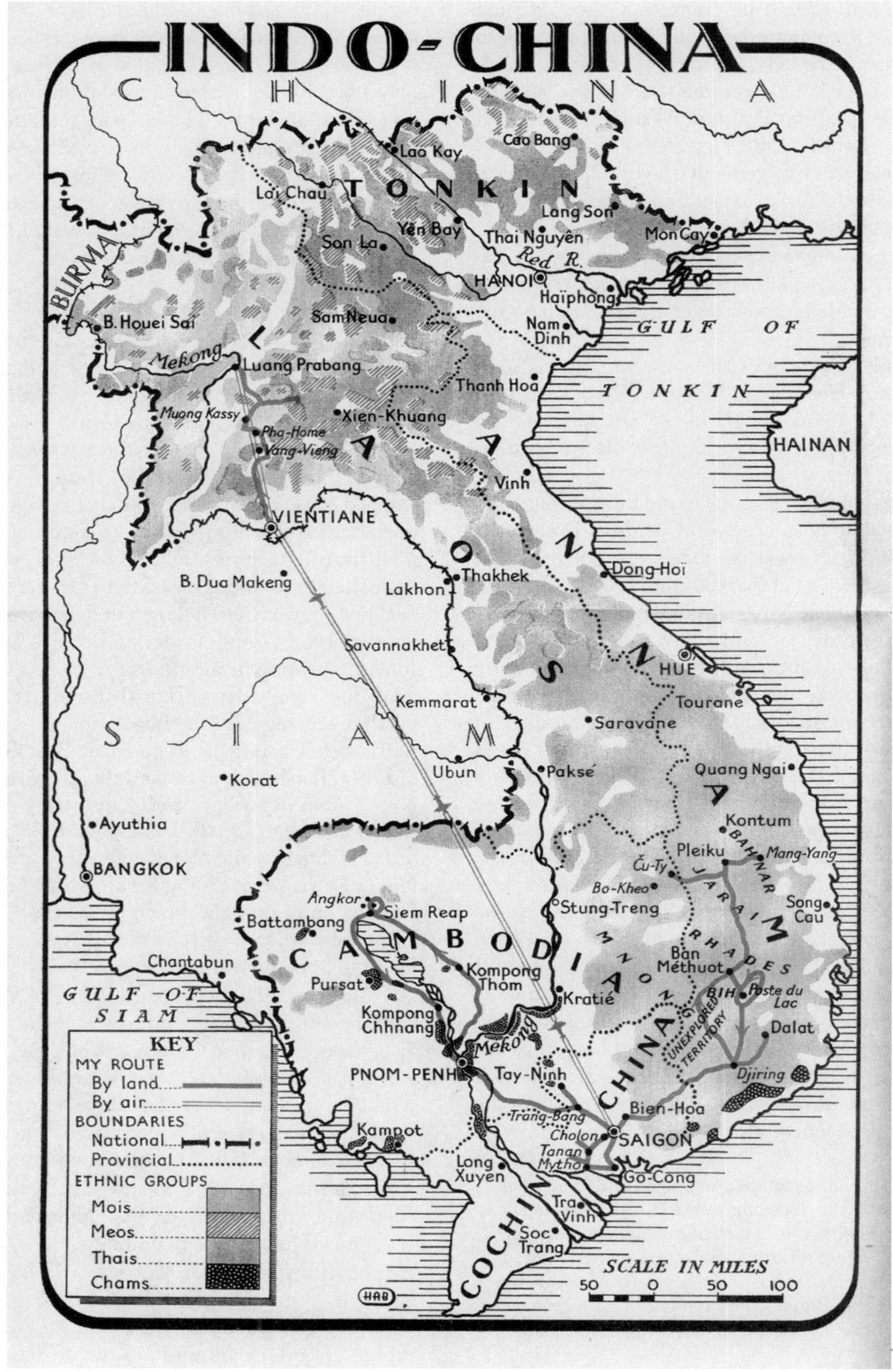

Map of the area through which Lewis traveled for A Dragon Apparent

ing Arab villages and becoming acquainted with the peoples and places of North Africa.

In "Memoirs of a Massacre Town," included in *The Changing Sky,* Lewis writes of his assignment in Philippeville (now Skikda), Algeria, from November 1942 to May 1943. As a member of the Port Security Section he was charged with maintaining surveillance on the attitude of the local Arabs toward the Allies. Certainly the Arab dockworkers were favorably disposed toward them, since the British had increased their wages tenfold. Most other Arabs also found ways to improve their lot under the new regime.

One of Lewis's informants was an Arab taxi driver named Hadef. The two became friends, and Lewis got to know the members of Hadef's family. When the Allied forces captured Tunis, Philippeville lost its strategic importance; most of the British, including Lewis, were moved out, leaving a skeleton garrison. In July 1943 bands of Senegalese "broke out of their barracks, seized weapons from the armory, which had mysteriously been left unlocked, and slaughtered every Arab they could find." Among those killed was Hadef.

On 9 September 1943 Lewis landed at Paestum, Italy, as part of the Allied invasion force. His Field Security Service unit was assigned to Naples, where he investigated possible enemy agents and sympathizers; he came to regard the task as pointless. His diary for the next year forms the basis for *Naples '44.*

"The war," Lewis writes in *Naples '44,* "had pushed the Neapolitans back into the Middle Ages." People, devastated of all resources and hope, resorted to drastic measures to survive. The city aquarium was ransacked for anything edible, and "the most prized item of the aquarium's collection," a baby manatee, was served with a garlic sauce at a banquet in honor of Gen. Mark Clark. Lewis was appalled to find a woman offering her thirteen-year-old daughter to soldiers; she had worked out "a revolting scale of fees" for various sexual services. Such depravity was brought on by rampant starvation and by epidemic illnesses spread largely by raw sewage after the sewers were destroyed in air raids. The only thriving enterprise was the black market in purloined military supplies. "At the opening of the San Carlo opera," Lewis notes, "every middle- and upper-class woman arrived dressed in a coat made from a stolen army blanket."

Yet, in the midst of this desperate spectacle Lewis still found examples of the indomitable human spirit. One was Caesar Rossi, who had been the Fascist dictator Benito Mussolini's press secretary. When Lewis arrived at Rossi's home with orders for his arrest, Rossi accepted his fate with magnificent poise. "He was," Lewis says, "one of the most dignified men I had ever met, with inner reserves that enabled him to face calamity of this kind without the slightest outward sign of distress." Lewis perceived the same quality in an impoverished lawyer, Vincente Lattarullo, one of the thousands of surplus doctors and lawyers in Naples who were "the end-product of the determination of every middle-class Neapolitan family to have a uselessly qualified son." Lewis marvels at Lattarullo's ingenuity in staying alive on a pittance, with an occasional windfall from impersonating an "uncle from Rome" at funerals to add dignity and stature to otherwise plebeian events. Lattarullo remained stoic and uncomplaining about his lot, choosing to starve rather than to abase himself in any of the multitudinous ways to which other Neapolitans resorted in order to eat.

On 22 October 1944 Lewis was ordered to escort three thousand Soviet prisoners back to the USSR; he recounts his assignment in his essay "The Cossacks Go Home," included in *A View of the World.* The men were Uzbeks, Kirghiz, and Kazakhs who had composed the Turkoman Infantry Division, organized in 1942 by a German general. The division had fought the Soviets in the Ukraine in 1943, then had been sent to northern Italy. In July 1944 American tanks had broken up the division, and most of the soldiers had surrendered. Afraid that the Americans would mistake them for Japanese, they had surrendered to Partisans. In the prisoner-of-war camps they endured abominable conditions, surviving only through cannibalism. Lewis sailed with the prisoners from Taranto, aboard the *Reina del Pacifico.* Soon he realized that a mutiny was brewing, led by a mullah called "Haj el Haq" (The Pilgrim of Truth) by the other prisoners. When they docked at Port Said, Egypt, and transferred to the HMS *Devonshire,* Lewis had British uniforms and other supplies issued to the prisoners. The effect was immediate: military discipline was reestablished among the men, the authority of Haj el Haq was quashed, and the prisoners busily converted the army-issued equipment into "a variety of musical instruments." The following evening they presented a performance "unlike anything I had ever seen before, or have seen since," full of "mime and masquerade." The entertainment "lifted the mind clear away from unacceptable reality to glowing new worlds of the imagination." Lewis felt the rich complexity of the life that had gone on in much the same way for millennia in the homelands of these men.

When the ship arrived in Khorramshahr, Iran, the prisoners were transferred to the Soviets, who loaded them onto trains normally used to transport pigs. Later that day Lewis learned from an interpreter what was going to happen to them: "They're going to be shot. Most of them anyway." To the Soviet officers, any countryman who had fought for the Germans was a traitor and had to be executed.

Dust jacket for Lewis's 1978 account of his experiences serving in the British army in wartime Italy, based on the diary he kept from October 1943 to October 1944

Lewis ended his tour of duty in Austria and Cologne, Germany, where he saw the overwhelming destruction of the Allied air attacks. On his discharge he sailed to Guatemala to join Ernestina, who had moved there several years earlier. They soon determined that they had little in common after seven years of separation, and they were divorced.

Lewis found much of interest in Guatemala, which, he declares in *Jackdaw Cake,* "was, and has remained for me, the most beautiful country in the world." He began assembling materials for a major study of its pre-Columbian culture, and he worked on a manuscript for many years. He says in *The World, the World,* however, that he finally realized that "its range was so vast that it could never be brought to completion," and he abandoned it.

Soon after returning to England, Lewis was advised by his doctor to lead a more vigorous outdoor life. In mid 1947 he rented St. Catherine's Fort in Tenby, Pembrokeshire, West Wales, which had been built at great expense in the mid nineteenth century to defend the coast against a French invasion; in *Jackdaw Cake* Lewis calls the project "a military folly." There he found pleasant solitude, writing in the cavernous banqueting hall and rattling around the sixteen rooms in the four turrets. The peacefulness was periodically broken by the Welsh hymn-singing of a mother and daughter who came to clean and cook.

Lewis's doctor had recommended that he take up rock climbing, but Lewis, "being a bad performer at sports of all kinds," quickly gave up that activity in favor of hiking and birdwatching. His friend Loke came to search for a unique species of wren that reputedly inhabited an island about thirty miles from Tenby.

In the spring of 1948 the prestigious publisher Jonathan Cape accepted Lewis's first novel, *Samara,* based on his experiences in Algeria during the war. It was the beginning of a relationship between the writer and the publishing house that continues to the present day. *Samara* was published in 1949.

In 1948 Lewis spent the first of three summers in the tiny fishing village of Farol, Spain. He recorded his experiences in the elegiac *Voices of the Old Sea* (1984). He chose Farol because it was "the least accessible coastal village in north-east Spain" and, therefore, a refuge from the rest of the world. He was also attracted by the low cost of living and the fishing. Few of the villagers had ever traveled outside of Farol; they believed that "those who were obliged to leave the village were instantly exposed to evil influences which increased mile by mile." This sort of thinking predisposed them to ascribe the worst motives to a stranger who came from a country they could only imagine. But Lewis worked his way into the routines and rhythms of village life, making himself useful in various ways–such as adding up figures for the merchants, who always had found calculating totals troubling and time-consuming. He knew that he had been accepted when the owner of the tavern placed "a fine ruin of a chair outside his bar for my personal use, in this way denoting the conferment of native status."

Lewis grew to enjoy the strange stews that were cooked for him out of revolting ingredients and the local wine that was so bitter as to resemble vinegar. When a pet goat urinated in the home of a prominent villager, Lewis notes with delight, "It occurred to me, subjected to what I should once have found the overpowering fetor of these surroundings, but which now provoked in me no disgust, that I had made considerable progress in the last two months."

The economy of the village depended on fishing, with activity increasing to a frenzy when sardines or tuna were running between March and October and slowing to near cessation for the rest of the year. The people were used to eking out each winter in the expectation of more and larger catches in the coming season, but for several years before Lewis arrived the fishing had been poor: "This was a village under threat of death." An apparent reprieve came during Lewis's second summer in Farol when a man who had made his fortune in the black market bought the local mansion, which had long stood empty, and turned it into a hotel. It was the first step in his plan to turn the village into a tourist destination along the emerging Costa del Sol. When Lewis returned for the third summer, he was astounded at the transformation the village had undergone. Many of the old buildings had been demolished; a Moorish-style café had been built on the beach; and many of villagers, lured by wages much higher than the incomes their fishing yielded, were working as maids, cooks, and waiters. They were, nevertheless, convinced that Farol would return to its previous state: "Everyone proclaimed their faith that, re-equipped by the chance of foreign bounty, the little fishing armada would sail again in a rejuvenated form, prepared–in their own words–to 'overwhelm the sea' and wrest from it those great harvests of fish, those miraculous catches awaiting them when the shoals returned." Lewis knew that no such day would ever come and that for all intents and purposes the fishing village had ceased to be.

During these years Lewis finished another novel, *Within the Labyrinth,* based on his experiences in Naples; it was published by Cape in 1950. At the suggestion of the publisher Lewis decided to make his next book a travel narrative about Indochina. "Nothing's been written about the place for years," Cape pointed out. "There's certainly a book in that." *A Dragon Apparent: Travels in Indo-China,* with twenty-seven photographs, established Lewis among the foremost travel writers of the day. It recounts his experiences in Indochina from January to March 1950, just before that part of the world was changed forever. Most of Vietnam was "unpopulated, jungle-covered, and looking much the same as China itself must have looked several thousand years ago, before the deforestation began." In the jungles of central and southern Vietnam, Lewis found the Moïs (Vietnamese for "savages"), indigenous Malayo-Polynesian tribes whose days were numbered by encroaching colonization. Lewis was taken with their gentle, peaceful ways and their manner of celebrating life and death. Drunkenness was a form of respectful behavior for the dead: "Passers-by are begged to join in Moïs orgies of eating and drinking, and it is bad taste–that is offensive to the spirits–to eat or drink less than is provided by the fearsome liberality of the hosts." Isolated in their villages, the Moïs had fared well for hundreds of generations; but contact with the French inevitably turned them into "dirty, degenerate, and miserable" creatures, stripped of their culture and unmercifully exploited. Lewis found an extreme example of exploitation in a group of Moïs working off their fifty days of yearly "taxes" to the French by building a road so that "the Emperor would be able to drive his specially fitted-up jeep, with a wooden platform built up, throne-like, in the back, right into the heart of what is supposed to be the richest hunting country in the world."

Other forms of exploitation were more common and more entrenched. At a rubber plantation Lewis and a sympathetic French colonial official encountered a group of nearly fifty Moïs who wanted to leave but could not do so because they had signed contracts to work for a year. Lewis notes that the rubber produced by this plantation, "which is regarded as essential to the conduct of our civilization," is "often only to be obtained by turning a blind eye to illegalities and oppression," and that "there is little difference in practice between the secret gangsterism of these days and the open slavery officially abolished in the last century."

The Moïs did not resist their oppressors; resistance was offered, however, by the Vietminh, the revolutionary movement led by Ho Chi Minh that controlled four-fifths of the country by day and virtually all of it after dark. Lewis learned firsthand of the presence of the Vietminh on his first evening in Saigon (today Ho Chi Minh City) when a hand grenade exploded in the sidewalk café across the square from his hotel, resulting in fifteen casualties; it was one of eight such attacks that evening. So accustomed were the residents to such events that the café was back in full operation ten minutes later.

Lewis was introduced to members of the Vietminh by a nightclub "taxi" girl he met in Cholon, Saigon's Chinatown. He was taken to a nearby military headquarters, hidden in a riverbank, that was in radio contact with a center that was tracking all movements of French troops and the exact number of soldiers in each unit. Later that evening he witnessed a Vietminh attack on a Vietnamese government guard tower; in less than half an hour the occupants of the tower had surrendered. Lewis was struck by the selfless devotion and heedless heroism of these revolutionary nationalists. A Vietminh captain told Lewis, "If it is only by becoming communists that we shall achieve our liberty, then we shall become communists."

Lewis had several close calls during his travels through Indochina. One occurred when he was on a bus going through bandit country on its way to Phnom Penh, Cambodia. To hide him from the bandits, who would certainly have killed him if they had found him, the driver made a hollow mound of baggage in the back of the bus and instructed Lewis to worm his way inside it. He anxiously remained there for the next several hours. The bus made it through without incident. Another close call came in Vietnam when a French lieutenant, taking a curve too fast, flipped their Citroën, throwing himself, Lewis, and their Vietnamese aide from the car. None sustained serious injuries, but they

Dust jacket for Lewis's 1989 collection of travel essays

were forced to hike to safety through dangerous territory. At one point they were menaced by two tigers. They pressed on, "expecting at every moment to see the animals come bounding down into the road in front of us." A third narrow escape occurred when Lewis was riding with a military convoy bound for Laos. As the convoy climbed up a road flanking a hill, the truck in front of Lewis's jeep veered off the road and into a precipice. The next moment seemed to happen in slow motion: "Gently, almost, [the truck] was lowered from sight amongst the bamboos. Up till the last fraction of a second before a thousand graceful stems screened it from our view it was still upright and quite level. The soldiers in it had hardly risen from their seats and raised their arms not so much in alarm, it seemed, as to wave farewell." The gesture was as delicate as the "swan-like movements" of the young Vietnamese women bicycling in the Jardins Botaniques in Saigon on a Sunday, movements "of unearthly elegance."

Most reviews of *A Dragon Apparent* were enthusiastic. Peter Fleming in *The Spectator* (20 July 1951) called it "a travel book of unusual interest and distinction." Arthur Marshall in *The New Statesman and Nation* (25 August 1951) said it was "an absorbing and fascinating book, on no account to be missed," and Richard Tregaskis in *The New York Times* (25 November 1951) called it "a full meal of adventure . . . vivid and written with careful craftsmanship." Perelman, a longtime traveler in Asia, wrote to a friend on 19 October 1951 that he had been reading *A Dragon Apparent* "with enormous pleasure" and called it "one of the best things of the sort I've read in years. It gives a very up-to-date, extremely graphic and penetrating, and often very funny picture of conditions there." In a letter to the same correspondent six weeks later Perelman added, "the book . . . is a model of what travel writing should be. It's superb–funny, packed with real observation, and written out of true experience in areas of Indochina almost nobody has penetrated for years." *A Dragon Apparent* was a popular success, as well; according to Michael S. Howard's *Jonathan Cape, Publisher* (1971), "It was the highlight of Cape's spring season" and sold "tens of thousands to an eager public."

On the heels of this success, Lewis and Cape agreed that Lewis should return to Asia and write another book about the region. This time he concentrated on Burma (today Myanmar), arriving late in 1951 and staying for three months. *Golden Earth: Travels in Burma* appeared in 1952.

Lewis found traveling in Burma "almost as slow as in the days of Marco Polo, and probably more hazardous." The country was riven by insurrection and factionalism. To prevent Lewis from consorting with rebel leaders, the government used every bureaucratic device it could to bar him from his desired destinations. Lewis found an ally in the permanent secretary of the Ministry of Information, an earnest young man named U Thant (who served as Secretary General of the United Nations from 1961 to 1971), but he was helpless to overcome the red tape. In desperation, Lewis secured an appointment with a general. When he entered the general's office, he found the man attempting to translate an anachronistic British military manual into Burmese. Lewis explained the unfamiliar terms to the general, and in gratitude the officer signed a pass for Lewis. Lewis had no problems with the government after that.

The physical difficulties of traveling in Burma were not as easily solved as the bureaucratic ones. The only way Lewis could get from Tatkón to Pyinmana was by riding on top of a truckload of potatoes along a severely shelled road; Lewis called the trip "a memorable torture." When he bought a ticket on the Rangoon Express in Mandalay, he learned that the train "went in the direction of Rangoon, and it might travel five, ten, or fifty miles before the line was dynamited, or a bridge blown up, or with good luck it might even reach Tatkón, which was about 150 miles away." The train was stranded several hours into the trip when explosions damaged the rails in front of and then behind it.

In spite of the difficulties, Lewis saw a great deal of Burma and was entranced by the country and its people. He found the easy acceptance of strangers by the Burmese remarkable, especially "when it is remembered that through failure to spend a token period as a novice in a Buddhist monastery, the foreigner has never qualified as a human being." The Buddhist abhorrence of killing produced various perplexities noted by Lewis. For instance, fishermen claimed that they did not kill their catch; rather, they "put them out on the bank to dry after their long soaking in the water. If in this process they should happen to die, there can be no harm in eating them." When a devout Buddhist caught Lewis killing a cockroach in a train compartment, he sternly asked if Lewis realized "that this poor, assassinated creature might quite well be my grandfather in another incarnation? The obvious answer to this was that had my grandfather indeed been reincarnated as a Burmese cockroach, I should have regarded it as an act of kindness to release him from what seemed to me–and would probably, from what I remembered of him, have seemed to him–an unsatisfactory existence."

The Buddhist attitude had not prevailed throughout the history of the country. Lewis learned that in the past people were buried alive under the foundations of a new building so that their spirits would protect it; fifty-eight sacrificial victims, for instance, lay beneath the walls and gatehouses of the citadel of Mandalay. This practice seemed to Lewis not just cruel but odd: "Why should it have been supposed that those who had died in such terrifying circumstances should be content, after death, to guard the city of their murderers?"

In the far reaches of the country Lewis saw the Kachins dressed in their traditional cloth, woven with beautiful designs incorporating the history of their tribe. Lewis expected, however, that when commercial printed cottons arrived in the area the typical Kachin woman would "renounce with contempt the gorgeous creations of her own hands, which are the result of the communal artistic imagination of her tribe throughout the centuries. . . . Art is sometimes protected by poverty, and civilization can be the destroyer of taste."

Golden Earth produced reviews even more enthusiastic than those of *A Dragon Apparent.* Margaret Parton in the *New York Herald Tribune Book Review* (23 November 1952) called it "a highly diverting travel book in which politics and economics are kept in the background and ordinary (and extraordinary) human beings emerge on every page." Tregaskis in *The New York Times* (9 November 1952) praised the "brilliant descriptive passages," and the anonymous reviewer for *The New*

Dust jacket for the second of Lewis's four autobiographical works, published in 1985

Yorker (22 November 1952) called the work "a superb travel book." Derrick Sington declared in the *Manchester Guardian* (9 September 1952): "It is hard to remember any better travel book published during the last twenty years than Mr. Norman Lewis's *Golden Earth.*"

Cape persuaded Lewis to return to Indochina in 1953 to gather experiences for a third book on the region. Lewis did have more adventures. At a festival in Thailand he threw grenades at moving targets of toy tanks, guns, and soldiers and was given a bedside lamp fashioned from a shell case for, as the inscription read, "dashed good effort." In a newly constructed French bunker at Hoa Binh, near Hanoi, he enjoyed a sumptuous lunch that was interrupted by a Vietminh attack. The commanding officer had proclaimed during the lunch that "we are here to stay forever," but at a press conference in Hanoi five days later a general announced that "Hoa Binh, which is now without value to us, has been evacuated." Such incidents were not sufficient to fill a book, however; the most Lewis could make of the journey were several essays. One of them, "The Road from Hoa-Binh," is included in *The Changing Sky.*

By the early 1950s Lewis had established a permanent residence in a flat on Orchard Street in London. Perelman, in a letter to his wife dated 23 December 1953, says that he has had dinner with Lewis three times in London and goes on to describe Lewis as "slightly taller than I am"–Perelman was quite short–with "feverish black eyes, hair, and mustache," and a "pallid face." Perelman concludes: "In short, he's a wack, extremely good company (and very funny, as his books suggest), and a man I know you'd take to." The two remained good friends until Perelman's death in 1979.

After Farol was transformed into a tourist attraction, Lewis found a new unspoiled summer spot on the island of Ibiza. In March 1954 he rented Casa Ses Estaques (House of the Mooring Posts), overlooking Santa Eulalia and the Mediterranean. It was another curious abode, with useless sinks, broken chandeliers, smashed furniture, and an intact but monstrously huge gilt mirror inherited from the previous occupant, an eccentric known as the Turkish Princess. Lewis was able to return to Casa Ses Estaques for a second season before land prices began to climb and the house was destined to be replaced with a "stark white cube of a hotel," as he calls it in his essay "Ibiza" in *The Changing Sky*.

Later in 1954 Lewis returned to Guatemala to see the drastic changes the country was undergoing. The events provided the basis for his novel *The Volcanoes above Us,* published in 1957. In January 1955 he made another trip to Guatemala to gather more material for the novel. In the mountains in the north, near the border of the Mexican state of Chiapas, he found a region so remote that, as he writes in "A Quiet Evening in Huehuetenango" (included in *The Changing Sky*), "even the onslaught of the Spanish Conquistadors faltered and collapsed." At a village festival Lewis was nonplussed when the high moment of the evening turned out to be a deafening rendition of "If You Were the Only Girl in the World" played on a gigantic marimba by nine men. The locals' love of marimba music appeared again in a tavern later when three "hard-muscled *ladinos,* half-breeds who carried in their faces all the Indian's capacity for resentment but none of his fear," asked Lewis, with extreme politeness, to punch the jukebox button for "Mortal Sin," a marimba tour de force. The *ladinos* played the record at full volume, listening in adoration, five times before an earthquake cut off the electricity. Of "Mortal Sin" one of the *ladinos* said, "It is remarkable and most inspiring. I do not think it can be bettered."

In addition to *The Volcanoes above Us,* Lewis produced two other novels during the 1950s. *A Single Pilgrim* (1953) is set in contemporary Thailand and draws heavily on his knowledge of the country, and *The Day of the Fox* (1955) takes place in a Spanish fishing village similar to Farol.

Lewis traveled widely and extensively throughout the 1950s and 1960s, often on assignment for newspapers or magazines such as *The Sunday Times, The New Statesman, The Independent, The Observer, The New Yorker,* and *Granta.* He collected many of the articles in *The Changing Sky, A View of the World,* and *To Run across the Sea.* In March 1957 he was in Ghana to see the country celebrate its independence, then in Liberia, where he watched a wife accused of adultery undergo trial by ordeal: a heated piece of iron was placed on her tongue several times; because she was not burned, she was declared not guilty. Later that spring Lewis was in Andalusian Spain, where he saw bullfighting in Sanlúcar.

In December 1957 Lewis went to Cuba at the behest of Ian Fleming, who was then foreign manager of *The Sunday Times* (but, Lewis believed, still connected with British Intelligence). Fleming suspected, contrary to the current reports, that Fidel Castro's revolutionary movement was a serious threat to the Fulgencio Batista regime, and he thought that Ernest Hemingway would be the best source of information in Cuba. Lewis met Hemingway at Hemingway's home, La Vigia, outside Havana. Hemingway, a literary god to Lewis, was full of suspicion and arrogance and had not aged well. About Castro and the revolution he was tight-lipped, dismissing the question with the comment, "I live here." Lewis says in *The World, the World* that after the interview he wrote Fleming: "This man has had about everything any man can ever have wanted and to meet him was a shattering experience of the kind likely to sabotage ambition–which may or may not be a good thing. . . . He told me nothing, but he taught me more even than I wanted to know."

Lewis returned to Cuba in December 1959, after Castro's overthrow of Batista, to find that much had changed but much had remained the same. As usual, he sought out the bizarre; he found it in the official executioner of the Castro government, who was kept busy carrying out the death sentences imposed on minor officials of the fallen government. This man was Herman Marks, an American who had been an employee in Macy's accounts department and who had taken on the executioner's job because "I felt I had to do something to be of use in some way." In Lewis's essay "Fidel's Artist," included in *A View of the World,* Marks describes the humane manner in which he carries out his executions, complains about the poor marksmanship of the soldiers in the firing squads and the paperwork involved in his job, and speaks contemptuously of "guys whose names you read every time you pick up a newspaper" who pestered him to see an execution. About a year after their meeting Marks himself was executed.

Lewis also traveled to Belize, the Yucatan, Goa, Haiti, and the Dominican Republic during the 1950s. In the Dominican Republic he observed the many monuments to the dictator Generalissimo Rafael Trujillo. In *The Changing Sky* he singles out the inscription on one–"No statesman in the history of the world has done so much for his country"–and remarks, "This may be an exaggeration." The dry comment is vintage Lewis.

Nineteen travel essays compose *The Changing Sky,* which received generally favorable reviews. The subtitle of the book, *Travels of a Novelist,* indicates Lewis's view of himself at the time. *Darkness Visible,* a novel set in Algeria, appeared in 1960, and *The Tenth Year of the Ship,* a novel set on a small Spanish island resembling Ibiza, came out in 1962. Both novels reveal Lewis's ability to depict local color.

In 1958 Lewis married Maureen Lesley Burley, whom he describes in *The World, the World* as "an old friend who had been helping me to organize my books" while he was in the process of moving out of his London flat. They settled in Essex, and in the early 1960s they moved into The Parsonage in Finchingfield, where they have lived ever since except for a seven-month attempt at expatriate living in Isola Farnese, Italy, in the 1970s. They have three children.

In 1960 Lewis went to Sicily to begin research for a book on the Mafia. He received much help from several courageous investigators, most of whom would later be assassinated by the Mafia. When he had almost completed the manuscript for the resulting book, *The Honoured Society,* Lewis obtained through Perelman an audience with the editor of *The New Yorker,* William Shawn, who immediately purchased it for, Lewis says in *The World, the World,* "what seemed an unbelievable fee." It was published in the magazine in three installments in February 1964 and in book form later that year to widespread critical acclaim in Great Britain and the United States. *TLS* (18 June 1964) proclaimed that Lewis had "written a vivid and absorbing book, providing the most accurate assessment of the Mafia yet to have appeared in English." In 1966 and 1967, respectively, Lewis published *A Small War Made to Order,* a spy novel set in Cuba, and *Every Man's Brother,* a suspense novel set on a Welsh farm.

Lewis has called "Genocide in Brazil," published in *The Sunday Times* on 23 February 1969, the watershed of his career. This extensive account (at 12,500 words, it was the longest article that had ever appeared in the paper) of the systematic decimation of Indian populations by the Indian Protection Service of the Brazilian government to clear lands for the *fazendieros* (estate owners) came out of Lewis's investigations in Brazil in January 1969 and various agency reports. Lewis describes the methods used to carry out the campaign, which included giving Indians clothing impregnated with smallpox virus and food poisoned with arsenic, as well as dynamiting their villages from the air. The Indian population had dropped from several million to between fifty and one hundred thousand. Lewis's sympathies obviously lie with the Indians, but he also wonders whether the goals of the *fazendieros* will be achieved: "The conclusion of all those who have lived among and studied the Indian beyond the reach of civilization is that he is the perfect human product of his environment–from which it should follow that he cannot be removed without calamitous results." Today, many areas of the Brazilian rain forest that have been cleared of trees and aboriginal populations have become deserts, unable to sustain crops.

Public response to "Genocide in Brazil" was immediate and widespread, producing action from governments and grassroots groups and leading to the formation of Survival International, an organization dedicated to protecting and defending indigenous peoples. Lewis writes in *A View of the World* (in which "Genocide in Brazil" is reprinted) that he considers the article "the most worthwhile of all my endeavours, and I have reason to believe that it at least saved some lives, and probably even benefited the long-term prospects of the Amerindians."

During the next twenty years Lewis made several trips to Latin America to report on the treatment of Indians in Mexico, Peru, Paraguay, Bolivia, and Venezuela. On many of these trips he was accompanied by the photographer Donald McCullin, with whom he has formed what he calls in *The World, the World* "a working collaboration and a friendship." Zinsser quotes McCullin, who considers Lewis his substitute father: "When I'm in Norman's presence I immediately become younger because there's a gaiety about him."

In his investigations Lewis has found a ubiquitous enemy of the Indians in two evangelical missionary groups, the Summer Institute of Linguistics and the New Tribes Mission–"exceedingly powerful organizations," Lewis writes in *The Missionaries*–that were "virtually dividing the whole of Latin America, where tribal people remained to be reached, into their spheres of interest." Lewis found that the missionaries resorted to extreme measures, including murder and torture, to force the Indians to convert to Christianity. Some twenty years earlier, in *A Dragon Apparent,* Lewis had noted about an American evangelical missionary in Vietnam: "I realized quite sharply that the pastor was totally uninterested in the natives as a whole, but only in 'our Christians (we love them like children).' He collected souls with the not very fierce pleasure that others collect stamps." Lewis has been aware of this sort of zealous piety all his life. In *An Empire of the East: Travels in Indonesia* (1993) he remembers a service he had attended in Wales when he was nine: "I was old enough to be amazed to be compelled to listen to a sermon, acclaimed in the Tabernacle by a standing ovation, on 'the sin of forgiveness.'"

The Indians were regarded as a resource by the missionaries, just as the trees in their rain forests and the minerals in their mountains were considered resources by logging and mining companies. Because of their common interest in subduing the Indians, the governments of Latin America and the missionary organizations worked in close covert cooperation.

In 1974 Lewis and McCullin found deplorable conditions on an Aché reservation at Cecilio Baez, Paraguay; the Indians were sick, weak, demoralized, and completely under the control of the New Tribes Mission station. Lewis says in *The Missionaries:* "There was something in the atmosphere here–the smiling young missionaries, more and more of whom had appeared, gathering in the background to sing what might equally have been a hymn or a cheerleader's song, the stench of excrement, the suspicion that there might be many hidden graves in this place–that made this the most sinister experience of my life." At a mission station near Pailón, Bolivia, in 1978 Lewis and McCullin found that the missionary in charge had cut off the water supply to the Ayoreo Indians because someone had stolen several gallons of gasoline, and he would not restore it until the guilty party had been turned over to him for a public beating. It apparently did not matter to the missionary that he had deprived many sick children of water for several days. The missionary was offended by the Indians' lack of a notion of "corrective chastisement": he "spoke of this aversion to punishment as of some genetic defect inherited and shared by the whole race."

Lewis mixed the menace of missionaries into the plot of *Flight from a Dark Equator* (1972), a novel about a Central Intelligence Agency-supported attempted coup d'état in Colombia. While reviews were mixed, *TLS* (17 April 1972) said that Lewis's "concern for Latin America, and his knowledge of the area, is always in evidence, and without seeming to embark on a political diatribe he manages to make his own opinions felt and understood." He presents, according to the review, "a convincing, if depressing, picture of overt and clandestine oppression."

Lewis's next novel, *The Sicilian Specialist* (1974), was inspired by the suggestion of Boris Giuliano, chief of the Pubblica Sicurezza (Public Safety Force) in Palermo, that the Mafia was involved in the assassination of President John F. Kennedy. The claim was supported by an Italian whom Lewis believed to be associated with the Mafia. In 1978 Lewis published *Naples '44,* based on the diary he kept between October 1943 and October 1944 while he served in the Field Security Service of the British army. Ted Morgan in *The Saturday Review-World* (7 July 1974) called it one of the ten best books on World War II, and Raleigh Trevelyan in *TLS* (3 March 1978) said that Lewis had treated the Neapolitans "with sympathy and tolerance" in spite of their scurrility and degraded ways. Luigi Barzini in *The New York Review of Books* (7 February 1980) found "the taste and smell of truth" in the book and praised Lewis for writing "very well, inconspicuously well."

Lewis's novels of the late 1970s and the 1980s met a mixed critical reception. *The German Company* (1979), set in Bolivia, pits the owner of a trucking company against a powerful neo-Nazi enterprise. Ian Stewart in the *Illustrated London News* (October 1979) declared that the novel has "the shock-value quality of brilliant reportage." *Cuban Passage* (1982), set at the moment of Castro's coming to power in 1959, was praised by Nicholas Shakespeare in *TLS* (14 May 1982) for "catching, with all its colours and cigar smell, a jaunty, hip-swinging society which has half-digested the systems it purports to reject." Shakespeare, however, found fault with the novel's effigylike characters and lack of focus. *A Suitable Case for Corruption* (1984), involving a CIA plot to kill Libyan leader Mu'ammar Gadhafi that instead ends in the assassination of Egyptian president Anwar as-Sadat, left most critics unimpressed. Shakespeare was among them: "We are told," he wrote in *TLS* (4 May 1984), "that foreigners flying into Tripoli transform their whisky into bottles labelled fruit juice. *A Suitable Case for Corruption* tastes as if it has been decanted the other way round, leaving the impression of a novel spread very thinly over too wide a canvas." *The March of the Long Shadows* (1987), however, received strongly favorable reviews. Set in Sicily in 1947, it is narrated by a British Secret Service veteran who is drawn into the murky depths of the Mafia. Neville Shack wrote in *TLS* (5 June 1987) that the novel "succeeds as a fascinating and entertaining yarn" and "is a book rich in images for the landscape and local history. Details of mood impress themselves on the story, giving it a fuller meaning, creating a very particular resonance." Lewis has not published another novel since *The March of the Long Shadows.*

If Lewis's novels are uneven, his travel narratives are consistently high in quality. When *Voices of the Old Sea,* his account of his seasons in Farol, was published in 1984, the reviews were laudatory. Bill Greenwell wrote in *The New Statesman* (7 September 1984) that Lewis "lives up to his own high standards. His is a subtle, exacting art, controlling the finest of descriptive sentences . . . but subjugating them to the more pressing task of reporting what is said and done." Tony Lambert noted in *TLS* (4 January 1985) that the tone of the book "is not merely elegiac; with a novelist's eye for a rounded story as well as an anthropologist's nosiness, Lewis disinters memorable lives and presents a rich array of brave, comic, idiosyncratic and above all dignified characters." Barbara Probst said in *The New York Times Book Review* (14 July 1985) that Lewis "is great in evoking the essence of things."

In the 1980s Eland Books in London and Hippocrene Books in New York republished *A Dragon Apparent* (1982), *Golden Earth* (1984), and *The Changing Sky* (1984); Eland also republished *Naples '44* (1985). In March 1987 Lewis received an honorary degree from the University of Essex. *The Missionaries,* about the plight of Indians in Latin America at the hands of evangelical missionary organizations, was published in 1988. Reviewing an advance copy in *The New York Times Book Review* (25 December 1987), L. Elisabeth Beattie called *The Missionaries* "a brave and honest book written in the name of social justice." In *TLS* (1 July 1988) Paul Henley said that it evokes "a powerful sense of place

Dust jacket for Lewis's description of his travels in the Indian states of Orissa and Madhya Pradesh in 1990

and atmosphere" and compared it to "Gabriel García Márquez at his best."

In 1990 Lewis traveled to India to see the tribal villages in the central states of Orissa and Madhya Pradesh, regions still relatively untouched by modern civilization. This situation, Lewis writes in *A Goddess in the Stones,* published in 1991, is only temporary: "India's jungles and all that they contain are to be swept away. It was a thought that increased my feelings of urgency in writing this book." Travel in this part of India was difficult; the roads were deplorable, and there was no public transportation. "The fact is," Lewis writes, "that there is virtually no travel in the interior of India. There is nowhere to stay, nowhere to eat, and it is not particularly safe." In other words, Lewis found the conditions of travel to be those to which he was accustomed. And he found travel there particularly rewarding, for he had the sense that everything he saw was in its natural state and not on exhibition. He found the erotic sculptures at the Temple of the Sun God at Konarak "largely standardized and repetitive," like those of the saints on medieval cathedrals. "In both so widely sundered civilizations," Lewis reflects, "the boredom of a sculptor, deprived of all outlet for invention and condemned to the mass production of almost identical figures, must have been extreme." In Kangrapada, an isolated village, the people had no knowledge of or need for money and apparently followed a carefree, utopian existence. Beneath the surface, however, life was perhaps not so blissful: "Slowly I was coming to the realization," Lewis writes of watching a young man and woman exchanging flirtations, "that for all the apparent free loving and living of the so-called primitives they were in reality wanderers under watchful eyes in the labyrinth of custom." The village elders were keeping track, from a discreet distance, of everything the couple did. Constraints and cautions existed in full force in Kangrapada.

Reviewers of *A Goddess in the Stones* included C. A. Bayly in *TLS* (7 June 1991), who called it "a subtle elegy for the 'old India'" written with Lewis's "usual economy and elegance," and Robert Carver in *The New Statesman* (7 July 1991), who pointed to Lewis's "precisely nuanced" and "calmly resonant" writing. *A Goddess in the Stones* won the 1991 Thomas Cook Travel Book Award.

Early in 1991 Lewis embarked on a difficult trip to the archipelago of more than thirteen thousand islands that makes up the country of Indonesia. Lewis comments early in his 1993 book about the trip, *An Empire of the East,* that anyone who attempted to visit every Indonesian island "would find himself trapped in the bailiwick of old age before completing such an odyssey." Lewis himself was nearing his eighty-third birthday at the time he undertook this trip; perhaps for that reason his son Gawaine and his daughter Claudia accompanied him on various parts of it.

"In all probability," Lewis says in *An Empire of the East,* "Indonesia can still offer the greatest variety of primitive scenes and entertainments of any country on earth." He found most of what he was looking for in Irian Jaya (West Irian), which, he asserts, is, "after the polar regions, one of the least known areas of the globe." He found a stone-age tribe, the Yalis, who lived as they always had, "with the exception of the ball-point pens stuck through the holes in the septums of their noses." In another part of Irian Jaya he asked a guide what might be of interest in a certain village; the guide replied, "Scenery very good. Also you are seeing different things. There are women in Karubaga turning themselves into bats." "That's promising," Lewis said. In the event, he witnessed no such transformations.

Lewis was particularly eager to visit East Timor, a former Portuguese colony in the southeastern part of the archipelago that has staunchly resisted its inclusion in Indonesia. "Only a permanent presence of the army," Lewis writes, "will prevent it from declaring independence." He encountered much official resistance to his visit, waiting eight days in Bali before he was permitted to fly to East Timor. Once there, he found it difficult to collect reports of the slaughters of East Timor natives by Indonesian soldiers in the late 1970s. The survivors were still too traumatized or too terrified of retribution to give Lewis their eyewitness accounts.

In *The New Statesman* (17 December 1993) Carver called the section of *An Empire of the East* on Irian Jaya "vintage Lewis–dry, witty, tender, and perceptive." In *TLS* (7 January 1994) Peter Metcalf wrote that it showed "the raconteur's instinct for details that convey a whole scene." Rand Richards Cooper in *The New York Times Book Review* (5 June 1994) called *An Empire of the East* "a classic narrative of manners, history and scenery."

A standard complaint among reviewers is Lewis's dearth of personal details and emotional expression in his writing. Lewis might respond that his subject is the travels, not the traveler. Yet the same complaint might be made about his four volumes of autobiography, *Naples '44, Jackdaw Cake, The Missionaries,* and *The World, the World,* as well as about his autobiographical essays. In these works Lewis says nothing about any romantic relationships, and he is guarded about dates and about places where he has lived. For example, in his essay "In Essex," included in *To Run across the Sea,* he claims to have lived in this "ugliest county" in England for three years in the late 1940s or early 1950s, but he disguises place names and does not mention this residence anywhere else in his writings. In *The Missionaries* he mentions that he lived "for some years" in Banchory, Kincardineshire, Scotland, but says nothing more about it. The four autobiographical volumes mostly consist of accounts of Lewis's travels. He has always chosen to travel as unencumbered as possible; this freedom from encumbrances would seem to be one of the principal joys of travel for him. He has usually traveled alone, leaving his wife and children at home and disdaining traveling companions.

The Lewis who emerges from his autobiographical volumes is patient yet persistent, deferential yet quietly assertive, a serious student of humanity who is able to retain a sense of humor. An incident Lewis recounts in *The World, the World* brings out all of these qualities. One evening in the slums of Lima, Peru, Lewis came upon a boy of about twelve lying unconscious in the street. Bystanders told him that the boy had fallen from a three-story building. Nobody was doing anything for the boy, so Lewis drove him to a hospital. Because hardly anyone was on duty at the hospital, the boy lay unattended all night. After the boy was admitted, Lewis, having done all he could, left the hospital not knowing whether the boy would live or die. Several days later Lewis was boarding an airplane when three carefully dressed and groomed Indians approached him carrying three small bone fragments on a cushion:

> There was no way of knowing what these men wanted with me although it was clear that their presence was allied to the drama of the injured boy. It was evident, too, that an operation had taken place, but what had been the result? These obsidian Indian faces gave no clue to the answer.

Lewis did not know the language the Indians spoke. "All I could do, stiffening the muscles of my face in an attempt to match an Indian absence of expression, was to touch the bones with the tips of my fingers which the Indians watched unblinkingly. Then we all bowed and withdrew." The story is emblematic of many of Lewis's encounters in his travels: there is so much that cannot be understood or expressed between people of different cultures, yet they can still find ways to show respect and depth of feeling.

In his tenth decade Lewis continues to travel and write, seemingly unslowed by age. Although, as McCullin told Zinsser, "he looks as if a gust of wind would blow him away," he stands up to the rigors of travel under even the most difficult conditions. In 1996 Zinsser found him looking much younger than his years: "His body is trim and his hair is still dark; only his bristle mustache is gray. He has a thin face, with sharp, unmemorable features except for warm brown eyes that gaze out from behind large horn-rimmed glasses." Zinsser quotes Lesley Lewis as saying of her husband, "Norman has never given in to the idea that he's old."

Searching for an answer to the question of what has driven him to go to so many obscure places, Lewis reverts in *The World, the World* to his childhood restlessness. In Wales

> I would go exploring with the idea in my head that the further I was from home the better it would be. The next valley would always be wilder. The lake would be bottomless, and I would find a mysterious ruin, and there would be ravens instead of crows in all the trees.

His yearning for places that are fresh, vital, and exciting leads him to search continually for new destinations, for familiarity diminishes these qualities soon after one arrives. He says in *A View of the World,* "I cannot think of any single place that I have written about that did not appear to have gone down hill–sometimes disastrously so–on a subsequent visit." When the freshness and novelty of a place diminish, a traveler registers any change as a decline.

Whatever happens to the places Lewis has written about, his travel narratives have an enduring vitality. They form a testament to the authentic ways of life of indigenous peoples. Respectful of the integrity of these ways of life, the works also express mirth at their incongruities, bemusement over their limitations, and revulsion over their inhumanities. Lewis has built a collection of remarkable works of travel. He may well be the best travel writer of his time.

References:

Michael S. Howard, *Jonathan Cape, Publisher* (London: Cape, 1971), pp. 243–244;

Pico Iyer, "Norman Lewis: A Curious Collector of Curiosities," in his *Tropical Classical: Essays from Several Directions* (New York: Knopf, 1997), pp. 89–104;

Eric Newby, ed., *A Book of Travellers' Tales* (New York: Viking Penguin, 1985), p. 369;

S. J. Perelman, *Don't Tread on Me: The Selected Letters of S.J. Perelman,* edited by Prudence Crowther (New York: Viking, 1987), pp. 112–113, 120, 147;

William Zinsser, "A Gene for Adventure," *Travel Holiday,* 179 (March 1996): 60–65, 126–127.

Patrick Marnham

(15 August 1943 –   )

Joshua D. Esty
Harvard University

BOOKS: *Road to Katmandu* (London: Macmillan, 1971); republished as *Road to Katmandu: Traveled by a Bunch of Zombies–Like Us* (New York: Putnam, 1971);

Nomads of the Sahel, Minority Rights Group Report, no. 33 (London: Minority Rights Group, 1977; revised, 1979);

Fantastic Invasion: Notes on Contemporary Africa (New York: Harcourt Brace Jovanovich, 1979); republished as *Fantastic Invasion: Dispatches from Contemporary Africa* (London: Cape, 1980); revised as *Fantastic Invasion: Dispatches from Africa* (London: Penguin, 1987);

Lourdes: A Modern Pilgrimage (London: Heinemann, 1980; New York: Coward, McCann & Geoghegan, 1981);

The Private Eye *Story: The First 21 Years* (London: Deutsch, 1982);

So Far from God: A Journey to Central America (London: Cape, 1985; New York: Viking, 1985; revised edition, London: Bloomsbury Classics, 1996);

Trail of Havoc: In the Steps of Lord Lucan (London: Viking, 1987; New York: Viking, 1988);

The Man Who Wasn't Maigret: A Portrait of Georges Simenon (London: Bloomsbury, 1992; New York: Farrar, Straus & Giroux, 1993);

Crime and the Académie Française: Dispatches from Paris (London: Viking, 1993);

Dreaming with His Eyes Open: A Life of Diego Rivera (New York: Knopf, 1998; London: Bloomsbury, 1998).

OTHER: *Night Thoughts: The Spectator Bedside Book,* edited by Marnham (London: Chatto & Windus/Hogarth, 1983).

Patrick Marnham

In a career that began in the early 1970s, Patrick Marnham has written about the political and cultural life of nations on almost every continent, though his reputation as a travel writer rests mainly on a trio of books about the heartlands of the developing world–Asia, Africa, and Latin America. Like other British writers who have turned their literary energies to the world beyond Europe, Marnham describes his journeys in romantic terms while ruefully acknowledging the element of fantasy involved in most travel writing. His works do not ignore the political and economic problems surrounding exotic locations, nor do they shy away from a frank critical recognition of European imperialism's contribution to those difficulties. Marnham's writing often addresses complex cultural histories and tackles substantial questions about belief, skepticism, communal responsibility, and individual freedom. His best works move beyond the vivid immediacy of journalism and attain the more abiding literary qualities of first-rate travel writing.

It seems fitting that Marnham, a writer with a lust for exotic locales and political controversy, was born on 15 August 1943 in the Palestinian city of Jerusalem, soon to become the divided center of Israel. A British citizen, he was the son of Sir Ralph Marnham, a surgeon, and Helena Marnham, née Daly. He was educated at Downside School, a Benedictine school in Bath, and at Corpus Christi College, Oxford, where he earned an honors degree in jurisprudence. He took the bar at Gray's Inn in 1966, but shortly thereafter he began writing for the satirical magazine *Private Eye*. He never practiced law.

In the tradition of such anatomizers of late British imperialism as Graham Greene, Malcolm Lowry, and Evelyn Waugh, Marnham documents with tragic irony and self-deprecating wit the fate of parts of the world that were once administered–and are still in many ways controlled–by Europe and the United States. But Marnham also works in the more swashbuckling mode of travel writing defined by contemporaries such as Paul Theroux and Bruce Chatwin, whose adventurousness recaptures some of the old glamour of colonial exploration. In the classic formula of British travel writing, Marnham's works are driven by the dramatic and sometimes amusing encounters between a chaotic world and a dry English observer as he uses common sense and Orwellian honesty to puncture political illusions and cultural misconceptions about the Third World.

Marnham's travel-writing career began with *Road to Katmandu* (1971), an account of a trek from Istanbul, Turkey, to Katmandu, Nepal, in 1968. With an almost telegraphic spareness punctuated by rhetorical flourishes and pungent descriptions, the book retells the classic Western journey toward Asian peace and harmony as a hippie-era quest for nirvana. It is less about the destination than about the travelers, a new generation of *wandervögel* (ramblers) presciently described in Waugh's *When the Going Was Good* (1946), in a passage quoted by Marnham, as "lean, lawless, aimless couples with rucksacks, joining the great army of men and women without papers, without official existence." Marnham's companions on the eastward road are disaffected members of a generation in retreat from the values of industrial and secular Europe. Their journey, Marnham says, amounts to a "total rejection of the philosophy of money and of the world of timetables." They live by an admirable code of spontaneity, honesty, poverty, and the pursuit of happiness, although that pursuit depends on obtaining cheap drugs and free rides from local people.

Gathering in the cheap rooftop hotels of Istanbul, the "zombies" of Marnham's road to Katmandu are driven by a restless search for meaning and a need to leave behind the corrupt societies of home. In Marnham's view, these deserters from the West are not simply escapists; they are believers in a better version of themselves. The fulfillment they seek in the exotic realms of the East is, however, elusive and evanescent. For Marnham, at least, it cannot be separated from the guilt triggered by his awareness that Asian exoticism often comes at the cost of economic underdevelopment. One of the travelers, Rat, carries the book through several picaresque episodes, appearing alternately as a charismatic innocent longing for a meaningful existence and as a spoiled young man seeking easy gratification. Both versions–the noble and the venal–are true, as Marnham's finely tuned irony allows the reader to see. Throughout the journey Marnham maintains the delicate balance between participation and detached observation that is typical of his best writing.

Whenever the journey begins to seem vaguely heroic, Marnham inevitably introduces a note of ironic self-deprecation. The rigorous adventures of overland travel in central Asia give way to the mundane, the comic–even the ridiculous. While the travelers relish their semicelebrity status as Western tourists in the remote villages of Afghanistan, they are also eager to learn from alien cultures: "They were purged of pretensions by the achievement of their survival out here on the road. They were beggar forerunners of a pacific empire-building race, preaching the gospel of Kim; people who had decided that the only way of escape was down; the refugees of some distant spiritual battle." Although he often assumes the group identity of the "we," here Marnham writes about the travelers in the third person in an attempt to distance himself from the journey's more grandiose ambitions. Marnham sympathizes with the utopian impulses of the new *wandervögel,* but he is also at pains to make objective and precise observations about them. Often he joins the natives of Asia in their suspicion of these "pukka hippies" with their Christlike beards and tattered clothes that conceal, but only for a moment, the blue eyes and traveler's checks of neocolonial tourists who often survive by selling illegal drugs and other contraband–not to mention their own blood and their girlfriends' bodies.

Marnham is not just an ethnographer of the hippie subculture; he also captures details of life in Turkey, Iran, Afghanistan, Pakistan, and India. The book establishes several themes that run through all of Marnham's travel writing: the difficulties and rewards of overland travel, the valiant but possibly futile quest for meaning in the late twentieth century, and the wistful recognition that travelers almost inevitably destroy the fragile exoticism that they seek. The last point is especially true of travel writers who not only visit magical places but also tell the rest of the world about them. Marnham's thrill

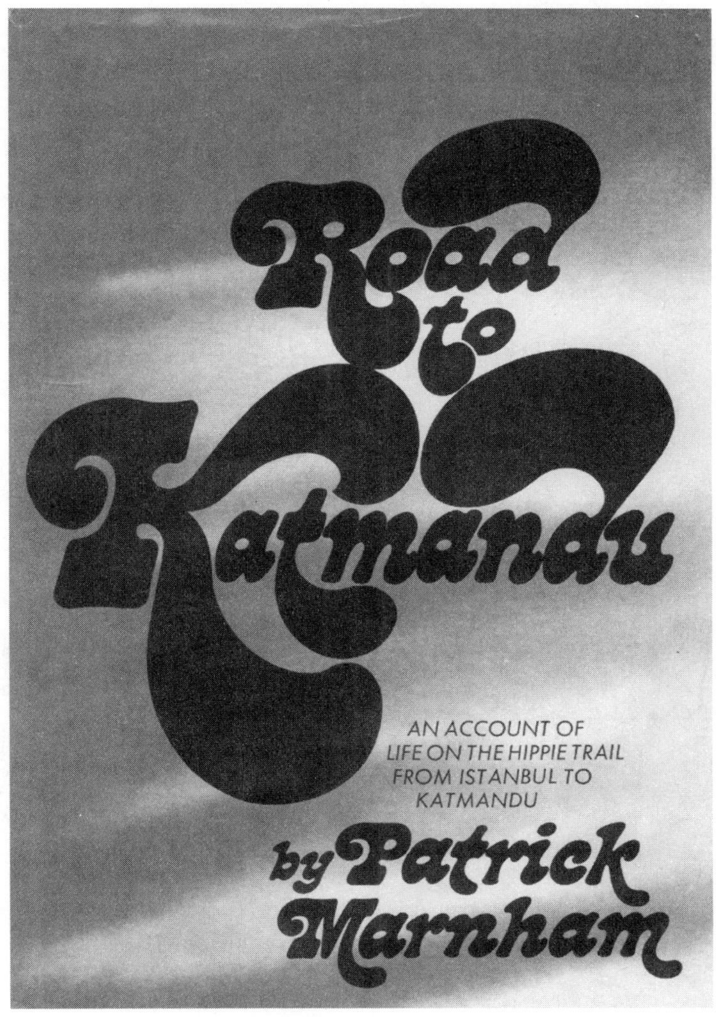

Dust jacket for the U.S. edition of Marnham's first book, published in 1971

of discovery is constantly undermined by his awareness that such discoveries can happen only once. Perhaps this realization accounts for his instant dislike of the Turkish modernizer who, to draw tourists to his picturesque hamlet, recast it in the mold of a Westernized town and thereby destroyed its appeal.

Road to Katmandu is a funny book, but it is not always comic or hopeful. Dangers and disillusionments dog the travelers from Turkey to Nepal. The dangers take the form not only of hunger, disease, boredom, thievery, and political corruption but also of the constant possibility that the West will catch up with them in their mad dash toward nirvana. As Marnham recognizes, the seeds of corruption are carried by the travelers themselves, making escape impossible even in the yawning deserts of Afghanistan or the lush valleys of Nepal. This bittersweet theme surfaces regularly as the travelers' idealism gives way to the touristic contingencies of time, money, hunger, and health. When Marnham and his companions reach Delhi, India, they discover, instead of the hoped-for guru on a mountaintop, a Hollywood movie starring Raquel Welch. At the end of the road in Katmandu, Marnham's unblinking eye reveals not the blissful inhabitants of Eden but wasted youths whose lives consist of begging and drug addiction. By the time readers encounter the pathetic, hepatic Englishwomen and the pathetic, emaciated Scandinavian, they are prepared for the possibility of rank disappointment. Still, in the book's final pages, Marnham gazes out at an enchanted Himalayan landscape with a feeling that approaches rapture: "On a clear day in Paradise, even the stones will sing." The singing stones of Nepal suggest that Marnham has caught a fleeting glimpse of nirvana.

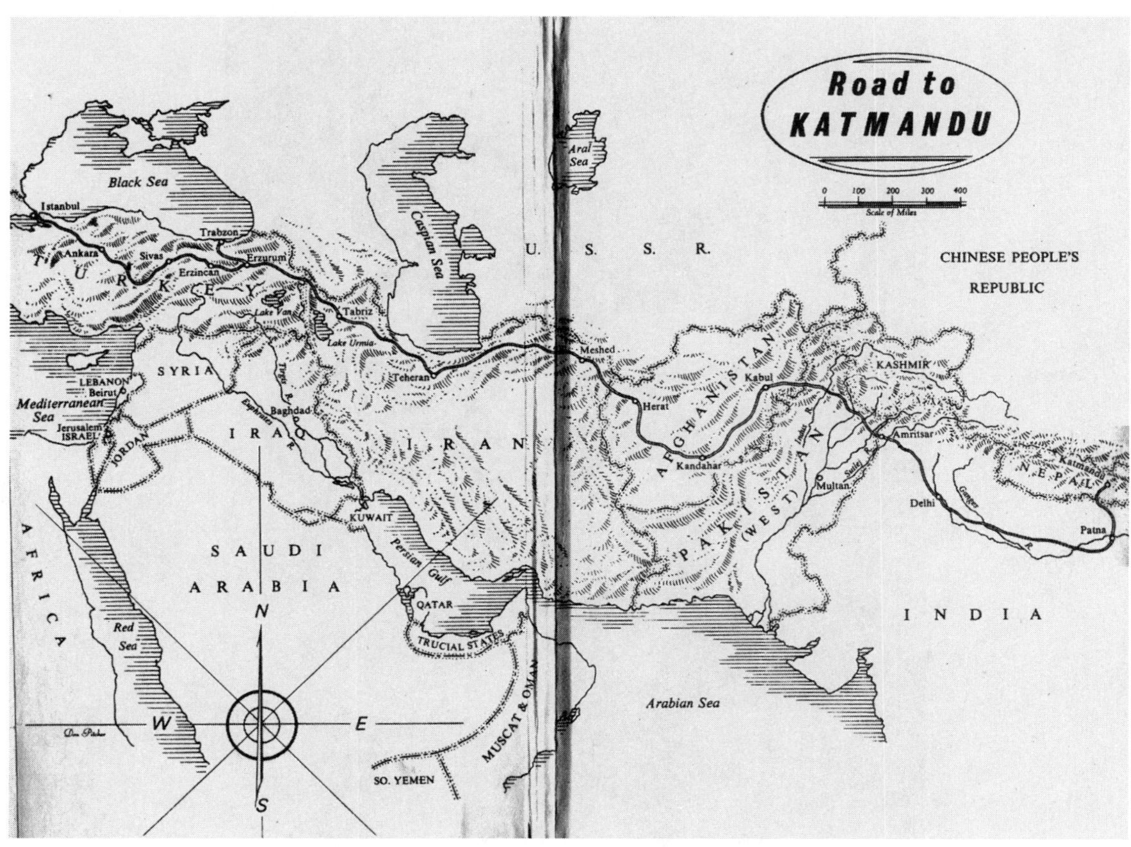

Map of the route followed by Marnham and his companions

Road to Katmandu was widely read as a dispatch to the West from the remote corners of Asia and to the mainstream reading public from the unknown world of hippie youth culture. The book spoke for a generation that seemed to many to be more interested in shiftless hedonism than in the metaphysical high road to fulfillment. It also secured Marnham's reputation as a promising journalist and travel writer. He worked as a journalist for the *Daily Telegraph* (London) from 1968 to 1970, and published articles in various British and American magazines. During this time he traveled widely in sub-Saharan Africa, amassing the experiences that form the basis for *Fantastic Invasion: Notes on Contemporary Africa* (1979).

Unlike *Road to Katmandu, Fantastic Invasion* does not narrate a single journey; instead, it offers a set of related observations, vignettes, and stories culled from many years of crisscrossing the continent. The central theme of the book, announced in the title, is the invasion of postcolonial Africa by "Northerners" of all kinds. Taking an epigraph from Joseph Conrad's *Heart of Darkness* (1902), Marnham investigates Africa's "ominous patience" as it waits "for the passing away of a fantastic invasion." In dozens of sharply narrated episodes he exposes the absurd and baleful influence of "Northern" neocolonialism. Whereas in *Road to Katmandu* he acknowledges that British imperial institutions were helpful as well as harmful in India, in *Fantastic Invasion* he sees virtually no redemptive value in Northern attempts to control or improve Africa. Europeans and Americans impose their institutions on a continent that cannot live on imported food, values, or technical aid. Marnham's relentless cataloguing of wrongheaded Northern schemes provides a bleak but richly detailed history of Africa in the 1970s, a decade when the first great hopes of decolonization were beginning to turn sour in the face of famine, corruption, and widespread political violence.

The book is divided into three sections: East Africa, West Africa, and "Parallel Africa," Marnham's name for places that have resisted or evaded Northern intervention. In a series of reports on East African game parks Marnham points out the tensions between Northerners and natives that continue to plague Africa in the twentieth century. Game reserves, he notes, serve Northern hunters, conservationists, and tourism promoters; but with the exception of an elite minority in the capital cities, Africans derive little benefit from these

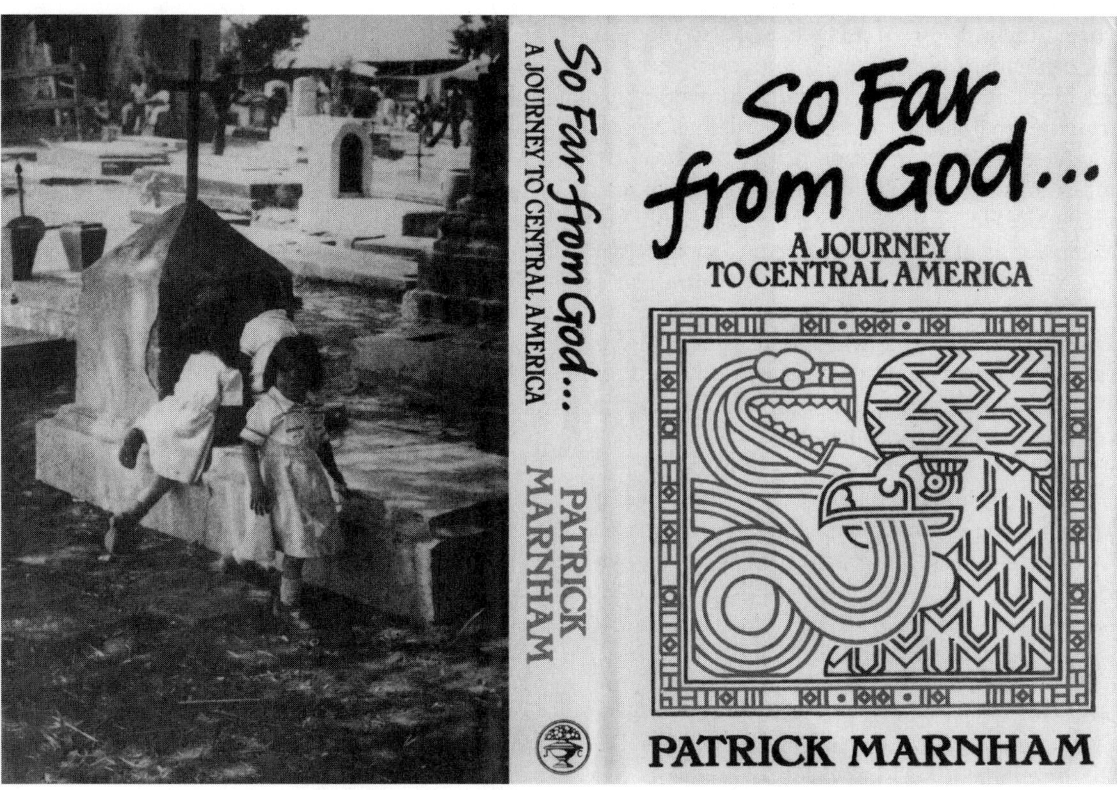

Dust jacket for Marnham's 1985 account of his travels from California to Nicaragua

enterprises. Marnham describes with grim irony the Kidepo valley in Uganda:

> Kidepo was consequently ruled off, the animals were protected from human pursuit by armed rangers, and a lodge was erected for tourists. What the far-sighted men had ignored was that these wild, thirsty plains were the hunting grounds, or meat larder, of the people of Kidepo, the Ik. Now, with their unrivalled view over the pleasant savanna from their "primitive settlements on the fringe of wooded hills," the Ik were in a unique position to count the seventy-odd mammals and two-hundred-odd bird species known to occur on the plain, while they starved to death.

Even seemingly benign Northern pursuits such as anthropology and paleontology seem suspect in their exploitation of African resources. With a deadly eye, Marnham observes the various Northerners who come to Africa looking for knowledge, diversion, or lucre. While sympathizing with their ambitious dreams and even their crackpot visions, he exposes their false assumptions and ethnocentric blind spots.

In the West African section of the book Marnham turns his attention to the ill-conceived nature of Northern altruism–in particular, famine relief in the Saharan border region known as the Sahel. In 1977 Marnham had been commissioned by the Minority Rights Group to write a report on the catastrophic conditions facing the Sahel's pastoral nomads; it had been published that year under the title *Nomads of the Sahel.* In *Fantastic Invasion* he provides a scathing picture of Northern policy in the economically dependent nations of the Sahel. For example, when the United States and European countries distributed supplies in the cities, Sahelian nomads came for the free food, leaving their starving herds behind and losing their livelihood. Again and again Marnham reveals the arrogant and misguided way in which Western aid programs displace local economies, to the permanent disadvantage of Africans. The book is explicitly polemical, and its arguments are substantiated by the horrifying scenes of corruption, chaos, and social disaster that Marnham observes in postcolonial Africa. But his tone is never strident; his outrage surfaces in the muted form of a deep and stinging irony as he juxtaposes such images as a Senegalese lunatic living in a sleekly modern but abandoned gas station or placidly inert policemen in starched uniforms watching ferry passengers scramble madly over a Gambian quay.

In the final section of *Fantastic Invasion* Marnham treats the shortcomings of Northern medical establishments that are more interested in researching Africans than in curing them. Western medicine fails so often in Africa, he contends, because of its imperviousness to the lessons of traditional African healing. In making his case Marnham rehabilitates one of the original Northern do-gooders, Albert Schweitzer. Schweitzer's saintly contributions to African medicine had been thrown into question by what Marnham sees as the myopic and ethnocentric consensus of official scientific medicine. What Schweitzer produced, however, Marnham claims, was a rare and effective adaptation of Western medicine to African conditions, a practice sensitive to local customs that ran athwart conventional medical wisdom–and, as Marnham notes in an aside, was also inimical to the interests of pharmaceutical companies.

For Marnham, imperial legacies and neocolonial interference in African politics have "poisoned everything that followed independence." Some readers have objected that this pessimistic vision discourages solutions and relies too heavily on the simplistic notion of leaving Africa to the Africans. Edward Hoagland in *The New Republic* (1 March 1980) found the book too pessimistic and too broadly aimed at political critiques of the North's role in African problems. Joseph Lelyveld in *The New York Times Book Review* (30 March 1980) largely echoed these sentiments. Also, Marnham is aware that his practice as a journalist is susceptible to the same criticism he launches at other Northerners who make their living in Africa; but he eschews sensationalized and graphic descriptions so as to distinguish himself from journalists who traffic in what he describes as a new "pornography of suffering."

Fantastic Invasion was met with acclaim in both England and the United States despite its bitter attacks on neocolonialism. Although Marnham compellingly exposes the North's failure to learn from Africa, his attempts to support the proposition that "when we leave it alone, it works" are overshadowed by the welter of social disaster that he depicts. The book was staunchly supported by important literary figures such as Doris Lessing, who described it as an "exhilarating Swiftian excursion into human folly," and Greene, who called it "an important book on independent Africa."

In *Lourdes: A Modern Pilgrimage* (1980) Marnham returns to a description of a specific journey. The road to Lourdes, France, like the road to Katmandu, is populated by pilgrims on a quest for religious meaning and spiritual healing. Marnham participates in this more formalized pilgrimage while maintaining the detachment and skeptical irony that tempered his belief in the Asian nirvana. He had traveled to Lourdes in 1978 along with more than four million pilgrims eager to be healed in the town where the Virgin Mary had supposedly appeared to a peasant girl named Bernadette Soubirous exactly 120 years earlier. Since 1858, he notes, sixty-four local miracles had been recognized by the Vatican. The journey to Lourdes represents the survival of faith and hope for those who have been afflicted by disease or social malaise, and, as in *Road to Katmandu,* Marnham finds himself drawn to people who genuinely believe that the pilgrimage will provide remedy and redemption. For Marnham the journey provides rich evidence of a living and powerful Christianity that survives in Europe almost in spite of organized religion. One of his recurrent themes in this book and elsewhere is the superiority of spontaneous, truly popular forms of religious worship to hierarchical religious institutions. Looking for the vital essence of European Catholicism beneath the composed surface of the Roman church, Marnham finds in Lourdes a genuine and robust folk religion.

Lourdes, however, is not simply a religious site but also a commercial business. Marnham's savage wit is perfectly suited to the task of revealing the tension between the holy shrine and the souvenir stand that pervades this provincial town that he calls "St. Disney's Land." Almost effortlessly he makes his satirical points simply by quoting from tourist brochures that offer "Budget, Weekend or Midweek pilgrimages." While many of the local citizens resent the intrusion of the devoted millions into their peaceful backwater, others avidly pursue the business of selling miracles:

> There are virgins in a snow storm, virgins in a television set, little cutie-doll bug-eyed half-witted virgins praying on velveteen mats; virgins in make-up, virgins in modern dress and the world-renowned hollow, plastic virgins whose crowns unscrew to turn into bottle stoppers. There are Virgins in Grottos, and there are virgins in grottos mounted on varnished Dutch clogs, an international two-horrors-in-one. If the wind got up you could be deafened by the tinkling cascades of medals which glitter and dangle in luxuriant clumps in shop after shop. When I finally summoned the courage to examine them, I found that half the medals bore the figure of Mary, and the other half the signs of the Zodiac. But you never got Mary on one side and Virgo on the other; that would be sacreligious.

Marnham continually muses about the persistence of belief in such a place, mixing the compassionate tone of a would-be believer with the deflationary tone of an observer who cannot help but notice the ersatz religious icons and dime-store elixirs that flow as copiously as Lourdes's celebrated holy water. He carefully preserves his dual position as participant and observer, bathing the narrative in a rich irony that neither ignores crass commercialism nor rejects the possibility of true religion.

In the early 1980s Marnham continued to work as a foreign correspondent, contributing to various

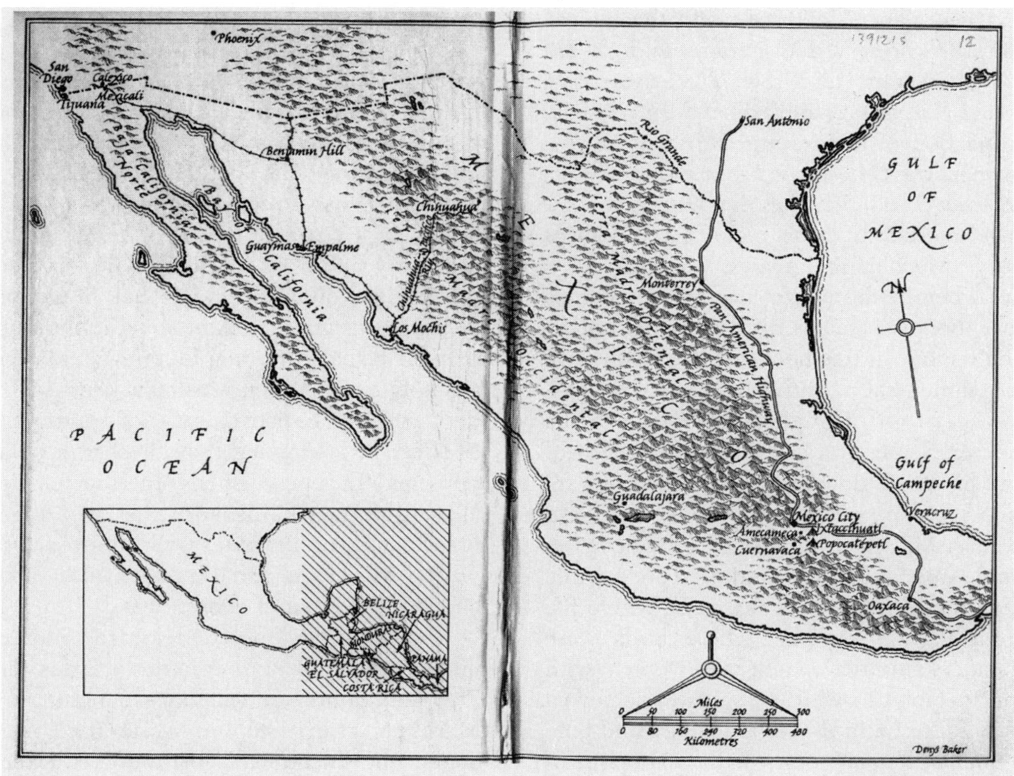

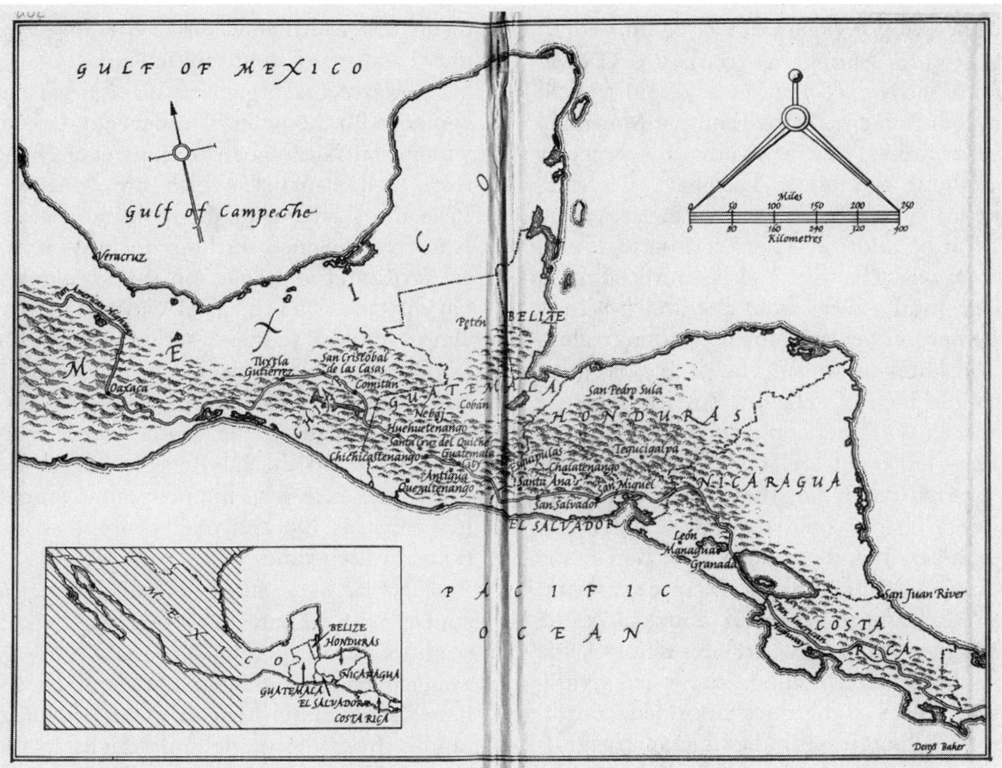

Maps of the region through which Marnham traveled on the journey described in So Far from God

magazines and newspapers in Britain and the United States. In 1981–1982 he served as literary editor of *The Spectator*. During this time he wrote *The* Private Eye *Story: The First 21 Years* (1982) and edited *Night Thoughts* (1983), a compilation of articles and stories from *The Spectator*. In his next travel book, *So Far from God: A Journey to Central America* (1985), he takes the perspective of a traveler who is interested in the region's post-Cortés cultural history. Marnham's greatest strength as a writer emerges when he dramatizes his own sometimes comic misconceptions, as well as his developing understanding of the region. In this book his anecdotal style is joined to a symmetrical narrative structure: the journey begins with a whiff of imperial adventure in the archives of Seville, Spain, and ends with the stench of imperial failure in the shadow of a rusty boat in Granada, Nicaragua.

At the outset Marnham reveals his romantic conception of Latin America as "the land of stained white suits and cheap dance music . . . the place where life was lived to a natural rhythm, where birds were devoured by spiders and men fought over women, with knives." From this point forward he seeks to achieve a clear-eyed appraisal of Latin American culture and politics that will qualify, but not destroy, the exoticism of his fantasy. Once again, his most important literary tool is the dry irony with which he captures both the political horror and the cultural vitality of the region.

The first stop on Marnham's journey is California, the "capital of the twenty-first century" and outpost of the decadent but influential kingdom that Marnham calls, after Frida Kahlo, "Gringolandia." At regular intervals throughout the book Marnham describes gringo interference in Central America in the same critical tone in which he addressed Northern neocolonialism in *Fantastic Invasion*. His tone and his purpose have, however, shifted subtly away from political polemics toward an attempt to understand the contrasting values of the Anglo and Latin cultures: "The people of North America have little idea of religion, but they have a strict public morality. The Latin people are without morality but they are highly religious. The two sides are attracted to each other, but they also feel mutual contempt." Such a claim would naturally elicit objections from specialists; but the reflection comes at the end of the journey, by which time most readers would grant Marnham the right to generalize about places he has observed so closely. The book adheres to the classic unspoken formula of travel writing: the writer vividly records his experiences and draws informed conclusions without pretending to speak the ultimate truth.

Marnham's claim about the religious quality of life in Central America constitutes one of the main themes of the book. As on the journey to Lourdes, he is always looking for populist and maverick variants of Catholicism, expressions of religious sentiment that are socially vital if not doctrinally pure. He is pleased to note, for example, that Mexican church officials have been unable to curb the excesses of self-flagellation and self-crucifixion that occur during Holy Week. Yet, Marnham does not paint Mexico as a land of pure credulity. In a characteristic episode, he initially ascribes the heavy traffic out of Mexico City on Good Friday to religious devotion, assuming that, like him, the hordes are on a pilgrimage to Amecameca; but it turns out that they are actually heading for a recreational area beyond the holy town. When Marnham crosses "the real frontier" into the Indian country of southern Mexico, he discovers a fascinating hybrid religion built on indigenous and European rituals. In rural Chiapas he finds Mayan idols in Christian niches and symbolic pagan fires burning on the outer walls of the churches. In such places, Marnham remarks, "the faith of the peasants had outlasted that of their priests."

While the most backward and dispossessed inhabitants of Central America express the most civilized kind of human behavior–spontaneous faith–when Marnham returns to the Westernized parts of "New Spain," he encounters corruption, thievery, and violence. Genuine faith and wanton violence are the two most important features of exoticism in the book: they distinguish Marnham's discoveries on the road from the gray comforts of modern England.

Marnham organizes his itinerary to maximize contact with the political violence of Guatemala, El Salvador, and Nicaragua; he skips over Honduras, Costa Rica, and Panama, which are "out of the battle." Instead of analyzing the political causes of Central American violence, the book focuses on its deep historical roots and its impact on the everyday lives of ordinary people. The threat of violence is treated in spare, almost muted, terms–a stylistic choice stemming not from the author's callousness but from the chilling familiarity of bloodshed in the region. In Marnham's deadpan narrative, the death squads who kill foreign journalists and the bus hijackers who shoot innocent passengers fuse with the petty annoyances of the journey, such as blocked mail chutes and hopelessly fictional bus schedules.

What does shock Marnham's sensibility is his contact with El Salvador's privileged elite, whose lives seem to consist of baby showers, beauty pageants, and military-school graduations. As in all his writing, Marnham uses juxtaposition to great advantage, switching rapidly from the tragic and serious to the comic and absurd. He captures many conflicting moods and messages within a single episode, such as an extended interview with the curator of reptiles at the San Salvador zoo: as uniformed schoolgirls look on, the curator handles poisonous snakes and denounces communism. The scene is rich in symbolic undertones and literary craft. No less shocking than the world of rich Salvadorans, however, is the Sandinista regime in Nicaragua, with its cobwebbed Marxist slogans, its corrupt acts of party patronage, and its arbitrary censorship of foreign publications, including the banning of a photograph of waterskiing elephants in Florida. In treating both countries Marnham alternates between objective journalistic description and a withering prosecutorial tone.

As a nonaligned, postimperial British traveler Marnham adopts a position of satirical neutrality in his evaluation of U.S. relations with Central America. He is also fascinated by the Spanish imperial legacy as a counterpoint to his observations of the "wreckage of the British empire" in Asia and Africa. Like earlier English writers such as Conrad and Greene, Marnham expresses the tragic and ironic political attitude of one who has seen the unfortunate and irreversible consequences of modern imperial history.

Since 1986 Marnham has been the Paris correspondent for *The Independent* (London). In 1987 he turned to the true-crime genre with *Trail of Havoc: In the Steps of Lord Lucan,* an account of a notorious English murder. In the 1990s he published two biographies–*The Man Who Wasn't Maigret: A Portrait of Georges Simenon* (1992) and *Dreaming with His Eyes Open: A Life of Diego Rivera* (1998)–and *Crime and the Académie Française: Dispatches from Paris* (1993), a collection of previously unpublished essays and pieces for *The Independent.*

Crime and the Académie Française is a work of journalistic travel writing set in a nation that, Marnham points out, is at once familiar and exotic to his English readers. He remarks at the outset that the book records the "impressions received by the innocent and sometimes bemused eye of a recently settled traveller, and continues to the point where the traveller began to notice so much about the country that he wondered whether he could be certain of anything at all." Ranging across France, he examines the absurd linguistic purism of the Académie Française, reports on the farmers of Briard who were evicted to allow the construction of Euro Disneyland, exposes the neocolonial abuses of the Paris-to-Dakar automobile rally, and considers the unlikely success of the xenophobic politician Jean-Marie Le Pen. The foibles and absurdities of French culture are on full display; yet, as the introduction notes, the book brims with an unmistakable affection for the country.

A fellow of the Royal Society of Literature, Marnham has widened his literary career substantially beyond the travel writing and exotic journalism with which he established his reputation. Like his predecessor Greene, who wrote about Cuba, Haiti, and Vietnam long before the world discovered their importance, he has displayed an almost prophetic ability to travel to the right places and to anticipate important issues. Exotic and uncharted zones of the planet have become increasingly rare; but if there remains an unbeaten track that promises new stories of faith, violence, mystery, absurdity, and beauty, there is a good chance that among the first to explore it will be Patrick Marnham.

Gavin Maxwell

(15 July 1914 – 7 September 1969)

Steven E. Alford
Nova Southeastern University

BOOKS: *Harpoon at a Venture* (London: Hart-Davis, 1952); republished as *Harpoon Venture* (New York: Viking, 1952);

God Protect Me from My Friends (London: Longmans, Green, 1956); republished as *Bandit* (New York: Harper, 1956);

A Reed Shaken by the Wind (London & New York: Longmans, Green, 1957); republished as *People of the Reeds* (New York: Harper, 1957);

The Ten Pains of Death (London: Longmans, 1959; New York: Dutton, 1960);

Ring of Bright Water (London: Longmans, 1960; New York: Dutton, 1960); abridged as *The Otters' Tale* (London: Longmans, 1962; New York: Dutton, 1962);

The Rocks Remain (London: Longmans, 1963; New York: Dutton, 1963);

The House of Elrig (London: Longmans, 1965; New York: Dutton, 1965);

Lords of the Atlas: The Rise and Fall of The House of Glaoua, 1893–1956 (London: Longmans, 1966; New York: Dutton, 1966);

Seals of The World, by Maxwell, John Stidworthy, and David Williams, World Wildlife Series, no. 2 (London: Constable, 1967; Boston: Houghton Mifflin, 1967);

Raven Seek Thy Brother (Harlow: Longman, 1968; New York: Dutton, 1969).

Gavin Maxwell, 1969

The name of Gavin Maxwell will be forever linked with his *Ring of Bright Water* (1960), a narrative of his experiences in keeping otters on the remote northwest coast of Scotland. Maxwell managed to infuse his account of his difficult, isolated, solitary existence in a cabin, bereft of electricity or plumbing, with a universal spiritual resonance matched by few nature writers in the twentieth century. His other books, praised by critics and beloved by readers, chronicle Maxwell's impractical schemes and peripatetic travels, from shark hunting in the sea around the Hebrides to shooting ducks among the reed islands of Iraq and mingling with the nobility of the remote Atlas Mountains of Morocco. The records of his travels and his involvement with the natural world are marked by a lyrical style rooted in the daily pains of making one's way in the world. While much of his work seems the product of a naturalist rather than a traveler, his achievement is comparable to that of Henry David Thoreau in his *Walden, or Life in the Woods* (1854), in which the exterior journey plots a complex relationship between inner discovery and external experience.

Gavin Maxwell was born into an aristocratic Scottish family on 15 July 1914 in Elrig, a house seven miles from his family's principal residence at Monreith, Wigtownshire, in Scotland. His mother was Lady Mary Percy, fifth daughter of the seventh duke of Northumberland, and his father was Lieutenant Colonel Aymer Edward Maxwell, heir to the baronetcy of Monreith. Gavin had two older brothers and an older sister. A few weeks after Gavin's birth, World War I began, and within three months Lieutenant Colonel Maxwell joined the British Expeditionary Force on the Continent. Barely three hours after he disembarked in Belgium in October 1914, Gavin's thirty-seven-year-old father was killed by German artillery. His bereaved mother bestowed her displaced affection on her youngest child, Gavin, who slept in her bed until he was eight. Raised in a remote area, surrounded by woods and animals, and meeting few human beings other than his siblings and the family servants, Maxwell developed a strong attachment to the environment and animals while also becoming a game hunter and skilled marksman.

From the age of ten Maxwell attended a series of boarding schools–Heddon Court, St. Cyphs, Hurst Court–moving from one to the other as his unhappiness increased and his inability to get along with his fellow students became more obvious. In September 1928 Maxwell was sent to public school at the newly opened Stowe. While at Stowe, on his sixteenth birthday, Maxwell contracted Henoch's purpura, a frightening disease whose symptoms include large purple spots, the result of blood collecting beneath the skin outside the vessels. This was the first of a series of serious health problems from which Maxwell was to suffer before his early death. Following a lengthy convalescence, Maxwell, with the aid of tutors, qualified for Hertford College, Oxford, which he entered in October 1933. Although his attendance was poor and his effort desultory, Maxwell–by cheating on his exit exam–managed to graduate in June 1937 with a Third Class Degree in Estate Management.

In the summer of 1938 he took his first trip, an ornithological expedition to the east Finnmark region of Norway, where he attempted to map the breeding ground of the Steller's eider duck. Seeing that the outbreak of World War II was imminent, Maxwell returned to Britain in June of 1939 and joined the Scots Guards on 2 September 1939 (the day before Britain and France declared war on Germany). In 1942 he became an instructor in small arms and field craft for the Special Operations Executive, stationed in Scotland, where he ultimately earned the rank of major.

Bored with the army, Maxwell wangled a medical discharge from the Army Medical Board in 1944 and resigned his commission on 24 February 1945. After leaving the army, Maxwell purchased the island of Soay, just south of the Isle of Skye, for £900. He devised a plan to hunt the basking shark, *Cetorhinus maximus,* and establish a shark processing plant on the island. Borrowing the money from his mother, he bought a boat (sight unseen) and other expensive tools, without doing any research. Hapless as a businessman throughout his life, he virtually exhausted his patrimony before his mother's death.

The shark-fishing business failed. Maxwell attempted to support himself as a society painter, but this enterprise failed as well. Thus by early 1948 he was broke, with no prospects. In October he rented a cottage at Sandaig, on the far western coast of Scotland, opposite the Isle of Skye, with no road or path leading to it, and came to stay there in 1949. By 1950 he had been persuaded by his friends to prepare a book synopsis about his shark-hunting venture. Although his synopsis was initially rejected, Maxwell continued to work on it, and *Harpoon at a Venture* was published by the firm of Rupert Hart-Davis on 26 May 1952.

From the outset *Harpoon at a Venture* was a critical and commercial success. As his biographer Douglas Botting notes, "*The Times* hailed Gavin as 'a man of action who writes like a poet'–praise to which he was to cling for the rest of his writing life." Much of the attraction of *Harpoon at a Venture* and his subsequent books lies in Maxwell's ability to present himself as an ordinary man, an amateur, who finds himself responding to a larger-than-life challenge. Not only did this style of writing endear him to his readership, but it also made him appear as an approachable, open person.

Following the success of *Harpoon at a Venture,* Maxwell made two trips to Sicily, in the autumn of 1952 and in the summer of 1953. He had first hoped to track down a long-lost relative and use her story for his next book. Once there, however, he became fascinated by the story of twenty-seven-year-old Salvatore Giuliano, a native of Montelepre in the northwest of Sicily, who had staged a seven-year-long campaign against the police. He was variously regarded as a bandit and as a Robin Hood, supporting the cause of the Sicilian poor. Giuliano's murder remained unsolved, with a multitude of possible assassins: the police, the Mafia, and perhaps one of his relatives. Maxwell became involved in a dispute with his publishers, Rupert Hart-Davis, and severed ties with them and moved to Longmans, where he was to remain for the rest of his writing career. In September 1954 Maxwell completed his book on Giuliano, *God Protect Me from My Friends* (1956). While critics applauded the book for the expressiveness and beauty of Maxwell's writing, it was not a commercial success. In addition, Maxwell's disregard for details and his negative portrayals in the book of several prominent Italian political figures were to haunt him later.

Boatmen in the Ma'dan reed marshes of Iraq during the 1956 trip Maxwell took with Wilfred Thesiger, the basis for Maxwell's 1957 book A Reed Shaken by the Wind *(Gavin Maxwell Enterprises)*

Returning to Sicily in May 1955, Maxwell had planned to write a book about the tuna fishermen in Scopello, an isolated fishing village near Castellammare del Golfo. A disastrous fishing season caused him to abandon the project and return to Scotland; however, his time with the poor and oppressed residents of Sicily made a deep impression on him, and he returned to these experiences in a later book, *The Ten Pains of Death* (1959).

Although fully capable of writing movingly about people, Maxwell's attachment to animals was invariably more passionate and long-standing than was his affection for human beings, even friends and lovers. Although he was loved throughout his life by his wife, Lavinia Renton, the poet Kathleen Raine, and a series of homosexual lovers, Maxwell's emotional capital was invariably spent on animals. In fact, following the death of his beloved dog, Jonnie, in 1955, Maxwell went into a depression requiring treatment by a London psychiatrist in early 1956.

Maxwell needed a change of scene. He had met the famous and tough-minded explorer, Wilfred Thesiger, known for his work among the marsh people of Iraq. Maxwell eventually persuaded Thesiger to allow him to accompany him, and in January 1956 they left for the marsh of Ma'dan, northwest of Basra. For weeks Maxwell accompanied Thesiger as they poled their way through the marshes, sitting cross-legged for hours in a low, flat boat, only to stagger onto the reed islands and sit cross-legged still longer in native huts. Thesiger, accompanied by a huge chest of medicines, cured tribesmen as he moved through their territory, winning their gratitude. Maxwell shot game for food but was otherwise very much a passenger and was miserable owing to his ignorance of the language and inability to interact with the people. In the book resulting from this trip, *A Reed Shaken by the Wind* (1957), Maxwell evokes perfectly the marsh and its people–along with his own disgruntled persona. Perhaps the most thrilling moment occurs when Maxwell is almost killed by a charging wild boar. At the last second, the pig falls into an unseen pit, and Maxwell is saved.

In retrospect, the most important aspect of this journey was his introduction to otters. Having bought a group of otter skins to take back to Britain, Maxwell acquired a baby otter, whom he named Chahala, and to whom he quickly became emotionally attached. Within days the otter fell ill and died, and Maxwell blamed himself for not having watched her diet more closely. On the eve of his departure in Basra, however, he was presented with another otter, Mijbil, whom he took back to London. Mijbil and his successors were to change Maxwell's life forever.

Dividing his time between London and Sandiag, Maxwell introduced Mijbil to both the wilderness of Scotland and the experience of being walked down London streets on a leash. His solution to the problem of Mijbil's traveling on a train was to declare him an "Illyrian poodle," which for some unaccountable reason mollified train officials. During their stay in London, Maxwell and Mijbil visited the British Museum, where a taxonomist attempted to classify the otter. Since Mijbil was a type of otter as yet unclassified, the taxonomist's designation bore Maxwell's own name: *Lutrogale perspicillata maxwelli.*

In London and in Sandaig, Maxwell worked on finishing the manuscript of *A Reed Shaken by the Wind.* Mijbil was given free reign at Sandaig, and while he often spent hours away from the house, he would always return. One day, however, he did not come home, and Maxwell discovered that the trusting otter had wandered into a village where he had been bludgeoned to death by a truck driver. Grief-stricken, Maxwell journeyed to Sicily in May 1957 hoping to resurrect his work on the tuna fishermen but was once again unsuccessful. In October 1957 *A Reed Shaken by the Wind* was published to positive reviews.

While enjoying the success of *A Reed Shaken by the Wind,* Maxwell was sued for criminal libel in Italy by Bernardo Mattarella, Italian minister of posts and telegraphs, on the basis of the characterization of Mattarella in *God Protect Me from My Friends.* Mattarella objected to passages that he claimed implied that he was a spy for the Allies during World War II and others that linked him to the Mafia. Mattarella won, and Maxwell was heavily fined and sentenced in absentia. Although he was later granted amnesty, this incident marked the end of his trips to Sicily.

Maxwell's sadness over the death of Mijbil was assuaged when he acquired another otter, Edal. Settling down with Edal at Sandaig, Maxwell began writing *Ring of Bright Water,* a celebration of Scotland, otters, dogs, geese, eels, and mackerel, as well as of solitude, isolation, and the joys of the natural environment. Not wishing to attract visitors, in his book he called Sandaig "Camusfeàrna": Gaelic for "The Bay of Alders."

While he was writing *Ring of Bright Water,* Maxwell's second book on Sicily, *The Ten Pains of Death,* was published. *The Ten Pains of Death,* in which Maxwell used his research into the tuna fishermen to tell a moving story of the Sicilian poor, was generally well-received by critics, although Maxwell's publishers were unhappy with the book, which had only modest sales.

In October 1959 Maxwell finished writing *Ring of Bright Water,* and it was published the following year. In his biography of Maxwell, Douglas Botting says, "*Ring of Bright Water* was one of those works that roused a perception of a different way of life and blazed a trail for the alternative life-style movement and for the conservation and whole-earth movements that followed in the sixties."

Maxwell's view of the relationship of humans to nature seems to be derived from traditional nineteenth-century Romanticism. He writes, "For I am convinced that man has suffered in his separation from the soil and from the other living creatures of the world; the evolution of his intellect has outrun his needs as an animal, and as yet he must still, for security, look long at some portion of the earth as it was before he tampered with it." This trite viewpoint appealed to many of his readers, particularly urbanites. Maxwell also expresses the commonplace idea about the difference between isolation and loneliness, claiming that few people on the British Isles ever experience true isolation. For Maxwell this type of solitude "is the very opposite of the loneliness a stranger finds in a city, for that loneliness is due to the proximity of other humans and the barriers between him and them, to the knowledge of being alone among them, with every inch of the walls wounding and every incommunicable stranger planting a separate bandillo." His experience at Sandaig, however, was "sharply exhilarating," he writes, it was "as though some pressure had suddenly been lifted, allowing an intense awareness of one's surroundings, a sharpening of the senses, and an intimate recognition of the teeming sub-human life around one." This passion for isolation, intense shyness around others, fear of their opinions, and profound involvement in nature are present in all of Maxwell's writing.

Ring of Bright Water traces the period from approximately April 1949, when Maxwell first came to stay at Sandaig, to 1959. Told in the first person, the narrative is as much about Maxwell–or Maxwell's literary persona–as it is about Camusfeàrna, which the narrator likens to Arthur's fabled Avalon, his island paradise in the western seas. The narrator tells of Maxwell's barren house and his "prospecting" the shore for useful washed-up goods, which he finds in abundance; of ferocious wildcats, twice the size of household cats; of a profusion of birds, including a group of greylag geese, raised from infancy, who drop from the sky and waddle up to Maxwell when he calls; of animal intruders into the house, including one cow that Maxwell discovered stuck in the stairway, unable to move; and of Jonnie the dog, whose death so affected Maxwell. One of the most memorable images of the book involves Maxwell's dis-

Maxwell in the Ma'dan marshes with his first otter, Chahala (Gavin Maxwell Enterprises)

covery of twin boys down at the shore, thigh deep in a huge school of herring fry:

> When I reached the water myself it was like wading in silver treacle; our bare legs pushed against the packed mass of little fish as against a solid and reluctantly yielding obstacle. To scoop and to scatter them, to shout and to laugh, were as irresistible as though we were treasure hunters of old who had stumbled upon a fabled emperor's jewel vaults and threw diamonds about us like chaff. We were fish-drunk, fish-crazy, fish-happy in that shining orange bubble of air and water; the twins were about thirteen years old and I was about thirty-eight, but the miracle of the fishes drew from each of us the same response.

More than anything else, however, the narrative is about otters. Maxwell retells the story, first told in *A Reed Shaken by the Wind,* of his discovery of Mijbil and the otter's tragic demise. He also relates how, while drinking in a hotel bar in Scotland, he happened to look out the window and see an otter stroll by on a leash. Stunned (and inebriated), he stumbled out onto the pavement, thinking it was a hallucination, but found that it was in fact a real otter, which a peripatetic British couple had obtained in Nigeria. The couple, about to travel abroad once more, gave Maxwell the otter, Edal, the central figure in *Ring of Bright Water.*

Maxwell estimated he received more than fourteen thousand fan letters following the publication of *Ring of Bright Water,* many of which expressed a longing for the Waldenesque life he had depicted in the book. In the two years following the book's publication, Maxwell grossed £55,000. Possessed of an aristocratic disdain for economy, however, he spent his windfall almost as quickly as he had earned it.

While still flush with his earnings from *Ring of Bright Water,* Maxwell left for North Africa in December 1960 with a brand new Land Rover. During this and subsequent trips Maxwell would gather the material for *Lords of the Atlas: The Rise and Fall of The House of Glaoua, 1893–1956,* published in 1966.

Returning to England in 1961, Maxwell produced a children's version of *Ring of Bright Water,* titled *The Otters' Tale,* which was published the following year. The shy, solitary man with homosexual proclivities then sought the stability and social approval of a heterosexual marriage. Maxwell had known Lavinia Renton for a number of years, as she was married to his wartime friend Edward Renton. After Lavinia divorced Edward, Maxwell proposed to her, and he and Lavinia, ten years his junior, were married on 1 February 1961. Following their marriage they went on a honeymoon to Morocco, the first time they had been in each other's company for any length of time. Maxwell was not writing and was not at all used to fulfilling the expectations of a heterosexual partner. Although they did not formally divorce until 1964, over the first fifteen months of their marriage they never spent more than three weeks together at one time.

Having spent his money, Maxwell was under serious financial pressure to publish. The result was *The Rocks Remain* (1963), a continuation of the story of Camusfeàrna begun in *Ring of Bright Water.* While it sold well, Maxwell thought the book hurried and lacking structure. Further helping to ease his money worries was a contract for an autobiography of his childhood–to become *The House of Elrig* (1965)–accompanied by a substantial advance. However, all was not well in Camusfeàrna.

In addition to Edal, Maxwell had received another otter, Teko, from a couple in the diplomatic service who were unable to keep him. There had been incidents when the otters had attacked people, causing serious injury with their powerful jaws, incidents Maxwell attempted to keep quiet since such news would have struck at his livelihood. Later he acquired two more otters–Mossy and Monday–and, until their departure from the house for the wilds around Sandaig, they provided further complications, expense, time, and concern. In addition, despite his attempt to conceal the location of Sandaig, the success of his book had brought hordes of tourists from all over the world who sought out–and thus destroyed–the idyllic locale of *Ring of Bright Water.* After Maxwell introduced electricity and telephone service to the house, operating expenses had increased substantially; Maxwell's income had not. He estimated at one point that it cost £7000 a year to keep Sandaig running. The outside world had come to Camusfeàrna, and various youthful male caretakers also complicated the environment.

In an effort to raise funds while striving to complete *The House of Elrig* and his book about Morocco, Maxwell bought two area lighthouses and their outbuildings, hoping to rent them out to rich vacationers. He contracted a friend and his wife to restore and decorate them, all at considerable expense.

Compounding his financial problems was a physical one. An automobile accident, when his Land Rover had collided with a stag near his house, had resulted in a serious problem with circulation in one of Maxwell's feet. A series of operations in late 1963 helped restore blood flow, but in the process he also contracted a serious infection, further slowing him down and weakening his constitution. Adding to his misery was a revival of the legal trouble surrounding *God Protect Me from My Friends.* Aware of the successful suit by Bernardo Mattarella, Italian M.P. Gianfranco Alliata sued Maxwell for libel in a British court, as Maxwell had published allegations that Alliata had been behind a 1947 massacre of communists. While Alliata won, the damages awarded were minimal. Maxwell was liable for court costs, however, which further depleted his already meager savings.

In December 1965 Maxwell completed the manuscript of his book tracing the fortunes of the Moroccan House of Glaoui. Published in October 1966, *Lords of the Atlas* traces the obscure and fantastic story of how this little-known Berber family, in the Atlas Mountains of southern Morocco, had succeeded in deposing two Moroccan sultans and had become fabulously rich. The following year *Seals of the World* was published. Although Maxwell is listed as an author, this reference work was a collaboration substantially completed by two London zoologists, John Stidworthy and David Williams. The text was also edited and rewritten by Maxwell's friend and biographer, Botting.

Back in Scotland, the practical problems Maxwell confronted in keeping up his home came to a crisis in January 1968, when an accidental fire destroyed Camusfeàrna, killing the otter Edal and destroying the contents of the house. Maxwell moved into one of the houses he had hoped to rent out, Eilean Ban, on White Island, northwest of Sandaig, within sight of the Isle of Skye.

Maxwell and his otter Edal (photograph by Terence Spencer)

Living on White Island proved difficult for Maxwell, given his partial lameness and the rugged terrain. There he wrote his final book, *Raven Seek Thy Brother* (1968), which covers the years from 1963 to 1968 at Sandaig. In this book he claims that many, if not all, of his problems had been brought about by a curse leveled at him by his friend, Kathleen Raine, following a serious argument. She purportedly did this seated underneath a rowan tree near his house. The rowan, he says, "is the guardian, the protecting power, the tree of life, infinitely malignant if harmed or disrespected; capable, too, of carrying within itself the good- or evil-wishes of those who have the power to communicate with it." Although Raine had done nothing more than speak angrily to Maxwell while under the tree, he was convinced that she was responsible for his misfortunes. Raine was deeply wounded by this bizarre accusation; however, it was characteristic of Maxwell to ascribe the causes of his mishaps to the malevolent workings of others.

Raven Seek Thy Brother, the final book in the trilogy about Camusfeàrna, traces its decline and ultimate demise. It also affords Maxwell an opportunity to review his life, to seek his motivations for hunting sharks, keeping otters, and chasing the stories of Sicilian bandits and Moroccan usurpers:

> During all my adult life I have had an almost compulsive urge to start something new; to try to be a pioneer; to essay fields either virgin or at least imperfectly explored. This, perhaps, has stemmed from an unconscious desire to avoid competition, so that nobody could say that I had failed where others had succeeded. "Educated" as I had been, I had always been unequipped for any life that I wanted to lead; while I was essentially an amateur in every sphere, others bore upon their banners the strange but powerful device "Qualifications." Whereas they had degrees in zoology, psychology, medicine, biology, and enviable letters after their names, I had emerged from Oxford with a degree in Estate Management, and the very fact that this course of action had been dictated against my wishes precluded me from ever managing an estate or wanting to.

The very quality that made his prose so engaging, that he was "an amateur in every sphere" confronted with an impressive physical challenge, was also the source of a deep sense of insecurity and anxiety, feelings that success did little to allay. This concluding book, forthright in its portrayal of Maxwell's sadness at Camusfeàrna's decline, lacks the inspirational tone and uplifting message of *Ring of Bright Water.* Published in December 1968, *Raven Seek Thy Brother* helped ease some of his financial problems but did not eliminate them.

In 1968, Gavin Maxwell, an alcoholic who smoked four packs of cigarettes a day, was diagnosed with cancer in the lung and femur. He died on 7 September 1969, only fifty-five years old. Botting calls Maxwell "a troubled and tempestuous but often hilarious terrier of a man, a flawed genius whose obvious faults of character were redeemed by a rare generosity of spirit, an undimmed utopian vision of life and nature, and a stoical courage that was undaunted even in the face of ultimate adversity." Maxwell seemed unable, or unwilling, to open himself to human affection, only comfortable in nature or with animals. In his writing, however, all the idiosyncrasies that made him such a difficult person melt away, leaving a persona that is warm, self-deprecating, humorous, and possessed of an uncanny skill to evoke nature and its creatures. Botting records that when Maxwell was asked by his boyhood friend Anthony Dickens to identify his greatest accomplishment, he replied, "Having a new species of otter, *Lutrogale perspicillata maxwelli,* named after me."

Biography:

Douglas Botting, *Gavin Maxwell: The Life of the Man Who Wrote* Ring of Bright Water (London: HarperCollins, 1993).

References:

Mark Cocker, *Loneliness and Time: British Travel Writing in the Twentieth Century* (London: Secker & Warburg, 1992), pp. 106–131;

Richard Frere, *Maxwell's Ghost: An Epilogue to Gavin Maxwell's Camusfeàrna* (London: Gollancz, 1976).

Alan Moorehead

(22 July 1901 – 29 September 1983)

David Callahan
University of Aveiro

BOOKS: *Mediterranean Front* (London: Hamilton, 1941; New York & London: Whittlesey House, McGraw-Hill, 1942);

A Year of Battle (London: Hamilton, 1942); republished as *Don't Blame the Generals* (New York & London: Harper, 1943);

The End in Africa (London: Hamilton, 1943; New York & London: Harper, 1943);

Eclipse (London: Hamilton, 1945; New York: Coward-McCann, 1945);

Montgomery: A Biography (London: Hamilton, 1946; New York: Coward-McCann, 1946);

The Rage of the Vulture (London: Hamilton, 1948; New York: Scribners, 1948);

The Villa Diana (London: Hamilton, 1951; New York: Scribners, 1951);

The Traitors: The Double Life of Fuchs, Pontecorvo, and Nunn May (London: Hamilton, 1952); republished as *The Traitors* (New York: Scribners, 1952; revised edition, New York: Harper & Row, 1963);

Rum Jungle (London: Hamilton, 1953; New York: Scribners, 1954);

A Summer Night (London: Hamilton, 1954; New York: Harper, 1954);

Winston Churchill in Trial and Triumph (Boston: Houghton Mifflin, 1955);

Gallipoli (London: Hamilton, 1956; New York: Harper, 1956);

The Russian Revolution (London: Collins/Hamilton, 1958; New York: Harper, 1958);

No Room in the Ark (London: Hamilton, 1959; New York: Harper, 1960);

Churchill: A Pictorial Biography (London: Thames & Hudson, 1960; New York: Viking, 1960); revised as *Churchill and His World: A Pictorial Biography* (London: Thames & Hudson, 1965);

The White Nile (London: Hamilton, 1960; New York: Harper, 1960; revised edition, London: Hamilton, 1971; New York: Harper & Row, 1971);

The Blue Nile (London: Hamilton, 1962; New York: Harper & Row, 1962; revised edition, London: Hamilton, 1972; New York: Harper & Row, 1972);

Alan Moorehead

Cooper's Creek (London: Hamilton, 1963; New York: Harper & Row, 1963);

The Fatal Impact: An Account of the Invasion of the South Pacific, 1767–1840 (London: Hamilton, 1966; New York: Harper & Row, 1966);

Darwin and the Beagle (London: Hamilton, 1969; New York: Harper & Row, 1969);

A Late Education: Episodes in a Life (London: Hamilton, 1970; New York: Harper & Row, 1971).

Editions and Collections: *African Trilogy, Comprising Mediterranean Front, A Year of Battle, The End in Africa: A Personal Account of the Three Years' Struggle against the Axis in the Middle East and North Africa, 1940–3* (London: Hamilton, 1944); abridged as *The Desert War: The North African Campaign, 1940–1943* (London: Hamilton, 1965); unabridged version republished as *The March to Tunis: The North African War, 1940–1943* (New York: Harper & Row, 1967);

The Blue Nile: Junior Edition, abridged by Lucy Moorehead (London: Hamilton, 1965); republished as *The Story of the Blue Nile* (New York: Harper & Row, 1966);

The White Nile: Junior Edition, abridged by Lucy Moorehead (London: Hamilton, 1966); republished as *The Story of the White Nile* (New York: Harper & Row, 1967);

The Fatal Impact: An Account of the Invasion of the South Pacific, 1767–1840, abridged by Lucy Moorehead (London: Hamilton, 1966);

Eclipse, abridged by Lucy Moorehead (London: Hamilton, 1967; New York: Harper & Row, 1968);

The Fatal Impact: The Invasion of the South Pacific, 1767–1840, preface by Manning Clark (New York: Harper & Row, 1987).

The principal quality that immediately stands out in Alan Moorehead's travel books, historical investigations, biographies, and fiction is his enthusiastic but level-headed curiosity. The eye for the immediate and for the telling detail that made Moorehead a successful journalist also characterizes his books. This talent serves his larger, more stimulating, although less immediately apparent, gift: the capacity to realize that a place is on the brink of important transformations. As a travel writer Moorehead is not so much interested in a "dream of an encounter with a pristine world"–as Dennis Porter formulates one of the motivations of travel writers in *Haunted Journeys: Desire and Transgression in European Travel Writing* (1991)–as he is in how people adapt to change and extremity. Moreover, travel writing formed a part of everything Moorehead wrote, whether or not his books appear to belong to the genre in conventional terms.

Alan McCrae Moorehead was born in Melbourne, Australia, on 22 July 1901. His father, Richard Moorehead, was a freelance journalist; his mother, Louise Moorehead, née Edgerton, was the daughter of a wealthy printer and publisher. Because his parents could not afford the university fees, after attending the prestigious Scotch College, Moorehead went to work in 1926 as an office boy in a small advertising agency. In 1928 he enrolled at Melbourne University, majoring in English. After receiving his B.A. in 1930 he decided to study law at the same university; but with the dramatic finality of a conversion, in 1933 he walked out of his final law examination and went straight to the editor of the *Melbourne Herald,* asked for a job, and was hired on the spot.

Moorehead reports in his memoir, *A Late Education: Episodes in a Life* (1970): "When I remembered the early part of my life–the first twenty-five years of which had been spent in Australia–it was not altogether with the sentimental glow which the exile is supposed to feel about his birthplace." Like many talented Australians of the period, Moorehead despised his native land and wanted to go to Europe. He left in May 1936. In *A Late Education* he says of sailing into Toulon harbor in June: "I date my life from this moment."

Through Australian contacts in London, Moorehead secured employment as a reporter at the *Daily Express.* Soon he was in Gibraltar covering the Spanish Civil War. He was the nearest reporter to the scene, although not an eyewitness, when the Republicans bombed the German ship *Deutschland.* Knowing that he had a story but not enough concrete information to report it, Moorehead fleshed it out with a descriptive enthusiasm that, according to his biographer, Tom Pocock, "convinced Moorehead that the way to success in journalism lay as much in descriptive writing as in the delivery of 'hard news.'"

After a series of assignments throughout the Mediterranean area Moorehead was stationed from 1937 to 1939 in Paris, which he preferred to England. Just before he left London for Paris, he met Lucy Milner, the editor of the women's pages of the *Daily Express.* He was sent to Rome in August 1939; within a month Germany invaded Poland. Moorehead brought Milner to Rome, where they were married on 29 October. They would have a daughter, Caroline, and two sons, John and Richard. In May 1940, with Italy about to enter the war on the side of the Axis powers, Moorehead, whose wife had by then returned to London, was evacuated to Athens and then to Cairo. From there he accompanied the Allied forces through North Africa, explaining to the readers of the *Daily Express* in admirably clear prose the confusing events of the war and reporting on individuals as well as on armies. He also described and reflected on his experiences in four successful books: *Mediterranean Front* (1941), *A Year of Battle* (1942), *The End in Africa* (1943), and *Eclipse* (1945). Although they are not conventional travel books, they describe ceaseless travel and thus, inevitably, display the central themes of travel writing: the physical and mental discomfort, as well as the fascination, of being placed in an alien environment.

In *Eclipse,* his narrative of the Allied campaigns in southern Italy, Normandy, and Germany, Moorehead writes, "I was after atmosphere more than fact . . . a book that was a half-way house to fiction." It is, he says, "not a war book, nor a history, nor a social treatise or a novel. You cannot expect accuracy or completeness or education and there is precious little romance." In this book Moorehead is reaching toward the sort of flexibility that the best travel writers have always employed.

For his war journalism Moorehead was awarded the Order of the British Empire in 1946. That same year he

Dust jacket for Moorehead's award-winning 1956 book, an account of the unsuccessful Allied campaign against Turkey during World War I

left the *Daily Express* to become a freelance writer and published a biography of Field Marshal Bernard Law Montgomery, first Viscount Montgomery of Alamein.

Moorehead's next book was a novel, *The Rage of the Vulture* (1948). It is set in the fictional state of Kandahar, identifiable as Kashmir during the British withdrawal from India. (Moorehead had visited India in 1942 and 1947.) In the first chapter there is no dialogue, but it is an excellent piece of travel reportage, a breathless succession of topographical, geographical, historical, economic, and political details alive with Moorehead's fascination for places that are undergoing transition and redefinition.

In 1948 the Mooreheads rented a house in central Italy. Its name provided the title for Moorehead's next book, *The Villa Diana* (1951), a collection of some of his *New Yorker* articles on Italy and a long essay on the poet Politian (Angelo Poliziano), who had lived in the villa during the time of Lorenzo de' Medici. Most of the pieces depict an Italy reconstructing itself physically and morally after World War II. The piece on the *Palio,* the semiannual horse race around the Piazza del Campo in the center of Siena, may be the best analysis of and response to the occasion ever written in English. Moorehead is interested in the morality of the event, the outcome of which is openly determined by bribery: "it is this complete cynicism with which the race is run—this bland assumption that all men are inherently bad—which probably gives the Palio its special fascination." He is also entranced by its color, observing participants "dressed in costumes that date from the Middle Ages, when taste in men's clothes was a deal more adventurous than it is now."

In 1950 Moorehead had accepted a position as a senior public-relations officer at the Ministry of Defence in London. The job lasted eight months and inspired him to write *The Traitors: The Double Life of Fuchs, Pontecorvo, and Nunn May* (1952), a nonfiction report on Soviet agents in Western defense establishments.

Moorehead's next book, *Rum Jungle* (1953), is a collection of travel pieces about his native country. There is a certain flatness about the work; Moorehead scarcely diverges from the "set" itinerary for the travel writer in Australia. Moreover, by saying at the outset that Australia is a country that possesses no lost cities, Moorehead perpetuates the Eurocentric perception of Australia as having been practically uninhabited when Europeans arrived: no cultural evidence other than cities counts. Although Moorehead perceives that the country is developing, even booming in parts, he misses the urgency and resourcefulness that he had seen in wartime and postwar Europe.

Moorehead's second novel, *A Summer Night,* set among the English-speaking expatriate community in

Italy, was published in 1954. Reflecting on his writing in his journal on 11 November 1948, he had accurately summed up his talents and limitations:

> I think I know myself as a writer now. Description of scenes, places, action: excellent. Readableness, continuity, tempo, construction: first class. Writing: often first class, sometimes better or worse. Dialogue: natural and fluent but without wit or any particular subtlety or inspiration. Characters: very bad with the exception of occasional flukes drawn from life. Plots: hopeless. Ability to state a meaning, a philosophy: hopeless.

The critics and the reading public agreed; the novel was not well received. After this disappointment, Moorehead did not publish another novel.

Since the heady days of his success as a war correspondent, Moorehead's career had not developed as he had hoped. He needed a new direction, and he soon found it in a mixture of historical re-creation, travel reportage, and intelligent summary. In 1956 he published *Gallipoli,* about the unsuccessful Allied campaign against Turkey during World War I. The work was an immediate success and has frequently been republished despite the subsequent appearance of more-scholarly books on the subject. While it is not a travel book, *Gallipoli* pays close attention to the geographical and topographical setting of the events described. The response of Drew Middleton, himself a well-known war correspondent, in *The New York Times Book Review* (16 September 1956) was typical: "The story is told superbly because Mr. Moorehead knows what a battlefield looks, smells and sounds like. . . . I have read no better piece of descriptive writing about either world war than Mr. Moorehead's account of life in the Anzac [Australian and New Zealand Army Corps] bridgehead on Gallipoli." *Gallipoli* received *The Sunday Times* (London) Gold Medal as book of the year and the Duff Cooper Memorial Award.

After another historical work, *The Russian Revolution* (1958), in 1959 Moorehead published *No Room in the Ark,* a collection of travel articles about Africa from *The New Yorker* and the *Sunday Times.* The central theme of *No Room in the Ark* is a plea for the preservation of wildlife in postcolonial Africa, but Moorehead lacks pomposity. He is aware that a large part of his motivation for traveling to the continent was "no more than the usual tourist thirst for the Africa of the tribal drums and the jungle in the raw, but it was nonetheless genuine for that." The book is suffused with the uncertainties of the postcolonial future of Africa, but Moorehead is always ready to look away from large issues to notice details such as the warthog, an animal that

> you find . . . in this part of Africa; he has a small trotting-on part in every other scene. The warthog is the clown of the jungle, and he has a certain awful charm. He is an extremely bothered animal about the size of a small pig, and he is furnished with two enormous tusks, a lion's mane and a tail and hind quarters which are quite uncompromisingly bare. He roots about the ground in family groups, and if surprised he stands and stares for a moment with deep concern written all over his appalling face. Then with a flick of his head, his tail rising like a railway signal bolt upright behind him, the father of the group is off into the scrub. . . . The warthog is not really ugly–it is the sort of countenance that is covered roughly by the French phrase "*une jolie laide*" [a handsome ugliness].

Along with Moorehead's interest in unglamorous animals such as the warthog and "the maribou stork with his hard hangman's eye" goes his genuine sympathy for practically everyone he meets. The only sins in Moorehead's eyes appear to be cruelty, selfishness, and the destruction of wild animals' habitats. He even writes understandingly of a type of traveler who excites most travel writers' disgust: those who try to cover as much territory as possible and are not particularly interested in their surroundings. Instead of writing them off as superficial, Moorehead is just as curious about their motives as he is about those who plunge fearlessly into the savanna. He surmises that such travelers "were not bad-tempered or even particularly disillusioned. They were tired. For the moment they had had enough. The realization of their dreams of traveling through the African wilds had arrived perhaps a little too late in life." The book was an immediate commercial success, selling thirty thousand copies in Britain within six months.

After *Churchill: A Pictorial Biography* (1960), Moorehead returned to the subject of Africa in his next two books. *The White Nile* (1960) deals with the late-nineteenth-century exploration of the sources of the White Nile and the resistance of the natives to European legal and military control. Before writing the book Moorehead retraced the steps of the Victorian heroes who people his pages; as a result the wanderings, erroneous suppositions, wrong turns, and hardships of the explorers assume an immediacy and impact that a mere retelling could not have accomplished. As Pocock notes, "few historians would have the stamina to undertake such journeys and few, if any, had the ability to describe places and people and choose the telling detail that he had acquired as a journalist." The book is, however, replete with ethnocentric value judgments that readers today will find jarring. From first to last Moorehead perceives European penetration of Uganda and the southern Sudan as a process of savagery giving way to civilization. At the center of this perspective, to be sure, lies condemnation of the slave trade, which was con-

Dust jacket for Moorehead's 1960 book, a history of the nineteenth-century European exploration of one of the two rivers that join at Khartoum to form the Nile

trolled by Arab traders with the collusion of African tribal chiefs. There is little evidence, however, that Moorehead was writing during the great wave of independence that had begun to wash over Africa, and his doubts as to the benefits of the Victorians' opening up of the river are only perfunctory. *The Blue Nile* (1962) ranges over a greater period of time, from the mid eighteenth century to 1868, and deals with a less intertwined set of personages. Here again Moorehead demonstrates his skill in describing terrain, feeling his way over the countryside and suggesting how its strangeness affected the Europeans.

Encouraged by friends to reconstruct an aspect of the early history of his own country, Moorehead wrote *Cooper's Creek* (1963) about the disastrous attempt by the Burke and Wills expedition to cross Australia from south to north in 1860–1861. As in the Nile books, he demonstrates an intimate knowledge of the flora, fauna, and meteorological conditions the expedition faced. Once again, however, as in *Rum Jungle,* Moorehead begins by claiming that the land "was absolutely untouched and unknown, and except for the blacks, the most retarded people on earth, there was no sign of any previous civilization whatever." The Aborigines, whose help proved crucial to knowledge of the fate of the expedition and whose comfortable drifting in and out of the struggling explorers' lives mocked the latter's ignorance and hubris, are merely a backdrop to the tribulations of the Europeans. The doyen of Australian historians, Manning Clark, said in the preface to an illustrated 1987 edition of Moorehead's next book, *The Fatal Impact: An Account of the Invasion of the South Pacific, 1767–1840* (1966), that Moorehead "always had the gift to anticipate the groundswells in public opinion" and that in "*Cooper's Creek* he was out in front of that huge swell of interest starting in the history of Australia."

Moorehead received the Royal Society of Literature Award in 1964. Mixing with central figures in the reconstruction of Australian postcolonial confidence such as Clark and the painters Sidney Nolan and Russell Drysdale, Moorehead found himself celebrated in the country he had rejected so determinedly thirty years previously.

Focusing on Tahiti, Australia, and Capt. James Cook's voyages to the Antarctic, *The Fatal Impact* describes the encroachment of Europeans into the Pacific Ocean from the mid eighteenth to the mid nineteenth century. His sympathies lie with the colonized, especially the Tahitians, but the title of the book reflects the old attitude toward indigenous peoples as dying races. That such peoples could survive colonization and fight to preserve their cultures seems not to have

Dust jacket for Moorehead's 1962 book, a companion volume to The White Nile

occurred to him. Still, the vigor of his denunciation of colonization is striking.

In late 1966 Moorehead suffered a stroke that partially paralyzed him and damaged parts of the brain that control verbalization. The two books he published after his stroke–*Darwin and the Beagle* (1969) and *A Late Education*–were completed by his wife. Moorehead was made a commander of the Order of the British Empire in 1968.

Darwin and the Beagle is a fluent recounting and reimagining of the momentous voyage from 1832 to 1836 that laid the groundwork for Charles Darwin's *On the Origin of Species by Means of Natural Selection* (1859). It is obvious that Moorehead was not as familiar with the territory covered by this voyage as he was with Africa, Australia, or Italy. When Brazil, Argentina, or Chile leap out at the reader, it is on account of the borrowed color of Moorehead's sources rather than the personal experiences that make the Nile books so vivid.

Moorehead's final book was his autobiography, *A Late Education.* Autobiography in Moorehead's case inevitably meant travel writing, and the book begins with a snapshot of the town of St.-Jean-de-Luz, France, near the Spanish border, at the time of the Spanish Civil War. Australia is depicted as a semipuritan, conventional moral straitjacket, without glamour, without drama, and without class.

Here, as elsewhere, Moorehead's strengths lie in his energy, his good-humored curiosity, and his gift for narrative. His representations of his time on the fringes of the Spanish Civil War and in Paris in the 1930s are vivid and full of the freshness of personal experience.

In 1978 Moorehead was awarded the Order of Australia, the highest honor the Australian government could bestow at the time. His papers were deemed sufficiently valuable to be acquired by the National Library of Australia that same year. In 1979 his wife was killed in a traffic accident on the road between Porto Ercole and Ansedonia, Italy, from which Moorehead escaped unhurt. He continued to live in London near his daughter, dying on 29 September 1983 from another stroke.

Writing to his wife from India in 1947, Moorehead tried to explain his passion for traveling: "It's simpler somehow; there seems more reason for living." He sometimes worried, however, that he traveled too much. In *A Late Education* he muses: "By moving about so much and attempting so many different things I had rejected life instead of discovering it." But he was never able to stop traveling and never able to stop writing about it until he had his first stroke. The best of his writing possesses a generosity of spirit and a genius for narrative that make it a matter of some regret that his works are rarely read today. His eyewitness account in *The Villa Diana* of Italian society undergoing readjustment after World War II is still useful. On the other hand, the books mixing travel writing and history for which he later became known, while excellent reconstructions of the events they narrate, have been largely superseded by subsequent scholarship and changing attitudes toward indigenous peoples. A book such as *The White Nile* has become a doubled text: it is both a history of the search for the origin of the White Nile and evidence of the attitudes of Western observers of Africa in the 1960s. Although he began his career by rejecting his native country, Moorehead is principally remembered for his books dealing with Australian themes: *Gallipoli, Cooper's Creek,* and *The Fatal Impact.*

Biography:

Tom Pocock, *Alan Moorehead* (London: Bodley Head, 1990).

Papers:

Alan Moorehead's papers are in the Australian National Library in Canberra.

Geoffrey Moorhouse

(29 November 1931 –)

Roy C. Flannagan III
Francis Marion University

and

Edward A. Malone
Missouri Western State College

BOOKS: *The Press* (London & Melbourne: Ward Lock Educational, 1964);

Britain in the Sixties: The Other England (Harmondsworth: Penguin, 1964; Baltimore: Penguin, 1964);

The Church, text by Moorhouse, drawings by William Papas (London: Oxford University Press, 1967);

Against All Reason (London: Weidenfeld & Nicolson, 1969; New York: Stein & Day, 1969);

Calcutta (London: Weidenfeld & Nicolson, 1971; New York: Harcourt Brace Jovanovich, 1972);

The Missionaries (London: Eyre Methuen, 1973; Philadelphia: Lippincott, 1973);

The Fearful Void (London: Hodder & Stoughton, 1974; Philadelphia: Lippincott, 1974);

The Diplomats: The Foreign Office Today (London: Cape, 1977);

The Boat and the Town (London & Toronto: Hodder & Stoughton, 1979; Boston: Little, Brown, 1979);

The Best-Loved Game: One Summer of English Cricket (London: Hodder & Stoughton, 1979);

San Francisco, by Moorhouse and the editors of Time-Life Books (Amsterdam: Time-Life Books, 1979);

Prague, by Moorhouse and the editors of Time-Life Books (Amsterdam: Time-Life Books, 1980);

Lord's (London: Hodder & Stoughton, 1983);

India Britannica (London: Harvill, 1983; New York: Harper & Row, 1983);

To the Frontier (London: Hodder & Stoughton, 1984; New York: Holt, Rinehart & Winston, 1985);

Rail across India: A Photographic Journey, by Moorhouse, Paul C. Pet, and Brian Hollingsworth (London: New Cavendish, 1985; New York: Abbeville, 1986);

Imperial City: The Rise and Rise of New York (London: Hodder & Stoughton, 1988); republished as *Imperial City: New York* (New York: Holt, 1988);

At the George and Other Essays on Rugby League (London: Hodder & Stoughton, 1989);

The Nile, photographs by Kazuyoshi Nomachi (London: Barrie & Jenkins, 1989);

Apples in the Snow: A Journey to Samarkand (London: Hodder & Stoughton, 1990); republished as *On the Other Side: A Journey to Soviet Central Asia* (New York: Holt, 1990);

Hell's Foundations: A Town, Its Myths, and Gallipoli (London: Hodder & Stoughton, 1992); republished as *Hell's Foundations: A Social History of the Town of Bury in the Aftermath of the Gallipoli Campaign* (New York: Holt, 1992);

OM: An Indian Pilgrimage (London: Hodder & Stoughton, 1993);

A People's Game: The Centenary History of Rugby League Football, 1895–1995 (London: Hodder & Stoughton, 1995);

Sun Dancing: A Medieval Vision (London: Weidenfeld & Nicolson, 1997); republished as *Sun Dancing: A Vision of Medieval Ireland* (New York: Harcourt Brace, 1997);

Sydney (London: Weidenfeld & Nicolson, forthcoming 1999).

OTHER: "The Nile: This Phenomenal Stream," in *Great Rivers of the World,* edited by Margaret Seeden (Washington, D.C.: National Geographic Society, 1984), pp. 32–67;

Alan Ross, *Ranji,* introduction by Moorhouse (London: Pavilion, 1988).

SELECTED PERIODICAL PUBLICATION–UNCOLLECTED: "The Moonies Invade Gloucester," *Harper's,* 262 (January 1981): 46–52.

Geoffrey Moorhouse (photograph by Tara Heinemann)

In an unpublished letter, Geoffrey Moorhouse describes himself as "simply a writer who happens to travel a lot, among other things, an inquiring generalist who has never felt the slightest inclination to become a specialist." Throughout his career Moorhouse has struggled to define himself as a writer, while resisting critics' and readers' occasionally facile classifications. His travel books, however, have won him international recognition. Those familiar with Moorhouse's work point to his books on Calcutta, the Sahara, New York, Pakistan, and the Soviet Union as his most significant achievements. Trained as a journalist, Moorhouse combines straightforward reporting with impressionistic narration in his best travel books, such as *The Fearful Void* (1974) and *To the Frontier* (1984). His other travel writings range from the expository and factual *Calcutta* (1971) to the deeply personal *OM: An Indian Pilgrimage* (1993).

Moorhouse was born Geoffrey Heald in Bolton, Lancashire, on 29 November 1931 to William Heald, a Congregational minister, and Gladys Heald, née Hoyle. After his parents were divorced, his mother married Richard Moorhouse, a clerk, and Geoffrey assumed his stepfather's last name. Moorhouse attended Bury Grammar School for eight years, then served in the Royal Navy from 1950 to 1952 before going to work for the *Bolton Evening News.* From 1954 to 1956 he worked for several newspapers in New Zealand: the *Grey River Argus,* the *Auckland Star,* and the *Christchurch Star-Sun.* He married Janet Marion Murray on 12 May 1956; they had four children: Ngaire Jane, Andrew Murray, Brigid Anne, and Michael John. After working briefly for the *News Chronicle* in Manchester, Moorhouse joined the staff of the *Manchester Guardian* in 1958 (the newspaper was renamed *The Guardian* the following year).

Moorhouse's first book, *The Press* (1964), published at the height of his journalistic career, describes in detail the business of newspaper journalism, from reporting and editing to issues of a free press. In the same year Moorhouse synthesized some of his pieces for *The Guardian* into a lengthy study of the lesser-known English districts. *Britain in the Sixties: The Other England* (1964) confronts the myopic assumptions that Londoners had about other parts of their homeland. The British media had typecast the North as one long stretch of industrialized wasteland and the South as a region of comparative wealth. Moorhouse refutes this picture by pointing to the actual characteristics of the various parts of England, from the cosmopolitan London suburbs to the idyllic Wordsworthian villages of the West Midlands to the slums of Newcastle upon Tyne. He supplies a portrait of the tourist industry in Cornwall that replaced mining as the primary means of survival. He notes that the Beatles in Liverpool caused the crime rate to drop as male gangs turned their attention to song-writing and playing music. He also pauses to acknowledge his background in Bury, a topic he later develops in *Hell's Foundation: A Town, Its Myths, and Gallipoli* (1992). Moorhouse moralizes over the social conditions of Pakistani immigrants, critiques the development of various cities, and digs up statistics at local government offices. He concludes this study with a condemnation of the obsessive English focus on London, which ignores the concerns of small communities around the country. *Britain in the Sixties* includes many of the features that characterize Moorhouse's travel books: anecdotes, scenic descriptions, statistics, and history. This research effort anticipates his meticulous preparation for his later travel books.

For his third book, *The Church* (1967), Moorhouse contributed the text for a series of drawings by William Papas. The work describes the hierarchy and mission of the Church of England. Moorhouse followed it with a seminal study of monastic life, *Against All Reason* (1969). Though he drew much of his information from published sources, he also surveyed one hundred monks and nuns "to find out why they became religious."

Retiring from journalism in 1970, Moorhouse began his career as a travel writer with *Calcutta.* The book is based on his observations during two trips to the Indian city in 1969 and 1970. His purpose in writing the work is to describe Calcutta comprehensively and to work out, in historical terms, how the city–which, he claims in the introduction, is "the so-called Third World in miniature"–came to be the way it is. Some of his descriptions are gruesome. A man is too weak to move while jackals devour parts of his body. A leprosy victim "uses the grey stump of her hand like a wooden spoon to stir a pot of steaming liquid, for it has no feeling left, and the ghastly image that comes to a Western mind is of some particularly hellish production of the witches' scene in *Macbeth.*" Moorhouse notices many ironic juxtapositions: a slum of lean-tos exists "where Job Charnock's famous tree once stood" (Charnock, an agent of the British East India Company, founded Calcutta in 1690); the Catholic nun Mother Teresa's refuge for the poor and sick is located next to a Hindu temple; an indigent is "lying prone and exhausted" and fanning himself under a huge sign advertising "the world's largest-selling air-conditioner." Most outsiders notice only the poverty of Calcutta, but there is also great wealth there. Moorhouse attempts to show both. He defends his delight in these incongruities: "To point out and enjoy these things is not to ignore the real horrors of this city, or in some obscure way to plead mitigation of them."

Moorhouse grapples self-consciously with the task of communicating famine to British and American readers. He mentions a quality in the eyes of starving people that the camera rarely catches and that the reporter cannot verbalize, and continues:

Moorhouse in the Sahara during the hardship-filled attempted crossing he describes in The Fearful Void *(1974)*

> It is very difficult for Westerners, certainly for the British, to understand quite what starvation means in terms of the person to whom it is happening. . . . It is also very hard to understand what the starvation and the other parts of Calcutta's poverty are like, at a distance, because of the effect they have on the man who is reporting them at first hand.

In a sense, Moorhouse is acknowledging his own inability to do justice to Calcutta's suffering.

Moorhouse is much more successful in describing the outward signs of the city's "imperial past," such as the buildings and monuments. He enumerates such less conspicuous but more important signs of the British occupation as the "vaunted rule of law," the city's parliamentary government, and the omnipresent English language. One might expect Moorhouse, a British subject, to adopt a pro-British position, but he does not. He indicts his country for its long-standing "indifference and incomprehension": "It was the British, after all, who started this place in order to tap the wealth of this land," but they have turned their backs, along with the rest of the world, on the city's problems.

Mainly on the strength of *Calcutta,* Moorhouse was elected a fellow of the Royal Geographic Society in 1972. His next book, *The Missionaries* (1973), is a history of the British missionaries in Africa from 1796 until after World War I. He shows that the missionaries accomplished few of their objectives because of their inability to understand African culture; on the other hand, they did explore Africa and reduce the slave trade, and their teachings infused the Africans with a desire to escape tyranny. His expository method in *The Missionaries* has much in common with that in his later travel writings: he dispenses a great amount of information, combining detailed descriptions with general observations.

The Fearful Void, one of Moorhouse's best-known and most critically acclaimed works, is an account of his attempt, beginning in October 1972, to cross the Sahara desert from the Atlantic to the Nile–a journey of about 3,600 miles. The title of the book refers to Moorhouse's fear of death, which he hoped to confront and overcome through his journey across the desert. While many travelers had crossed the Sahara from north to south, no foreign explorer had ever traversed the length of the desert; in the event, he made it only about halfway, to Tamanrasset, Algeria. Setting off from Nouakchott, Mauritania, with a guide and several camels, he twice almost died of thirst and suffered from lice, diarrhea, open sores, malnutrition, sleeplessness, exhaustion, and boredom. His pains were so constant and severe that he found it difficult to concentrate on the external aspects of his journey, such as the landscape; thus, the work is as much a record of his suffering as it is an account of travel in a foreign land. Moorhouse also had to negotiate his way through Arab social codes, violation of which could have led to imprisonment or death.

The Fearful Void begins and ends, unconvincingly, with Moorhouse trying to read a deeper meaning into his actions. In Tamanrasset he visits Jean-Marie, the hermit of Assekrem, in the nearby Ahaggar Mountains in an unsuccessful effort to have a religious experience that would make sense of his trip. Reviewing *The Fearful Void* in *The New York Times Book Review* (31 March 1974), Paul Zweig wrote: "Moorhouse has seen the desert better than he has seen himself. His motivations . . . are unconvincing; his sporadic mysticism seems shallow and sentimental. Yet the journey itself is magnificent, as is Moorhouse's harrowing account of it." This curious split between Moorhouse's theorizing about his trip and his account of the trip itself adds a narrative tension to the book that complements the death-defying suspense of the adventure. Moorhouse is primarily a writer, not a desert adventurer, and his attempts to combine the perspectives of both make for this book's odd fascination.

On 23 September 1974, his first marriage having ended in divorce, Moorhouse married Barbara Jane Woodward. For the following two years he conducted research for his next book, *The Diplomats: The Foreign Office Today* (1977). He then spent a year, from May 1976 to May 1977, working as a commercial fisherman in Gloucester, Massachusetts. The experience resulted in his first work of fiction: *The Boat and the Town* (1979) examines life in a small New England fishing community, focusing on the activities of the crew of one boat from the middle of summer to the following spring. In an "Author's Note" Moorhouse says that he originally intended "to produce a straight-forward documentary account of that year" but decided that he would have to "enlist imagination to describe adequately what was felt, and sometimes to fuse characteristics from half a dozen different people into one so that a reader might more fully understand a way of life." *The Boat and the Town* shows Moorhouse struggling to find an appropriate technique for his travel writing, something between the straightforward reporting of *Calcutta* and the subjective approach of *The Fearful Void.*

Moorhouse's second marriage ended in divorce in 1978. His next book, *The Best-Loved Game: One Summer of English Cricket* (1979), a collection of essays, won the Cricket Society book of the year award.

San Francisco (1979) and *Prague* (1980) were written for the Time-Life Books Great Cities series. The books are heavily illustrated with photographs and include brief essays on each city's history and scenery. Moorhouse writes of the easy optimism of San Francisco, the gold rush, the nineteenth-century railroad barons, the 1906 earthquake, and the hippie movement of the 1960s. In *Prague* he describes the brief flowering of freedom in the Prague Spring of 1968 and its crushing by the Soviet army–events to which he was an eyewitness. Written under the constraints of the Time-Life Books format, the volumes form a footnote in Moorhouse's oeuvre.

In December 1981 Moorhouse's younger daughter, Brigid, died of rhabdomyosarcoma a month before her seventeenth birthday. Her death would send Moorhouse on a quest for meaning that he would describe in *OM: An Indian Pilgrimage.* He was elected a fellow of the Royal Society of Literature in 1982. On 7 July 1983 he married his third wife, Marilyn Isobel Edwards. That same year he published two books. In an unpublished list of his writings he describes the first, *Lord's,* as "an anatomy of the world's most famous cricket ground and the international headquarters of the game." The second, *India Britannica,* is a history of British rule in India from the establishment of the East India Com-

Two of Moorhouse's guides leading their camels against strong winds during the Fearful Void *journey (photograph by Geoffrey Moorhouse)*

pany in 1608 to the British withdrawal from the subcontinent in August 1947, the "story of a complicated love-hate relationship that no other two peoples, so vastly different in origins and cultures, have ever known."

In *India Britannica* Moorhouse mentions that as a child he had written an adventure story set on the North-West Frontier; as an adult he lived out his childhood fantasy by traveling across the region with nothing but a haversack. He recounts the experience in *To the Frontier* (1984). Although he describes the hardships of the journey, as he did in *The Fearful Void,* this work is less focused than the earlier one as Moorhouse delves into the history of the region. Landing in Karachi in March 1983, he works his way on foot and in trains, jeeps, and broken-down buses through the nearly impassable mountain country of Sind, Baluchistan, Punjab, and the Northwest Frontier Province to the Kashmir border. Along the way he encounters the fierce martial races of the area–Sikhs, Punjabi Muslims, and Pathans. Moorhouse cheerfully makes a study of anything that comes his way. Meeting a band of Pakistani cricketers, he launches into a lengthy digression about the game. He discusses the war then raging in Afghanistan between the Marxist government, supported by Soviet troops, and Muslim guerrillas and the effect of the war on Baluchistan. He describes the architecture of tombs, the religions of the area, archeological digs, hotels, local entertainments, the beliefs of a vegetarian American couple who join him on a train ride through Sind, and the Kafkaesque bureaucratic bungling of the officials over his visas. The narrative takes on a more serious tone when he describes the political oppression practiced by the regime of Pakistani president Mohammad Zia-ul-Haq; there is a lengthy account of the torture of a writer. He questions experts in Islamic law about such practices as public stonings. Near the border with Afghanistan he comes across hospitals full of wounded and crippled Afghan rebels still maniacally eager to return to fighting the Soviet troops. In the Khyber Pass he finds opium smuggling, caves where gangs manufacture heroin, and elaborate codes of revenge. At the end of his travels he flies back to Karachi, worried that the torture account he is smuggling in his sock will be discovered; but the customs official prefers to chat with him about cricket, and he flies safely back to England.

However Moorhouse may have resisted being classified as a travel writer, he seems to enjoy the freedom this form of writing allows him to indulge his deliberately amateurish–in the sense of nonspecialized–interests in history, architecture, politics, religion, and nature. The serendipitous character of his adventures gives parts of his writing a haphazard, improvisational quality that offsets the more fully researched historical digressions. *To the Frontier* won the Thomas Cook Award as the best travel book of 1984.

On 31 October 1984 Moorhouse was boarding a plane for India at Heathrow Airport when he heard that Indian prime minister Indira Gandhi had been assassinated. He witnessed rioting in Old Delhi when he landed, and he watched the funeral on television in

Bombay. A few weeks later he joined the procession of mourners passing Gandhi's ashes in Bangalore. "I would not willingly have been anywhere else on earth at that time," Moorhouse confessed a decade later in *OM: An Indian Pilgrimage.*

Rail across India: A Photographic Journey (1985), by Moorhouse, Paul C. Pet, and Brian Hollingsworth, attempts to capture the immensity and diversity of India in photographs and prose. Moorhouse contributed the prologue, an introduction to India's history and culture. He repeats many of the sentiments that he had expressed in *Calcutta* and *India Britannica,* but here he takes a somewhat rosier view of the legacy of British imperialism. As in the earlier books, he enjoys pointing out India's contrasts and contradictions: the seasonal monsoon and the unbelievably dry Thar desert; the ancient temple of Shiva, god of reproduction, on Elephanta Island and the "large silvery domes" of India's first nuclear reactor on nearby Trombay Island; and India's sexually explicit past, exemplified by the *Kama Sutra* and the erotic decorations on ancient Hindu temples, and its sexually repressive present, as seen in rigid moral codes and movie censorship. Moorhouse lauds India's assimilation of British culture as "a gift that sets her far apart from others," citing the country's "parliamentary democracy, a rule of civilised law, a highly efficient civil service and, yes, the finest railway system in the world outside Europe and North America."

In January 1986 Moorhouse suffered a heart attack while driving his car. He tells the story of his near-death experience in *OM: An Indian Pilgrimage:*

> A policewoman just happened to be coming down the road and at once radioed for an ambulance which, by preposterous coincidence, was only a few hundred yards away. When I was hauled from the wreckage, surprisingly undamaged by the crash, my heart had been stopped for a couple of minutes: which is about the time limit allowed under the Geneva Convention. The policewoman told the ambulancemen they could forget about me, because I had obviously gone; but they said they'd give it a go, and got the heart pumping again. They had to do this five more times before they trundled me into intensive care, where I remained in a coma for the next thirty-six hours.

He received triple-bypass surgery and was able to resume his life with only minor changes in his routine.

Imperial City: The Rise and Rise of New York (1988) is Moorhouse's second book-length study of an urban center; but whereas *Calcutta* confronts the reader with the city's poverty, *Imperial City* celebrates the rich history and cultural diversity of America's great metropolis. Moorhouse is fascinated by the spectacle and energy of New York and its constant re-creation of itself. He begins with a description of the city from the vantage point of the Brooklyn Bridge, proclaiming the skyline of the "butt end" of Manhattan one of the most spectacular sights he has seen anywhere. He goes on to give the history of the building of some of the skyscrapers, including stories of welders leaning fearlessly into the abyss. He discusses the city's major ethnic groups, including the Irish, the Jews, and the Puerto Ricans. He characterizes the city as always on the move, relentlessly practical, greedy, aggressive, social-climbing, entrepreneurial, mercurial, and fast-paced. Moorhouse wants to like the city, but he recognizes its many problems: potholes, crime, skyrocketing rents, and an overall decline in the quality of life. The third volume in what Moorhouse calls his "metropolitan trilogy," a book about Sydney, Australia, is to be published in 1999.

In 1989 Moorhouse published *At the George and Other Essays on Rugby League* and collaborated with the photographer Kazuyoshi Nomachi on *The Nile,* a photographic essay on the river. In his introduction to the latter work, which is based on research he had done for an essay in *Great Rivers of the World* (1984), Moorhouse marvels at the length of the Nile–it is the world's longest river–and the diversity of its shores. No other river, he says, "traverses such a variety of landscapes, such a medley of cultures, such a spectrum of peoples." He uses one superlative after another as he describes the terrain through which the Nile passes and the history of the places along its course. Not satisfied with the river's humble ending in twin channels that enter the Mediterranean at Rosetta on the west and at Dumyāt (Damietta) on the east, he shifts attention to Alexandria, which lies just to the west of Rosetta, and its rich history as Cleopatra's death site and Alexander the Great's final resting place. In effect, he poetically alters the course of the river to have it end more auspiciously.

In 1989, thanks to the thawing effects of glasnost and the sponsorship of the National Geographic Society, Moorhouse was able to travel along the Silk Route of Soviet Central Asia; he recounts the trip in *Apples in the Snow: A Journey to Samarkand* (1990). As in his earlier travel books, his visits to various places–Kazakhstan, Tajikistan, Uzbekistan–become pretexts for discussing their histories. He is dismayed by the way the Soviets have destroyed the traces of history in the region by tearing down ancient buildings for new factories or dull suburban complexes. He shows how glasnost has transformed Soviet Asia: he is invited to judge a beauty contest in a village in Kazakhstan in which the contestants appear in their traditional kaftans and then dance erotically in Western garb to loud disco music. The contest provides Moorhouse with an apt emblem for the grow-

OM 136

the most sumptuous display of fantasy I had seen in India or anywhere else, of a variety and inventiveness that made the gargoyles and other images of the greatest Gothic churches in Europe seem sparse, inhibited and grey. A plaque on the wall of the West tower, which went up early in the fourteenth century, just as the building of Exeter Cathedral was getting into its stride, said that there were 1,124 sculptures on its facade; and all the other gopurams were as richly endowed. On one tier alone there were multi-headed personages facing three ways at once, a moustachioed godling in knee-breeches flexing his fourteen arms, mermaids reclining suggestively within the open lips of conch shells, sixteen sprites struggling to control a serpent which had coiled itself round the building, androgynous creatures bestriding bulls and horses and swans, characters wearing crowns or tiaras or haloes or vaguely pharaonic diadems, and figures that appeared to have been frozen in the middle of some elaborate choreography whose every dancer was performing an unrelated movement of its own. All [illegible] this was delicately coloured in pastel shades of pink and green and yellow and blue, with an artfully blended fleshy tint that made even the most grotesque apparition seem to be endowed with a disturbingly human personality. And this vividly crazy carnival of goblins and satyrs, nymphs and genies, demons and heroes, with glaring eyes and posturing limbs, with hands that beckoned and shunned and implied every conceivable emotion in between, this monumental hallucination reproduced itself again and again as the gopuram rose higher above the ground; until, at the very top of the building, an enormous and devilish face looked down with wide open mouth, from which every creature on the four walls had been disgorged in a magnificent, astonishing, terrifying, and tumbling extravaganza.

Page from the typescript for Moorhouse's OM: An Indian Pilgrimage, *published in 1993 (Collection of Geoffrey Moorhouse)*

ing East-West cultural split in the region after decades of drab communism.

The two major set pieces of the book concern the statues of the Bolshevik leader Vladimir Ilyich Lenin and the Mongol warlord Genghis Khan. After an extended description of Lenin's statues in their various studied poses, Moorhouse enjoys imagining other statues in which Lenin holds a chess piece or bends his knees in a Russian dance. As glasnost lowered Lenin's stature, Moorhouse revels in tweaking the self-importance of the statues. He gives a lengthy history of the Mongols, describing their aversion to bathing, their ruthless efficiency as warriors, and their practice of executing everyone in large cities to prevent later uprisings. Moorhouse is particularly fascinated with Genghis Khan and wonders what event in his youth led him to pursue world domination. In the midst of his guided travels from city to city in the frozen steppes Moorhouse allows his imagination to dwell on these two powerful figures.

Like *To the Frontier, Apples in the Snow* is uneven but often entertaining. More comfortable now, no longer living the adventures of his earlier travels, Moorhouse becomes more associative and playful in his writing, allowing the drama of history to make up for a desolate plain, looking for the oddities of remote cultures. He challenges a Muslim scholar with a discussion of Salman Rushdie. In Bukhara he records the story of a bear that gradually ate 411 men who had been paralyzed by drink from the local bandits. Moorhouse organizes this hodgepodge of impressions by beginning the book with a depiction of an Orthodox church service and closing it at a *lavra,* an Orthodox monastery. He leaves the region with a heightened appreciation of the people in Central Asia, their regional identities long obscured by communist rule.

The 1992 work *Hell's Foundations: A Town, Its Myths, and Gallipoli* grew out of Moorhouse's boyhood memories. It is, as the subtitle of the American edition says, a social history of the town of Bury in the aftermath of the Gallipoli campaign. As he writes in *India Britannica,* his childhood parish church was "pickled in my associations with my grandfather's old regiment, the Lancashire Fusiliers, who turned up *en masse* once a year to celebrate and lament the anniversary of their landing at Gallipoli in 1915." The book is a lovingly detailed portrait of a town coming to terms with a devastating and futile military campaign. He describes Bury before the war, with the soldiers doing bayonet exercises in the surrounding countryside; gives a brief description of the campaign, noting the anti-British sentiments of the Australians, New Zealanders, and other nationalities who fought in it; and then shifts back to Bury to recount the war's effects: the crippled and shell-shocked veterans, the shunning of conscientious objectors, the little patriotic plaques that the government gave to the widows, the Lancashire Fusiliers marching through town on Armistice Day and Gallipoli Sunday. One keeps looking for an acknowledgment of the absurdity of Gallipoli, but the people of Bury need to believe in the nobility of the campaign. All of the banal commemorative ceremonies form a necessary mythology of their loss. One is left with an impression of the humanity and dignity of the people of Bury.

Published in 1993, *OM: An Indian Pilgrimage* recounts Moorhouse's journey of self-discovery through southern India during the first three months of 1992; the book's title is a reference to the Hindu meditative chant "Ommmmmmm." Moorhouse travels from one holy place to another, seeking gurus and religious people of various faiths to answer his questions about the meaning of the premature death of his daughter and his own near-fatal 1986 heart attack. Along the way he discusses India's politics and history, but far less than in previous books. Moorhouse's trip takes the form of a pilgrimage, with chapters devoted to the various holy places on his itinerary. But Moorhouse is a pilgrim only in an ironic sense: as a skeptic in search of a religion. He considers Judaism, Hinduism, Catholicism, and Protestantism, rejecting them all. The last chapter finds Moorhouse in San Thomé Cathedral (the Cathedral of Doubting Thomas) in Madras. Tradition holds that Saint Thomas, the skeptical apostle, brought Christianity to the subcontinent. Moorhouse proclaims himself an eternal skeptic in the tradition of this saint:

> It was not that I found it difficult to accept divinity, to marvel at mystery, to believe in miracles; these had never been my stumbling blocks, for I was a naturally credulous man. But every faith I had examined, most of all that into which I had been born and in which I would die, insisted on something that I could not do: and that was to surrender myself to all that it offered of goodness, to all that it demanded of self. . . . my far too logical and sceptical mind became my shield and my defence.

Ever the wary reporter, Moorhouse cannot give himself over to blind faith. He says, however, that India, a society where everything–one's station in life, the inevitability of death, personal inadequacy, cruelty, poverty, hardship, and so on–is accepted without demur, has taught him to accept his mortality. Kneeling in Doubting Thomas's crypt, he prays to be allowed to return soon to India, his beloved land. A personal meditation in which an inner journey merges with a physical one, *OM* represents a step beyond travel writing into the realm of spiritual autobiography.

After *OM* Moorhouse wrote a second book on rugby, *A People's Game: The Centenary History of Rugby League Football, 1895–1995* (1995), before returning to a subject he had treated extensively in *Against All Reason:* monasticism. *Sun Dancing: A Vision of Medieval Ireland* (1997) combines fiction and explanatory essays to dramatize the six-hundred-year history of a community of monks who lived on an inhospitable rocklike island, Skellig Michael, off the west coast of Ireland. During the Dark Ages, Irish monasteries such as this one kept Western civilization alive while much of continental Europe succumbed to invading hordes. The book depicts the monks' struggles with the sea and with themselves in a series of stories that jump from generation to generation between 588 and 1222. The reader witnesses the founding of the monastery, the pagan Celtic rituals that persisted under Roman Catholicism, and the visions and sufferings of the anchorites in their cells. The second half of the book consists of chapter-length explanations of aspects of the stories. Putting his research on display, Moorhouse explores topics that range from the various versions of St. Anthony in painting and literature to the influence of the Vikings on monastic culture. Through this synthesis of imagination, hearsay, and fact he attempts to convey the essence of early Irish monasticism. The publisher, Weidenfeld and Nicolson, nominated the book for the 1997 Booker Prize.

In his later works Moorhouse has increasingly explored spiritual questions, but he continues to balance religious curiosity with journalistic skepticism. He will probably be remembered best for his books on the Sahara, Pakistan, and the crumbling Soviet Union, in which he plays the roles of observer and participant with equal enthusiasm. A versatile writer, he has crossed genres to produce competent nonfiction about sports, religion, history, and politics.

Interview:

Jacquelin Burgess and Alan Jenkins, "'This Is What It Is Like': An Interview with the Writer Geoffrey Moorhouse," *Journal of Geography in Higher Education,* 13, no. 2 (1989): 127–147.

Reference:

Mark Cocker, *Loneliness and Time: British Travel Writing in the Twentieth Century* (London: Secker, 1994), pp. 5, 104, 106, 134–135, 142–144, 162–163.

Jan Morris
(James Humphrey Morris)

(2 October 1926 -)

William Over
St. John's University

BOOKS: *Coast to Coast* (London: Faber & Faber, 1956); republished as *As I Saw the U.S.A.* (New York: Pantheon, 1956);

Sultan in Oman (London: Faber & Faber, 1957; republished as *Sultan in Oman: Venture in the Middle East* (New York: Pantheon, 1957);

The Market of Seleukia (London: Faber & Faber, 1957); republished as *Islam Inflamed: A Middle East Picture* (New York: Pantheon, 1957);

Coronation Everest (London: Faber & Faber, 1958; New York: Dutton, 1958);

South African Winter (London: Faber & Faber, 1958; New York: Pantheon, 1958);

The Hashemite Kings (London: Faber & Faber, 1959; New York: Pantheon, 1959):

Venice (London: Faber & Faber, 1960; revised edition, 1974; revised edition, 1983; revised edition, 1993); republished as *The World of Venice* (New York: Harcourt, Brace & World, 1960; revised edition, New York: Harcourt Brace Jovanovich, 1974; revised edition, New York: Harcourt Brace, 1995);

South America, A Guardian Pamphlet (London: Manchester Guardian and Evening News, 1961);

The Upstairs Donkey, and Other Stolen Stories, illustrations by Pauline Baynes (London: Faber & Faber, 1962; New York: Pantheon, 1962);

Cities (London: Faber & Faber, 1963; New York: Harcourt, Brace & World, 1963);

The Outriders: A Liberal View of Britain (London: Faber & Faber, 1963);

The Road to Huddersfield: A Journey to Five Continents (New York: Pantheon, 1963); republished as *The World Bank: A Prospect* (London: Faber & Faber, 1963); republished as *The Road to Huddersfield: The Story of the World Bank* (New York: Minerva, 1968);

The Presence of Spain (London: Faber & Faber, 1964; New York: Harcourt, Brace & World, 1964); republished as *Spain* (London: Faber & Faber, 1970; revised edition, London & Boston: Faber & Faber, 1979; New York: Oxford University Press, 1979);

Jan Morris (photograph © Jerry Bauer)

Oxford (London: Faber & Faber, 1965; New York: Harcourt, Brace & World, 1965; revised edition, Oxford & New York: Oxford University Press, 1978);

Pax Britannica: The Climax of an Empire (London: Faber & Faber, 1968; New York: Harcourt, Brace & World, 1968);

The Great Port: A Passage Through New York, photographs by Albert Belva (New York: Harcourt, Brace & World, 1969; London: Faber & Faber, 1970);

Places (London: Faber & Faber, 1972; New York: Harcourt Brace Jovanovich, 1973);

Heaven's Command: An Imperial Progress (London: Faber & Faber, 1973; New York: Harcourt Brace Jovanovich, 1974);

The Preachers, illustrations by Tom Huffman (New York: St. Martin's Press, 1973);

Conundrum (London: Faber & Faber, 1974; New York: Harcourt Brace Jovanovich, 1974);

Travels, illustrations by Nicholas Hall (London: Faber & Faber, 1976; New York: Harcourt Brace Jovanovich, 1976);

Farewell the Trumpets: An Imperial Retreat (London: Faber & Faber, 1978; New York: Harcourt Brace Jovanovich, 1978);

Destinations: Essays from Rolling Stone (New York: Oxford University Press, 1980; Oxford: Oxford University Press, 1980);

My Favourite Stories of Wales (Guildford, U.K.: Lutterworth, 1980);

The Venetian Empire: A Sea Voyage (London: Faber & Faber, 1980; New York: Harcourt Brace Jovanovich, 1980);

A Venetian Bestiary (London: Thames & Hudson, 1982; New York: Thames & Hudson, 1982);

The Spectacle of Empire: Style, Effect and the Pax Britannica (London & Boston: Faber & Faber, 1982; Garden City, N.Y.: Doubleday, 1982);

Wales: The First Place, photographs by Paul Wakefield (London: Aurum, 1982; New York: Potter, 1982);

Stones of Empire: The Buildings of the Raj, photography and captions by Simon Winchester (Oxford & New York: Oxford University Press, 1983);

Journeys (New York & Oxford: Oxford University Press, 1984);

The Matter of Wales: Epic Views of a Small Country, photographs by Paul Wakefield (Oxford & New York: Oxford University Press, 1984);

Among the Cities (London: Viking, 1985; New York: Oxford University Press, 1985); abridged as *From the Four Corners* (London: Penguin, 1995);

Last Letters from Hav (London: Viking, 1985; New York: Random House, 1985);

Scotland: The Place of Visions, with Paul Wakefield (London: Aurum, 1986; New York: Potter, 1986);

Manhattan '45 (London & Boston: Faber & Faber, 1987; New York: Oxford University Press, 1987);

Hong Kong: Xianggang (London: Viking, 1988; New York: Random House, 1988); revised as *Hong Kong: Xianggang: The End of an Empire* (London: Penguin, 1990); revised as *Hong Kong: Epilogue to an Empire* (Harmondsworth: Penguin, 1993; revised edition, London: Penguin, 1997);

Pleasures of a Tangled Life (London: Barrie & Jenkins, 1989; New York: Random House, 1989);

City to City (Toronto: Macfarlane, Walter & Ross, 1990);

Ireland, Your Only Place, photography by Paul Wakefield (London: Aurum, 1990; New York: Potter, 1990);

Over Europe, text by Morris, photography by Torbjorn Anderson, edited by Mary-Dawn Earley and Jane Frasier (London: Times Books, 1991; New York: Mallard, 1992);

Locations (Oxford & New York: Oxford University Press, 1992);

O Canada!, illustrated by Barry Britt (London: Hale, 1992; New York: HarperCollins, 1992);

Sydney (London: Viking, 1992; New York: Random House, 1992);

A Machynlleth Triad (Newtown, Wales: Gwasg Gregynog, 1993; New York & London: Viking, 1993); enlarged as *A Machynlleth Triad = Triawd Machynlleth,* Morris and Twm Morys (London & New York: Viking, 1994);

Fisher's Face, or, Getting to Know the Admiral (London: Viking, 1995; New York: Random House, 1995);

The Princeship of Wales, Changing Wales Series (Llandysul, Wales: Gomer, 1995);

Fifty Years of Europe: An Album (London: Viking, 1997; New York: Villard, 1997).

OTHER: Tobias Smollett, *Travels through France and Italy,* introduction by Morris, Traveller's Classics (Fontwell, U.K.: Centaur, 1969);

The Oxford Book of Oxford, edited by Morris (Oxford & New York: Oxford University Press, 1978);

My Favourite Stories of Wales, edited by Morris (Guildford, U.K.: Lutterworth, 1980);

John Ruskin, *The Stones of Venice,* edited, with an introduction, by Morris (Boston: Little, Brown, 1981; London & Boston: Faber & Faber, 1981);

Wales, edited by Morris (Oxford & New York: Oxford University Press, 1982);

"In Quest of the Imperial Style," in *Architecture of the British Empire,* edited by Robert Fermor-Hesketh (London: Weidenfeld & Nicolson, 1986), pp. 10–31;

Michael Weir, *Images of Egypt,* introduction by Morris (London: Pyramid, 1989);

Riding the Skies: Classic Posters from the Golden Age of Flying, introduction by Morris (London: Bloomsbury, 1989);

Fergus M. Bordewich, *Cathay: A Journey in Search of Old China,* introduction by Morris (New York: Prentice Hall, 1991);

Janet Davies, ed., *Compass Points: Jan Morris Introduces a Selection from the First Hundred Issues of Planet,* introduction by Morris (Cardiff: University of Wales Press, 1993);

Frontispiece by Ansel Adams and title page for Morris's first book (1956), a narrative of his trips through America in the early 1950s

Virginia Woolf, *Travels with Virginia Woolf,* edited by Morris (London: Hogarth Press, 1993).

SELECTED PERIODICAL PUBLICATIONS–UNCOLLECTED: "Itchy Feet and Pencils: A Symposium," by Morris, Russell Banks, Robert Stone, and William Styron, *New York Times Book Review,* 18 August 1991, pp. 1, 23, 24;

"The World According to Baedeker," *Travel Holiday,* 179 (February 1996): 54–59;

"Clive's Castle," *Granta,* 57 (Spring 1997): 249–255;

"The Naughty Girl Next Door," *Time,* 150 (15 September 1997): 50;

"Travel Lit's Novel Pursuit," *Nation,* 265 (6 October 1997): 37–38.

A prolific and innovative travel writer, Jan Morris has, paradoxically, always rejected the label of travel writer. Known for incorporating local history and lore, literary and personal anecdotes, and geographical description into her travel narratives, Morris approaches her writing comprehensively, defying conventional genre distinctions. This defiance of labeling has extended to her personal life; although born a man, she realized at an early age that she was in fact a woman and eventually underwent a sex change operation. In her major works, Morris successfully combines a cultural map of inhabitants with a keen and compelling sense of their physical environment to form a clear conception of locale, sympathetically depicting the cultures and people that she encounters during her travels.

Jan Morris was born James Humphrey Morris on 2 October 1926 in Clevedon, Somerset, England to Walter and Enid Payne Morris. The nine-year-old James Morris began a lifelong love affair with Oxford University, where he attended the choir school of Christ College. He later attended Lancing College in Shropshire, of which Morris writes in the autobiographical *Conundrum* (1974): "I was not really unhappy there, but I was habitually *frightened.*" There Morris enjoyed lighthearted romances with fellow students and was flattered when pursued by the "best-looking senior boy," but found pederasty "aesthetically . . . wrong."

In 1944 Morris left Lancing and became a member of the editorial staff of the *Western Daily Press* of Bristol. Later that year he joined the army, serving from

1944 to 1947 in a tank regiment and rising to the rank of lieutenant. In *Conundrum,* Morris writes, "I think I learned my trade in the Ninth Lancers, for I developed in that regiment an almost anthropological interest in the forms and attitudes of that society; . . . I evolved the techniques of analysis and observation that I would later adopt to the writer's craft."

Morris served with the Ninth Queen's Lancers in Italy and later in Palestine as an intelligence officer with the regiment during the last years of the British mandate. After his discharge from the army and with time to spare before study at Oxford University, Morris joined the British-operated Arab News Agency in Cairo, Egypt, from 1947 to 1948, writing editorials and international news stories that were distributed to newspapers and magazines throughout the Arab world.

After returning to England in 1948, Morris entered Christ Church College, Oxford University, earning the B.A. degree with second-class honors in 1951 and an M.A. in 1961. In 1949, James Humphrey Morris married Margaret Elizabeth Tuckniss, and thus entered into what Morris characterized in *Conundrum* as "a marriage that had no right to work, yet it worked like a dream." They had five children: Mark, Henry, Tom, Susan, and Virginia (who died in infancy). Their marriage was trusting and open, with "partners . . . free to lead their own lives, choose their own friends if they wish, have their own lovers perhaps, restrained only by an agreement of superior affection and common concern." They remained together through Morris's sex change and, although they later divorced, sustained their friendship throughout the years.

From 1951 to 1956, Morris was on the editorial staff of *The Times* (London), working as special correspondent in Scandinavia, the Netherlands, India, the United States, and Egypt. He was on the *Manchester Guardian* editorial staff from 1956 to 1961 but was allowed six months off each year to write. During the 1950s, Morris traveled widely on assignment, often in difficult wilderness areas or reporting on "hot spots" of the Cold War era, but also producing meticulous travel accounts. Of the years 1947 to 1962, Morris writes in *Heaven's Command: An Imperial Progress* (1973), "I found myself vocationally engaged in the dissolution of the [British] empire."

In 1956 Morris published his first travel book, *Coast to Coast,* about a series of trips through the United States during the years 1953–1954. Its vivid style and affirming tone reveals an attraction to America, a fascination that would grow in subsequent decades. Morris was not uncritical, however, lamenting the shortcomings of the traditional South, with its racial segregation and everyday prejudices. His journeys through the United States were abruptly interrupted in 1953 when *The Times* sent Morris to cover the British Mount Everest expedition, recognizing that he was the most physically fit of the staff journalists, an "agile twenty-six."

Morris accompanied the expedition team to the 22,000-foot level and gained recognition as a journalist with his scoop of Edmund Hillary and Tenzing Norgkay's successful assault of the summit. His real achievement, however, was the clever communications system devised to pass the news to Europe. His reportage formed the basis for his book *Coronation Everest* (1958), a personal account of news reporting amid secrecy in an inhospitable climate.

Other books based on travels for *The Times* include *Sultan in Oman* (1957), which describes Morris's journey through the hinterlands of Muscat and Oman in December 1955; and *The Market of Seleukia* (1957), which is based on observations in Egypt, Sudan, Lebanon, Syria, Jordan, Saudi Arabia, Iraq, and Iran. Although Morris's political observations are often overly general and uninformed, the accounts reveal a penchant for travel writing.

Sent by the *Manchester Guardian* in 1957 to report on the political and social situation in South Africa, Morris produced *South African Winter* (1958). His contact with local people reveals a willingness to listen and an occasional effort to report their conditions, but Morris frequently retreats into his own travel concerns when confronted with the horrors of apartheid. Still, throughout the chapters Morris demonstrates an affinity for Africans, later writing in *Conundrum,* "I came to regard black Africa as a solace, and . . . Africans revealed to me more frankly a deeper stillness of their spirit. This growing empathy has been very good for me."

As a journalist for the *Guardian,* Morris was inspired to tell the story of the House of Beni Hashem while he was in Jordan attending King Hussein's press conference in July 1958 that announced the assassination of Hussein's cousin, King Faisal II of Iraq. More an intimate history than travel account or political analysis, *The Hashemite Kings* (1959) vividly profiles the family members Morris had observed as correspondent during his stint with the Arab News Agency.

Venice (1960) became Morris's first full-length travel work to achieve major success. In 1960 he was undergoing a major career transition, changing from journalist to travel essayist, writing in the preface to the first U.S. edition, "I was a foreign correspondent then, and I planned this book as a dispatch about contemporary Venice." A reviewer in the 12 August 1960 issue of *The Times Literary Supplement* (*TLS*) praised Morris's ability to convey the experiential aspects of the city. The *TLS* reviewer, however, called Morris's treatment of the magnificent artwork in Venice inadequate, even irrever-

Morris in the early 1960s

ent–"On painting and sculpture his comments are at best perfunctory, at worse intolerantly pert." Morris's appreciation and knowledge of the city, however, are evident. The author's foreword to the 1993 edition expresses a strong regret that much of what was available to the visitor in 1960 has since disappeared. This addendum expresses what has become a familiar sentiment to Morris readers, an elegiac nostalgia.

In *Venice,* the writer's persona intrudes throughout the chapters on art, architecture, neighborhoods, and Venetian social types, as he records interactions between people and place. Morris writes that a Venetian

> goes to St. Mark's for no definite purpose, to meet nobody specific, to admire no particular spectacle. He simply likes to button his coat, and sleek his hair a little, assume an air of rather portentous melancholy and stroll for an hour or two among the sumptuous trophies of his heritage.

Often these interactions are described in phrases that evoke Venice's long history, such as "he only shrugs his shoulders and smiles a separate, melancholy smile, as a Doge might smile at an importunate emperor, or a great sea-captain patronize a Turk." Exploring the boundaries between history and travel writing, Morris devotes much of *Venice* to social and cultural studies, although the social history is often only superficial. The chapter titled "On Women," for example, chiefly concerns the sexual practices of the upper classes, with little commentary on the conditions of Venetian poor and working women.

Morris uses Venice's long and illustrious history–as a prominent port linking East and West, as a cultural and fine arts center, and as a political power–to meld time with place, a strategy he had used in his earlier journalistic reporting. The historical accounts are often disjointed, but Morris's real strength as a historian is an ability to associate contemporary realities with the past. Morris's keen social eye and talent for teasing out the nuances of cultural development by focusing on physical setting–in this case, the architecture, city planning, and civic services of a unique urban environment–keep the book afloat.

Venice demonstrates Morris's technique of throwing lists at the reader to create a cycloramic effect, recreating a kind of sensory overload of objects and people, as in his extensive catalogue of types of boats used in the Venetian canals and on the lagoon. The use of Italian names adds to the specificity–he describes such boats as the *sandolo, vaporetto, motoscafo, topo, trabaccolo, cavallina, vipera, bissona, barcobestia,* and the *bucintoro*. A listing of lion symbols evident in Venetian streets and public buildings uses a rhetorical device that Morris would repeat years later in listing castles in *Wales: The First Place* (1982); that is, he defines a category for the listed item in such a way that it offers an immediate impression: "the most imperial lion," "the ugliest pair," "the silliest lion," "the most unassuming," and so on.

In *Venice,* the writer gropes for the essentials of the city through explorations of its hiddenness. Morris gives the Venetian term for wandering in the small covered passages that wend between houses, *andare per le fodere*–"to move along the lanes." The phrase might apply in general to Morris's exploratory method in the book, as he seeks the secret of the city, consciously leaving the well-trodden boundaries of the guidebooks. In fact, the frequent allusions to nineteenth-century and early twentieth-century guidebooks establish a dichotomy between popular preconceptions and the sort of adventurous uncovering Morris wishes to undertake.

In *Venice,* Morris attempts too much and fails in the perhaps impossible task of defining the unique atmosphere of the city. Still, the book's shortcomings fade before the author's stunning vision: *Venice* is honest, witty, and perceptive, a precursor of Morris's more personal full-length works.

The year 1960 was an important one in Morris's career. He received the prestigious Heinemann Award from the Royal Society of Literature in England for *Venice* (1960), as well as the George Polk Memorial Award in 1960, given by Long Island University for journalism in America. In 1962 he published his first juvenile fiction, *The Upstairs Donkey, and Other Stolen Stories,* a multicultural collection of folktales from across the globe.

Following these achievements, Morris became a full-time freelance writer in 1961, and an impressive number of books soon appeared. *The Road to Huddersfield: A Journey to Five Continents* (1963) was commissioned by the International Bank for Reconstruction and Development; however, in the preface Morris declares that he is unbiased in his reportage. Morris is less concerned with individual financiers, statistics, and policies than with on-site descriptions of that organization's projects in third-world countries. *Cities* (1963), a collection of articles that were mostly originally published in *The Guardian, The Times* (London), and *Life* magazine, includes pieces on seventy-six metropolitan areas–from Accra in Ghana to Wellington in New Zealand–and tests the writer's ability to present brief vignettes of diverse locales.

The Presence of Spain (1964) is a volume featuring the photographs of Evelyn Hofer. William Barratt, reviewing the book in *The Atlantic* (January 1965), found Morris moving beyond travel reporting to attempt a definition of the Spanish character, but Morris seems aware of the elusive nature of the task and reveals a certain self-conscious irony, knowing the reader will find the book a failure. For a 1979 revision titled *Spain,* the writer revisited the country after the dictator Francisco Franco's death in 1975 and updated some information and commentary but added no significant new observations.

Oxford (1965) became one of Morris's most successful full-length travel books. Along with *Spain,* this study has achieved the status of a travel classic. While working on the book, Morris lived with his family at their pied-à-terre in the city, and he used the University College common room, which allowed close contact with Oxford students and dons. The five main chapters are further divided into unusual oblique perspectives on the university and its community. Morris melds history and geography, presenting, for example, not just the stories of eccentric dons through the centuries, but, in the subchapter "Fauna and Flora," discussing their pets and favorite gardens.

In the first chapter Morris orients the reader to Oxford through use of a familiar device: lists. To the obligatory list of graduates from Sir Walter Ralegh to Beau Brummel, Morris adds lists of those who would have liked to have gone to Oxford; of those who hated it there; of eponymous places and things, from Henry Morgan's pirate ship to the twenty-one towns named Oxford in the United States; of famous objects left at Oxford; of famous buildings; of famous disciplines that began there; of famous world leaders who wanted Oxford as their capitals. This associative approach underscores the significance of Oxford as cultural icon, but it also speaks to its diversity.

Morris's novelistic modifications to the travel essay appear throughout *Oxford;* for instance, in a broad conceit pondering where Oxford's many treasures would be sold if the sudden need arose, Morris writes:

> The books would no doubt go first, quick as a flash across the Atlantic, and the Old Masters next; and the glass would be distributed among missions, youth clubs and churches in new Industrial towns; and the portraits would dribble away down the market, leaving a Lawrence in this art gallery, a Henry Lamb in that, until at last the dimmest and most obscure of the ecclesiastics showed up dusty in the corners of junk shops for the sake of the frames. Up to Sotheby's would pour the astrolabes, and the great silver salt cellars, and the beautiful furniture from Master's Lodgings. . . .

Morris once again responds subjectively as he walks around Christ Church College meadows in winter. "The meadows," he writes, "felt downright primeval, so subdued and muffled were the trees, so empty was everything, so silent: I almost expected to see the thin smoke of a Neolithic fire rising above the elms." Overall, the many literary quotations and allusions reveal his confidence as a travel writer, and the concise flashes of description, apparent throughout the book, establish his mastery of the genre.

Morris's method merges geography and history to establish the origins of a place, while defining its long-standing character. Thus, he considers the most reliable accounts of Oxford's origins by describing early archaeological sites beginning with prehistory through the Roman, Saxon, and Norman eras. Morris then situates these sites within a travel context by indicating the contemporary buildings that have now replaced them–for instance, the grave of the early iron-age chieftain superseded by the walls of the Examination Schools.

Morris's eye for human character enhances his descriptive prose. People at the annual St. Giles Fair, for example, are vividly profiled in elegant parallel sentences:

> The academics go with their burbling children, eating iced lollipops and arguing the toss with indulgent showmen in piping cultured accents. The factory families go, trailing balloons and sweet papers, and hugging flowery vases they have won at shooting galleries. The farmers go, stumping stoically through the hubbub with kind wives in blue hats. . . .

Indeed, the clarity and abundance of his character sketches allow the reader to forget that Morris is, after all, an outsider at Oxford.

Spanish countrymen in New Castile; photograph by Evelyn Hofer in Morris's The Presence of Spain *(1964)*

Oxford exhibits a mastery of expository prose, aided in part by the writer's aphoristic and concise sentence structure—"In manners it seems to me much less polished than Harvard or Princeton, and in personnel it ranges from the exquisite to the downright boorish, by way of a thousand dullards." Although critical, his statements seldom mislead, and his style encompasses an insider's aplomb and a certain cavalier affection.

In 1968, Morris published *Pax Britannica: The Climax of an Empire,* the second volume (but the first written, and the first to appear) of an historical trilogy about the British Empire. The first volume, *Heaven's Command,* was published in 1973; and the concluding volume, *Farewell the Trumpets: An Imperial Retreat,* was published in 1978.

The three volumes span the decades of Britain's empire at its greatest extent, describing the conception of the empire as it arose from the early Victorian era into the twentieth century. Morris did research for the project largely in England but also at such places as the National Archives in Salisbury, Rhodesia. Approaching historical narrative in a now-familiar style, Morris paints a pointillist picture, impressive in its meticulousness and descriptive detail, of the "muddled grandeur" of the British Empire at its height. Such a subject lends itself well to Morris's keen-eyed journalistic intent to set the distant scene. Adroit at devising oblique perspectives on the subject, the whole unfolding into a clear point of view, in *Pax Britannia* Morris offers such chapters as "Life-Lines," about transportation innovations; "Pioneers," about the frontier towns of each continent; "The Glory," about conceptions that justified the aggressiveness of colonialism; and "Tribal Lays and Images," about the fine arts within colonial countries. The large number of chapters—eighty-one in the three volumes—allows Morris to investigate both microhistory and the general policies of empire.

A reviewer of the first volume of the trilogy noted, in the *TLS* (7 November 1968), a "grave ambiguity" in it: how is the reader to take Morris's nostalgic tone about colonial exploitation? In the introduction to *Pax Britannia,* Morris anticipates objections to what could well be taken as a celebration of European colonialism; he says that "I have not tried to hide a sensual sympathy for the period, haunted as it is in retrospect by our knowledge of tragedies to come." Morris offers a short apology: "I have tried only to recall what the Empire was . . . and how the British themselves then saw it–for what it meant to their alien subjects, it would be presumptuous of me to conjecture."

The seventeen essays comprising *Places* (1972) focus upon locales featured in the *Pax Britannica* trilogy, although European travel haunts such as Baden-Baden are included. Morris acknowledges an outsider's perspective, "from the outside, detached and unembroiled." The collection is perhaps Morris's most exotic, including such unusual destinations as Swaziland, but the entries are too brief to cover such radically different cultures.

In 1972 James Morris underwent a sex change operation, the culmination of a process begun in 1964. She recounted the history of this decision in her autobiographical *Conundrum,* published in 1974 under her new name, Jan Morris. The unprecedented recognition–and certain negative reactions–her account received from critics and public derived from Morris's characteristic ability to analyze her personal life and decision to become a woman physically, with honesty and comprehensiveness. She makes some sweeping comments about British boys' schools, for instance, that caused controversy; and she argues for a definition of gender that is not accepted by many people.

In *Travels* (1976) Morris continues the project begun in *Places* of exploring sites within the fading British Empire. The eleven essays in the book often involve historical topics, such as the travels of Ibn Batuta, a fourteenth-century Arab travel writer; Canadian railway travel in the 1920s; and nineteenth-century guidebook commentary. In these essays Morris merges cultural history with contemporary travel writing and indicates the diverse ways people have experienced travel.

Intended to mark the 500th anniversary of the founding of the Oxford University Press, *The Oxford Book of Oxford* (1978), edited by Morris, comprises eyewitness accounts of the university from its founding to 1945. With concise commentary, Morris links the extracts from several hundred authors, which discuss themes such as town-and-gown fights, the vagaries of class distinction, and peculiar college rituals.

Destinations: Essays from Rolling Stone (1980) is Morris's most incisive and independent statement as a writer. Its language is confident and fluent, while its perspective is the most combative and well defined among her writings. In these essays she achieves an independence that enables a more critical perspective. No longer considering herself a mere travel reporter, Morris often takes a decidedly oppositional stance, creating tension between subject and writer that challenges preconceptions of place, culture, and political reputation.

A prime example of this new approach is "The Morning After," the essay on Washington, D.C., wherein she establishes at the outset a critical dichotomy between herself and her subject. Noting that the mayor of Washington, D.C., is Mayor Washington, the treasurer of the White House Correspondence Association is Edgar A. Poe, and the doorkeeper of the House of Representatives is William (Fish Bait) Miller, she comments:

> A concomitant of power is the privilege of eccentricity, and though in recent years Americans may have pined for rulers of more orthodox method, still to visitors from smaller and less potent states an early intimation of quirk is more a comfort than a threat–the gods make their victims mad, but their favorites unconventional.

Morris establishes from the beginning of the collection a new, more polemical approach. No longer the quasi-anonymous Baedeker traveler of *Venice,* she instead insinuates herself into the locale, becoming the anomalous outsider, the visitor "from smaller and less potent states."

Along with this new point of view is a leaner, less forgiving, more cutting prose, less concerned with how natives regard her than with how the cultural locale has affected her. In a description of residential streets in the fashionable Georgetown section of Washington, D.C., she writes that "Georgetown is an innocent exterior disguising an immensely worldly, not to say tigerish community." She finds the homes "poky, inconvenient and unbeautiful," but she senses a "rich inner glue of common interest and influence" that pulls them together, forming "wings of some awkwardly dismembered mansion." Morris does not care for huge bureaucracies, especially those of world powers. Washington–immensely powerful, systemically corrupt, unresponsive to ordinary people–incites Morris. Her ideal is Wales, which represents for Morris all that is positive about the pre–Cold War era (innocence, tradition, and natural connectedness). Washington inspires her writing: she deftly defines the character of a people by observing what they have done with their private and collective environments.

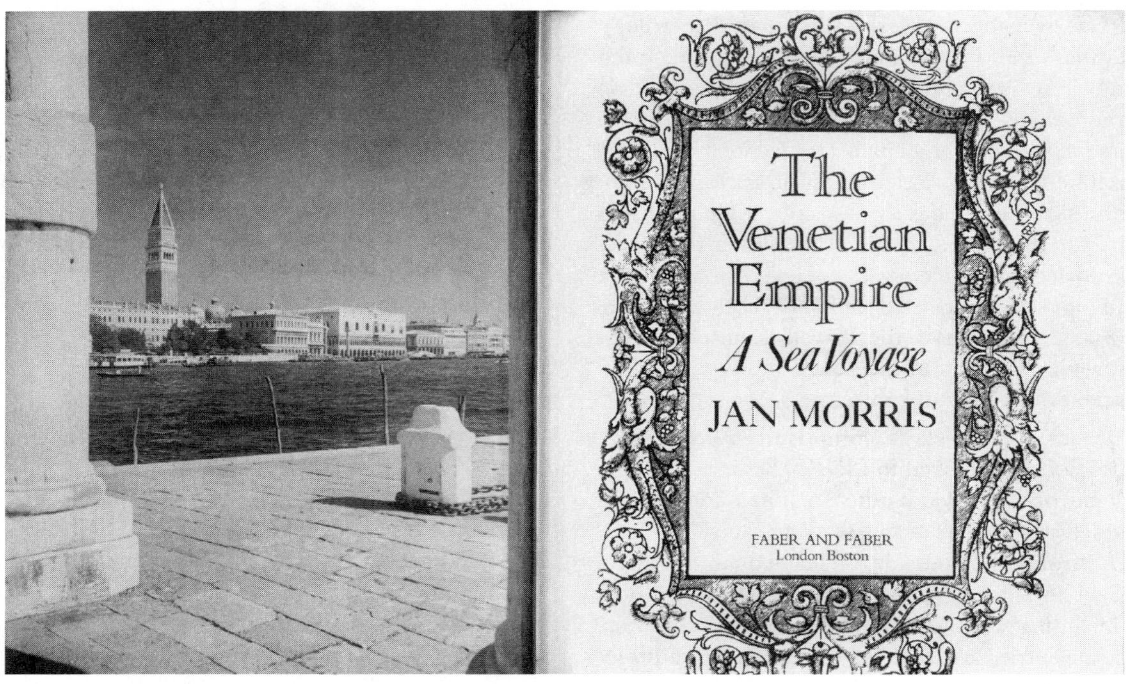

Frontispiece by Olive Cook/Saffron Waldon and title page for Morris's 1980 history of Venice

In *Destinations,* Morris substitutes insightful general impressions at the expense of her instinct for investigative reporting; however, her purpose is not to disclose specifics but to reveal the implications of personal observation. In "Mrs. Gupta Never Rang," her essay on India, Morris describes a highly nuanced tension between the individual traveler and the world, but the occasional hasty conclusion creeps in. Explaining the lack of response by passersby to a large red boil on her nose, for example, she at first ascribes it to tact, but then concludes, "They *really* did not notice. They thought my face quite normal. For what is a passing grotesquerie, in a land of deformities?"

"An Imperial Specimen," the essay on Panama, is less insightful, as Morris does not comment significantly on U.S. political involvement in that country; however, her close scrutiny of individuals and groups is occasionally brilliant, as when she muses on the "American pride of achievement" that she finds among the Americans in the Canal Zone: "This gives the Zone community a very old-fashioned, almost touching air, a nostalgic assertion of myth that is a kind of mirror image of Panamanian aspirations across the border–the one people hungering for a chimerical fulfillment, the other pining for a half-legendary past." Although Morris does comment on the political history of U.S. intervention in Panama and the strategic significance that the Canal Zone had for U.S. military domination of Latin America, she is more interested in recording general impressions of what she recognizes as an anachronistic outpost of imperialism. The reader may wish that in *Destinations* Morris had mustered her instincts for international journalism and written the sort of investigative reportage of third-world countries that launched her career; however, she remains the hesitant outsider rather than the independent investigator.

Los Angeles seems to fascinate Morris. In "The Know-How City" she describes how she enjoys the freeways of Los Angeles much more than British motorways, finding something quintessentially Californian about them. Her descriptions at times wax poetic, as when she calls the freeways "the city's grandest and most exciting artifacts." She continues: "Snaky, sinuous, undulating, high on stilts or sink in cuttings, they are like so many concrete tentacles, winding themselves around each block, each district, burrowing, evading, clambering, clasping every corner of the metropolis as if they are squeezing it all together to make the parts stick." In general, the cityscape of Los Angeles coaxes figurative language from Morris–"The civic landmarks of L.A., such as they are, display themselves conveniently for you, the pattern of the place unfolds until, properly briefed by the experience, the time comes for you to unlock from the system, undo your safety belt, and take the right-hand lane into the everyday life below." Her response to the vagaries of southern California lifestyles is enthusiastic and exploratory, as though, appreciating the ambience more than understanding it, she is drawn by what is different.

Perhaps the most penetrating analyses in *Destinations* are in her paired essays, "The Siege States," on South Africa and Rhodesia. In "Black, White and Fantasy in South Africa," Morris confronts the complexities of apartheid, going further than most of her white contemporaries in eliciting the private and public disclosures of a culture living in denial. She works with a special eye for the obscure and tentative, making subtle observations that at times seem novelistic. Her description of the exuberant, though unrealistic, mood soon after the Xhosa Republic of the Transkei was declared an independent state is typical:

> Not a single country in the world has recognized the independence of the Transkei, on the grounds that it is no more than a political fraud, a trick of apartheid. Yet in some ways it is *true*. . . . Black men throng all the bars, ordering quarts where pints were once the measure, and a heady feeling of liberation really does brighten little Umtata, the new capital. National flags fly all over the place, Transkeian Army officers stump about in unexpected uniforms; from his fine new hilltop mansion, the Prime Minister . . . makes encouraging declarations about freedom, cooperation and South African generosity.

The descriptions of black youth are often appreciative; Morris enjoys their company and listens to what they have to say. Aware of the centrality of black youth movements within the South African political struggle, she captures their varied voices, if not always their individuality.

Morris's treatment of South Africa has limitations. Her careful and ample discussion of Afrikaner mentality, cultural and political history, for example, is not juxtaposed with an equally full discussion of the attitudes and heritage of indigenous Africans. Generally, Morris seems content with recording offhanded remarks from blacks about their social history and her main focus is on the European struggle for empire.

In "The Stage-City," her article on London, Morris demonstrates a fine ability to capture the fleeting moment. She can concisely epitomize a particular place or urban circumstance through selective observation, conveyed in well-constructed sentences. Of the wealthy Arabs who have "colonized" London, she writes, "they seem a kind of dour unity, as Europeans once appeared to them, from the black-veiled ladies silent in the dentist's waiting room to the plump, small boys in expensive grey flannel ogling the shopgirls at Selfridge's, or . . . the princelings, perfectly at ease in their beautiful tweeds, who offer . . . slinky half-smiles in hotel lobbies."

Her idiosyncratic and complex response in "Behind the Pyramids," the essay on Cairo, presents a striking picture of an ancient city moving toward the twenty-first century. Sympathetic to Arab aspirations, Morris grants Egyptians space to be themselves and explain themselves. Moreover, her knowledge of Egyptian political and class struggles is impressive, helped by her early years in residence in the British army and news bureaus.

In 1980 Morris published two books. In *My Favourite Stories of Wales,* Morris offers an anthology suitable for adults as well as children, with an appreciative introduction. *The Venetian Empire: A Sea Voyage* profiles the imperial years of the Republic of Venice, the twelfth through eighteenth centuries. More a travel guide than chronicle of the empire, it describes the varied peoples ruled by Venice, the enemies of Venice–chiefly the Ottoman Turks–and the demise of the republic under Napoleon. Morris draws close parallels with the British Empire, which also depended upon ruling the sea.

Edited and introduced by Morris, *The Stones of Venice* (1981) is an abridgment of John Ruskin's 1853 work. Morris's continuing fascination with Venice also inspired *A Venetian Bestiary* (1982), a short volume about animals in that city, accompanied by seventy-seven illustrations drawn from historical artwork and contemporary photographs.

In *The Spectacle of Empire: Style, Effect and the Pax Britannica* (1982), Morris returns to the theme of Britain's nineteenth-century colonial grandeur that she had treated earlier in the *Pax Britannica* trilogy. Here she attempts a much more subjective, experiential treatment of the subject by relating history through an extremely detailed and photographic descriptiveness. The result is a travel narrative through time, an imaginative evocation of life under British colonialism. Although this ambitious topic has interest, it comes with built-in limitations. Morris is basing much of her visual impressions on photographs of the period, and such an approach depends upon preconceptions and a stereotyping of the past. Still, Morris's historical understanding of the visual environment is impressive. Her sensibility and knowledge as a foreign journalist enable thoughtful meditations on the European colonialist world. These reflections are given more immediacy by the use of the first person plural:

> There it lies to port now, the generic Imperial Island, and though it may be steaming and fretted in the equatorial heat, or bundled against the Atlantic cold, still it looks, as we approach the lighthouse on its harbour mole, unmistakably disciplined . . . from the yard-arm of the flagpole above the Custom House . . . the Union Jack flies as a guarantee of common-sense and punctual meal-times.

Afrikaner woman preparing to defend her home, an illustration for an article by Morris collected in her 1980 book, Destinations: Essays from Rolling Stone *(photograph by Alon Reininger/Contact)*

Such subjectivity, of course, allies fiction with nonfiction.

The Spectacle of Empire represents an attempt at the cultural study of nostalgia. Morris's thematic presupposition that "splendour worked" in maintaining the British Empire is offered to the reader early in the book. As in her earlier *Pax Britannica* trilogy, in *The Spectacle of Empire* Morris opens herself to criticism for apparently sentimentalizing the colonial era and neglecting the viewpoints of indigenous populations. Morris generally remains silent on subject peoples, occasionally implying complicity or parenthetically quoting famous leaders, such as Jawaharlal Nehru, who is quoted as calling the "overweening extravagance" of the British rule "vulgar ostentation." Moreover, Morris seldom qualifies her statements about collective memory; for example, the colonialists who traveled first class may have seen the old railway stations as orderly and neat, but not the natives, who were largely relegated to the chaos and squalor of third class.

Morris accepts the truism that colonialism depended on the colonizers' promotion of spectacle and style to impress native people, ignoring other explanations for colonialist high style, such as that elaborate pomp and circumstance were exercises in self-flattery. Still, Morris's portrayals of nineteenth-century British officials and their families, European entrepreneurs and bureaucrats, are often critical and insightful. Although critics generally commented favorably on the book, Jamie James, in a review for *The Nation* (13 November 1982), called Morris's project too ambitious and the book only "a serviceable sketch" of the "seductive romanticism of its imagery."

Paul Wakefield's evocative photographs are primary in the short book *Wales: The First Place* for which Morris contributes a sensitive commentary on the beauty of her country. In *Stones of Empire: The Buildings of the Raj* (1983), she examines British architecture in India and Pakistan, particularly Sir Bartle Frere's designs. Morris's appreciative presentation of late-nineteenth-century civic buildings further demonstrates her interest in the imperialist image of itself. While occasionally critical of the British colonial presence, Morris remains fascinated by the grandeur of its public buildings, avoiding deeper explorations of how colonialized people may have perceived such undertakings and how British planners may have wanted such buildings to be perceived.

In *The Matter of Wales: Epic Views of a Small Country* (1984), Morris moves decidedly further toward an exploratory merging of cultural memory and physical setting. For Morris, an exposition of Wales cannot begin with the conventional narrative form of the travel essay. "I see it [the book] not as a continuum," she writes, "but timeless, one kind of Welshness blurring into another, one influence absorbed into the next, the whole bound together, often unconsciously, by the age, strength, and fascination of the Welsh tradition, and the spell of the Welsh landscape." Morris uses the tradition of Owain Glyndwr (Owen Glendower), heroic rebel against English domination, as a "symbolic index."

In practice, however, the Glyndwr references become only one of many devices through which Morris handles the formidable task of the book. Her chapters include an initial meditation on the geography and natural environment of Wales, an extensive history of the Welsh as a people always adjusting to foreign dominance, chapters on religious practices and the mental world, reflections on the national character, a chapter on resistance movements through the centuries, a description of Welsh emigration patterns, and chapters on Welsh architectural and technological development. Throughout the main text, Morris juxtaposes quotations that explain or challenge traditional notions of Wales and the Welsh. Her wide use of Welsh terms and phrases adds to the sense of particularity of the book, but she avoids alienating the non-Welsh reader by the thoughtful clarity of their references and with a special preface on the language. In this book, Morris successfully defies categorization, mingling the genres of travel writing, history, and cultural study.

Apparent throughout *Wales* is Morris's ability to find the significant feature of a locale and define its character. Perhaps more self-referential in this book than in any other of her travel works, she frames the journey with the stated goal of exploring "corners . . . insidiously Welsh." The chapters are not just about landscape; they depict a Welsh person recovering her roots.

Typically creative in her approach to the particularities of culture, Morris meticulously informs the reader of the many types of traditional animals, livestock, and pets in Wales. Typical also is Morris's use of listing to create ambience through the spectacle of everyday details. Her list of merchandise in the Abergavenny market juxtaposes people and farm produce in such a way as to create a poignant specificity of place:

> Twelve pounds of gleaming Usk salmon lies in the window of Vin Sullivan's, the posh food store, along with laver bread from the coast, potatoes from Dyfed, Brazilian papaws and East African chillis; people peer over one another's shoulders at the property announcements in J. Straker Chadwick's–Magnificent Livestock Farm, 1000 Yards Both Bank Fishing, Lovely Position But in Need of Improvement, Well-Restored Georgian Country House. . . . the saddler's in Cross Street is busy with breezy women buying snaffles; farmers in pairs inspect the second-hand volkswagens in the yard at Whittall Williams'.

Another use of listing is the full catalogue of Welsh castles in the chapter "Building Wales," which shows the centrality of ancient buildings in the culture. Each castle is introduced through its designated epithet, which Morris devises: the most brutal (Chepstow); the most astonishing (Caerphilly); the most insensitive; the nastiest, jolliest, silliest, and so on. The accompanying comments on each castle, brief and flippant for the most part, interpret the ancient edifices in common travelogue parlance; this highly personalized response situates them in their modern environments.

The ability to discern and interpret the subtler points of culture (and cultural difference) within a fluent, often wry, sentence marks Morris as a supremely confident writer. Thus, her encapsulation of an English residential section outside Monmouth is: "Delectably encouched in their gardens the little villas lie, trellised, rose-embowered, with lazy fat Labradors lying on their verandahs, reached by nooky lanes and given authentic Ooty names (Cedars, Rosedale, Lilac Cottage, or Mountain Home). Far, far away is the jabber of the natives!" Such ironic constructions run throughout the chapters. Morris's superb narrative prose creates the intimacy necessary in a genre that deals with the unfamiliar. Often such descriptions are vivid profiles of an event or social interaction, such as the brief anecdote about some Welsh people on a bus excursion, the various neatly defined individuals and groups suddenly united in choral harmony en route.

Morris's forceful characterizations are achieved through her ability to pick up on telling snippets of private dialogue, as in the "all-but-English businessmen" in the pubs, who scoff at the Welsh language but add, "Though mind you, I'm as good a Welshman as any one of them. . . ." In such profiles she emphasizes a strong theme of the book, the contemporary chauvinism and cultural dominance threatening Wales. Cultural and political intrusions are recorded throughout *Wales,* such as the tank gunnery range of the British and German armies in Castlemain. Morris's critical tone takes on a clarity at such moments, as she writes,"Such sadnesses, such squalours, such wasted loyalties!" She continues, "Historically Wales is doomed to be a satellite of England. . . ."

The historical narratives in *Wales,* which blend local description with vignettes of history, are among her most vivid. In "Holy Country," Morris melds place, incident, and religious history from Celtic Christianity to Methodism in a concisely readable style. Her discussions of church polity, differences in creed, and the social struggles underlying them are masterful.

The cement of the book is Morris's personal involvement with her subject, in a way that approaches the confessional:

> And not just Wales today, either, but all of the once-and-future kingdom glides within the parish of my care. Not an episode I have described in these pages but I have felt some part of me tugged into participation . . . whether it be at the soup kitchens of Maerdy or beneath the castle walls of Harlech. I am all Wales in one!

Morris thus presents herself as a living example of Wales through her personal identification with the landscapes and people of her home.

Although praising *Wales* overall, Geraint H. Jenkins, who reviewed the book for the *TLS* (1 March 1985), found it "untidy, digressive, and maddening." While such charges have some validity, Morris's indirection in Wales was deliberate, as she attempted a method more subjective and evocative than standard travel prose. The book is illustrated with black-and-white photographs by Paul Wakefield that present lonely, barren landscapes, and ethereal images that recall German romantic painting in their moodiness and heavy chiaroscuro.

In her introduction to *Journeys* (1984), Morris describes the book as a "mystery tour" of diverse places, all visited in the early 1980s. Collected from original publications as various as *The Times* (London) newspaper, the magazines *Connoisseur, Encounter, Texas Monthly,* and most especially *Rolling Stone*, these essays are good examples of her later tone and writing style. Her fifth anthology of travel essays, their completion elicited a brief epilogue of personal closure from Morris: "I bring to fulfillment a jejune ambition–to have seen and described, before I died, the whole of the urban world."

Morris maintains a critical tone in *Journeys,* expressing her dislike for the European Common Market, for driving imported cars, and for commuting across the most populous and prosperous part of England. In "Not So Far," an account of a short trip on the Continent, Morris adopts the persona of a mainstream Briton, anxiously driving on the motorways, mistreated by jaundiced customs officials, herded onto a channel boat, part of the indistinguishable load of tourists.

Morris seems to regret the social realities of late-twentieth-century consumerism and multinational capitalism, and she strives, with difficulty, to escape its manifestations, finding that France has been strangely changed by its sudden prosperity, while Switzerland no longer represents the placid retreat of bygone years. Morris's metaphors remain vivid: of 1980s Geneva, she writes, "It suggests to me one huge airport lounge, sleepless, dissatisfied, inhabited by world-weary duty-free concessionaires and slightly jet-lagged transients, coming and going night and day in a time-zone haze beside the lovely lake."

Structurally, "Not So Far" retains a nimble conciseness, as Morris bounces from one country to another, profiling and critiquing. Morris uses a technique of focusing on minor or fleeting instances to describe the whole. Thus, the slickness of Venice's renaissance of tourism and economic activity is encapsulated in the reference to how the famous bronze horses of St. Mark's were replaced with inferior plastic replicas.

Although capable of seeing the negatives within radically different cultures, Morris nevertheless enjoys her self-orchestrated confrontations with otherness. For instance, in "Fun City," the chapter on Las Vegas, Morris is highly anecdotal about the fantasy culture of American consumerism. When a fellow guest gives her "a little souvenir of my visit," she finds it to be a photograph of a sculpture: "It showed a naked girl of total innocence sleeping side by side with an adorable little fawn, and it was called 'The Dream.' 'Kinky postcards, huh?' said a man looking over my shoulder." Morris presents such moments with little or no comment, allowing her readers to interpret the people and situations.

Michael Leapman, in the *New Statesman* (25 January 1985), praised *Journeys* for this critical approach: "Starting with the superficial, Ms. Morris penetrates, layer by layer, to the often ugly truth." Morris's method is more indirect than blatant, more minimalist than meticulous. With seeming effortlessness, she incorporates keen observation and selectivity, always, however, avoiding interpretive voice-overs.

Running throughout the essays in *Journeys* is a balanced critical perspective, maintained, sometimes gingerly, to allow natives the space to be themselves. This balance, however, does not prevent Morris from probing her subjects' cultural ambiguities. She notices, for instance, that adult theaters and bookstores are outlawed in Fun City and that the suburbs of this gambling center reflect the "wholesome conformity" of bourgeois values. Morris usually balances such explorations, however, with admiring apologetics–"Las Vegas really does contain a decent enough western town within it, struggling to get out, at least to reveal or fulfill itself."

In *Journeys,* Morris establishes mood through an imaginative selection of images and events that convey the deeper colors of location in brief vignettes. Thus, the description of a train approaching Beijing station in "A Chinese Journey" is both succinct and factual, evoking subjective dimensions of character. She writes:

> With a triumphant blast of its whistle it came majestically to Beijing, the three engineers in their cab sitting there like a trio of admirals on a flagship bridge, and the waiting people clapped, and cheered, and waved newspapers, as the doors opened and from Mongolia or Siberia, Omsk or Moscow itself, their travel-worn loved ones fell home into China.

Morris seems most at home in third-world or other impoverished settings where the marginalized and disadvantaged inspire her poetic muse. Such moments elicit poignant observations and associations. A poor Mexican American family bathe themselves in the holy soil within the *santuario* (sanctuary) of a small church in Chimayo, New Mexico. The pilgrims wash in the soil as if it were water, covering their bodies with handfuls,

> The father gravely reverent, the mother shy but happy, and the little boy on his knees enthusiastically disregarding the injunction on the wall that says PLEASE

> DO NOT THROW HOLY DIRT OUTSIDE THE HOLE. They smiled at me with a kind of confidential ecstasy; as if to imply that we at least, the lucky four of us, whatever went on in that crisscross town below, knew where to scoop the simple truth.

Morris's empathy for those on the bottom of society allows such moments of connectedness, defying the "corrosions of tourism."

In *Journeys,* expressions of longings for bygone days when consumer culture and commercial tourism were less prevalent often appear at the end of chapters, becoming self-disclosures. For example, at the conclusion of "A Visit to Barchester," Morris comments, "Atavist though I am, yearning sometimes for the austerity of Wales, for some of the gorgeous and heedless assurance . . . nostalgic in this way for the England I am just old enough to remember, I miss the purple swagger and swank." Morris ends with a general assessment of the traveler's dilemma–the quest for the holy grail of the imagination proves anticlimactic: "For it was partly the conceit of it, Trollope's hubris of the cloth, that captured our imaginations once–now gone it seems, for better or for worse, as utterly from Barchester as from Simla or Singapore." Herein lies a major tension within Morris's writing. While at times iconoclastic, to the point of alienating traditionalists of all stripes, she remains a self-described "atavist," longing for a vanished past.

In "Houston, U.S.A.," in commenting on the conformist atmosphere of that Texas city, Morris attempts a modest reference to her political sensibilities: "and for myself, as an anti-nuclear neutralist, animal liberationist, Welsh nationalist and aspiring anarchist, I am seldom altogether at ease with the stern Free World exhortations of the Houston *Post* or *Chronicle.*" Rather than venture into explicit political discussion, however, she merely provides the reader with this list of political labels.

Among the Cities (1985) includes selections from Morris's five previous travel essay collections. Published between 1956 and 1984, they are wide-ranging in time and geography. The author's fascination with cities stems from her lifelong quest for difference, as she remarks in her introduction: "living as I myself always have deep in the countryside, it is above all among the cities . . . that my long journey took me."

The novel *Last Letters from Hav* (1985) draws upon Morris's travel experience commissioned by the magazine *New Gotham* and presents a series of travel letters from a fictional city in the eastern Mediterranean. The book received overwhelming praise; although a first novel, it was nominated for the prestigious Booker Prize in Britain. In "Itchy Feet and Pencils: A Symposium," published in *The New York Times Book Review* (18 August 1991), Morris writes, "It always seemed to me that if I led a more domestic life, I would have probably have become a writer of fiction, of more normal fiction, more obvious fiction."

After *Scotland: The Place of Visions* (1986), a brief pictorial work featuring the evocative photographs of Paul Wakefield, came the highly original experiment in writing a travel monograph on a particular decade and place, *Manhattan '45* (1987). Of the title, Morris has commented (in *American Heritage,* July 1987) "it sounded partly like a kind of gun, and partly like champagne, and thus matched the victorious and celebratory theme of my book." Exploring a city fast emerging as a world center at a critical turn in modern history, Morris combines history and geography, cultural studies and personal responses, an approach familiar to her readers. However, by defining the essence of a particular year–really the mid 1940s–she must explore the relatively difficult subject of zeitgeist without the advantage of chronological narrative as preparation. Only a few writers, such as David Halberstam in *The Fifties* (1993), have attempted similar studies.

Something of the minimalist's approach is evident in Morris's chapters, which are not arranged to cover a theme, but to profile it and to contribute to an overall impression of a city in a particular time. Thus, her chapters "On Style" and "On System" deal with the particularities of how New York organizes itself for living, but what she attempts is not so much an explication of how things work in a big city, but how and why New Yorkers create a certain style and rhythm. The chapters "On Race" and "On Class" show impressionistically the uniquely heterogeneous characteristics of a city that, in 1945, had just gained the title "Capital of the World, the future site of the United Nations."

The reader learns in the acknowledgments that *Manhattan '45* is really a labor of love for Morris. In the prologue Morris writes that she is intrigued by the permanence of a city that is never finished, but even this confession has within it contradictions–"But looking back now on the splendid relaxation of 1945, it seems that just for a spell the city *was* finished, *was* staying the same, as it contemplated its new status in the world and breathed the long sigh of victory."

According to Morris, *Manhattan '45* is an "outsider's book," not because she is an outsider, but because it is "about the public rather than the private city." The work succeeds by remaining with the surfaces, like the best journalistic photography, conjuring inner realities by creating images from the surface of things. After the innovative explorations of *Wales,* Morris is well equipped for such impressionist pursuits. She is fully aware, however, that to create compelling

View from the Welsh mountains; photograph by Paul Wakefield in Morris's The Matter Of Wales: Epic Views Of A Small Country *(1984)*

impressions and to capture the mood and heart of a time and place, she must avoid generalities and stick with specifics. Her background preparation is, typically, impressive. Morris's prodigious research, culled from special collections in Manhattan, anchor the chapters in historical fact and contemporary opinion. The real strength of the book depends upon Morris's brilliant visual sense, her ear for dialogue and telling phrases, and the interjection of illuminating personal responses.

Literary quotations are used amply and cogently, such as Cyril Connolly's description of Rockefeller Center as "the sinister Stonehenge of economic man," followed by his comment on Manhattan in general as "concrete Capri." Local names gain special focus. Morris's adroit use of onomastics enhances the sense of place and indicates the local pride in naming and nicknaming familiar sites. For example, in "On Class," the derivative upper-middle-class ostentation of Manhattan is revealed through a list of private apartment building names on the Upper East and West Sides: Majestic, Embassy, Chatsworth, Trianon, Kenilworth, Kipling Arms, St. Rita, and so on. Also specially featured are abundant notes, which introduce related details and further digressions. One footnote in "On Pleasure," for example, documents the longevity of Rockette chorus girls (some not retiring until they were past sixty) and describes their dormitories in Radio City Music Hall.

Morris's concern for the minutia of urban mass culture indicates an underlying thesis: that New York has been the capital of twentieth-century mass culture, raising it to prominence even before the city invented pop art. In fact, Morris has consistently shown a fondness for popular forms of expression. Her use of statistics on the conditions of New York poor in 1945 is incisive, and it reveals the contrasting undercurrents of social inequality within the finance capital of the world.

No group is exempt from Morris's empathy, however. Her presentation of the public response to Wall

Street financiers shows a certain tolerance for the gusto of the wealthy, as do her vivid descriptions of banking executives residing in their opulent financial houses. In treating the more venal element of New York, in fact, Morris's openness and urge toward inclusiveness at times lead to an uncritical, seemingly naive attitude. Similarly, the treatment of New York's high society lacks a certain critical perspective and lapses into vagueness at times.

On the other hand, in *Manhattan '45* Morris demonstrates an acute visual sense not without cultural discernment. She describes an "extremely churchy Episcopalian church, here a stupendously club-like club, and far down to the south, beyond the end of the avenue, rises the distant raggety cluster of towers, spike-topped, pyramidical, slim or hefty, which is the downtown financial district." In "On Style" buildings are shown to match the lifestyle and pace of the city. Noting that the early skyscrapers were regarded with quasi-religious reverence, with nicknames such as "the Cathedral of the Skies" (the Empire State Building), and "the Cathedral of Commerce" (the Woolworth Building), and that the lighting was kept appropriately low and reverent in their public spaces, below gargoyles and other features of religiosity, Morris relates such instances of ocular ambience to the milieu of 1945: "All in all it was an architecture simultaneously fanciful, swanky and strong, and as such it perfectly suited the mood of Manhattan in victory."

The meticulous method of the writer's earlier travel studies is well matched in *Manhattan '45;* the sheer size and diversity of the city supply much material for an impressive selection of cultural detail, ranging from the types of trolley repair vehicles to the distinct smell of New York books in the shops. Overall, Morris succeeds at unfolding the formidable panoramas of the city, and where she falls short, she admits her limitations, as when she acknowledges in a footnote the shallowness of most white responses to the Harlem of the 1940s.

In *Manhattan '45,* Morris establishes a tension between conventional conceptions of early postwar New York and the city that she herself has experienced. The city of the 1940s had changed vastly by the 1980s, when Morris was writing her book, and part of the understanding of place results from the ongoing tension between past and present. Intruding into the historical research is a traveler, Morris, who tests the statements of the popular chronicles and urban legends, bringing a later judgment based on firsthand experience. The result is a document of change, of social transformation, as well as a portrait of a particular time and place.

Morris's second venture into autobiography, *Pleasures of a Tangled Life* (1989), is more frank and reflective than her first autobiography, *Conundrum.* Again, the general response was sharply divided; negative reviewers criticized her forthright explanation of her decision to undergo a sex change operation. However, Martin J. Hudacs in *Library Journal* (15 October 1989) observed, "The memories here are in random order, but the style and vivid imagery that have won Morris acclaim . . . are evident."

Morris continued to be a prolific writer in a variety of genres. *City to City* (1990), a short collection of travel essays on Canada originally commissioned by the Toronto magazine *Saturday Night,* was followed by the brief pictorial work, *Ireland, Your Only Place* (1990), which continues Morris's collaboration with the photographer Paul Wakefield. A sense of the past predominates in her next travel book, *Sydney* (1992). Australia's frontier origins are evident beneath the city's urbanity.

Another anthology of essays, *O Canada!* (1992), presents ten cities, from St. John's to Vancouver. In the introduction, Morris admits a critical tone, and her comments on Canadian urban life are often frank and irreverent. For example, she finds Ottawa a panoply of architectural clichés.

The title of Morris's next collection of travel essays, *Locations* (1992), suggests the art of film, and the essays are, in a sense, scripted. Morris arrives at each place about which she writes in *Locations* with a stated set of preconceptions (always particular and developed) that establish a tense relationship between what she expects to find and what she discovers. She thus leaves room for being surprised, shocked, fascinated, or disappointed. Often what she documents are interpersonal contacts. "Vermont" reconfirms her view that it is, in fact, a quite un-American place, in spite of the Norman Rockwell scenes that she finds there.

Morris astutely discerns the laconic and curmudgeonly tendencies of native Vermonters, saying that "they are totally untouched by the cosmetic veneer of contemporary American convention (the instant sincerity, the compulsory smile." She fails to notice, however, the many Americans from elsewhere (particularly New York City and Boston artists and intellectuals) who have claimed Vermont as their own. Nor is she bothered by the development of the tourist and leisure industries in Vermont small towns, markedly more advanced than in other northern New England states. This is surprising for Morris, who usually shuns beaten trails and disclaims any desire to promote local tourist franchises.

One of the few third-world settings described in *Locations* is Oaxaca, Mexico. There Morris

> realized (not for the first time) the fantastic nature of these Spanish colonial towns. In no other modern

> empire was building done with such ebullient sophistication at such remote and improbable sites. The British built no Oaxaca in India, the French created nothing so exquisite in Indo-China. And we must look to the dominions of the ancients . . . to find a civilization recreating itself with similar art and craftsmanship in foreign parts.

Nostalgic yearnings pervade these essays, a regret for old values represented in older landscapes and traditional social interactions. In the essay "London," for example, Morris juxtaposes the spirit of commitment and sacrifice evident in the Churchill War Cabinet rooms (of "amateur and comradely order") to the "usual gaping crowds" at London tourist sites. The rituals at Buckingham Palace still attract enormous crowds, but their significance as "an organic part of the life of the city" is gone, Morris finds.

In the essay "Glasgow" she recognizes positive social change in her astute assessment of the successful elimination of the notorious Gorbals, the crime-ridden slum areas of the city. "Life wasn't all statues in Glasgow's Victorian prime," she writes, "when social contrasts were fearful and many of those picturesque tenements were among the worst slums in Europe." Certainly, Morris's economic and cultural analyses of the cities she visits are discerning. Her discussion of the anomalous nature of San Francisco is a case in point. Shaken by the capabilities of the modern U.S. military as displayed in Operation Desert Shield, Morris finds a happy contrast in the city: "I find here older aspects of the American genius, like tolerance, and quirk, and gentlemanliness, and kindness, and a touch of the rapscallion lazy." While Morris may yearn for the older, more orderly and genteel days as she envisions them, her real love is the freedom of lifestyle and thought represented in the kindly and magnanimous identity of San Francisco, home of the flower children and social nonconformity. At such personal discoveries or rediscoveries, she can become uncommonly humorous: "SUCKS TO RUDE U.S. IMMIGRATION OFFICERS, I wrote on a wall as I walked back to the hotel that night. . . . Well, I didn't actually. But another couple of days in San Francisco, and I might have." Morris's special affection for Los Angeles and San Francisco may result from their embodiment of tolerance, from their potential freedom from social strictures, qualities that, paradoxically, Morris also finds in traditional rural Wales.

Morris's prose is vivid, clear, and rife with inner spectacle and narrative exposition. She moves successfully beyond established literary genres to encompass the travel essay, cultural and social history, narrative, and description. Morris has always avoided opinionated or tendentious essays, yet her style has evolved constantly throughout her career, from more impersonal to more personal. Morris's gender change may have influenced a more personal approach; however, other factors may have contributed to a more intimate style, such as writing for progressive publications; and the rise of postmodern relativism in the 1970s and 1980s, which has encouraged more particular responses.

Easily recognizable is the writer's penchant for integrating ample historical detail with her travel narrative. While such an approach is certainly not unique among British travel writers–authors as diverse as H. V. Morton and John Prebble have incorporated lengthy historical anecdotes into their texts–Morris seeks an uncommonly intimate connection between historical fact and personal observation. With roots in international journalism, which requires historical and cultural exposition to acquaint readers with situational developments, Morris has regarded history as "an essential part of good travel writing." Dervla Murphy's comment, in her review of *Locations* for the *TLS* (23 October 1992), may be extended to all of Jan Morris's writing: "One does not need to have a prior interest in the places she writes about to enjoy her apparently effortless virtuosity."

Reference:

David Holden, "James and Jan," *New York Times Magazine* (17 March 1974): 18–19.

Dervla Murphy

(28 November 1931 –)

Carol Huebscher Rhoades

BOOKS: *Full Tilt: Ireland to India with a Bicycle* (London: Murray, 1965; New York: Dutton, 1965);

Tibetan Foothold (London: Murray, 1966; New York: Transatlantic Arts, 1966);

The Waiting Land: A Spell in Nepal (London: Murray, 1967; New York: Transatlantic Arts, 1968);

In Ethiopia with a Mule (London: Murray, 1968);

On a Shoestring to Coorg: An Experience of South India (London: Murray, 1976; Woodstock, N.Y.: Overlook, 1989);

Where the Indus Is Young: A Winter in Baltistan (London: Murray, 1977);

A Place Apart (London: Murray, 1978);

Wheels within Wheels (London: Murray, 1979; New Haven: Ticknor & Fields, 1980);

Race to the Finish: The Nuclear Stakes (London: Murray, 1981); republished as *Nuclear Stakes: Race to the Finish* (New Haven & New York: Ticknor & Fields, 1982);

Eight Feet in the Andes (London: Murray, 1983; Woodstock, N.Y.: Overlook, 1986);

Changing the Problem: Post-Forum Reflections (Gigginstown, Mullingar, Ireland: Lilliput, 1984);

Muddling through in Madagascar (London: Murray, 1985; Woodstock, N.Y.: Overlook, 1989);

Ireland, text by Murphy and photographs by Klaus Francke (London: Orbis, 1985);

Tales from Two Cities: Race Relations in Britain (London: Murray, 1987);

Cameroon with Egbert (London: Murray, 1989; Woodstock, N.Y.: Overlook, 1990);

Transylvania and Beyond (London: Murray, 1992; Woodstock, N.Y.: Overlook, 1993);

The Ukimwi Road: From Kenya to Zimbabwe (London: Murray, 1993; Woodstock, N.Y.: Overlook, 1995);

South from the Limpopo: Travels through South Africa (London: Murray, 1997);

Visiting Rwanda (Dublin: Lilliput, 1998);

One Foot in Laos (London: Murray, 1999).

Dervla Murphy (photograph by Tara Heinemann)

SELECTED PERIODICAL PUBLICATIONS–UNCOLLECTED: "Mannas from Heaven," *Cornhill,* 175 (Spring 1966): 175–181;

"Unease in Addis Ababa," *Cornhill,* 176 (Spring 1968): 349–358;

"In a Half-Forgotten Corner," *Blackwood's,* 313 (January 1973): 52–64;

"The Brighter Side of 'Black Amid,'" *Blackwood's,* 313 (March 1973): 248–255;

"The Loves of Isabella Bird Bishop," *Blackwood's,* 314 (November 1973): 385–395;

"Leaves from a South Indian Diary," *Blackwood's,* 316 (August 1974): 97–112;

"The Mound of the Dead," *Blackwood's,* 318 (December 1975): 500–514;

"A Taste of California," *Blackwood's,* 326 (August 1979): 100–111;

"The Reality of Nuclear Power," *Blackwood's,* 326 (September 1979): 193–211;

"A Return," *Blackwood's,* 327 (January 1980): 38–46;

"India and British Portraiture: 1770–1825," *Blackwood's,* 327 (May 1980): 372–380;

"Foot Notes: Reflections on Travel Writing," *Wilson Quarterly,* 16 (Summer 1992): 122–129.

Dervla Murphy is most often described in terms of strength: she is intrepid, strong-minded, compulsive about traveling and writing, and able to endure hunger and exhaustion to reach her goals. She is also a woman of strong opinions who has love and compassion for her fellow humans and a strong Irish sense of humor. Often compared to the intrepid women travelers of the nineteenth century, such as Isabella Bird Bishop and Mary Kingsley, Murphy is, in fact, a decidedly twentieth-century traveler. Like her predecessors, Murphy relates her adventures and misadventures humorously, but she is much less self-deprecating than early women travelers. She more often places herself in the foreground and has no compunctions about appropriate dress or undress, other than the consideration of ease for rough travels or in proving her gender. Her fondness for cigarettes and sampling every sort of alcoholic beverage also separates her from the lady travelers, who would not have written about tastes like Murphy's even if they had them.

Murphy's zest for the independence of travel, however, directly connects her with the lady travelers of the nineteenth century. This enthusiasm is freshest in her first book, *Full Tilt: Ireland to India with a Bicycle* (1965), the continuing popularity of which has made it a travel classic. Later books, although bearing the marks of greater authorial control and manipulation, still retain an inherent honesty and sense of wonder that bonds the reader to Murphy, just as she forms bonds with the peoples met on her journeys. Whether or not readers agree with Murphy's assessments of political or social situations, they appreciate her willingness to understand, in layman's terms and with the perspective of the average person, the complexities of societal systems and their problems in the late twentieth century. Murphy's writings are fresh, exciting, and thought provoking, justifying the claims that she is one of the great travel writers of her time.

Born in Cappoquin, County Waterford, Ireland, on 28 November 1931, Dervla Murphy (named Dervilla Maria on her birth certificate) is the only child of Fergus Joseph Murphy and Kathleen L. Rochfort-Dowling Murphy. Her father worked as county librarian in nearby Lismore from 1931 until his death on 25 February 1961. Until her daughter's birth, Kathleen Murphy assisted her husband in setting up a rural library service and worked as an unpaid library assistant. She loved walking the hills and fields of Blackwater Valley near their home and imparted that fondness to Dervla. Diagnosed with rheumatoid arthritis at the age of twenty, however, Kathleen Murphy was completely crippled by the disease by the time she was twenty-six. Because of her mother's need for constant care and the family's limited income, Dervla Murphy spent most of her first thirty years at home.

Murphy was intermittently educated at home, at an Irish-speaking co-educational school (where she was unhappy), and at a convent school. From an early age she was a voracious reader and had access to a larger range of books than most children. Nevertheless, she admits to having been an indifferent student except when applying herself to English and history. When she was fourteen, she left school to care for her mother and did so until her mother died on 25 August 1962.

When she was twelve Murphy's "Picking Blackberries" won first prize in the *Cork Weekly Examiner* competition for writers under sixteen. She then won the competition five weeks running. Despite the awards, she sensed that her writing was not high quality, and she worked diligently toward improvement. Later, in *Wheels within Wheels* (1979), she wrote that while at the convent school she produced several "full-length, lurid adventure stories set in nameless Foreign Parts where the political crises were even more ambiguous than in Ireland and led to a profusion of warm sticky blood, choking emotions and gallant last-minute rescues."

On her tenth birthday Murphy had received a bicycle and an atlas, and soon afterward she decided that she could bicycle to India. Over the next few years she built up strength and endurance by cycling through the mountains and valleys near her home. In 1951, when she was nineteen, her parents encouraged her to take her first cycling trip abroad. She spent three weeks cycling through Wales and southern England and published her first travel essays–impressions of Stratford, London, and Oxford–in *Hibernia.* The next year, she took a five-week journey through Belgium, Germany, and central France. Her essay on Paris, also published in *Hibernia,* omitted a kidnapping from which she quickly escaped, focusing instead on the enchantment of the city. Murphy's fascination with the places she visits, even those that others might view as dismal, is a hallmark of her works.

In the winter of 1952–1953 Murphy wrote her first novel, about an illegitimate girl in Ireland. The novel might have been published if she had agreed to change the tragic ending to a happier one. She refused

Kesang, Juliet Maskell, Murphy, and Sister Sawnay at the Tibetan refugee camp in northern India where Murphy served as a volunteer for five months in 1963 (from Murphy's Tibetan Foothold, *1966; courtesy of Dervla Murphy)*

to do so because she felt that, despite its mawkishness, her work had a certain integrity that would be lost by the change. She then wrote a second novel for her own entertainment and did not send it to a publisher.

During the 1950s Murphy's already difficult relationship with her mother worsened, and she felt the need to break free temporarily from the constraints of constantly attending an invalid. In the spring of 1953 she set off for Spain, inspired by *Spanish Raggle-Taggle: Adventures with a Fiddle in Northern Spain* (1935), by Walter Starkie, whose attitude toward travel later inspired her journey to Transylvania in 1990. Murphy published twelve essays on Spain based on her diary entries in the *Irish Independent* newspaper, but her attempts to publish the expanded essays in book form failed. In spite of publishers' rejections, Murphy felt that she had written a reasonably good travel book, and she determined to pursue a writing career.

Murphy returned to Spain in 1956 for a month's visit that reinforced her already developing sense that generalizations about national characteristics should be avoided. The lingering cheerfulness that she usually experienced after her return home was quickly obliterated by her mother's increasing needs and demands.

After her mother's death in 1962, Murphy was free to pursue her dreams of traveling and writing. Her long-deferred trip to India by bicycle began on 14 January 1963, when she set out on a bicycle, which she called Roz. Still the most popular of her travel books, *Full Tilt: Ireland to India with a Bicycle* (1965) is dedicated "to the peoples of Afghanistan and Pakistan"–an indication of the parts of the journey Murphy enjoyed most thoroughly and to which she returned in later travels. The beginning of the journey also became a touchstone for later works, a reminder of the hardships endured by intrepid travelers.

The first three months on the route to India, from Dunkirk to Tehran, were not at all what Murphy imagined and are summarized in an introduction to the book. The winter of 1963 was one of the coldest ever in Europe, and Murphy struggled through ice, snow, and floods, and the humiliation (for her) of having to ride trains, buses, and trucks instead of bicycling as she had intended. She was forced to use her pistol to ward off attacking wolves, lustful men, and thieves, and she vowed that she would never again visit Azerbaijan alone. Yet, she was treated with immense kindness by strangers all along her route.

In the foreword to *Full Tilt* Murphy claims, "Apart from burnishing the spelling and syntax, which are apt to suffer when one makes nightly entries whether half asleep or not, I have left the diary virtually unchanged." She also resisted the urge, common among travel writers, to interpolate statistics, historical information, or essays on the sociology, art, culture, or politics of an area. As Murphy's reputation has grown, however, she has supplemented her authority as a traveler by including more detailed background reading.

Throughout Murphy's works, she makes it clear that she does not consider Europe or cities appropriate destinations for true travel tales, but scattered references indicate that she did spend time in those locales. In *Full Tilt* Murphy distinguishes between what does and does not count as part of the "real" journey by summarizing the first two months in an introduction distilled from letters. The true journey begins with a diary entry dated Tehran, 26 March.

In Iran, Murphy found in the intense blue skies and wild mountains a solitude and a beauty that were far more magnificent than she imagined possible. She was particularly impressed by "the unique purity of the light" which she perceived as an entity in itself rather than simply as a medium for seeing other objects. Murphy's sensitivity to the qualities of light is reiterated throughout many of her works, most often those on travels in the Himalayas and other mountainous regions.

Murphy's enjoyment of the landscape, which she feels cannot be experienced when one is whizzing by in a motor vehicle, causes consternation for others. While cycling on unbeaten tracks, she must constantly watch the ground, which is often not made for smooth cycling. To see the landscape she walks or stops. She also has to convince others that traveling alone to non-tourist areas is desirable, exciting, and within the realm of possibility. Getting visas for a long enough stay in such places becomes the foremost obstacle in these journeys, and Murphy's works abound with visa and border tales.

Murphy quickly develops strong feelings about each country she visits, although she is rather ambivalent about Iran. She has more pity than liking for the people, whom she considers undermined by inbreeding and malnutrition. While tending to find individuals characterless, she senses a collective dignity in them that comes from being part of an old and rich civilization. In *Full Tilt* she describes Herat as "a city of absolute enchantment in the literal sense of the word. It loosens all the bonds binding the traveller to his own age and sets him free to live in a past that is vital and crude but never ugly."

Within a few days, despite intense heat, a miserable bus ride, and seeing atrocious treatment of women, Murphy was delighted with the character of the Afghans, declaring "I'm in love with Afghanistan–with its simplicity, its courtesy and its leisureliness and with the underlying *sanity* of an area fortunate enough to have remained very backward indeed." Later journeys have revealed the disadvantages of such a lack of modernization to Murphy, but she remains charmed by life without the encumbrances of modern Western notions and appliances.

While in an Afghani hospital with a broken rib Murphy reflected on the differences between West and East and became increasingly convinced that Muslims are more tolerant, honest, and kinder than Christians, and that, for the most part, Westerners are incapable of accepting the great wisdom of cultures other than their own. She realizes that her understanding of the East was acquired gradually as she cycled into areas of deeper poverty and became more accustomed to primitive conditions, such as polluted and dirty water, fleas, and insect-infested cheeses and breads. It is surprising, then, to read that about two weeks later Murphy was in Peshawar declaring that the city is well compensated for British colonial exploitation by schools, hospitals, efficient transportation, reliable communication systems and electricity, a functioning bureaucracy, and proper roads. Later in the book she makes a similar observation about India.

During the remainder of her journey, Murphy experienced extremes in landscape, climate, and peoples. She stayed with Pakistani colonels and rajas as well as villagers so poverty-stricken that they have only stewed clover to eat. She freezes in glacial areas and several times becomes ill from heat exhaustion. The Gilgit and Indus valley region, to which she returned on a later journey with her daughter, is one of the most extraordinary areas through which she traveled and acutely affected her perceptions. The loneliness of the gorges freed her from awareness of the outside world and her past life, and the eerie surroundings blotted out her sense of self. Throughout Murphy's narratives are moments in which she allows the presence of colors, light, and crystalline air to permeate the reader's senses. Yet, she also answers the reader's desire for adventure with descriptions such as scenes of crossing raging torrents.

As Murphy bicycled south toward New Delhi, the heat took its toll, and she became alternately giddy and grumpy from the climate and exhaustion. Having become as attached to Pakistan as she was to Afghanistan, she sensed that she would be less comfortable among the Hindus than the Muslims. Not until she stayed in south India several years later did Murphy better understand and thus become more tolerant of Hindu strictures and attitudes. On this first trip, however, she was happy to reach her destination and to transform herself from an unwashed tribeswoman back into an Irishwoman among British friends. Like Murphy's later narratives, *Full Tilt* does not describe her city experiences. Her instincts about why people read travel narratives are echoed by reviewers who focus on how intrepid, resourceful, and determined, yet amusing and naively trusting she is. They cite the hazardous or ridiculous scenes as enticing readers to the book. Occasional negative criticisms characterize Murphy's reflections on political and social situations as simplistic.

Following the success of *Full Tilt,* Murphy published the diary she kept in northern India during July-November 1963, after the cycling trip. *Tibetan Foothold* (1966) chronicles the five months Murphy served as a volunteer in a Tibetan refugee camp and then took a short bicycle journey to inspect the conditions of workers and children in road camps. Because it is in diary form, *Tibetan Foothold* has a more intimate quality than some of Murphy's other books. One senses that the diary was originally kept to share with close friends rather than for publication. It is likely that the success of *Full Tilt* convinced Murphy that a quick follow-up to the book would bolster her status as a professional travel writer.

The book focuses on the plight of Tibetan children who are crowded into inadequate buildings and have limited food, medical care, and education. As in subsequent works Murphy criticizes relief agencies that treat refugees as logistical problems rather than as needy humans. Yet, she praises the extraordinary dedication of the people with whom she worked. She immediately fell in love with the Tibetans and worked to improve the lot of the children under her care. With no particular training she concentrated on a cleanliness campaign that greatly alleviated the children's skin infections and parasitic afflictions.

Occasionally the book changes focus, and Murphy the travel writer re-emerges. As in nearly all her travels, she encountered sudden, intense, awe-inspiring storms. Throughout Murphy's works bad weather is not simply a hazard; it stimulates the imagination as do the landscapes and vistas. The roads provide the main hazards, creating obstacles that prove Murphy's mettle. They also provide thrills, as when she takes off again on Roz, delighting in the icy air while speeding around hairpin turns.

Murphy is usually disdainful of tourists, whom she distinguishes from travelers. Travelers take risks, are bold about finding shelter, and persevere. They also rapidly alter their plans when unforeseen opportunities arise. On the way to another camp in the Kula valley Murphy saw a sign for a village near the almost inaccessible settlement of the Malana, a community of primitive Hindus whose language and culture separate them from other Indians. As a white woman, she was considered an untouchable and allowed only on the outskirts of the village. The excitement of being in such a remote area amply rewarded the risks she took by traveling the treacherous route to the village and her frustration at being segregated within it.

Murphy setting out on a tour of road camps in northern India, 1963 (photograph from Tibetan Foothold; *courtesy of Dervla Murphy)*

The main section of the book ends with the diary entry for 31 December 1963, which expresses her surprise at learning that arriving at and staying in a place has its own deep rewards. The people met on the journey are as important as the journey itself. Murphy established her identity as traveler through her desire to follow only in the tracks of remote villagers and to communicate, despite language barriers, on as equal a footing as possible with them.

Murphy returned to work as a volunteer with the Tibetan refugees in 1965. Conditions for the Tibetans had improved so much in India that her services were superfluous, but a newly opened camp in Pokhara, Nepal, needed assistance. Her diary entries from this period were published as *The Waiting Land: A Spell in Nepal* (1967).

The flight from London to India took Murphy over the route she had previously bicycled, and she gained an appreciation for air travel as she gazed at mountains and lakes from a new perspective. Arrival in New Delhi gave her a sense of peace. In the book she wrote of her primary reason for traveling to economically undeveloped areas: "People may jeer at this phrase as romantic nonsense, yet to arrive suddenly in India after a fortnight's immersion in an affluent society does induce a strong sense of liberation from some intangible but threatening power." Later Murphy better appreciated the benefits of affluence when she realized how inadequate nutrition and disease lead to permanent suffering and stunted mental development.

Murphy usually enjoys traveling rough, but she revised her opinions somewhat after enduring a few hours crammed into a small train compartment with seventeen Gurkha soldiers and mounds of equipment. While Murphy for the most part avoids contact with Europeans on her journeys, she is appreciative of their presence when she is injured or ill, or has lost her passport, money, or plane tickets.

Because Murphy usually mailed her diaries to correspondents in Ireland, she was concerned with the peculiarities of foreign post offices. A scene in an Indian post office on the border with Nepal is typical of difficulties she encountered in other countries as well. She claims that her request to mail a packet to Ireland caused "unprecedented chaos" because none of the clerks had any idea where Ireland is and then spent an inordinate amount of time looking up registration information in ancient volumes, weighing the packet on unreliable scales, and laboriously copying the address in a foreign script. The scene could be read as an indirect slur on the lines of "funny, inefficient foreigners," but any reader familiar with the ways of the Irish bureaucracy would understand the implied similarities between clerks at home and abroad.

Murphy has often declared that she is more determined than courageous, and she is not afraid to admit when she is frightened or has failed to achieve an expected goal. In her travels with some Tibetan refugees through a mountainous area with flooding rivers, Murphy was definitely not intrepid as she sat astride and pulled herself along a log over a raging river that the Tibetans had just crossed by foot. Likewise, the Tibetans were not meek, helpless refugees as they laughed at Murphy's fears.

Unable to leave Nepal without seeing more of that country, Murphy arranged a modest two-week trek north of Kathmandu, taking so few provisions that her Sherpa guide was uneasy about the wisdom of accompanying her. The point of the trek was relaxation, and she wandered happily up and down mountains, spending nights in what seemed to be remote hamlets until she came across a wrapper from Lifebuoy soap. One of Murphy's strongest desires, expressed on every journey, is that the places she visits remain pristine without the help of western cleansers. In the epilogue to *The Waiting Land* Murphy acknowledges the contradictory characteristics of the countries north of India: "Nepal weaves a net out of splendour and pettiness, squalor and colour, wisdom and innocence, tranquillity and gaiety, complacence and discontent, indolence and energy, generosity and cunning, freedom and bondage."

Murphy's next journey linked a childhood fascination with the legends of Abyssinia to her desire for exploring. Although the highlands of Ethiopia were considered too filled with bandits for solitary travel, Murphy is granted a six-month visa for a 1,024-mile trek that proved her toughest and most dangerous journey. As preparation, she read extensively, finding Donald N. Levine's *Wax and Gold: Tradition and Innovation in Ethiopian Culture* (1965) the best guide to understanding Amharic culture. Her research is incorporated in the text and in footnotes, supplementing her observations with historical and cultural information.

Because of the nature of her journey, *In Ethiopia with a Mule* (1968) is more serious than other Murphy works. Her initial romantic outlook quickly turned to reservation as she sensed that as an alien she would not be readily accepted. Having also decided to switch from cycling to walking for this journey, she had difficulty adjusting to the physical demands and had to take a break after only a few days on the trail. Carrying a fifty-pound pack is a serious strain when one is walking from three thousand to eight thousand feet, and Murphy's feet were reduced to pulp after she tried to walk off blisters. While she recuperated, friends introduced her to Leilt Aida Desta, the granddaughter of Heile Selassie, who not only assisted Murphy in finding a mule but made sure she had protection along her route.

Setting out again on 29 December 1966, Murphy realized that she would be dependent on strangers for help with packing the mule, which she named Jock, after her publisher, "Jock" Murray. Used to the friendliness of Asians, Murphy was perplexed by the "mixture of hostility, suspicion, and contempt" with which she was viewed and which boded ill for a journey on which she had been advised always to sleep in a compound or village. Her way was further complicated by a police escort, as she would rather have faced bandits than travel at the pace of others. After a few days she dismissed her bodyguards, found friendlier people, and had the happiest sort of day: "seeing only hoof prints in the dust, with all around the healing quiet of wild places, unbroken save by bird-song." She savored the

Buying Jock
Loading
Ready to start, with Leilt Aida and Christopher
On the road

Photographs by Murphy of preparations for 1966-1967 tour of Ethiopia (from In Ethiopia with a Mule, *1968)*

softened light and glowing reds, browns, and yellows that colored the cliffs as the heat haze of day lifted in early evening.

Murphy's carefree traveling did not last long, and she found that she had to accept protection from villagers, partly because of their sense of duty but also to allay their suspicions of a foreigner so far off the beaten track. Murphy believes that she was the first white person many peasants in the highlands had seen.

Murphy's trekking in the High Semien (Simyen) Mountains was exhilarating and exhausting, as were her encounters with the people of the area. Meeting some British men who were also climbing in the area, Murphy argued about the merits of staying with local people rather than separating oneself and not interacting. Murphy always prefers to observe people closely and to allow them to observe her. In Ethiopian towns Murphy stayed in hotels but still managed to meet people. She enjoyed the company of well-educated Ethiopians but became exasperated with half-educated youths who are removed from village life yet not at ease with modern life. Murphy so cherishes the simple life that she seems to forget how privileged she is to be able to take it or leave it as she pleases.

Because of Murphy's reputation, the local police quickly ferreted out the men who stole equipment from her at Lake Tana. Having recuperated from this mishap, Murphy went on with her journey, exploring the uplands, where she felt more comfortable: "There are two phases of enjoyment in journeying through an unknown country–the eager phase of wondering interest in every detail, and the relaxed phase when one feels no longer an observer of the exotic, but a participator in the rhythm of daily life." The world of the highlanders became as familiar and normal to her as her Irish community, but she viewed their society as static and stylized. Their way of life, of course, seems static only to the traveler passing through. Murphy's contentment vanished as the way became more difficult. She and Jock were both injured, and food became scarce, so she was forced to stay in a town for a while. Eventually Murphy had to leave Jock with a caring family, and she completed her trek with an unobliging donkey she named Satan.

For Murphy the mountain areas are the "real Ethiopia." Even if some of the people were suspicious of her or unfriendly, she had a better chance of interaction with them than with the Ethiopians in Addis Ababa, who distance themselves from foreigners. Nevertheless, since the language barrier prevented her from carrying on all but the simplest conversations, her bond with the villagers is mainly spiritual:

> A traveller who does not speak their language cannot presume to claim any deep understanding of the Ethiopian highlanders. But it is the gradual growth of affection for another race, rather than the walking of a thousand miles or the climbing of a hundred mountains, that is the real achievement and the richest reward of such a journey.

This statement applies equally well to the people Murphy has met on all her journeys.

Murphy spent six weeks in Addis Ababa before returning home to write *In Ethiopia with a Mule,* which mixes a diary format with historical interpolations and footnotes. Murphy has revealed little about the next two years of her life. Just before the birth of her daughter, Rachel, on 10 December 1968, she took a three-month trek around Turkey. In 1976 she revealed the name of Rachel's father, whom she did not marry. He was Terence de Vere White, Irish novelist, biographer, and critic, who died in June 1994. For the next five years, she limited her travels to Europe, as she felt that a child needs stable surroundings and routines. She and Rachel did, however, travel rather extensively around continental Europe. To supplement the income from her books Murphy wrote a regular column for the *Irish Times* and her autobiography, *Wheels within Wheels* (1979), which focuses on her childhood, her difficult relationship with her mother, and her early travels.

When Rachel was five, Murphy decided that her daughter should be initiated into "real" traveling, which for Murphy means non-European. Murphy had settled on central Mexico when a friend visiting from India persuaded her that no place would be more suitable or enticing than southern India. Murphy and Rachel traveled there in November 1973.

On a Shoestring to Coorg: An Experience of South India (1976) is aptly titled. Murphy has perfected the art of essentials-only travel. For four months in India she decided that Rachel could take a tin box with seven tiny rubber animals, crayons and felt pens, a toy squirrel, *Squirrel Nutkin,* and six schoolbooks. For herself Murphy took a swimsuit, sleeping bags, books, notebooks, and maps plus first-aid supplies and vitamins. Since clothing costs so little in India, they took only a change of underwear with them. Originally Murphy was worried that traveling with a child might be tiresome, but she found that Rachel was a good companion and helped her meet people that she might not have otherwise. Another worry was Murphy's lack of sympathy with Hindu culture. She did not embrace the culture by the end of her journey but felt that she had achieved a greater understanding of it.

Murphy had not planned on a two-month stay in the Coorg region of southwestern India. She began the journey by wandering down the southwest Indian coast, traveling primarily by bus. Each of the chapters includes diary sections, which were rewritten and edited. Murphy thanks "Diana Murray who tactfully but relentlessly de-purpled many passages, and provided endless inspiration and comfort during the darkest hours of Revision." One expects that historical information is added during the postjourney writing, and that the development of sensibilities and cultural observations are also the products of posttravel reflection and study. These observations must be carefully integrated into the text, as they are in *On a Shoestring to Coorg,* so that they simulate the deeply felt experience of the traveler.

Despite her rather happy-go-lucky attitude at the beginning of the book, Murphy clearly intended to translate her travels into a book that would allow her to examine seriously her own and her readers' prejudices about India. Much historical information and many suggestions for further reading are included, and Murphy meticulously describes the surroundings and the people. It was perhaps her desire to empathize that led her to overcome her discomfort with Hindu taboos and strictures on castes and to examine respectfully and deeply the meanings and effects of Hindu culture. Rachel's delighted acceptance of the scene counterbalanced her mother's more-complex reactions and helped Murphy gain a wider perspective.

While the historic information relies on secondary sources, the travelogue features Murphy's dreamy visions of the sights and smells of the landscape, a harmonizing of the luminescent colors of the land, the sky, and people's clothing. Murphy's romantic India is epitomized in Bandipur:

> undulating, cultivated land, where dark red earth glowed in the hazy golden light and the glossy green of palms, plantains and wayside banyans stood out against a deep blue sky. Then a purple-pink tinge dramatically suffused the whole scene as the sun dropped lower, and its last slanting rays burnished the classical brass water-jars that were being carried across the fields on the heads of slim women in vivid, graceful saris. At such moments the simple, timeless beauty of rural India can be very moving.

The personal travelogue examines Rachel's reactions to travel and a different culture and Murphy's difficulties in facing the fact that, as a woman in India, she was "an essentially inferior person." While Murphy thinks that by eschewing the gadgets and transport of other travelers, she creates an equality between herself and the people she meets, she also enjoys being thought of as the interesting foreigner and "one of the men." The circumstances in India disrupted her accustomed identity and authority as traveler but led to a more diverse narrative. In India Murphy was not so much the intrepid traveler as the curious visitor who acknowledges that her views are sometimes naive.

Murphy was delighted by the integrity that keeps Hindu culture from catering to tourists while also making it less impervious to travelers: "it is too individual, too absorbent, too fortified by its own curious integrity, to be vulnerable to those slings and arrows of outrageous vulgarity which have killed the loveliness of so many places since tourism became big business." When Murphy participated in Hindu festivals or ceremonies, she had to do so as one who is engaged with the spirit of the occasion, even if she did not share Hindu religious beliefs. She fell so much in love with Coorg that these ceremonies became meaningful to her. On all her journeys, Murphy has had the occasional day when the world seems perfect to her, and in Coorg she was profoundly satisfied by the vitality of colors and clarity of light in a land saturated with golden sunshine. Both she and Rachel were quite reluctant to leave.

By November 1974 Murphy was ready for a return visit to the subcontinent, opting for Pakistan, with which she feels a greater empathy than India. She was also quite confident that six-year-old Rachel was hardy and stoic enough for a true journey, so they spent the winter in Baltistan, one of the least developed places in Asia.

In *Where the Indus Is Young: A Winter in Baltistan* (1977) Murphy mentions political situations such as the division of India and Pakistan, the imminent division of Pakistan and Bangladesh, the military dictatorship of Pakistan (which she calls benevolent), and the position of women in an Islamic society. Yet, her main focus is trekking in a remote and poverty-stricken area. Early on she expresses her fascination by the possibility of being the first outsider to visit an area:

> Actually I do feel that travel-snobs, of which I am such a shameless example, are much less blameworthy than most other kinds of snob. If one of the objects of a journey is to observe how the other half lives, then it is essential to travel in areas where the other half remains uncontaminated by one's own half.

Dust jacket for Murphy's 1976 book, about her 1973 journey to India with her five-year-old daughter, Rachel

In Baltistan, however, she was constantly amazed and dismayed by the extent of Western infiltration, finding, for example, a Charlotte Yonge novel in a mud hovel. She wishes that living standards could somehow be raised without any taint of the West.

Murphy emphasizes the remoteness of Baltistan by the occasional use of a question mark for an unknown town or village name. She acknowledges previous visitors to the region by using quotations from their writings as chapter epigraphs. *Where the Indus Is Young* again includes excerpts from Murphy's diary. Rachel also kept a diary, and some snippets from it are also included. (Larger pieces of Rachel's diary are included in Murphy's later books.) While Rachel was, overall, an adventurous and observant companion, her overstimulated curiosity sometimes tried her mother's nerves. Murphy is honest in her admissions that she was too short tempered and unreasonable in her expectations of what a six-year-old could do. Rachel's ability to cope with high altitudes, extreme cold, and rugged conditions was remarkable for one so young and inexperienced.

To make the trek easier Murphy bought a horse, Hallam, for Rachel to ride and spent several weeks acclimatizing in the relatively urban town of Skardu.

Here she learned how to crack apricot stones (an essential food of the region), how to hammer large bits of rock salt into usable bits, and how to concoct a version of shortbread with the local grain flours and ghee. The capital of Baltistan, Skardu provided a base from which to take short journeys and was also the site of Murphy's first dental problems. Toothaches bring out the weakest and worst in Murphy, and she readily admits: "I was reminded of the last lines of my favourite travel-book, when Eric Newby and his companion, after their short walk in the Hindu Kush, meet Thesiger and are dismissed by him as a couple of pansies." Her self-image as the hardy traveler was shattered by a pain so severe that she could not even write. Her usual empathy, which normally prevents her from caricaturing people, disappeared when an inept dentist, whom she designates as "Oaf," botched a filling.

Another doctor attempted sexual assault, which in retrospect seemed humorous to Murphy, who described herself as "unwashed for five weeks; in filthy shapeless garments; greying hair stiff with dust, sweat and grease; nails black and broken; hands like emery paper and cracked and bleeding." This sudden sight of herself as a filthy stranger, a scene that is repeated in several of her travel books, contrasts with the immaculate grooming of the Victorian lady travelers with whom she is often compared.

Murphy's great respect for Islam was shaken by the extensive self-scourging displayed in the Muharram rituals. Her lack of sympathy with religious fervor derives from the grief she has seen it cause in her own country. She also encountered bigotry against non-Muslims, which she had previously come across only in eastern Turkey. Nevertheless, she tried to align herself with the spirit of the region and thanked Allah whenever she was lucky or grateful.

After a month in Skardu, Murphy and her daughter began their trek through the Indus River valley, following barely discernible tracks and resting wherever they could find shelter, from filthy hovels to a raja's palace. The journey was both arduous and exhilarating. Murphy was more conscious of risks on this trip, but already her intrepidity had been instilled in Rachel, who frequently wanted to show that she was brave like her mother.

On this journey Murphy became more fond of the place than the people. She found the people cheerful and likable but decided that they do not have a distinctive personality, perhaps a consequence of the extreme poverty, scarcity of food, and widespread disease–all of which tend to dampen energy and intellectual curiosity. Toward the end of the journey Murphy began to feel that some of the Baltis have more in common with their animals than they do with other humans. She sensed that she was truly away from the outside world. When she rested on the trail observing the vast solitude of the Himalayas, she achieved the greatest satisfaction of her journey: experiencing the peace of a world that has no sounds other than the roaring of deep cold rivers and the cracklings of ice in the mountains, a place where the light and air are crystalline.

Rachel's schooling took them back to Ireland and gave Murphy the opportunity to examine the causes of the fighting between Catholics and Protestants in Northern Ireland. Beginning in June 1976, Murphy made several trips to Northern Ireland "to be able to clarify the present Northern Irish turmoil for the ordinary citizens of Britain and the Republic." *A Place Apart* (1978) begins as a travel account in diary format, which is followed by essay-chapters on historical background and critical analysis. She returns to the diary format toward the end of the book, with accounts of several short excursions to Northern Ireland.

While the importance of *A Place Apart* lies in Murphy's analysis of the political situation, the brief descriptions of her journeys in Northern Ireland are worth examining as travel literature. Although Murphy had already successfully completed arduous journeys on other continents, her proposed bicycle tour through the six counties of Northern Ireland caused her friends great concern for her safety and gave her "sick little spasms of fear." Nevertheless, she set out, enjoying the lush countryside of the Republic of Ireland and being surprised that the border was unmarked in the peaceful rolling farmlands. Ironically, when Murphy entered a town and noticed that no cars were parked on the streets (because of the fear of car bombs) and that pub patrons were guarded, she felt more relaxed. The realization that the situation was more or less commonplace helped her somehow to put aside her fears; yet, she was often surprised at the resilience and good spirits of many of the people she met. Murphy's trust in the inherent goodness of all people eased her way into discussions with an extensive cross-section of people in Northern Ireland. It took time for her to discover that an outwardly peace-loving and caring person can kill for the sake of an ideal.

Murphy quickly recognized the cultural split between Northern and Southern Ireland. As a citizen of the Republic of Ireland she remained an outsider, examining the six northern counties with a traveler's eye that enabled her to view the issues anthropologically, as tribal differences. She emphasizes the myths and rituals of the various groups within the region as the root causes of the continuing inability to compromise and sees no chance for a political solution to the problems until the tribal unconscious is exhumed and examined critically. Murphy concludes that the "Northern Irish

Dervla and Rachel Murphy setting off from London on their 1978 journey to Peru (from Eight Feet in the Andes, *1983; courtesy of Dervla Murphy)*

may not be comprehensible" to outsiders or themselves. Nevertheless, she also finds them "addictive" and sees hope for an area to which she plans to return for pleasure journeys. In acknowledgment of her efforts to understand the ordinary people of Northern Ireland, Murphy was awarded the first Christopher Ewart-Biggs Memorial Prize for *A Place Apart* in 1978.

Wanting to take one final long journey with Rachel before she went to boarding school, Murphy chose to explore Central and South America in 1978. *Eight Feet in the Andes* (1983) covers only part of their journey, their September to December trek in Peru from Cajamarca to Cuzco. Their route was similar to Francisco Pizarro's 1533 conquest route through the Inca territory. The historical information in *Eight Feet in the Andes* focuses almost exclusively on the conquistadores and tends to give the reader the impression that no other Europeans traversed the route in the four centuries between the two journeys. Citing the difficulties the terrain posed for the conquistadores also underscores the Murphys' intrepidity.

To ease the difficulties of carrying packs and walking the 1,300-mile route for the nine-year-old Rachel, Murphy purchased a mule, Juana. While trekking, she wondered if the high altitudes and extreme poverty were the reason that the Andean peasants "seem to lack that potent spiritual dimension to daily life which sustains even the poorest Hindu peasant." In the attempt to understand the Andeans, she looked for similarities between Tibetans and the Andeans, but she found little other than certain physical characteristics. The Andean Indians' lack of interest in the Murphys annoyed her somewhat. Later Murphy was told that she was never invited into homes because of the fear that she might steal.

Clearly one of the delights of traveling for Murphy is to be observed. She sometimes makes fun of herself, as when she describes taking foolish short cuts. Her traveler's humor is apparent in names she gave their campsites in the Andes and later used as headings in the book: names such as "Camp amidst Cactus beside Stream," "Camp on Sloping Ledge on Mountainside," and "Camp on Balcony of Chicmo Municipal Offices." Yet, she is nonetheless perceived as an intrepid traveler. During their Andes trek Rachel pointed out to her mother that she would disappoint her readers if she got disoriented.

Murphy's honesty precludes omitting the scenes in which she has behaved like the tourists she disdains. While admitting to be ashamed of herself afterward, Murphy used letters of introduction and threatened children who have stolen from her with prison. The importance of completing the trek took precedence over qualms about the recovery of stolen clothing and equipment or having to rely on the extremely poor for food. Murphy was conscientious about paying for food but only occasionally recognized that the money has little significance for those who are starving. Her admission that "our treks are just playing with hardship" has a double-edged significance in a country where hardship is a way of life.

Murphy continues to exhibit her heightened sensitivity to landscape: a green, many-hued lake; the depths of the blues in the sky; and the brilliant orange sunsets that would look fake if painted. The splendors she describes include menacing cactus and thorn plants as well as eerily jagged peaks and sudden, violent storms. Even before she left, Murphy became nostalgic for "the black-and-silver world" of the Andes in moonlight, a land "held in a stillness that seems holy." The images stay with the reader. Murphy ends the book before the end of their journey. The reader is given only a brief view of Cuzco and the scrubbed and newly attired Rachel and Dervla Murphy. Their sojourn in Lima and their subsequent expulsion from Peru for having expired visas are not mentioned.

On her way back to Ireland, Murphy traveled by bus to San Francisco and then across the United States. A brief account of this quick bus journey across the United States was published as "A Taste of California" in the August 1979 issue of *Blackwood's Magazine*. The amount of history that she condensed in the article suggests that she might have been contemplating a larger work. Usually negative about cities, Murphy was charmed by San Francisco. What strikes her most about the United States is the violation of the land, not only by overdevelopment but also by ardent nature-lovers who want dependable trails even in the wilderness.

Murphy was staying with friends in Williams Corner, Pennsylvania, at the end of March 1979, when the accident at the Three Mile Island nuclear facility occurred. The incident confirmed Murphy's antinuclear sentiments and reinforced her urgent sense that a general discussion of the issue was imperative. After collecting media information throughout the crisis period and consulting with antinuclear organizations in Washington, D.C., and Boston, Murphy published a long article in the September 1979 issue of *Blackwood's Magazine*. The negative response to the article convinced her that she had presented the issue too simply. Murphy then put aside work on her account of her trip to the Andes to write *Race to the Finish: The Nuclear Stakes* (1981), the product of considerable research. Written in layman's terms, it is an attempt to convince ordinary citizens that the nuclear industry poses dangers to safety, health, and the economy.

Murphy and her daughter once again traveled light during their summer 1983 trip to Madagascar, which resulted in the appropriately titled *Muddling through in Madagascar* (1985), often described as Murphy's funniest travel book. While spending the summer on the red island with fourteen-year-old Rachel, Murphy suffered more accidents and illnesses than she had on longer and more dangerous travels. The journey is presented in retrospect, in chapters rather than in diary format, and the book includes a considerable amount of historical information. Particularly in the opening chapters, personal observations are mixed with information gleaned from postjourney reading, giving the reader a fuller perspective on the culture and peoples than in the usual Murphy book. The mixture of history and firsthand experience is distracting, however, as details of a day's journey are separated by long passages on culture and history.

Casting herself in the role of *vazaha* (foreigner), Murphy quickly learned that she had to respect the many *fady* (taboos) if she were to be received warmly by the local people. Despite their many rules, the Malagasy described in the book are relaxed, cheerful, and welcoming. Their warmth made what might seem a horrendous journey bearable and even fun.

Even so, the first night she was the guest of a village Murphy unwittingly broke several taboos and caused anxiety because her diary writing was suspected to be a spy report on the people with whom she was staying. She was cajoled out of a book and had to hide portions of the vast mound of unappetizing rice she was served to avoid hurting anyone's feelings. She describes the incident and much of the journey humorously, but there is an uneasy undertone. She calls the people "friendly and generous" but not "relaxed or spontaneous," an assessment that typifies the ambiguities underlying the book, which veers from respectful descriptions to caricatures.

Where earlier Murphy felt that relying on villagers for food and shelter engendered a bond of common humanity, by the time she went to Madagascar she had come to see herself as a wealthier, independent outsider, who has to be more considerate and must be reluctant to impose. This change of attitude from previous journeys meant that she and Rachel often trekked on empty stomachs.

Murphy's sensitivity fluctuated during the journey. Madagascar is often displaced by Dervla Murphy the famous travel writer. The entire adventure was cut short when mother and daughter got hepatitis. Despite their various mishaps, Murphy took a vial of Madagascar's red earth to ensure that she would return some day.

Murphy originally conceived of writing *Tales from Two Cities: Race Relations in Britain* (1987) as she bicycled from London to Edinburgh in 1966. At the time she did not feel she had the expertise to tackle a book on black and brown immigrants to Great Britain, but by 1983 she had decided to attempt the work. Her bout with hepatitis and then a broken back delayed the start of the project until January 1985. For almost a year Murphy resided in inner-city areas, spending six months in Manningham (a neighborhood of Bradford, England) and the rest of the time in Handsworth, Birmingham. Her purpose was not to gather statistics or to be objective about the situations of brown (mostly Pakistani) and black (Afro-Caribbean) immigrants. Instead she wrote about her perceptions of the lives and feelings of the nonwhite population of Great Britain.

Tales from Two Cities has more in common with travel works than with sociological studies. The book is anecdotal and includes occasional diary excerpts as well as historical information. During her stay in Bradford and Birmingham, Murphy took an anthropologist's stance: the outsider who lives within a culture, participating enough to become friends with residents but making it clear that she is "on duty" and needs time and distance to write reports from the field. Like the travel writer though, she did not allow herself to become invisible. The reader sees her boldly stepping into "unknown" territory and recording her perceptions. While many of the blacks and browns among whom she lived are second- and third-generation British, they are still seen as foreigners and regarded with distrust and disdain a decade after the book was published. *Tales from Two Cities* thus remains pertinent and compelling.

Throughout the book Murphy presents herself as genuinely neutral because she sympathizes with a multitude of often conflicting viewpoints. By the end of her urban residence she felt that she could neither forget her visit nor neatly remedy the complex problems of racial relations. She admitted in the preface to her next travel work, *Cameroon with Egbert* (1989), that "I was then rather below par: exhausted, distressed and bewildered after an intense two-and-a-half-year involvement in Britain's confused and confusing inner-city-cum-race-relations scene. As our Aeroflot plane took off I felt a sense of liberation. . . ."

While Murphy originally planned to travel alone in Nigeria, friends convinced her that Cameroon would be more to her liking, and Rachel convinced her mother to take her as companion. They decided to purchase a packhorse, Egbert, for carrying travel essentials. As Rachel remarked, "we invested £250 in a pack-horse so that we could have plenty to read." Among the books they took were two of Dervla Murphy's favorite travel works: Mary Kingsley's *Travels in West Africa* (1897) and Mungo Park's *Travels in the Interior Districts of Africa* (1799).

The adventures Murphy described in *Cameroon with Egbert* began with the quest for a three-month visa and information about Cameroonian history. The introduction offers a synopsis of Cameroonian history and includes careful observations on the geography and peoples.

Murphy's worries about inadequate visas faded as she began the journey through the highlands of Cameroon. On the first day of the trek she "experienced pure happiness," and it seemed that "uncomplicated months stretched ahead." Nonaggressive black ants, lush scenery, golden light, and a useful dream about how to load a packhorse all contribute to the travelers' happiness. Soon, however, the heat of the plains on the way to the Mbabo Mountains, sudden heavy rainstorms, the ethical problems of paying bribes, and landscapes devastated by badly planned foreign-aid projects, dispel the romance. Nevertheless, Murphy's characteristic buoyancy was reinforced by the affability and good humor of the people she met.

Murphy was intrepid, and Rachel was stoic as they made their way, getting lost several times. Their persistence rewarded them with enchanting views and extremely kind villagers but also malaria and illness from a river that looked uncontaminated but was not. Lack of water, little feed for Egbert, and the threat of attacks by lions prevent them from following their planned itinerary. At one point Rachel reminded her mother of her duties as a travel writer: "You're letting down your fans–they like to imagine you're brave. They'll hate to hear about your scooting away in panic at the first rumour of a possible lion." Of course, Murphy does not let her readers down. Only a few pages later she describes her pleasure in seeing baboons, warthogs, monkeys, and antelope in a natural environment uninhabited by humans, on the Mbabo escarpment, which surrounds primeval forest and rock-wall ravines.

By the following morning mother and daughter forgot the magnificence of the scene when they discovered that Egbert had bolted, an event which Murphy considered the worst in her twenty-five years of traveling. His loss meant that they had to change their travel plans again, which Murphy does not normally do. Yet, years of travel have taught her that one must be adaptable. It is the journey, not the arrival, that interests readers.

The going was quicker without Egbert, but they suffered "book starvation" because their reading materials had to be left with friends in Bamenda. Murphy's

-138-

Chapter Nine

The Great Karoo

Travellers have complained of the taciturnity of these Karoo people who would sit for hours without speaking many words. An occasional yes or no was often advanced during a conversation but when it drifted to matters relating to farming interests, then the host was a good conversationalist. The lack of conversation on matters pertaining to the latest European news or to the outer world generally was merely the result of ignorance. It was the consequence of the absolutely isolated life led and the very little reading indulged in. The only book read and known thoroughly was the Holy Bible.

C. Graham Botha, Social Life in the Cape Colony, 1926.

The Great Karoo, being extreme, evokes extreme reactions. 'Avoid it!' said most South Africans. 'It's hundreds of miles of dusty nothing - horrible to drive through, madness for a cyclist!' My friends, however, envied me and approved of my carefully chosen route; by keeping to dirt roads I could escape from traffic for days on end.

The further south the darker the mornings and we left Griquatown by Venus-light; never have I seen that planet so large and luminous. The sky was clear, the cold air herb-scented and heavy with the aromas of wet earth unaccustomed to rain. Then a brillian object flashed meteorite-like above the southern horizon, something lime-green and bigger than any meteorite - space-junk, no doubt. Beyond the ridge above Griquatown the gravel road continued to climb; for the first time since leaving Johannesburg I was in mountainous country - mildly mountainous.

The slow pastel dawn revealed a surprising landscape: Scottish moors in mid-winter rather than African semi-desert. As the light strengthened a strange blueness suffused the scene; this 'moorland' lay under a blanket of grey-blue brackbosch, growing densely, covering miles of shallow valleys and gradually sloping mountains with long sinuous crests. When the terrain became more broken - the valleys deeper, the hills steeper - several huge holes marked the spots where eager diamond-seekers, on their way to what was not yet Kimberley, had paused to dig hopefully. A few miles away is the river-bank on which those children found such pretty playthings in 1867.

This miniature mountain-range is the gateway to the Great Karoo; soon after 8.0 I was freewheeling fast towards a plain that extends almost to the Atlantic coast. In the eighty miles to Prieska I passed only five farm entrances - the homesteads invisible, miles off the road - and met only four farmers' bakkies. All day it remained cold, the cloudless sky an intense cobalt blue - to me an intoxicatingly beautiful colour. The clarity of the light seemed other-worldly; isolated koppies forty miles ahead, rising from the plain like gigantic buildings, looked quite close. This plain is not platteland-flat but very slightly undulating; an easy five-mile rise may be followed by a slow five-mile freewheel.

Pages from the revised typescript for Murphy's 1997 book, South from the Limpopo *(Collection of Dervla Murphy)*

-139-

For arcane geological reasons, the beauty of the colours and contours of this landscape is truly unique. So is the silence. It is a rich, alive silence. It feels like a blessing, It is a religious experience. But why is it so different from the equally flawless and awesome silence of very high and never inhabited mountain regions? Is it too fanciful to think back to the San? The Karoo was not always so sparsely inhabited, the remains of many San paintings smudge the rocks and San stone tools litter the ground; one doesn't have to search for them and a collection now adorns my desk. This silent place is desolate yet companionable; mysteriously, one never feels alone as one does in the high Andes or Karakoram. The Karoo is another sort of experience with an underlying sadness, a much more complicated experience than the liberating exhilaration bestowed by the stillness of high mountains.

If the Great Karoo feels mysterious to travellers, to scientists it is mysterious. Between 200 and 300 million years ago, - the scientists guesstimate - layers of sandstone-forming sediment were deposited one upon another, layer after layer after layer. Then came the Big Melt, causing an ocean to cover the region. Time passed - a lot of time, like seventy million years, during which the ocean was reduced to a swamp. Next, an unimaginable cataclysm convulsed the area. From the burning bowels of the earth basalt lava spewed forth, covering thousands of square miles. Then erosion set to work on the sandstone lower layers, leaving the volcanic dolerite to form those hauntingly beautiful hills (koppies) peculiar to the Great Karoo.

One should never talk of the Karoo's 'mountains'; that word suggests a complex of depths and heights, a road rising and falling, a confining of the horizon. The Karoo's koppies are lowish hills, dramatic because of the unconfined immensity of space in which each stands alone, emphasising the surrounding vastness. Oddly, most writers refer to 'table-topped hills' - and leave it at that. This, too, is misleading. Many koppies are indeed table-topped but one of the Karoo's enchantments is the infinite variety of these rocky configurations. Some are great piles of loose, rough-hewn, red-brown rock, precariously piled - jutting slabs outlined preposterously, irrationally against that cobalt sky as though here Nature had gone mad. (Doubtless that volcanic cataclysm, aeons ago, was Nature going mad.) And Erosion - what an artist! - has also produced some masterpieces of precision. Two pointed, breast-like hills, identical in size and form, rise on either side of a flat-topped koppie - a carefully arranged tableau, formal, dignified, in contrast to the chaos of piled boulders. Other hills are symmetrically crowned by serrated grey-brown rock, each crown quite perfect as though wrought by a royal jeweller. And sometimes by the wayside lie jumbles of jagged boulders, angular and multi-coloured - ochre, silver-grey, pale brown, brick-red, black, fawn - with an occasional mighty, many-sided

Dervla Murphy (photograph by Gypsy P. Ray)

enthusiasm was dampened when her ideas proved disquieting to Cameroonians, who were not willing to agree with her that Africa has lost its own cultures to rampant materialism and would be better off with the precolonial village system.

The last part of the journey included exhilarating climbing, ending in a scene of breathtaking beauty and utter horror. Lake Nyos, at first inviting after the long climb, proved eerie, and they hastened away, careless of thorn cuts and unsure of their way. They passed charred homes, dead cattle, and overgrown fields before finally reaching the ominously silent Nyos village. Eight months before, gas from the lake had exploded, killing about two thousand people. An encounter with a lone survivor is one of the most haunting scenes in Murphy's works. Despite the uneven pacing of the narrative, *Cameroon with Egbert* is a lively book that bears the hallmarks of the best travel writing: the adventures and misadventures of the narrator, memorable portraits of the peoples and landscapes, and thoughtful commentary on the issues facing the people met along the way.

Murphy's plan of returning to Africa for a journey through Uganda was put aside when travel to Romania suddenly became possible in January 1990. *Transylvania and Beyond* (1992) describes three journeys to Romania during 1990 and 1991. On hearing the news of the fall of Communist leader Nicolae Ceausescu in December 1989, Murphy planned a Transylvanian trek, for pleasure not for book material. Nevertheless, she traveled with notebooks and pens (which were all she had left after border officials stole her backpack). Her loss became a metaphor for shedding preconceptions and losing the security derived from attachments to particular possessions.

Despite feeling vulnerable without her equipment and suitable winter clothing, Murphy trekked through the Mures valley, contrasting her experience of constant vigilance against reckless truck drivers with Patrick Leigh Fermor's visions of bucolic bliss during his 1934 travels in the area. Murphy's second trek came to an abrupt end when she injured her back in a car accident. Her contact with the people of Timisoara and the pain of walking convinced her to remain in the country to write a book. At this point in the narrative, the book ceases to be a traveler's journal, becoming instead that of a political observer. The reader learns nothing about the remainder of Murphy's second journey other than that she had "a series of nightmare hassles at Belgrade airport."

When Murphy slipped back into her traveler self on her return to Romania in March 1990, she was shocked to be attacked by a farmer as she photographed the countryside. In fact, she was more welcome in the cities than in rural areas. Traveling in nontourist areas in Romania during the off-season is dangerous, and Murphy was viewed with suspicion by hotel staff and officials throughout her travels in Transylvania.

In Cluj-Napoca with the fading beauty of its historic city center surrounded by ugly housing and industrial blocks, Murphy quickly became absorbed into intellectual circles. Her conversations with students and university professors reveal some of the complexities of revolutionizing Romanian society, as well as anti-Semitic and antigypsy sentiments and a callousness about beggars and orphaned children.

A solidarity rally showed Murphy a more positive spirit and gave her hope that eventually reconciliation between all the nationalities and races in Romania might take place. The description of the scene also reminds the reader of the constant presence of the travel writer. While other observers may report the scene without revealing the reporter as participant or observer, travel writers, such as Murphy, tend to include themselves in the narration of the action. For the "close-ups" of the demonstration, the reader sees not jubilant Romanians but Murphy as she alternately observes and participates.

For a time Murphy concentrated on the concerns and scenes around her, vividly describing village life, contrasting relatively prosperous sheep farms and unproductive collectivized farms. Those villages, which managed to survive despite Ceausescu's fervor for obliterating them, appeared to have preserved the life and color that had been drained from the cities, where even the food was gray and tasteless. Murphy rejoiced to find delicately flavored apricot *tuica,* and her description gives the reader an appreciation of its color and taste, which become a metaphor for village life in general.

By April 1990 Murphy had become exhausted by the problems of Romania and longed for an interlude of quiet. She chose northern Moldavia for its mountains and picturesque villages, once again experiencing the beauties that the armchair traveler longs to experience vicariously: "a fairyland of fragile pennants of ice, streaming from every hoar-whitened blade." Another injury immobilized her for several weeks in Cluj.

The penultimate chapter of *Transylvania and Beyond* is a traveler's tale of hazardous, glass-strewn roads, and vicious sheepdogs in the Carpathians. Pausing on the Borzont Pass, Murphy was grateful for the well-maintained road to it, but she mused on the awfulness of tourist facilities in places where travelers would be content to enjoy undeveloped nature.

Reviewers of *Transylvania and Beyond* appreciated Murphy's gradual exposition of the sobering reality that followed the initial exuberance of the Romanian revolution. It is not surprising that the final chapter reveals the sadness of her return to Romania in 1991. Despite the great resilience and kindness of the Romanians, she concluded that they were unable to grapple with the complications of the movement toward democratization and with the legacies of the disastrous economic and social policies of the Ceausescu regime.

In the opening to her next book, *The Ukimwi Road: From Kenya to Zimbabwe* (1993), Murphy admits to having suffered from stress for several years. As therapy, she decided to take a carefree, solitary cycling tour through southeast Africa, refusing to reveal her route to anyone. She took her sixtieth birthday treat, a deluxe, twenty-one-speed bicycle that she named Lear. The journey gave her days of exalting cycling and the satisfaction of reaching goals despite rough going; her entire trip, however, is overshadowed by the specter of AIDS, and to a lesser extent the sight of the devastating effects of badly executed aid projects.

It would be unreasonable for the reader to expect Murphy's account of this journey to be lighthearted and filled only with descriptions of the natural beauty. Like *Transylvania and Beyond, Ukimwi Road* uneasily balances serious concerns with a traveler's focus on the self and the journey.

Often mistaken for an aid worker or government agent, Murphy quickly dissociated herself from them, feeling that she was more open-minded than the typical white person. Nevertheless, she was still criticized and admonished by African women, who forthrightly informed her that she had no understanding of their position. She also reveals her biases in attributing "exasperating mental inflexibility" to Africans who would not let her have her way.

Murphy learned a great deal about AIDS and what she calls the AIDS industry during her four-month journey from Kenya through Uganda, Tanzania, Malawi, and Zambia to Zimbabwe. Her opinion that the treatment of AIDS by Western scientists is clinically detached and ignores African culture is as controversial as her views on development projects, which she expressed in her writings about Tibetan refugees and her travels in Ethiopia and Madagascar. She strongly believes that development projects and other foreign aid undermine the recipients' self-confidence and further drain economies already weakened by first-world appropriation of resources. She considers aid another form of colonialism, which–together with the allure of the Western lifestyle–creates unrealizable desires for material goods. In reviewing *The Ukimwi Road* for *TLS: The Times Literary Supplement* (14 January 1994), Catherine Bond responded by arguing that "it is arrogant to deny them [Africans] the right to try to attain some of its [the West's] advantages." In fact, Murphy is ambivalent about Europeans' effect on nonwestern cultures, and, as she often admits, she is romantic about the virtues of village economies and peasant cultures.

The history of British imperialism in Africa serves as background to *The Ukimwi Road,* and, when Murphy follows the routes of past explorers, it creates a mild sense of danger and suspense, as though nineteenth- and twentieth-century travel conditions were similar. Murphy's venture sometimes seems like a parody of exploring. Instead of being carried by bearers, she often had to carry or push her transport, as the roads were too atrocious for her bicycle. While she is as intrigued by witch doctors as her predecessors, she also expects to find bicycle repairmen in remote villages.

Malawi was to be the height of Murphy's journey. She was particularly keen to avoid tourists; yet, some contact with tourists allowed her to criticize the latest craze in tours: overlanding. She realized that her ten-day visa could not be circumvented and, unusually, carefully planned her route along a nineteenth-century road into a remote, sparsely populated mountain area. She tested her strength and endurance and enjoyed the admiration of villagers who could not imagine anyone traveling the distance she had on a particular day. Murphy's greatest enjoyments are typical of people who deem themselves travelers: exhilarating treks, expansive views, solitude on the trail, and being the center of village attention and hospitality.

Dust jacket for Murphy's 1998 book, an account of her 1997 journey to examine the lingering effects of the 1994 civil war in Rwanda

The stance of the Western traveler in third-world countries is ambivalent, and Murphy exemplifies the paradoxes. On the one hand, she journeys to remote areas so that she can experience "authentic" culture that has not become distorted by Western values and tourist desires. She travels as a friend, not an imperialist, wanting to meet the local people on their terms, eating what they eat and sleeping as they do. She admits, however, that she quickly becomes "memsahibish" when she is impatient or ill, and she is glad to have access to British embassies around the world. In Africa, when she was stricken with malaria, she was relieved to be taken care of by strangers, rather than having to rely on her own resources. She ends up seeing her collapse as she crossed into Zimbabwe as providential because she realizes that the country is more appropriately a beginning for the exploration of South Africa than it is an end to exploring sub-Saharan Africa.

Murphy resumed her African journey with a pre-election visit to South Africa from March to August 1993, a return for the elections in April and May 1994, and a postelection tour from June to September 1994. In light of the momentous changes taking place in South Africa, Murphy was eager to see the country from multiple viewpoints. *South from the Limpopo: Travels through South Africa* (1997) presents complex, though sometimes quite naive, images and analyses. While researching the book, Murphy traveled the length and breadth of South Africa physically, psychologically, and historically, searching for the roots of apartheid and its dissolution. For those unfamiliar with South African history and the many political groups active in the struggle over apartheid, the book, which is liberally sprinkled with acronyms, can be difficult to follow.

Cycling through a country unused to and suspicious of anyone on a bicycle, especially an older white woman traveling alone, Murphy quickly learned that her traveler's eye was not only inadequate but offensive. On the first day she was told "for your own sake you should know as a white you're intruding here. This is *our* place. It's not a zoo for tourists to see how 'natives' live." The landscapes she cycled through–often parched and harsh, sometimes rich in color and intensity–as well as the weather, which shocked her with cold and heat, serve as metaphors for the people she was discouraged from observing. Murphy eventually decided that she must see the country through the eyes of its inhabitants and, after approval by the ANC (African National Congress), she temporarily settled in a Cape township. Here she found a normal everyday life that contrasted with the incidents of murder and mayhem reported by the media and by proponents of apartheid, who used a prevailing sense of lawlessness to rationalize their actions.

The tension between her desire to observe intensely and objectively and to participate constructively posed a dilemma for Murphy: "Am I being an obtuse outsider, unaware of all the nuances? Or as an outsider am I sensing something the South Africans themselves have lost sight of under the pressure of day-by-day destabilizations?" Murphy's maneuverings between factions and her stance as insider/outsider cause her viewpoints to shift occasionally. Yet, her attempts to be open-minded about even the most close-minded people she met opens up the complexities of South African society and history for the readers.

Originally traveling to South Africa with optimism about the ability of its diverse population to overthrow the past, Murphy came almost full circle by the end of her journey. The exhilaration caused by the elections and the inauguration of President Nelson Mandela was deflated almost immediately on her return for her postelection tour, when she found that she was still not welcome to work in South Africa without the proper permits. On finding her application lost, she simply began her 2,140 miles of cycling through the Zulu and Griqualand areas. Alternately energized by chill morning air and exhausted by excessive heat, Murphy came to see that the disparities in South African society are not merely between but within the races. She was distressed to discover the emergence of a wealthy black class no more concerned than its white counterpart with the lives of poorer blacks. Her final disillusionment came when she finds that her friends in the Capetown township saw her return as the opportunity for gifts, which she gave willingly. She was shocked when a day at the beach became a demonstration of blood lust. She could not comprehend the thrill her friends felt in witnessing the severe beating of a mixed-race woman by three black youths. Murphy always travels with a positive outlook, hoping to see the best in the people and societies she visits. Her fears about South Africa contradict a lifetime of fearless journey. Nevertheless, she returned to central Africa to write *Visiting Rwanda* (1998).

At an age when many people retire, Murphy has not slackened the pace of her traveling or her writing. John Murray will publish her book on Laos in 1999 and her book on Ireland in 2000.

While some of Murphy's contemporaries are content to follow in the literal and literary footsteps of illustrious travelers of the past (see, for example, recent retracings of the routes of Samuel Johnson, John Keats, and Mary Kingsley) or to travel with sound and camera crews, Murphy has always forged her own routes. As she wrote in "Foot Notes: Reflections on Travel Writing" (*Wilson Quarterly,* Summer 1992), she differentiates herself from her contemporaries by pointing to her independence: "Although I was to become a professional writer, I have remained an amateur traveller. By nature I am only interested in wandering that can be undertaken alone or with my daughter; unshackled by media subsidies or publishers' commissions, independent of newfangled equipment, and free of intrusive publicity."

Murphy is enchanted with the simple life, feeling that she can best partake of it by traveling light and seeking food and shelter without planning ahead. While she desires solitude on her travels, she also relishes communication with the people she meets. She freely admits that she has a tendency to romanticize the lives of villagers who have no modern conveniences. Nevertheless, she has come to acknowledge the deleterious effects of malnutrition and to revise her views on the status of women in rural cultures. Although she has voracious reading habits herself, she sees no reason for literacy among "simple folk." Perhaps because she uses a great deal of physical energy on her own trips and savors the pleasure of a body pushed to the limits, she glamorizes the sight of people working in the fields with their hands or primitive tools.

What differentiates Murphy from other travelers who present similar pictures of third-world life is her honesty in speaking for no one but herself. She is aware that wherever she travels, she carries the baggage of a white, first-world person, but she tries as much as possible to dispel preconceptions and bridge the gaps between herself and people of different cultures and outlooks.

Murphy has often been likened to the Victorian lady travelers, particularly Isabella Bird Bishop, but she is not as categorical as her forebears. In the less-certain world of the twentieth century, Murphy embodies its contradictions. Called "Ireland's most intrepid woman traveller" by A. A. Kelley, Murphy can also seem naive and deliberately dependent on others–she never forgets to remind readers that she is hopeless about learning languages and bicycle repair. While she clearly strives to be honest in her writing, she also seems compelled to remind the reader frequently that she is a "famous travel writer." At the same time, however, she finds that designation humorous. Less insistent than many Western travelers on clearly defined perspectives, Murphy allows her narratives to encompass the incongruities of the journey, and for this reason alone, they merit reading and re-reading.

A member of the Asiatic and Tibet Societies, Murphy is also a fellow of the Royal Geographical Society and has been short-listed for the Thomas Cook Travel Award. She continues to review books for *TLS,*

The Guardian, The Observer, and *The Irish Times*. She makes her home in County Waterford, Ireland, and she intends to continue traveling and writing as long as she lives.

Interviews:

Liz Hodgkinson, "Relative Values: Travels with my Daughter," *Sunday Times Magazine* (London), 15 December 1985, pp. 17–18;

Mary Russell, "No Home away from Home," *Times* (London), 13 November 1987, p. 21;

Clive Davis, "Adventures of a Literary Vagrant," *Times* (London), 19 August 1989, p. 33;

Shirley Kelly, "Into the Unknown," *Writers' Monthly* (April 1992): 4–6.

References:

A. A. Kelley, "Dervla Murphy," in her *Wandering Women: Two Centuries of Travel out of Ireland* (Dublin: Wolfhound, 1995), pp. 189–195;

Sonia Melchett, *Passionate Quests: Five Modern Women Travellers* (Boston & London: Faber & Faber, 1991), pp. 7–55;

Mary Russell, *Blessings of a Good Thick Skirt: Women Travellers and Their World* (London: Collins, 1986), pp. 159–160, 167–169, 191–192.

V. S. Naipaul

(17 August 1932 –)

Sura Prasad Rath
Louisiana State University in Shreveport

BOOKS: *The Mystic Masseur* (London: Deutsch, 1957; New York: Vanguard, 1959);

The Suffrage of Elvira (London: Deutsch, 1958; New York: Vintage, 1985);

Miguel Street (London: Deutsch, 1959; New York: Vanguard, 1960);

A House for Mr. Biswas (London: Deutsch, 1961; New York: McGraw-Hill, 1962); republished with a new foreword by Naipaul (New York: Knopf, 1983; London: Deutsch, 1984);

The Middle Passage: Impressions of Five Societies, British, French and Dutch, in the West Indies and South America (London: Deutsch, 1962; New York: Macmillan, 1963);

Mr. Stone and the Knights Companion (London: Deutsch, 1963; New York: Macmillan, 1964);

An Area of Darkness (London: Deutsch, 1964; New York: Macmillan, 1965);

The Mimic Men (London: Deutsch, 1967; New York: Macmillan, 1967);

A Flag on the Island (London: Deutsch, 1967; New York: Macmillan, 1967);

The Loss of El Dorado: A History (London: Deutsch, 1969; New York: Knopf, 1970; revised edition, Harmondsworth: Penguin, 1977);

In a Free State (London: Deutsch, 1971; New York: Knopf, 1971);

The Overcrowded Barracoon and Other Articles (London: Deutsch, 1972; New York: Knopf, 1973);

Guerrillas (London: Deutsch, 1975; New York: Knopf, 1975);

India: A Wounded Civilization (London: Deutsch, 1977; New York: Knopf, 1977);

A Bend in the River (London: Deutsch, 1979; New York: Knopf, 1979);

A Congo Diary (London: Sylvester & Orphanos, 1980);

The Return of Eva Perón; with The Killings in Trinidad (London: Deutsch, 1980; New York: Knopf, 1980);

Among the Believers: An Islamic Journey (London: Deutsch, 1981; New York: Knopf, 1981);

Finding the Center: Two Narratives (New York: Knopf, 1984); republished as *Finding the Centre: Two Narratives* (London: Deutsch, 1984);

V. S. Naipaul

The Enigma of Arrival: A Novel in Five Sections (Harmondsworth & New York: Viking, 1987); republished as *The Enigma of Arrival: A Novel* (New York: Knopf, 1987);

A Turn in the South (London: Viking, 1989; Franklin Center, Pa.: Privately printed for the Franklin Library, 1989; New York: Knopf, 1989);

India: A Million Mutinies Now (London: Heinemann, 1990; New York: Viking, 1991);

Bombay: Gateway of India, photographs by Raghubir Singh (New York: Aperture, 1994);

A Way in the World: A Sequence (London: Heinemann, 1994); republished as *A Way in the World: A Novel* (New York: Knopf, 1994);

Beyond Belief: Islamic Excursions among the Converted Peoples (London: Little, Brown, 1998; New York: Random House, 1998).

OTHER: Seepersad Naipaul, *The Adventures of Gurudeva,* foreword by Naipaul (London: Deutsch, 1976).

SELECTED PERIODICAL PUBLICATIONS–UNCOLLECTED: "Letter to Maria," *New Statesman,* 56 (5 July 1958): 14;

"The Regional Barrier," *Times Literary Supplement,* 15 August 1958, pp. 37–38;

"Caribbean Medley," *Vogue,* 134 (15 November 1959): 90;

"New Novels," *New Statesman,* 59 (26 March 1960): 461–462;

"The Little More," *Times* (London), 13 July 1961, p. 13;

"Living like a Millionaire," *Vogue,* 138 (15 October 1961): 92–93;

"Jamshed into Jimmy," *New Statesman,* 65 (25 January 1963): 129–130;

"Castles of Fear," *Spectator,* 211 (5 July 1963): 16;

"Sporting Life," *Encounter,* 21 (September 1963): 73–75;

"Speaking of Writing," *Times* (London), 2 January 1964, p. 11;

"Trinidad," *Mademoiselle,* 59 (May 1964): 187–188;

"Words on Their Own," *Times Literary Supplement,* 4 June 1964, p. 472;

"The Documentary Heresy," *Twentieth Century,* 173 (Winter 1964): 107–108;

"Australia Deserta," *Spectator,* 213 (16 October 1964): 513;

"They Are Staring at Me," *Saturday Evening Post,* 238 (10 April 1965): 82–84;

"East Indian, West Indian," *Reporter,* 332 (17 June 1965): 35–37;

"Images," *New Statesman,* 70 (24 September 1965): 452–453;

"What's Wrong with Being a Snob?" *Saturday Evening Post,* 240 (3 June 1967): 2, 18;

"Comprehending Borges," *New York Review of Books,* 19 (19 August 1972): 3–6;

"A Country Dying on Its Feet," *New York Review of Books* (4 April 1974);

"Argentina: The Brothels behind the Graveyard," *New York Review of Books,* 21 (19 September 1974): 12–16;

"Conrad's Darkness," *New York Review of Books,* 21 (17 October 1974): 16–21;

"Letters to a Young Writer," *New Yorker,* 71 (26 June 1995): 144–153;

"Notebooks," *Granta,* 57 (Spring 1997): 194–203;

"After the Revolution," *New Yorker,* 73 (26 May 1997): 46–69.

In a 1994 interview with John F. Baker, V. S. Naipaul said: "I'd like to travel some more before the body shuts down completely. But I can't travel without writing. I love to see things come out of the darkness, and if I can't do that I'll feel I've lost something vital. I have to do that." Things coming "out of the darkness"–unraveling the mystery of the unknown and rediscovering the meaning of the known in a new light–are central to Naipaul's traveling and writing. His explorations of the geographical territories of the earth are so intricately intertwined with his probing of the psyche of the people–real and fictional–whom he describes that one might rephrase his words and claim that he cannot write without traveling.

For this Trinidad-born grandchild of an East Indian indentured laborer, a trip to Oxford in 1950 opened the doors to a vast new world that expanded as he recorded his experiences in fiction and nonfiction. Since then Naipaul has visited and written about Africa, Asia, North and South America, and Europe. In many of his books the boundaries between the journalist Naipaul and his fictional narrators become blurred, mixing up memory and history, the genres of the travelogue and the novel.

Naipaul is heir to three major cultures: his grandparents' north Indian Hindu culture; colonial British culture; and Trinidadian culture, which itself includes African black culture and South American Hispanic culture. Each culture has been integral to his growing sense of self-identity, and his travel to various parts of the world is closely tied to his search for this identity. The farther he has traveled abroad, the more deeply he has penetrated into himself. Naipaul's travel writing is a hybrid form, bringing together the journalistic realism of conventional travelogue and the realistic portrayal of fictional characters.

The second of seven children–two boys and five girls–of Seepersad and Bropatie Capildeo Naipaul, Vidiadhar Surajprasad Naipaul was born in Chaguanas, Trinidad, on 17 August 1932. His grandparents on both sides had been indentured laborers from Uttar Pradesh, India, and were of the Brahman caste. Naipaul attended the Chaguanas Government School until 1938, when the family moved to Port of Spain; there he attended the Tranquility Boys' School. Naipaul's father, although he had only an elementary-school education, had become a reporter for the *Trinidad Guardian.* In 1943 he published *Gurudeva and Other Indian Tales,* a critical and satiric depiction of the decay of the immigrant community separated from its root culture. The proof copy of

Dust jacket for the 1973 U.S. edition of a collection of Naipaul's essays written over a fifteen-year period; the title piece is about the island of Mauritius.

the privately published book is now in the V. S. Naipaul Archive in the McFarlin Library at the University of Tulsa. In 1976 he wrote the foreword to a republication of the book under the title *The Adventures of Gurudeva.*

Naipaul studied at the prestigious Queens Royal College from 1943 to 1949. In 1948 he won a Trinidad government scholarship to study abroad; two years later he began studying English literature at University College, Oxford. After taking his degree in 1954 he worked briefly in the cataloguing department of the National Portrait Gallery in London and then as an editor for the British Broadcasting Corporation program *Caribbean Voices* and a reviewer for the *New Statesman.* In 1955 he married Patricia Ann Hale, whom he had met at Oxford. After her death in 1996, he married Nadira Alvi.

The search for a home and the trauma of homelessness have been central to Naipaul's writing. His first four books explore this rootlessness in fictional form. The protagonist of the novel *The Mystic Masseur* (1957), Pundit Ganesh, after failing as a schoolteacher, a faith healer, a scholar and author, and a technical wizard, ends up mimicking colonial values by changing his name to G. Ramsey Muir, Esq., M.B.E., and being elected to the Trinidad Legislative Council. The book won the prestigious John Llewellyn Rhys Memorial Prize in 1958. *The Suffrage of Elvira* (1958) focuses on a backward country holding its second election; self-governance becomes a mockery in the hands of people who are unprepared to accept the responsibilities of democracy. *Miguel Street* (1959) is a collection of short stories in which the narrator is a boy who learns about life on the street in colonial Trinidad. The narrator calls his people "romancers," though what he sees in their lives is the stark realism of poverty and despair in which American movies influence the popular culture and the men try to salvage their dignity through physical and mental abuse of women. The book won the W. Somerset Maugham Award in 1961. Considered by many Naipaul's masterpiece, *A House for Mr. Biswas* (1961) is a story of the pain and hardship of immigrant life in Trinidad. Mr. Biswas dies unemployed and unable to pay off the mortgage on his new house; the husbands of Mr. Biswas's in-laws, the Tulsis, have to move into Hanuman House, the Tulsi home, because they cannot afford to build their own homes; and the Tulsi sons marry into non-Hindu families, ushering in the decay of the family's Hindu religious practices.

In 1960–1961 Naipaul spent five months visiting Trinidad, British Guiana, Surinam, Martinique, and Jamaica on a scholarship from the government of Trinidad. The trip resulted in *The Middle Passage: Impressions of Five Societies, British, French and Dutch, in the West Indies and South America* (1962). The title is derived from the middle leg of the trade route that brought slaves to the New World. The transition from fiction to travel writing was not easy for Naipaul. In the foreword to *Finding the Center: Two Narratives* (1984) he says: "When more than twenty years ago I began to travel as a writer, I was uneasy and uncertain. My instinct was toward fiction; I found it constricting to have to deal with fact." The glamour of the "idea of the long journey" appealed to him, but he wondered how he might "set about looking at a place in a way that would be of value to other people." Also, "To arrive at a place without knowing anyone there, and sometimes without an introduction; to learn how to move among strangers for the short time one could afford to be among them; to hold oneself in constant readiness for adventure or revelation; to allow oneself to be carried along, up to a point, by accidents; and consciously to follow up other impulses–that could be as creative and imaginative a procedure as the writing that came after." The possibility of failure in reaching an insight about a people or a place, alternating with the moments when a place would begin to clear up and experiences yield new meanings, gave every arrival a "gambler's excitement." Ultimately, travel "broadened my world-view; it showed me a changing world and took me out of my own colonial shell; it became the substitute for the mature social experience–the deepening knowledge of a society–which my background and the nature of my life denied me."

In the West Indies, Naipaul sees that the immigrant communities suffer from a self-contempt that kills their potential for achievement; in British Guiana the missionaries even preach self-contempt to the natives in an attempt to convert them. In Surinam residents boast of their real or affected ignorance of local customs and traditions as a sign of their social status. In Martinique, a French territory, most consumer goods are imported from France, and even locally produced merchandise is marketed through French agents. In all of the islands the slavery of the colonial past is replaced by economic slavery as descendants of the former slaves sell themselves and their country to the package tour operators. Naipaul sees little or no plan for sustained economic development, no indigenous models for growth, and no vision. The shadows of colonial life linger in these places and keep the people in darkness.

Critical response to Naipaul's unrelenting exposé of the postcolonial decadence in the Caribbean was divided. In *Conversations with V. S. Naipaul* (1997) Bharati Mukherjee, an expatriate Indian author living in the United States, is quoted as saying that Naipaul "travels to confirm his Eurocentric prejudices," that he is "a mass of defenses, a personality in knots, obsessed with his own expatriation, with his in-bred cultural distance from what is, for him, the center of the universe, London." But in the same work Robert Hass says that Naipaul

> is the supreme writer of disenchantment that we have now. Most Western writers grew up in a rationalized world hungry for enchantment, whereas he grew up in an enchanted world and was hungry for rationality. The targets of his contempt are almost always people who have some sort of delusion–he *hates* them.

In 1961 Naipaul made a year-long tour of his ancestors' homeland, India. He writes about the trip in *An Area of Darkness* (1964). Traveling via Greece and Egypt, he arrived at Bombay to encounter an unfriendly, incomprehensible bureaucracy, but soon "some little feeling for India as the mythical land of my childhood was awakened." "India is the poorest country in the world," he observes; but "to see its poverty is to make an observation of no value," for "a thousand newcomers to the country before you have seen and said as you." He traveled extensively, visiting his ancestral village in the north Indian state of Uttar Pradesh, the Dal Lake in Kashmir, and the holy cave of Amarnath in the Himalayas. Places and people are described in vivid detail, but the narrative soon evolves into introspection and self-analysis:

> I had seen Indian villages: the narrow, broken lanes with green slime in the gutters, the choked back-to-back mud house, the jumble of filth and food and animals and people, the baby in the dust, swollen-bellied, black with flies, but wearing its good luck amulet. I had seen the starved child defecating at the roadside while the mangy dog waited to eat the excrement. I had seen the physique of the people of Andhra, which had suggested the possibility of an evolution downwards, wasted body to wasted body, Nature mocking herself, incapable of remission. Compassion and pity did not answer; they were refinements of hope. Fear was what I felt. Contempt was what I had to fight against; to give way to that was to abandon the self I had known.

Naipaul is keenly aware of the ambivalence with which he approaches his ancestral land. In the "India of my childhood, the land which in my imagination was an extension, separate from the alienness by which we ourselves were surrounded, of my grandmother's house, there was no alien presence," he reminisces, but he also finds that the old India has eroded, that "what was whole was the Idea of India." His hope of blending into the Indian crowd is undercut by his Western upbringing. "It was like being denied part of my reality," he realizes. "I had been made by Trinidad and England; recognition of my difference was necessary to me. I felt the need to impose myself, and didn't know how."

An Area of Darkness was followed by three works in which the line between fiction and travel writing becomes blurred. Bruce King calls *The Mimic Men* (1967), a psychological portrait of a transplanted Indian, Ralph Kripal Singh, the author's "attempt to understand how his own personal and colonial past has shaped his character, vision and approach to writing." Instead of the linear chronological narrative of the earlier novels, it uses memory and flashback to develop Singh's character. *A Flag on the Island* (1967) is a collection of stories, the earliest of which, "The Mourners," dates back to 1950. In the title story Naipaul offers vignettes of life on a Caribbean island after independence, as American influence replaces the former British presence. The nonfiction *The Loss of El Dorado: A History* (1969) is an examination of the early history of Trinidad that King calls "a study in the greed and mistaken idealism which produced colonial empires."

Naipaul traveled in east Africa from December 1965 to September 1966; in the Caribbean, Central America, and the United States from October 1968 to September 1969; and in India in early 1971. The African tour provided the background for *In a Free State* (1971), which comprises a prologue and epilogue describing Naipaul's experiences in Egypt and three short stories. In the prologue Egyptian businessmen humiliate an Englishman; in the epilogue an Egyptian tries to humiliate some poor people. In the first story,

Advertisement for Naipaul's controversial 1981 book about the rise of Islamic fundamentalism in Iran, Indonesia, Malaysia, and Pakistan, based on his travels there in 1979–1980

"One out of Many," Santosh, an Indian diplomat's servant, leaves his employer in Washington, D.C., and becomes an illegal immigrant to the United States. Fearing deportation, he marries an African American woman but soon finds that he is out of place in an alien setting that neither accepts him as its own nor respects his Hindu sense of racial purity. His freedom from Indian servitude turns out to be merely a delusion as it brings him confusion and loss of self-respect. The protagonist of the second story, "Tell Me Who to Kill," is an expatriate West Indian in London, and the central characters in the title story are two expatriate English civil servants in a recently independent African state in the midst of a civil war. *In a Free State* won the prestigious Booker Prize. *The Overcrowded Barracoon and Other Articles* (1972) is a collection of essays written over a fifteen-year period; the title essay is about Mauritius, a British colony that became independent in 1968 and that Naipaul visited in early 1971. The new nation has to cope with scanty resources and growing population; it remains an "agricultural colony, created by empire in an empty island" now left to itself as "an abandoned imperial barracoon, incapable of economic or cultural autonomy." *Guerrillas* (1975) is a novel set in the West Indies.

Naipaul recorded his 1971 visit to India in *India: A Wounded Civilization* (1977). "India is for me a difficult country," he says in the preface. "It isn't my home and cannot be my home; and yet I cannot reject it or be indifferent to it; I cannot travel only for the sights." Naipaul sees a living spirit in the geography of the land through which he travels:

> India in the late twentieth century still seems so much itself, so rooted in its own civilization, it takes time to understand that its independence has meant more than the going away of the British; that the India to which Independence came was a land of far older defeat; that the purely Indian past died a long time ago of a new Indian dissolution.

Naipaul notices what the ordinary tourist does not: blind obedience to rules and rituals, the decay of traditional religious and political ideals, the celebration of destitution and deprivation, the failure of the doctrine of karma as a sustaining principle for progress, the collective amnesia of a people languishing in a stupor, stagnation, the defeat of the common people's dreams, and the death of the intellect, "spiritually annulling the civilization out of which it issues, India swallowing its own tail." He ends on a prophetic note:

> While India tries to go back to an idea of its past, it will not possess that past or be enriched by it. The past can now be possessed only by inquiry and scholarship, by intellectual rather than spiritual discipline. The past has to be seen to be dead; or the past will kill.

In 1979 Naipaul traveled to Iran, Indonesia, Malaysia, and Pakistan to research *Among the Believers: An Islamic Journey* (1981), an in-depth analysis of the rise of Islamic fundamentalism. The book received angry reviews. Edward Said wrote in the *New Statesman* (16 October 1981) that Naipaul "carries with him a kind of half-stated but finally unexamined reverence for the colonial order," an attitude that "the old days were better, when Europe ruled the coloureds and allowed them few silly pretensions about purity, independence, and new ways." This "East/West dichotomy," according to Said, "covers up a deep emptiness in Naipaul the writer, for which Naipaul the social phenomenon is making others pay, even as a whole train of his present admirers applauds his candour, his telling-it-like-it-is about that Third World which he comprehends 'better' than anyone else." Fouad Ajami said in *The New York Times Book*

Review (25 October 1981) that instead of trying to understand the Muslims, Naipaul is "ready to judge them":

> In his desire to discover their hidden vulnerabilities and point out their contradictions, their need for outside goods and approval, he tends to miss the drama and the real meaning of their situation. He forgets that it is part of the painful process of history that people are always made by the world they reject and that the rage at it they express is in large measure rage at themselves.

Ajami called *Among the Believers* Naipaul's thinnest and least impressive book. Julio Marzan wrote in *The Village Voice* (4–10 November 1981) that Naipaul traveled to the Islamic countries "to confirm about Islam the third world flaws he knew he would find: institutionalized hypocrisy, blind idealism, and the failure to match lofty ideology with performance." He said that *Among the Believers* is less about the countries visited than about Naipaul among the believers, "over whom, in a civilized manner, his personality looms as the hero embodying a presumed, schematically articulated Westernism." In *The Hudson Review* (Spring 1982) Marvin Mudrick called Naipaul "a one-idea writer (How do these barbarians have the *nerve* to set themselves up against the West?)." Still other critics pointed to Naipaul's blindness toward the faults of the West.

The first part of *Finding the Center: Two Narratives,* "Prologue to an Autobiography," combines an account of Naipaul's beginnings as a writer with reminiscences of Trinidad and his father, who died in 1953. The second narrative, "The Crocodiles of Yamoussoukro," is a report on Naipaul's visit to the Ivory Coast at the end of 1982. Written between April and June 1983, it expresses his wonder and joy at the Ivorian community and its mysteries, finding there a heartland, a center, rather than a suburb, of the world. D. A. N. Jones commented in *The London Review of Books* (3–16 May 1984) that "what Naipaul seems to have found among the Ivorians is an intriguing, encouraging reflection of the ex-colonial, ancient-and-modern dilemma faced both by his real-life father and by Mr. Biswas: the Ivorians had their own equivalent of the choice between vaccinating the cattle or sacrificing to Kali, and they had the confidence to reconcile the two."

In 1984 Naipaul traveled to the United States to observe the Republican Convention in Dallas for an article commissioned by *The New York Review of Books.* While he was in Dallas the idea for a book on the American South came to him, and in 1987 he returned to the United States. In *A Turn in the South* (1989) he examines America's past and present from the perspective of his experiences in Trinidad and India. Visiting the restored Middleburg Plantation in the former rice country of South Carolina, Naipaul remarks both on the fidelity of the restoration and its most significant omission:

> The land and the past were being honored, the plantation and the river at its back which had made for the rice paddies, as in the East Indies. But what was missing were the slave cabins. The plantation house, even with its surviving dependencies, was without what would have been its most important–and most notable–feature.

The landscape he surveys has been cleansed of the most damning evidence of the past. The slave cabins are gone; only an avenue of oaks remains. He finds it difficult "to set the cabins in that grandeur that spoke more of old European country houses." In Charleston he meets an elderly woman who tells him that according to family legend, her "Burke ancestors from Philadelphia had been left the island of Trinidad." Incredulous, Naipaul asks, "The whole island?" She replies, "That is the story. Southern people like to feel that, once upon a time at least, they were rich. But they died, the Burkes, in the Windward passage, when they were going down to claim the land." Naipaul muses on what might have happened had the Burkes been able to claim their holdings: "How strange to reflect that the black people of Trinidad I grew up among might, with another twist, have been born in the Carolinas and might have had a different history."

Slavery ended in the British colonies in 1834; by the 1980s "150 years separate the black people of the British caribbean from slavery." Although slavery officially ended in the American South during the Civil War, Naipaul remarks, American blacks only began to acquire their freedom in 1954: "In those thirty years American blacks have grown to see opportunity; while the larger independent territories of the British Caribbean–Trinidad, Jamaica, Guyana–have in their various ways been plundered and undone." Naipaul comes to appreciate the American South's palpable sense of history and defeat. It is this "sense of a special past, the past as a wound," that he misses when he drives north into Virginia. History in Virginia, the land of Thomas Jefferson and Monticello, is a celebration of achievement and wealth, while the people of the deep South are "coming to terms with a more desperate kind of New World history."

In 1988, twenty-seven years after his first visit to India, Naipaul, as he says in *India: A Million Mutinies Now* (1990), "succeeded in making a kind of return journey, shedding my Indian nerves, abolishing the darkness that separated me from my ancestral past." An optimistic book, *India: A Million Mutinies Now* lets India define itself through the experiences of its people rather than

Dust jacket for Naipaul's 1989 account of his travels in the southern United States in 1987

depicting it through Naipaul's reactions. Places such as Bombay, Goa, Calcutta, and Delhi are described by the men and women with whom he talks. A cross section of Indian society is presented: Muslims living in ghettoes, Hindu and Sikh leaders, slum dwellers, gangsters, terrorists, radical conservative Brahmans, politicians, scientists, writers, journalists, publishers of women's magazines, and former princes. One of the individuals is a Brahman from Madras whom Naipaul had first met in 1962 on a Himalayan trip taken during the annual pilgrimage to the ice lingam, symbol of Shiva, in the cave of Amarnath. No longer a young man, no longer living in the house of his middle-class parents, and with the Brahmans no longer rulers of the area, the man Naipaul calls Sugar occupies a one-room ground-floor apartment. Yet Sugar is neither bitter nor despairing, despite his ill health and changed circumstances. Instead, in his apartment he receives many who come "just for peace," for the gifts of his spirit. Naipaul observes that he was "perhaps more protected, more looked-up to, than he had ever been in the family house where he had grown up." The horror and degradation that characterize India in the two earlier travel books have been replaced by glimmers of hope. The old darkness lingers in India, and what Naipaul had described as its self-inflicted wounds continue to fester, but he sees among educated Indians a willingness to discuss the issues of history and challenge the previously unquestioned path of national destiny.

Naipaul was knighted in 1990. In *A Way in the World: A Sequence* (1994) he sketches his life as a boy in Trinidad, a student at Oxford, a struggling writer, and a world traveler. These vignettes frame portraits of two earlier travelers, Sir Walter Ralegh and Francisco Miranda, whose lives were destroyed by their attempts to exploit the places they visited. The work is part autobiography, part fiction, and part travel narrative.

In 1995 Naipaul returned to Indonesia, Iran, Pakistan, and Malaysia, revisiting many of the social, political, and cultural issues, and interviewing some of the same people, presented in *Among the Believers.* The record of this five-month trip is *Beyond Belief: Islamic Excursions among the Converted Peoples* (1998). The book focuses on the "effects of the Islamic conversion" on people in the four non-Arab Muslim countries. "This is a book about people," Naipaul says in the prologue. "It is not a book of opinion. It is a book of stories." But in his usual way he presents his views about the "Imperial Arabizing demands" Islam makes on its converts. In Indonesia he sees many changes in Imanuddin, the lecturer in electrical engineering and Islamic preacher he had met in 1979. The scientist-preacher now hosts a Sunday morning television program: "The very mixture of science and Islam that had made him suspect to the authorities in the 1970s now made him desirable, the model of the Indonesian new man, and had taken him up to the heights, had taken him very near to the fount of power." In Iran he observes that the Muslim fundamentalists' tyranny is no less than that of the Shah in earlier years. In Pakistan he sees a populace obsessed with fantasy and neurosis about their imaginary Arab ancestry. In Malaysia the Muslim Youth organization thrives, but the people struggle to keep their faith in the face of spiritual decline. *Beyond Belief* shows a more mature and more balanced Naipaul, and as a supplement to *Among the Believers,* offers a map of the changes that the Asian region has undergone in nearly two decades.

For Sir Vidia Naipaul, who has traveled throughout the world for nearly half a century, every new place has a mystery to unfold, a new truth to deliver. As the unnamed narrator says in *The Enigma of Arrival:* "After all my time in England I still had that nervousness in a new place, that rawness of response, still felt myself to be in the other man's country, felt my strangeness, my solitude. And every excursion into a new part of the country–what for others might have been an adventure–was for me like a tearing at an old scab." He is the traveler for whom the horizon is never reached, for whom the unknown others out in the unseen corners of the world hold the key to his ever unknowable self.

Interviews:

Dileep Padgaonkar, "The Hindu Awakening. (On Soul of the World Order)," *New Perspectives Quarterly,* 10 (Fall 1993): 60–62;

K. Sharma, "Indians Have Never Talked about India in This Way Before," *Times of India,* 5 December 1993;

Mel Gussow, "V. S. Naipaul in Search of Himself: A Conversation," *New York Times Book Review,* 24 April 1994, pp. 29–30;

John F. Baker, "Interview with V. S. Naipaul," *Publishers Weekly,* 241 (6 June 1994): 44–45;

Aamer Hussein, "Delivering the Truth," *Times Literary Supplement,* 2 September 1994, pp. 3–4;

Feroza Jussawalla, ed., *Conversations with V. S. Naipaul* (Oxford: University Press of Mississippi, 1997).

Bibliographies:

Kelvin Jarvis, *V. S. Naipaul: A Selective Bibliography with Annotations, 1957–1987* (Metuchen, N.J. & London: Scarecrow, 1989);

Jarvis, "V. S. Naipaul: A Bibliographical Update (1987–94)," *Ariel,* 26 (October 1995): 71–85.

References:

Ian Baucom, "Mournful Histories: Narratives of Postimperial Melancholy," *Modern Fiction Studies,* 42 (Summer 1996): 259–288;

Roger A. Berger, "Writing without a Future: Colonial Nostalgia in V. S. Naipaul's *A Bend in the River,*" *Essays in Literature,* 22 (Spring 1995): 144–156;

Selwyn R. Cudjoe, *V. S. Naipaul: A Materialist Reading* (Amherst: University of Massachusetts Press, 1988);

Wimal Dissanayake and Carmen Wickramagamage, *Self and Colonial Desire: Travel Writings of V. S. Naipaul,* Studies of World Literature in English, volume 2 (New York: Peter Lang, 1993);

Robert D. Hamner, *V. S. Naipaul* (New York: Twayne, 1973);

Dolly Zulakha Hassan, *V. S. Naipaul and the West Indies* (New York: Peter Lang, 1989);

Graham Huggan, "V. S. Naipaul and the Political Correctness Debate," *College Literature,* 21 (October 1994): 200–206;

Peter Hughes, *V. S. Naipaul* (New York: Routledge & Kegan Paul, 1989);

Shashi Kamra, *The Novels of V. S. Naipaul: A Study in Theme and Form* (New Delhi: Prestige Books in association with Indian Society for Commonwealth Studies, 1990);

Bruce King, *V. S. Naipaul* (New York: St. Martin's Press, 1993);

Judith Levy, *V. S. Naipaul: Displacement and Autobiography,* Garland Reference Library of the Humanities, volume 1781 (New York: Garland, 1995);

Peggy Nightingale, *Journey through Darkness: The Writing of V. S. Naipaul* (St. Lucia, Australia & New York: University of Queensland Press, 1987);

Rob Nixon, *London Calling: V. S. Naipaul, Postcolonial Mandarin* (New York: Oxford University Press, 1992);

William S. Pritchard, "Naipaul's Written World," *Hudson Review,* 47 (Winter 1995): 587–596;

Stephen Schiff, "The Ultimate Exile," *New Yorker,* 70 (23 May 1994): 60–71;

Paul Theroux, *Sir Vidia's Shadow: A Friendship across Five Continents* (Boston: Houghton Mifflin, 1998);

Timothy F. Weiss, *On the Margins: The Art of Exile in V. S. Naipaul* (Amherst: University of Massachusetts Press, 1992);

Weiss, "V. S. Naipaul's 'fin de siecle': *The Enigma of Arrival* and *A Way in the World,*" *Ariel,* 27 (July 1996): 107–124;

Sarah Lawson Welsh, "The West Indies," *Journal of Commonwealth Literature,* 31 (Winter 1996): 177–186;

Christopher Wise, "The Garden Trampled: Or the Liquidation of African Culture in V. S. Naipaul's *A Bend in the River,*" *College Literature,* 23 (October 1996): 58–72.

Papers:

Many of V. S. Naipaul's early manuscripts, which were stored in two boxes in a London warehouse, were destroyed because of a confusion in labeling. In the United States the V. S. Naipaul Archive at the University of Tulsa holds the author's surviving papers, including prepublication notes, drafts, manuscripts, and typescripts before 1986. All of the papers except some notebooks related to *A Turn in the South* and *India: A Million Mutinies Now* are available to scholars.

Eric Newby

(6 December 1919 –)

Kenneth A. Robb
Bowling Green State University

and

Harender Vasudeva
Bowling Green State University

BOOKS: *The Last Grain Race* (London: Secker & Warburg, 1956; Boston: Houghton Mifflin, 1956);

A Short Walk in the Hindu Kush (London: Secker & Warburg, 1958); republished as *A Short Walk: A Preposterous Adventure* (Garden City, N.Y.: Doubleday, 1958);

Something Wholesale (London: Secker & Warburg, 1962);

Time Off in Southern Italy: The Observer Guide to Resorts and Hotels (London: Hodder & Stoughton, 1966);

Slowly Down the Ganges (London: Hodder & Stoughton, 1966; New York: Scribners, 1967);

Grain Race: Pictures of Life before the Mast in a Windjammer (London: Allen & Unwin, 1968); republished as *Windjammer: Pictures of Life before the Mast in the Last Grain Race* (New York: Dutton, 1968);

Wonders of Britain: A Personal Choice of 480, by Newby and Diana Petry (London: Hodder & Stoughton, 1968); republished as *Wonders of Britain and Where to Find Them* (New York: London House, 1971);

Wonders of Ireland: A Personal Choice of 484, by Newby and Petry (London: Hodder & Stoughton, 1969; New York: Stein & Day, 1970);

Love and War in the Apennines (London: Hodder & Stoughton, 1971); republished as *When the Snow Comes, They Will Take You Away* (New York: Scribners, 1971);

The Mitchell Beazley World Atlas of Exploration (London: Mitchell Beazley, 1975); republished as *The Rand McNally World Atlas of Exploration* (Chicago: Rand McNally, 1975); republished as *The World Atlas of Exploration* (South Melbourne, Australia: Macmillan / London: Mitchell Beazley, 1975);

Great Ascents: A Narrative History of Mountaineering (Newton Abbot, U.K.: David & Charles, 1977; New York: Viking, 1977);

The Big Red Train Ride (London: Weidenfeld & Nicolson, 1978; New York: St. Martin's Press, 1978);

A Traveller's Life (London: Collins, 1982; Boston: Little, Brown, 1982);

On the Shores of the Mediterranean (London: Harvill, 1984; Boston: Little, Brown, 1984);

Round Ireland in Low Gear (London: Collins, 1987; New York: Viking, 1988);

What the Traveller Saw (London: Flamingo, 1989; New York: Viking, 1990);

A Small Place in Italy (London: HarperCollins, 1994);

A Merry Dance around the World: The Best of Eric Newby (London: HarperCollins, 1995).

OTHER: *My Favourite Stories of Travel,* edited by Newby (London: Lutterworth, 1967);

Ganga: Sacred River of India, photographs by Raghubir Singh, introduction by Newby (Hong Kong: Perennial Press, 1974);

A Book of Travellers' Tales, edited by Newby (London: Collins, 1985; New York: Viking, 1986).

In his early works Eric Newby shows the spirit of adventure and endurance–spiced by more than a pinch of foolhardiness–that is requisite for a great explorer. He was born after most of the blank spaces on the maps had been filled in, however, and consequently he became a traveler and travel writer. After books about his sea voyage to Australia and his travels in Afghanistan and India, he focused on the British Isles and the Mediterranean, but he also made a trip through the Soviet Union on the Trans-Siberian Railroad, and he has traveled and written on other areas in the Eastern Hemisphere. His books convey his knowledge with informality and wit. Usually a companion–in his later travels his wife, Wanda–provides a realistic, sometimes caustic foil when Newby's persona fails to describe adequately the discomforts and inconveniences of their adventures. Newby's books are often excellent guides to

Eric Newby, 1942 (courtesy of Eric Newby)

little-known, relatively unvisited places in otherwise familiar geographical contexts.

George Eric Newby was born in London on 6 December 1919 to George and Hilda Pomeroy Newby. After attending St. Paul's School in London, he worked at an advertising agency in 1937 and 1938. The loss of a major account and the resulting threat of cuts in salaries and jobs led him to sign on with the Grain Fleet, thirteen three- and four-masted sailing ships that carried grain from South Australia to Europe. Their last voyage was in 1938, the year Newby sailed aboard the Finnish ship *Moshulu.* Nearly twenty years later he described the details of that journey in *The Last Grain Race* (1956), his first travel book. He sailed in September 1938 and was back in England the following June. That autumn World War II began, and he joined the British Army.

After serving in India and the Middle East, Newby was sent to Italy, where he became a prisoner of war in August 1942. He recalls in *Something Wholesale* (1962) that to escape the feeling of confinement he talked with prisoners who were amateur explorers about fantastic journeys they might someday undertake. In September 1943, after the Italians surrendered and the Germans had tightened their grip on Italy, Newby and other prisoners escaped from the orphanage where they were being held, near Parma. Abandoned by the others because he had a broken ankle, Newby credits his survival to "the ordinary Italian people who helped prisoners of war at great personal risk" and Wanda Skof, a young Slovenian woman. He was recaptured in January 1944 and spent the rest of the war in prisoner-of-war camps in Germany. He wrote about his experiences in Italy in *Love and War in the Apennines* (1971) and in *A Traveller's Life* (1982).

After the war ended in 1945, Newby's parents involved him in the family business, Lane and Newby, which specialized in expensive ready-made women's clothing. He performed various jobs at the headquarters on Great Marlborough Street, briefly traveling abroad to thank the Italians who had helped escaped Allied prisoners during the war, but especially to see Wanda Skof. They were married in Florence on 4 April 1946 and eventually had two children, Sonia and Jonathan. Newby worked at the garment trade through the gradual decline of Lane and Newby. In 1954 Newby went to work for Worth-Paquin, a couture house in Grosvenor Street.

The Moshulu *in Belfast Lough and Newby as an apprentice aboard that ship during the 1938 round trip from England to Australia that he described in his 1956 book,* The Last Grain Race *(courtesy of Eric Newby)*

While at Worth-Paquin, Newby wrote his first book, *The Last Grain Race,* the story of his 1938 voyage to Australia. He had signed on as an apprentice on the *Moshulu* and left from Belfast for Port Lincoln, Australia. They almost immediately ran into heavy weather in the Irish Sea. Thus, Newby learned his duties under the worst of conditions. After that storm the voyage proceeded rapidly if not always smoothly. Most of the crew members spoke a heavily accented English. The food was unpalatable. The crew's pranks were often inhumane to a stomach-churning degree, and the captain was unsympathetic and distant. On the other hand, there were moments of great beauty, such as the view the sailmaker pointed out to Newby as they were leaving Spencer Gulf in Australia. The book includes photographs by Newby, most of them showing the seamen at their routine jobs.

Newby survived it all, including his initiation when the ship crossed the Equator (during which his head was shaved and painted), skinned arms, ulcers in his mouth from excessively salty food, and a mysteriously lame leg. Reviewers were generally enthusiastic. The reviewer for *The New Yorker* (6 October 1956) called the book "an admirably taut and indelibly explicit narrative," while Martin Levin described it as "filled with information, nostalgia and unusual wit" in *Saturday Review* (20 December 1956). Although sometimes overly technical (Newby invites the reader to skip a "technical interlude"), this first work is indispensable to understanding Newby's persona as the traveler; and he returns to the memory of the voyage repeatedly in his writings.

In 1952 Hugh Carless, a friend of Newby's in the British Foreign Service, wrote him from Afghanistan about having "just returned from an expedition to the borders of Nuristan, The Country of Light." In 1956 Newby suddenly decided to quit Worth-Paquin and sent a telegram to Carless at the British embassy in Rio de Janeiro: "CAN YOU TRAVEL NURISTAN JUNE?" After Newby received Carless's positive response a few days later, the preparations began at a frantic pace. The result of this journey was *A Short Walk in the Hindu Kush* (1958). Carless ordered a station wagon to be delivered at Brighton so that Newby could drive it to Istanbul, where Carless was to join him. Initially, Newby was "filled with profound misgivings. . . . I had never climbed anything. I had never been anywhere that a rope had been remotely necessary." With

Newby, Donald Shaw, and "Doc" Caraher, escaped prisoners of war in Italy, winter 1943 (courtesy of Eric Newby)

only four days to learn mountain climbing Carless and Newby underwent a brief course at "an inn situated in the wilds of Caernarvonshire."

Eric and Wanda Newby then drove to Istanbul, where they spent several days sightseeing, and Newby had his wallet stolen. Then the Newbys and Carless started for Kabul in their station wagon. Many misadventures occurred along the road to Kabul, Afghanistan–some of them comic in retrospect. Not only did they lose their way, but near Bayazid, Carless was falsely accused of a vehicular homicide, and there was the threat of a trial. The charges were dropped, however, and the party proceeded to Tehran, where Wanda Newby left the two men and returned to Europe. Next, their car broke down in Meshed (Mashhad), Iran, where the proprietor of the repair shop, "a broken-toothed demon of a man, conceived a violent passion for Hugh." After some hair-raising experiences with him Newby and Carless continued on, reaching Kabul on 5 July, five days later than they had planned.

On 10 July they left for the Panjshir valley and Mir Samir in the Hindu Kush mountain range. With the aid of three helpers Newby and Carless made several unsuccessful attempts to reach the summit of Mir Samir. They suffered various hardships: Carless injured his hands with a rope; new boots caused bleeding sores on Newby's feet; and both suffered diarrhea at different times.

After their failure to climb Mir Samir, Newby and Carless decided to venture into Nuristan, where their experiences offer further evidence of Newby's endurance and, sometimes, his sense of humor, which made that endurance possible. Fearing for their lives, Newby and Carless's guides at first refused to accompany the two Englishmen, but eventually the guides agreed. After entering Nuristan through the Chamar Pass and crossing the Chamar River, they met a group of men from the Ramguli Katir tribe, who surrounded them, mistaking them at first for Russians. These Nuristanis served them cold milk and attempted to keep Carless's telescope and Newby's waterproof Rolex watch. Newby and Carless's second encounter was with two armed men, one of whom looked "really sinister." Later, a young man named Aruk offered to accompany them to Pushal, the capital of the Ramguli Katirs. There Newby and his party were the guests of Sultan Muhammad Khan, a former captain of the Royal Afghan Bodyguard. During their stay Newby and Carless visited Lake Mundal, where Newby's expensive camera was ruined when the pack on one guide's horse was submerged as he forded the river flowing into the lake. Later, in Linar, one of their guides, Shir Muhammad, received "a fearful beating" from a woman and "her son and two hefty daughters" when he was caught stealing their mulberries. On 1 August, as the party passed through the Arayu Pass on the way out of Nuristan, Newby had "the sensation of emerging from a country that would continue to exist more or less unchanged whatever disasters overtook the rest of mankind."

The story of Newby and Carless's remarkable and arduous journey is at times awe-inspiring and always engaging. They suffered great hardships and risked their lives many times during the expedition, but, ironically, when they met the well-known explorer Wilfred Thesiger in Panjshir at the end of their journey, he called them "a couple of pansies" because they had brought air mattresses. As Mark Cocker envisages the meeting, it was as though two heroes from "modern picaresque comedy" encountered "the archetypal old-style travel hero and foil to Newby's new man." Throughout the book the arduous nature of the journey and the beauty of Nuristan are often foregrounded against the irony and self-mockery of Newby's narration. Many reviewers noted Newby's wit, including Cyril Ray in *The Spectator* (23 January 1959): "Without being in the least facetious, the book is very funny. . . . One of the most engaging travel books since Colonel Fleming was in his globe-trotting heyday." Speaking of Newby, the reviewer for *The Times Literary Supplement (TLS)* discussed the rise of amateurism among travelers since World War II, saying that "equipment, training, acclimatization, expertise–all has gone by the board, to be supplanted by a rugged ability to endure and to cope, which active service in the last war implanted" (14 November 1958). This reviewer also noted resemblances between Newby's tone and Peter Fleming's, but he noted some significant differences as well. Calling Newby an "amateur" and Fleming a "hobo," he continued, "one takes nobody except himself seriously, the other includes himself in the universal offbeat." Jeanette Wakin, in a short review for *Saturday Review* (13 June 1959), described the book as "immensely literate and one of the most unusual exploration books of recent years. . . . an extremely witty and funny book." *A Short Walk in the Hindu Kush* has remained popular and has been republished in several paperback editions.

On his return to England, Newby went to work for the publishing house of Secker and Warburg, remaining with them until 1959. Then he returned to the garment trade and worked for the John Lewis Partnership as the central buyer for model dresses until 1963. While working for John Lewis, he published *Something Wholesale* (1962) about his earlier work in the garment business. The only travels described in the book are trips for business purposes or long walking excursions for pleasure. An amusing, aggravating journey to Edinburgh and Glasgow to show the firm's clothes to buyers is described at length.

After seven years of working and writing in England, Newby and his wife celebrated his forty-fourth birthday, 6 December 1963, on a boat in India. In *Slowly Down the Ganges* (1966) Newby describes the twelve-hundred-mile journey he and Wanda undertook on the Ganges, the holiest river in India for Hindus. Although the river is small compared with the Nile and the Yangtze (Chang), Newby views the Ganges as "a great river." While in India during World War II, Newby had spent some time on its banks and concluded that the Ganges was "the most memorable river of all."

The Newbys' journey began at the holy city of Hardwar in a boat borrowed from the local irrigation department. Accompanying them were three boatmen and a companion whom Newby refers to as "Mr. G." The first part of the journey was punctuated by groundings and other hardships. At Sukarthal a bridge master refused to open the drawbridge for them, so they were forced to haul their boat out of the water and carry it overland to a point down river. It took them five and a half days to reach Raoli, which was only "about thirty-five miles as the crow flies" from their starting point. During this time, Newby says, the party "had been stranded sixty-three times and crossed thirty-six rapids." Because the boat had to be sent back to Hardwar, the next leg of the journey was by bus. Soon, despite Newby's attempts to dissuade him, Mr. G. decided to return home. When travel by boat was impossible or inconvenient, the Newbys used any other means of transportation available: train, bus, and even bullock cart. They were able, however, to complete the last two segments of their journey by boat. A tugboat took them to Calcutta from Bandel, and they traveled by steamship from Bandel to Sandheads in the Bay of Bengal.

Newby's claim that this book is not about India but "is about the river as we found it" seems to be an expression of modesty on his part. The book is replete with descriptions of not only the river but also of the people. He writes about their culture, religion, and everyday life. The vast cultural differences in how the price of goods or services was negotiated frustrated and annoyed the Newbys. The lack of adequate sanitation at most places was discomforting to them. In Banaras they were appalled at the exorbitant prices charged by a hotel for extremely poor service. At times they were angered by some people's indifference and the lack of courtesy, but at others they were touched by the hospitality and generosity that many people extended to them.

There were many instances in which Newby detected contradictions between what people professed and what they practiced. At Hardwar he discovered that the brothel area was patronized by the religious men in charge of performing prayers and other rites. In addition to being a "great hive of whores," this section of the city was also "the rendezvous of secret drinkers, eaters of fish and fowl, eggs and meat" –things forbidden to Hindus. At Banaras the Newbys met a young university student who rode away in a rickshaw after lecturing them against the use of rickshaws as "disgraceful." Here they also met a holy man who drank liquor and ate eggs at their expense.

Newby's earlier stay in India and his knowledge of its history lend personal and historical dimensions to his account. At many points in the narrative he

Newby (center) with attendants during the 1956 travels he described in his 1958 book, A Short Walk in the Hindu Kush *(courtesy of Eric Newby)*

recounts the history of a place he visited. For example, writing about Balawali, he recalls how Timur Leng (Timur Lenk, known to Westerners as Tamburlaine or Tamerlane) crossed the Ganges at a nearby place in the fourteenth century before capturing Delhi. When he describes his return visit to Fatehgarh, where he had been stationed as an army officer, he recounts his earlier experiences, including his visit to a brothel in the company of two fellow officers.

The Newbys suffered many tense moments and reacted differently to hardships. In *Slowly Down the Ganges* Wanda Newby often speaks from emotion, whereas her husband suffers in silent stoicism. Newby portrays this British couple traveling through a land vastly different from their own as sometimes comic and sometimes heroic, suffering adversity with wry humor, tenacity, and the traditional English stiff upper lip.

Reviewing *Slowly Down the Ganges* for *Newsweek* (14 August 1967), Saul Maloff called the book a "bizarre, funny, charming, awesome account" and offered insight into Newby's point of view:

> Simultaneously enthralled and disenchanted, wry and ironic, he perceived everything and participated vitally in everything he perceived. Newby's India–the India spread out along the river's banks–is radically *other,* absolutely alien, and yet by submitting himself lovingly, openly, and fully to the "spell of the Ganges," he was able to bring it all home.

The *TLS* reviewer (24 November 1966) referred to the Newbys as "intrepid amateurs" and believed that "no journey into an unmapped interior to carry the word or find a lost explorer was more obstinately seen through to its end than this do-it-yourself pleasure trip." The reviewer added that Wanda Newby "doggedly stayed the course and stays in our memories as the real heroine of the affair."

In 1964 Newby began a nine-year stint as travel editor for *The Observer* (London) and also became general editor of the *Observer* series of Time Off travel guides, writing *Time Off in Southern Italy* (1966) as part of the series. He later wrote two other guide books with Diana Petry: *Wonders of Britain: A Personal Choice of 480* (1968) and *Wonders of Ireland: A Personal Choice of 484*

"Pilgrims on the great sandbank at Allahabad," photograph by Newby in his Slowly Down the Ganges *(1966)*

(1969). These books tell the traveler how to visit the selected sites, many of them rather remote and rarely visited by the ordinary tourist. Each place is located on excellent maps and described in two or three paragraphs. There are also many interesting illustrations, including old drawings and contemporary photographs.

During the late 1960s Newby also compiled the collection *My Favourite Stories of Travel* (1967) and published *Grain Race: Pictures of Life before the Mast in a Windjammer* (1968), a retelling of his voyage to Australia with additional photographs.

Love and War in the Apennines (1971) is Newby's account of his adventures in Italy during World War II. The book helps the reader to understand Newby's later devotion to Italy and the blend of foolhardiness and caution that characterizes his subsequent life. At one point in the book he recalls the experience of climbing a steep mountain in the snow while burdened by a forty-pound sack of rice and realizing that the physical and emotional strain had broken "something in me." He goes on to explain: "It was not physical; it was simply that part of my spirit went out of me, and in the whole of my life since that night it has never been the same again."

Newby's narrative and descriptive skills find full expression when he writes about the people. He relates how, after his escape from the prisoner-of-war camp near Parma, friendly Italians took him high into the mountains, where he began a long period of service to Signor Zanoni, spending months disguised as a simple laborer clearing a field of stones. Throughout the book the peasants, especially his fellow farm workers, are vividly individualized. Newby's later descriptions of the Po and its valley as well as the mountains through which he trekked and in which he hid after leaving the farm are most effective. In a review for *New Statesman* (14 May 1971) Vernon Scannell found Newby's portrayal of and dedication to the Italian people "touching" and "very enjoyable" but felt the narrator was rather emotionless in describing his suffering and his falling in love with Wanda. The reviewer for *TLS* (21 May 1971) similarly praised Newby's "admirable collection of portraits of admirable men and women" and assured readers that "admirers, which means readers, of his last book, *Slowly Down the Ganges,* will find that he has improved even on that."

Newby's next book, *The Mitchell Beazley World Atlas of Exploration* (1975), also published as *The Rand McNally World Atlas of Exploration* and *The World Atlas of Exploration,* is a comprehensive history of exploration and explorers from the time of Irish monks such as St. Brandon to the space era. The work is filled with maps, old drawings, and modern photographs. Many illustrations employ unusual perspectives, as when a drawing of Drake's *Golden Hind* is superimposed "athwart a modern giant supertanker, the 'Esso Northumbria' (250,000 tons)," both on the same scale. The text is generally factual, readable, interesting, and straightforward.

The book received mixed reviews, mostly in publications for librarians. The reviewer for *Library Journal* (15 February 1976) called it "superficial," and said it "falls uneasily between the coffee table and the reference shelf," while the *Choice* reviewer (March 1976) said Newby had chosen his material well and called the atlas "an intriguing book." A long, generally favorable review in *Booklist* (15 May 1976) concluded that the atlas "is an easily understood basic textual and pictorial guide to world exploration. It is primarily a browsing item and secondarily a reference source."

In *Great Ascents: A Narrative History of Mountaineering* (1977) Newby's purpose is to recapture some of the excitement in the history of mountain climbing from dusty, largely forgotten tomes on library shelves. The bibliography of narratives of mountain climbing at the end of this book is impressive; many of the works listed were written by the principals of historically important expeditions, including Edward Whymper, who in 1865, with Michael Croz, was the first to reach the summit of the Matterhorn. Newby emphasizes the importance to the development of mountaineering of Victorian art critic John Ruskin, who wrote about the sublime beauty of the Alps, and Newby also notes the significant participation of women such as Lucy Walker and Meta Brevoort in early mountain climbing.

Newby's book covers climbing on four continents and in New Zealand, and it spans the time period from the arrival of Richard Pockocke's party in Chamonix in 1741 to the climbing of the south face of Annapurna in the Himalayas in 1970. The narratives are detailed and often quite dramatic. Except in the introduction, Newby holds his wit in abeyance, often allowing the mountaineers to express their feelings and reactions in their own words. Maps of routes show the options open to the mountaineers, the routes chosen, and the outcomes. The book also includes excellent photographs of mountains and mountaineers.

Newby's inspiration for his next book, *The Big Red Train Ride* (1978), came in 1964, while he was making a comfortable, eight-and-a-half hour train trip from Leningrad to Moscow (410 miles). A Russian passenger with whom Newby drank a good deal of vodka suddenly suggested that he should take the Trans-Siberian Railway to Nakhodka on the Sea of Japan. (At that time Vladivostok was closed to foreigners.) Newby was immediately taken by the idea, but other obligations intervened. Finally, in May 1977, the Newbys, a German photographer named Otto, and Mischa, their guide from the official Soviet tourist agency ("regarded by Western intelligence services as an arm of the KGB"), boarded the *Rossiya.* The 5,900-mile train trip, which took eight days and crossed seven time zones, was sometimes less comfortable than Newby's earlier railroad journey from Leningrad to Moscow. The train kept fairly well to the schedule, arriving at most stops about ten minutes late.

In addition to a wide assortment of clothing, the Newbys took with them a considerable number of books, two large maps, and a store of food and drink, which was renewed whenever possible at one of the ninety-three, often brief, stops along the way, usually by Wanda. Fortunately their compartment was fairly comfortable and had plenty of storage space. In *The Big Red Train Ride* Newby divides his attention about equally among the train personnel and passengers, the view outside, and historical background gleaned from his reading of the "barely portable library of Siberiana" that he brought with him.

When Newby showed Mischa a book describing all the bridges, with photographs of the biggest, Mischa protested that such information was confidential, even after Newby pointed out that it was published in 1900 and recently reprinted in England. He also said Newby should not have brought all the current magazines they had with them; yet, Newby pointed out, Mischa had already read their *Observer.*

A comic encounter with train personnel occurred in Novosibirsk, after the Newbys found their window would not open. Eventually Mischa, the two formidable conductresses (whom Newby called "Wardresses"), and the "Brigadier in charge of the train" crammed into the Newbys' compartment. After removing all the window screws with a key failed to produce the desired results, they used an ax to pry open the window, which, of course, could not be shut again when the night grew cold.

Writing about their approach to Omsk, on the steppes, Newby describes the towers and storage tanks of a modern petrochemical plant in a modern satellite city; then he gives historical background on Omsk and points out that few of his sources have anything good to

Wanda Newby (seated second from left) during an outing on Lake Baikal; photograph by Newby in his 1978 book, The Big Red Train Ride

say about the city. Anton Chekhov, whose letters Newby frequently cites, "ignored or bypassed it completely." Mrs. Lucy Atkinson, a British traveler, recorded a bad experience with the police master there in 1849 in her *Recollections of Tartar Steppes and their Inhabitants* (1863), and Italian journalist Luigi Barzini, on the 1907 Great Trans-Continental Automobile Race from Peking to Paris, found it rather middle-class and provincial. Then Newby tells how during their stop in Omsk "the usual one-reel comedy was made under Russian direction." Otto, who was working on a project of his own, not with the Newbys, tried to take photographs at the station:

> The big scene, which should have been played in bathing costumes with horizontal stripes, was with what was, presumably, the deputy female station-master, a person of uncertain age who was wearing a truly terrible grey skirt which made her look as if she was imbedded in a block of concrete. She managed to get one hand over the front of his 28mm, Perspective Control Lens, the whole point of which was to exclude undesirable objects, and the other under his chin, shoving his head back for the final neck-break–what she was doing with her knee was not clear–all of which, presumably, was to stop him photographing the place where the front of the station building would have been if someone hadn't taken it away and replaced it with scaffolding and lots of plastic sheeting.

The comic touch in this present perspective adds a piquant detail to the associations Newby has built up through his historical background.

Stopovers and side trips in Novosibirsk, Irkutsk, Ulan-Ude, and Khabarovsk gave some variety to the trip and allowed Newby a little more insight into Soviet life than he could have obtained from a train window. His explorations were limited, however, because Mischa was almost always present to determine what they could see. (The Newbys did manage to sneak out of their hotel in Khabarovsk.) The hotels at their stopovers were generally comfortable, though somewhat old-fashioned, and the people were friendly.

Although one reviewer, J. H. Dreisbach, described the work as "a rather dull picture in various tones of grey"–its dullness caused not by the author nor the style but by the "lack of color available to form the literary picture" (*Best Sellers,* May 1979)–*The Big Red Train Ride* is vintage Newby. As a travel guide it may be dated in some details, but as travel writing it is not dated at all. Newby expertly moves from realistic observation to historical background and summary of other travelers' impressions, often exercising his characteristic wit and never becoming pedantic. The book includes twenty-six photographs taken by the Newbys and a good map at the beginning of the text.

At the end of the book Newby extends his insight into people to Wanda, whose low level of tolerance for discomfort inspires her as usual to make critical comments that qualify Newby's enthusiasm and stoicism. She is given almost the last word in the book:

> "I've had enough Nakhodka," Wanda said. Her teeth were chattering. "It's a hell of a place. What's more I've had enough of Siberia, and we've all had enough of Mischa, and I'm fed up with your damn maps. I want to go home."

Newby concludes: "So we did."

In *A Traveller's Life* (1982), which begins with Newby's birth and ends in 1973, Newby often writes about events covered in his earlier books, but he adds accounts of other journeys, such as a trip on the Orient Express in 1969, an exploration of the London sewers in 1963, and his travels during his wartime service mapping landing sites in Lebanon in 1942. In his discussion of reasons for travel at the beginning of the book, he finds his own reasons basically at one with those Evelyn Waugh expressed in his preface to Newby's *A Short Walk in the Hindu Kush:* the urge to satisfy "the longing, romantic, reasonless, which lies deep in the hearts of most Englishmen, to shun the celebrated spectacles of the tourist and, without any concern with science or politics or commerce, simply to set their feet where few civilized feet have trod."

Such places, however, are becoming rare. Mark Cocker quotes Newby's lament in *A Traveller's Life* that "the time was not far off when there would be no place on earth accessible to ordinary human beings in which they would be able to feel themselves alone under the sky without hearing the noise of machines." Newby also foresees a time "when the desire to be alone has finally been extinguished from the human heart." Reviewing the book favorably in *Newsweek* (23 August 1982), Gene Lyons quoted Newby's comment that in a world where tourists are "moved around the world en masse rather like air freight," real travel has been lost. Lyons hoped that the sentiment "proves wrong." Most other reviewers liked *A Traveller's Life,* and some took the occasion of its publication to sum up Newby's career. In *TLS* ((20 August 1982) Joseph Hone praised Newby's style and concluded, "He . . . is one of the few travel writers who make you want to follow in his footsteps."

On the Shores of the Mediterranean (1984) begins with Newby's description of the small house, near Carrara in northern Tuscany, that he and Wanda had owned for eighteen years: it is "exactly like almost any one of the various houses in which Italian peasants had hidden me high up in the Apennines in the winter of 1943–4 when I had been an escaped prisoner-of-war." The Newbys usually visited the house twice a year to care for the vineyards Newby had planted, harvesting grapes with their neighbors about 1 October and making wine. When Newby decided to use the house as a starting point for traveling around the Mediterranean, he vacillated about where to go first. He considered Gibraltar or the Great Pyramid, but, typically, Wanda Newby settled it. Reminding him that he had always said he wanted to go back to Naples, she said, "Well why don't you start in Naples and go clockwise round the Mediterranean instead of dashing off in all directions like a lunatic?" Newby writes, "So we did."

During their visit to Naples, Newby noted similarities and differences between the present-day city and the one the Newbys had visited twenty years previously to do research for *Time Off in Southern Italy:* the dock area had been automated; nightlife had changed to such an extent that "the heart of Montecalvario is gone"; yet Neapolitan driving had retained its distinctive characteristics, and sitting in the Piazza Sannazzaro to watch people still provided endless entertainment. For the most part, however, Newby's emphasis on the quality of the changes and his frequent references to the pollution of the Mediterranean introduce a pervading theme of deterioration.

After a return to their Tuscan farmhouse, the Newbys' next stop was Venice. There, unhappy with the winter weather, they decided to go home to England and resume their clockwise journey around the Mediterranean in the spring. They began the major part of the journey by leaving Victoria Station in London on the inaugural run of the Venice-Simplon-Orient Express. Detraining at Venice, they traveled by van into the Kras area of Slovenia (then part of Yugoslavia), Wanda's homeland. They proceeded down the coast of Yugoslavia, made a side trip to Montenegro, where they found the capital and major port devastated by the great earthquake of 1979, and then visited "Albania Wild and Stern," as the chapter is titled. In Greece they had planned to spend several days exploring the monasteries of the Meteora, but once there they found they were twenty years too late. It had become a tourist attraction, with "a huge coach park outside the Monastery of the Transfiguration" and lines of stalls "selling junk." They moved on to Mount Olympus, which Newby climbed, and then went to the Hellespont and Istanbul. (Newby includes an excellent background chapter on the harem at Topkapi and Turkish harems in general.) Next they visited the plains of Troy, Jerusalem, the Great Pyramid, and Tobruk, Libya, where

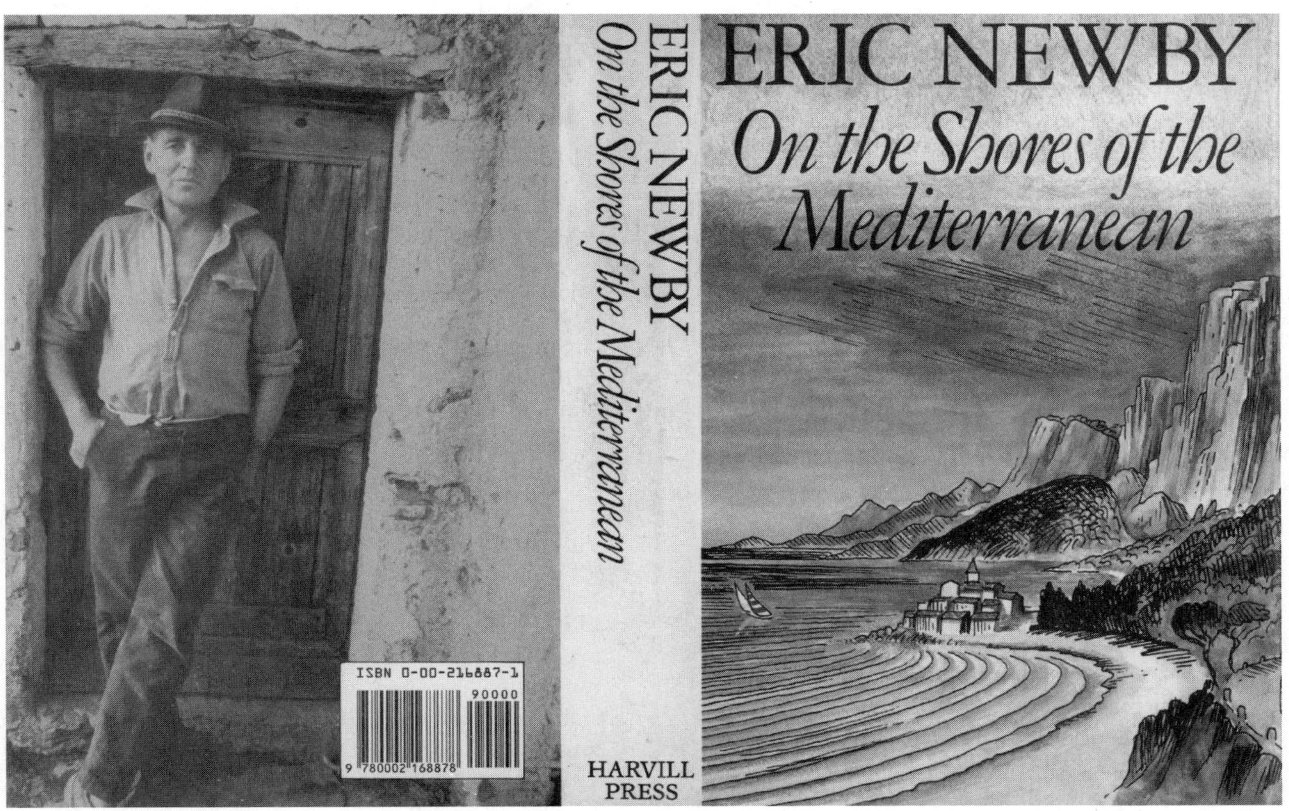

Dust jacket, illustrated by Jonathan Newby, for Eric Newby's 1984 book, an account of a clockwise journey around the Mediterranean that began and ended at his farmhouse in Tuscany

some of Newby's friends had fought and died during World War II. The Newbys completed their circuit with stops in Tunis, Fez, Gibraltar, Seville, and Nice before finally arriving back at their house in Tuscany.

Occasionally, Newby gives prominence to the process of traveling, writing, for example, about bus rides from Tripoli in Libya to Sfax and then Tunis in Tunisia and including an account of the maddening and lengthy process of passing through customs in both countries. Often, however, a chapter begins at the destination announced at the end of the preceding chapter. The chapter on Fez, Morocco, for example, begins with the description of the early morning chanting. There is no description of how the Newbys traveled there from Nefta, Tunisia. As in earlier books, Newby gives excellent historical background. In the section on Seville, for example, such information gives depth and significance to his close observation of the Holy Week processions. Throughout the book Newby reports his exchanges with Wanda in his usual witty manner.

In general reviewers found *On the Shores of the Mediterranean* uneven. Colin Thubron (*TLS,* 4 January 1985) said the book proceeded "like a firecracker, spluttering damply through Tuscany and Venice, bursting into life in Slovenia." Bruce Hepburn wrote that Newby "doesn't really get into his stride–and what a stride!–until he reaches the Eastern and Southern Mediterranean." (*New Statesman,* 21 September 1984).

A Book of Travellers' Tales (1985), edited with an introduction and commentary by Newby, is a collection of short excerpts from the writings of travelers from Pliny to Samuel Johnson to Paul Theroux. After the first section, "Advice to Travellers," the book is arranged geographically–Africa, Europe, Great Britain and Ireland, Near Asia, Middle Asia, Far Asia, North America, Central and South America and the Caribbean, Australia and New Zealand, the Arctic and the Antarctic. Within each of these sections the excerpts are arranged chronologically according to author's birth date when known. This book is good for browsing and is well suited for any would-be traveler's nightstand.

Round Ireland in Low Gear (1987) is about the Newbys' bicycle excursions in Ireland, including trips from Limerick to Galway Bay, from Cork to the Dingle Peninsula, and from Dublin to Galway. These trips took place over the course of about a year, which may have contributed to the "unsatisfactory formlessness" that Dervla Murphy mentioned in her review of the book for *TLS* (9 October 1987). Occasionally, the Newbys visited places Newby and Petry described in *Wonders of Ireland,* discovering that some of them were not only different but also not as wonderful. For example, *Wonders of Ireland* includes a description of Danganback, a fortress house of the Macnamaras. In *Round Ireland in Low Gear* Newby reports that he and Wanda were unable to find Danganback. The track "eventually delivered us into a farmyard filled with liquid mud and policed by a pair of ferocious amphibious sheep dogs," and they were forced to give up their attempt. In other cases Newby describes places in greater detail in *Round Ireland in Low Gear* than he did in *Wonders of Ireland.*

Although Newby describes notable sites and charming people in *Round Ireland in Low Gear,* the prevailing impression many readers retain is that of Wanda's misery, caused by encounters with fierce dogs, cycling up long inclines against wind, rain, or snow, and arriving in villages where the decent restaurants are either closed or no longer existent. All Newby's wit, curiosity, and endurance cannot make bicycling in Ireland during the off-season seem like anything except an almost unbearable ordeal. For Murphy only "the indefinable but potent Newby charm" saved the book from being "a disaster." Writing for *The New York Times Book Review* (21 August 1988), Evelyn Toynton commented that "the living people he describes seem flat, dull and undifferentiated one from another. Even the famous Irish love of language . . . seems to have departed." Nevertheless, the book was popular enough to warrant republication as a paperback in the Penguin Travel Library (1989).

Newby reviews and sums up his travels from 1938 to 1977 in *What the Traveller Saw* (1989), which, he says, "essentially commemorates the past, and, in many cases, a world that has changed beyond all recognition." In the first essay, "Round the Horn Before the Mast," he recounts the experiences he had described more fully in *The Last Grain Race* (1956). Another essay goes back over his experiences as a prisoner of war in Italy. In all, the twenty-one books cover a wide range of peoples and visits to countries such as Italy, Ireland, Portugal, East Africa, India, Fiji, and Bali in words and photographs.

The excellence of Newby's writing style is usually in its transparency, but at times some readers find it too impersonal. As Joseph Hone said in his review of *A Traveller's Life,* "A lot of his effects lie between the lines." Many readers find his wit engaging, but some feel that it contributes to the impersonality. His voice is usually informal, sometimes slangy, and even when technical he rarely sounds pedantic. In the works in which she appears, the persona of Wanda Newby is a wonderfully effective complement or foil for Newby's own persona. She is the voice of common sense, comfort, security, which Newby, the "intrepid amateur," wishes to forswear but cannot quite. The Newbys live in Bucknowle, Wareham, Dorset. Newby has occasionally used the pseudonym James Parker for magazine and newspaper contributions.

As time goes on, Newby has noticed changes in the places he visits, concluding that not only has tourism smothered travel but the urge to travel has been stifled by modern life. As he said in *Something Wholesale,* his books and photographs are an attempt to preserve a way of life that has disappeared–that of the true traveler.

Reference:

Mark Cocker, *Loneliness and Time: The Story of British Travel Writing* (New York: Pantheon, 1992).

Jonathan Raban

(14 June 1942 –)

James J. Schramer
Youngstown State University

BOOKS: *The Technique of Modern Fiction: Essays in Practical Criticism* (London: Arnold, 1968; South Bend, Ind.: University of Notre Dame Press, 1969);

Mark Twain: Huckleberry Finn (London: Arnold, 1968);

The Society of the Poem (London: Harrap, 1971);

Soft City (London: Hamilton, 1974; New York: Dutton, 1974);

Arabia through the Looking Glass (London: Collins, 1979); republished as *Arabia: A Journey through the Labyrinth* (New York: Simon & Schuster, 1979);

Old Glory: An American Voyage (London: Collins, 1981; New York: Simon & Schuster, 1981);

Foreign Land (London: Collins Harvill, 1985; New York: Viking Penguin, 1985);

Coasting: A Private Voyage (London: Collins Harvill, 1987; New York: Simon & Schuster, 1987);

For Love & Money: Writing, Reading, Travelling, 1969–1987 (London: Collins Harvill, 1987); revised and enlarged as *For Love & Money: A Writing Life, 1969–1989* (New York: Harper & Row, 1989);

God, Man & Mrs. Thatcher (London: Chatto & Windus, 1989);

Hunting Mister Heartbreak: A Discovery of America (London: Collins Harvill, 1990; New York: HarperCollins, 1991);

Bad Land: An American Romance (London: Picador, 1996; New York: Pantheon, 1996).

TELEVISION: *Square,* teleplay by Raban, Granada Television, 1971;

Snooker, teleplay by Raban, BBC-TV, 1975;

The Water Baby, teleplay by Raban, BBC-TV, 1975.

RADIO: *A Game of Tombola,* radio play by Raban, BBC Radio 3, 1972;

At the Gate, radio play by Raban, BBC Radio 3, 1973;

The Anomaly, radio play by Raban, BBC Radio 3, 1974;

The Daytrip, radio play by Raban, BBC Radio 3, 1976.

Jonathan Raban (photograph © 1989 Fay Godwin)

OTHER: *Robert Lowell's Poems: A Selection,* edited, with an introduction and notes, by Raban (London: Faber & Faber, 1974);

The Oxford Book of the Sea, edited, with an introduction, by Raban (Oxford & New York: Oxford University Press, 1992).

Jonathan Raban is one of the handful of British writers born during or shortly after World War II who revitalized British travel writing in the 1970s and 1980s. Along with Bruce Chatwin, William Dalrymple, Nicholas Cruse, Redmond O'Hanlon, Colin Thubron, and Gavin Young, Raban transformed British travel writing from an often unabashedly imperialist genre into a post-modern form of personal narrative. As Bill Buford observes in his introduction to *In Trouble Again* (1986), a special travel-writing issue of *Granta,* "contemporary travel writing is generically androgynous: it borrows from the memoir, reportage, and most importantly, the novel." Raban's work fits this definition, revealing as much about Raban as it does about the places to which he travels and about which he writes.

Jonathan Raban was born in Fakenham, Norfolk, England, on 14 June 1942 to Peter Raban, an Anglican clergyman, and Monica Sandison Raban. In *Soft City* (1974) Raban later wrote of the difficulties of growing up in a vicarage in provincial Norfolk, commenting that the local mental hospital "was a terminus for villagers not up to the strenuous moral art of villaging." At age eleven he was sent to the King's School, Worcester, where he studied from 1953 to 1958, an experience he recalls in *Coasting* (1987):

> The school . . . had started life in the Dark Ages and claimed the Venerable Bede as its founder. But its character was wholly nineteenth-century, a shoestring model of Thomas Arnold's Rugby. Since the middle of the nineteenth century it had been preparing the sons of clergymen, solicitors and the better sort of tradesmen for the tough business of Empire.

Raban also remembers doorless toilet cubicles, cold showers, and a total lack of privacy and realizes that his "compulsive fictionalizing" during these years was a form of escapism that only increased his misery and isolation: "I wasted the greater part of my time at this school in drawing the bars of my cage. I went there at eleven, on a state scholarship, and was mercifully withdrawn when I was sixteen." Escaping King's School "with a handful of mediocre O-levels," he entered sixth form at a co-educational grammar school in Lymington, Hampshire, where his family had moved.

Raban later attended the University of Hull, graduating with a B.A. in 1963. His literary idols at the time were American writers: Henry Roth, Nathanael West, Bernard Malamud, and Saul Bellow. Planning to pursue a doctorate, Raban explains in *For Love & Money* (1987) that he stayed on at Hull for what he calls "a three-year wallow in the most exciting contemporary fiction that was being written in English." Although he scrapped his plans to write a thesis titled "Variations on the Theme of Immigration and Assimilation in the Jewish American Novel from 1870 to the Present Day," Raban found academic employment with relative ease. As he recalls in *For Love & Money,* "In the early and mid-dling 1960s, there was a lot of higher education about." New universities at Essex, East Anglia, Sussex, and Warwick were eager to hire even "if one started from an unfashionable place like Hull."

Raban taught English and American literature at the University College of Wales, Aberystwyth, in 1966–1967 and English literature at the University of East Anglia, Norwich, in 1967–1969. Finding his "gentlemanly and donnish" teaching duties left him an "ocean of leftover time," Raban wrote a short textbook, *The Technique of Modern Fiction* (1968).

The Technique of Modern Fiction is a thin volume of slightly more than two hundred pages. In his introduction Raban compares his arrangement of the book to making a sandwich: each chapter features a morsel from a mid-twentieth-century story or novel "surrounded by two slices of critical discussion." Debts to Roland Barthes's *Writing Degree Zero* (1953; translated, 1967) and Raymond Williams's *Culture and Society 1780–1950* (1958) and *The Long Revolution* (1961) are evident in Raban's structuralist methodology and his emphasis on the political and social contexts of contemporary fiction. In addition to working on this book Raban found ample time to write "a handful of articles with footnotes for journals that paid with parcels of offprints."

The firm of Edward Arnold next commissioned Raban to write *Mark Twain: Huckleberry Finn* (1968), a short study for its Studies in English Literature series. Writing about *Adventures of Huckleberry Finn* (1884) was a labor of love for Raban, who had daydreamed in his childhood that a nearby brook was the Mississippi River. Raban's fondness for Mark Twain and his fascination with the Mississippi later led to *Old Glory: An American Voyage* (1981), an account of his voyage down the river from Minneapolis to New Orleans.

While he was teaching at the University of East Anglia, Raban met novelists Malcolm Bradbury, who was a senior lecturer in American literature, and Angus Wilson, who divided his time between "teaching in the summer term and starring at parties during the rest of the year." These two writers and their students, who included Rose Tremain and Ian McEwan, made the University of East Anglia what Raban describes as an unusual academic environment, "a place that had a place for writers, whether they were students or teachers."

In 1969 Raban found that with some scrimping he could make a living by writing book reviews and freelance material for radio programs on the arts. He decided to leave the relative financial security of a university lectureship and to live in London as a freelancer. In *Soft City* (1974) he describes his move from provincial England to metropolitan London and his first foray into travel writing. "The city," Raban argues, "is soft, ame-

Dust jacket for Raban's 1979 book, about a journey motivated by the growing number of Arabs in his London neighborhood

nable to a dazzling and libidinous variety of lives, dreams, interpretations." Its plasticity can liberate the human spirit by allowing people to create identities that would be forbidden in the more rigid worlds of country or village life. Yet it is not without problems. The same elastic qualities "which make the city the greatest liberator of human identity also cause it to be especially vulnerable to psychosis and totalitarian nightmare." Violence is not peculiar to the city, however. As Raban notes, based on per capita rates for murder, a "remote, low density area like Cardiganshire in West Wales can more than hold its own against London." It is the anonymity of violence that makes the city frightening: "In a city, you can be known, envied, hated by strangers."

Still, Raban notes, for all of their random violence, cities attract newcomers. These "greenhorns" come to cities such as London "more often from suburbs or other cities than from villages," as they might have in the past. Still, the greenhorn as "prototypical stranger" remains the "central figure in the mythology of initiation into the city." Despite, perhaps even because of, feeling out of place, the greenhorn rushes to assimilate, to adopt urban dress and manners. The first step "is to buy himself a suit of city clothes." (As Raban notes, this sartorial process also works in reverse: "When weekending Londoners, randy for Tudor beams and flagstone floors, descended on the Hampshire village where I grew up, their first rural gesture was to rig themselves out in ghastly pepper-and-salt tweeds.") In the city the greenhorn discovers that "city clothes are quite unlike the occupational or class uniforms of the countryside and small town." City clothes do not so much proclaim one's profession as one's desire to fashion a new identity. According to Raban, "the city offers" newcomers "a destiny and identity that have lain chrysalid-like in the heart, waiting for the sudden blast of heat and light and change of scale to set them free."

Not all newcomers to the city are in a rush to assimilate. Some people stubbornly cling to the culture of their native land or home county, forming "the soft city into the rural mould of a nostalgic dream life." The regulars in Ward's Irish House in Picadilly Circus, for example, have never made the mental move to London; "they drink and talk in Ireland not in London." Other Londoners fiercely re-create a vanished England. The "community of ardent villagers" in Highgate "wear country clothes–riding macs and headscarves, tweeds and Wellington boots–and talk in gentry voices, braying bravely over the tops of taxis." A city such as London allows for this sort of folly precisely because there is no set form for city life.

As Raban lived longer in London, he began to realize that it is many cities, "sequestered places with clear boundaries . . . of tribal castes and styles." In the Earls Court section of London to which he finally moved, Raban finds no solid center: "Everybody here is marginal–and to be old, or poor, or have a regular job is to be both as odd and as ordinary as to be a drag quean [*sic*] or a leather freak." Earls Court is a temporary stop on the route to other places and other lives. Few people remain there for long. Because its inhabitants change so frequently, Earls Court is a social barometer revealing the economic climate in England and the rest of the world.

Earls Court as a social barometer is the starting point for Raban's first international travel book, *Arabia through the Looking Glass* (1979), published in the United States as *Arabia: A Journey through the Labyrinth.* In the mid 1970s, as Arab oil money started to flow into England, Raban and other Britons began to take note of the strangers in their midst. At first the influx of Arabs and Arab money into England produced little more than a bumper crop of anti-Arab jokes. Commenting on British xenophobia, Raban writes that the jokes were "at least a change from the staple diet of jeers against the Irish and Pakistanis; and the Arabs were so evidently rich, so patently fair game, that they somehow seemed to be beyond the scope of the Race Relations Act." Soon there were changes on Earls Court Road. At first it was the "beak-shaped foil masks" of the Arab women that caught his eye, the women reminding him of "hooded falcons." Then he noticed a sudden "blossoming of Arabic signs," announcing "a calligraphic revolution" in the area.

The growing number of Arabic signs on Earls Court Road motivate Raban to learn Arabic and to read about Arabia. He buys a translation of the Koran but is disappointed by its lists of "bloodcurdling threats" about the fate of infidels. The English version, he writes, "manages to be boring and frightening in equal parts." His readings in the classics of British writing about Arabia proved equally unenlightening. Reflecting on T. E. Lawrence's *Seven Pillars of Wisdom* (1922), Wilfred Thesiger's *Arabian Sands* (1959), "and a clutch of books by Freya Stark," Raban writes that "British Arabism is an old romantic love affair in which a faint glimmer of the perverse is never far from the surface." He finds that some of these works reveal more about tastes formed in English boarding schools than in the empty quarters of Arabia. Of Thesiger and Lawrence he observes that "one is sometimes alarmingly close to the tone of the school captain of Hellenic inclinations doting on the wiry young heroes of the under-14s rugby team."

Only when he began to study Arabic did Raban start to learn about his new neighbors on Earls Court Road. Although he readily admits that his spoken Arabic is "limited to greetings, street directions, words for food and thank-yous," Raban says that his excursion into the labyrinthine mysteries of Arabic taught him more about the Arabs in London "than either Thesiger, Lawrence, or the Koran." Intrigued by the glimpse of Arabic culture that his study of Arabic had provided, he resolved to travel to Arabia to learn about the region firsthand. He soon learned that the labyrinth of the Arabic language is matched in complexity by the twists and turns of obtaining permission to travel to Arab countries. Bahrain proved easy. He did not even need a visa. North Yemen, Jordan, and Egypt also admitted him. Qatar and the United Arab Emirates insisted on paying his hotel bills and caring for him as if he were a guest. Saudi officials, however, completely frustrated his efforts to visit their nation.

Writing about his flight to the Gulf, Raban reflects on the distortion of time and space that characterizes modern air travel:

> Jet travel makes a twisted nonsense of geography. In time, Bahrain is a good deal closer to London than West Wales is, and the seemingly motionless speed of the Boeing 747 renders all the small, crucial distinctions of climate, culture and topography illegible.

From the air Europe slips by beneath "like a giant suburban golf course." As the plane crosses over Turkey, Raban notices topographic changes below: "After the barbered green of Europe, Turkey comes as a peremptory reminder that the earth is really just a crust of cooled lava on which our own native patches are no more than happy, untypical geological accidents."

Raban's first stop is the oil-rich island of Bahrain. Unlike salespeople or consultants who are funneled into a narrow route that runs from the Gulf Hotel to the business district, Raban wanders about Manama, the capital city, as "a lucky trespasser." In the diverse neighborhoods–each dedicated to a different craft or trade–he finds an Arabic response to Western "monoculture." He describes Manama as a city "in a state of delirious flux." The streets echo with a "babble" of tongues: "a snatch of Hindustani, a bellow of Pidgin English across a building site, a rapid interchange in Arabic, a burst of Chinese." Everyone is in a rush to make the most of opportunities in Bahrain before the oil runs out.

Although Bahrain is scarcely the size of Martha's Vineyard, Pakistani and Korean laborers and Western technicians and businessmen in Bahrain see little of this tiny nation. Most of the consultants keep to their clubs. The British Club is "a little imaginary England, a pretty, watercolour world where the roses are always in bloom and the year is always 1927." In the "mock Tudor" bar the air is "pungent with homesickness." The expatriates look up from their pints of British ales to ask Raban if he is "Just out from the Youkay?" Raban describes the bar as "a memorial shrine to Youkay–the country of the rambler rose, the thatched cottage and the Ploughman's Lunch." Yet the expatriates in the bar are "not thatched-cottage men." They are technical advisers who have learned their trades in apprenticeships and at polytechnical colleges. The "Youkay" they memorialize is a fiction. It is England with "no drizzly ring roads, no blocks of high-rises, no miles of corrugated iron and chimneys . . . no standing-room-only rush hour trains."

Raban does run across an occasional Englishman who refused to retreat to the mock-Tudor refuge of the English Club. On the flight to his next destination, Qatar, Raban sits next to Mr. Roland Moon, a sales representative for a British electrical-engineering firm who deplores the loss of the Arabia he has grown to love:

> The Gulf had been his territory for fifteen years, and he was jealous of it. He disliked the new wave of brash young men, the freeloaders, the quick operators who got contracts signed during refueling stops and who could be in and out of a dozen Middle Eastern countries in a week.

Ironically, Mr. Moon brings to the Gulf the same sort of changes he regrets: "power cables, electric light, air conditioning, dynamos, turbines, elevator shafts, pylons."

According to Raban, the people of the Gulf region are rushing toward a future they can scarcely comprehend. This mad rush into modernity distorts one's perception of time. In Abu Dhabi, Raban observes, change progresses with dizzying speed; time itself seems compressed:

> Two years in the gulf have roughly the same weight as a decade in Europe. They represent as much of the past as can comfortably be remembered, as much of the future as any sensible man would dare to anticipate. In two years, cars turn to scrap, contracts expire, investments come home, and the whole vastly accelerated cycle of life starts up again. This biennial whirligig gives an insistent edge of temporariness to everything.

Raban compares Abu Dhabi to a hotel, a place where nothing seems permanent and people are always in transit. This instability provides him with an insight into the codes and rituals developed by the nomadic Bedouins:

> Their social code, with its ritual language and elaborate formalities, was a highly developed instrument for negotiating a passage through other people's territories. Their family structure, with its rigid roles and divisions, had been designed to withstand the stress of constant motion and the consequent threat of dissolution. In a sense, the Bedu had been better prepared for a world of cars and skyscrapers and jet travel than anyone in Europe or the United States.

From Abu Dhabi, Raban travels to Dubai, a journey that takes him across a featureless desert that seems as boring as "a flat Sunday afternoon." Sharing the taxi ride with a Jordanian television journalist who lives part of the year in Surrey makes Raban homesick: "suddenly I found myself longing for that imaginary, expatriate's England which I had found half touching, half comic when I had glimpsed it in the British clubs." Wrenching him from his reverie, the Jordanian tells Raban a story about what had happened to him and his wife and child as they waited at Gatwick for a vacation flight to Crete. A group of British holiday travelers had cooed appreciatively over the baby and, guessing that the family was French or Italian, had asked them where they were from. When the journalist said they were Jordanian Arabs, the group "just gaped, and you watched their faces freeze. You know, they didn't speak to us again once."

Raban often finds that Arabs are more accepting of him than his countrymen are of them. In Dubai he discovered the joy of getting lost in an all-male Arab crowd, which differs little, Raban concludes, from the regulars in a British pub:

> The inside of White's is much like the street-café society of Dubai. . . .The great difference lies in the fact that the Dubai crowd make no fuss about membership; the only qualification is that you have to be male.

After a while, however, this incessantly male world becomes tiresome.

Occasionally Raban does manage to add a feminine perspective to his observations, as in his description of his meeting with Ayysha Sayyar, the director of Social Services for Dubai, who is known as the "Gulf's token Emancipated Woman." Through an interpreter, Raban asks Sayyar if she can imagine a time when women in the region would begin to express their frustration and anger through literature. Sayyar, whose face reflects the strain of her "lonely prominence," responds that if such writing existed, it "would be a secret writing–a hidden writing, in a box." Raban wants to ask her if she has ever considered writing this kind of book but decides that "the question would have been a trespass."

In Cairo, which Raban describes as having "been the intellectual center of the Arab world," he again brings up the subject of women writers. A male poet tells Raban that despite Egyptian women's reputation for being the "most liberated" women in the Arab world, their "freedoms are very small; they are not really freedoms at all. . . . It's not the *angry* freedom of the West. It's not the freedom which makes people write. I think we are a very long way from seeing a Women's Novel of the kind you have in England or America."

Ironically, the woman writer from whom Raban gains most insight about Cairo is British writer Jan Morris, who first visited Cairo in the 1950s, when she was still James Morris. Raban meets Morris during her first visit to Cairo "since she changed gender," and he notes that she seems "nervous about what Jan might see in James's city." Morris says she is "so frightened of going back to places and finding that I liked them better as I was than I do as I am." Raban compares Morris to "some enviable, distant female cousin whose ability to cope with the world is always putting the rest of the family to shame." He wonders "if James Morris–whom I'd never known–had been an altogether more obviously haunted and muddled figure" and if Morris's cheery take on the changes in Cairo "was really more a reflection of the differences between the temperaments of James and Jan than it was any measure of a change in the city itself."

Raban's experiences in Yemen and Jordan represent the polarities that he detects in Arabic culture. Both countries have low per-capita incomes, but each deals with its poverty differently. With a per-capita income of $120 when Raban visited there, Yemen also has a high rate of illiteracy and a widespread addiction to a narcotic leaf called *qat.* Raban compares chewing *qat* to chewing a bunch of privet leaves. All the best land in the country, which has some of the finest arable land in the entire Gulf region, is given over to growing *qat.* According to Raban, Yemen lives on a "client economy," producing little, exporting its people as laborers, and importing almost everything: "What was Yemen's own was the air of glazed fatigue . . . the dirt which stuck in our throats, and the presence, everywhere in sight, of the makeshift, the gimcrack and the tumbledown." Despite the kindness of the Yemeni with whom he chewed *qat* and played cards, Raban was relieved when he left Yemen.

In contrast to Raban's dislike for Yemen is his obvious love for Jordan, which he compares to a middle-eastern Switzerland. He "had been wary of coming to Jordan" because he "hadn't liked the look of its Gross National Product." (The per capita income at the time was less than $500.) Raban ends up being charmed by the tidiness and the European outlook of Amman, where he feels at ease. He notes with obvious pleasure that the *Jordan Times* gave equal coverage to the war in Beirut and the death of English literary critic F. R. Leavis. He admires the Jordanian national habit of "being all right": "Everywhere I went in Jordan, I met a determined ebullience, a refusal to be done down by anyone; it was the kind of place where people were always whistling, whether or not they had anything to whistle about." The reader, however, cannot help but wonder if Raban's affection for Jordan is not owing in part to its so closely reflecting his own values.

Returning to England from Jordan, Raban ends his book where it began, on Earls Court Road. He realizes that Earls Court Road serves much the same function for the Arabs in London as the British clubs do for the expatriate technicians in the Gulf:

> Between the hotel, the kebab house, the Arab newsagent's, the Oriental Grocery and the Arab cinema, it was possible to forge a temporary life which much resembled the one they had left behind. . . . Like the expatriates, they [the Arabs in London] were tiptoeing so lightly over the top of an alien culture that their feet barely touched this foreign ground.

After his return from Arabia, Raban began planning a journey in search of a boyhood dream. In *Old Glory: An American Voyage* (1981), for which he won the Heinemann Award of the Royal Society of Literature and the Thomas Cook Award, he recounts his trip down the Mississippi from Minneapolis to New Orleans in a sixteen-foot open boat. The cover illustration on his copy of the book was the stuff of dreams:

> The picture on its cover, crudely drawn and coloured, supplied me with the raw material for an exquisite and recurrent daydream. It showed a boy alone, his face prematurely wizened with experience. . . . The sheet of water on which he drifted was immense, an enameled pool of lapis lazuli. Smoke from a half-hidden steamboat hung over an island of Gothic conifers. Cut loose from the world, chewing on his corncob pipe, the boy was blissfully lost in this stillwater paradise.

As a seven-year-old, Raban had dreamed that he was a more timid version of Huck Finn. While the fictional Huck was off having adventures on the dangerous shore, young Jonathan stayed on the raft, "alone on that unreal blue, watching for 'towheads' and 'sawyers' as the forests unrolled, a mile or more across the water." Thirty years later, when he arrives in Minneapolis to begin his voyage, he finds that his first task is to locate the river, which has been dammed, channeled, and locked into an urban existence by a city that has turned its back on the river: "Minneapolis behaved toward the Mississippi as if the river were the skeleton in the city's family closet." Finally, after crossing "a potter's field of ancient railroads," he finds the river. It is not the Mississippi of his boyish daydreams. "It wasn't the amazing blue of the cover of my old copy of *Huckleberry Finn*. . . . It was just a river. . . . Its color was much the same as that of my domestic Thames: a pale dun, like iced tea with a lot of mosquito larvae wriggling in the glass."

Once he gets the *Raban's Nest* (named by the boatyard crew) on the water, Raban begins to see the real Mississippi–a working river. Near St. Paul the shore is "solidly blocked in with cranes, derricks, huge steel drums, gantries, chutes, silos and brick warehouses." South of St. Paul, near Lake Pepin, in the early morning light, Raban momentarily recaptures the river of his boyhood dreams:

> There was one other early bird about: on the north side of the channel, a fisherman stood in his flat skiff, casting plugs for walleyes. As the sun came up, his reflection sharpened until he joined it to make a single cruciform pattern on the water. For me, the moment was unalloyed magic. The picture in my head had been real after all.

For much of his journey downriver Raban seems to spend more time ashore than afloat. He readily accepts the kindness of strangers and just as readily includes unflattering verbal sketches of them in his book. When Bob, the master at the lock near Winona, Minnesota, insists that he see Winona, Raban reluctantly accepts and hates the tour: "It went on for hours. I was shunted through the suburbs of Winona in the night rain, seeing them only as smears and blotches through the streaming windshield of one car after another."

Finally, he is dropped off at Bob's house, where he waits with Bob's wife, Beverley, for Bob to come home from his night shift at the locks: "She looked like a lady wrestler. Slack-jawed, her eyes hidden behind the thick lenses of her glasses, she filled her outside stretch pants to the last stitch." Bob fares no better. Playing on Beverley's comment that Bob is an amateur radio operator–"a real big ham"–Raban writes that Bob is "indeed a real big ham. Only a cartoonist . . . could have managed the bell-shaped curve of his basic construction. An ellipse of bristled stomach showed between his T-shirt and his jeans." His hosts, in fact, "were of one flesh. They must have had six hundred pounds of the stuff between them." Later, after a long day of being a local celebrity, a sleepy Raban is shown to Beverley's bedroom, which she has surrendered to her guest.

He repays her kindness by sneaking a look at her journal, which contains verses she copied from the Gospels. The passages surprise him: "I thought that I had

Raban at the time of Arabia through the Looking Glass *(photograph by Amer Al-Zuhair)*

met an enormous slut. That was not the person revealed here. Few of her favorite passages were consoling ones." In *Old Glory* Raban turns his surprise at discovering depths to Beverley's character into a telling comment about the hazards of relying on surface impressions: "As I traveled, glancingly, through the lives of other people, I had learned to trust to surface appearances, as travelers must. Reading Beverley's private book, I felt chastened."

The next morning Bob takes Raban for a trip around Winona in his Bronco pickup truck and gives him a lesson in old-fashioned American hatred. Bob hates government, tax-exempt religious schools, Madison Avenue advertisers, and "beautiful people." After spewing out all his frustrations, he turns to Raban and asks, "You ever get the feeling you was born in the wrong time?" Bob's idea of the "right time" is an idealized version of the West in which he is a well-armed, sure-shot frontiersman. Bob then takes Raban back to the house to show off his prized arsenal, including an automatic rifle. As he focuses the telescopic sight and adjusts the crosshairs, Raban imagines what Bob has wanted him to see: "Washington politicians, Madison

Avenue jerks, college presidents, and beautiful people. One by one they staggered to their knees like struck deer." Like Huck Finn, Raban has strayed onto a violent shore. Days after leaving Beverley and Bob in Winona, he finds that they have "taken up a fully furnished apartment" in his mind.

Despite its twists, turns, and threatening currents, the river becomes Raban's endlessly fascinating haven. Recalling that a New York journalist had told him the river would be "kind of samey" and that a London friend had assured him he would find it boring, Raban concludes that the "Mississippi could terrify, enchant, delude, but it was beyond the range of its character to bore or disappoint." After traveling scarcely more than a hundred miles downriver from Minneapolis, he already finds himself "in the river's grip."

The grandeur of the river stands out in stark contrast to Raban's often-bleak portraits of life in the towns along its banks. In the old river towns he visits–La Crosse and Prairie du Chein in Wisconsin; Buffalo and Burlington in Iowa–he meets soured people living stale lives. For Raban nothing symbolizes the depressing atmosphere of these river towns more than the view from the Gateway Arch in T. S. Eliot's hometown–St. Louis:

> Pushing one's face against the glass, one could see all that any human being could reasonably bear of St. Louis: mile after mile of biscuit-colored housing projects, torn-up streets, blackened Victorian factories and the purplish urban scar tissue of vacant lots and pits in the ground. It was The Waste Land.

Yet, despite the forlorn appearance of St. Louis, Raban falls in love there and eventually finds himself loving the city itself. Sally helps Raban see the city from a new perspective: "Old genteel St. Louis–T. S. Eliot's city–thought of itself as a slice of cultivated Europe. It seemed mystified as to how it had landed here, stranded on the wrong side of the big American river."

Eventually Raban and Sally drift apart, and he resumes his voyage downriver, picking his way through snags and eddies and reflecting on his running away from commitments. Raban mentions that he was once married, but the marriage lasted less than a year, and he decides that he has become an escape artist: "Running away was something that had started as simple compulsion; now it was what I was good at." He also sees parallels between river navigating and writing:

> One could lose oneself in the delicate business of keeping afloat and on course in just the same way as one could lose oneself in the pleasure and hazard of inching along through the words on the page. . . . One needed a degree of disengagement to do either. Maybe Sally was right, and it was a streak of cowardice that impelled me to do both.

Old Glory turns out to be as much about writing and living as it is about traveling. In New Orleans, sitting morosely watching the joyless gaiety of a city bent on selling itself to tourists, he tries to sum up what the voyage has meant to him: "Riding the river, I had seen myself as a sincere traveler, thinking of my voyage. . . . as a scale model of a life." New Orleans laughs at his self-image:

> I wasn't a traveler at all; I was just another rubberneck in a city that made its living out of credulous rubbernecks. Go buy a guidebook! Take a buggy ride! . . . Eat *beignets!* Listen to the sounds of Old Dixie . . . then *go home* schmuck!

In his next book, the novel *Foreign Land* (1985), Raban explores how difficult it can be to go home, especially if one has become estranged. The main character, George Gray, returns to England after spending two decades in the former Portuguese colony of Montedor in West Africa. Living in his deceased parents' house on the Cornish coast, he finds it difficult to adjust to life in England and to an adult daughter he scarcely knows. During the years that he ran a marine refueling station in Bom Porto, Africa had become home: "Africa was where he was whenever he forgot himself: it was the place where he slept, and brushed his teeth." England is the "foreign land" of the title:

> It was England, not Africa, that was so far away. The country was all around him, dark and mossy, littered with his parents' ancestral junk. Yet it was like a thin charcoal smear on the horizon of an enormous lake.

Increasingly restless, George buys the *Calliope,* a remodeled fishing ketch. With its suggestions of epic poetry and Odyssean voyages, the *Calliope* symbolizes George's desire to escape. He worries about his friends in Montedor and agonizes over the unsolicited payoff he received from the president of that nation. (George had been away at a business conference in Nigeria when revolutionary forces blew up a Portuguese patrol boat.)

When bloody fighting breaks out in Montedor and no one in England seems to care, George accepts their indifference: "It wasn't surprising. The place didn't have any oil fields, or British 'kith and kin' to give it human interest; Montedor was the sort of country where you could have a massacre without anyone minding much." When the newspapers refer to Montedor as a "small West African state," however, George becomes annoyed: "It was twice as big as England."

Raban at the time of Old Glory, *his 1981 book about his travels down the Mississippi River from Minneapolis to New Orleans (photograph by Sigfried Estrada)*

Ignoring the dry rot in the stern post of his boat, he loads it with provisions and runs away to sea, steering for Africa. The reader never finds out if he makes it safely to Bom Porto.

With its portrait of a man trying to come to terms with his past and finally escaping to sea, *Foreign Land* is a rehearsal for Raban's own escape to sea, which he documents in *Coasting: A Private Voyage* (1987). The title refers both to the literal act of sailing around the coastline of England and to the figurative "coasting" Raban did as a young boy in an English public school: "Raban has coasted through yet another term, and I can hold out little hope for his prospects in the forthcoming Examinations," the housemaster had informed his father, who looked up from the report and asked, "Wouldn't you say old boy . . . that it was about time that you put a pretty abrupt end to this . . . coasting?" At age thirty-nine Raban bought the *Gosfield Maid* and "With all the ardent solemnity of a thirteen-year-old" embarked on a voyage around England.

The voyage is Raban's way of understanding and encompassing Britain, which he has always felt was more his father's country than his own. By the 1980s it had been more than a century since England had had an inland tract that was truly wild. The sea is the English wilderness. It once puzzled Raban "that in every corner newsagent's in every English big city I visited, there would be a stack of yachting magazines." Soon he realized there was no mystery at all in their appeal:

> In high-rise flats on Inkerman Streets everywhere, where the plane trees below are choked with blue exhaust fumes, where people live tight-packed as football crowds, someone is dreaming himself to sleep over stories of hurricanes, wet sleeping bags and sunset anchorages of idyllic, empty calm.

On April Fool's Day 1982 Raban began his three-thousand-mile voyage around Britain. At the same time Britain was getting ready for a voyage of its own: "I was pointing east by north for the Dover Straits; England was headed west and south for the Falkland Islands." The war reports on the radio and the screen of the portable television on his boat are the background for the book. England seems to have gone mad for war. Switching off the radio after listening to a live broadcast from the House of Commons, Raban feels as if he had "been eavesdropping on the nastier workings of the national subconscious." When he goes ashore, he discovers that "the whole country was out on a field day." In Brixton a spray-painted sign proclaims in six-foot-high letters, "SMASH ARGENTINA!" He momentarily mistakes it for "a football slogan."

As he did on his voyage down the Mississippi, Raban spent more time ashore than afloat as he circumnavigated Great Britain. One appealing shore vignette is Raban's account of visiting his parents. Like many adult children returning home, he finds his parents changed. His mother "had somehow managed to regain the bobbed boyish figure of the girl in the 1930s photographs." His father, now retired, has grown a full beard, and his hair, "no longer barbered to Church or Army regulations," flows over his shirt collar. His father was part of the Church of England in the 1950s, when "the smart cliché about the Church of England was that it was the Conservative Party at prayer." His father and the Church have changed. His father opposes the Falklands war, and from the pulpit "prayers were being said for the Argentinean as well as for the British forces." His father has "emerged as a dissenter, a hot-water man, in a Church which had itself been reinvigorated by getting into hot water."

Coasting is not all family visits and soggy patriotism. At times Raban is reminded that the sea only tolerates those who travel or toil on it. While sailing in the Irish Sea and passing through Calf Sound near the Isle of Man, he has the odd sensation of the sea beyond appearing "lower" than the sea on which he was floating: "Calf Sound was a hill of water, a chute through which one half of the Irish Sea was doing its damnedest to fill up the other." After getting safely through this churning passage, he enters a calm sea "as still and black as a monastery fishpond." The calm is broken only by the droning sound of an RAF Nimrod aircraft crossing and recrossing the sea from Ireland to Wales. Later he hears a radio report about a missing trawler, the *South Stack,* out of Holyhead. An empty life raft is found about a week after the search ended; no trace of the boat is found. It is a common tragedy:

> There was nothing unusual in the disappearance of the *South Stack.* Every day the seaman's paper, *Lloyd's List,* carries hundreds of such entries in its Casualties columns; boats announced as Overdue, then as Missing; boats known to have foundered on rocks; boats presumed lost "due to stress of weather."

What "makes one shiver," Raban writes, is the casualness with which ships disappear: "First you are steaming along under a blue sky, and then you are sunk. For a few minutes you leave a trail of bursting bubbles–then nothing. Not even bubbles."

In "Envoi: A Peculiar People," the concluding chapter of *Coasting,* Raban reflects on his three years of coastal voyaging while sitting out a winter storm in a seventeenth-century cottage on the Essex marshes. On this "boggy fringe of things, where England petered out into water and water petered out into England," Raban daydreams about another voyage. Referring to a woman companion, he writes, "There are two of us now, and weather-bound in an anchored house, we fret our time away as ship's crews do, waiting for the rumble of chain on the winch and the inspiriting busywork of making a departure." Only people who live on continents think of the ocean as a boundary, the end of a journey. "For people who live on islands, especially on small islands, the sea is always the beginning." The *Gosfield Maid* has been refitted and repainted. Another voyage is in the offing.

Raban's next voyage was on a huge containership, the *Atlantic Conveyor,* on which he sailed to America. His account of a contemporary emigrant's voyage was published as *Hunting Mister Heartbreak: A Discovery of America* (1990). One sentence stands out so often from the soiled pages of emigrants' journals that Raban feels it deserves to be set in italics: *"Having arrived in Liverpool, I took ship for the New World."* Although he admits that "the modern emigrant" is "more likely to fly the Pacific in the cramped vinyl pod of a 747, cross the Rio Grande, or sneak ashore among the mangroves on a Florida key, than to make the journey to New York by ship," Raban wanted to make his passage to America by ship. After a spiritless goodbye to his wife (of whom the reader is told no more), Raban searches for his ship amid the "smoking heaps of brickdust" that had been the Victorian docks along the Mersey River.

The *Atlantic Conveyor* is impossible to miss: "Nine hundred-and-something feet long, fifty-six-thousand tons gross, the *Conveyor* was a custom-built marine pantechnion. It had a toppling Hilton hotel mounted on its back end, with a long city block of slotted containers stretching out ahead of it." The ship was "gorged with exports." If a container ship were to run aground off a desert island, a modern Robinson Crusoe, after salvaging the cargo, "could drive around his island in an XJS, clad in Dior . . . blind drunk on Courvoisier and armed with enough high explosives to blow an unsightly mountain to smithereens."

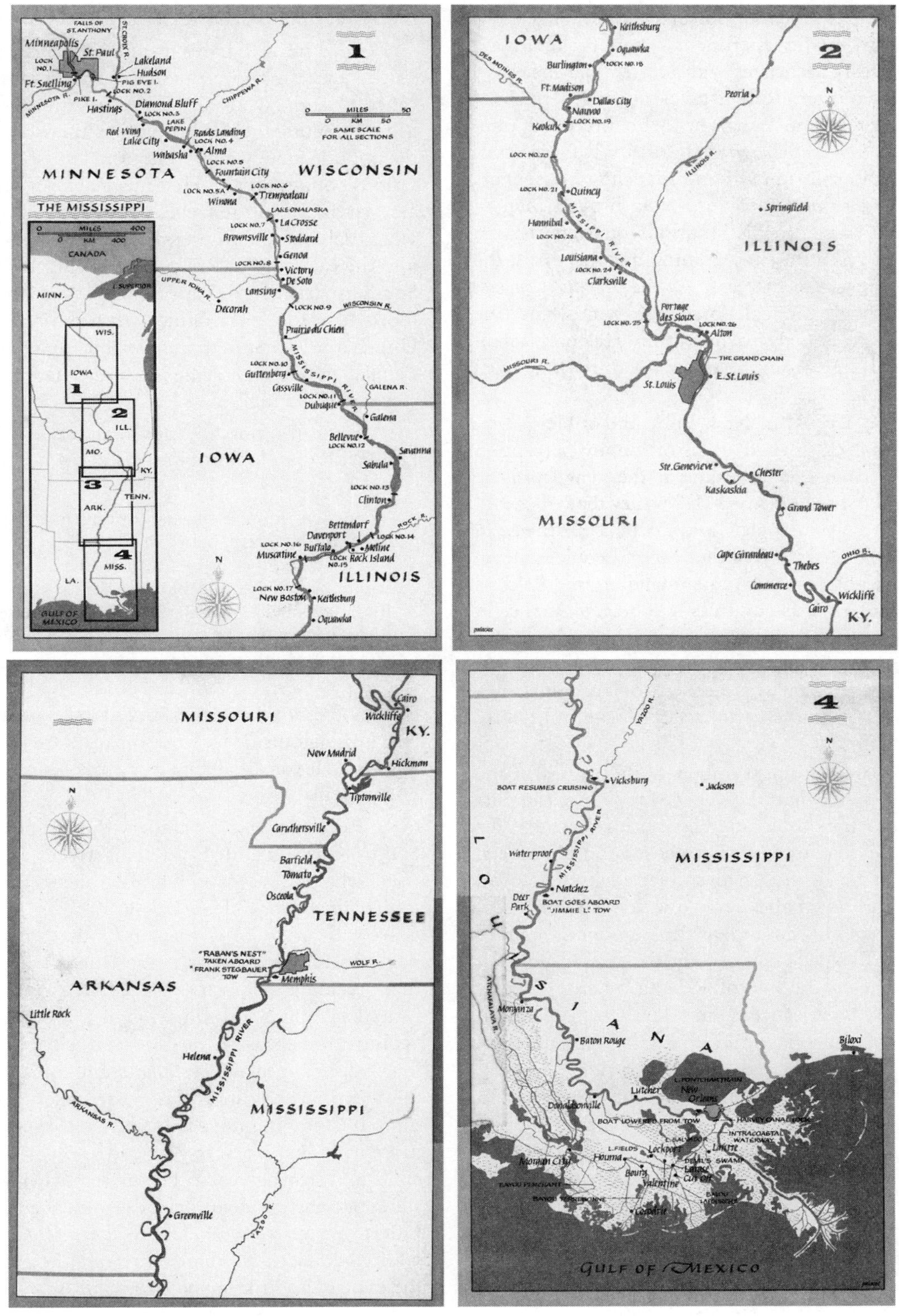

Maps of Raban's journey down the Mississippi (from Old Glory, *1981)*

Raban's quarters are luxurious. As a guest of the ship owners, he is given an officer's cabin that is more like a "roomy studio apartment" than the cramped space one usually associates with crews' quarters. Ever the bookish voyager, Raban takes aboard a stack of works by writers and emigrants who preceded him, including *The Amateur Emigrant* (1895) by Robert Louis Stevenson, who calls himself and his fellow passengers in steerage, "a shipful of failures, the broken men of England." As he sits in his luxurious quarters, Raban "felt a tide of resentful envy coming my way from the voyagers on the bookshelves." As the *Atlantic Conveyor* slammed through the gale-force-nine winds and the huge waves generated by hurricane Helene, Raban marvels at the view from the bridge. A thirty-foot swell seems miniscule.

Once he arrived in New York and sublet a tiny apartment, Raban noticed a distortion in perception and scale that is just as unsettling as the view from the towering bridge of the *Conveyor.* He writes that Alice and her friends are "Air People," and far beneath them, in the caverns of the city, dwell the "Street People." Elevators, Raban argues, are "as fundamental to middle-class culture in New York as gondolas had been to Venice in the Renaissance." It scarcely matters how high up one lives; "access to the elevator was proof that your life had the buoyancy that was needed to stay afloat in a city where the ground was seen as the realm of failure and menace."

To Raban, nothing symbolizes the values of the "Air People" better than the "new Macy's" and its line of Ralph Lauren clothing and accessories. In the 1970s and 1980s the department store whose motto had been "It's smart to be thrifty" had converted itself into an upscale emporium of the new American dream. Lauren, the son of an immigrant Russian housepainter named Frank Lifshitz, "had become the arbiter of urban American taste in the age of Reagan." Lauren represents the new American dream: "The world of Ralph Lauren was a version of the pastoral. With besotted unrealism, Lauren idolized the countryside, the past, and a class system that America had never experienced at first hand." As Mark Ford observes in a review essay on *Hunting Mister Heartbreak* (*London Review of Books,* 24 January 1991), "Raban is particularly good at exposing . . . the bizarre process by which the polo-playing, grouse-shooting lords who once symbolized all that was wrong with Europe have somehow been converted into instantly recognisable emblems of American success." The title *Hunting Mister Heartbreak* alludes to Michel Guillaume Jean de Crèvecoeur (also known as J. Hector St. John de Crèvecoeur), whose *Letters from an American Farmer* (1782) was one of the earliest books to explore what it meant to be an American. Crèvecoeur, Raban implies, would surely have been puzzled by America in the 1980s and its slavish emulation of indolent nobility.

Ford finds Raban's portrait of contemporary New York "prudish and reductive," commenting: "The so-called 'friends' whose life-styles he mercilessly analyses as representing the Air People's pettiness and blindness" do not adequately represent "the city's teeming multifarious communities." He finds Raban far more at ease and far more himself when he writes about Guntersville, Alabama. In Guntersville, where he easily slipped into the role of John Rayburn–a name given him by his Southern friends–Raban confronts an America much more like the one about which Crèvecouer wrote. Unlike the denatured atmosphere in which the "Air People" live, Guntersville is close to nature, and nature still carries a sting.

From the porch of his rented cottage in Polecat Hollow, Raban looks out on a still-savage America:

> There was more savagery lurking in my plot–in the water, up the trees, under the dead leaves, in the woodwork, behind the shower curtain–than there was in the whole of Europe put together; and if the Crèvecoeur hypothesis held good, I had lit on the cradle of American savagery, in the state that harboured more venomous creatures than any other in the Union.

The thought of the snakes, bugs, and poisonous vegetation lurking outside his door makes Raban nervous, but it was religion that finally drove him away from Guntersville.

Recalling that "Flannery O'Connor called the South 'Christ-haunted,'" Raban writes, "In Guntersville, religion was continually bubbling up to the surface of everyday life. . . ." Raised in "the well-bred Episcopal brand of Christianity" that "handled death with satisfyingly gloomy pomp," he is not prepared for the forcefulness of evangelicalism in a region visited by tornadoes and crawling with poisonous snakes: "Nature here was so profuse and violent that only a magical, or a religious, explanation could match up to the weird splendours of one's own backyard." Finding himself "drifting into a habit of mind more instinctive, more irrational" than any he had known since he was a child and fearing that if he stays much longer he will start praying, Raban decides to leave Guntersville. Offering twenty-five dollars to the high-school student who could write the best essay on "the rival merits of the big city and the small town," he awards the prize to a girl who wrote, "It's simplicity itself to make a mistake in a small town that will follow you for the rest of your life." Feeling Guntersville closing in around him, he decided "that if I stayed much longer, I would make that one mistake."

Raban's next stop was Seattle, where he finds a congenial home. In his hotel room, in a drawer beneath the telephone, he finds a Gideon Bible and *The Teaching of Buddha.* Listing names of American writers who had been influenced by Buddhism–from Ralph Waldo Emerson and Walt Whitman to Jack Kerouac and Robert M. Pirsig (author of *Zen and the Art of Motorcycle Maintenance,* 1974)–Raban concludes that "in every phase of postcolonial American history, Buddhism has offered a rhetoric of dissent; and on the Pacific coast it has coloured the fabric of the culture."

Raban realizes that *The Teaching of Buddha* has found its way to his hotel room for reasons that have more to do with economics than dissent. In the late 1980s Seattle had once again become a boomtown. The reason for this latest boom was Japan: "Seattle was close to Japan in exactly the same way that it had been close to Nome and close to the European theaters of war–close enough to get the benefit of the action and plenty far enough to feel provincially detached from it." Assuming the climatologically appropriate sobriquet of Rainbird, Raban settles into this quiet and well-mannered boomtown.

In deciding to stay in Seattle, he is not alone. Every day hundreds of others come to this latest American Eden: "New Yorkers on the run from the furies of Manhattan; refugees from the Rustbelt; Los Angelenos escaping their infamous crime statistics . . . and jammed and smoggy freeways. Then there were the Asians–Samoans, Laotians, Cambodians, Thais, Vietnamese, Chinese, and Koreans." The Korean immigrants fascinate Raban, and Ford observes that Raban's "encounters with these dogmatic, proud, fiercely-motivated Koreans . . . constitute the book's only really original contribution to the literature of immigration."

The Korean immigrants to Seattle embrace the Puritan work ethic with an evangelical fervor. They are the new Puritans, eagerly creating and then protecting their vision of the Puritans' "City upon a Hill." In Mountlake Terrace, a bedroom community fifteen miles north of downtown Seattle, Raban talks to Pastor Kim of the Korean Presbyterian Church about America: "From Pastor Kim's puritan fastness in Mountlake Terrace, America stretched away below us, a nation of backsliders, lazy and corrupt." These immigrants expect the impossible from their children. "Every Korean child was designed," Raban writes, repeating an often rehearsed local anecdote, "to become a brain surgeon by day and a concert pianist by night."

For all of its funny moments–as when Raban describes trying to come to terms with Christ-ridden and snake-infested Guntersville–or its serious ones–when he is documenting the angst of Korean American teenagers trying to live in two worlds–*Hunting Mister Heartbreak* is an uneven book. The final chapter, in which Raban writes about deciding to leave Seattle and live for a while in the Florida Keys, seems contrived. As Ford points out, "At this moment one's sense of the artificiality and scrappiness of his whole journey's–and book's–trajectory is uncomfortably acute." Raban's adventures in Key West, including a fantasy about living the life of a drug smuggler, seem, as Ford puts it, "willfully worked up for the sake of copy."

After writing *Hunting Mister Heartbreak,* Raban edited *The Oxford Book of the Sea* (1992), a collection of stories, poems, and essays. According to Raban, these selections chart "an arbitrary course across an ocean of writing, on which the solo editor carries his own limited horizon with him as he goes." The introduction provides insightful comments on the differences between British and American writing about the sea, arguing that American writers do not have to carry "the weight of sea-history that the British carried on their shoulders." To demonstrate the differences between British and American sea literature, Raban compares Frederick Marryat's *Mr. Midshipman Easy* (1836) and Richard Henry Dana's *Two Years Before the Mast* (1840). Both works are about "an induction into manhood and the exemplary society of the ship," but the American Dana can be realistic in a way that Marryat–tied to the British tradition of maritime masochism–cannot: "Dana can spend a paragraph on the difficulty of drying out socks and trousers, and on the leakiness of composition boot-soles, in a way that must have struck many of his British readers as deplorably unmanly." Dana can also take the time to describe icebergs as looking "like little floating fairy isles of sapphire." " It is," writes Raban, "hard to imagine Marryat ever allowing the sea off the Horn to be 'smooth'; and harder still to imagine one of his young heroes thinking in terms of 'little fairy isles of sapphire.'" He concludes that American sea literature, unlike its British counterpart, is "contiguous with 'nature writing,' as if the sea offered not so much a counterworld as a liquid extension of the green fields and forests within the land itself."

In *Bad Land: An American Romance* (1996) Raban turns to the great inland sea of the American imagination: the western prairie. As Raban has said in a recent on-line interview, "One of the most interesting things about the prairie is that it's dotted with wrecks. Houses, many of them built with the same care and affection that ships were built with." The prairie about which Raban writes is not the lush long-grass prairie of the Middle West. It is the short-grass prairie of the Dakota and the Montana plains. For years labeled the Great American Desert, this region is more properly steppe land, best suited to raising livestock, hay, and wheat–in those years when there is enough rain.

During the years 1911–1913 the settlers on the plains of eastern Montana were greeted with above average rainfall and milder temperatures than in normal winters. This rain, an exceptional amount of it for these dry parts; the theories of Hardy W. Campbell, author of *Campbell's Soil Culture Manual* (1902); and pamphlets distributed by the railroads drew immigrants to homestead this semi-arid region:

> The pamphlet-readers, innocent of the reality of America, brought to the text both a willing credulity and a readiness to fill in the spaces between the words with their own local, European experience. They had no more idea of Montana than they had of the dark side of the moon. But they were devout believers and imaginers.

Their faith was further enhanced by what they read in *Campbell's Soil Culture Manual.* Raban describes Campbell's system of soil management as a homiletic to conservation and thrift: "It brought to farming a strict, Presbyterian ethic of saving, husbanding, and staying home on your own plot." Campbell assured his readers that if they compacted the soil at the root level of the crop (purchasing a Campbell Sub-Surface Packer would help them accomplish this task) and tilled the top few inches to a dustlike mulch they could succeed at dryland farming: "The pulverized soil would collect the rain; the packed soil would store it for future use." Campbell's ideas were pure pseudoscience. During years in which there was slightly above average rainfall, especially during the growing season, the new settlers fared rather well. "Then the weather broke. It had not been cured, as the optimists claimed. It had only been in remission."

Raban's experience of walking a little less than a mile on a clear, cold, January night in Montana attests to the rigors of the climate:

> I had never felt my bones *as* bones before–the dry clacking of the joints of the skeleton. My kneecaps, thin and brittle as sand-dollars, came to my attention first, followed by my wrists, knuckles, shoulder-blades and ankles. I rattled as I walked, my trouser-legs flapping around bare white shinbones.

Trying to imagine what it must have been like to sit out a three-week cold spell in a tarpaper shack on the treeless prairie, Raban admits that his experiment in roughing it left him even "further out of touch with the homesteaders."

Yet Raban's writing does put readers in touch with the homesteaders, their dreams, and their disappointments. It is a distinctly American story: "These people came over, went broke, quit their homes, and moved elsewhere? So? This is America, where everyone has the right to fail–it's in the Constitution." As he drives back to Seattle, he is mindful that this cool, green, Emerald City was the "elsewhere" to which many of the dryland farmers migrated. Recalling the black-and-white images of Kansas in the movie version of *The Wizard of Oz* (1939), Raban concludes that "Dorothy's dream of a green city is rooted in the exigencies of life in a dry, brown land."

A central concern in all of Raban's writing is mutability. His description in *Soft City* of the changing signs on Earls Court Road is a metaphor for the changing world through which he travels. His account of his meeting in Cairo with Jan Morris in *Arabia through the Looking Glass* has a similar theme. In his travels Raban often meets people who lament changes in favorite places. In *Old Glory* Raban explores his version of Heraclitus's dilemma. Can he travel on two rivers at the same time: the river of his boyhood imagination and the real Mississippi? *Foreign Land* examines what it is like to return to a homeland that no longer seems like home. One response to change is to keep changing. In *Hunting Mister Heartbreak* Raban becomes a shape-shifter, taking on the colors of his surroundings. Willingly assuming identities that others create for him, he becomes Rayburn in the South and Rainbird in Seattle. This restless need to keep moving, to keep changing, lies behind much of Raban's travels and his travel writing. In a world of rapid change, one needs to keep moving. Raban, who now lives in Seattle, seems comfortably settled there, but the reader of his books suspects that Raban still feels the need to travel.

Reference:

Roger George, "A Boat Swamped with Abstractions: Reading Raban's River," in *Temperamental Journeys: Essays on the Modern Literature of Travel,* edited by Michael Kowaleski (Athens: University of Georgia Press, 1992), pp. 249–263.

Bettina Selby

(25 August 1934 –)

Jane Claspy Nesmith
Coe College

BOOKS: *Riding the Mountains Down* (London: Gollancz, 1984); republished as *Riding the Mountains Down: A Journey by Bicycle to Kathmandu* (London: Unwin, 1985);

Riding to Jerusalem (London: Sidgwick & Jackson, 1985; New York: Bedrick, 1986); republished as *Riding to Jerusalem: A Journey through Turkey and the Middle East* (London: Abacus, 1994; Boston: Little, Brown, 1995);

Riding the Desert Trail (London: Chatto & Windus, 1988); republished as *Riding the Desert Trail: By Bicycle up the Nile* (London: Chatto & Windus, 1989);

The Fragile Islands: A Journey through the Outer Hebrides (Glasgow: Drew, 1989);

Riding North One Summer (London: Chatto & Windus, 1990);

Frail Dream of Timbuktu (London: Murray, 1991);

Beyond Ararat: A Journey through Eastern Turkey (London: Murray, 1993);

Pilgrim's Road: A Journey to Santiago de Compostela (London & Boston: Little, Brown, 1994);

Like Water in a Dry Land: A Journey into Modern Israel (London: HarperCollins, 1996).

Bettina Selby

Bettina Selby, a former schoolteacher and photographer turned freelance writer, writes about traveling by bicycle across many parts of the world. Selby travels alone, braving hostile truck drivers, extremes of weather, and even landslides to reach her destinations. Her humble mode of travel and her interest in the inhabitants of the lands she visits allow Selby intimate and unusual experiences in the Indian Subcontinent, Africa, the Middle East, Europe, and the British Isles. Selby's books are not just travel guides to remote areas. Living close to nature wherever she travels, Selby often turns a critical eye on how the land and indigenous peoples have been neglected and abused in the name of progress.

Bettina St. Claire was born 25 August 1934 in Southsea, Hampshire, England, to Sydney Thomas St. Claire (an insurance agent) and Emma Cecilia Desmonde. Evacuated to a coal mining village in south Wales during World War II, Selby coped with the separation from her parents by making up stories and discovered a talent for writing. She left school at age fifteen and, after a series of casual jobs, joined the Women's Royal Army Corps, where she served from 1952 to 1954. After leaving the military, she began working as a freelance photographer.

She married Peter Max Selby, a film producer, on 1 September 1958. The couple had three children: Jonathan, Catherine, and Anna. Selby raised her children while continuing to work as a freelance photographer. She went back to school, receiving a B. Ed. degree ("with Honours") from the University of London in

1974. From 1974 to 1981 she taught at primary schools in London.

Selby was forty-seven years old before beginning her career as a travel writer. As she explains it in an autobiographical note posted on her webpage, "with the children off my hands, I decided it was at last time to see something more of the world." She began bicycling on a holiday trip to Ireland and fell in love with this mode of travel. "Moving quietly along at gentle speeds allows me to see, hear, and smell the country, in a way which isn't possible encapsulated in a motor car or bus," she writes in *Riding to Jerusalem* (1985). Selby travels on a strict budget, usually with camping gear or information about local hostels, leaving her dependent on the charity of strangers wherever she goes. Her journeys by bicycle are strenuous; they include a trek across a desert and into the Himalaya Mountains, a voyage from London to Jerusalem, and trips in equatorial Africa. She manages them all, however, with humor, stamina, and an observant eye for the landscape and people around her.

Selby's first book, *Riding the Mountains Down* (1984), is a travelogue of her five-month, four-thousand-mile bicycle trip from Karachi in Pakistan to Kathmandu in Nepal. The trip required endless resourcefulness and stamina, as Selby faced terrible riding conditions, illness, angry crowds, and dehydration; yet, she also describes the wild and harsh beauty of desert and mountain and tells stories of the unexpected kindness of local people, who offer food and hospitality in a land of sparse resources.

Selby had a bicycle custom-made for the trip (the specifications appear in an appendix to the book) and flew to Karachi on the Arabian Sea to begin the long trek through the Sindh desert and across the flat Punjab to the Himalayas. She recounts hardships straightforwardly. Throughout the trip she often had little food or water, riding up steep mountain grades and once over loose rock scattered by an avalanche. At one point, in a desolate region of northern India, she mended a tire by stuffing it with spare clothing.

Though descriptions of the physical experience of the journey are vivid, the real charm and insight of the book come from Selby's tales of encounters with indigenous peoples. Welcomed by Christian Pakistanis in Karachi, Selby is sent along a trail of "safe houses," where a network of strangers provides lodging and hospitality, often despite a language barrier. Chance encounters prove serendipitous: hungry and worn down by riding through congested northern Indian cities, she is cooked an omelet dinner by an elderly and poor Sikh who calls her "my daughter." Stranded in a small town with a punctured tire, she is helped by a group of young men who find a translator and give her tea while they locate someone to repair her bicycle. Selby also tells, however, of long hours spent dealing with corrupt government officials and frightening encounters with mobs of young boys who chase and threaten her.

Despite the hardships of the long journey, Selby reaches her destination in the lofty Himalayas, which she finds as magnificent as she had imagined them to be. While visiting a nearby school she declares that "If I hadn't had a husband back home who was expecting me to return shortly, I would have been tempted to take up the offer of a permanent post."

In her review of the book for *TLS: The Times Literary Supplement* (22 June 1984) Dervla Murphy pointed out that Selby is sometimes too ready to view all of Islamic Pakistan as "enemy territory" based on her many negative encounters with hostile Muslim men. Overall, though, Murphy noted Selby's perceptivity, resourcefulness, and stamina, praising the book's use of "detail that no one travelling by motor vehicle would be likely to observe."

In her second book, *Riding to Jerusalem,* first published in 1985, Selby travels the route of the eighth century missionary and pilgrim St. Willibald from London to Jerusalem. With her bicycle standing in as a "humble and innocent . . . pilgrim's staff," she is "as dependent on local goodwill as were the early pilgrims."

As in her first book, Selby details the scenery and areas of historical significance, especially as she travels across Turkey, where Roman ruins and remnants of crusaders' fortresses dot the landscape. Once again, her mode of transportation brings her close to the people of the countries she visits, and the heart of her book is the stories of the moments of connection with local people, who insist on giving her fruit and buying her cups of strong Turkish tea. Selby is especially fascinated with crossing from Europe into Asia and continually contrasts the two cultures in her account. Selby writes of trying times with "the Turk," especially men; she tells of difficulties with a self-important bus driver who refuses to take care of her bicycle and with threatening young men who harass her. These experiences lead Selby to contemplate the anger and violence that contribute to political strife in the region. "No amount of reading news accounts or seeing television reports had prepared me for the realities of such a situation," she writes. The remains of fortresses she sees along the Turkish coast remind her poignantly that crusaders from western Europe added to this violence in their determination to rid the land of "the infidel."

Political tensions between Israel and Jordan make it difficult for Selby to cross the border, and she waits in frustration, contemplating the armed guards. Eventually, she is allowed to bicycle triumphantly through to

Jericho and then into Jerusalem. At the end of the book Selby reflects that the troubles of the Middle East are not so different from the ones St. Willibald had seen more than one thousand years earlier. *Riding to Jerusalem* has proved one of Selby's most popular books: a U.S. edition was published in 1986; the book was republished in Glasgow by R. Drew in 1989; British paperback editions were published in 1994 and 1995 by Abacus and Little, Brown UK; and a U.S. paperback edition was published by Warner in April of 1995.

Selby's 4,500-mile trip up the Nile River described in *Riding the Desert Trail* (1988) was inspired by a visit to the Egyptian antiquities room at the British Museum on a cold, wet autumn day. *A Thousand Miles up the Nile* (1877), an account of a journey written by Victorian novelist and travel writer Amelia B. Edwards, also intrigued Selby, who quotes from it often in her own book. Selby begins her trip in the sophisticated city of Cairo, travels through Islamic fundamentalist Sudan, and continues on through war-torn Uganda to Lake Victoria.

While visiting Sudan, Selby visits the various relief agencies attempting to aid the people whose land is gripped by drought. At one point, she is almost arrested for photographing a homeless street boy sleeping near a police station in Khartoum. Selby's Sudanese guide extricates her from the hands of the police, who are apparently highly suspicious of foreign relief agencies. The photographs that Selby has included in her book bear witness to the poverty in Khartoum that these agencies are trying to battle.

Along with the usual difficulties of riding a bicycle long distances over badly maintained roads in the desert, finding food and shelter in poor rural areas, and contending with corrupt local police forces, Selby fears stray bullets as she rides through politically unstable Uganda. Distracted by the beauties of the Ugandan countryside, Selby fails to notice "the rusty upturned wheelbarrow which constituted an army road block" and rides past it:

> The first intimation that I had committed a grave error was the look of fear on an old woman's face as she gestured at me with flapping movements of her hands to go back. In the same moment I realised that the grunts behind me, which had been rising in pitch and volume, might have something to do with me. As I turned round I saw a soldier bearing down fast towards me, his rifle aimed at my middle and his finger trembling on the trigger. His face was contorted with anger and his shouts had by now become screams and bellows of rage; it was clear that he was preventing himself from firing only with great difficulty. Realising what I had done I hurried back towards him and even as I was taking in the situation, it came to me that here at last was the other side of things–the root of the fear I had felt in crossing the border. It was my first encounter with the terrifying violence that had ruined this land.

Selby manages to placate the soldier and get on with her ride. Her view of the Ugandan people is not much colored by this incident, and she finishes her trip marveling at how welcoming and friendly the majority of Ugandans are, despite their political strife. *Riding the Desert Trail* was enthusiastically reviewed in *The Scotsman* and by Richard West of the *London Sunday Telegraph,* who pronounced it "a travel book of extraordinary fascination and charm." The book was successful: Chatto & Windus published a second edition in hardcover in 1989, and the book was republished in paperback form in May of that year, and again in 1990 and 1993. It was also the subject of an episode in the *Art of Travel* television series.

In *The Fragile Islands: A Journey through the Outer Hebrides* (1989) Selby takes an all-terrain bicycle and her tiny one-person tent to Scotland's Outer Hebrides where she tours the islands' half-deserted roads, towns, and farms. As the title suggests, the book emphasizes the way economic development has taken its toll on these remote islands. Throughout the book Selby points out that humans and the natural world have coexisted for a long time on the Hebrides, but late-twentieth-century development has scarred these fragile islands, and the islanders have increasingly been forced to abandon their ancestral homes.

An accident early in the trip leaves Selby's ankle in a cast, but this does not slow her down much. She finds she can still ride a bicycle. As usual, her mode of travel and her outgoing manner bring her into contact with many interesting people–tourists, new residents, and natives of the land. From these people and from rainy-day trips to local libraries, Selby learns about the history and present conditions of these northern islands.

Throughout her travels in Scotland, Selby is aware of the natural beauty of the Hebrides. Even when she stays in comfortable, sociable surroundings–at youth hostels or in the homes of people she meets–she is anxious to return to the solitude of bicycle riding by day and camping under the stars by night. "No matter how sad I feel at parting from new friends or from places I would like to stay in longer," she writes, "there is always a sense of freedom in setting off again that never palls."

Returning again to her own part of the world for her fifth bicycle trip and book, Selby sets off from London on a tour of northern England, recounted in *Riding North One Summer* (1990). Nostalgia inspired by "memories of lakes and hills, moorland and meadows, hedgerows, seashores and rivers" fuels her desire to see if the

Dust jacket for Selby's 1988 book about her trip to Africa

northern part of England is still unspoiled. Selby bicycles through the Severn River valley, over the hills of the Cotswolds and the mountains of the Pennine Chain, across the Lake District, through the counties on the border with Scotland, and back along the northeast coast of England. Her knowledge of local histories adds depth to her descriptions of places such as Hawkshead, where the poet William Wordsworth attended grammar school; Hadrian's Wall; Lindisfarne, or Holy Island, an important religious center in the seventh century; and Whitby, an historic port town on the North Sea.

She turns her attention to the afflictions of industrialization on this land. One target is the Sellafield nuclear plant, whose sinister appearance on the horizon makes her uneasy. Conversations with local people reveal their worries about the dangers posed by the plant. A more immediate threat, perhaps, is the scourge of polluting factories that ravage the old and new industrial towns set among the rolling hills and areas of historical interest. After visiting the peaceful island of Lindisfarne, Selby must bicycle through the industrial town of Teeside, where "Monstrous cooling towers, huge chimneys and pipes belched forth black rivers of smoke." Selby, the former schoolteacher, wonders about the effect of such an environment on local children, but the book ends on a hopeful note, as Selby visits Whitby, which she finds charming and unspoiled, and spends her last night under the stars on the nearby moors.

In *Frail Dream of Timbuktu* (1991) Selby describes a return to Africa for a bicycle trip of more than one thousand miles along the course of the Niger River through remote, semidesert regions of Niger and Mali to the city of Timbuktu (the traditional name for Tombouctou). Selby's trip is not easy. There are many hazards along the Niger for bicycles, perhaps more in this undeveloped part of Africa than along the Nile. Selby's bicycle becomes mired in deep sand called *fesh-fesh* and later its tire is pierced by hundreds of sharp thorns. Selby becomes progressively more dehydrated in this land of desiccating heat and contaminated water, and eventually falls ill of bilharzia, a waterborne disease. As usual, she takes it all in stride and relishes the adventure, often turning down rides or luxurious housing despite the hardships.

Because the Niger River is such an important feature of the landscape, Selby takes advantage of this "royal road" to Timbuktu, traveling part of the way in a small, canoe-like pirogue, which is poled by a young African man named Boubcar. Lively descriptions of the cheerful Boubcar, inhospitable western missionaries, and energetic Peace Corps workers almost overshadow her account of crumbling, decrepit Timbuktu, once an important center for trade caravans.

Traveling on a slow-moving bicycle and bypassing luxurious hotels for the solitude and freedom of her tent, Selby becomes aware of the sufferings of people in western Africa. She sees the results of urban drift, where overfarmed land and drought lead to poverty, disease, and child beggars in overcrowded city streets. In an episode that illustrates her active compassion, Selby describes a visit to the Dogan people, whose ancient ways of life are threatened by a drought caused by nearby communities that are tapping into the water table that feeds the Dogan wells. Selby acts as a secretary for the Dogan on her visit, transcribing an eloquent plea for assistance into a letter to UNICEF officials, who promise to forward the letter to the appropriate government agencies. Selby views this promise with equal measures of skepticism and hope.

Inspired by the story of Noah's Ark, Selby decided to brave the mountains of eastern Turkey and bicycle to Mount Ararat, a journey she recounts in *Beyond Ararat: A Journey through Eastern Turkey* (1993). "No ascents, not even the steepest Swiss passes or the Himalayas exacted the degree of sweat and toil as did these Pontic Alps," she writes. Often, she is unable to manage the steep gradient and, "bent almost double and panting fit to burst with the effort," she has to push her heavily laden bicycle. Selby's journey takes her past many significant Turkish historical sites: the Hagia Sophia in Istanbul, the ancient Sumela Monastery, and the haunting ruins of the ghost town of Ani, a former Armenian capital. This second visit to Turkey allows her to experience Turkish hospitality again. In one town she is "auctioned" off to potential hosts, while elsewhere women practically suffocate her with interest and some men refuse to believe a woman can use tools or bicycle up steep inclines and gallantly offer their "help."

Selby learns firsthand about the situation of the Kurds as she bicycles through territory where the Kurdish resistance movement is active. The rural Kurds are poor and desperate, and several people confide in her about their plight, though she is hesitant to choose sides in the complex conflict between separatist Kurds and the Turkish government. While waiting in the government-controlled Kurdish town of Hakkari for a bus, however, Selby reflects on the tensions underlying the "superficial air of normality":

> Fierce-looking men with hooked noses, huge black moustaches and dark flashing eyes, wearing the traditional voluminous trousers and rough turbans, sat drinking tea and avidly watching cartoons on the outdoor television. A few were in western garb, and I thought these might well be government agents for they were not interested in the cartoons, but watched the viewers over the top of their newspapers. . . . At the very summit of the town just beyond the tea garden sat Atatürk in bronze on a mettlesome charger, and above him was a banner with the over familiar sentiment "HOW WONDERFUL TO BE ABLE TO SAY I AM A TURK" writ large. I wondered idly how the Scots, the Welsh or the Irish would react to banners with "HOW WONDERFUL TO BE ABLE TO SAY I AM AN ENGLISHMAN" adorning their main squares and carved into mountain sides?

Selby's ambivalence about the political situation in Turkey sometimes extends to the country itself. Trash litters the roadsides and beaches that would otherwise be strikingly beautiful, and the noise of televisions, pop music, and the calls of the muezzins shatter the nighttime peace of cities and towns. Children gang up on her and pelt her with stones as she bicycles through rural areas where outsiders are regarded with fear and anger. Selby's genuine interest in others and in the historical importance of the land she visits carry her through a strenuous trip. She ends her narrative in Harran, within the Fertile Crescent, picturing Abraham and Sarah as they set off on their own long journey.

Affixing a scallop shell–the emblem of St. James and the traditional sign of the pilgrim–to her bicycle, Selby once again follows a medieval pilgrimage route in her book *Pilgrim's Road: A Journey to Santiago de Compostela* (1994). Santiago de Compostela, where the remains of the apostle St. James are said to rest, was a tremendously important destination for pilgrims in the Middle Ages, and a revival of religious and historical interest since the 1970s has made it popular again among vacationers. Neither pilgrim nor tourist, Selby sets off on the Camino Santiago, a route running from the middle of France to Santiago de Compostela, a town near the western coast of Spain. She had long wanted to visit the area with its historic towns, Romanesque churches, and rugged mountains.

Selby shapes the narrative of her journey by describing a change of attitude toward the trip after many days of strenuous travel and nights in the spartan lodgings offered to pilgrims. At a church service in Roncesvalles, she finally realizes that she is a "real if reluctant" pilgrim, drawing spiritual sustenance from the difficult journey and from the spirit of St. James. As a pilgrim, she finds herself the recipient of much attention. Tourists want to photograph her with her bicycle and scallop shells. Fellow pilgrims share their dreams and stories, and local people entreat her to *"priez pour nous"* (pray for us). All of this attention, and the growing sense of being on a spiritual journey, gives Selby a feeling of connection with the thousands of pilgrims who have gone before her. A television documentary was made of Selby's journey; this and the growing popularity of the pilgrimage route helped sales of her book, which went into a paperback edition a year after its first publication.

Selby's next book, *Like Water in a Dry Land: A Journey into Modern Israel* (1996), chronicles her return to the Holy Land. Encouraged by an audience with King Hussein and the peace treaty between Jordan and Israel, Selby hopes to find more stability in the land she came to love on her earlier visit.

A long journey from Cyprus through Lebanon, Jordan, and Syria provides Selby with many face-to-face encounters with ordinary people of the region: a Greek ship's captain who arranges her passage from Cyprus to Lebanon; Armenian high-school girls who bicycle with her through Beirut; and a group of Bedouin women who feed her olives, bread, and cheese on a rooftop in Syria. At the River Jordan, Selby faces the inevitably difficult border crossing, then bicycles through the countryside, and finally thrills to the sight of road signs for the biblical Jerusalem, known as the Old City. Selby finds the diversity of the Old City, with its jealous territorial claims, a change from "the apathy that characterizes so much of modern church life back home."

In the occupied West Bank, territorial claims seem more disruptive and unjust. There, Israeli rule means unfair taxation, continuous harassment, and even torture for those Palestinians who resist Israeli policies. Despite her desire to see the country from the Israeli viewpoint as well as the Palestinian, she becomes convinced of Israel's injustice. She writes of hearing ordinary Israelis remark that Palestinians should just leave their homeland for one of the surrounding Arab countries: "If they don't like it here, they should go," many people tell her. Attitudes such as this, and the many frightening encounters with Israeli police and soldiers Selby either has or is told about, lead her to compare modern Israelis to the Romans who occupied the Holy Land in Jesus' time. Visiting the Jabalia refugee camp, Selby is infuriated by what she sees:

> Conditions were appalling. We drove through lakes of sewage, between housing that was shacks cobbled together with disparate scrap materials, while little children, the third generation of refugees who had been forced to live here, picked a cautious, painful route on bare feet through the ravaged littered ground that passed for streets. The dust and dirt were terrible causing all sorts of eye infections and health problems. I found it all far worse than refugee camps I had visited in Africa and the poorer parts of India, mainly because civilization had advanced so much further here that the destruction of it made for a greater degradation. Nor was it drought or any natural calamity that had brought about these conditions but the deliberate policy of an occupying force.

Selby's bleak view of the Holy Land is brightened, though, by the people she meets: the Palestinians of Beit Sahour devoted to nonviolent resistance, the many international aid workers providing medical and legal assistance to refugees, and those Israeli Jews willing to question their government's policies. In the end, Selby focuses on these "people of goodwill," the only promise of peace in a troubled land: "Like water in a dry land they were the basis for hope and new beginnings."

Bettina Selby is an important voice in late-twentieth-century British travel writing, a counterpoint to the distanced realism of some of her contemporaries, whose cynical descriptions of distant lands and peoples seem to suggest travel writers should not enjoy traveling. Selby's books appeal to a variety of readers: Christians who are moved by her thoughtful spiritualism, bicycling enthusiasts who appreciate the hardships she has overcome, women inspired by her matter-of-fact feminism, and armchair adventurers of all persuasions. Her books have been translated into Dutch, German, and Japanese. In the *Irish Independent,* reviewer Dervla Murphy declared: "Each of Bettina Selby's books is better than the last; and that cannot be said of many travel writers. . . . Being such an enthusiastic, perceptive, and sympathetic traveller, she makes it possible for us not simply to read about her enjoyment, but to share in it and be refreshed by it."

Timothy Severin

(25 September 1940 –)

Scott R. Christianson
Radford University

BOOKS: *Tracking Marco Polo* (London: Routledge & Kegan Paul, 1964; New York: Peter Bedrick Books, 1986);

Explorers of the Mississippi (London: Routledge & Kegan Paul, 1967; New York: Knopf, 1968);

The Golden Antilles (London: Hamilton, 1970; New York: Knopf, 1970);

The African Adventure: A History of African Explorers (London: Hamilton, 1973); republished as *The African Adventure: Four Hundred Years of Exploration in the "Dangerous Continent"* (New York: Dutton, 1973);

The Horizon Book of Vanishing Primitive Man (New York: American Heritage Publishing, 1973); republished as *Vanishing Primitive Man* (London: Thames & Hudson, 1973);

The Oriental Adventure: Explorers of the East (London: Angus & Robertson, 1976; Boston: Little, Brown, 1976);

The Brendan Voyage (London: Hutchinson, 1978; New York: McGraw-Hill, 1978);

The Sindbad Voyage (London: Hutchinson, 1982; New York: Putnam, 1983);

The Jason Voyage: The Quest for the Golden Fleece (London: Hutchinson, 1985; New York: Simon & Schuster, 1985);

The Ulysses Voyage: Sea Search for the Odyssey (London: Hutchinson, 1987; New York: Dutton, 1987);

Crusader: By Horse to Jerusalem (London: Hutchinson, 1989);

In Search of Genghis Khan (London: Hutchinson, 1991; New York: Atheneum, 1992);

The China Voyage: Across the Pacific by Bamboo Raft (London: Little, Brown, 1994; Reading, Mass.: Addison-Wesley Publishing, 1995);

The Spice Islands Voyage: In Search of Wallace (London: Little, Brown, 1997); republished as *The Spice Islands Voyage: The Quest for the Man Who Shared Darwin's Discovery of Evolution* (New York: Carroll & Graf Publishers, 1998).

photograph by Ian Yeomans

Tim Severin

MOTION PICTURES: *The Brendan Voyage,* script and photography by Severin, privately produced, 1978;

The Sindbad Voyage, script by Severin, produced by Severin, Sultanate of Oman Television, 1981;

Crusade, script by Severin, produced by Severin, Mediac International, 1989;

In Search of Genghis Kahn, script and photography by Severin, produced and directed by Severin, RTE Irish Television, 1991;

The China Voyage, script and photography by Severin, produced and directed by Severin, Atlantic Film/ ZDF German Television/RTE Irish Television, 1995;

The Spice Islands Voyage, script and photography by Severin, produced and directed by Severin, 1997.

Tim Severin (as he has signed his books since 1978) is an intrepid traveler and a prolific writer about travel. Severin is distinguished among late-twentieth-century travel writers because he is a professional historian of travel and exploration, with a research degree from Oxford University. He demonstrates an eclectic command of history, geography, politics, and biography based on extensive research into primary documents of travel and exploration, including personal memoirs, logs, and journals.

For many of his books, Severin supplements historical research with travel and exploration of his own, verifying details of climate, geography, and other conditions with his firsthand experience. More dramatically, for several of his books Severin has duplicated historic or legendary voyages as he has followed the paths of such travelers as Marco Polo, St. Brendan of Ireland, Sindbad the Sailor, Jason and the Argonauts, Ulysses.

Giles Timothy Severin was a world traveler almost from the moment of his birth. He was born on 25 September 1940 in Jorhat, Assam, India to Maurice Rimington Watkins, a tea planter, and Inge Severin, a writer. He attended Tonbridge School in England, and later Keble College of Oxford University, where he earned a B.A. degree in 1962, and the degrees of M.A. and B. Litt. in 1968. In 1997 Trinity College, Dublin awarded Severin an honorary D. Litt. He studied in the United States and lives in Timoleague, County Cork, Ireland. Since 1961 Severin has been a professional scholar, writer, and traveler and has received the Founders Medal from the Royal Geographical Society, the Livingstone Medal from the Royal Scottish Geographical Society, and the Sir Percy Sykes Medal from the Royal Asiatic Society.

Although Severin's works focus on widely separated subjects in the history of the literature of travel and exploration, he repeats several themes and concerns in his writing. One of these is the passion for travel–his own, as the motivating force behind much of his research, and that of the travelers and explorers about whom he writes. Severin's passion for travel embodies those features as well as another aspect, prevalent throughout his books: his love and respect for the past. Severin's enjoyment and enthusiasm for his travels are always highest at moments when he can connect what he sees or experiences with past places, events, and discoveries. He embraces past modes of travel and exploration–of living and being in the world–and he does not believe that modern methods and technologies are superior to those of the past. Historical texts of travel and exploration receive close attention by Severin; another constant in his books is an appreciation of travel writing throughout history and his insistence upon the influence and accuracy of such accounts, however personal or unscholarly they may be.

Tracking Marco Polo (1964), Severin's first book, embodies his passion for travel; his love and respect for the past; and his interest in travel writing, in this case, Marco Polo's narrative of his journey to Cathay, or China, as recorded in *Divisament dou monde* (*A Description of the World,* 1298). Severin's interest in the account of the Venetian trader's journey began when he was a student at Tonbridge preparatory school; it was renewed by the Honours School syllabus on the History of Geography at Oxford, where Severin was a Trevelyan Scholar at Keble College. In the foreword to the first U.S. edition (not published until 1986), Severin reflects, "from the outset, *Tracking Marco Polo* was both an old-fashioned, and an undergraduate book." The Marco Polo Route Project was concocted at Oxford by Severin and an Exeter College man named Stanley Johnson. They accepted a volunteer, Michael de Larrabeiti, a Londoner who was an experienced cameraman and world traveler. They raised minimal funding; and with Brian Watkins, Severin's older brother, agreeing to act as "Home Agent," or support liaison, in England the three set off on two B.S.A. motorcycles–in spite of the fact that Severin and Johnson had failed to qualify for English motorcycle operator's licenses. Undeniably, the most "undergraduate" features of the book involve hair-raising incidents and reckless driving of the two motorcycles. The motorcycles, however, allowed the Marco Polo Route participants more immediate access to the terrain and conditions Polo would have experienced travelling with horse and camel caravans, at the same time that their motorized speed allowed the team to cover ground more quickly.

The Marco Polo Route Project was a writer's project. As Severin proudly notes in the foreword to the U.S. edition, "the former members of the Marco Polo Route project have produced a total of more than twenty-five books between them," including Johnson's poetry, de Larrabeiti's novels, and Severin's books of history and travel. In the concluding chapter of *Tracking Marco Polo,* Severin notes that all three members felt "the lack of books" was as serious a problem as poor provisions. The general enthusiasm for books and writing centered upon Polo's *A Description of the World,* which

Stanley Johnson, Severin, and Michael de Larrabeiti during the trip Severin wrote about in his first book, Tracking Marco Polo *(1964; photograph by de Larrabeiti)*

guided every aspect of the project and its travels. Severin and his companions were never happier than when they had, through their own experiences, clarified or proven some fact in Polo's account of his travels. Discounting the disbelief of both Polo's contemporaries and later scholars, Severin argues throughout for the historical and factual accuracy of the Venetian trader's account.

The expedition ground to a halt in Afghanistan when the travelers could not secure permission from the authorities–because of tensions with neighboring Pakistan–to enter the Wakhan Corridor, the ancient caravan route into China. They could not have gone much further, in any case–Severin and Johnson were due back at Oxford for the new term, the team had only £40 left, and their one surviving motorcycle was nearly defunct. They had, however, documented both the exact trail of Polo's travels and substantiated the veracity of many of his descriptions. They had endured treacherous mountain passes in the Balkans and Pamirs, desert conditions in Turkey and Iran, and hostile natives and national bureaucracies. Overall, their lean-and-mean mode of travel actually provided them with fewer amenities than Marco Polo, scion of a wealthy Venetian merchant family, could command–and far less than those taken for granted by modern travelers and tourists. In the course of their journey, Severin broke his foot in a motorcycle accident; members of the expedition were variously thrown in jail out of general suspicion or because their papers were not in order; and they were set upon by vicious dogs belonging to wasteland nomads. Throughout the trip they trusted to luck and to the humanity and generosity of the diverse people they encountered. Severin and his companions regularly encountered peoples and conditions largely unchanged from the time of Marco Polo; they perceived such continuities as not only documentation of Polo's veracity, but also as an affirmation of ways of life that date back to the Middle Ages.

As Severin details in the foreword to the first American edition, *Tracking Marco Polo* launched his career as researcher, traveler, and writer: "When the type-script was accepted . . . it encouraged me to continue with post-graduate studies in the history of exploration and discovery, and to try to make my living as a writer on the subject." Moreover, *Tracking Marco Polo* documents not only Severin's tolerance for personal hardships, but his appreciation of the endurance of ancient ways in the face of modern civilization.

Upon his graduation from Oxford with a degree in the history of medieval Asian exploration, Severin accepted a Commonwealth Fund (Harkness) Fellowship in 1964 to study in the United States at the University of California at Berkeley, the University of Minnesota, and Harvard University. While at Harvard, he met Dorothy Virginia Sherman, whom he married on 24 March 1966; the couple had one daughter, Ida. The marriage was dissolved in 1979.

His experience in North America led him to investigate the history of the exploration of the Mississippi–"the Father of Waters"– from the point of view of the explorers, which Severin was surprised to find had not yet been done. These investigations–which included a journey by boat from the source to the mouth of the Mississippi in the summer of 1965–culminated in *Explorers of the Mississippi* (1967). Severin's second book, and his first written as a professional writer and researcher, evinces his keen interest in the history and genre of travel writing and his preoccupation with the truth (or lack thereof) of travelers' and explorers' accounts of their journeys and experiences.

From Harvard University, Severin traveled to Jamaica accompanied by his American wife, Dorothy, and began researching his third book, *The Golden Antilles* (1970). Grounded in his research and knowledge of Renaissance history, exploration, and travel writing and supplemented by his travels throughout the Caribbean and Central America, *The Golden Antilles* is Severin's narrative of swashbucklers, pirates, and colonists in the sixteenth and seventeenth centuries.

Severin's next book, *The African Adventure: A History of African Explorers* (1973), continues his interest in the history of travel. With this book, Severin began his association with "picture researcher" Sarah Waters who supplied period illustrations, engravings, and illuminations for *The African Adventure* and subsequent works. The illustrations from throughout the history of European exploration of Africa provide a fit accompaniment to Severin's often vivid prose.

In appearance, *The African Adventure* is different from Severin's three previous works. Published in an oversized coffee-table book format, it is clearly intended for a general audience. It is a popular history of African exploration with chapters and sections on such popular figures of legend and history as the mythical African Christian king Prester John, the Scottish missionary and explorer David Livingstone, and the British journalist and explorer H. M. Stanley.

Severin's admiration for the feats of explorers and travelers is evident throughout the book but is tempered by his pragmatic understanding of their motivations. In *The African Adventure* Severin captures the adventurous aspects of that travel and exploration and writes admiringly of the travelers and explorers who opened Africa to Europe. In this respect, it is typical of traditional accounts of European exploration in the African continent. It is atypical, however, for its time, in its serious consideration of more popular and less scholarly accounts of African exploration and colonization. Prefiguring new historicist and post-colonial scholars and critics, Severin observes how the writings of travelers and explorers shaped and influenced popular and official conceptions of and policies toward Africa. While he may emphasize the motivations of geographical curiosity, missionary zeal, and the desire for adventure, Severin also acknowledges the colonialist and imperialist motivations of African explorers and their European commercial and nation-state sponsors.

Severin followed *The African Adventure* with *The Horizon Book of Vanishing Primitive Man* (1973), which is not a work of travel writing or the history of travel, but a work of popular anthropology. In *Vanishing Primitive Man,* published first by the American Heritage Society for a wide American audience, Severin shows himself aware of and attentive to developments in cultural theory and history–especially the anthropological studies of Claude Lévi-Strauss, who was important to cultural theory in the post–World War II period.

The Oriental Adventure: Explorers of the East (1976), Severin's next history of travel and exploration, demands comparison with Edward Said's influential *Orientalism,* published two years later. There are important similarities between Severin's text, a book aimed at a general audience, and Said's scholarly work, which has been widely credited with inaugurating post-colonial theory and studies. Both writers argue that the idea of the Orient has, in Said's words, "helped to define Europe (or the West) as its contrasting image, idea, personality, experience." Said, however, focuses on the Orient as the lands of North Africa, the Middle East, and India that were (and are) most subjected to European influence and colonization, and Severin instead focuses on Asia proper, from Siberia eastward through Mongolia to Manchuria, and from Afghanistan through northern India and Tibet to China.

Another difference between the two projects is that Said draws on scholarly texts produced by "Orientalists," the European scholars who collected data about the Orient and codified it into a body of knowledge called "Orientalism," while Severin focuses on the narratives, notes, and reports of travel and exploration written by Europeans who actually journeyed to the East. The difference in selection yields remarkably different results and perceptions. Severin's Asia emerges as a vast and diverse space resistant both to change and to the influence of Europeans, replete with self-contained and autonomous peoples and cultures. Said, on the other hand, argues that the West has continually dominated Asia and that relations of knowledge and power have worked almost exclusively for the benefit of Europe and the West at the expense of the freedom and self-determination of the East. Severin's sympathetic approach is signaled in his wry disclaimer of comprehensiveness:

> Certainly an overall history of Asian exploration is not intended, because the very idea of Europeans "exploring" Asia is something of an impertinence. In most cases the Asians knew very well where they lived and they had a shrewd idea of who their neighbours were, long before the Europeans arrived and put them in another perspective.

Severin's work has generally been neglected by scholars of the history of colonization and decolonization. His research, however, explores and documents the firsthand experiences of travelers and explorers, many of whom were motivated primarily by curiosity and wanderlust, as much as by commercial or colonial interests. Severin argues persuasively that accounts written by travelers and explorers played a significant role in European knowledge and understanding of Asia.

With his next book, *The Brendan Voyage* (1978), Severin embarked on a new phase of his work as a historian of travel, traveler, and travel writer. The idea for the book came, as Severin describes in the book, when his wife, Dorothy–a scholar of medieval Spanish literature–remarked, "There's something odd about the Saint Brendan text." The text to which Dorothy referred was the *Navigatio Sancti Brendani Abbatis,* known simply as the *Navigatio Brendani* or *The Voyage of Brendan.* St. Brendan–also called Brendan of Clonfert or Brendan the Voyager–was an Irish monk who lived between about A.D. 486 and 578 and who supposedly made a voyage between A.D. 565 and 573 across the Atlantic to North America, although scholars had long dismissed the *Navigatio Brendani* as fantasy. The oddity the Severins discussed, after dinner across their kitchen table in their house in Courtmacsherry in southwest Ireland, was the abundance of "practical details" of geography, progress of the voyage, times and distances that give the text a different "feel," as Dorothy put it, than narratives of other early medieval saints.

> "Well, I don't see why Saint Brendan couldn't have got there," said my wife firmly.
>
> "No, neither do I. You and I know that it's possible to cover enormous distances in small vessels. We've done it ourselves. Perhaps it's time someone tried to find out whether Saint Brendan's voyage was feasible or not."

After all, Severin reasoned, he and his wife–and their three-year-old daughter–had sailed their small sloop, *Prester John,* "as far afield as Turkey."

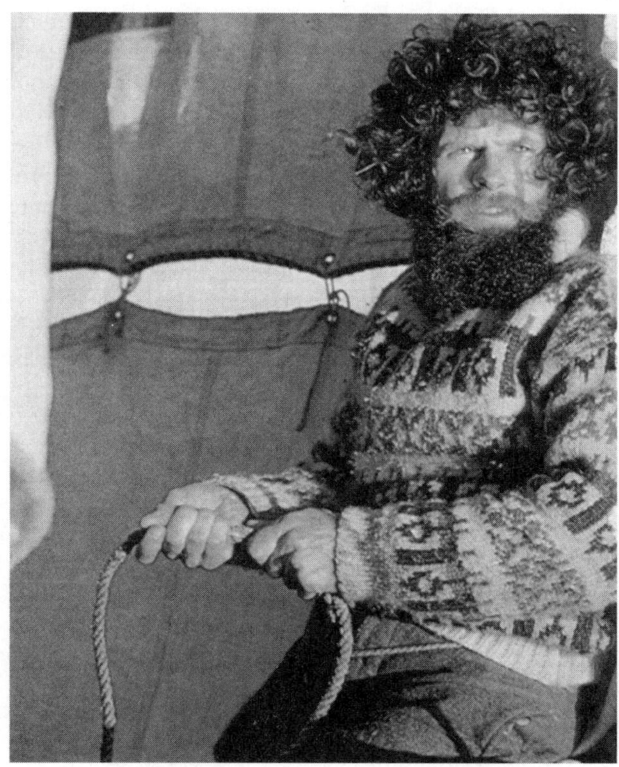

Trondur Patursson, the Faeroese artist who joined Severin on the trip described in his 1978 book, The Brendan Voyage *(photograph by Cotton Coulson)*

As he had done in *Tracking Marco Polo,* Severin decided to re-create an ancient voyage using a travel narrative as his guide. The *Navigatio* was a more dubious guide, however, than *A Description of the World* had been: it is full of accounts of fabulous happenings and creatures encountered by St. Brendan; and it posits that an Irish monk could have reached the New World hundreds of years before the Vikings and a thousand years before Columbus.

Severin determined that the best way to test his theory that the account of St. Brendan's voyage was based on an historical voyage was to attempt to sail to America in a craft as much as possible like Brendan's. So began the long and intensive effort of research, gathering of authentic "medieval" materials, and the design and building of *Brendan,* a medieval-style boat similar to an Irish fishing curragh but whose hull was oak-bark-tanned leather. On 17 May 1976 the *Brendan* left *Cuas an Bhodaigh,* or Brandon Creek, in western Ireland. With what Severin was to call "Brendan Luck"–the "stroke after stroke of good fortune" the crew experienced during the project–the *Brendan* sailed north, through the Hebrides to the Faeroes, a cluster of islands halfway between Scotland and Iceland, and on to Iceland itself where "Brendan Luck" temporarily ran out and the boat had to be wintered. The voyage resumed in May 1977, and after rough seas and ice floes off Greenland that punctured the leather hull, "Brendan Luck" returned. Severin and his crew were able to repair the puncture and sail free of the ice, and reached "the New World at 8:00 p.m. on June 26 on the shore of Peckford Island in the Outer Wadham Group some 150 miles northwest of St. Johns, Newfoundland."

The Brendan voyage showed that it was possible for a medieval-type leather boat to sail across the North Atlantic from Ireland to North America. Perhaps most importantly, in Severin's view the voyage "demonstrated that the *Navigatio* is more than a splendid medieval romance." He argues that

> It is really a story hung upon a framework of facts and observation which mingles geography and literature, and the challenge is how to separate one from the other. This mixture is hardly surprising. Scholars of epic literature know from experience that many of the truly durable legends, from the *Iliad* to the *Romance of Alexander,* are founded upon real events and real people which the later storytellers have clothed in imaginative detail.

The Brendan Voyage was the first of many ventures by Severin to test the veracity of the "durable legends" of Western culture. The "Brendan hypothesis," the theory that St. Brendan had reached America, and its framework of facts were strengthened by the experience of the crew, who found in the course of their voyage that it was the medieval materials, clothes, tools, and methods that served them best as most of their modern and high-tech equipment rusted or ripped into uselessness in the open boat. Severin discovered that "historians do not realize just how well the medieval seafarers were equipped for their endeavors."

The book Severin wrote about the trip, *The Brendan Voyage,* resembles a detective story; in his piecing together of clues collected during a remarkable voyage, he establishes the validity of the hypothesis. The photographs that accompany the text complement Severin's writing, and the drawings of Trondur Patursson–a Faeroese seafarer and artist who joined the crew at the Faeroe Islands–capture impressions of every facet of the voyage. Although some scholars, such as John O'Meara, who reviewed the book for *TLS: The Times Literary Supplement* (14 July 1978), strongly disagreed with Severin's analysis of the *Navigatio,* even O'Meara acknowledged that *The Brendan Voyage* was "a thrilling story of adventure and suspense," and the book was awarded the Christopher Prize in 1980. An educational motion picture of the project and voyage was made, and a crucial showing of this motion picture produced unhoped-for benefits for Severin's next project.

The powerfully built Patursson joined Severin for his next "historic" voyage, tracing the seven voyages of Sindbad the Sailor, which Severin recorded in *The Sindbad Voyage* (1982). As Severin notes in the foreword to the book, the voyage took nearly five years to plan and execute, and he gratefully acknowledges the indispensability of Sarah Waters, who had researched illustrations for *The African Adventure* and *The Oriental Adventure* and who for the first time would serve Severin as his home agent. Severin describes how the idea for the project came to him in June 1977 as he smelled the pine forests of Newfoundland just before successfully completing the Brendan expedition. "The Brendan Voyage had demonstrated that the technique of building a replica of an early vessel was a useful research tool," Severin writes, and fifty miles off the coast of Newfoundland, he decided to use the same technique "to investigate another, apparently mythical, figure connected with the sea"–Sindbad the Sailor. Could a re-creation of the legendary voyages of Sindbad, in a replica of a medieval Arabian ship, help "to establish a dividing line between truth and fiction in the adventures" and determine "just how much of Sindbad the Sailor's voyages was based on the real achievements of Arab seamen"?

In preparing for the project, Severin examined "all the source material relevant to the creation of the Sindbad stories." He researched medieval Arab navigation and the Arab sea trade, and he began the "research, design and construction of a full-sized sailing ship." Severin determined that the design of the ship would resemble an Arab *boom,* assembled without a single nail and literally stitched together, sporting two masts and a total of 2,900 square feet of sail with a hull of 80 feet. A showing of the movie of the Brendan Voyage during a visit to Oman to research the building of the ship led to the full financial support for the project by the Sultan of Oman.

After seven months and several visits by Severin to India, hunting for suitable shipbuilding timber, *Sohar*–named after the Omani seaport that claims Sindbad as a native son–was built in only 165 days. On 23 November 1980, trimmed and freshly painted for the Omani National Day, *Sohar* set sail on its proposed voyage in the tracks of Sindbad the Sailor. When *Sohar* reached China in June 1981, having sailed 6,000 miles, elaborate receptions and celebrations awaited Severin and his crew in Canton. They had demonstrated that a medieval Arabian ship could sail from Arabia to China, as recounted in the Seven Voyages of Sindbad. They did not establish the historical reality of Sindbad, but rather that the legends of Sindbad the Sailor are probably based on the real stories of many intrepid medieval Arab sailors.

The success of the Sindbad Voyage persuaded Severin to undertake two voyages based on Greek

Severin and his crew approaching Newfoundland in his replica of a medieval curragh, near the end of the transatlantic journey he described in The Brendan Voyage *(photograph by Cotton Coulson)*

epics: that of Jason and the Argonauts and the *Odyssey*. In 1981, Severin began planning both expeditions. While doing research, he discovered that the tales of Jason and Ulysses (the Latin name for Odysseus) "are closely intertwined." Because Homer mentions Jason and his voyage and scholars concurred that Jason's voyage on the *Argo* pre-dated that of Ulysses, Severin focused first on the voyage of the Argonauts. Severin writes in *The Jason Voyage: The Quest for the Golden Fleece* (1985) that, "as a historian of exploration, studying the great voyage epics of literature, I began to realize just how important the Jason story is. It holds a unique position in western literature as the earliest epic story of a voyage that has survived."

Severin was surprised to find that scholars were generally in agreement about the geography of the legend–that the voyage started in Iolcos, in northern Greece, went to the far eastern end of the Black Sea, and arrived in Colchis, an ancient kingdom located in modern Georgia (part of the Soviet Union at the time Severin led his Jason voyage). From there, however, the agreement ended: "Some authorities saw the tale as pure fabrication, an engaging myth invented to amuse its audience"; others argued that no text survived from the thirteenth century B.C. and that later reconstructions of the tale therefore had to be unreliable; and many insisted that such a voyage would have been impossible given the state of maritime knowledge at the time. No one, however, had attempted to test the veracity of the Jason voyage by building and sailing a ship of the type used by the ancient Greeks along the 1,500-mile route agreed upon by scholars. Severin decided to make that test.

As with the previous two projects that re-created the voyages of Brendan and Sindbad, crucial first stages of the Jason Voyage project were ship design and building. When Severin's vessel, the *Argo*–named for her famous predecessor–splashed into the sea of the Old Harbor at Spetses, south of Volos (Iolcos in Jason's day) in the summer of 1984, she was the proud product of three years of research, planning, and building. Fifty-four feet long, the *Argo* sported a "snout-like ram" in front painted with two malevolent eyes, a graceful tail, a single mast, and twenty oars. After completing the accepted route of Jason and having proved the factual possibility of Jason's voyage, *Argo* arrived in Georgia where, he writes, the "story of the quest for the Golden Fleece is far better known . . . than anywhere else in the world. They learn the tale as young children when it is a fairy story. At school they read it as a basic text. At university they can study it as a source for Georgian history. . . ." Severin claims that his researches and the journey of the new *Argo* confirm that the story of Jason's journey and theft of the Golden Fleece conform to available archaeological evidence, and he argues that the Golden Fleece itself "was precisely that: a fleece from the Caucasus mountains, used in the gold-washing technique, and impregnated with gold dust."

Once again Severin had proven that a ship built according to period design and with comparable materials could be sailed along the established route of a "literary" voyage, which could have been, in fact, historical. The project was again guided by Severin's longtime associate and home agent, Sarah Waters, and Trondur Patursson sailed with Severin once again. At its last stage it was facilitated through Turkish customs by Severin's Turkish friend, Irgun Akca, who had earlier helped Severin on his Marco Polo trek and who met the modern Argonauts after the *Argo* was towed through the Bosphorus by a Soviet merchant ship, the *Tovarisch.* The mayor of Istanbul proclaimed that *Argo* was to be the guest of the city, and the twenty-oared boat spent the winter in a boat park opposite Bebek. The voyage of the modern Argonauts was, thus, an international collaboration, and *The Jason Voyage* documents this remarkable journey through Severin's characteristically dynamic writing, drawings by Patursson, and many photographs by John Egan, Seth Mortimer, and Tom Skudra. A documentary movie was also made of the journey.

Near the end of *The Jason Voyage,* Severin writes, "Having unravelled the story of Jason and the Argonauts, I intended the following spring to set sail with *Argo* again, this time to try to trace the voyage of Ulysses as he came home from Troy, the voyage told by Homer in the *Odyssey.*" So in 1985 Severin launched *Argo* yet again, with the ever-reliable Sarah Waters as his home agent, recording the adventure in *The Ulysses Voyage: Sea Search for the* Odyssey (1987).

The first edition of *The Ulysses Voyage* resembles a lavishly illustrated and oversized coffee-table book (like *The African Adventure, Vanishing Primitive Man,* and *The Oriental Adventure*) and represents an even more determined effort than *The Jason Voyage* to integrate, for a general audience, discussion of a classical epic of adventure with a contemporary reenactment of that voyage. Even more than do Severin's earlier books, *The Ulysses Voyage* reads like a detective story.

Severin decided to follow Ulysses's homeward passage from Troy along "the track that a Late Bronze Age sailor would have chosen if he was a prudent man." He writes about the project's goals: "My approach would be practical–geographical and maritime. It would be from a commonsense viewpoint–the stern deck of a replica Bronze Age galley."

The *Argo* sailed to its logical starting point, the archaeological site of the City of Ilium, or Troy. Severin had decided to use nineteenth-century admiralty charts, including maps made by Captain Thomas Spratt whose charts had guided Heinrich Schliemann to the historical site of Troy. These 150-year-old maps and charts proved doubly useful: by comparing them with changes in coastlines and currents encountered on *Argo*'s late-twentieth-century voyage, Severin and his crew could gauge the even more dramatic changes that would have occurred between their voyage and that of Ulysses. This comparative knowledge helped Severin chart the course of *Argo*'s voyage of detection.

A lesson learned at Troy was that it was Schliemann's amateur and romantic faith in the underlying truth of Homer's epic of Troy that had made him succeed in his search for the historical site of Troy where other, more scholarly, experts had failed. The actual site of Troy, as Severin wandered among the ruins, offered also a more sobering and commonsense lesson. As Severin remarks, Troy was actually no larger than a village: "you could stroll around the circuit of the ancient walls in less than ten minutes." Thus emerged for Severin "the basic rule of epic writing":

> The epic poet does not take large sites and major personalities and make them smaller by reducing them in size and importance. His method is quite the opposite. He takes human figures and transmutes them into heroes. He inflates ordinary places so as to make them seem vast and impressive.

Severin realized that he would have to keep a sharp eye out for smaller, seemingly insignificant clues and evidence of Ulysses's journey, given the epic poet's tactics of inflation and exaggeration: "Our task was to try to judge them through the magnifying imagination of the poet."

Following in the tracks of Ulysses, *Argo*'s experiences under sail and oar postulated and strongly supported a more circumscribed original Odyssey than most scholars entertained. For example, directly experiencing the *meltemi*–sudden miniature typhoons that could push a Bronze Age vessel off course and then force it to drift slowly for days on end–Severin reasons that Ulysses had encountered such a *meltemi* off Cape Malea, the southernmost point of the Peloponnisos peninsula, and had drifted to the "land of the Lotus Eaters," straight south to Libya. "Ulysses' track from Malea is not guess-work," Severin insists, and he argues that when the northerly winds finally shifted around to the south, Ulysses would have left the land of the lotus-eaters and sailed almost straight north to Crete, where he would encounter Polyphemus, the man-eating cyclops.

On Crete, Severin learns that local folk legends could give important clues as to the route of the Odyssey when aspects of folk legend corresponded with details of Greek myth, incidents in the *Odyssey,* and the experience of actually sailing *Argo* as the "prudent" Ulysses would have done. Severin discovers the Cretan folk legend about the *triamates,* man-eating giants with *three* eyes–an omniscient eye located on the backs of their heads–who behaved much as did the Greek cyclopes of myth. When he tours one of Crete's many caves, sits in a natural formation that resembles a giant's throne that looks toward an entrance that could be covered by an enormous boulder (and was), and sees the Cretan sheep pens and an enormous limestone stalagmite that looks precisely like an eye, Severin exults, "The cave was *exactly* as Homer described," adding, "If a carpentry crew from a film studio had been asked to dress a set for the Cave of Polyphemus, it could not have done a better job. The place was perfect." Severin concludes:

> The key to understanding the wanderings of Ulysses might lie in the link between practical seafaring and regional folklore. The *Odyssey* was a chain of tales–further along his voyage Ulysses was to meet such legendary beings as the sirens, Scylla the man-snatcher, and the Charybdis the swallower–and perhaps each story might turn out to be associated with a particular coastal locality. If we could identify the places the folklore came from, then we might have a shrewd idea of the places Ulysses visited.

In *The Ulysses Voyage* Severin pointedly contrasts the efforts of traditional scholars with those of more adventurous spirits, such as himself and his crew. Their journey strongly supports the archaeological and historical value of practical testing of hypotheses. In its modest and commonsensical approach, pursuing a shorter and more localized route for the *Odyssey* than posited by earlier scholars, Severin's detective work deserves serious notice. As an exciting modern *Odyssey,* written in Severin's typically gripping prose style, interspersed with Severin's retelling of the Homerian epic, *The Ulysses Voyage* enacts a happy fusion of classical literature and scholarship, high seas adventure, archaeology, geography, and history. With many photographs by Kevin Fleming, Nazem Choufeh, and Rick Williams and drawings done by crew member Will Stoney, who imaginatively sketched the scenes of the *Odyssey* from his modern observations, carefully deleting modern seacraft, towns, roads, and other post-Homeric additions to the land- and seascapes, *The Ulysses Voyage* captured, for a general late-twentieth-century audience, something of the personal, intellectual, historical, and epic excitement that Ulysses's adventures have instilled in generations of readers.

After undertaking four successive sea journeys, Severin decided that his next two forays into reenacting of historical travels should be overland. The first of these involved following the path of the First Crusade (which lasted from 1096 to 1099), an eight-month journey on horseback that Severin first wrote about in "Retracing the First Crusade," a *National Geographic* article published in September 1989. For the second journey Severin covered nearly 5,000 miles riding with modern day Mongol horsemen in an attempt to recapture the historical milieu of Genghis Khan, the near-legendary Mongol leader.

All of Severin's journeys offer a unique blend of the personal and impersonal. Severin adopts the impersonal and objective stance of the scholar who desires to know how and why past explorers traveled and explored, and who attempts to sort out the fact and the fiction from the explorers' narratives of travel, many of which shaped popular conceptions of distant places and peoples and some of which found their way into epics and classics of Western literature. He also, however, evinces the personal passion of the traveler who wants to see and experience things for himself, who needs to make a personal connection with the people, places, and travails encountered by the historic travelers and explorers. Severin fuses these two impulses in his scholarly and personal re-creations of historic voyages, testing the claims of scholars and his own endurance and ingenuity by following in the tracks of past explorers, using the forms of travel they would have employed.

In *Crusader: By Horse to Jerusalem* (1989) Severin recounts his 2,500-mile-long journey on horseback from Belgium to Jerusalem, following the route of Duke Godfrey of Bouillon, a leader of the First Crusade. He followed this personal venture with one that he recorded in the 1991 book, *In Search of Genghis Khan.* In it Severin recounts his experiences in Mongolia, invited there by the post-communist authorities as a "window of opportunity" opened for Western observation and travel. He again affirms the endurance and value of ancient ways of life, through his experience riding with Mongol herdsmen whose life has remained largely unchanged since the time of their great leader Genghis Khan, who lived between 1162 and 1227.

Severin's passion for travel and for the East again led him back to Asia for his most perilous journey, described in *The China Voyage: Across the Pacific by Bamboo Raft* (1994). In 1990, intrigued by the Sinologist Joseph Needham's theory that the ancient Chinese had influenced the development of Meso-American civilizations, Severin began to consider seriously whether or not a voyage on a boat designed like Chinese bamboo rafts of the first century A.D. would be worth the risks that a Pacific voyage of over 6,000 miles would inevitably entail.

In the *Hsu Fu,* a Vietnamese-built 60-foot replica of a 2,000-year-old raft, Severin and his small crew, which included the photographers Joe Beynon and Rex Warner, sailed from Hong Kong to within 1,000 miles of America before the raft disintegrated, demonstrating that ancient Chinese could have made transpacific voyages on bamboo rafts. The perils of the journey also suggested, however, that few would have landed on the western coast of the New World, and those that did would probably have died or at best been assimilated into Native American cultures, since the Asians would have arrived with little or nothing left aboard their meager bamboo boats after so long a journey.

In the first months of 1996 Severin embarked on yet another voyage in a replica vessel, this time to retrace the route the naturalist Alfred Russel Wallace took in his 1854 journey through the Spice Islands of eastern Indonesia that formed the basis for his book *The Malay Archipelago* (1869). Severin's expedition was connected by computer with school classrooms around the globe through a site on the World Wide Web.

To duplicate Wallace's voyage as closely as possible, Severin commissioned local boatwrights on Kei Island in the Moluccas to construct a replica of a nineteenth-century Malay prau. Named the *Alfred Wallace,* the forty-eight-foot vessel was built according to traditional practices, although the boat was equipped with the latest satellite communications equipment, with which Severin sent communiqués about his trip that were read by schoolchildren across the world, and responded to questions posted by classes participating in the project.

Wallace's trip was made with the main intent of gathering specimens of strange birds and animals for transport back to England; its historical significance, however, is that from it he gained inspiration for the concept independently devised by his colleague, Charles Darwin, with whom it is most associated: that in evolution "the inferior would inevitably be killed off and the superior would remain–that is, the fittest would survive."

In retracing Wallace's journey, Severin, accompanied once again by his old friend Patursson, as well as the photographers Joe Benyon and Paul Harris, the artist Leonard Shiel, and Indonesian crewman, Yannis, hoped to assess how well the flora and fauna that Wallace had documented had survived. The book that Severin wrote about this trip, *The Spice Islands Voyage: In Search of Wallace* (1997), is both an attempt to revive the reputation of the now largely forgotten Wallace and an exploration of the marvelously diverse ecology of the region.

Tim Severin's work has received little scholarly attention. His books have been well received by readers and reviewers, selling in the thousands and going through multiple printings and translations and serving as the basis for several educational movies and videos. He has received at most incidental mention in scholarly works on the subjects he investigates in his hands-on, practical, and adventurous fashion. Perhaps his unorthodox mode of scholarship–reenacting historic voyages in replicas of period modes of transportation–has failed to impress more serious scholars. His style of writing, too, tries to capture the feeling of real and lived adventure for a general audience, as opposed to the measured writing for academic publication by experts and scholars. It may be that Severin's writing is too lively, his adventures too vivid, and his passion for travel and exploration too much in evidence to suit the tastes and standards of academic audiences.

Reference:

Edward Said, *Orientalism* (New York: Pantheon, 1978).

Wilfred Thesiger

(3 June 1910 –   )

M. D. Allen
University of Wisconsin–Fox Valley

BOOKS: *Arabian Sands* (London: Longmans, 1959; New York: Dutton, 1959);

The Marsh Arabs (London: Longmans, 1964; New York: Dutton, 1964);

Desert, Marsh and Mountain: The World of a Nomad (London: Collins, 1979); republished as *The Last Nomad: One Man's Forty Year Adventure in the World's Most Remote Deserts, Mountains, and Marshes* (New York: Dutton, 1980);

The Life of My Choice (London: Collins, 1987; New York: Norton, 1988);

Visions of a Nomad (London: Collins, 1987);

The Thesiger Collection: A Catalogue of Unique Photographs (Dubai & London: Motivate, 1991);

Wilfred Thesiger's Photographs: A "Most Cherished Possession." An Exhibition at Pitt Rivers Museum, University of Oxford, 16 June 1993 – 27 February 1994 (Oxford: Pitt Rivers Museum, 1993);

My Kenya Days (London: HarperCollins, 1994);

The Danakil Diary: Journeys through Abyssinia, 1930–34 (London: HarperCollins, 1996).

Wilfred Thesiger (photograph by Marion Kaplan)

OTHER: Mark Allen, *Falconry in Arabia,* foreword by Thesiger (London: Orbis, 1980; Brattleboro, Vt.: S. Greene Press, 1982);

Richard Trench, *Arabian Travellers,* foreword by Thesiger (London: Macmillan, 1986; Topsfield, Mass.: Salem House, 1986);

Hilary Hook, *Home from the Hill,* foreword by Thesiger (London: Sportman's, 1987; New York: St. Martin's Press, 1987);

Nigel Pavitt, *Kenya: The First Explorers,* foreword by Thesiger (London: Aurum, 1989; New York: St. Martin's Press, 1989);

Clinton Bailey, *Bedouin Poetry from Sinai and the Negev: Memoir of a Culture,* foreword by Thesiger (Oxford: Clarendon Press / New York: Oxford University Press, 1991);

Pavitt, *Samburu,* foreword by Thesiger (London: Cathie, 1991; New York: Holt, 1991);

Peter Clark, *Thesiger's Return,* photographs by Thesiger (Dubai: Motivate, 1992).

SELECTED PERIODICAL PUBLICATIONS–UNCOLLECTED: "The Awash River and the Aussa Sultanate," *Geographical Journal,* 85 (January 1935): 1–23;

"A Camel-Journey to Tibesti," *Geographical Journal,* 94 (December 1939): 433–446;

"Across the Empty Quarter," *Geographical Journal,* 111 (January 1948): 1–21;

"A Further Journey across the Empty Quarter," *Geographical Journal,* 113 (January 1949): 21–46;

"Desert Borderland of Oman," *Geographical Journal,* 116 (December 1950): 137–171;

"The Ma'dan or Marsh Dwellers of Southern Iraq," *Royal Central Asian Journal,* 41 (January 1954): 4–25;

"The Marshmen of Southern Iraq," *Geographical Journal,* 120 (September 1954): 272–281;

"The Hazaras of Central Afghanistan," *Geographical Journal,* 121 (September 1955): 312–319;

"A Journey in Nuristan," *Geographical Journal,* 123 (December 1957): 457–464.

In a career that spans the twentieth century from the confident days of the late Edwardians to the anxious, postcolonial age, Wilfred Thesiger has earned wide acknowledgment as his era's greatest explorer and the author of two travel classics, *Arabian Sands* (1959) and *The Marsh Arabs* (1964). Immensely distinguished, both revered and despised, and a figure of awkward, if imperfectly consistent, integrity, Thesiger–who has frequently been called "the last explorer"–has raised important questions about the modern world's relationships to developing countries and to the environment.

The eldest of three brothers, Wilfred Patrick Thesiger was born on 3 June 1910 in a wattle-and-daub hut within the British legation in Addis Ababa, the capital of Abyssinia (present-day Ethiopia), to Capt. the Honourable Wilfred Gilbert Thesiger and Kathleen Mary Thesiger, née Vigors. His father was His Britannic Majesty's Consul-General and Minister Plenipotentiary to the emperor of Abyssinia, Lij Yasu. His grandfather, Maj.-Gen. (later Gen.) Frederic Augustus Thesiger, second Baron Chelmsford, broke Zulu power under the legendary Cetywayo in 1879. His uncle Frederic John Napier Thesiger, third Baron Chelmsford, served as governor of Queensland and then of New South Wales before becoming viceroy of India from 1916 to 1921, in which year he was created the first Viscount Chelmsford. Wilfred Thesiger wrote in his autobiography, *The Life of My Choice* (1987): "My father was intensely and justifiably proud of his family, which in his own generation produced a viceroy, a general, an admiral, a Lord of Appeal, a High Court judge and a famous actor." Thesiger's biographer Michael Asher says that the family "were aristocrats of the British Empire" who "had found their niche in service to the Crown. Not of old landed gentry, they belonged to the new class of plutocrats raised to the peerage in Victorian times."

In 1916 Lij Yasu was deposed because he had shown himself to be sympathetic to Islam, a move that was unacceptable to his Christian subjects. Ras Tafari was proclaimed regent and given the task of defeating the forces loyal to Lij Yasu. Ras Tafari left his baby son for safekeeping at the British legation, Thesiger's father feeling unable to refuse what Thesiger calls this "most embarrassing proof" of Ras Tafari's confidence. Fortunately for the Thesigers, Ras Tafari's army emerged victorious from the battle of Sagale, fought in late October sixty miles north of Addis Ababa. Thesiger and his brother had watched "the chivalry of Abyssinia going forth to war, unchanged as yet from the armies of the past. It was an enthralling, unforgettable sight for a small, romantically minded boy." After Sagale he watched the victory parade in Addis Ababa:

> I had been reading *Tales from the Iliad.* Now, in boyish fancy, I watched the likes of Achilles, Ajax, and Ulysses pass in triumph with aged Priam, proud even in defeat. I believe that day implanted in me a life-long craving for barbaric splendour, for savagery and colour and the throb of drums, and that it gave me a lasting veneration for long-established custom and ritual, from which would derive later a deep-seated resentment of Western innovations in other lands, and a distaste for the drab uniformity of the modern world.

On a visit to his uncle, the viceroy of India, in 1918, Thesiger was impressed by the splendid ancient buildings and awed by the sight of Lord Chelmsford in his viceregal robes. As guests of the maharajah of Jaipur, the Thesigers hunted tigers and "were surrounded by an opulence and splendour little changed since the time of Akbar."

As a boy Thesiger read works such as *Jock of the Bushveld* (1907), "that marvellous book by Sir Percy Fitzpatrick about hunting in South Africa"; Annie and Eliza Keary's *Heroes of Asgard* (1857); Rudyard Kipling's *Jungle Books* (1894, 1895) and *Puck of Pook's Hill* (1906); and–a favorite–*A Sporting Trip through Abyssinia* (1902) by Percy H. G. Powell-Cotton. In 1919 he began four unhappy years at a preparatory school in Sussex, followed by four more-palatable ones at Eton. During his first year at Eton he met Ras Tafari, who was on a state visit to Britain. To the romantic Thesiger's comment, "My dearest wish, sir, is that one day I should be able to return to your country," the regent replied, "One day you shall come as my guest." Thesiger continued to read about big-game hunting and enjoyed novels by John Buchan, Joseph Conrad, and H. Rider Haggard, in addition to Kipling. Eton confirmed Thesiger's sense of his own uniqueness and his feeling that admirable qualities thrive best in "traditional" societies. "No wonder that in this setting, during these impressionable years," he writes in *The Life of My Choice,* "I acquired lasting respect for tradition and veneration for the past. Here, too, from masters and boys alike, I learnt responsibility, the decencies of life, and standards of civilised behavior."

In late 1928 Thesiger enrolled at Magdalen College, Oxford. In mid 1930 he received an invitation to attend Ras Tafari's coronation as Emperor Haile

Selassie, along with a letter from the Foreign Office informing him that he would be attached to the British royal party. On 2 November he saw Ras Tafari crowned in St. George's Cathedral in Addis Ababa. "This was the last time that the age-old splendour of Abyssinia was to be on view," he writes in *The Life of My Choice*. "Already it was slightly tarnished round the edges by innovations copied from the West," including the khaki uniforms of the emperor's bodyguard, the cars in the streets, and the "brash, noisy journalists." Despite the reservations of the British ambassador, he went hunting around Bilen, half a dozen miles from the Awash River and near the territory of the ferocious Danakil or Afar people, who judged a warrior's worth by the number of men he had killed and castrated. The river provided Thesiger with a conundrum: what happened to it between Abyssinia and the Gulf of Aden, which it never reached?

Returning to Oxford, Thesiger began to plan for an expedition along the Awash. He read about the previous expeditions to Danakil country; all had been attacked, and some had been wiped out. He obtained permission from Haile Selassie, sponsorship from the Royal Geographical Society, and grants. He left Oxford in June 1933 with a reputation as a good boxer and an undistinguished third-class degree in history, and with a friend who soon had to drop out of the mission for health reasons, he arrived in Addis Ababa in September.

Thesiger's first attempt at exploration was aborted when the government ordered the immediate return of his military escort because of the unsettled state of the area. After weeks of discussion, Thesiger was permitted to try again. His party traveled north along the Awash. As he neared the Sultanate of Aussa, he sent messengers ahead to warn of his approach and was allowed to enter. In *The Life of My Choice* he writes almost rhapsodically of his meeting with the sultan:

> As I looked round the clearing at the ranks of squatting warriors and the small isolated group of my own men, I knew that this moonlight meeting in unknown Africa with a savage potentate who hated Europeans was the realization of my boyhood dreams. I had come here in search of adventure: the mapping, the collecting of animals and birds were all incidental. The knowledge that somewhere in this neighbourhood three previous expeditions had been exterminated, that we were far beyond any hope of assistance, that even our whereabouts were unknown, I found wholly satisfying.

Thesiger was given permission to cross Aussa guided by the sultan's vizier, who attempted to limit Thesiger's wanderings by representing a nearer lake as that into which the Awash finally drained. Thesiger saw

Thesiger during his expedition through Danakil country in Ethiopia, 1934

through the trick and went on to Lake Abhebad (or Abe, Abbe, or Abhe), thus reaching in April 1934 the Awash's true end. The party went on through the deserts of French Somaliland (today Djibouti) to Tadjoura on the coast. Thesiger, only twenty-three years old, had made a contribution to European knowledge of Africa. More important in his eyes, he had managed men of a different culture well and endured hardship.

"I'd wanted to join the Sudan Political Service since I was about fourteen," Thesiger told Asher, "possibly even younger than that, because my ambition was to get back to Abyssinia." As a boy he had talked to "Consuls and officials on the frontiers who had come up to see my father in Addis Ababa and I'd heard a good deal from them about what was going on–armed raids and lion hunting." He had thought that "this was the life for me, and that the best way to do it would be to join the Sudan Political Service and then get transferred to a post in Abyssinia." The Sudan Political Service had been created to administer the Sudan; the territory was officially an Anglo-Egyptian condominium, but Egyptian officials had been forced to withdraw in 1924. In the summer of 1934 Thesiger became assistant district commissioner in Kutum, an isolated town in the desert Darfur province in west central Sudan bordering present-day Chad.

Thesiger would dedicate *Desert, Marsh and Mountain: The World of a Nomad* (1979) to his superior in Kutum, Guy Moore, "who taught me to appreciate the desert, its people and their ways." The legendary Moore was district commissioner in northern Darfur from 1930 to 1946. He traveled around his district by camel, had no objection to native food, and dined with the Sudanese chiefs–"not aloof in a chair like most DCs." Moore and Thesiger discussed great figures of Anglo-Arabian relations, such as Charles M. Doughty and T. E. Lawrence, during their evenings in Kutum.

Thesiger with his lion cubs in front of the house at Kutum where he lived while serving in the Sudan Political Service in the mid 1930s

Yet Moore never doubted that the British belonged in the Sudan as benevolent, paternalistic administrators, at least for the foreseeable future, and that the conquered should exist in a clearly understood and unquestioned hierarchical relationship with their imperial rulers. Thesiger absorbed Moore's attitudes.

Thesiger's years in Kutum were happy ones. He hunted game almost obsessively, acquiring the nickname "Samm al 'Usuud" (Lion's Poison). During leaves he visited Syria and Palestine in 1936 and Morocco in 1937. In the latter year he was transferred to the Western Nuer District on the Upper Nile. He continued to travel, visiting French Equatorial Africa in 1938, but he was unhappy in his new post: he found the Nuer people–naked tribesmen and women who dyed their hair with cow urine–culturally alien. He was, accordingly, delighted to learn in 1939 that he would be posted again to Kutum. But in September, World War II broke out, and all transfers were canceled.

Commissioned at the rank of Bimbashi (captain) in the Sudan Defence Force, from June 1940 to June 1941 Thesiger helped liberate his beloved Abyssinia from its incorporation into Italian East Africa. During the later part of the period he fought alongside the celebrated British officer Maj. (later Gen.) Orde Charles Wingate. If Thesiger made mistakes during these months–at one point, for example, urging trust in an Abyssinian leader who had been bought over to the enemy–he also had notable successes. At the end of the campaign he was recommended for the Distinguished Service Order for his part in the defense of the fort of Wagidi and his safe delivery to Wingate of two thousand Italian prisoners of war.

Thesiger was named second in command of the Arab Legion under the famous Glubb Pasha (Sir John Bagot Glubb), but on arriving in Cairo he was informed that the job had gone to someone else. Instead, he was made second in command of the Druze Legion, a cavalry unit fighting the Vichy French and commanded by the only slightly less celebrated Arabist Gerald de Gaury. A year passed with no action, and Thesiger grew impatient. In October 1942 he drove to Cairo and talked himself into the Special Air Service Brigade, which went behind enemy lines and destroyed hundreds of German aircraft. Fighting from jeeps compared unfavorably for Thesiger with his experiences in Abyssinia:

> One owed nothing to the country or to the people who were there. We carried our water and our food and it was simply good or bad going. I felt utterly and completely dissociated from the whole thing. It meant nothing to you. Whereas when I was fighting in Abyssinia it had meant living with the people and I was dependent on them for food and had to persuade them to fight and everything else.

At the end of the war the Middle East Anti-Locust Unit needed someone to search for locust breeding areas in the deserts of Arabia. Thesiger expressed regret to the unit's director that he was not an entomologist and received the reply, "Oh, but I'm not looking for an entomologist. I'm looking for someone who knows about deserts." Thesiger knew about deserts, and he longed to explore the Rub' al-Khali, or "Empty Quarter," nearly a quarter of a million square miles in the southeast corner of the Arabian Peninsula. He told Asher:

Thesiger's porters cutting up an elephant he shot on a trek through Nuer country on the Upper Nile in 1938 (photograph by Wilfred Thesiger)

> I thought the Empty Quarter was completely out of our reach. I'd always wanted to go there, but I'd never thought I'd get permission. It had always been the sort of "desert of deserts," and the most exciting challenge, because it was unexplored and the tribes there were completely unadministered. It was almost the last corner of the earth that was unexplored.

Asher adds that the fact that Thesiger's new job did not require him to explore the Empty Quarter hindered his ambition not at all, for his "own priorities, like those of all born adventurers, were highest in his list of needs."

Thesiger spent most of the next five years in Arabia and crossed the Empty Quarter twice; he was the third Westerner to cross it, after the pioneering Bertram Thomas and the greatest of all Arabian explorers, H. St. John Philby. On 25 October 1946 Thesiger and an escort of twenty-four men from the Bayt Kathir tribe set off from Salalah on the south coast of what is now Oman, entering the Empty Quarter proper on 23 November. Despite hunger, thirst, and heat, all went well until Sultan, the leader of the Bayt Kathir, refused to go on. In *Arabian Sands* Thesiger says: "His nerve had gone. He had always been the undisputed leader, with a reputation for daring. It was a reputation not easily acquired among the Bedu," but now he "looked an old and broken man and I was sorry." Asher, however, interviewed Thesiger's companions or their descendants, and they presented a different perspective. Sultan's son, supported by others, claimed that his father had orders from the sultan of Muscat and Oman "not to take the Christian beyond the borders of his territory. . . . He said to me later that to cross the border into Sa'udi Arabia would mean trouble for us" and for the sultan. "My father . . . was the Sheikh and the responsibility lay on his shoulders." Another of Thesiger's companions realized that the single-minded Englishman had tricked the ruler, implying that he wished to travel only in those areas of "the Sands" under Sultan's authority, not that he intended to make an extended journey into the domains of the king of Saudi Arabia.

Thesiger's ambition was not thwarted by Sultan's defection, and his romantic view of the Arabs survived what he perceived as the cowardice of an individual Arab. A smaller party continued north. With difficulty, they crossed the massive dunes of the Uruq al Shaiba:

> We led the trembling, hesitating animals upward along great sweeping ridges where the knife-edged crusts crumbled beneath our feet. Although it was killing work, my companions were always gentle and infinitely patient. The sun was scorching hot and I felt empty, sick, and dizzy. As I struggled up the slope, knee-deep in shifting sand, my heart thumped wildly and my thirst grew worse. I found it difficult to swallow; even my ears felt blocked, and yet I knew that it would be many intolerable hours before I could drink.

Thesiger as a captain in the Sudan Defence Force, talking to the exiled Ethiopian emperor Haile Selassie in Khartoum in December 1940

When the party reached the well of Khaba, the danger of death from thirst was over. Although the return journey still lay ahead, Thesiger felt that he had done what he had set out to do:

> For years the Empty Quarter had represented to me the final, unattainable challenge which the desert offered. . . . Now I had crossed it. To others my journey would have little importance. It would produce nothing except a rather inaccurate map which no one was ever likely to use. It was a personal experience, and the reward had been a drink of clean, nearly tasteless water. I was content with that.

As the party approached Liwa Oasis, the northernmost point it would reach before swinging eastward, it was short of food. A visit to Liwa by some of the Arabs–to his regret, Thesiger could not enter this oasis that no Westerner had ever seen–produced only some flour and dates, not the meat for which Thesiger longed.

Although he suffered greatly from hunger, Thesiger remained loyal to his commitment to a premechanical age and the courage, endurance, and solidarity such a world represented to him: "No, I would rather be here starving as I was than sitting in a chair replete with food, listening to the wireless, and dependent upon cars to take me through Arabia." The physical demands of desert life and what Thesiger saw as the strength of character bred by that life were illustrated by an incident on the homeward route. One of the party caught a hare. In mounting anticipation, the meat-starved travelers watched the soup cook. Suddenly, three Arabs approached:

> We greeted them, asked the news, made coffee for them, and then Musallim and bin Kabina dished up the hare and the bread and set it before them, saying with every appearance of sincerity that they were our guests, that God had brought them, that today was a blessed day, and a number of similar remarks. They asked us to join them but we refused, repeating that they were our guests. I hoped that I did not look as murderous as I felt while I joined the others in assuring them that God had brought them on this auspicious occasion.

The journey had taken Thesiger north and east to Mughshin on the edge of the desert, farther north and then in a westerly loop into the depths of the desert, and finally eastward and southward almost to his starting point–a route more arduous than Thomas's and in an area uncovered by Philby. After traveling in less-demanding regions of the Arabian peninsula, he went to London. Drawn back to the Empty Quarter in 1948, he arranged a journey across the western part, traveling a route not previously used by Thomas or Philby. This journey resulted in his being detained by one of King Ibn Sa'ud's emirs; he was released at the behest of Philby, who was a longtime confidant of the king.

The disapproval of Arab rulers and incidents of religious fanaticism made it impossible for Thesiger to remain in the land where he had spent the happiest years of his life. Forty-one years old, without a career, and unsuited to life in increasingly democratic and consumerist England, in 1951 he went to live among the Ma'dan people in the marshes of southern Iraq, where the Tigris and Euphrates rivers meet. He spent most of each year there until 1958, traveling in the summers, when the climate in the marshes became "intolerable," to Iran, Iraqi Kurdistan, Pakistan, and Afghanistan.

In 1957 Thesiger acceded to the urging of his mother, of the publisher Mark Longman, and of the literary agent Graham Watson that he write a book about

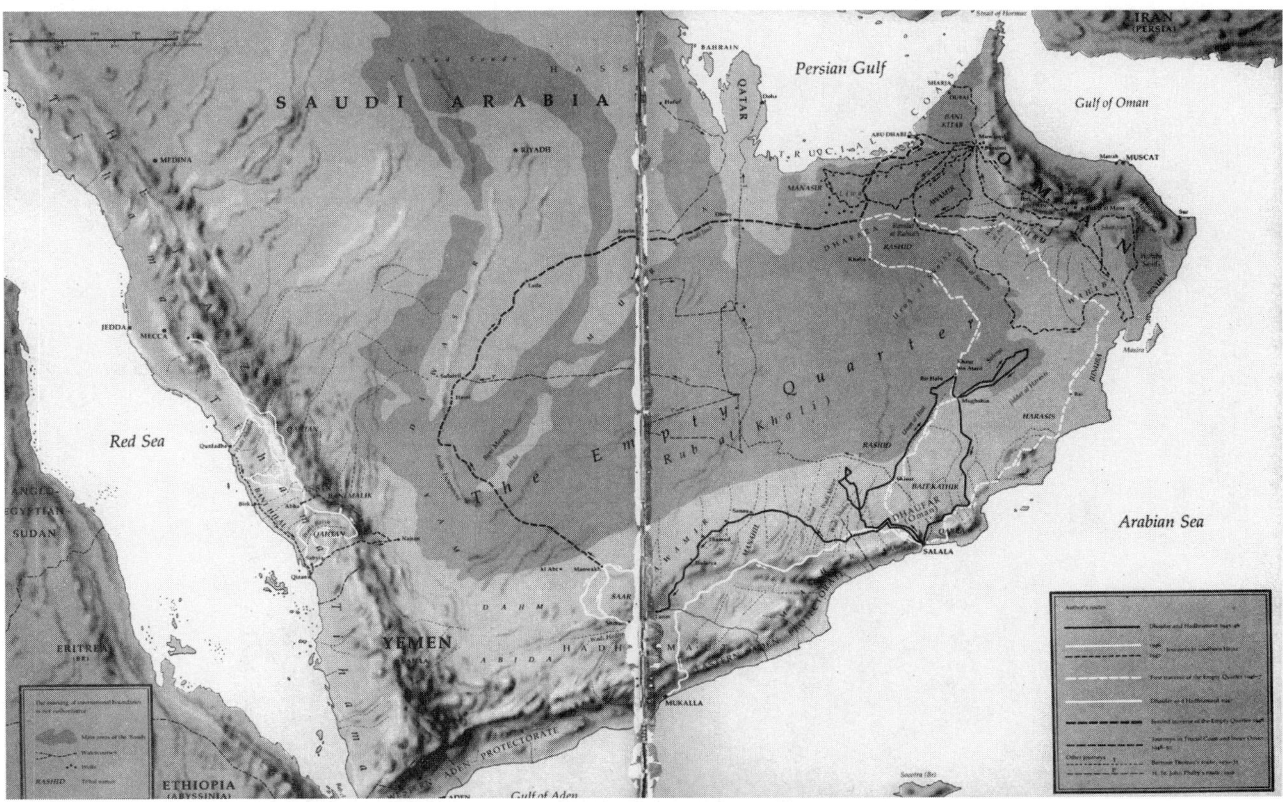

Map of Thesiger's travels in the Empty Quarter of the Arabian peninsula in the late 1940s

his travels in Arabia. Although he had published a dozen articles in specialist journals–most of them in *The Geographical Journal,* the organ of the Royal Geographical Society–since 1935, he was unenthusiastic about the project; he associated literary endeavor with schoolwork. Nevertheless, he spent most of 1957 in Copenhagen, where he sat down in the Park Hotel at 8:30 each morning intending to write until lunch. But, using the brief notes he had made, his photographs, and his *Geographical Journal* articles, he sometimes found himself absorbed in composition for sixteen hours a day.

Published in 1959 and still the book for which Thesiger is best known, *Arabian Sands* is a paean of praise to ancient virtues only imperfectly reachable by the sophisticated Thesiger and, simultaneously, a lament for their inevitable passing in an age of technological progress. It is written in an unpretentious prose that occasionally rises to a slightly self-conscious tragic nobility suitable to its theme of the disappearance of Iliadic greatness before a crass machine worship. Within the framework of a travel narrative it presents fascinatingly abstruse information about the Arabs and their ways and memorable scenic descriptions. Mark Cocker, noting that Thesiger averaged only 250 words a day when writing *Arabian Sands,* lauds his "hard-won, word-perfect style, whose economy is well matched to the task of describing desert life." As an example of Thesiger's use of synecdoche and "almost epigrammatic concision" Cocker cites: "The values of the desert have vanished: all over Arabia the transistor has replaced the tribal bard." Scenes are hauntingly rendered in lists of vignettes, a technique that is reminiscent of Thesiger's gift for catching moments on film:

> When I returned to Oxford the pictures crowded back into my mind. I saw once more a group of Danakil leaning on their spears, slender graceful figures, clad only in short loin-cloths, their tousled hair daubed with butter; an encampment of small dome-shaped huts and the sun's rays slanting through the cloud of dust as the herds were brought in at sunset; the slow-flowing muddy river and a crocodile basking on a sandbank. . . .

There are five more such "pictures" before the sentence ends.

The work met with a highly favorable reception. Peter Quennell described *Arabian Sands* in the *New York Times Book Review* (1 November 1959) as "a work of considerable art"; Simon Raven in *The Spectator* (23 October 1959) called it "Moving, fascinating." V. S. Pritchett said in *The New Statesman* (24 October 1959) that Thesiger "has the power to disclose the extraordi-

Sand dunes in the Empty Quarter (photograph by Wilfred Thesiger)

nary experience, physical and mental, that has been shut up in himself with stern determination for half an active life-time." "Among the classics of Arabian exploration," said *The Saturday Review* (9 January 1960) . One of the few dissenting voices was that of Peter Worsley in *The Guardian* (13 November 1959): Worsley acknowledged that "Thesiger's descriptive prose conveys a vivid sense of living in a very insecure world" but confessed that "I did not find the quality of great literature in this work that the publishers claim."

Thesiger spent his years in the marshes helping the Madan by killing dangerous boars, circumcising young men, and acting as a sort of traveling doctor; on one occasion he cured the infant son of a favorite canoe boy of vomiting and diarrhea by injecting the baby with penicillin. But the Englishman who laughed at rumors that he was a British spy, saying that he only wanted to live privately, had savoir-faire and money enough to threaten government action to procure for that same canoe boy a truce in a blood feud. He thus brought the prospect of official power into a country that charmed him by its anachronistic, unadministered isolation.

In the summer of 1958 Thesiger was having tea with friends in Ireland when he was told that a revolution had taken place in Baghdad. The British-sponsored royal family had been butchered and the British embassy had been burned by the mob. "I realized that I should never be allowed back, and that another chapter in my life had been closed," he says in *The Marsh Arabs*.

Although Thesiger would never feel the satisfaction in the marshes that he got from the Empty Quarter, their appeal was profound. In a yearningly beautiful paragraph of his second book, *The Marsh Arabs,* he recalls

> firelight on a half-turned face, the crying of geese, duck flighting in to feed, a boy's voice singing somewhere in the dark, canoes moving in procession down a waterway, the setting sun seen crimson through the smoke of burning reedbeds, narrow waterways that wound still

Thesiger in the Empty Quarter

deeper into the Marshes . . . peace and continuity, the stillness of a world that never knew an engine.

The Marsh Arabs, Thesiger points out, is not really a travel book, nor is it an account by a trained anthropologist. Rather it is a "picture of the Marshes and of the people who live there." It is written in crisp, exact, sometimes poetic, occasionally schoolmasterly prose and is filled with his characteristic prejudices and predilections. Critical response was favorable, although less so than for *Arabian Sands.* Robert Payne, a biographer of Lawrence, wrote in *The New York Times Book Review* (4 October 1964): "It would be unfair to pick out the plums: the feuds, the battles royal and the harsh sufferings. There are magnificent descriptions of weddings and mass circumcisions, of boar hunts, of endless nights spent under the stars." Asher, however, considers the book less successful as an evocation of marsh life than Gavin Maxwell's *A Reed Shaken by the Wind* (1957). The young men to whom Thesiger was closest in Iraq do not emerge with the same vividness as do bin Kabina and bin Ghabaisha in *Arabian Sands.* In a review in the *Journal of the Royal Geographical Society* James (later Jan) Morris praised Thesiger's "perplexing, beautiful and haunting book" but was unimpressed by Marsh Arab civilization, with its "Diseases, blood-feuds, crippling superstitions, robberies with violence, bullying Sheikhs, filth, caste-prejudices, graft, and the perpetual risk of being savaged by wild pigs." *The Marsh Arabs* won the W. H. Heinemann Award.

Unable to return to Iraq, Thesiger lived in Kenya with the Samburu and Turkana tribes, of whom he characteristically remarked to Asher, "They are pagans and at times slightly uncouth, but I much prefer to be with them than a more sophisticated tribe. You can establish a relationship with them that is quite impossible once a group has been exposed to the outside world."

Thesiger comments in the final chapter of his autobiography that a "tin-roofed, mud-walled house" in Maralal, Kenya, was his base in the years immediately before the book's publication in 1988; it remains his

A Ma'dan village in the marshes of southern Iraq, an area in which Thesiger spent several months of most years from 1951 to 1958 (photograph by Wilfred Thesiger)

home today. Thesiger came across Maralal on a safari in 1961. Before settling down there, he traveled to an extraordinary number of places. *Desert, Marsh and Mountain,* a largely photographic account of his life to 1978, is prefaced by a "Biographical Summary and List of Principal Travels." One reads there that Thesiger climbed Mount Kilimanjaro in 1962, that he was in "Persia" (Iran) in 1964, in Afghanistan in 1965, in Addis Ababa in 1966 for the ceremony commemorating the twenty-fifth anniversary of its liberation from Italian occupation, and then spent five months with the Royalist forces during the Yemeni civil war. From 1968 to 1976 he was in Kenya for nine months each year, "mainly on safari." He wore out the cartilages of his knees with voyages that included a two-week expedition to Sarawak in 1977 and three months in India in 1978.

Failing eyesight required Thesiger to dictate *My Kenya Days* (1994) to his friend Alexander Maitland, to whom the book is dedicated. Simpler in style than his previous books–at times almost choppy–it is the least considerable of his major works. In 1996 HarperCollins published the notes he had made more than sixty years earlier in Abyssinia as *The Danakil Diary: Journeys through Abyssinia, 1930–34.*

Thesiger's honors include the Founder's Medal of the Royal Geographical Society in 1948, the Lawrence of Arabia Medal of the Royal Central Asian Society in 1955, the Livingstone Medal of the Royal Scottish Geographical Society in 1962, the Burton Memorial Medal of the Royal Asiatic Society in 1966, honorary D.Litt. degrees from Leicester University in 1967 and Bath University in 1992, and an honorary fellowship of the British Academy in 1982. He was made a commander of the Order of the British Empire (CBE) in 1968 and was knighted in 1995. In his review of *The Life of My Choice* and *Visions of a Nomad* (1987), a collection of Thesiger's photographs, in *The New York Review of Books* (30 June 1988) Ian Buruma described him as a "cult figure" in Britain, perceived there as a "Great Man, a *real* traveler, unlike those smart-alecky young writers today who parachute in and out of places; Thesiger really *knew* the people he wrote about; he lived with them; he loved them."

But if the plaudits increased, so did the criticisms. Critics have disliked what they see as an almost fascist admiration for physical power and what Buruma calls "racial macho." As Buruma puts it, Thesiger scorns the world of the town, where men settle their differences in debate, preferring an aristocratic warrior code possible only to untamed tribesmen in untamed regions of the world. *Arabian Sands* includes several accounts of internecine tribal feuds that are related by Thesiger with no evident disapproval. Reviewing *The Life of My Choice* in *The New York Times Book Review* (20 March 1988), Michael Mewshaw accused Thesiger of hypocrisy and bigotry:

> Indifferent to slavery, female circumcision, random brutality and even butchery among tribes, he fell into paroxysms of fury whenever any modern state, except England, acted with the same savagery. While he professed "veneration for long-established custom and ritual," what he actually liked was exotic pageantry and bellicose behavior reminiscent of his favorite H. Rider Haggard stories.

Asher and Stephen E. Tabachnick point out that Thesiger can and does leave the desert at will, returning to the comfort of his flat in Chelsea and his club in Pall Mall and to Western standards of medical care.

Frank McLynn's response to *My Kenya Days* in *The Guardian Weekly* (5 June 1994) was positively venomous. For McLynn, Thesiger represents "the dark side of the English elite–the Establishment 'id,' so to speak." He is "a hero to the Establishment" because "he dares to articulate the rabid, John Bircher, life-denying ideas that the more ultramontane of them nurture in their secret hearts." The "characteristic features of his half-dozen books" are "a kind of death-driven rage and aggression, and political views of the extreme right."

Sometimes wrong-headed, often inconsistent, and in his old age apparently despairing of the future ("I see absolutely no hope for the human species," he told Asher), Thesiger remains a great writer and explorer and a fascinating man. In *The Life of My Choice* he records that during his time in the Sudan a superior wrote of him that if he was a "misfit" it was because of "excess of certain ancient virtues and not because of any vices–a brave, awkward, attractive creature." One notices the oddness of a writer publicly quoting such a description of himself; but one feels, too, the justness of the observation.

Biographies:

Timothy Green, *The Adventurers: Four Profiles of Contemporary Travellers* (London: Joseph, 1970); republished as *The Restless Spirit: Profiles in Adventure* (New York: Walker, 1970), pp. 51–113;

Michael Asher, *Thesiger: A Biography* (London & New York: Viking, 1994).

References:

Peter Brent, *Far Arabia: Explorers of the Myth* (London: Weidenfeld and Nicolson, 1977), pp. 219–226;

Mark Cocker, *Loneliness and Time: British Travel Writing in the Twentieth Century* (London: Secker & Warburg, 1992); republished as *Loneliness and Time: The Story of British Travel Writing* (New York: Pantheon, 1992), pp. 52–71;

Stephen E. Tabachnick, "The Man Who Would Be Last," *Contention,* 2 (Fall 1992): 181–196;

Richard Trench, *Arabian Travellers* (London: Macmillan, 1986; Topsfield, Mass.: Salem House, 1986), pp. 212–215.

Papers:

Wilfred Thesiger has donated his papers to Eton College. The archive includes early drafts of *Arabian Sands; Desert, Marsh and Mountain; The Life of My Choice;* and *Visions of a Nomad,* as well as travel diaries, family photographs, and letters written to his mother when he was on his travels. He has given his collection of photographs, prints, and negatives to the Pitt Rivers Museum, Oxford.

Colin Thubron

(14 June 1939 -   )

Julia M. Gergits
Youngstown State University

and

James J. Schramer
Youngstown State University

BOOKS: *Mirror to Damascus* (London: Heinemann, 1967; Boston: Little, Brown, 1968);

The Hills of Adonis: A Quest in Lebanon (London: Heinemann, 1968; Boston: Little, Brown, 1969);

Jerusalem, photographs by Alistair Duncan (London: Heinemann, 1969; Boston: Little, Brown, 1969);

Journey into Cyprus (London: Heinemann, 1975; New York: Atlantic Monthly Press, 1990);

Jerusalem, by Thubron and the editors of Time-Life Books, photographs by Jay Maisel (Amsterdam: Time-Life Books, 1976);

The God in the Mountain: A Novel (London: Heinemann, 1977; New York: Norton, 1977);

Emperor: A Novel (London: Heinemann, 1978);

Istanbul, by Thubron and the editors of Time-Life Books (Amsterdam: Time-Life Books, 1978);

The Venetians, by Thubron and the editors of Time-Life Books (Alexandria, Va.: Time-Life Books / Morristown, N.J.: School and library distribution by Silver Burdett, 1980);

The Ancient Mariners, by Thubron and the editors of Time-Life Books (Alexandria, Va.: Time-Life Books, 1981);

The Royal Opera House Covent Garden, text by Thubron, photographs by Clive Boursnell, picture-edited by Mia Stewart-Wilson (London: Hamilton, 1982);

Among the Russians (London: Heinemann, 1983); republished as *Where Nights Are Longest: Travels by Car through Western Russia* (New York: Random House, 1984);

A Cruel Madness (London: Heinemann, 1984; New York: Atlantic Monthly Press, 1984);

Behind the Wall: A Journey through China (London: Heinemann, 1987; New York: Atlantic Monthly Press, 1988);

The Silk Road, China: Beyond the Celestial Kingdom (London: Pyramid in association with *Departures,* 1989); republished as *The Silk Road: Beyond the Celestial Kingdom* (New York: Simon & Schuster, 1989);

Great Journeys: 20th-Century Journeys along the Great Historic Highways of the World, by Thubron, Philip Jones Griffiths, Naomi James, William Shawcross, Norman Stone, and Hugo Williams (London: BBC Books, 1989; New York: Simon & Schuster, 1990);

Falling (London: Heinemann, 1989; New York: Atlantic Monthly Press, 1991);

Turning Back the Sun (London: Heinemann, 1991; New York: Burlingame, 1991);

The Lost Heart of Asia (London: Heinemann, 1994; New York: HarperCollins, 1994);

Distance (London: Heinemann, 1996).

Colin Thubron is a versatile writer whose carefully honed novels have been well received by critics; his travel literature has also attracted critical acclaim, as well as such honors as the Hawthornden Prize and the Thomas Cook Travel Book Award. His books, both fiction and travel, display a keen sense of history and place; he excels at portraying the changes and contradictions caused by the passing of time. He maintains a careful distance in his travel writing, revealing little about himself while fully describing the places he visits and the people he meets. Thubron began his career as a travel writer, and he has evolved a pattern of writing a travel book, then a novel or two, and then returning to travel writing. In a 1992 interview with Barth Healey Thubron said that travel books are easier to write than novels because "they are about the outside world. They need only curiosity. Novels don't hinge on the outside

Colin Thubron

world, but on the inner landscape. I spend two or three years writing a travel book, and then I look inside myself for a novel."

Colin Gerald Dryden Thubron was born in London on 14 June 1939 to Gerald Ernest Thubron, an army brigadier, and Evelyn Dryden Thubron, a descendant of the seventeenth-century poet John Dryden. Apparently he is proud of this lineage, since it is one of the few biographical facts he includes in the prefatory material of each of his books. After attending Eton College from 1953 to 1957 he joined the editorial staff of the publishing firm Hutchinson and Company in 1959. Leaving Hutchinson in 1962, in 1962–1963 he wrote and photographed freelance television documentaries on Turkey, Morocco, and Japan for the British Broadcasting Corporation. In 1964–1965 he worked on the editorial staff of the Macmillan Company of New York. Since 1965 he has been a freelance writer.

Thubron's first book, *Mirror to Damascus* (1967), is his most personal and detailed travel work, reflecting the intimate knowledge of Damascus that he gained as a resident of the city in the fall and winter of 1965 (he had made a brief visit to the city in 1963). He guides the reader from the newly arrived visitor's impression of the city's chaotic formlessness to an appreciation of its subtle organization:

> To gaze down on Damascus is to view confusion. The streets are artifacts from different ages, contorted and overlapping. Even from a height the city takes pains to conceal her identity; enmeshing the eye with walls, enigmatic trees and alleyways curling in irrational directions; for here it is the custom that beauty be veiled.

Thubron travels by whatever conveyance will take him to interesting sites, but he favors means that allow him to view Damascus from an intimate angle. He buys a bicycle and relishes the freedom it affords him, even though it comes at a risk: "Bicycling, even in the modern part of Damascus, is a specialised art." Traffic laws are irrelevant: "No notice need be taken of traffic-lights or one-way streets; but a floppy hand dangled out of a car window is a common signal meaning that its owner will, some time soon, do something outrageous." He enjoys this apparent chaos and notes that, "as the bicycle-vendor murmured, we are all in the hand of God." He is continually lost: "My maps and diagrams, which unfolded in disordered sheets, attracted every passer-by. Helpers would form into factions, debating the best way to reach a place." Forming factions is natural for the Damascenes, he points out; it is an ancient inheritance of an area overrun perpetually by invaders, including Abbassids, Egyptians, Seljuk

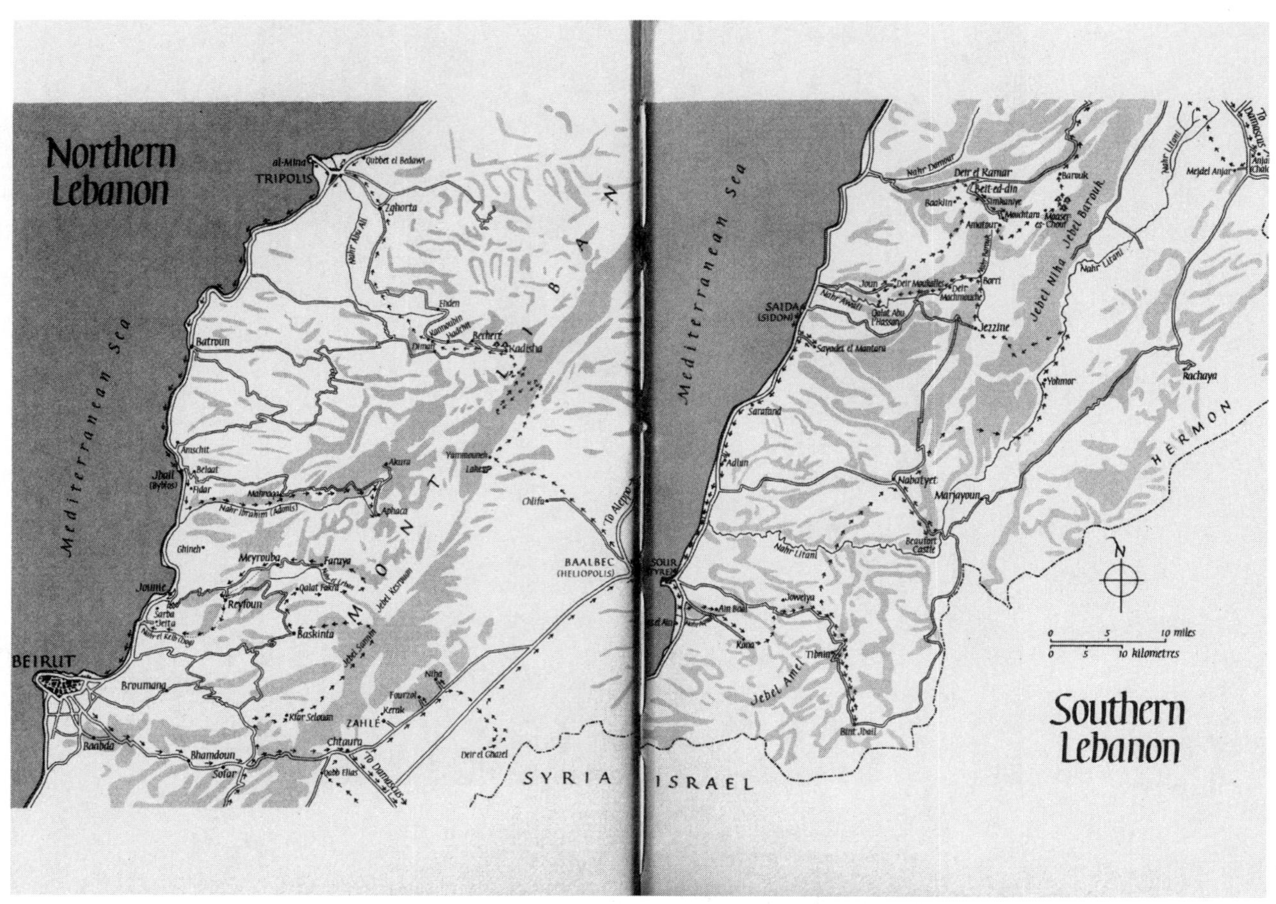

Maps of the route Thubron followed in the journey described in The Hills of Adonis *(1968)*

Turks, and Crusaders. Thubron presents the complex history and landscape of Damascus deftly and sensitively. Instead of the straightforward physical movement from place to place that is familiar to readers of travel literature, he depicts a movement from age to age and culture to culture. He visits the Christian, Jewish, and Muslim sections of the city, staying at the Greek Orthodox nunnery of Couvent de Notre Dame de Seidnaya in Maloula and hearing a peasant recite the Lord's Prayer in Aramaic. He develops a respect for these people living in a crossroads of conquerors, noting that the Damascenes "flourished, accommodating themselves to the whims of their conquerors" by producing and trading luxuries such as fabric, damascened copper and brass, ivory, glassware, inlaid furniture, even snow; they "forged Damascus blades, which were so highly polished that if a man wished to correct the angle of his turban he would hold up his sword as a mirror."

Thubron's next book, *The Hills of Adonis: A Quest in Lebanon* (1968), narrates his four-month hike in 1967 northward from Tyre through Sidon, eastward into the mountains, and back to Baalbek and Byblos. Thubron makes his tour on foot because to "drive through such a country is to receive no sense of it." Although both Christians and Muslims occasionally greet him with suspicion, during the early part of his journey he finds a great deal of kindness and hospitality, and he reminds readers that the Lebanese were once legendary for their willingness to succor travelers. Mahmoud, a Palestinian refugee who works occasionally as a watchman and is the proud owner of a radio and a television set, brings Thubron into his community. Bedawi farmers in Ain Baal find him camping in the hills and insist on sharing their homes and food with him. At a Maronite monastery he meets a garrulous and depressed Frenchman; in Druze territory he meets Wazeem, a goatherd with eight children and a wife with striking light eyes. In just a few lines he sketches his hosts' personalities, captures a scene, or recalls a conversation that epitomizes an aspect of Lebanon and its people. Mountain children, he writes, are well loved, but they develop a hardness to death that makes him uneasy:

> I once found a crowd of children who were watching a butcher kill a calf. If they understood that it was afraid, they accepted this as natural, and without nervousness or gloating merely looked, with the same brown eyes as the calf, and saw the red fountain from its throat, unmoved.

Thubron weaves together observations of the modern Lebanese countryside with ruminations on the region's past; he finds nature "desolate without history." He realizes, however, that he cannot really recapture the past:

> Sitting below the tombs of El Awatim, sleepy with clover and the sun on the cliffs, I felt all this impossible to understand. I might learn the past of ancient peoples, but I could never perceive nature or divinity as they had. Our worlds were irreparably divided.

He camps "in the mazes of Qalat Fakra, where Byzantine columns clustered like daffodils and the Roman road spread directionless." Chance and chaos leave picturesque ruins that evoke dreamlike reveries. At Baalbek he reflects: "that so much survives of what is rare and fragile is a miracle."

The Arab-Israeli War of 5–10 June 1967, even though it did not directly involve Lebanon, changes the tone of the book. Thubron becomes uncomfortable meditating on the distant past: "It was decadent to find significance in anything but the tragic present." He ignores the British consul's warning to leave the country immediately, even though "hostility, imagined or genuine, surrounded" him and other Europeans, who were perceived to be pro-Israeli: "Faces which had smiled were now turned away or pretended not to see: the little slights of war." He no longer speaks of individual Lebanese; the general unfriendliness makes him feel vaguely threatened as he walks alone in the hills. The book ends abruptly with reflections on resurrection and rebirth, a theme that has pervaded the work in its fascination with the ancient gods of the region such as Aphrodite and Adonis.

Thubron followed *The Hills of Adonis* with *Jerusalem* (1969), a straightforward travelogue with excellent maps and photographs. He writes about the quality of the city that has led Jews, Romans, Muslims, and Christians to struggle for control of it:

> This dream of the divine, strong yet not easily found in its proper purity, is the genius of the city still. Half-hidden in her history and in her people, the essence is there to seek–a tradition spun through many tones and depths, which I could feel only lightly in a single spring and summer: a parable perhaps revealing more of man than of God, but without which Jerusalem has lost her meaning.

Thubron has many small adventures as he reviews the history and geography of the city: he stays with the Polish Sisters of St. Elizabeth and marvels at their dedication; he meets an American Jesuit who keeps snakes and demonstrates how to help them shed their skin. Thubron grows to "love the Hellenistic [architecture] passionately, not because it was more beautiful than elsewhere–often it was coarse and hybrid–but because it shone through a tangle of servility and mindlessness, in art and life." The book was praised by Richard Church in *Country Life* (27 November 1969), by N. K. Burger in *The New York Times Book Review* (7 December 1969), and by Gerald Kaufman in *The Listener* (London).

Journey into Cyprus (1975) led to Thubron's election as a fellow of the Royal Society of Literature. It relates a six-hundred-mile walking tour in a zigzag pattern that takes him end-to-end and back and forth across the island, crossing and recrossing the boundaries between the warring Greek and Turkish areas. As in his walking tour of Lebanon, he chooses this mode of travel deliberately: "To go on foot was to entrust myself to the people, a gesture of confidence, and to approach the land as all earlier generations had known it, returning to its old proportions." He is generally greeted as an eccentric, harmless wanderer. The British colonization of Cyprus, which ended in 1960, remains alive in people's memories; but, although a few soldiers bluster at him and civilians occasionally revile the British, he is welcomed into many homes. Hamid, a carpenter, takes him home after soldiers are rude to him. Hamid's nine children, who look like "Renaissance angels," stare unremittingly at Thubron, laughing and scattering when he makes faces at them. Few people challenge his right to walk alone through the countryside. Much of his journey is through meadows and along barely discernible paths in areas frequented only by shepherds and farmers. His sleeping places include a medical clinic, monasteries, a flophouse, and a pigsty. He finds the most colorful hotels, such as one in Paphos that is "the caravanserai for a dying race: travelling conjurors, country violinists, lute-players." During his stay "a gypsy fortune-teller came, a mendicant strong-man, a lapsed priest; and three Syrian prostitutes slopped about the corridors in carefully disarrayed dressing gowns." If he is not near a town, farm, or monastery when night falls, he unrolls his sleeping bag and sleeps beneath the stars, often chilled into wakefulness to find himself wet with dew.

As in all of his travel narratives, Thubron spends much of his time pondering history; he seeks evidence of the successive civilizations and the nearly endless waves of domination and colonization of Cyprus. Piles of rocks evoke poetic reflections:

Ruins of an altar and tower at Qalat Fakra in northern Lebanon (photograph by Colin Thubron)

> And it is true, these ruins are little more than the foundations of walls built with rocks carried from the winter stream eight thousand years before. But they mark a beginning. Laid down unhewn for streets and houses, they once enclosed the island's earliest men, and my own journey, which is to be a voyage through time as well as space, begins in this archaic twilight.

He wanders through an ancient copper mine, examines ruined monasteries, peers into Roman sewers–he even crawls through one, frightening a British woman–and climbs around inside Crusaders' castles. He maintains a balance between the past and the present, moving comfortably between historical analysis and vignettes of the kindness he receives from strangers.

Thubron's next two works were novels; they were not widely noticed, but they allowed him to experiment with tone, description, and characterization. In these works he develops a cool, restrained style reminiscent of Ernest Hemingway's. *The God in the Mountain* (1977) is a story of a doomed love affair set in an unnamed region of the eastern Mediterranean; at its heart is a clash between secular modernity and religious tradition. *Emperor* (1978) is an historical novel about the Roman emperor Constantine and his wife, Fausta, whom he eventually kills. Thubron compared travel writing and fiction writing in a 25 July 1985 interview:

> The mechanics of writing about something you have actually experienced is completely different. In a travel book you devote your energies to expressing that which already exists, to remembering the quality of a city, the texture of a wall. In a novel there are no parameters. You create the wall. The same curiosity that is projected outwards in travelling is turned inwards in fiction. The one is a great delight at what is over the horizon, the other is an excavation of one's own inner guts.

After a ten-thousand-mile journey through part of the Union of Soviet Socialist Republics in a battered Morris Marina, in the questionable company of tour guides whom he suspected of being spies and drunken friends of friends, Thubron wrote one of his most influential and popular travel books: *Among the Russians* (1983; republished as *Where Nights Are Longest: Travels by Car through Western Russia,* 1984). He writes: "I had been afraid of Russia ever since I could remember. When I was a boy its mass dominated the map which covered the classroom wall; it was tinted a wan green, I recall, and was distorted." He finds the "sheer size of the country" disturbing: "Wherever you touch it, you are conscious of a giant, alienating hinterland. You are always, somehow, on the periphery." He is better prepared for his trip than many travelers: he insists that his Russian is not very good, but his anecdotes suggest that he is fairly fluent in the language; and he has prearranged as much of his itinerary as possible: "I had tickets for camping, tickets for petrol, tickets for hotels." His route takes him "eastward to Moscow, north to Leningrad (today St. Petersburg) and the Baltic Sea, south to the Caucasus and the Turkish border, back across the Ukraine and the Crimea"–travels that, he says, comprise "only the historic edge of a mighty wilderness."

Thubron is highly critical of the communist system: "This country, after all, had dared to set itself as the exemplar of the future, the lost paradise remaking, and I judged it automatically by the light of its own ideals." He sees disillusionment and frustration in every part of the country: "In Russia, I was starting to think, the suppression or distortion of history had persuaded a whole people of their virtue." Soviet buildings are hideous because Russians "do not see their buildings aesthetically, but symbolically." Communism, which replaced religion as a "usurping creed," resulted in the creation of public structures during Joseph Stalin's reign that "subconsciously strained for religious effect, and frog-marched into service half the paraphernalia of classical paganism." Communism is condemned to failure because it insists on its infallibility and its right to destroy all traces of opposition. By attempting to stifle dissent, it undermines its own ideals:

> the dissidents . . . disturb the Kremlin not because of their numbers, which are tiny, but because they embody a truth. This truth accuses and makes guilty the whole system. It expresses what everyone in fact knows: that Communism is smaller than life. It dissolves the myth of the Soviet paradise. And for this, it cannot be forgiven.

But communism is not the only problem. In Thubron's eyes the Russians, in their waywardness, are unable to implement it. He argues that Russians envy the West and fear the East, with Leningrad symbolizing "the paradoxical leaning of Russia towards the West, spurred by an atavistic dread of China and a centuries-old longing for civilized recognition." The signs of incipient barbarity appear everywhere. Muscovites, despite their Western clothes and attempts at modern culture, are peasants at heart, driven by impulse and superstition. The Russians strike Thubron as naive, but he appreciates their tenacity and their dedication to their country and culture: "Patriotism is Russia's heart and womb, whereas Communism is merely–and not always–its head."

Drunkenness is woven through the book, providing surreal images and bizarre adventures:

> Vodka–that colourless innocence! It's the curse and liberation of Russia, a self-obliterating escape from tedium and emptiness, from interminable winter nights, and the still longer, darker nights of the soul. It is drunk in furious, catatonic debauches, with the full intention of rendering its drinkers virtually insensible.

Alcohol has led to increases in traffic accidents, wife beating, divorce, infant mortality, and murder, yet the only way to participate in the culture is to share in its drunkenness. Thubron engages in nearly superhuman bouts of drinking with his various hosts and friends; in many scenes the description and narration become blurry as the prose mimics his gradual descent into oblivion. One evening in Pyatigorsk he and his hosts get drunk on champagne and then move on to a seriously drunken party. Misha, who talks about himself in the third person, babbles:

> It's true there are no girls in Pyatigorsk . . . not after Moscow. Misha enjoyed himself in Moscow. But it's not a good city for the personal relationships. . . . *Bye-bye, baby, bye-bye.* . . . Russian girls, let me tell you sir, make very good wives, excellent in the home, very tender and not very sexually experienced. . . . What is your father's job?

Thubron strives to maintain a "tiny, watchful fragment of myself . . . refusing to get drunk"; he covertly pours some of his vodka into planters and empty vases. Nevertheless, he feels his head floating to the ceiling and his limbs becoming numb. Drunkenness, for Thubron, aptly symbolizes the absurdity and chaos of Russia.

Thubron's sense of danger, oppression, and lack of privacy increases as he is shadowed by the mulish guides imposed on him by the Soviet authorities, guides who know little about their own land. He feels invaded and haunted. This paranoid feeling invests the book with a nervous energy. His hotel room is searched; he is arrested and, absurdly, forced to read a medieval Latin manuscript to prove that he is English; and he is followed by the KGB. Finally, his notes are almost confiscated at the border:

> Without them, I might not believe that I had entered the Soviet Union at all. And there are times even now when this land reverts to the enigma which hung on my classroom wall when I was a boy–Mercator's projection, its proportions distorted–until it seems to be less a physical country than an area of mingled tenderness and unease in my mind.

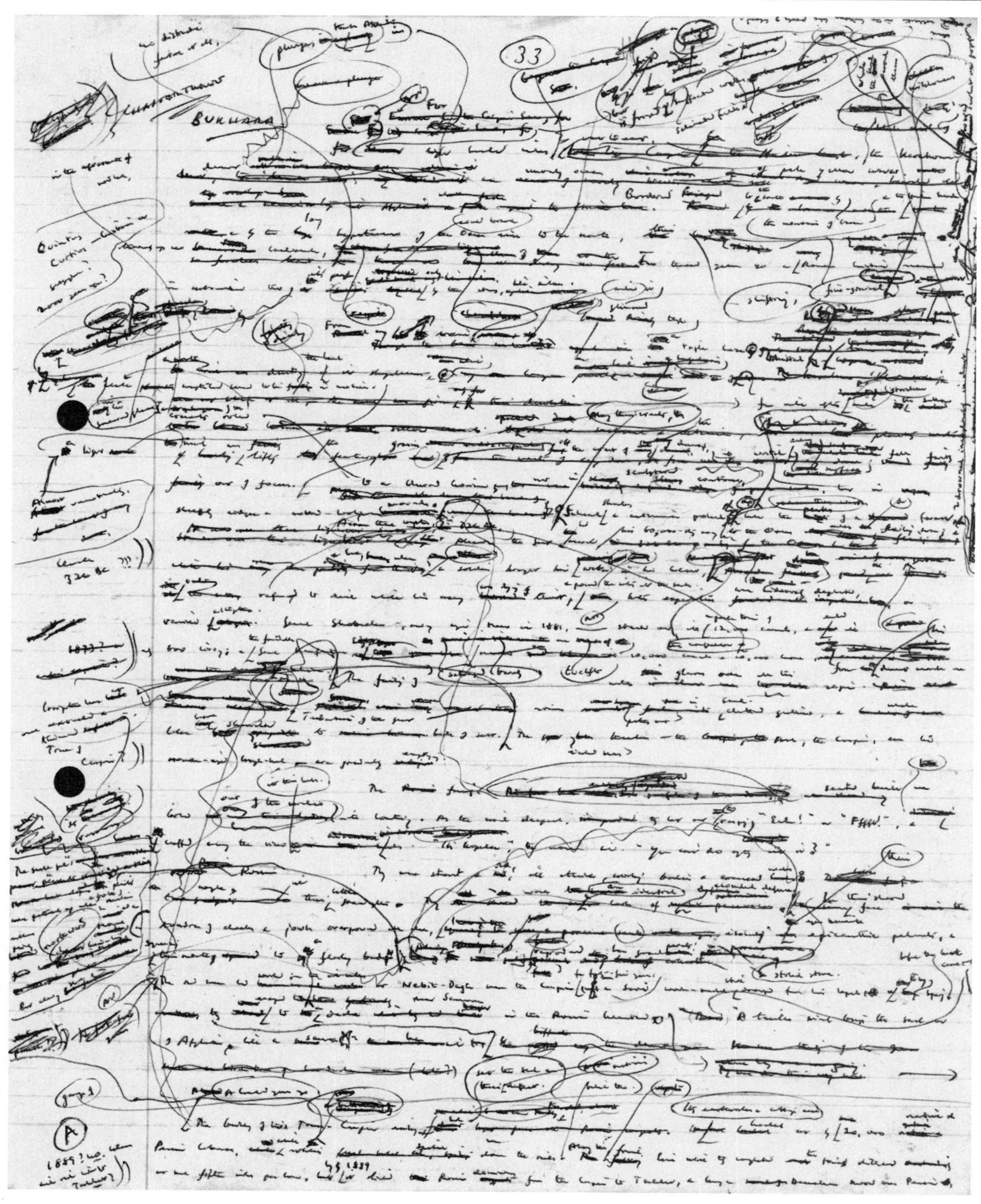

Front and back of a leaf from the manuscript for Thubron's 1994 book, The Lost Heart of Asia *(Collection of Colin Thubron)*

After working hard to prepare himself for Russia, Thubron has been nearly overwhelmed by its complexity and diversity. He captures well the bewilderment of the outsider faced with Russian history and self-definition. In *The Times* (London) for 15 December 1983 Nikolai Tolstoy said that Thubron's writing "has an enchanted, lyrical quality which never falters" and that it "is hard to think of a book more warmly to be recommended to anyone with the slightest interest in Russia and her people, or who simply wishes to read some of the very best English prose."

Thubron's next book was the novel *A Cruel Madness* (1984). The narrator, Daniel Pashley, a schoolteacher who volunteers to teach the inmates at a local insane asylum on weekends, discovers that his former lover, Sophia, is a patient there. As he recalls their affair her voice occasionally replaces his. The reader eventually realizes that Daniel is himself a patient at the asylum and that his "memories" may be delusions. Anthony Thwaite in *The Observer* (26 August 1984) called the novel "Torturous and absorbing. . . . It moves on into a maze of falsities, delusions, haunted memories and distorted mirrors." Fionnuala McHugh in *The Literary Review* (September 1984) proclaimed it "a triumph of imaginative prose." *A Cruel Madness* won the 1985 P.E.N. Silver Pen Award for the best book written in English.

Thubron followed *A Cruel Madness* with another travel book, *Behind the Wall: A Journey through China* (1987), which won both the Hawthornden Prize and the Thomas Cook Travel Book Award. It combines a trip that "took place over a single autumn and early winter" with episodes from an earlier brief visit to China; Thubron calls the book "a compression of experience."

Unlike the Soviet Union, China does not intimidate Thubron; its vast distances make it a "luminous puzzle" rather than a threat. Although he attempts to learn Mandarin so that he can communicate without a translator, he finds himself shut out of much of Chinese life. He is, irrevocably, an outsider, a representative of an alien and distant culture. Like Isabella Bird, his Victorian precursor, who complained of being a spectacle wherever she went in China, Thubron finds himself constantly the center of attention: "But over the past weeks I had become inured to this relentless staring. Even in shops and offices I would turn to find layers of noses squashed at the glass behind me."

Thubron carefully distinguishes the various Chinese provinces and cities, noting regional differences in dialect, diet, and customs. In Canton

> Table manners joyfully endorse the ecstasy of eating. Diners burp and smack their lips in hoggish celebration. Bones are spat out in summary showers. Noodles disappear with a sybaritic slurping, and rice-bowls ascend to ravenously distended lips until their contents have been shovelled in with a lightning twirl of chopsticks.

He sees an "old Chinese mercilessness" in the Cantonese habit of eating all parts of nearly all animals on the planet: "pig stomach, lynx breast, whole bamboo rats and salamanders." In Beijing he observes that the Chinese "conspired to fulfill Western clichés of themselves: inscrutable and all alike." In Shanghai he reflects: "This. . . is what is meant by 'the masses'–something not plural at all, but monolithic. It goes in a white shirt and black trousers. It looks alike. It owns one character and one will." In a public bath he finds the naked bodies of Chinese men disconcerting, "lapidary, almost polished" because of their hairlessness. He bicycles to out-of-the-way tombs and ruins; he buys fourth-class train tickets so that he can mingle with the common people; he wanders into sites that are not normally seen by tourists. Like his Victorian predecessors, he visits hospitals, a zoo in which "everything unusual seemed to be asleep," a medical college, a mental hospital, a boarding nursery, temples, the Forbidden City, the Great Wall, the town of Qufu (the home of Confucius), and so on. Unlike them he travels without companions, not even the guides and translators that the Victorians deemed as essential as food and clothing. At the medical college he visits Professor Yang, who specializes in diseases of the tongue and has more than two hundred wax tongues illustrating various disorders: "There were stunted tongues and swollen, translucent ones, yellow-coated gastric tongues, ghoulish opaline ones and wicked little dried-up red forks–tongues filmed over, tongues cleft, tongues fissured–greenish, retracted, putrid, carbuncled." The tongues are so lifelike that Thubron becomes concerned about the condition of his own tongue.

China's version of communism captures much of Thubron's attention. Thubron heartily disapproves of communism, as was made clear in *Among the Russians,* and he finds ample evidence of decadence, repression, and illogic throughout the country. The vast majority of the 650 million Chinese (the population at the time Thubron was there) are locked out of the political decision-making process by the old men who run the party. Men are not allowed to marry until they are twenty-five, women until they are twenty-three; couples may have only one child. People have to live and work where and at what the government decrees. A man named Dengming tells Thubron that he seldom sees his wife, because they are required to work so far apart; their son lives with the wife's parents. The effects of the

Cultural Revolution of 1966 to 1976 still haunt art. Ordinary citizens are kept out of stores that are reserved for tourists and upper-echelon party members. Families have to adapt to rigid regulations and rationing. Near the tomb of Dr. Sun Yat-sen, the father of modern China, Thubron meets a banker who had been brought up to hate Americans but, on traveling to the United States, had discovered that "everything we'd been told had been a lie. . . . I was invited into more than twenty private houses and I couldn't believe it . . . televisions, carpets, air-conditioning, cars. And the houses were all separate."

Thubron finds himself becoming pettish and annoyed as the Chinese bombard him with questions, make patently absurd assumptions about his life and income, and insist on versions of historical facts that contradict those of the West. He begins lying to his questioners, telling them that he has a wife and daughter back in England and that he hates his job. By the end of his journey he has lost considerable weight and become downright snappish: "In the scrimmage for tickets and bedrooms I had become dourly irritable."

In *The Silk Road, China: Beyond the Celestial Kingdom* (1989) Thubron recounts his 1988 journey along the ancient trade route west from Xinjiang (formerly known as Sinkiang) in western China into East Turkistan and on to the fabled cities of Samarqand and Bukhara in the Uzbek Soviet Socialist Republic (today Uzbekistan). Of the Chinese far west Thubron writes: "The Chinese, who grew up along the great eastern rivers, feared wilderness and despised nomadism. Within their Great Wall, they believed, spread all true civilisation. . . . Beyond was only a barbarian dark, haunted by robbers and drifting herdsmen of inexplicable habits." Comparing the Chinese who have migrated west into Xinjiang with the indigenous Uighur, Thubron describes the Chinese as "conventional, bureaucratic, and collective," the Uighur as "relaxed, sensuous, and individualistic." Even though the Uighur have been settled around the oases for some eight centuries, Thubron characterizes them as possessing the nomadic spirit.

"Through the schizophrenic landscape the tarmac highway links oases of wheat and orchards where Chinese and Uighur cohabit uneasily, and the fields and poplar avenues, nourished by snowfed streams, sprawl over the sand," Thubron writes. To the north of the Silk Road are the Tian Shan mountains; to the south is the Taklimakan desert, which the Uighur call the place "you go in and never return." Perhaps the fact that the book was published in conjunction with *Departures,* the official magazine of American Express, accounts for the passage at the end of the work in which Thubron uncharacteristically praises tourism and modern conveniences:

> The Road today is a comfortable and beautiful way into the Middle Kingdom, leading straight to its most remote and fascinating province, Sinkiang. What used to be a scree path a few feet wide, clinging to a precipice with bridges often no more than a rope to be taken hand-over-hand, is now the superb Karakorum highway. It is possible to take luxury tours . . . in air-conditioned comfort through this savage and beautiful landscape.

The Silk Road, China was followed by two novels, *Falling* (1989) and *Turning Back the Sun* (1991). *Falling* is narrated by Mark Swabey, prisoner number 63176, as he mulls over the events that led to his one-year sentence for manslaughter. Mark loved two women: Katherine, a stained-glass artist, and "Clara the Swallow," a high-wire circus performer who works without a net. The title refers to the characters' falling in love; to Katherine's greatest artwork, a depiction of Lucifer's fall from heaven; and to Clara's actual fall from the tightrope, which leaves her a quadriplegic. Mark's accession to her request that he help her to die has led to his imprisonment. *Turning Back the Sun* is set in an unnamed colonial country in the 1930s. The protagonist, Dr. Rayner, has been exiled to a frontier outpost after failing his examinations. Nostalgic for his sophisticated boyhood home, "the Capital," a thousand miles away, and in love with a local stripper named Zoe, Rayner has to deal with a mysterious rash that is turning the white colonists' skin as dark as that of the natives. The colonists blame the natives for their affliction, a drought frays tempers even further, and a massacre of the natives is narrowly averted. *Turning Back the Sun* was shortlisted for Britain's most prestigious literary award, the Booker Prize.

Thubron's next travel book was *The Lost Heart of Asia* (1994). The author's note at the beginning of the work says that this journey, taken "during the first spring and summer of Central Asia's independence from Moscow" after the breakup of the Soviet Union, is the "final, most elusive piece" in a "personal jigsaw" that began with his trip to the "nearer Moslem world, then the European Soviet Union . . . and eventually China."

Thubron's first view of the Central Asian landscape reveals a featureless void:

> The sea had fallen behind us, and we were flying above a desert of dream-like immensity. Its sands melted into the sky, corroding every horizon with a colourless light. Nothing suggested that we were anywhere, or even moving at all. The last solid objects in the universe were the wing-tips of the plane.

Ancient peoples had filled this terrifying emptiness "with their inner demons." From here had come the "Cimmerian hordes," the Scythians, the Huns, the Turks, the Mongols. After the breakup of the Mongol empire in the fifteenth century and the death of the Silk Road, Central Asia ceased to be a source of terror or treasure for the West. In the nineteenth century the Russian empire "easily devoured it." Now, with the dissolution of the Soviet Union, Thubron wonders what will happen to the "shadowy Moslem nations" and their newborn independence: "Would they hurl themselves into the Islamic furnace . . . or reconvene in a Communist mass? I could conceive of their future only in the light of powers which I already knew: Islam, Moscow, Turkey, and the West."

Throughout his travels in the region Thubron is hampered and frustrated by his European concepts of space and culture. Of Turkemenistan he complains, "I longed to find some geographical heart to this diffused nation, but there was none. It owned no Vatican, no Acropolis." The only monument he discovers is the town of Geok-Tepe, the site of unsuccessful resistance to Russian expansion in 1881 and thus a symbol of "heroic failure." When Thubron mentions Geok-Tepe to his host's son, Bairam, the young man insists on driving him there. The expedition soon turns into a riotous party. In a "vodka-soaked trance" Thubron listens to Bairam's re-creation of the history of his people, the Turkomans: "He had reconstructed them in this land, as if they were the pure descendants of Neolithic men. He had reconstructed them . . . as an ancient, homogeneous people steeped in early wisdom."

As he does on all of his travels, Thubron seeks out friends of friends, strikes up conversations with strangers, and finds himself invited to weddings, parties, and dinners. He is not always treated well: he is robbed of a great deal of money; people revile the British in his presence; he is badgered about conditions in the West. Throughout the middle part of his journey he travels with the mercurial Oman, who reveals "many Omans": "the inveterate merchant, the embittered drunk, the tea-house philosopher, the poignant friend, the sentimentalist, the hedonist." Despite his companion's foibles–drunkenness, insulting KGB agents, wearing crimson briefs–in Oman's company Thubron sees aspects of Turkistan that would otherwise have been hidden from him. Oman has access to ordinary people and can explain the meaning of their customs.

In Samarqand, Thubron meets a Russian woman, Tania, who is married to a Muslim. She feels displaced by the death of the Soviet Union; she has lived in Turkistan for many years, yet she is still an outsider. She is angry with the Muslims for not appreciating what the Soviets had given them. Thubron reflects, "Here, too, was the inborn colonial expectation that people be grateful for what they had never requested. My own nation had made the same mistake."

The region, which Thubron imagines as being shaped like a crouching dog, is a hopeless mixture of races, religions, and cultures:

> The Uzbeks overlapped their Kazakh borders, and were numerous in every other state, comprising one quarter of the population of Tajikistan. But the Tajiks formed the bedrock of Uzbek Samarkand and Bukhara, while the little Karakalpak nation, ethnically close to the Kazakhs, lodged discomfitingly in the dog's groin. Russians littered every nation, of course, especially Kazakhstan, alongside Tartars, Ukrainians, Germans, Koreans, Chinese, Uighurs, Arabs and a host of others.

He worries about the impact of Islamic fundamentalism, noting that "it was this potential ferment which licensed the diehard government in Tashkent to limit democracy." Thubron asks people what will happen to the region in the aftermath of the Soviet breakup; many seem to be unaware of the perilousness of their situation, but some reflect carefully on the complex problems facing the newly independent countries. A university professor, who burns "with patriotic longings," believes that the future will be bright. Thubron is skeptical, noting that "this belief in the future was ardent and mercurial, like him, rooted more in his desires than in reason."

One of the most valuable aspects of *The Lost Heart of Asia* is Thubron's reflections on the travel experience. Toward the end of the book he describes the mysterious process of becoming familiar with a city, a process of demystification and domestication:

> It is strange. You arrive in a city by night, and staring down from a hotel balcony on its light-glazed streets, looking more secret and seductive than they will by day, you wonder how you will ever decipher it. But within a morning the puzzle unravels with desanctifying speed. A few hours' walk locates the main avenues, elicits a conversation or two, uncovers a mood, and you return to a hotel no longer swimming among mapless lights and possibilities, but anchored, grey and unlovely, on the corner of Gogol and Krasin streets.

In an earlier passage he muses about how the strangeness of a new place makes one forget one's home–until an image of home comes to mind with surprising forcefulness:

> For a long time, immersed in the challenge and strangeness of a new country, I imagine missing nothing of my own. Then an intruding memory–a chance thought, a facial resemblance–ignites a transient but overwhelm-

> ing homesickness, like some unacknowledged weariness, and I try to return for a moment into my own mislaid tradition.

Annette Koback in *The New York Times Book Review* (4 December 1994) praised the book: "Interweaving the history of the area with conversations he has along the way, Mr. Thubron gives a strong overall impression of the . . . pervasive unfocused homesickness of the new republics . . . [and] tracks down key leftovers from Central Asia's colorful past."

Following his usual pattern, Thubron next wrote a novel, *Distance* (1996). The main character, Edward Sanders, is a graduate student in astronomy who is "suffering from associative amnesia." He has become obsessed with the fear that a star will appear where he has predicted a black hole. The novel recounts his gradual recovery of his memory–particularly of the deaths of his mother and of the woman he loved. The novel is evocative, mysterious, and filled with symbolism.

Colin Thubron's place in the forefront of modern travel writing is secure. His work evokes the mood of the traveler encountering and seeking to understand a new place. He skillfully weaves historical narratives and mysteries into his unfolding journey. His style is clear, direct, and descriptive; it is also surprisingly reticent. Thubron creates the illusion of intimacy, but the reader learns little about him. His travel books are not autobiographies; they are elaborately woven blends of narrative, history, and description.

Interviews:

Nicholas Shakespeare, "The Vital Importance of Going Solo," *Times* (London), 25 July 1985, p. 11;

Ian Thomson, "Solitary Travels in Strange Lands," *Independent,* 30 September 1989;

Sheila McNamara, "A Solitary Quest," *Observer,* 15 September 1991;

Bridget Frost, "Passing Through," *Writer's Monthly* (March 1992);

Barth Healey, "The Taint of Reality," *New York Times Book Review,* 2 August 1992, p. 7;

Maggie Parkham, "Lonesome Voyager," *Independent,* 17 September 1994;

Julia Llewellyn Smith, "Strange Taste of Turkic Delight," *Times* (London), 9 October 1994.

Barbara Toy

(11 August 1908 -)

M. D. Allen
University of Wisconsin–Fox Valley

BOOKS: *Lifeline: A Play of the Merchant Navy in Three Acts,* by Toy and Norman Lee, as Norman Armstrong (London: S. French, 1943);

A Fool on Wheels: Tangier to Baghdad by Land-Rover (London: Murray, 1955);

A Fool in the Desert: Journeys in Libya (London: Murray, 1956);

A Fool Strikes Oil: Across Saudi Arabia (London: Murray, 1957);

Columbus Was Right!: Rover around the World (London: Murray, 1958);

In Search of Sheba: Across the Sahara to Ethiopia (London: Murray, 1961);

The Way of the Chariots: Niger River–Sahara–Libya (London: Murray, 1964);

The Highway of the Three Kings: Arabia–from South to North (London: Murray, 1968);

Rendezvous in Cyprus (London: Murray, 1970).

OTHER: *Agatha Christie's Murder at the Vicarage,* dramatized by Toy and Moie Charles (London: S. French, 1950);

Random Harvest, by James Hilton, dramatized by Toy and Charles (London: S. French, 1950);

The Man in Grey: A Play in Three Acts from the Novel by Lady Eleanor Smith, dramatized by Toy and Charles (London: Evans, 1953).

Elected a fellow of the Royal Geographical Society in 1950 for her visits to Iceland, Yugoslavia, Greece, and Lebanon, Barbara Toy later became the first Westerner to set foot on the summit of Mount Wahni in Ethiopia and received the Rover Award for her transit of North Africa from the Niger River northeast to the Mediterranean, a journey "of outstanding initiative and enterprise." This award had only been granted once before by the Long-Distance Land-Rover Association. Described by Phillip Llewellin, who interviewed her in 1962 for *The Observer* (London), as a "traveller in the most full-blooded and old-fashioned sense of the word," she has recorded eight of her journeys in informal and highly readable books.

Barbara Toy

Toy was born on 11 August 1908 in Sydney, Australia, to Bert F. Toy, literary editor of the *Sydney Bulletin,* and Nellie Frederica Toy, née Lowing. In an unpublished letter of 11 October 1994 Toy says that "the biggest influence in my life was my father, whom I adored. We went off on holiday together. There was a great affinity and looking back I realise I had a real father-complex which probably didn't help my relations with other men!" Perhaps Toy obtained her self-reliance and longevity from her mother, who, though she came from a wealthy family, still studied to be a nurse and died at 103. Toy's yen for traveling may have come from a grandfather who reportedly ran away to sea at the age of six though she says that it was seeing the Russian ballerina Anna Pavlova dance that sent her "wandering"–at least in her imagination.

In her 11 October 1994 letter Toy describes her education as "very elementary" and comments that her

Toy in the Sahara, on the hood of the Land Rover that replaced her beloved Pollyanna, during the trip that provided material for In Search of Sheba *(1961)*

"father's theory was that one learnt more from the school of life." But she reaped the advantages of being the daughter of an editor, for she had "the run of my father's library and had read most of Havelock Ellis before I was twelve." She also read the works of such authors as Sir Walter Scott, Virginia Woolf, Robert Nathan, Henry Williamson, Ronald Firbank, Rom Landau, Ernest Hemingway, Aldous Huxley, Michael Arlen, and F. Scott Fitzgerald. Toy describes most of these selections as "a rather predictable choice for a late teenager" of her time. The discovery of travel literature came later: "From my first journey onwards I have read Wilfred Thesiger, Freya Stark, [Charles Montagu] Doughty, Henri Lhote, or anything that relates to my one and only love–the desert!"

At fifteen Toy went to work at what she calls "a very fine book and art shop," the Roycroft, on Rowe Street. The owner, Frances Zabel, taught her about art, literature, and music. In April 1930 Toy married Ewing Rixson, "a member of a well-known New York Quaker family" whom *The Sun* (Sydney) described as an "ardent booklover" and "an inveterate traveller" who was serving as consul for Panama in Sydney. In October 1930 he was elected a fellow of the Royal Geographical Society, which listed his qualifications for the honor as having "travelled extensively in Lapland, Australia and the South Sea Islands, explored in New Caledonia, Society, Sandwich and Loyalty groups, and Ricatea Island." In her 11 October 1994 letter Toy says that she and her husband traveled together for some years, visiting "most countries in Europe and China, Bangkok, Ceylon, Lapland, Finland." Eventually they "drifted apart–quite amicably."

After separating from her husband, Toy settled in England. To earn her living, she went on the stage. In her 1994 letter she says of her acting that "the only good thing anyone ever said about it was that at least I looked as if I was enjoying myself." Before long, "like all bad actresses," she "migrated backstage": "War broke out and like all struggling actresses I had to take anything to pay the rent." She became assistant stage manager at the Richmond Theatre, taking over as stage director when her predecessor was called up for military service. When a bomb fell nearby and the theater was closed, Toy found work at a film studio in Welwyn Garden City, Hertfordshire, where she met the director Norman Lee. Under the pseudonym "Norman Armstrong" the pair wrote *Lifeline* (1943), a well-received play about the merchant navy. Toy spent most of the war years in London, where she served as an air-raid warden. Toward the end of the conflict she visited Belgium and Holland to report on the state of theaters in

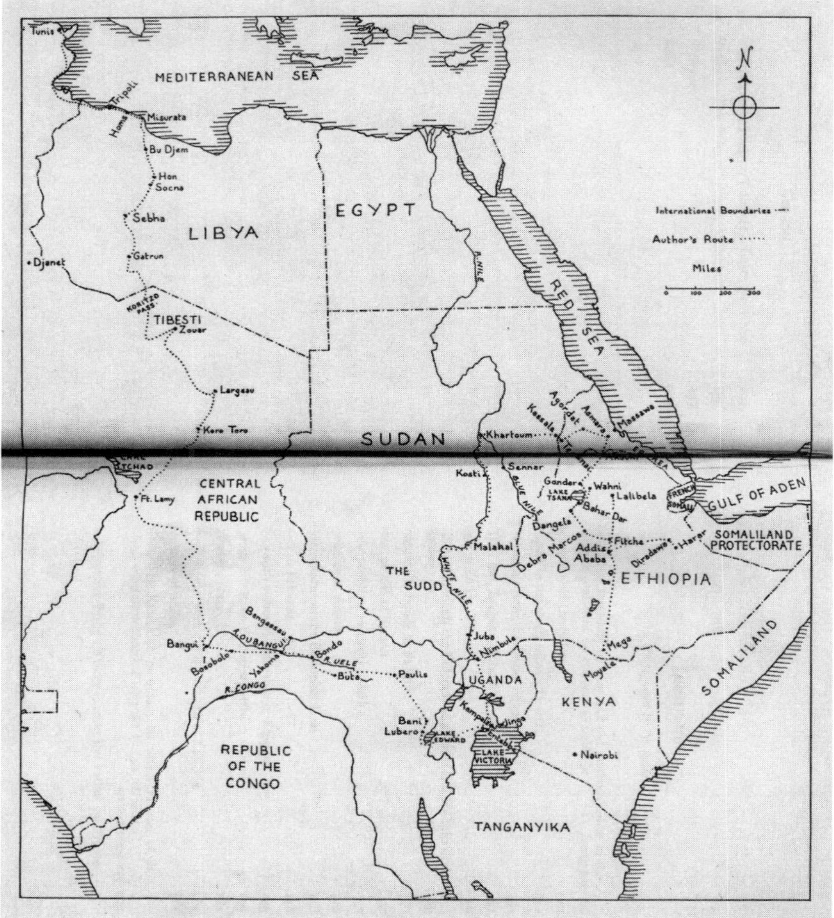

Map of Toy's route from In Search of Sheba

liberated western Europe for E.N.S.A. (Entertainments National Service Association).

After the war Toy dramatized three novels with her friend Moie Charles: Agatha Christie's *The Murder at the Vicarage* (1930) and James Hilton's *Random Harvest* (1941) in 1950 and Lady Eleanor Smith's *The Man in Grey* (1942) in 1953. Toy and Charles became directors of a new theater production company, Farndale, which put on plays and acquired theaters in Worthing, Bromley, and Tunbridge Wells.

Toy continued to direct plays after the war, settling down into what Llewellin calls "a comfortable rut." Toy's most complete explanation of her break from this routine into the sort of life she had dreamed about in childhood is given in that interview. "One evening," she told Llewellin, she encountered "a group of youngsters in a pub" who

> were grizzling about having won the war but lost the peace–this was 1949–and how you just couldn't get away from it all. I said that was ridiculous. Why the hell couldn't they just get up and go if they really wanted to? That sort of thing was fine for someone like me, they said. Good job to come back to, all expenses paid, no problems. . . . Well–I'm always doing this sort of thing, never learn to keep my mouth shut–I found myself saying I would cut loose, give up the job, get a car and drive to see an old friend in Baghdad.

Toy did exactly that. She bought a Land Rover and named it Pollyanna because "it sounded so very square and solid, and therefore very appropriate." She had it shipped to Gibraltar and then drove from Tangier, Morocco, to Baghdad, Iraq–the journey she narrated in her first travel book, *A Fool on Wheels: Tangier to Baghdad by Land-Rover* (1955). From then until the publication of *Rendezvous in Cyprus* in 1970, Toy wrote eight books about her travels.

The first three–*A Fool on Wheels, A Fool in the Desert: Journeys in Libya* (1956), and *A Fool Strikes Oil: Across Saudi Arabia* (1957)–deal with trips in Arab North Africa and the Middle East. The "fool" motif, abandoned after the third book, had its origin in a conversation that is recorded in an epigraph to the first volume: "'What's this I hear about you going off across North Africa alone? They ought to stop you! Haven't you got a husband, or someone to put his foot down?' 'It's quite an easy journey. . . .' I began. 'Easy? Don't know what you're talking about! A fool, that's what you are, traipsing off alone–a fool on wheels.'" Toy was counting on chivalric protectiveness and the status of honorary man that Western women are accorded in the Arab world. She told Llewellin: "When you arrive you either play the silly old woman who is looking for rock carvings, or, if the light's very flattering, the younger one who doesn't really know where she is. You play it by ear."

A Fool on Wheels recounts Toy's trip from Tangier along the North African coastline, then, via Cyprus, through Syria, Jordan, and Jerusalem to Baghdad. *The Spectator* accurately described the account as "a casual, highly readable book." The casualness ensures the readability, as in Toy's description of the Krak des Chevaliers (Castle of the Knights) in Syria, the most splendid of the Crusader castles:

> It is a really mighty structure and an amazing piece of medieval architecture. It was capable of housing a huge army, complete with equipment and horses, within its walls and was almost impregnable. Even Saladin, I believe, was unable to capture it. I wandered through the great halls, the vaults, the horses' stables and along the ramparts and it took me over two hours to see it all.

Some travel writers would have provided a full description of, as well as an elaborate response to, this celebrated castle; others might have fallen into pretentiousness. If Toy does not do the former–"an amazing piece of medieval architecture" is rather superficial–at least she avoids the latter. Her breeziness is further illustrated by her refusal to expend the energy to ascertain whether Saladin captured the castle in which she has spent only a little "over two hours."

On other occasions, however, Toy's style too closely resembles a travel agent's brochure. Of the fortified city of Constantine she writes, "Nobody who comes to Algeria should miss this beautiful place, there is so much to see in and around the town; the walk along the fantastic Rhummel Gorge, the swimming pools of Sidi M'Cid, the native quarter where the dwellings have a solid squat air about them and are roofed with lovely red-brown tiles." The reader is told that in Cyprus "many of the villages retain much of their ancient charm, and the Cypriot of today is a friendly, pleasant person; he smiles readily and often and has an upward turn to the sides of his mouth, a mark of good humour and generosity."

The book is a pleasure to read because Toy is an astute observer. During a sandstorm in Libya she notes that "food is out of the question. . . . The fine sand filters into the pores of the bread, a film settles on water or tea, and the hole in the condensed milk tin has a gritty crust around it." She can also turn a phrase. At an expensive Egyptian hotel, well-dressed women sip their drinks "and hotel 'wolves' prowled round with their usual air of concentrated detachment."

The 1,800-foot summit of Mount Wahni, Ethiopia, where Toy spent the night alone during the trip described in In Search of Sheba *(photograph by Barbara Toy)*

Hopelessly romantic, Toy describes a world that she first perceived in childhood and that is more glamorous than any reality. She writes that "one soon forgets the flies, heat, dirt, smells, the modern tawdriness and those interminable visas" and one "begins to recapture the colour and excitement of youthful impressions one had when reading the *Thousand and One Nights*." She feels as though the "spirit of Harun-al-Rashid still sits disguised in some quiet corner, away from the screeching clamour of the car-packed Baghdad streets; and the lilting lines of 'Hassan' come continuously to the mind." Toy sees Baghdad through lenses tinted by Scheherezade, the heroine of *The Thousand and One Nights' Entertainments,* and the works of the English poet James Elroy Flecker. Another aspect of her unwillingness to accept the limitations of everyday life, especially as manifested in a highly organized Western–or Western-

Dust jacket for Toy's 1964 account of her trip through northern Africa

izing–society, is Toy's growing interest in the desert, her "one and only love."

In *A Fool in the Desert* Toy writes about her seven months traveling in the three provinces of Libya, a trip undertaken "to find out why [the desert] had never been long out of my mind" after her trip across North Africa. Her expression of this fascination may sometimes be clichéd–"There is no escape for those who have come under its spell; once the magic has worked, they will return"–and occasionally she is credulous, in a Western sort of way, about the spiritual benefits the desert may have on its inhabitants. Cold-eyed realism about a "one and only love" is not to be expected, and her sincerity is undeniable.

A Fool in the Desert captures well, as its immediate successor would also, a country at a certain moment in its history. Libya still bore the scars of the war, and the best chapter grimly describes a German War Graves Commission unit searching for the final resting places of missing German soldiers. Later Toy watches charcoal being burned on an old Italian land mine to make tea: she hopes that it has been disabled. "Many strange things are used as tea-trays: soldiers' helmets, shattered bits of bomb, and flattened jerry-cans." One feels admiration for Toy's courage and good humor when she accepts an invitation to descend in a diver's suit into the waters of Benghazi harbor. A *Sunday Times* (London) reviewer found *A Fool in the Desert* "lively and entertaining," and a writer in the *Daily Post* (Liverpool) described the book as "gay, intelligent, and illustrated with sun-drenched photographs."

A Fool Strikes Oil describes a trip from Kuwait across Saudi Arabia to Jidda on the Red Sea. Although Toy betrays no profound knowledge of the past or present of the Arabian Peninsula, her account is a congenial, sometimes perceptive, portrait of a society in an acute phase of transition because of newfound oil profits. The book includes entertaining vignettes of the people she met, among them King Saud, who "had a small moustache over a rather soft mouth with full lips" and "was the sort of person from whom unpleasant things should be kept"; H. R. P. Dickson, an expert Arabist, and his wife, Violet; H. St. John Philby, the illustrious British explorer of Arabia; and an obscure schoolmaster who told Toy that his favorite book was Charles Dickens's *David Copperfield* (1849–1850), because "I understand him so well . . . his life has been so like mine." Toy agonizes over the mistreatment of animals by her Arab companions; she experiences "absolute contentment" while drinking tea during a desert sunset. *A Fool Strikes Oil* reveals her interest in the lives of the secluded but pampered Saudi women, and this scrutiny led the *Arab World* magazine to recommend it highly "for the picture it gives of the women in a Moslem country passing through a social and economic revolution." The *Daily Post* (Liverpool) called *A Fool Strikes Oil* a "fantastic tale about a fantastic part of the world" and noted that "the problems that have come to these primitive countries through the quite recent headlong rush of riches are vividly revealed."

In her late forties Toy returned to Sydney on a trip that she describes in *Columbus Was Right!: Rover around the World* (1958). The chapter on New South Wales gives glimpses of a happy childhood:

> The first recollection in my life was walking down steep steps towards a small jetty. We passed through a glaring white arch, towering high. It was a whale's jaw-bone set on end. I was holding my mother's hand and, when we came to the wooden jetty, I could see the bright blue water and the wriggling stones beneath the slats of wood. The wind caught the flags and they flipped and cracked; and the little white craft lay alongside, waiting for us. My mother, with her incredibly white skin and slim waist had laughed for the sheer joy of living and the beautiful scene. It was a yacht in Sydney harbour and I was, my mother tells me, just two years old.

She remembers childhood visits to the Jenolan Caves, seventy miles west of Sydney: "All the sun colours of the world are captured here, as though some giant had taken a handful of the great shimmering sun outside and let it loose in this fairyland. No child who has ever seen these caves can fail to believe in fairies." She recalls that "the trams still clattered round the winding streets" of Sydney. But "it was the ferry boats running across the harbour that brought back a rush of memories. There had been journeys all through my childhood into 'town.'" John Murray, the publisher, claimed on the book's dust jacket that "for anyone attempting the same exploit [driving around the world], her book is the ideal guide."

Toy's next two books can be considered her best. *In Search of Sheba: Across the Sahara to Ethiopia* (1961) immediately strikes the reader as a more ambitious and accomplished work than the previous ones. Gone is the jaunty tone, and the guidebook-style summaries are rarer. But the book has many of the familiar elements of Toy's narratives: sketches of people she encountered, with a particular feeling for children, and of places she passed through. The unpretentious and detailed account of an obviously experienced traveler, *In Search of Sheba* is divided into two parts. In the first, "The Sahara and Onwards," Toy records her journey south through Libya and the Central African Republic, east through the Belgian Congo in its last days before independence, and back north through Uganda and southern Sudan to Khartoum. Pollyanna had been donated to a technical college in England, and Toy has a new, higher-powered Land Rover. Nor is the car all that is different about this trip. Until her departure from Bangui, the largest city in the Central African Republic, Toy travels not alone but with company–first with two incompetent desert voyagers who venture into the Sahara in a "little grey Renault," then with a French colonel and his party, who save Toy's expedition by arriving on the scene just when a broken speedometer, which would make it impossible to measure distance covered, has persuaded her to turn back.

Part two of the book, "Ethiopia," ends on a–literally–high note. Toy had wanted to investigate the legend of the Queen of Sheba, who allegedly traveled north from Ethiopia to visit King Solomon in the tenth century B.C.; the emperor of Ethiopia, Haile Selassie, was reputed to be a direct descendant of the two rulers. If Toy forgivably fails to settle that question once and for all, she has the adventure of a lifetime as compensation when she is ferried by a skilled and daring helicopter pilot to spend a night on Mount Wahni, which is "not a mountain at all . . . just a pinnacle of rock" that rises "sheer out of the valley to a height of 1,800 feet." Since every prince, including illegitimate ones, had some claim to the throne, all except the direct heir were incarcerated on the mountain. Nevertheless,

> for many decades its very existence had been queried, for none of the earlier travellers and writers, while referring to it, had ever seen the mountain. Its presence, however, was always felt and no prince of royal blood was ever free from the threat of being banished to its high peaks; just as from time to time a prince, reputed to have been imprisoned there, was brought down to the capital to be crowned king. Its direction lay somewhere deep in the Belesa Hills and it is doubtful if even the returning princes knew the exact location, for it was several days' journey away.

Only the inhabitants of the valley in which the pinnacle rises knew of its existence until its rediscovery in the twentieth century. Toy became the first European–and probably the first human–to set foot on its summit since its abandonment two centuries earlier.

Here, indeed, was a feat–"the most fantastic thing of my life," she told Llewellin–to satisfy the dreamer who wanted Baghdad to be more like *The Thousand and One Nights* and who found solace in the desert. Toy examines the remains of the fortress, the ruined church, the foundations of the governor's house, and the princes' cells. She finds "the large wooden door" of the guardhouse still hanging "dramatically on its hinges"; she builds a fire, and "legends would build up about the high ribbon of smoke that . . . was seen for the first time in living memory." When, with difficulty, she is taken off the next morning, Toy carries a wine jug, which she donates to the University College Museum in Addis Ababa, and droppings of a carnivorous animal, probably a leopard, the thought of which had alarmed her during the night, as she was armed only with a truncheon.

Three years later Toy published the account of another significant achievement, for which she received the Rover Award "for an expedition of outstanding initiative and enterprise." *The Way of the Chariots: Niger River–Sahara–Libya* (1964) begins with her arrival in the legendary city of Tombouctou (traditionally, Timbuktu), Mali, by the Tanezrouft route, south through west-central Algeria. She then progresses northeast through Mali and Algeria to Tripoli, crossing the three Saharan mountain ranges on the way. Toy explains in her introduction that the purpose of her trip was to seek evidence that horse-drawn chariots once traveled the same route. The idea came from a French officer's discovery in 1933 of rock carvings depicting elephants, giraffes, lions, and other animals no longer seen in the Sahara, along with "paintings of exquisite beauty in many varied styles." Henri Lhote later led an expedition to record these carvings and paintings, and Toy quotes from Alan Houghton Brodrick's translation of his book, *The Search for the Tassili Frescoes: The Story of the Prehistoric Rock-Paintings of the Sahara* (1959). The central

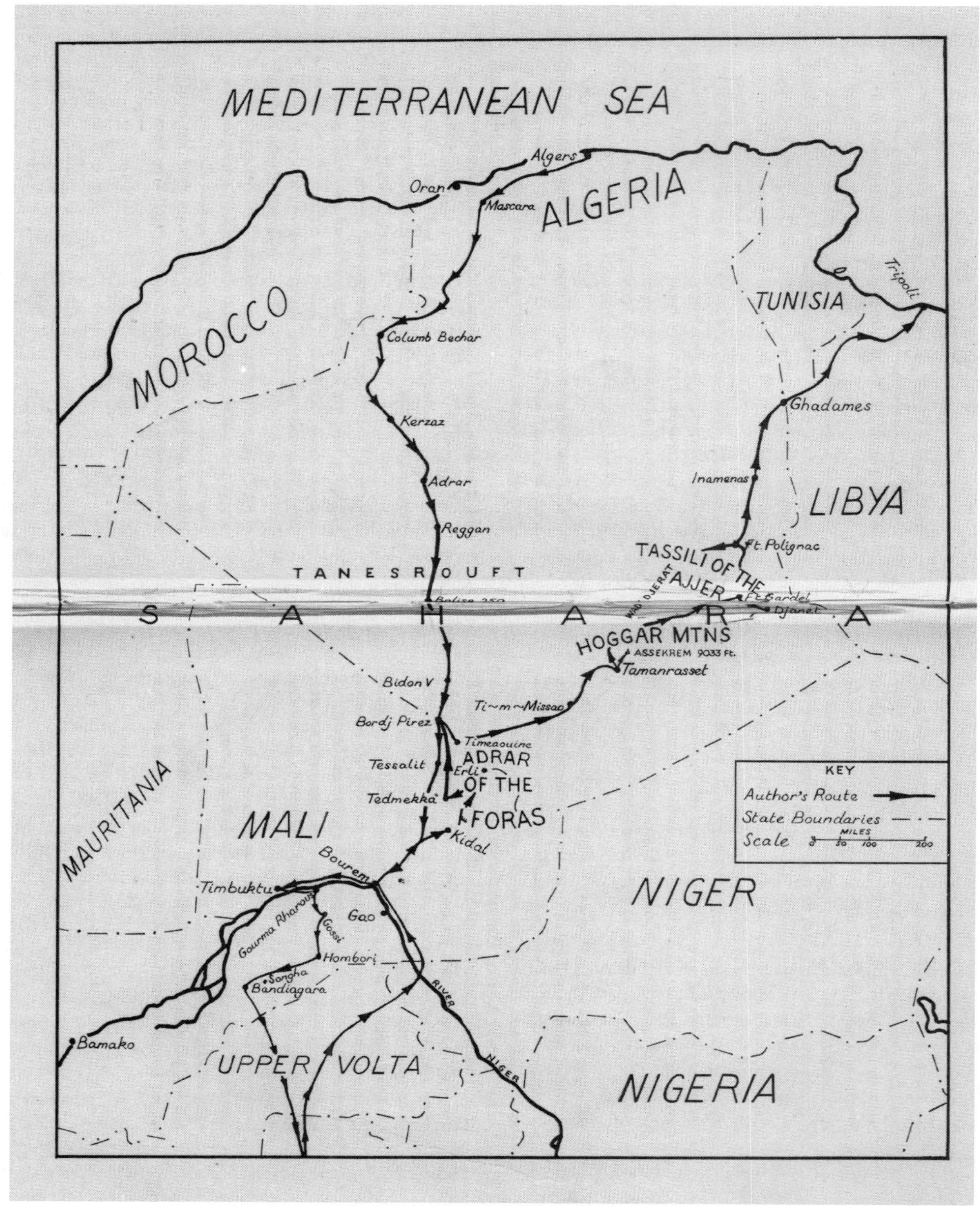

Map of Toy's route from The Way of the Chariots

Sahara was once, argues Toy, a thoroughfare between the Mediterranean and Black Africa: "Could a vehicle drawn by a horse have made this trip? For me, it was certainly worth taking the journey–to find out."

Toy's response to the rock paintings–"the oldest art gallery in the world"–is perhaps the least satisfactory aspect of her book. An admitted nonspecialist, she adds little more to the reader's knowledge of the drawings than she did to that of Sheba. Closer to the real raison d'être for the journey is her interest in–even infatuation with–the Sahara and the experiences of European explorers of and adventurers in the desert. On the first page of her narrative she notes that "this is a famous stretch of country used by most of the travellers and explorers as their approach to Timbuktu." Readers who share Toy's interests will find many familiar names in *The Way of the Chariots,* including René Caillé, Lieutenant Colonel Flatters, Maj. Alexander Laing (there is a photograph of Toy standing outside the house in which Laing stayed in Tombouctou), Gen. Henri Laperrine d'Hautpul, and Charles-Eugène Foucauld. Foucauld was an aristocratic French soldier who resigned his commission to become a priest in the Sahara; the desert changed a worldly playboy into a religious mystic and, finally, a martyr. *The Way of the Chariots* reflects Toy's own somewhat mystical response to the desert:

> I was parked away from the lorry and sat for a while watching the light fade. The silence closed in. How to explain this moment of suspension, of freedom, so hardly won in a crowded civilized world? Is the desert flat, uninteresting? It is a place where the mind rises from the perpetual repetition of civilization; nothing pulls you back, nothing beckons you on, giving this moment of suspension, so that time is petrified, arrested–and you with it. These moments of fixed time, the sudden freeing of spirit and identity, which others find perhaps in drugs, sex, or danger, are absolute; and there is no aftermath or complication, which is true of all reality. But perhaps it is a drug after all and as insidious as any other, for once having experienced it there is no real return.

Toy also writes of meeting Dr. Frances Wakefield, who gave up medicine "to concentrate on what became her life's work, translating the Bible into Tamahaq," the language of the desert people, the Tuaregs. *The Way of the Chariots* includes Toy's explanation of her own search for God, delivered in an evening conversation with friends: "I look for Him all the time. It is, I suppose, the real reason I travel." The celebrated traveler and author Laurens van der Post said of *The Way of the Chariots:* "Of all the intrepid journeys Miss Toy has undertaken this is the most remarkable." He praised the book as "not just an account of an exacting physical journey"–it is also

The goal of Toy's journey in The Way of the Chariots: *some of the prehistoric rock paintings discovered in the Sahara in 1933*

"the record of a profound inner search, a highly personal participation in the past and present of unusual men and women in one of the most forbidding environments on earth."

The Highway of the Three Kings: Arabia–from South to North (1968) does not pursue this mystical vein. The story of her trip from Aden, north via Jidda, Aqaba, and Amman to Damascus on the old Incense Route is somber in its implications for travelers. Toy closed *The Way of the Chariots* with a lament: the fort at Sinalouen had only the "ghosts of the Foreign Legionnaires who had entertained me on my very first journey. I can still see . . . the officer in charge advancing to meet me in a sweeping cloak of black and gold. Where is the colour going? Why is it fading everywhere, even in this great continent?" For Toy the color seems to be fading by the late 1960s in the great Peninsula. In Egypt, President Gamal Abdel Nasser spouts anti-British propaganda; "increased traffic" in Mukalla, Yemen, requires a policeman to direct it; and American tourists have arrived in Tarim in east central Yemen. Halfway along the coast, "the veneer of modern Jeddah [Jiddah] has gone deeper now; it has become cosmopolitan with the anonymity of a large city." In the north, at Aqaba, Jordan, she observes that "the magic of the untouched, the colour has gone." She continues:

> But am I not being contrary? Haven't I advocated just this state of affairs as a means of opening up the rest of Arabia? And aren't such luxuries the first buds of any rehabilitation? This is the continuous mental tug-of-war that travellers like myself experience, for on the one hand we want things to stay as they are and on the other know it is not practical in the world today. But it is painful to watch the corruption of transition; and the resulting period of uncertainty, feeling of inferiority and doubt. . . . Petra, for all its beauty, was slightly shop-worn and "tourist." Previously I had slept in a cave and dined in a large and colorful tent, but now there is a hastily erected hotel with a cafe attached, and boys with boxes of cooled orange squash wait at various points for the tourists.

Toy's next book, *Rendezvous in Cyprus,* was the product of an eight-month stay on the island during 1967–1968. She spoke with Turkish and Greek Cypriots and to Archbishop Makarios III, the first president of the Republic of Cyprus. She toured the country and lived in two villages; one of them was Ayios Philon in the eastern peninsula, a little-known area. The book is, however, somewhat insubstantial.

Although she has not written another volume since *Rendezvous in Cyprus,* Toy continues to travel. In 1989 she bought Pollyanna back from a museum for £3,500 (she had paid £640 for it in 1957). In June 1990 Toy began driving toward Australia, but in Turkey she met two "British intelligence types" who warned her not to cross into Kuwait. Iraqi president Saddam Hussein's troops invaded Kuwait not long afterward. Toy drove back to Greece, where the captain of a container-ship heading for Fremantle took her and Pollyanna on board. Toy was entered in the logbook as "Assistant to Land-Rover." But Australia, too, was getting tame, she complained: "There are too many made-up roads. Instead of going from homestead to homestead, it's all motels now." Toy and Pollyanna later returned to England via the United States.

Barbara Toy knows that her books have given pleasure to many readers, but she has no overwhelming urge to write any more of them. In a private letter she notes that "It's just that I don't travel to write–just travel to travel which means about half the journeys have not been recorded." A comment in *The Times Literary Supplement* (10 October 1968) about *The Highway of the Three Kings* may stand for nearly all her books and, indeed, her life: it was "a fascinating experience, a proper adventure, and any amount of guts."

Interview:

Phillip Llewellin, "The World's Most Adventurous Woman Motorist," *Observer,* 1962.

Reference:

Sun (Sydney), 23 November 1930.

Laurens van der Post

(13 December 1906 – 15 December 1996)

Kenneth A. Robb
Bowling Green State University

BOOKS: *In a Province* (London: Hogarth, 1934; New York: Coward-McCann, 1935);

Venture to the Interior (New York: Morrow, 1951; London: Hogarth, 1952);

The Face Beside the Fire (London: Hogarth, 1953; New York: Morrow, 1953);

A Bar of Shadow (London: Hogarth, 1954; New York: Morrow, 1956);

Flamingo Feather: A Story of Africa (London: Hogarth, 1955; New York: Morrow, 1955);

The Dark Eye in Africa (London: Hogarth, 1955; New York: Morrow, 1955; republished with new introduction (London: Hogarth, 1960);

Race Prejudice as Self-Rejection: An Inquiry into the Psychological and Spiritual Aspects of Group Conflicts, compiled and edited by Nathan Sherman, Martha Jaeger, and Roger Lyons (New York: Workshop for Cultural Democracy, 1957);

The Lost World of the Kalahari (London: Hogarth, 1958; New York: Morrow, 1958);

The Heart of the Hunter (London: Hogarth, 1961; New York: Morrow, 1961);

Patterns of Renewal, edited by Elizabeth Vining, Pendle Hill Pamphlets, no. 121 (Wallingford, Penn.: Pendle Hill, 1962);

The Seed and the Sower, edited by Ingaret Gifford (London: Hogarth, 1963; New York: Morrow, 1963);

A View of All the Russias (London: Hogarth, 1964); republished as *Journey into Russia* (New York: Morrow, 1964); republished with new introduction (Cevelo, Cal.: Island, 1984);

The Hunter and the Whale: A Tale of Africa (London: Hogarth, 1967; New York: Morrow, 1967);

A Portrait of All the Russias, text by van der Post and photographs by Burt Glinn (London: Hogarth, 1967; New York: Morrow, 1967);

A Portrait of Japan, text by van der Post and photographs by Glinn (London: Hogarth, 1968; New York: Morrow, 1968);

African Cooking, Foods of the World series (New York: Time-Life, 1970);

Laurens van der Post (photograph by Howard Coster)

Recipes: African Cooking, Foods of the World series (New York: Time-Life, 1970);

The Night of the New Moon (London: Hogarth, 1970); republished as *The Prisoner and the Bomb* (New York: Morrow, 1971);

Man and the Shadow, Conway Memorial Lectures, no. 23 (London: South Place Ethical Society, 1971);

A Story Like the Wind (London: Hogarth, 1972; New York: Morrow, 1972);

A Far-Off Place (London: Hogarth, 1974; New York: Morrow, 1974);

Jung and the Story of Our Time: A Personal Experience (New York: Pantheon, 1975; London: Hogarth, 1976);

A Mantis Carol (London: Hogarth, 1975; New York: Morrow, 1976);

Intuition, Intellect and the Racial Question (New York: Myrin Institute, 1976);

First Catch Your Eland: A Taste of Africa (London: Hogarth, 1977; New York: Morrow, 1978);

Yet Being Someone Other (London: Hogarth, 1982; New York: Morrow, 1983);

Testament to the Bushmen, by van der Post and Jane Taylor (Harmondsworth, U.K.: Penguin, 1984; New York: Viking, 1984);

A Walk with a White Bushman: Laurens van der Post in Conversation with Jean-Marc Pottiez, by van der Post and Jean-Marc Pottiez (London: Chatto & Windus, 1986; New York: Morrow, 1986);

About Blady: A Pattern Out of Time (London: Chatto & Windus, 1991; New York: Morrow, 1991);

The Voice of the Thunder (London: Chatto & Windus, 1993; New York: Morrow, 1994);

The Admiral's Baby (London: Murray, 1996; New York: Morrow, 1997);

The Secret River: An African Myth, text by van der Post and illustrations by Larry Norton (Bath, U.K.: Barefoot Books, 1996).

Collection and Edition: *The Collected Works of Laurens van der Post,* nine volumes (London: Chatto & Windus, 1985–1987);

Feather Fall: An Anthology, edited by Jean-Marc Pottiez, assisted by Jane Bedford (London: Chatto & Windus, 1994; New York: Morrow, 1994).

VIDEO: *King Lear; and The Tempest,* BBC-TV *Shakespeare in Perspective* series, Films Incorporated, 1984;

Laurens van der Post Remembering Jung, Bosustow Video, 1993.

TELEVISION: *The Lost World of the Kalahari,* written and narrated by van der Post, British Broadcasting Films, 1955;

The Story of Carl Jung, written and narrated by van der Post, British Broadcasting Films, 1972.

OTHER: Ray Parkin, *Out of the Smoke,* introduction by van der Post (New York: Morrow, 1960);

Eliot Elisofson, *The Nile,* introduction by van der Post (London: Thames & Hudson, 1964; New York: Viking, 1964);

William Plomer, *Turbott Wolfe,* introduction by van der Post (London: Hogarth, 1965);

Ian MacDonald Horobin, *Collected Poems: Ian Horobin,* introductions by van der Post and Sir John Betjeman (London: Jameson Press, 1973);

Michael Wood, *Go an Extra Mile: The Adventures and Reflections of a Flying Doctor,* foreword by van der Post (London: Collins, 1978);

Voorslag: A Magazine of South African Life and Art, edited by van der Post, Roy Campbell, and William Plomer, with an introduction and notes, by Colin Gardner and Michael Chapman (Pietermaritzburg, South Africa: University of Natal Press / Durban, South Africa: Killie Campbell Africana Library, 1985).

The impact of Laurens van der Post's books, lectures, and documentary motion pictures has been immense. In his 1969 book on van der Post, for example, Frederic I. Carpenter notes that the best comparison that van der Post's writing and personality suggest is with Lawrence of Arabia: "An almost legendary aura attaches to both men." Jan Morris, concluding an adverse review in *The Spectator* (21 December 1974) of van der Post's novel *A Far-Off Place* (1974), wrote, "Laurens van der Post's absurdities are other men's achievements, and one of his doubts is worth a dozen of our poor certainties." Perhaps Jean-Marc Pottiez summarized best and most positively when he wrote in his introduction to *Feather Fall: An Anthology* (1994), "Laurens van der Post has a unique capacity to inspire, to heighten awareness and fire the imagination."

Laurens Jan van der Post was born 13 December 1906 in Philippolis, Orange Free State, South Africa, to Maria Magdalena (Lubbe) and Christian Willem Henrick van der Post, a barrister by training. He was the thirteenth and youngest of the children who survived of the fifteen his mother bore. His mother's family had been in Africa a long time and had participated in the Boers' Great Trek northward in the late 1830s; in his writings van der Post often referred to his maternal grandfather's huge estate, *Boesmans Fontein* ("Bushman's Springs"), near the Orange River. His father had been born in the Netherlands and immigrated to South Africa with his family in the mid nineteenth century. Christian van der Post served as chairman of the Executive Council of the *Volksraad* (legislature) of the old Republic of the Orange Free State and fought against the British during the South African War of 1899. After the republic lost its independence in 1902, he gradually withdrew from public life and became devoted to reading European literature; he died in 1914. Afrikaans was Laurens van der Post's first language, but he soon learned to read the Dutch, French, and German books in his father's library, and when he was about ten he learned English in school.

As he passed into adulthood, van der Post rebelled against the family tradition of gaining a university education, rejected the vocation of farming, and–rejecting his native Afrikaans–adopted English as the language in which he would write. He discusses this youthful rebellion in the autobiographical *Yet Being Someone Other* (1982). He traveled to Durban in Natal province and obtained a job on an English-language newspaper, the *Natal Advertiser,* where he received "an intensive and exacting course of classical newspaper training," including shorthand and typing, legal studies, and court reporting.

As a consequence of his assignment to cover the shipping news, he came into contact with a much larger and more diverse world than he had experienced on his family's farms in the Orange Free State. He received permission to sail on a whaler for three seasons and report on the experience. He also became friends with the novelist William Plomer and the poet Roy Campbell, and the three of them edited the magazine *Voorslag*–whose title he translated as *The Lash of the Whip* in a 2 November 1963 interview with Roy Newquist. The ideas about race and racial justice that the editors promulgated in that journal were quite advanced for the South Africa of that time. They were ideas developed from van der Post's childhood relationships with black Africans. Increasing tension over the direction *Voorslag* was taking, personality conflicts, and poor management led van der Post, Plomer, and Campbell to withdraw as editors.

Thus, van der Post was free in 1926 to accept an invitation to sail to Japan on the first ship in the newly instituted monthly service between Durban and Osaka. The invitation arrived as a consequence of an incident in a coffee shop a few months previously, when the waitress had tried to refuse service to two Japanese journalists. Van der Post intervened because of his opposition to racial prejudice and made friends with these visiting reporters, who later arranged that van der Post be invited to visit Japan. After visiting the *Canada Maru* and meeting its captain, Katsue Mori, van der Post agreed to sail, provided his friend Plomer could accompany him, which was soon arranged.

On the long trip to Japan, as the ship went first up the coast of Africa, stopping at ports along the way, van der Post became imbued with Japanese culture, learning the language and coming to realize that "travelling into a new external world in the *Canada Maru* mean[t] so much to me because it was helping me to go thereby into a great undiscovered country of my own imagination, which I could not have entered any other way." By the time he returned to South Africa, van der Post's perspective had changed, and he was so disturbed by the racial situation in the country that for a while he alternated between trying to live in England and in South Africa. In 1928 he married Marjorie Wendt, whom he had met in South Africa; they subsequently had two children, a daughter, Lucia, and a son, Jan Laurens.

Van der Post wrote his first book, the novel *In a Province* (1934), during one of his periods in England when he was running a dairy farm in Gloucestershire.

Dust jacket for the British edition of van der Post's 1951 account of a trip through Nyasaland

It was in part inspired by his friend Plomer and reiterated through fiction the opposition to South African racial prejudice van der Post had earlier expressed in *Voorslag* and in an article published in *The Realist* in England in 1929. Van der Post vividly portrays the dilemma of his Afrikaaner hero, van Bredepoel, as he observes his black friend, Joseph Kenon, fall victim to the racist legal system. *In a Province* was well received and has been republished several times. Based on observations van der Post had made while a journalist in South Africa, the novel is rich in realistic detail, and this realism led the writer Ezekiel Mphahlele, in his study *The African Image* (1962), to value this novel above van der Post's later works.

In 1938 van der Post, who was living in England, became convinced that war was imminent. He sent his wife and children to safety in South Africa, and attempted to write a book, provisionally titled "The Rainbow Bridge," warning of the coming disaster. The book was never finished, and the manuscript was destroyed by German bombs during World War II.

Enlisting in the British Army in 1939, van der Post was soon given a commission, and he served in North Africa, Abyssinia (now Ethiopia), Syria, and the Dutch East Indies (now Indonesia). While leading a guerrilla group behind enemy lines on the island of Java in 1942, he was captured by the Japanese. Released from the prisoner-of-war camp in 1945, van der Post resumed his military career, serving under Louis, first Earl Mountbatten. Attached to 15 Indian Army Corps, Java, van der Post attempted to maintain order after the Japanese capitulation when Indonesian nationalists rebelled against the returning Dutch colonial authorities. He attained the rank of lieutenant colonel before leaving active service in 1947.

When he returned to London, van der Post was made Commander of the Order of the British Empire in recognition of his wartime service. In 1947 he tried to resume his career as a journalist in South Africa, working for a year as editor of the *Natal Daily News* (Durban). In 1948, however, the Nationalist Party gained a majority in the South African parliament and set about institutionalizing apartheid, the policy of social and economic discrimination against nonwhite South Africans. Disgusted by these racist policies, van der Post returned to England, where his first marriage ended in 1948. The following year he married Ingaret Giffard, an actress and writer who was so interested in the work of the Swiss psychologist Carl Gustav Jung that she went to consult a Jungian analyst in Zurich (she would later become a Jungian therapist herself). Van der Post had read some of the works of Jung and Sigmund Freud before the war, and, when he joined his wife in Zurich, he quickly became a close friend of Jung and an adherent of his theories, which played an important role in almost all of van der Post's subsequent books.

Venture to the Interior (1951), van der Post's first postwar publication, had its roots in a mission he undertook in 1949 to Nyasaland (now the Republic of Malawi) for the Colonial Development Corporation, a British government agency. He was to explore thoroughly two little-known areas near Lake Nyasa to see if they could be developed to produce food in case an anticipated food shortage developed. Van der Post makes clear early in his narrative that his motives in accepting the commission were to regain a sense of Africa, to regain a sense of spiritual wholeness within himself, and to achieve a relationship between himself and Africa. As the book proceeds, the ambiguity of the title is revealed: the venture was to an African physical interior, Nyasaland, to an African spiritual interior, the "soul" of Africa, and to van der Post's own soul. He describes the roots of his conflict as deriving partly from the differences between his parents. After characterizing them, van der Post summarizes his conflict as between "on the one side, under the heading 'AFRICA,' . . . unconscious, female, feminine, mother; and under 'EUROPE' on the other: conscious, male masculine, father."

As he recounts his flight south across the continent, stopping briefly for refueling or staying overnight, van der Post describes such cities as Khartoum, Nairobi, and Salisbury as boring and lacking character, unlike the surrounding countryside, probably because the cities were centers of European influence. Once he arrives in Blantyre in Nyasaland, van der Post is ready to comment sarcastically on non-African phenomena, such as the lawns in a residential section of the town and the lack of success the British "exiles" have in growing European flowers in their gardens, although zinnias, native to Africa, grow quite well. On the other hand, flying over the country and viewing it by day, van der Post was often deeply moved, as when he looks down on Kampala and Lake Victoria: "With the view I felt a rush of affection for Africa. Africa is great and majestic in all it does; there is nothing mingy or mean in its methods, no matter whether it is producing desert, mountain, lake or plain." Furthermore, he contrasts the "spontaneous, pure and immediate laughter" of ordinary Africans with the "melancholy . . . learned, self-conscious gloom" of educated blacks who serve as clerks under the British.

Van der Post's first assignment, the subject of the third part of the book, "Encounter with the Mountain," was to explore Mlanje, a mountainous region of between 120 and 190 square miles in the extreme south of Nyasaland. With the cooperation of several British colonial administrators, he organized and equipped an expedition. While doing so, van der Post experienced feelings of foreboding and of being an intruder. Although they professed the admirable goal of making Mlanje a fine forestry reserve, forestry officials often showed possessiveness toward the region and were suspicious of van der Post and the government's motives for sending him on this mission.

Van der Post traveled into Mlanje accompanied by Peter Quillan, the Chief Forestry Officer for the province, twenty carriers, a cook, and a "personal boy." Their first goal was Chambe, the home of Richard "Dicky" Vance, the forestry officer for the area, and the center of a Mlanje cedar-logging operation. Despite their appearance, these trees were not really cedars, but "a conifer of a unique and very ancient sort, which [had] their roots in the most antique of antique African botanical worlds." Chambe is permeated with the smell of sawed Mlanje cedar, "a strange, thick, resinous, spiced, oily scent," a scent that van der Post characterizes as uniquely African.

At the same time, however, van der Post confirms one administrator's description of Chambe as "like a glen in Scotland," and Vance proudly shows him the home he had built for his family, a "genuinely Tudor building." Thus, van der Post continues the juxtaposition of the essentially African and the essentially European. Although English, Vance and his wife, Val, concur in their judgment that the place is "absolutely perfect" for them and their baby, Penelope, and they seem to have fully committed themselves to Africa, to Chambe, and to Vance's job of managing the forest reserve. Van der Post feels strong misgivings, however, when Vance decides to join the expedition and the two young people say goodbye: "I felt desperately afraid for them."

The climax of van der Post's narrative comes when the group is driven down from the mountains by a sudden fierce storm and encounters a torrent they have to cross just above its fall into a deep gorge. Vance undertakes to ford it slowly with a rope around his waist, feeling for footholds ahead with a stout stick. All goes according to plan until he draws near the opposite shore, when suddenly he lets go of the stick and tries to swim the rest of the way. He is immediately swept over the waterfall; the rope chafes, then breaks, and Vance falls to his death. His body was never found.

When Quillan and van der Post break the news to Val back in Chambe, they learn how unhappy Vance had been as a child and how Val, his baby daughter, and his job at Chambe–all "perfect"–had finally brought him happiness. He had found his Eden, but Mlanje was not to be domesticated.

Even as van der Post goes north to investigate the Nyika Plateau, he continues to contemplate Vance's death. One of his conclusions is that a "split in ourselves produces a split in the pattern of our lives, creates this terrible gash down the middle, this deep, dark Mlanje gorge, through which disaster runs and the devil drives. Accident and disaster without feed on accident and disaster within." When van der Post lies back in the grass as the exploration party waits for the darkness and mist to lift from Nyika, he thinks again of Vance's death and remembers a significant episode in his own life (a near-death experience when he was a prisoner of war). He comes to a second, illuminating conclusion: "I had a vision of the universe and myself, in which the circumference was reduced to a mere mathematical abstraction, and in which all was Centre–one great unfailing Centre, and myself, in the heart of Africa, in the heart of the Centre."

The overall impression van der Post creates in his description of the expedition is that of great beauty and an abundance of life, as when he writes, "We walked from there, I reckoned, through ten square miles of irises. When this heraldic field of gold and purple ended we came to an altitude in which the grass glowed with the orange, red, blue and gold of wild gladiolus." It is almost as though van der Post found the Eden from which Vance was expelled. As van der Post emphasizes more than once in the work, "The design of our outward life . . . reflects and confirms our deepest and most private purposes," and in contrast to Vance, who was

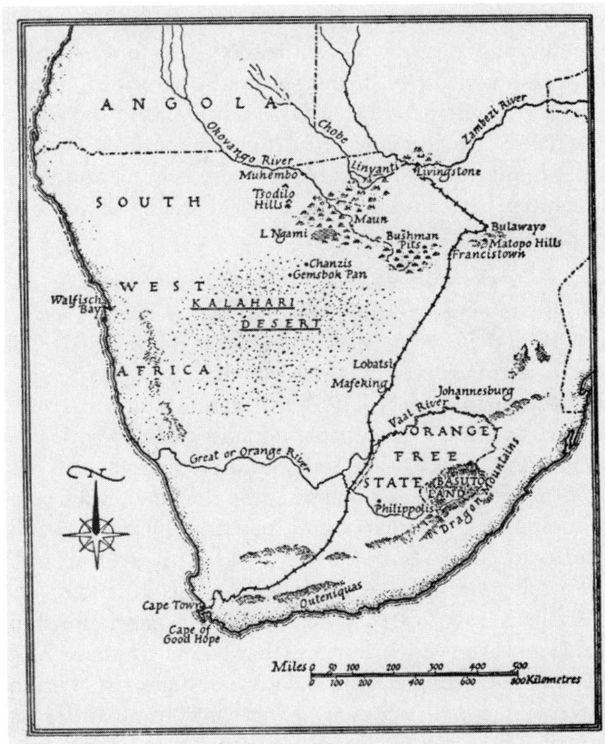

Map of southern Africa showing places van der Post visited in the search for South African Bushmen he described in The Lost World of the Kalahari *(1958)*

divided and in conflict, van der Post felt himself to be whole.

According to Mark Cocker in his *Loneliness and Time: The Story of British Travel Writing* (1992), "Richard Vance is intended to symbolize the European self divided by personal experience and cultural background." Vance, in Cocker's reading, is "cut off from the dark half of his own being, and therefore capable of only a lop-sided understanding of life." As such, Vance serves as a foil to the older and wiser narrator.

The elaborate construction of the work and van der Post's recurrent premonitions of Vance's impending death contribute to an impression that the line between fiction and travel writing is being blurred. Cocker justly describes *Venture to the Interior* as "one of the most elaborately constructed travel books in the post-war period"; and in his Twayne study of van der Post, Carpenter analyzes that construction expertly, discussing it in terms of both the exterior venture to Nyasaland and the interior venture into the human heart and spirit. Carpenter concludes of van der Post's writing that, "Best of all, he has narrated these experiences in a book free of all moralism and abstraction." Some experienced travel writers and reviewers, however, criticized van der Post for vagueness. In his review of the book for *The Specta-*

tor (22 February 1952), Peter Fleming characterized the expedition's goal as exceptionally nebulous. Others were also distrustful of the spiritual or mystical aspect of the work, an aspect that Hassoldt Davis in the *Saturday Review of Literature* (10 November 1951), on the other hand, found admirable: "There is great and grim adventure here, and a quasi-mystical seizing of it which recalls St. Exupéry in his simplest prose."

Van der Post's next three works were fictions: *The Face Beside the Fire* (1953), the novella *A Bar of Shadow* (1954), and *Flamingo Feather: A Story of Africa* (1955). All are to some degree autobiographical and bear some connection to Africa. The hero of the first is a South African painter who becomes dissatisfied with his native land, goes to England, and there marries and has children. He becomes increasingly alienated from conventional English society and his family, however, and returns to Africa. Subsequently, he returns to England, gains self-confidence even as he loses his artistic drive, and falls in love with a different woman, a relationship which promises to bring him happiness ultimately. *A Bar of Shadow* centers on the nature of Sergeant Hara, a powerful Japanese prisoner-of-war camp commander, as one of his prisoners, John Lawrence, experienced it. *Flamingo Feather* is an action-adventure story about the discovery and eventual frustration of a Russian plot to subvert an African tribe.

The Dark Eye in Africa (1955) is based on a lecture originally titled "Mata Kelap, or the Appearance of the Dark Eye in Africa: A Talk on the Invisible Origins of African Unrest," which van der Post delivered in March 1954 at a joint meeting of the C. G. Jung Institute and the Psychological Club of Zurich. Van der Post addresses the problem of unrest in Africa in *The Dark Eye in Africa,* centering on the Mau-Mau and Kikuyu uprisings and emphasizing the African's perspective, to which he felt particularly qualified to speak. Although not a travel book, *The Dark Eye in Africa* is an important explication of van der Post's feelings about Africa and the relationships between races there, as well as an explicit statement of his Jungian assumptions.

Van der Post explains the post–World War II change in Africans' relationship to Europeans by applying to it the Malayan term *mata kelap,* which refers to the behavior of an individual who has been obliging all his life and then suddenly rebels and "goes out and murders everyone who imposed such goodness upon him, father, mother, wife, children, head of the village. . . ." In short, "his eye has darkened within him." Africans have experienced this universal phenomenon; and, according to van der Post, African unrest is clearly an extension of modern individual unrest, for the outer is a mirror of the inner.

In 1955 van der Post undertook the expedition he later described in *The Lost World of the Kalahari* (1958). In the first chapter of that book, van der Post reviews the popular South African conceptions about the character of the San tribe, the people commonly referred to as the Bushmen. He recounts the long history of their decimation and exploitation at the hands of blacks and whites in South Africa, and recalls his personal experiences regarding Bushmen and other blacks on his family's estate. He emphasizes, for example, the important role Klara, his Bushman nurse, played in his early life. Out of a mixture of motives, among them remorse over the role his ancestors may have played in exterminating the Bushmen, he had earlier resolved to seek the remnants of the San tribe, but his trip had been postponed by World War II.

At last, he arranged financing for an expedition to the Kalahari Desert to film the Bushmen and their surroundings for the British Broadcasting Corporation. He was accompanied on this expedition by his friends Wyndham Vyan and Ben Hatherall, and an acquaintance, Eugene Spode, whom van der Post chose to be in charge of the filming. Van der Post decided to undertake the expedition in early August because at that harsh time of the year all other people except the "pure" Bushmen left the desert. Relieved of the intruders, the true Bushmen were more likely to emerge and be found. First, however, van der Post led the expedition from Muhembo into the swamps along the rivers on the north edge of the Kalahari in search of the River Bushmen. On this long, unsuccessful foray, the greatest irritations for van der Post were Spode's inability to handle the physical and mental stresses to which they were all subjected and the cameraman's refusal to do any filming.

Tension built until the party returned to Muhembo and van der Post discharged Spode. Then van der Post had to fly to Johannesburg to find a new photographer. He was fortunate to be able to take on Duncan Abraham, who joined the party at Muhembo. The expedition's next journey was to the Tsodilo Hills (or "Slippery Hills") southwest of Muhembo in the northern part of the Kalahari. Eventually, they made contact with one Bushman who arranged for them to camp near a settlement of about thirty other Bushmen. Van der Post had ample opportunity to study the Bushman paintings on the hills and to observe the way they lived and assay their character. Gradually, the members of the expedition were truly accepted by the Bushmen, and the expedition members left with regret.

In *The Lost World of the Kalahari* van der Post waxes lyrical in his descriptive passages: "Three amazed giraffes in harlequin silk watched us go by, and suddenly far below we saw vast herds of game grazing up

Van der Post and Tshekid Khana, a South African chief, in the Kalahari Desert with young Bushmen, who are filling ostrich eggshells with water for use as canteens

to their chins in the grass between the sparkling mopane forest and the pink and mauve mists drawn up, steaming, from the molten marshes." As in *Venture to the Interior,* the line between fiction and travel narrative seems blurred, and van der Post often finds experiences archetypal or resonant with meaning that the reader may not be able to identify, as in his description of an encounter with a buffalo about which he had dreamed all his life and that he then refused to shoot even as it charged him.

In her 15 November 1958 review in the *New Statesman,* the South African novelist Doris Lessing observed that van der Post "has fallen under the spell of persuasive Papa Jung" and ends by citing the comment of an African who told her that the white man's really unforgivable crime was that "even the best of you use Africa as a peg to hang your egos on." Lessing's criticism is ameliorated, however, by her observation that not only is van der Post open to this charge, but "so are all the rest of us." The book was awarded the American Literary Guild Choice Award in 1958.

Van der Post undertook the first of several trips to the United States in 1956, in response to requests for him to conduct seminars and give lectures. The trip also enabled him to overcome "a complete block in my imagination," as he puts it in *A Mantis Carol* (1975), at the time he was writing *The Heart of the Hunter* (1961), the sequel to *The Lost World of the Kalahari.* On this first trip he started in New York City, proceeded to Montreal, Kingston, Toronto, and Manitoba, thence to California, Texas, New Orleans, Washington, D.C., and back to New York, where he conducted a series of seminars, and then to the Society of Friends (Quaker) training center in Pendle Hill, Pennsylvania, where he conducted further seminars. In these lectures van der Post brought together some of his experiences in Africa, principally among the Bushmen, and Jungian psychology. *Race Prejudice as Self-Rejection: An Inquiry into the Psychological and Spiritual Aspects of Group Conflicts* (1957) is a compilation of van der Post's New York lectures, while *Patterns of Renewal* (1962) collects van der Post's Pendle Hill seminars.

The Heart of the Hunter, dedicated to Jung, is a continuation of the story of the expedition chronicled in *The Lost World of the Kalahari,* tracing the group's journey out of the Central Desert. Van der Post says that the shape of the book comes from the real sequence he experienced of the physical journey leading him to insight into his own mind, thought, and experience and thence into the Bushman mind. The progression is effective, though it turns the book more emphatically into anthropology than travel writing, and the last part seems verbose and dull. In contrast, the writing in the first part is often as poetic as that of *The Lost World of the Kalahari* or *Venture to the Interior,* as in van der Post's description of the clouds over the Kalahari: "The last red glow in the west died down behind the purple range of cloud, and it went utterly dark beyond our camp. Our own fire rose higher than ever, straining like a Gothic spire towards the stars which were,appearing in unusual numbers."

Van der Post frequently compares aspects of the culture of the Bushmen to aspects of various other cultures he has known, such as the sense of time in Bushmen and Javanese cultures and the devastation that contact with Europeans has brought on indigenous peoples. He criticizes the lack of knowledge both Europeans and other Africans have of Bushman culture and living conditions. Neighboring tribes oppress them, even enslave them, and the government prosecutes and imprisons them for killing "protected" animals that they have used for food for centuries. Van der Post argues that with knowledge comes greater understanding and sympathy. He attributes the enthusiasm of audiences he has addressed throughout the world to the idea that the Bushman represents "some elemental common denominator" in a diverse humanity.

In the last section of the book van der Post presents and interprets–from what is frequently a Jungian perspective–the myths, folklore, and beliefs of the Bushmen, thus entering the mind of the Bushmen. If the Bushman is a hunter, van der Post concludes, then he is a "hunter not of big game but of greater meaning," much like van der Post himself.

Writing a quarter of a century later in *The Spectator* (22 December 1984) in a review of *Testament to the Bushmen* (1984), Christopher Booker referred to the documentary movies van der Post brought back from this expedition as "the only television series which, rather than simply passing on existing information, actually added in an important sense to our store of knowledge" and called the series possibly "the most significant television series ever made."

In *The Seed and the Sower* (1963), van der Post republished the previously published novella *Bar of Shadow* with two additional novellas (*The Seed and the Sower* and *The Sword and the Doll*) all centered around the character John Lawrence, and all derived from van der Post's experiences on Java during World War II. *Bar of Shadow* is generally understood to be the most successful of the three. It was later adapted and produced by Jeremy Thomas as the stage drama *Merry Christmas, Mr. Lawrence* (1983). Japanese director Nagisa Oshima and Paul Mayersberg adapted the story into a motion picture of the same title, which was released the same year, starring David Bowie and Tom Conti.

Van der Post's relationship with *Holiday* magazine had begun with an article, "Africa," published in the March 1954 issue. In 1961, the year *The Heart of the Hunter* was published, *Holiday* arranged van der Post's next journey, a tour of Japan, and the resulting article, "Journey Through a Floating World," was published in the October 1961 issue. Next followed a *Holiday*-sponsored journey to the Soviet Union and a series of articles, which were expanded to become *A View of All the Russias* (1964).

In *A View of All the Russias,* van der Post continuously contrasts the Russian bureaucracy, Intourist guides, and restrictions to the people he meets and talks with as he travels on a series of trips from Moscow. Indeed, his aim on this trip was, as he states, "to learn something of the humanity of their people." Consequently, the sights of Moscow receive far less regard than those of the first trip to Central Asia, in which he traveled to Tashkent, then Bukhara, the Caspian and Black Seas, then to Kharkov, Kiev, and Moscow. Van der Post truly came into contact with "the people" and gloried in their diversity in Tashkent and Baku. The people there, he believed, showed a character that related them much more closely to the Mediterranean world than to that of Moscow.

Subsequently, van der Post traveled east on the Moscow-Peking Express and found himself at ease in central Russia, for he "felt more at home in a pioneering community that had many affinities with the world in which I had grown up in Africa." A later trip from Moscow to Riga to Leningrad and back gets short shrift, the emphasis being on visiting churches.

Van der Post tells of his experiences with interesting people, such as his meeting a bootblack in Irkutsk who asks if van der Post knows Marilyn Monroe and encountering a group of young people in Yalta with whom he spends hours discussing England and America. Few books give a better look into the Soviet Union of the 1960s, particularly as to what ordinary people said and thought at that time. In the *Saturday Review* (2 May 1964), Russian expert Harrison E. Salisbury lauded van der Post's work, finding it "a pure joy." Although clearly attached to Western ideas, Salisbury said, van der Post is "a man who regards all humans as part of the whole, one who is prepared to meet and talk with Russians as one man to another and not within the context of an interminable debating match." *A Portrait of All the Russias* (1967), based on the same journey, is more superficial and repeats some of the same ideas and even phrasing of *A View of All the Russias.* The text is enhanced, however, by the photographs of Burt Glinn, which emphasize the diversity of the Russian people.

The Hunter and the Whale: A Tale of Africa was also published in 1967. In this novel van der Post combines his knowledge of whaling, gained when he was a journalist at the port of Durban, and his knowledge of hunting game in Africa with his concern about race relations in South Africa. The narrator, Peter, is a seventeen-year-old Afrikaner who becomes friends with a Zulu stoker, Mlangeni, aboard a whaling ship sailing out of Durban. The action reaches a climax after a famous elephant hunter comes on board to join the captain of the ship in a compact to hunt a sperm whale, nicknamed "Caesar." The hunt is reminiscent of that in Herman Melville's *Moby-Dick* (1851). In his review of the book for the *Saturday Review* (4 November 1967), Henry Beetle Hough found that van der Post's theme was "rather evenly compounded of Africa and of whaling, a unity that gives his book its special quality and interest."

A Portrait of Japan (1968) follows the format of *A Portrait of all the Russias,* with Glinn again providing photographs. In *A Portrait of Japan* van der Post often alludes to his impressions on his 1926 visit and compares them to those of the trip of 1961. For example, that first trip aboard the Japanese ship *Canada Maru* took several weeks, but in 1961 van der Post flew to Tokyo by jet on a trip that took only several hours. Of course, signs of Japan's modernization are everywhere, especially on the Ginza and along the main streets of Kyoto with their modern lights, crowds in predominantly Western dress, and traffic congestion.

These, however, are external changes, and although van der Post acknowledges that "other approaches might convey more of what the modern Japanese 'has,'" he aims to "indicate more of what she 'is'"–the fundamental selves of the Japanese. Thus, he finds the Japanese gift for miniaturization in the small size but simple beauty of hotel rooms as well as in their production of fine camera lenses and transistor radios. To him, the Japanese adaptation of Chinese pictograph writing is beautiful. In Zen Buddhism, he finds an attempt to make humans whole and to transcend the "clash of opposites in human nature," which is universal. Most of all, he perceives the spirit of Japan, in, for example, the temple of Tofuku-ji or in Mount Fuji, which remained as it had been when he first saw it:

> The first time I saw it was at dawn from the railway line along the shore of Tokyo Bay, and at once it made the most wonderful music in my senses, rising like a vortex of purple sound out of the wine-red sea of dawn to achieve a white cone of elegance and perfection in the blue sky. It expressed the thing about true mountains, which makes them sacred in the natural symbolism of the human spirit.

On a darker note, van der Post acknowledges the high rate of suicide in Japan, a result of many causes, among them a loss of one's feeling important as an individual and simply ennui.

Van der Post makes no effort to be inclusive in this relatively brief book. He describes Tokyo by day and by night, and traveling the Tokaido Road to the former capital of Kyoto. He devotes attention to Kyoto itself and the city of Nara and concludes with a few comments on Kyushu and the island of Hokkaido. Some of his remarks seem prophetic, as when he says regarding the skill and originality of the Japanese, "indeed, had they raw material and physical resources as they have imagination, skill and will, they would sweep the markets of the world." In his review of the book in the *New Statesman* (25 October 1968), Plomer recounted his own memories of the trip to Japan with van der Post in 1926 and summarized well his friend's analysis of Japanese character, justly concluding that this book is "a pleasant travelogue which keeps indicating that depths exist."

In *African Cooking* (1970), illustrated by Richard Jeffrey's photographs, and the accompanying volume, *Recipes: African Cooking* (1970), van der Post returns to the Africa he knew so well, this time from a gustatory perspective. Although a volume in the Time-Life Foods of the World series, *African Cooking* comprises a good deal of personal reminiscence as well. Van der Post describes a typical dinner at his grandfather's large dining table in Boesmans Fontein, then digresses with the account of how his mother's side of the family participated in the Great Trek of the 1830s and settled on farms near the Orange River.

Van der Post divides sub-Saharan Africa into five regions. After describing the ecology and culture of each, he combines description of their foods with tales of his personal experiences of them. For example, he describes his first taste of *ortej,* Ethiopian honey wine, curds and whey, and millet bread when he entered Ethiopia leading a camel train from the Sudan during World War II to arm those rebelling against the occupying Italians.

After touring and tasting in West Africa, East Africa, and Mozambique and Angola with their Portuguese influences, van der Post arrives at Southern Africa, first emphasizing Malay cooking at the Cape and then, in a particularly interesting and authoritative way, the culture and foods of his native province, the Orange Free State. For example, van der Post writes:

> This for me was always one of the most moving aspects about the pioneers: although they had rejected the Cape forever and there never was any thought of turning back, they were pursued by a dream of all they had left behind. Wherever they went and as soon as they could, they reproduced in miniature the gardens that had been the main purpose of the original Cape settlement.

African Cooking exhibits van der Post's style at its most concrete, most engaging, and most direct. Food is obviously a favorite topic for him, and he expertly synthesizes the dishes he discusses and the cultures and circumstances from which they spring. *First Catch Your Eland: A Taste of Africa* (1977) expands on some of the personal experiences of *African Cooking* and supplements them, but omits the pictures and recipes of the earlier volumes.

In most of the nonfiction books that followed, van der Post engaged in remembering. In "The Other Journey," an essay he wrote for *The Voice of the Thunder* (1993), he distinguishes between "looking back," which has universally negative connotations, as in the experiences of Lot's wife or Orpheus, and memory: "looking back tends to make the present a past, whereas remembering makes what is valid in the past part of the present."

The genesis of *The Night of the New Moon* (1970), published in the United States as *The Prisoner and the Bomb* (1971), for example, lay in what he saw, twenty-five years after atom bombs were dropped on Hiroshima and Nagasaki, as a tendency to consider the Japanese only as victims and not the aggressors they were. His aim is to remember in detail his experience as a prisoner of war of the Japanese on Java during World War II and to argue that had the atom bombs not been used he and thousands of other Allied prisoners of war would probably have been massacred by their captors. William Beauchamp, reviewing the book in *Saturday Review* (13 March 1971), found "the style . . . egocentric, pompous, affected, and complacent," and suggested "to this add a sense of superiority and divine mission, even if only metaphorical."

In the 1970s, van der Post published works on Jung and Jungian psychology, *Jung and the Story of Our Time: A Personal Experience* and *A Mantis Carol* (both published in 1975), and two novels set in Africa, *A Story Like the Wind* (1972) and *A Far-Off Place* (1974). In his 19 September 1974 review for *The Listener* of *A Far-Off Place,* Kenneth Graham found "impossible episodes, ungainly prose, fossilized character-types, and wooden dialogue," while Jan Morris declared in her review for *The Spectator* (21 September 1974) that "in this book the message is the medium," with all the literary aspects overwhelmed by "the spectacle of Colonel van der Post trying to come to terms with a world apparently determined to block his every path of enlightenment." Despite these negative reviews, the novels sold fairly well and were adapted into a Walt Disney Pictures motion picture, *A Far Off Place,* directed by Mikael Solomon and released in 1993.

In 1976 van der Post appeared on the BBC-TV series *Shakespeare in Perspective,* and discussed his interpretation of William Shakespeare's play *The Tempest.* Van der Post returned to a focus on travel in *Yet Being Someone Other.* Van der Post describes this work as "not an autobiography but a story of a special relationship with the sea." Telling this story, however, involves telling a good deal about his life. Two important themes of the book are his early rebellions and his consequent restlessness, travel, and exposure to other peoples and cultures.

In *Yet Being Someone Other* van der Post recounts the story of his 1926 trip to Japan, and the trip he and Plomer made by train throughout the country. Van der Post describes the people, shrines, a *Noh* theater piece, and other aspects of Japanese culture in detail. Rebellion against his family's expectations and South African prejudice led van der Post to the experience of traveling and learning about another culture.

Back in Durban, van der Post writes, he found himself changed, his perspective altered by the voyage to Japan, and he narrates his beginning the trips between Africa and England that were to continue for most of his life, meeting in England many writers of the time and writing articles, and trying to become a writer himself. He describes his wartime service in Africa, and how he was asked to go to Indonesia in December of 1941. There, on the slopes of Mount Djaja-Sempoer in 1942, he found himself surrounded by Japanese soldiers. Certain he was about to be killed, he suddenly blurted out, "Would you please condescend to be so kind as to wait an honourable moment?" in perfect Japanese–which he had been taught years earlier by the *Canada Maru*'s Captain Mori–so that he was taken captive instead. Van der Post seems to see these events as more than a series of coincidences, but rather, a pattern like destiny, which provides retrospective justification for some of the decisions he made and actions he took earlier in his life.

Far from being simply "a story of a special relationship with the sea," as van der Post terms it, *Yet Being Someone Other* provides the reader with much information important to an understanding of this writer. Brian Martin, reviewing the book in the *New Statesman* (14 January 1983), found that not only had van der Post led a "remarkable life," but that "his writing about it is visionary and lyrical." He described *Yet Being Someone Other* as "a long, elegant book which demands leisure to be fully appreciated."

The act of remembering continues in van der Post's contribution to Jane Taylor's 1984 book, *Testament to the Bushmen,* the essay "Witness to a Last Will of Man." Van der Post had inspired and encouraged Taylor to produce a television series on the Bushmen, and this book was pub-

Van der Post with a praying mantis (photograph by Jonathan Stedall)

lished in conjunction with the airing of Taylor's documentary. In addition to writing the essay that constitutes the last fourth of the book, van der Post agreed to narrate the programs. "Witness to a Last Will of Man" is a somewhat rambling essay, in which van der Post reiterates many of his ideas about the Bushmen. Once again, he laments the destruction of the Bushman civilization and its values, and he denounces the superficiality, materialism, and rootlessness or estrangement of modern culture and modern man. He expresses again his conviction that the Bushmen represent the primitive in all humans and that they live "on as a ghost within ourselves."

Testament to the Bushmen is well illustrated, and Taylor's part of the book updates van der Post's earlier books. Although van der Post's essay adds little that is new, he sums up his reflections on the Bushmen well, writing that the "essence of this being, I believe, was his sense of belonging: belonging to nature, the universe, life and his own humanity."

A Walk with a White Bushman: Laurens van der Post in Conversation with Jean-Marc Pottiez (1986) had its origins in a series of wide-ranging conversations van der Post had between 1982 and 1985 with Pottiez, who originally intended to broadcast the interviews on French radio or television. He decided to transcribe and publish them instead, and van der Post agreed to edit them. The resulting text, with short queries or interjections by Pottiez and long passages by van der Post, recaptures the sense of the original conversations as van der Post discourses on almost every topic he had considered in his long life.

About Blady: A Pattern Out of Time (1991) is overtly and frankly digressive, and it is far from clear where van der Post intends to take the reader. The book as a whole is an exploration and meditation on "that one-ness of life we are meant to share," and is shaped by a tracing out of insights or lines, which van der Post argues extend throughout a person's life and suddenly, inexorably, achieve a significant pattern. In this respect, it bears a similarity to *Yet Being Someone Other*.

Turning to a single narrative line in the last part of the book, van der Post begins to draw the various threads together as he tells of a visit he paid to friends in Spain. As van der Post and the couple are driving past a farmer's field, the wife, devoted to horses, sees a horse plowing a field and recognizes his potential as a jumper. She purchases the horse, Blady, from the farmer and undertakes to train him.

The climax of the book is at a fiesta in Castellona. Here, van der Post's skills as a travel writer become most prominent, as he describes the small city at fiesta time, the hotel where the visiting nobility and the horse fanatics gather, and a bullfight. Toward the end of the fiesta, tension builds as the woman and Blady compete in a series of races over several days. The tension, as well as the whole series of problems van der Post has raised and themes he has traced, reaches a resolution in the last gathering of the guests in the hotel dining room, where "the Baron" presides with sensitivity, understanding, and nobility.

Of the three essays that comprise *The Voice of the Thunder,* published in 1993, two were previously published. Van der Post's essay in *Testament to the Bushmen* appears here, retitled "The Great Memory," while the essay "The Great and the Little Memory" of the 1988 republication of *The Lost World of the Kalahari* appears as "The Little Memory." The first essay in the collection, "The Other Journey," is a heretofore unpublished explication of an Odyssean pattern in the unconscious of all human beings. Van der Post finds that the symbolic significance of the journey Teiresias prophesied Odysseus would take after his return to Ithaca illuminated his own life and that events in his own life illuminated the Odyssean pattern: "this epic of individuation and search for wholeness in individual man." In the course of his discussion, van der Post deplores contemporary society's loss of an historical sense and indifference to history, the degeneration of language, and modern man's loss of contact with "the image-making part of himself."

Published in 1994, *Feather Fall* is an anthology of passages from van der Post's fiction and nonfiction writing, edited by Jean-Marc Pottiez and Jane Bedford and arranged thematically in twelve chapters. The passages in *Feather Fall* range in length from a sentence taken from *The Hunter and the Whale* or *Yet Being Someone Other* to the entire essay against racial prejudice van der Post wrote for *The Realist* in 1929 and the previously unpublished letter of 1989 to Hioaki Mori paying tribute to his recently deceased father, Commander Katsue Mori.

Many of van der Post's observations and much of his wisdom and insight are of great value, and he shared them freely. Pottiez notes in a brief biographical sketch at the beginning of *Feather Fall* that "He has always been discreet about his confidential role as a political and personal adviser, but the services he has given to the public life of his country were recognized with a Knighthood in the New Year's Honours List of 1981."

A close confidant of former British prime minister Margaret Thatcher, van der Post was also called a "guru" or "mentor" of Charles, the Prince of Wales, with whom he traveled to Africa for a five-day retreat in the Kalahari in 1987. Earlier, van der Post served as godfather to Prince William. In his judicious review of *A Walk with a White Bushman* for *The Spectator* (15 November 1986), Colin Welch noted that van der Post "is certainly a man who seeks influence," and who "could be ridiculed as self-important, officious, thrusting, interfering." The tone of the self-important guru or of the prophet often intrudes into van der Post's writing, particularly in his late works, although, as Welch also noted, through the "dark impenetrable swirling fogs of words" that comprise van der Post's prose, also come flashes of revelation, which "momentarily illuminate for us vast tracts of unfamiliar landscape."

Laurens van der Post died in his London home on 15 December 1996, two days after his ninetieth birthday. His autobiographical account of his experience in Indonesia immediately following World War II, *The Admiral's Baby,* was published in October of 1996. Van der Post had lived long enough to see the dismantling of the apartheid system in South Africa with the elections of 1994. The basic apartheid laws were repealed in 1991–the same year in which his family home in South Africa, where he was born, was declared a national monument by the South African government.

Interview:

Roy Newquist, "Laurens van der Post," in his *Counterpoint* (Chicago: Rand McNally, 1964), pp. 603–612.

References:

Isadore Lewis Baker, *Laurens van der Post: Venture to the Interior* (Bath, U.K.: Brodie, 1963);

Frederic I. Carpenter, *Laurens van der Post* (New York: Twayne, 1969);

Mark Cocker, *Loneliness and Time: The Story of British Travel Writing* (New York: Pantheon, 1992), pp. 72–95; 135–139, 154;

Cyril Kemp, *Notes on Van der Post's* Venture to the Interior *and* The Lost World of the Kalahari (London: Methuen, 1980);

Ezekiel Mphahlele, *The African Image* (London: Faber & Faber, 1962), pp. 128–129;

Richard Peck, "The Liberal Tradition in South African Writing: Alan Paton and Laurens van der Post," in his *A Morbid Fascination: White Prose and Politics in Apartheid South Africa,* Contributions to the Study of World Literature, no. 78 (Westport, Conn.: Greenwood Press, 1997), pp. 93–107.

Gavin Young

(24 April 1928 -   )

Craig Loomis
Sacramento City College

BOOKS: *Return to the Marshes: Life with the Marsh Arabs of Iraq* (London: Collins, 1977);

Iraq: Land of Two Rivers (London: Collins, 1980);

Slow Boats to China (London: Hutchinson, 1981); republished as *Halfway around the World: An Improbable Journey* (New York: Random House, 1981);

Slow Boats Home (London: Hutchinson, 1985; New York: Random House, 1985);

Worlds Apart: Travels in War and Peace (London: Hutchinson, 1987);

Beyond Lion Rock: The Story of Cathay Pacific Airways (London: Hutchinson, 1988);

In Search of Conrad (London: Hutchinson, 1991);

From Sea to Shining Sea: A Present-Day Journey through America's Past (London: Hutchinson, 1995);

A Wavering Grace: A Vietnamese Family in War and Peace (London: Viking, 1997);

Eye on the World (London: Viking, 1998).

OTHER: Asterisk [R. J. Fletcher], *Isles of Illusion: Letters from the South Seas,* edited by Bohun Lynch, introduction by Young (London: Century/Hutchinson, 1986);

Lucas Bridges, *Uttermost Part of the Earth,* introduction by Young (London: Century, 1987);

Indonesia: A Voyage through the Archipelago, text by Edward Behr, captions by Paul Zach, foreword by Young (Paris: Millet Weldon Owen, 1990; London: Collins, 1990);

"A Search for the Soul of Malaysia," in *Malaysia, Heart of Southeast Asia* (Singapore: Archipelago Press, 1991), pp. 92–107;

Paul Bowles by His Friends, edited by Gary Pulsifer, essay by Young (London: Peter Owen, 1992), pp. 153–156;

Joseph Conrad, *Lord Jim,* introduction by Young (London: Folio Society, 1996).

Gavin Young (photograph by Hubert Van Es)

As they neared Karachi, Pakistan, the *nakhoda* (captain) of the launch, Ghani Adam, turned to Gavin Young and asked, "Why do you travel with us on *Al Raza* when you can fly?" Young says that he could have answered by quoting Graham Greene ("the universal desire to see a little further, before the surrender to old age and the blank certitude of death") or Rudyard Kipling ("For to admire an' for to see, / For to be'old this world so wide"). Instead, he said simply, "To meet you." This anecdote from *Slow Boats to China* (1981) captures Young's essence as a journalist and travel writer: it is this interest in people that makes his works so readable, entertaining, and instructive.

Gavin David Young was born in London on 24 April 1928. His father, army Lt. Col. Gavin David Young, was an avid swimmer, yachtsman, cricketer, rugby player, and horseman whose love of the sea

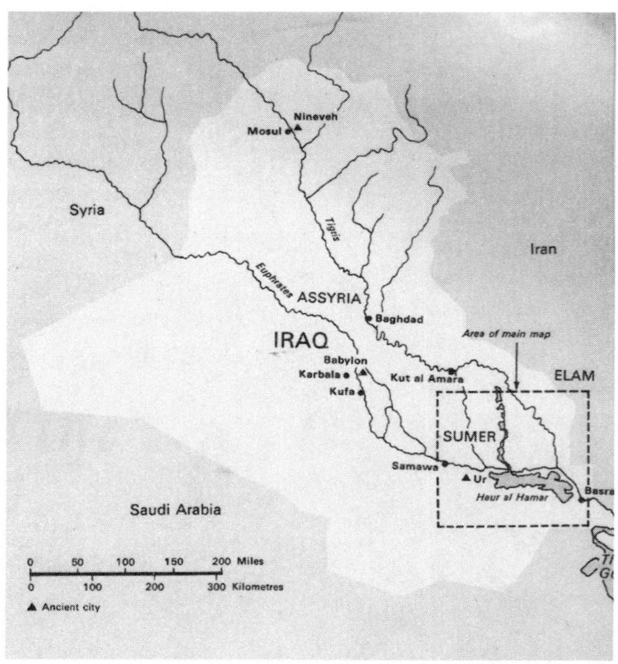

Map in Young's Return to the Marshes *(1977), showing the area inhabited by the Marsh Arabs with whom he lived from 1952 to 1954*

played an important role in shaping Young's quest for adventure and exploration. Young's mother, Daphne, was the daughter of a longtime member of Parliament for Monmouth, South Wales, Sir Leolin Forestier-Walker, Bt.

As a boy Young spent many summers in the small harbor town of Bude on the infamous Wrecker's Coast of north Cornwall, where his father, who was of Scottish descent, had been raised. Young was mesmerized by the sea, with its promise of adventure and travel. He was even more entranced by the books he found in his grandmother's attic by such authors as Kipling, Robert Louis Stevenson, Jack London, Frederick Marryat, R. M. Ballantyne, and Joseph Conrad. Here was food for his boyhood dreams.

After finishing his studies at Rugby School in 1946 Young joined the army as a lieutenant in the Welsh Guards; he was stationed in Palestine in 1947–1948. After his military service, which he thoroughly enjoyed, he enrolled at Trinity College, Oxford. Graduating in 1950 with an M.A. in modern history, he took a position as a clerk at £5 a week with Ralli Brothers, an international trading firm. He was soon sent to the company's branch office in the port city of Basra in southern Iraq.

Young immediately threw himself into the new culture, taking Arabic lessons and reading the works of T. E. Lawrence, Bertram Thomas, and Gertrude Bell. He conceived the idea of riding a camel across the Arabian Peninsula from the Persian Gulf to the Red Sea. About this time, however, he met Wilfred Thesiger, one of the last of the great Arabian travelers and Arabists. Thesiger convinced Young that the political situation at the time made his camel journey across Arabia impractical and directed his attention to the Ma'dan, or Marsh Arabs, who inhabit some six thousand square miles of marshland in the vicinity of the Tigris and Euphrates rivers in southern Iraq. Young's fascination with the Marsh Arabs became so all-consuming that he left Ralli Brothers in 1952 and went to live with the Ma'dan. In 1954 he moved to southwestern Saudi Arabia to stay with the Bedouins; while there he became involved in the United Nations–sponsored Desert Locust Control project. During his time in Iraq and Saudi Arabia he wrote occasional articles for periodicals such as *The Royal Asian Magazine.*

In 1956 Young took a part-time position with Radio Morocco's English Service in Rabat. Around this time he became friends with Ian Fleming, the creator of James Bond, who advised him to go into journalism. In 1959 Young was hired as a Tunis-based stringer on North Africa and the Middle East for *The Observer* (London). "I fell into journalism as a drunken man falls into a pond," he says in the preface to *Worlds Apart: Travels in War and Peace* (1987). Within six months he was promoted to foreign correspondent, which greatly enlarged the scope of his reporting duties. He covered the Nagaland revolt in India in 1961 and was stationed in New York City in 1962–1963 and in Paris in 1967. He spent several years covering the Vietnam War and was there during the Tet Offensive of 1968. In 1971 he shared the Journalist of the Year citation of the IPC National Press Awards with Peter Hazelhurst of *The Times* (London) for his coverage of the Indo-Pakistan War.

Young had never forgotten the marshes of southern Iraq, but it was not until 1973 that he was able to travel there again. The visit was the basis for his first book, *Return to the Marshes: Life with the Marsh Arabs of Iraq* (1977), with photographs by Nik Wheeler. *Return to the Marshes* exemplifies Young's ability to capture the essence of a place through a mixture of history, observation, and commentary. He first takes an historical look at the Ma'dan, starting with the Sumerians, who arrived in the region before 3,000 B.C., and winding his way through a long list of kingdoms, regimes, and invasions. Aside from an occasional report or letter from a soldier, explorer, or merchant such as Col. Francis Chesney, J. Baillie Fraser, and Sir Austen Henry Layard, the Marsh Arabs were virtually unknown to Europeans until the British arrived in 1915. A proud, independent people divided into tribes led by sheikhs, the Ma'dan use the marsh reeds to build their homes and feed their livestock; their only means of transportation is by boat. Young reports on their wedding ceremonies, their methods for settling neighborhood feuds, their pig-hunting expeditions, and their warfare rituals. Having been away since the mid 1950s, he sees many changes: there is a new sugar factory and a new school; the Ma'dan have access to ice and better food; and their taxes are lower. Young's personal tone and his willingness to mingle with the Ma'dan and participate in their culture allow readers to know, respect, and care about a people most of them never knew existed. The book was not widely reviewed, but *The Economist* (24 July 1977) praised Young's personal, enthusiastic approach to his subject. In 1979 *Return to the Marshes* became the basis for a BBC documentary of the same title. Young wrote the script and appeared in this segment of *The World about Us* series.

Young's second book, *Iraq: Land of Two Rivers* (1980), an account of a journey through Mesopotamia, comments on almost every aspect of the country–its weather, food, schools, religious centers, even its barber shops. Young's intimate style is on display once again as he meets and talks with individual Iraqis. Thanks to Wheeler's photography, the land of the ancient cities of Babylon, Habbaniyah, and Samarra is captured in pictures as well as in words. Like Young's first book, *Iraq: Land of Two Rivers* was not widely reviewed, but most of those who did review it considered it the premier introductory book on Iraq.

Slow Boats to China, published in the United States as *Halfway around the World: An Improbable Journey* (1981), propelled Young into literary notoriety. His plan, he tells the reader, is to travel alone from Europe to China by sea, avoiding anything that resembles a tourist cruise or vacation package; he will take whatever vessel he can find that is headed in a generally eastward direction. Travel agents and shipping officials tell him that this ship-hopping project is impossible: booking one person on one ship would be difficult enough, but making arrangements for several different vessels is out of the question. This sort of bureaucratic denial only spurs him on: since they say that it cannot be done, he has to do it. His quest for information about travel to Asia brings him into contact with John Swire of Swire and Sons, one of the biggest trading and shipping conglomerates in the Far East. The meeting leads to a lasting friendship between the two men.

Equipped with notebooks, pens, two cameras, and reading material that includes Conrad's *Mirror of the Sea: Memories and Impressions* (1906) and *Under Western Eyes* (1911) and Ford Madox Ford's *Memories and Impressions: A Study in Atmospheres* (1906), Young takes a four-month leave of absence from *The Observer* in August 1979, certain that he has given himself more than enough time to complete his expedition. He selects Athens as the starting point for his journey. On the first leg he has to endure politics and bureaucratic red tape–endless waiting, postponements, and cancellations confront him at every port, especially in the Middle East. During his stopover in Cyprus he offers the reader a short history of the Turkish-Greek conflict that has divided the island since 1974. He captures the atmosphere of the places through which he travels largely by describing the people he encounters: the nonsensical hotel receptionists in Port Said; the friendly, carefree ship captain in the Red Sea; the arrogant Saudi port officer; and the slow-moving but efficient crewmen in Dubai.

The village of Saigal in the marshes of southern Iraq (photograph by Nik Wheeler)

The second part of the book, "Dubai to Singapore," is a collage of heat and humanity; of boat engines that stall, sputter, and break down; and of Western expatriates–in every hotel lobby and bar in almost every port there seems to be at least one leftover American hippie, German drifter, or British alcoholic. Young talks with them, jokes with them, and buys them drinks. There is beauty, but there is also danger. The launch Young takes to the Maldives is almost swamped in a sudden storm. Later, as he crosses the Sulu Sea

Young getting into a canoe for a shooting expedition during his return visit to the Iraqi marshes in 1973 (photograph by Nik Wheeler)

headed for the Philippines, his boat is boarded by Moro pirates, but Young avoids robbery by giving the pirates Polaroid snapshots of themselves.

A mood of homecoming permeates the last section of the book as Young approaches Southeast Asia, for much of his journalistic activity has been centered in Vietnam, Cambodia, Thailand, and Indonesia. In Hong Kong he and some old drinking and writing buddies relive their experiences in Asia, and it is not long before they turn to the Vietnam War. They recall the journalists and photographers who were killed, and Young tells the story of the young South Vietnamese soldier who died in his arms. Eight months and twenty-three vessels–including a Greek island steamer, a Turkish motor ship, a French freighter, a Persian Gulf tugboat, an Indian schooner, and a Hong Kong hydrofoil–after leaving Athens, Young reaches his destination: Canton.

Most critics thought *Slow Boats to China* an intelligent blend of history, memoir, and scholarship. Young's energetic yet informal and relaxed style was also applauded. In *TLS: The Times Literary Supplement* (27 November 1981) the travel writer Jan Morris said, "Young's evident gift for friendship gives the book a curious sense of running comradeship." Some reviewers, however, found the book, although well written, cluttered with remembrances and good-old-boy stories.

Because of the Iran-Iraq war, Young was unable to return to the marshes of southern Iraq until March 1984. He found the marshland devastated by the war and many of his friends maimed or dead.

Slow Boats Home (1985) describes Young's journey from China back to England, which takes him the rest of the way around the world. Still insisting on taking the next vessel that is headed eastward, no matter what its size or condition, he leaves Hong Kong and hop-

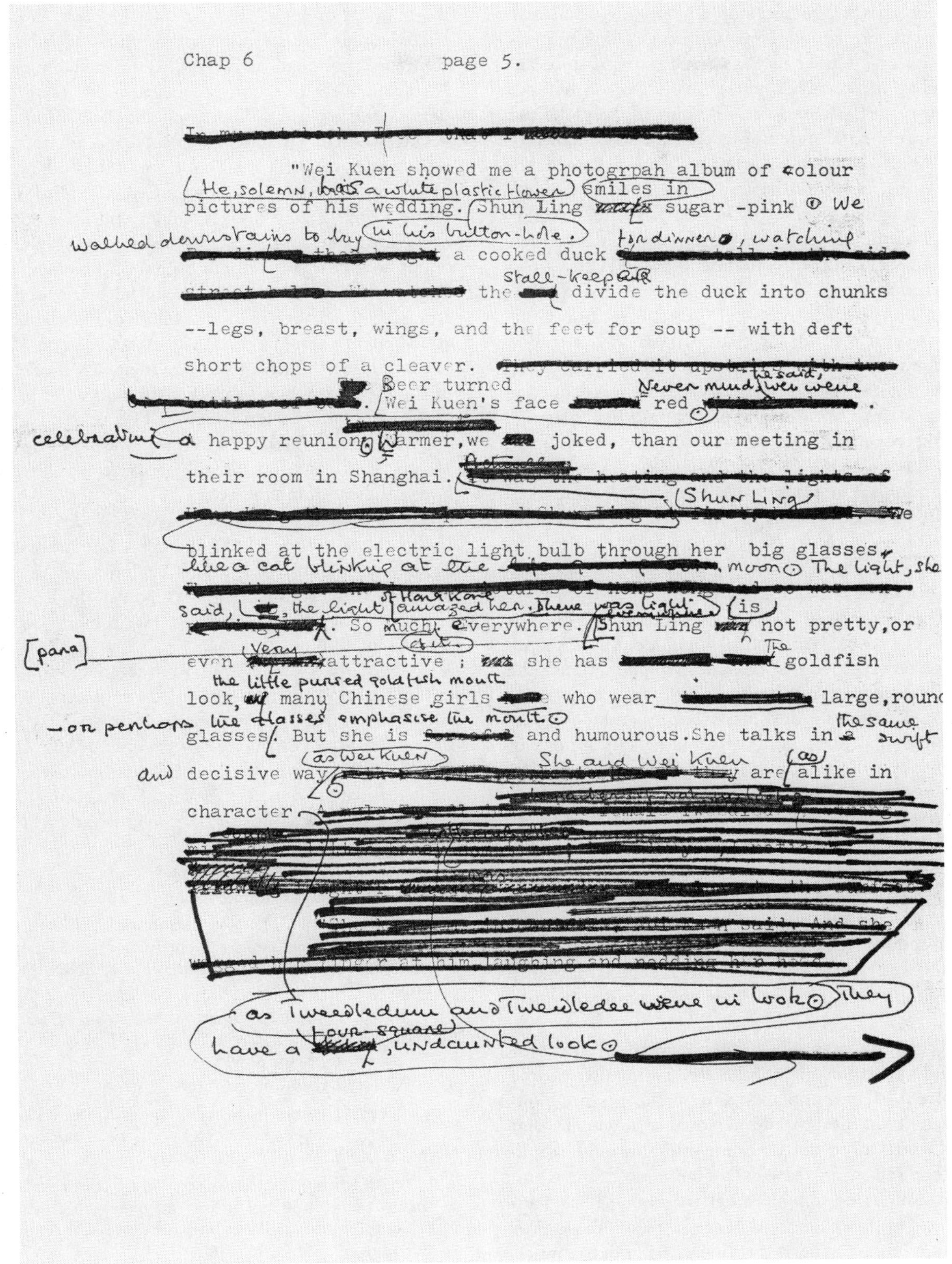
Chap 6 page 5.

"Wei Kuen showed me a photogrpah album of colour pictures of his wedding. Shun Ling sugar -pink a cooked duck the divide the duck into chunks --legs, breast, wings, and the feet for soup -- with deft short chops of a cleaver. Beer turned Wei Kuen's face red . a happy reunion, warmer, we joked, than our meeting in their room in Shanghai.

blinked at the electric light bulb through her big glasses. So much everywhere. Shun Ling not pretty, or even attractive ; she has goldfish look, many Chinese girls who wear large, round glasses. But she is and humourous. She talks in swift and decisive way are alike in character.

Page from the typescript for Young's 1985 book, Slow Boats Home *(Collection of Gavin Young)*

scotches across the Pacific, stopping at New Britain and Bougainville in Papua New Guinea, Viti Levu and Ovalau in Fiji, Upolu in Western Samoa, Tahiti, and Nuku Hiva in French Polynesia. This part of the book is the story of Paradise Lost, of a part of the globe that has been robbed of much of its charm and romance by World War II and the "progress" that followed. He goes on to South America, visiting with Chilean marines assigned to one of the most isolated military outposts on the planet, Cape Horn Island. From Argentina he crosses the South Atlantic to South Africa–stopping at the Falkland Islands shortly after the end of the April–June 1982 war between Argentina and Great Britain–then travels up the coast of West Africa to Portugal, Spain, France, and, finally, England.

As before, among the necessities he has packed in his metal case is an ample supply of reading material, including Stevenson's *The Master of Ballantrae* (1889) and *Vailima Letters* (1895), Herman Melville's *Typee* (1846), Jack London's *The Cruise of the Snark* (1911), and Paul Gauguin's *Intimate Journals* (1921), translated by Van Wyck Brooks. As he makes his way from port to port and from country to country, he quotes relevant passages from these and other books.

The characters Young encounters during his Hong Kong–to–England journey include tough Australian managers of sordid Melanesian plantations, the soft-spoken prime minister of Fiji, an overzealous Mormon missionary, and many happy-go-lucky tourists, soldiers, drifters, and vagabonds. His modes of transportation range from an uncomfortable containership to a luxurious Russian cruise liner filled with Germans who cannot stop talking about World War II. As in *Slow Boats to China,* there are irritants, misadventures, and delays–always delays. Occasionally, there is real danger, as when he is stranded off the coast of Brazil in a South African ship with a Zulu crew that is on the brink of mutiny. Given his unorthodox traveling methods, however, and the unsavory types he continually encounters, Young's experiences are remarkably positive.

Reviewers generally praised *Slow Boats Home* for its friendly, relaxed style; for the way Young uses people to capture the flavor of places; and for the mixture of literature, politics, history, and personal commentary that he works into his narrative. Some critics found his optimistic tone refreshing, especially compared to the whining and condescension of travel writers such as Paul Theroux. On the other hand, there were still those who complained that Young was trying to cram in too much material.

Published in 1987, *Worlds Apart: Travels in War and Peace* is a collection of Young's articles; most were written for *The Observer. Worlds Apart* takes readers on a tour of the many "hot spots" and personalities that Young has encountered during his more than thirty years as a foreign correspondent. In early 1961 he visits little-known Nagaland, a swath of jungle wedged in between the borders of Burma and China in northeastern India, as the Nagas struggle for independence; he is in Bangladesh during its successful 1971 war for independence from Pakistan; he enters the gang-infested Walled City in Hong Kong. Young finds Vietnam and its people especially intriguing. Some of his most moving pieces are about how Hue, the ancient capital of the country, and, in particular, a Vietnamese family he befriended there, struggled to survive the war. There are also interviews with Cuban president Fidel Castro and Prime Minister Ian Smith of Rhodesia (today Zimbabwe), a celebration of the mystery writer John Buchan, and an exploration of the gaudy and materialistic side of southern California ("Getting 'Laid Back' in Hollywood"). The same year *Worlds Apart* came out, Young became a fellow of the Royal Society of Literature.

Young's next book, *Beyond Lion Rock: The Story of Cathay Pacific Airways* (1988), is a corporate history of the airline controlled by his friends Sir John and Sir Adrian Swire. In 1989 Young became a fellow of the Royal Geographical Society of London. He retired from *The Observer* in 1990.

In Search of Conrad (1991) retraces Conrad's travels in the East and unveils some of the real people, places, and events that are fictionalized in such works as *Almayer's Folly: A Story of an Eastern River* (1895), *Lord Jim* (1900), and "The Secret Sharer" (1910). In the weed-choked Bidadari cemetery in Singapore, Young asks the caretaker to direct him to the grave of the "real" Lord Jim:

> "The writer, Lord Jim?"
>
> "Well," I said, "he was a character in Joseph Conrad's novel of that name. . . . The man who was the original Lord Jim–the real Lord Jim–is buried here. At least I hope so."
>
> Mr. de Souza had not read *Lord Jim,* but he remembered now that he had seen the feature film of the novel: "Who was the actor now?"
>
> "Peter O'Toole," I answered.
>
> "Peter O'Toole! Now, we know what we're looking for–the grave of Peter O'Toole! We'll try all the harder to find the tomb, Mr. Young!"
>
> With renewed vigour we set about clearing grass and shrubs. And suddenly it was all over. There it was, calf-deep in grass and needing to be swept: the grave of Lord Jim.
>
> Augustine Podmore Williams
>
> Born 22nd May 1852
>
> Died 17th April 1916
>
> "Thy Will be Done"

Young goes to the strip of sand where Lord Jim was last seen alive; he travels down the Berau River in Borneo, which became the Patusan in Conrad's fiction; he stands on the grave of Charles Olmeijer, the model for Almayer, in Surabaya, Indonesia; and he writes about Capt. William Lingard, a well-known personality in Singapore at the end of the nineteenth century on whom Conrad closely modeled Capt. Tom Lingard, Almayer's boss at the trading post. Part journal and part literary detective work, *In Search of Conrad* shared the Thomas Cook Travel Book Award for 1992 with Norman Lewis's *A Goddess in the Stones.*

In *From Sea to Shining Sea: A Present-Day Journey through America's Past* (1995) Young again uses literature to direct his travels. He begins in Sag Harbor on Long Island in search of the lost whaling life portrayed in Melville's *Moby-Dick* (1851). In Georgia he follows Gen. William Tecumseh Sherman's route to the sea during the Civil War, quoting extensively from Sherman's memoirs and papers. In his chapter on San Antonio he retells the story of Davy Crockett and the Battle of the Alamo, adding a humorous portrait of Antonio López de Santa Anna, the Mexican general who defeated the American defenders of the fortified mission in 1836. Young then travels to Los Angeles: "To me–to a great many people, I suppose–Los Angeles means Raymond Chandler and his private-eye hero, Philip Marlowe, one of the first and toughest of that breed." He continues up the California coast to Carmel and Monterey, John Steinbeck country. In Montana, Young visits the site of the 1876 Battle of the Little Bighorn, reporting what historians have written about the event and about Gen. George Armstrong Custer. *From Sea to Shining Sea* ends with Young in the Yukon, seeking guidance in the works of Jack London.

From Sea to Shining Sea received mixed reviews. His eye for detail and ability to sum up a person, place, or event in a few words continued to receive praise, but some critics were disappointed that Young felt the need to review the more-familiar scenes of American history when so much remained untapped. The reviewer for *The Economist* (6 May 1995) complained, "Once Young has chanced on something that tickles him (such as the fact that William Tecumseh Sherman liked Dickens, or that Davy Crockett called his rifle Betsy), he repeats it again and again."

A Wavering Grace: A Vietnamese Family in War and Peace (1997) is the story of the family of Madame Bong, with whom Young stayed in Hue during the 1968 Tet Offensive. He describes the changes he found in Madame Bong, her family, and her country on his return visits to Vietnam in 1985 and 1995, as well as the assistance he provided to younger members of the family in immigrating to the United States. In 1998 he published *Eye on the World,* a collection of his photographs and reminiscences from his five decades of wandering.

Gavin Young is constantly searching for glimpses of a tough, individualistic way of life that has largely been lost in the fast-paced, high-tech modern world. His writing has always been concerned with reporting sightings of this rugged spirit, whether in the marshes of southern Iraq, the crowded backstreets of Saigon, the barren wasteland of Cape Horn, or the glitz of Los Angeles.

British Travel Writing, 1940–1997

Alexander, Michael. *Offbeat in Asia: An Excursion.* London: Weidenfeld & Nicolson, 1960.

Allen, Benedict. *Hunting the Gugu: In Search of the Lost Ape-Men of Sumatra.* London: Macmillan, 1989.

Allen. *Into the Crocodile Nest: A Journey Inside New Guinea.* London: Macmillan, 1987.

Allen. *Mad White Giant: A Journey to the Heart of the Amazon Jungle.* London: Macmillan, 1985.

Allen. *The Proving Grounds: A Journey Through the Interior of New Guinea and Australia.* London: HarperCollins, 1991.

Allen. *The Skeleton Coast: A Journey Through the Namib Desert.* London: BBC Books, 1997.

Allen. *Through Jaguar Eyes: Crossing the Amazon Basin.* London: HarperCollins, 1994.

Andrews, Kevin. *Athens.* London: Phoenix House, 1967.

Andrews. *The Flight of Ikaros: A Journey in Greece.* London: Weidenfeld & Nicolson, 1959. Republished as *The Flight of Ikaros: Travels in Greece during a Civil War.* Harmondsworth, U.K.: Penguin, 1984.

Asher, Michael. *A Desert Dies.* London: Viking, 1986.

Asher. *Impossible Journey: Two Against the Sahara.* London: Viking, 1988.

Asher. *In Search of the Forty Days Road.* Harlow, U.K.: Longman, 1984.

Asher. *The Last of the Bedu: In Search of the Myth.* London: Viking, 1996.

Balfour, Patrick, Baron Kinross. *Europa Minor: Journeys in Coastal Turkey.* London: Murray, 1956.

Balfour. *The Innocents at Home.* London: Murray, 1959.

Balfour. *The Orphaned Realm: Journeys in Cyprus.* London: Marshall, 1951.

Balfour. *Portrait of Egypt.* London: Deutsch, 1966.

Balfour. *Portrait of Greece.* London: Parrish, 1956.

Balfour. *Within the Taurus: Journey in Asiatic Turkey.* London: Murray, 1954.

Banham, Reyner. *Scenes in America Deserta.* London: Thames & Hudson, 1982.

Barley, Nigel. *The Duke of Puddle Dock: Travels in the Footsteps of Stamford Raffles.* London: Viking, 1991.

Barley. *The Innocent Anthropologist: Notes from a Mud Hut.* London: British Museum, 1983.

Barley. *Not a Hazardous Sport.* London: Viking, 1988.

Barley. *A Plague of Caterpillars: A Return to the African Bush.* Harmondsworth, U.K.: Viking, 1986.

Bass, Catriona. *Inside the Treasure House: A Time in Tibet.* London: Gollancz, 1990.

Beaton, Sir Cecil. *Chinese Album.* London: Batsford, 1946.

Beaton. *The Face of the World: An International Scrapbook of People and Places.* London: Weidenfeld & Nicolson, 1957.

Beaton. *Far East.* London: Batsford, 1945.

Beaton. *India Album.* London: Batsford, 1946.

Beaton. *Japanese.* London: Weidenfeld & Nicolson, 1959.

Beaton. *Near East.* London: Batsford, 1943.

Bedford, Sybille. *The Sudden View: A Mexican Journey.* London: Gollancz, 1953.

Bell, Gavin. *In Search of Tusitala: Travels in the Pacific After Robert Louis Stevenson.* London: Picador, 1994.

Bibby, Geoffrey. *Looking for Dilmun.* London: Collins, 1970.

Birkett, Dea. *Serpent in Paradise.* London: Picador, 1997.

Blair, Lawrence, and Lorne Blair. *Ring of Fire: Exploring the Last Remote Places of the World.* London: Bantam, 1988.

Blanch, Lesley. *Under Lilac-Bleeding Star: Travels and Travellers.* London: Murray, 1963.

Bonington, Chris. *Annapura, South Face.* London: Cassell, 1971.

Bonington. *Chris Bonington's Lake District.* Skipton, U.K.: Dalesman, 1997.

Bonington. *Everest, South West Face.* London: Hodder & Stoughton, 1973.

Bonington. *Everest, the Hard Way.* London: Hodder & Stoughton, 1976.

Bonington. *Everest the Unclimbed Ridge.* London: Hodder & Stoughton, 1983.

Bonington. *Kongur, China's Elusive Summit.* London: Hodder & Stoughton, 1982.

Bonington. *Mountaineer: Thirty Years of Climbing on the World's Greatest Peaks.* Leicester, U.K.: Diadem, 1989.

Bor, Eleanor. *Adventures of a Botanist's Wife.* London & New York: Hurst & Blackett, 1952.

Bordewich, Fergus M. *Cathay: A Journey in Search of Old China.* London: Grafton, 1991.

Bowen, Elizabeth. *A Time in Rome.* London: Longmans, 1960.

Bower, Ursula Graham. *The Hidden Land.* London: Murray, 1953.

Bower. *Naga Path.* London: Murray, 1950.

Brenan, Gerald. *The Face of Spain.* London: Turnstile Press, 1950.

Brenan. *South from Granada.* London: Hamilton, 1957.

Brook, Elaine. *In Search of Shambhala.* London: Cape, 1996.

Brook. *Land of the Snow Lion.* London: Cape, 1987.

Brook, and Julie Donnelly. *The Windhorse.* London: Cape, 1986.

Brooke, Sylvia. *Queen of the Headhunters.* London: Sidgwick & Jackson, 1970.

Burns, Jimmy. *Beyond the Silver River: South American Encounter.* London: Bloomsbury, 1989.

Burns. *Spain: A Literary Companion.* London: Murray, 1994.

Buruma, Ian. *God's Dust: A Modern Asian Journey.* London: Cape, 1989.

Cameron, James. *An Indian Summer.* London: Macmillan, 1974.

Cameron. *Mandarin Red: A Journey Behind the Bamboo Curtain.* London: Joseph, 1955.

Cameron. *Touch of the Sun.* London: Witherby, 1950.

Carrington, Dorothy. *Granite Island: A Portrait of Corsica.* London: Longman, 1971.

Carrington, Richard. *East from Tunis: A Record of Travels on the Northern Coast of Africa.* London: Chatto & Windus, 1957.

Carrington, Richard. *Great National Parks.* London: Weidenfeld & Nicolson, 1967.

Carrington, Richard. *The Tears of Isis: The Story of a New Journey from the Mouth to the Source of the River Nile.* London: Chatto & Windus, 1959.

Carson, Anthony. *Carson Was Here.* London: Methuen, 1962.

Carson. *On to Timbuctoo.* London: Methuen, 1958.

Carson. *Poor Man's Mimosa; or, Journeys in Modern Europe.* London: Methuen, 1962.

Carson. *A Train to Tarragona.* London: Methuen, 1957.

Carson. *Travels Near and Far Out.* New York: Pantheon, 1963.

Chapman, F. Spencer. *Helvellyn to Himalaya: Including an Account of the First Ascent of Chomolhari.* London: Chatto & Windus, 1940.

Chapman. *The Jungle is Neutral.* London: Chatto & Windus, 1949.

Chapman. *Lightest Africa.* London: Chatto & Windus, 1955.

Chapman. *Living Dangerously.* London: Chatto & Windus, 1953.

Chetwode, Penelope. *Kulu: The End of the Habitable World.* London: Murray, 1972.

Chetwode. *Two Middle-aged Ladies in Andalusia.* London: Murray, 1963.

Chichester, Francis. *Alone Across the Atlantic.* London: Allen & Unwin, 1961.

Chichester. *Along the Clipper Way.* London: Hodder & Stoughton, 1966.

Chichester. *Gipsy Moth Circles the World.* London: Hodder & Stoughton, 1967.

Christmas, Linda. *The Ribbon and the Ragged Square: An Australian Journey.* Harmondsworth, U.K.: Viking, 1986.

Cohn, Nik. *The Heart of the World.* London: Chatto & Windus, 1992.

Coleridge, Nicholas. *Around the World in 78 Days.* London: Heinemann, 1984.

Conrad, Peter. *Down Home: Revisiting to Tasmania.* London: Chatto & Windus, 1988.

Conrad. *Where I Fell to Earth: A Life in Four Places.* London: Chatto & Windus, 1990.

Crane, Nicholas. *Atlas Biker: Mountainbiking in Morocco.* Sparkford, U.K.: Oxford Illustrated Press, 1990.

Crane. *Bicycles up Kilimanjaro.* Yeovil, U.K.: Oxford Illustrated Press, 1985.

Crane. *Clear Waters Rising: A Mountain Walk Across Europe.* London: Viking, 1996.

Crewe, Quentin. *In the Realms of Gold: Travels Through South America.* London: Joseph, 1989.

Crewe. *Touch the Happy Isles: A Journey Through the Caribbean.* London: Joseph, 1987.

Dalrymple, William. *City of Djinns: A Year in Delhi.* London: HarperCollins, 1993.

Dalrymple. *From the Holy Mountain: A Journey in the Shadow of Byzantium.* London: HarperCollins, 1997.

Dalrymple. *In Xanadu: A Quest.* London: Collins, 1989.

Daniels, Anthony. *Coups and Cocaine: Two Journeys in South America.* London: Murray, 1986.

Daniels. *Monrovia, Mon Amour: A Visit to Liberia.* London: Murray, 1992.

Daniels. *Sweet Waist of America: Journeys Around Guatemala.* London: Murray, 1990.

Daniels. *The Wilder Shores of Marx: Journeys in a Vanishing World.* London: Hutchinson, 1991.

Daniels. *Zanzibar to Timbuktu.* London: Murray, 1988.

Danziger, Nick. *Danziger's Adventures: From Miami to Kabul.* London: HarperCollins, 1992.

Danziger. *Danziger's Britain: A Journey to the Edge.* London: HarperCollins, 1996.

Danziger. *Danziger's Travels: Beyond Forbidden Frontiers.* London: Grafton, 1987.

Davidson, Basil. *Ghana: An African Portrait.* London: Gordon Fraser Gallery, 1976.

Davidson. *Turkestan Alive: New Travels in Chinese Central Asia.* London: Cape, 1957.

Davison, Ann. *By Gemini, or Marshmallows in the Salad . . . A Coast-wise Cruise from Miami to Miami.* London: Davies, 1962.

Davison. *Florida Junket: The Story of a Shoestring Cruise.* London: Davies, 1964.

Davison. *Home Was an Island.* London: Davies, 1952.

Davison. *Last Voyage: An Autobiographical Account of All That Led up to an Illicit Voyage and the Outcome Thereof.* London: Davies, 1951.

Davison. *My Ship Is So Small.* London: Davies, 1956.

Deacock, Antonia. *No Purdah in Padam: The Story of the Women's Overland Himalayan Expedition 1958.* London: Harrap, 1960.

Debenham, Frank. *Kalahari Sand.* London: Bell, 1953.

Dew, Josie. *Travels in a Strange State: Cycling Across the U.S.A.* London: Little, Brown, 1994.

Dew. *The Wind in My Wheels: Travel Tales from the Saddle.* London: Little, Brown, 1992.

Downer, Lesley. *On the Narrow Road to the Deep North: Journey Into a Lost Japan.* London: Cape, 1989.

Drysdale, Helena. *Alone Through China and Tibet.* London: Constable, 1986.

Drysdale. *Dancing with Death: A Journey to Zanzibar and Madagascar.* London: Hamilton, 1991.

Drysdale. *Looking for Gheorghe.* London: Sinclair-Stevenson, 1995. Republished as *Looking for George: Love and Death in Rumania.* London: Picador, 1996.

Dunsheath, Joyce. *Guest of the Soviets: Moscow and the Caucasus.* London: Constable, 1959.

Dunsheath, and Eleanor Baillie. *Afghan Quest: The Story of the Abinger Afghanistan Expedition.* London: Harrap, 1961.

Dunsheath, and others. *Mountains and Memsahibs. By the Members of the Abinger Himalayan Expedition, 1956.* London: Constable, 1958.

Durrell, Gerald. *The Aye-Aye and I: A Rescue Expedition to Madagascar.* London: HarperCollins, 1992.

Durrell. *The Bafut Beagles.* London: Hart-Davis, 1954.

Durrell. *Birds, Beasts, and Other Relatives*. London: Collins, 1969.

Durrell. *Gerald and Lee Durrell in Russia*. London: MacDonald, 1986.

Durrell. *My Family and Other Animals*. London: Hart-Davis, 1956.

Durrell. *The Overloaded Ark*. London: Faber, 1953.

Durrell. *Three Singles to Adventure*. London: Hart-Davis, 1954.

Durrell. *Two in the Bush*. London: Collins, 1966.

Durrell. *A Zoo in My Luggage*. London: Hart-Davis, 1960.

Dyson, John. *The South Seas Dream: An Adventure in Paradise*. London: Heinemann, 1982.

Edwards, Ted. *Beyond the Last Oasis: A Solo Walk in the Western Sahara*. London: Murray, 1985.

Edwards. *Fight the Wild Island: A Solo Walk Across Iceland*. London: Murray, 1986.

Fairfax, John. *Britannia: Rowing Alone Across the Atlantic: The Record of an Adventure*. New York: Simon & Schuster, 1971; London: Kimber, 1972.

Farson, Negley. *Behind God's Back*. London: Gollancz, 1940.

Farson. *Caucasian Journey*. London: Evans, 1951.

Farson. *Last Chance in Africa*. London: Gollancz, 1949.

Fawcett, Percy Harrison. *Exploration Fawcett,* edited by Brain Fawcett. London: Hutchinson, 1953.

Fenton, James. *All the Wrong Places: Adrift in the Politics of the Pacific Rim*. New York: Atlantic Monthly Press, 1988. Republished as *All the Wrong Places: Adrift in the Politics of Asia*. London & New York: Viking, 1989.

Fiennes, Sir Ranulph. *Atlantis in the Sands: The Search for the Lost City of Ubar*. London: Bloomsbury, 1992.

Fiennes. *The Feather Men*. London: Bloomsbury, 1991.

Fiennes. *The Headless Valley*. London: Hodder & Stoughton, 1972.

Fiennes. *Hell on Ice*. London: Hodder & Stoughton, 1979.

Fiennes. *Ice Fall in Norway*. London: Hodder & Stoughton, 1972.

Fiennes. *Living Dangerously: The Autobiography of Ranulph Fiennes*. London: Macmillan, 1987.

Fiennes. *Mind Over Matter: The Epic Crossing of the Antarctic Continent*. London: Sinclair-Stevenson, 1993.

Fiennes. *A Talent for Trouble*. London: Hodder & Stoughton, 1970.

Fiennes. *To the Ends of the Earth: Transglobal Expedition, 1979–82*. London: Hodder & Stoughton, 1983.

Forbes-Boyd, Eric. *Aegean Quest: A Search for Venetian Greece*. London: Dent, 1970.

Forbes-Boyd. *In Crusader Greece: A Tour of the Castles of the Morea*. London: Centaur Press, 1964.

Francis, Clare. *Come Hell or High Water*. London: Pelham Books, 1977.

Francis. *Come Wind or Weather*. London: Pelham Books, 1978.

Frater, Alexander. *Chasing the Monsoon*. London: Viking, 1990.

Frater. *Stopping-Train Britain: A Railway Odyssey*. London: Hodder & Stoughton, 1983.

Gebler, Carlo. *Driving Through Cuba: An East-West Journey.* London: Hamilton, 1988.

Gelder, Stuart, and Roma Gelder. *Long March to Freedom.* London: Hutchinson, 1962.

Gelder and Gelder. *Memories for a Chinese Grand-daughter.* London: Hutchinson, 1967.

Gelder and Gelder. *The Timely Rain: Travels in New Tibet.* London: Hutchinson, 1964.

Glazebrook, Philip. *Journey to Kars.* Harmondsworth, U.K.: Viking, 1984.

Glazebrook. *Journey to Khiva.* London: Harvill, 1992.

Golding, William. *An Egyptian Journal.* London & Boston: Faber & Faber, 1985.

Goodall, Jane (Baroness von Lawick-Goodall). *In the Shadow of Man.* London: Collins, 1971.

Goodall. *My Friends, the Wild Chimpanzees.* Washington, D.C.: National Geographical Society, 1967.

Goullart, Peter. *Forgotten Kingdom.* London: Murray, 1955.

Goullart. *The Monastery of Jade Mountain.* London: Murray, 1961.

Goullart. *Princes of the Black Bone: Life in the Tibetan Borderland.* London: Murray, 1959.

Graves, Robert. *Majorca Observed.* London: Cassell, 1965.

Grimble, Arthur. *A Pattern of Islands.* London: Murray, 1952.

Grimble. *Return to the Islands.* London: Murray, 1957.

Hamilton, Genesta. *A Stone's Throw: Travels from Africa in Six Decades.* London: Hutchinson, 1986.

Hampton, Charles, and Janie Hampton. *A Family Outing in Africa.* London: Macmillan, 1988.

Hanbury Tenison, Marika. *For Better, for Worse: To the Brazilian Jungles and Back Again.* London: Hutchinson, 1972.

Hanbury Tenison. *A Slice of Spice: Travels to the Indonesian Islands.* London: Hutchinson, 1974.

Hanbury-Tenison, Robin. *Mulu: The Rain Forest.* London: Weidenfeld & Nicolson, 1980.

Hanbury-Tenison. *A Pattern of Peoples: A Journey Among the Tribes of Indonesia's Outer Islands.* London: Angus & Robertson, 1975.

Hanbury-Tenison. *A Ride Along the Great Wall.* London: Century, 1987.

Hanbury-Tenison. *Spanish Pilgrimage: A Canter to St. James.* London: Hutchinson, 1990.

Hanbury-Tenison. *Worlds Apart–an Explorer's Life.* London & New York: Granada, 1984.

Hansen, Eric. *The Curse.* Upton-upon-Severn, U.K.: Hansen-Page, 1990.

Hansen. *Motoring with Mohammed: Journeys to Yemen and the Red Sea.* London: Hamilton, 1991.

Hansen. *Stranger in the Forest: On Foot Across Borneo.* London: Century, 1988.

Harding, Mike. *Footloose in the Himalaya.* London: Joseph, 1989.

Harding. *Footloose in the West of Ireland.* London: Joseph, 1996.

Harding. *Tales from the Towpath: A Canalside Amble through Central Manchester.* Manchester, U.K.: Central Manchester Development Corporation, 1992.

Harding. *Walking the Peak and Pennines.* London: Joseph, 1992.

Hardyment, Christina. *The Candy-Coloured Cart: One Family's Search for Storybook Europe.* London: Heinemann. 1987.

Harvey, Andrew. *A Journey in Ladakh.* London: Cape, 1983.

Henfrey, Colin. *The Gentle People: A Journey among the Indian Tribes of Guiana.* London: Hutchinson, 1964.

Henfrey. *Manscapes: An American Journey.* London: Deutsch, 1973.

Herbert, Marie. *The Reindeer People.* London: Hodder & Stoughton, 1976.

Herbert. *The Snow People.* London: Barrie & Jenkins, 1973.

Hickman, Katie. *Dreams of the Peaceful Dragon: A Journey Through Bhutan.* London: Gollancz, 1987.

Hickman. *A Trip to the Light Fantastic: Travels with a Mexican Circus.* London: HarperCollins, 1993.

Hillaby, John. *Journey Home.* London: Constable, 1983.

Hillaby. *Journey Through Britain.* London: Constable, 1968.

Hillaby. *Journey Through Europe.* London: Constable, 1972.

Hillaby. *Journey to the Gods.* London: Constable, 1991.

Hillaby. *Journey to the Jade Sea.* London: Constable, 1964.

Hillary, Sir Edmund. *From Ocean to the Sky.* London: Hodder & Stoughton, 1979.

Hillary. *High Adventure.* London: Hodder & Stoughton, 1955.

Hillary. *No Latitude for Error.* London: Hodder & Stoughton, 1961.

Hillary. *Schoolhouse in the Clouds.* London: Hodder & Stoughton, 1965.

Holman, Alan. *White River, Brown Water: A Record-making Journey Down the Amazon.* London: Hodder & Stoughton, 1985.

Holmes, Richard. *Fatal Avenue: A Traveller's History of the Battlefields of Northern France and Flanders, 1346–1945.* London: Cape, 1995.

Holmes. *Footsteps: Adventures of a Romantic Biographer.* London: Hodder & Stoughton, 1985.

Holmes. *Riding the Retreat: Mons to the Marne 1914 Revisited.* London: Cape, 1995.

Holt, Peter. *The Big Muddy: Adventures up the Missouri.* London: Hutchinson, 1991.

Holt. *In Clive's Footsteps.* London: Hutchinson, 1990.

Hone, Joseph. *Children of the Country: Coast to Coast Across Africa.* London: Hamilton, 1986.

Hone. *The Dancing Waiters: Some Collected Travels.* London: Hamilton, 1975.

Hone. *Duck Soup in the Black Sea: Further Collected Travels.* London: Hamilton, 1988.

Hone. *Gone Tomorrow: Some More Collected Travels.* London: Secker & Warburg, 1981.

Hudson, Mark. *Our Grandmothers' Drums.* London: Secker & Warburg, 1989.

Hudson, Peter. *A Leaf in the Wind: Travels in Africa.* London: Columbus Books, 1988.

Hudson, Peter. *Travels in Mauritania.* London: Virgin, 1990.

Hudson, Peter. *Two Rivers: In the Footsteps of Mungo Park.* London: Chapmans, 1991.

Hyland, Paul. *The Black Heart: A Voyage Into Central Africa.* London: Gollancz, 1988.

Hyland. *Indian Balm: Travels in South West India.* London: HarperCollins, 1994.

Iyer, Pico. *Falling Off the Map: Some Lonely Places of the World.* London: Cape, 1993.

Iyer. *The Lady and the Monk: Four Seasons in Kyoto.* London: Bodley Head, 1991.

Iyer. *Video Night in Kathmandu and Other Reports from the Not-so-far East.* London: Bloomsbury, 1988.

Jackson, Monica. *The Turkish Time Machine.* London: Hodder & Stoughton, 1966.

Jackson, and Elizabeth Stark. *Tents in the Clouds: The First Women's Himalayan Expedition.* London: Collins, 1956.

Jaffrey, Madhur. *A Taste of India.* London: Pavilion, 1985.

James, Clive. *Flying Visits: Postcards from The Observer 1976–83.* London: Cape, 1984.

Jukes, Peter. *A Shout in the Street: An Excursion Into the Modern City.* London: Faber & Faber, 1990.

Keay, John. *Into India.* London: Murray, 1973.

Kewley, Vanya. *Tibet: Behind the Ice Curtain.* London: Grafton, 1990.

Kirkup, James. *Filipinescas: Travels Through the Philippine Islands.* London: Phoenix House, 1968.

Kirkup. *Streets of Asia.* London: Dent, 1969.

Kirkup. *These Horned Islands: A Journal of Japan.* London: Collins, 1962.

Kirkup. *Tropic Temper: A Memoir of Malaya.* London: Collins, 1963.

Lancaster, Osbert. *Classical Landscapes with Figures.* London: Murray, 1947.

Lancaster. *Sailing to Byzantium: An Architectural Companion.* London: Murray, 1969.

Lee, Laurie. *As I Walked Out One Midsummer Morning.* London: Deutsch, 1969.

Lee. *A Rose for Winter: Travels in Andalusia.* London: Hogarth Press, 1955.

Leith-Ross, Sylvia. *Stepping Stones: Memoirs of Colonial Nigeria, 1907–60,* edited by Michael Crowder. London & Boston: Peter Owen, 1983.

Levi, Peter. *A Bottle in the Shade: A Journey in the Western Peloponnese.* London: Sinclair-Stevenson, 1996.

Levi. *The Hill of Kronos.* London: Collins, 1980.

Levi. *The Light Garden of the Angel King: Journeys in Afghanistan.* London: Collins, 1972.

Levin, Bernard. *Hannibal's Footsteps.* London: Cape, 1985.

Liddell, Robert. *Aegean Greece.* London: Cape, 1954.

Liddell. *Byzantium and Istanbul.* London: Cape, 1958.

Liddell. *Mainland Greece.* London: Longmans, 1965.

Linklater, Andro. *Wild People: Travels with Borneo's Head-Hunters.* London: Murray, 1990.

Lister, Charles. *Between Two Seas: A Walk Down the Appian Way.* London: Secker & Warburg, 1991.

Lloyd, Sarah. *Chinese Characters: A Journey Through China.* London: Collins, 1987.

Lloyd. *An Indian Attachment.* London: Harvill, 1984.

Macaulay, Rose. *Fabled Shore: From the Pyrenees to Portugal.* London: Hamilton, 1949.

Macaulay. *A Pleasure of Ruins.* London: Weidenfeld & Nicolson, 1953.

Mackenzie, Compton. *All Over the Place: Fifty Thousand Miles by Sea, Air, Road and Rail.* London: Chatto & Windus, 1948.

Mackenzie. *Greece in My Life.* London: Chatto & Windus, 1960.

Mainwaring, Marcus. *Nor any Drop to Drink: England to Australia, May 1987–January 1988.* London: Bloomsbury, 1988.

Markham, Beryl. *West with the Night.* Boston: Houghton Mifflin, 1942; London & Toronto: Harrap, 1943.

Marriott, Edward. *The Lost Tribe: A Search Through the Jungles of Papua New Guinea.* London: Picador, 1996.

Mayle, Peter. *Toujours Provence.* London: Hamilton, 1991.

Mayle. *A Year in Provence.* London: Hamilton, 1989.

Mayne, Peter. *The Alleys of Marrakesh.* London: Murray, 1953.

Mayne. *Friends in High Places: A Season in the Himalayas.* London: Bodley Head, 1975.

Mayne. *The Narrow Smile: A Journey Back to the North-west Frontier.* London: Murray, 1955.

Mayne. *The Private Sea.* London: Murray, 1959.

Mayne. *Saints of Sind.* London: Murray, 1956.

Mear, Roger, and Robert Swan. *In the Footsteps of Scott.* London: Cape, 1987.

Miles, Beryl. *Attic in Luxembourg.* London: Murray, 1956.

Miles. *Candles in Denmark.* London: Murray, 1958.

Miles. *Islands of Contrast: Adventures in New Zealand.* London: Murray, 1955.

Miles. *Spirit of Mexico.* London: Murray, 1961.

Miles. *The Stars My Blanket.* London: Murray, 1954.

Milnes Walker, Nicolette. *When I Put Out to Sea.* London: Collins, 1972.

Moffat, Gwen. *Hard Road West: Alone on the California Trail.* London: Gollancz, 1981.

Moffat. *Space Below My Feet.* London: Hodder & Stoughton, 1961.

Moffat. *The Storm Seekers: A Journey in the Footsteps of John Charles Frémont.* London: Secker & Warburg, 1989.

Monbiot, George. *No Man's Land: An Investigative Journey through Kenya and Tanzania.* London: Macmillan, 1994.

Monbiot. *Poisoned Arrows: An Investigative Journey through Indonesia.* London: Joseph, 1989.

Morin, Nea. *A Woman's Reach: Mountaineering Memoirs.* London: Eyre & Spottiswoode, 1968.

Morland, Miles. *The Man Who Broke Out of the Bank–and Went for a Walk in France.* London: Bloomsbury, 1992.

Myers, Wendy. *Seven League Boots: The Story of My Seven-Year Hitchhike Round the World.* London: Hodder & Stoughton, 1969.

Naipaul, Shiva. *North of South: An African Journey.* London: Deutsch, 1978.

Newman, Bernard. *American Journey.* London: Hale, 1943.

Newman. *Baltic Background.* London: Hale, 1948.

Newman. *British Journey.* London: Hale, 1945.

Newman. *Bulgarian Background.* London: Hale, 1961.

Newman. *Far Eastern Journey: Across India and Pakistan to Formosa.* London: Jenkins, 1961.

Newman. *Mediterranean Background.* London: Hale, 1949.

Newman. *Middle Eastern Journey.* London: Gollancz, 1947.

Newman. *Morocco Today.* London: Hale, 1953.

Newman. *North African Journey.* London: Hale, 1955.

Newman. *Oberammergau Journey.* London: Jenkins, 1952.

Newman. *Portrait of Poland.* London: Hale, 1959.

Newman. *Portrait of the Shires.* London: Hale, 1968.

Newman. *Report on Indo-China.* London: Hale, 1953.

Newman. *Ride to Rome.* London: Jenkins, 1953.

Newman. *Round the World in Seventy Days.* London: Jenkins, 1964.

Newman. *South African Journey.* London: Jenkins, 1965.

Newman. *Spain on a Shoestring.* London: Jenkins, 1957.

Newman. *Spain Revisited.* London: Jenkins, 1966.

Newman. *Still Flows the Danube.* London: Jenkins, 1955.

Newman. *Tito's Yugoslavia.* London: Hale, 1952.

Newman. *To Russia and Back.* London: Jenkins, 1967.

Newman. *Turkey and the Turks.* London: Jenkins, 1968.

Newman. *Turkish Crossroads.* London: Hale, 1951.

Newman. *Unknown Yugoslavia.* London: Jenkins, 1960.

Nicholl, Charles. *Borderlines: A Journey in Thailand and Burma.* London: Secker & Warburg, 1988.

Nichols, Beverley. *The Sun in My Eyes, or, How Not to Go Round the World.* London: Heinemann, 1969.

Nicholson, Michael. *Across the Limpopo: A Family's Hazardous 4,000-mile Journey Through Africa.* London: Robson, 1985.

Nicolson, Nigel, and Adam Nicolson. *Two Roads to Dodge City.* London: Weidenfeld & Nicolson, 1986.

Norwich, John Julius. *Sahara.* London: Longman, 1968.

Norwich, and Reresby Sitwell. *Mount Athos.* London: Hutchinson, 1966.

O'Hanlon, Redmond. *Congo Journey.* London & New York: Hamilton, 1996.

O'Hanlon. *Into the Heart of Borneo: An Account of a Journey Made in 1983 to the Mountains of Batu Tiban with James Fenton.* Edinburgh: Salamander Press, 1984.

O'Hanlon. *In Trouble Again: A Journey Between the Orinoco and the Amazon.* London: Hamilton, 1988.

Page, Robin. *Dust in a Dark Continent.* London: Claridge, 1989.

Page. *Journeys Into Britain.* London: Hodder & Stoughton, 1982.

Paine, Sheila. *The Afghan Amulet: Travels from the Hindu Kush to Razgrad.* London: Joseph, 1994.

Paine. *The Golden Horde: Travels from Himalaya to Karpathos.* London: Joseph, 1997.

Pakenham, Thomas. *The Mountains of Rasselas: An Ethiopian Adventure.* London: Weidenfeld & Nicholson, 1959.

Palin, Michael. *Around the World in 80 Days.* London: BBC Books, 1989.

Palin. *Full Circle.* London: BBC Books, 1997.

Parks, Tim. *An Italian Education: The Further Adventures of an Expatriate in Verona.* New York: Grove, 1995; London: Secker & Warburg, 1996.

Parks. *Italian Neighbours: An Englishman in Verona.* London: Heinemann, 1992.

Paxman, Jeremy. *Through the Volcanoes: A Central American Journey.* London: Joseph, 1985.

Pern, Stephen. *Another Land, Another Sea: Walking Round Lake Rudolph.* London: Gollancz, 1979.

Pern. *The Beach of Morning: A Walk in West Africa.* London: Hodder & Stoughton, 1983.

Pern. *The Great Divide: A Walk Through America Along the Continental Divide.* London: Phoenix House, 1987.

Pern. *Masked Dancers of West Africa: The Dogon.* Amsterdam: Time-Life Books, 1982.

Pilkington, John. *An Adventure on the Old Silk Road: From Venice to the Yellow Sea.* London: Century, 1989.

Pilkington. *An Englishman in Patagonia.* London: Century, 1991.

Pilkington. *Into Thin Air.* London: Allen & Unwin, 1985.

Portway, Christopher. *The Great Railway Adventure.* Yeovil, U.K.: Oxford Illustrated Press, 1983.

Portway. *Indian Odyssey: Around the Subcontinent by Public Transport.* London: Impact, 1993.

Portway. *Journey Along the Spine of the Andes.* Yeovil, U.K.: Oxford Illustrated Press, 1984.

Portway. *A Kenyan Adventure: Tailing the Tana–The Story of a River Expedition.* London: Impact, 1993.

Potter, Ursula Barnett. *I'll Fly No More: An Airwoman's Diary.* London: George Allen, 1951.

Powell, Anthony. *The Empire Revisited.* London: Cleveland Press, 1985.

Powell, Dilys. *Remember Greece.* London: Hodder & Stoughton, 1941.

Powell, Dilys. *The Villa Ariadne.* London: Hodder & Stoughton, 1973.

Prentice, James K. *Time, Chance and Change.* Braunton, U.K.: Merlin, 1984.

Pritchett, V. S. *At Home and Abroad: Travel Essays.* Berkeley, Cal.: North Point Press, 1989; London: Chatto & Windus, 1990.

Pritchett. *Dublin.* London: Bodley Head, 1967.

Pritchett. *Foreign Faces.* London: Chatto & Windus, 1964. Republished as *The Offensive Traveller.* New York: Knopf, 1964.

Pritchett. *London Perceived.* London: Chatto & Windus, 1962.

Pritchett. *The Spanish Temper.* London: Chatto & Windus, 1954.

Pryce-Jones, David. *Next Generation: Travels in Israel.* London: Weidenfeld & Nicolson, 1964.

Pye-Smith, Charlie. *In Search of Wild India.* London: Boxtree, 1992.

Pye-Smith. *The Other Nile: Journeys in Egypt, the Sudan and Ethiopia.* Harmondsworth, U.K.: Viking, 1986.

Pye-Smith. *Rebels and Outcasts: A Journey Through Christian India.* London: Viking, 1997.

Pye-Smith. *Travels in Nepal: The Sequestered Kingdom.* London: Aurum Press, 1988.

Rankin, Nicholas. *Dead Man's Chest: Travels After Robert Louis Stevenson.* London & Boston: Faber & Faber, 1987.

Reid, Alastair. *Whereabouts: Notes on Being a Foreigner.* Edinburgh: Canongate, 1987.

Reynolds, Reginald. *Beware of Africans: A Pilgrimage from Cairo to the Cape.* London: Jarrolds, 1955. Republished as *Cairo to Cape Town: A Pilgrimage in Search of Hope.* Garden City, N.Y.: Doubleday, 1955.

Rhodes, Anthony Richard Ewart. *The Dalmatian Coast.* London: Evans, 1955.

Rhodes. *A Sabine Journey to Rome in Holy Year.* London: Putnam, 1952.

Rhodes. *Where the Turk Trod: A Journey to Sarajevo with a Slavonic Mussulman.* London: Weidenfeld & Nicolson, 1956.

Ridgway, John M. *Amazon Journey: From the Source to the Sea.* London: Hodder & Stoughton, 1972.

Ridgway. *Cockleshell Journey: the Adventures of Three Men and a Girl.* London: Hodder & Stoughton, 1974.

Ridgway. *Journey to Ardmore.* London: Hodder & Stoughton, 1971.

Ridgway. *Road to Elizabeth: A Quest in the Mountains of Peru.* London: Gollancz, 1986.

Ridgway, and Andy Briggs. *Round the World Non-stop.* Wellingborough, U.K.: Stephens, 1985.

Ridgway, and Chay Blyth. *A Fighting Chance.* London: Hamlyn, 1967.

Ridgway, and Marie Christine Ridgway. *Round the World with Ridgway.* London: Heinemann, 1978.

Ridgway, Marie Christine Ridgway, and Rebecca Ridgway. *Then We Sailed Away.* London: Little, Brown, 1996.

Ross, Alan. *The Bandit on the Billiard Table: A Journey Through Sardinia.* London: Verschoyle, 1954.

Ross. *Time Was Away: A Notebook in Corsica.* London: Lehmann, 1948.

Rushdie, Salman. *The Jaguar Smile: A Nicaraguan Journey.* London: Pan/Cape, 1987.

Sansom, William. *Away to It All.* London: Hogarth Press, 1964.

Sansom. *Blue Skies, Brown Studies.* London: Hogarth Press, 1961.

Sansom. *The Icicle and the Sun.* London: Hogarth Press, 1958.

Scott, Sheila. *I Must Fly: Adventures of a Woman Pilot.* London: Hodder & Stoughton, 1968.

Scott. *On Top of the World.* London: Hodder & Stoughton, 1973.

Seth, Vikram. *From Heaven Lake: Travels Through Sinkiang and Tibet.* London: Chatto & Windus, 1983.

Sewell, Brian. *South from Ephesus: Travels in Aegean Turkey.* London: Century, 1988.

Shand, Mark. *Queen of the Elephants.* London: Cape, 1995.

Shand. *Travels on My Elephant.* London: Cape, 1991.

Shepherd, Anthony. *Arabian Adventure.* London: Collins, 1961.

Shepherd. *The Flight of the Unicorns.* London: Elek, 1965.

Shipton, Diana. *The Antique Land.* London: Hodder & Stoughton, 1950.

Shipton, Eric. *Land of Tempest: Travels in Patagonia, 1958–62.* London: Hodder & Stoughton, 1963.

Shipton, Eric. *The Mount Everest Reconnaissance Expedition, 1951.* London: Hodder & Stoughton, 1952.

Shipton, Eric. *Upon That Mountain.* London: Hodder & Stoughton, 1943.

Shukman, Henry. *Sons of the Moon.* New York: Scribners, 1989; London: Weidenfeld & Nicolson, 1990.

Shukman. *Travels with My Trombone: A Caribbean Journey.* London: HarperCollins, 1992.

Sillitoe, Alan. *Road to Volgograd.* London: W. H. Allen, 1964.

Simon, Ted. *Jupiter's Travels.* London: Hamilton, 1979.

Simon. *Riding Home.* Harmondsworth, U.K.: Viking, 1984.

Simpson, Joe. *Storms of Silence.* London: Cape, 1996.

Simpson, Joe. *Touching the Void.* London: Cape, 1988.

Simpson, Myrtle. *Due North.* London: Gollancz, 1970.

Simpson, Myrtle. *Greenland Summer: Based on a True Expedition.* London: Gollancz, 1973.

Simpson, Myrtle. *Home is a Tent.* London: Travel Book Club, 1964.

Simpson, Myrtle. *White Horizons.* London: Gollancz, 1967.

Sinclair, Ronald. *Adventures in Persia: To India by the Back Door.* London: Witherby, 1988.

Sitwell, Sacheverell. *Arabesque and Honeycomb.* London: Hale, 1957.

Sitwell. *The Bridge of the Brocade Sash: Travels and Observations in Japan.* London: Weidenfeld & Nicolson, 1959.

Sitwell. *Golden Wall and Mirador: From England to Peru.* London: Weidenfeld & Nicolson, 1961.

Smeeton, Beryl. *The Stars My Blanket.* Victoria, B.C.: Horsdal & Schubart, 1995.

Smeeton, Beryl. *Winter Shoes in Springtime.* London: Hart-Davis, 1961.

Smeeton, Miles. *Because the Horn is There.* Lymington, U.K.: Nautical Publishing / London: Harrap, 1970.

Smeeton, Miles. *The Misty Islands.* Lymington, U.K.: Nautical Publishing / London: Harrap, 1969.

Smeeton, Miles. *Once is Enough.* London: Hart-Davis, 1959.

Smeeton, Miles. *The Sea Was Our Village.* Lymington, U.K.: Nautical Publishing / London: Harrap, 1973.

Smeeton, Miles. *Sunrise to Windward.* London: Hart-Davis, 1966.

Smith, Janet Adam. *Mountain Holidays.* London: Dent, 1946.

Spender, Stephen, and David Hockney. *China Diary.* London: Thames & Hudson, 1982.

Staley, John. *Words for My Brother: Travels Between the Hindu Kush and the Himalayas.* Karachi & Oxford: Oxford University Press, 1982.

Stevens, Stuart. *Malaria Dreams: An African Adventure.* London: Simon & Schuster, 1990.

Stevens. *Night Train to Turkistan: Adventures along China's Ancient Silk Road.* London: Macmillan, 1988.

Stewart, Stanley. *Frontiers of Heaven: A Journey Beyond the Great Wall.* London: Murray, 1995.

Stewart. *Old Serpent Nile: A Journey to the Source.* London: Murray, 1991.

Swale, Rosie. *Back to Cape Horn.* London: Collins, 1986.

Swale. *Children of Cape Horn.* London: Elek, 1974.

Tanner, Marcus. *Ticket to Latvia: A Journey from Berlin to the Baltic.* London: Dent, 1989.

Templeton, Edith. *The Surprise of Cremona: One Woman's Adventures in Cremona, Parma, Nantua, Ravenna, Urbino, and Arezzo.* London: Eyre & Spottiswoode, 1954.

Thompson, Dorothy Evelyn. *Climbing with Joseph Georges.* Kendal, U.K.: Titus Wilson, 1962.

Thomson, Alex, and Nick Rossiter. *Ram Ram India.* London: Collins, 1987.

Tilman, H.W. *China to Chitral.* Cambridge: Cambridge University Press, 1951.

Tilman. *Ice with Everything.* Lymington, U.K.: Nautical Publishing, 1974.

Tilman. *In "Mischief's" Wake.* London: Hollis & Carter, 1971.

Tilman. *Mischief Among the Penguins.* London: Hart-Davis, 1961.

Tilman. *Mischief Goes South.* London & Sydney: Hollis & Carter, 1968.

Tilman. *Mischief in Greenland.* London & Sydney: Hollis & Carter, 1964.

Tilman. *Mischief in Patagonia.* Cambridge: Cambridge University Press, 1957.

Tilman. *Mostly Mischief: Voyages to the Arctic and to the Antarctic.* London: Hollis & Carter, 1966.

Tilman. *Mount Everest, 1938.* Cambridge: Cambridge University Press, 1948.

Tilman. *Nepal Himalaya.* Cambridge: Cambridge University Press, 1952.

Tilman. *Two Mountains and a River.* Cambridge: Cambridge University Press, 1949.

Tilman. *When Men & Mountains Meet.* Cambridge: Cambridge University Press, 1946.

Toynbee, Arnold Joseph. *East to West: A Journey Round the World.* London: Oxford University Press, 1958.

Tracy, Honor. *Silk Hats and No Breakfast: Notes on a Spanish Journey.* London: Methuen, 1957.

Tracy. *Spanish Leaves.* London: Methuen, 1964.

Tracy. *Winter in Castille.* London: Eyre Methuen, 1973.

Trench, Richard. *Forbidden Sands: A Search in the Sahara.* London: Murray, 1978.

Tullis, Julie. *Clouds from Both Sides.* London: Grafton, 1986.

Ward, Francis Kingdon. *Return to the Irrawaddy.* London: Melrose, 1956.

Waugh, Alec. *Bangkok, The Story of the City.* London & New York: W. H. Allen, 1970.

Waugh, Alec. *The Sugar Islands: A Collection of Pieces Written About the West Indies between 1928 and 1953.* London: Cassell, 1958. Republished as *Love and the Caribbean: Tales, Characters and Scenes of the West Indies.* New York: Farrar, Straus & Cudahy, 1959.

Waugh, Alec. *The Sunlit Caribbean.* London: Evans, 1948. Republished as *The Sugar Islands: A Caribbean Travelogue.* New York: Farrar, Straus, 1949.

Waugh, Daisy. *A Small Town in Africa.* London: Heinemann, 1994.

West, Rebecca. *Black Lamb and Grey Falcon: A Journey Through Yugoslavia,* 2 volumes. London: Macmillan, 1941.

White, Don. *Get Up and Go: Round the World on Twenty-five Pounds.* London: Wingate, 1959.

Williams, Hugo. *All the Time in the World.* London: Alan Ross, 1966.

Williams. *No Particular Place to Go.* London: Cape, 1981.

Wilson, Angus. *Reflections in a Writer's Eye: Travel Pieces.* London: Secker & Warburg, 1986.

Winchester, Simon. *Outposts.* London: Hodder & Stoughton, 1985.

Young, Geoffrey. *Country Eye: A Walker's Guide to Britain's Traditional Countryside.* London: George Philip, 1991; London: Hodder & Stoughton, 1982.

Checklist of Further Readings

Adams, Percy G., ed. *Travel Literature Through the Ages: An Anthology.* New York & London: Garland, 1988.

Adams. *Travel Literature and the Evolution of the Novel.* Lexington: University Press of Kentucky, 1983.

Aitken, Maria. *A Girdle Round the Earth.* London: Constable, 1987.

Allen, Benedict, and others. *More Great Railway Journeys.* London: BBC Books, 1996.

Apostolopoulos, Yiorgos, Stella Leivadi, and Andrew Yiannakis, eds. *The Sociology of Tourism: Theoretical and Empirical Investigations.* London & New York: Routledge, 1996.

Bathe, Basil W. *Seven Centuries of Sea Travel: From the Crusaders to the Cruises.* London: Barrie & Jenkins, 1972.

Bishop, Peter. *The Myth of Shangri-La: Tibet, Travel Writing, and the Western Creation of Sacred Landscape.* Berkeley: University of California Press, 1989.

Brent, Peter. *Far Arabia: Explorers of the Myth.* London: Weidenfeld & Nicolson, 1977.

Brinnin, John Malcolm. *The Sway of the Grand Saloon: A Social History of the North Atlantic.* London: Macmillan, 1972.

Burkart, A. J., and S. A. Medlik. *Tourism: Past, Present, and Future.* London: Heinemann, 1974.

Callaway, Helen. *Gender, Culture and Empire: European Women in Colonial Nigeria.* Urbana: University of Illinois Press, 1987.

Cameron, Kenneth M. *Into Africa: The Story of the East African Safari.* London: Constable, 1990.

Clark, Ronald William. *Men, Myths and Mountains.* London: Weidenfeld & Nicolson, 1976.

Cocker, Mark. *Loneliness and Time: British Travel Writing in the Twentieth Century.* London: Secker & Warburg, 1992.

Cole, Garold L. *Travels in America from the Voyages of Discovery to the Present: An Annotated Bibliography of Travel Articles in Periodicals, 1955–1980.* Norman: University of Oklahoma Press, 1984.

Crossley-Holland, Kevin, ed. *The Oxford Book of Travel Verse.* Oxford: Oxford University Press, 1986.

Dodd, Philip, ed. *The Art of Travel: Essays on Travel Writing.* London: Frank Cass, 1982.

Eisner, Robert. *Travelers to an Antique Land: The History and Literature of Travel to Greece.* Ann Arbor: University of Michigan Press, 1991.

Feifer, Maxine. *Going Places: The Ways of the Tourist from Imperial Rome to the Present Day.* London: Macmillan, 1985. Republished as *Tourism in History: From Imperial Rome to the Present.* New York: Stein & Day, 1986.

Fowler, Marian. *Below the Peacock Fan: First Ladies of the Raj.* New York: Viking, 1987.

Fraser, Keath. *Bad Trips.* New York: Vintage, 1991.

Frater, Alexander. *Beyond the Blue Horizon: On the Track of Imperial Airways.* London: Heinemann, 1986.

Fussell, Paul. *Abroad: British Literary Traveling Between the Wars.* New York & Oxford: Oxford University Press, 1980.

Fussell, ed. *The Norton Book of Travel.* New York: Norton, 1987.

Greenhill, Basil, and A. Giffard. *Women Under Sail: Letters and Journals Concerning Eight Women Travelling or Working in Sailing Vessels Between 1829–1949.* Newton Abbot, U.K.: David & Charles, 1970.

Grewal, Inderpal. *Home and Harem: Nation, Gender, Empire, and the Cultures of Travel.* Durham, N.C. & London: Duke University Press, 1996.

Hassan, Ihab. "Motion and Mischief: Contemporary British Travel Writing," in his *Rumors of Change: Essays of Five Decades.* Tuscaloosa & London: University of Alabama Press, 1995, pp. 208–227.

Hatt, John. *The Tropical Traveller: The Essential Guide to Travel in Hot Climates,* enlarged edition. London: Pan, 1985. Hindley, Geoffrey. *Tourists, Travellers and Pilgrims.* London: Hutchinson, 1983.

Hollander, Paul. *Political Pilgrims: Travels of Western Intellectuals to the Soviet Union, China, and Cuba, 1928–1978.* New York: Oxford University Press, 1981.

Hopkirk, Peter. *Trespassers on the Roof of the World: The Race for Lhasa.* London: Murray, 1982.

Hudson, Kenneth. *Air Travel: A Social History.* Bath, U.K.: Adams & Dart, 1972.

Jakle, John A. *The Tourist: Travel in Twentieth-Century North America.* Lincoln: University of Nebraska Press, 1985.

Jameson, Fredric. *The Political Unconscious: Narrative as a Socially Symbolic Act.* Ithaca, N.Y.: Cornell University Press, 1981.

Kabbani, Rana. *Europe's Myths of Orient: Devise and Rule.* London: Macmillan, 1986.

Kaplan, Caren. *Questions of Travel: Postmodern Discourses of Displacement.* Durham, N.C.: Duke University Press, 1996.

Keay, John, ed. *The Royal Geographical Society History of World Exploration.* London: Hamlyn, 1991.

Kelly, A. A., ed. *Wandering Women: Two Centuries of Travel Out of Ireland.* Dublin: Wolfhound, 1995.

Kowalewski, Michael, ed. *Temperamental Journeys: Essays on the Modern Literature of Travel.* Athens & London: University of Georgia Press, 1992.

Lambert, Richard S. *The Fortunate Traveller: A Short History of Touring and Travel for Pleasure.* London & New York: Melrose, 1950.

Lawrence, Karen R. *Penelope Voyages: Women and Travel in British Literary Tradition.* Ithaca, N.Y.: Cornell University Press, 1994.

Leed, Eric J. *The Mind of the Traveler: From Gilgamesh to Global Tourism.* New York: Basic Books, 1991.

Lomax, Judy. *Women of the Air.* London: Murray, 1986.

Löschburg, Winifried. *A History of Travel,* translated by Ruth Michaelis-Jena and Patrick Murray. Leipzig: Edition Leipzig, 1979.

MacCannell, Dean. *The Tourist: A New Theory of the Leisure Class.* London: Macmillan, 1976.

MacGregor, John. *Tibet: A Chronicle of Exploration.* London: Routledge & Kegan Paul, 1970.

MacKenzie, John, ed. *Imperialism and Popular Culture.* Manchester, U.K. & Dover, N.H.: Manchester University Press, 1986.

Mahood, M. M. *The Colonial Encounter: A Reading of Six Novels.* London: Rex Collings, 1977.

Marsden-Smedley, Philip, and Jeffrey Klinke, eds. *Views from Abroad: The Spectator Book of Travel Writing.* London: Grafton, 1988.

Massingham, Hugh and Pauline, eds. *The Englishman Abroad.* London: Phoenix House, 1962.

Michael, Maurice Albert, ed. *Traveller's Quest: Original Contributions Towards a Philosophy of Travel.* London: Hodge, 1950.

Mills, Sara. *Discourses of Difference: An Analysis of Women's Travel Writing and Colonialism.* London & New York: Routledge, 1991.

Morgan, Susan. *Place Matters: Gendered Geography in Victorian Women's Travel Books About Southeast Asia.* New Brunswick, N.J.: Rutgers University Press, 1996.

Morris, Mary, ed. *Maiden Voyages: Writing of Women Travellers.* New York: Vintage, 1993.

Newby, Eric, ed. *A Book of Travellers' Tales.* London: Collins, 1985.

Norwich, John Julius, ed. *A Taste for Travel.* London: Macmillan, 1985.

Oliver, Caroline. *Western Women in Colonial Africa.* Westport, Conn.: Greenwood Press, 1982.

Ousby, Ian. *The Englishman's England: Taste, Travel, and the Rise of Tourism.* Cambridge & New York: Cambridge University Press, 1991.

Porter, Dennis. *Haunted Journeys: Desire and Transgression in European Travel Writing.* Princeton, N.J.: Princeton University Press, 1991.

Pratt, Mary Louise. *Imperial Eyes: Travel Writing and Transculturation.* London & New York: Routledge, 1992.

Rice, Warner G., ed. *Literature as a Mode of Travel.* New York: New York Public Library, 1963.

Robinson, Jane. *Wayward Women: A Guide to Women Travellers.* Oxford: Oxford University Press, 1990.

Robinson, ed., *Unsuitable for Ladies: An Anthology of Women Travellers.* Oxford & New York: Oxford University Press, 1994.

Said, Edward. *Culture and Imperialism.* New York: Knopf, 1993.

Said. *Orientalism.* New York: Pantheon, 1978.

Sigaux, Gilbert. *History of Tourism,* translated by Joan White. London: Leisure Arts, 1966.

Smith, Valene, ed. *Hosts and Guests: The Anthropology of Travel.* Philadelphia: University of Pennsylvania Press, 1977.

Spurr, David. *The Rhetoric of Empire: Colonial Discourse in Journalism, Travel Writing, and Imperial Administration.* Durham, N.C.: Duke University Press, 1993.

Stefoff, Rebecca. *Women of the World: Women Travelers and Explorers.* New York: Oxford University Press, 1991.

Strobel, Margaret. *European Women and the Second British Empire.* Bloomington: Indiana University Press, 1991.

Tinling, Marion. *Women Into the Unknown: A Sourcebook on Women Explorers and Travelers.* New York: Greenwood Press, 1989.

Trench, Richard. *Arabian Travellers.* London: Macmillan, 1986.

Urry, John. *The Tourist Gaze: Leisure and Travel in Contemporary Societies.* London & Newbury Park: Sage, 1990.

Wallraff, Barbara. "A World of Books: Reading Matter to Enhance and Inspire Travel," *Atlantic Monthly,* 274 (November 1994): 46–50.

Contributors

Steven E. Alford . . . . *Nova Southeastern University*
M. D. Allen . . . . *University of Wisconsin–Fox Valley*
John Boening . . . . *University of Toledo*
David Callahan . . . . *University of Aveiro, Portugal*
Victoria Carchidi . . . . *Massey University*
Scott R. Christianson . . . . *Radford University*
Marcia B. Dinneen . . . . *Bridgewater State College*
Joshua D. Esty . . . . *Harvard University*
Suzanne Ferriss . . . . *Nova Southeastern University*
Roy C. Flannagan III . . . . *Francis Marion University*
Julia M. Gergits . . . . *Youngstown State University*
Anita G. Gorman . . . . *Slippery Rock University of Pennsylvania*
Syrine C. Hout . . . . *American University of Beirut*
Sherrie A. Inness . . . . *Miami University*
Cecile M. Jagodzinski . . . . *Illinois State University*
Craig Loomis . . . . *Sacramento City College*
Edward A. Malone . . . . *Missouri Western State College*
Jane Claspy Nesmith . . . . *Coe College*
William Over . . . . *St. John's University*
Sura Prasad Rath . . . . *Louisiana State University in Shreveport*
Dennis M. Read . . . . *Denison University*
Brian D. Reed . . . . *Case Western Reserve University*
Carol Huebscher Rhoades . . . . *Austin, Texas*
Kenneth A. Robb . . . . *Bowling Green State University*
James J. Schramer . . . . *Youngstown State University*
Harender Vasudeva . . . . *Bowling Green State University*
Hariclea Zengos . . . . *American College of Greece*

Cumulative Index

Dictionary of Literary Biography, Volumes 1-204
Dictionary of Literary Biography Yearbook, 1980-1997
Dictionary of Literary Biography Documentary Series, Volumes 1-19

Cumulative Index

DLB before number: *Dictionary of Literary Biography,* Volumes 1-204
Y before number: *Dictionary of Literary Biography Yearbook,* 1980-1997
DS before number: *Dictionary of Literary Biography Documentary Series,* Volumes 1-19

A

B

C

D

E

F

G

H

I

J

K

L

M

O

P

Q

R

S

T

U

V

X

Y

Z

ISBN 0-7876-3098-5
90000
9 780787 630980